CRUSADERS
IN THE COURTS

CRUSADERS IN THE COURTS

HOW A DEDICATED BAND OF LAWYERS FOUGHT FOR THE CIVIL RIGHTS REVOLUTION

JACK GREENBERG

BasicBooks

A Division of HarperCollins*Publishers*

Copyright © 1994 by Jack Greenberg.
Published by BasicBooks, A Division of HarperCollins Publishers, Inc.

Library of Congress Cataloging-in-Publication Data

Greenberg, Jack, 1924–
    Crusaders in the courts : how a dedicated band of lawyers fought for the civil rights revolution / by Jack Greenberg.
    p.   cm.
    Includes bibliographical references and index.
    ISBN 0–465–01518–2 (cloth)
    ISBN 0–465–01519–0 (paper)
    1. Afro-Americans—Legal status, laws, etc.—History—20th century. 2. Race discrimination—Law and legislation—United States—History—20th century. 3. Civil rights movements—United States—History—20th century. 4. NAACP Legal Defense and Educational Fund—History. 5. Greenberg, Jack, 1924–   6. Lawyers—United States—Biography.
I. Title.
KF4757.G699 1994
342.73″0873—dc20
[347.302873]

                                                                93–45972
                                                                CIP

95 96 97 98 ❖/HC 9 8 7 6 5 4 3 2 1

For Debby

CONTENTS

PART III
BROWN DECIDED: EYES ON THE FUTURE

PART IV
THE MOVEMENT TAKES OFF

PART V
THE ERA OF THE CIVIL RIGHTS ACT

PART VI
CHANGING THE GUARD AGAIN

FOREWORD

I first became involved in the work of the NAACP Legal Defense and Educational Fund in 1948. Thurgood Marshall and my colleague at Howard University James Nabrit, Jr., asked me to serve as the "expert witness" in the case of *Lyman Johnson v. the University of Kentucky*. Johnson had applied to the university to pursue graduate studies in U.S. history. He was denied admission on the basis of his being an African American and told that whatever he needed he could get at the public institution for his race, Kentucky State College at Frankfort.

Marshall and Nabrit asked me to provide evidence that the black institution was no match for the University of Kentucky. After comparing the two institutions in library and faculty resources, I was prepared to support the plaintiff's argument that the University of Kentucky was far superior in every respect. Marshall, however, had other things in mind. After my report to him, and after the preliminary statements before the court by the counsel for the university, Marshall requested Judge H. Church Ford to render a verdict ordering the University of Kentucky to admit Johnson "forthwith." Judge Ford, no foe of segregation but a strong believer in the equal protection clause of the Fourteenth Amendment, agreed and ordered the admission of Johnson. I was delighted with the decision but regretted that the early disposition of the matter precluded my testimony.

The next opportunity I had to work with the LDF, or the "Ink Fund" as it was widely known, came in 1953. The Fund was preparing a brief in response to the questions raised by the United States Supreme Court in *Brown v. Board of Education* regarding the intent of the Congress, members of state legislatures, and other contemporaries as to whether they understood that the Fourteenth Amendment prohibited racial segregation in the public schools. Upon the invitation of Thurgood Marshall, I joined the non-legal research staff of the LDF and worked on a regular basis, commuting weekly from Washington to New York from September to December 1953. I did research, wrote papers, and participated in discussions related to the history of segregation in the public schools. Historians can rightly claim that they gained a new level of respect as attorneys on both sides waited for the historians to tell them what actually happened during the period the Fourteenth Amendment was under consideration.

As I came and went in and out of the LDF offices, several younger lawyers impressed me as being very bright and deeply committed. One was Constance Baker Motley, who had joined the staff in 1945, even before she graduated from Columbia Law School, which she did the following year. Motley's versatility and courage were apparent as she moved from one type of civil rights case to another and as she returned from the "field of battle" to regale us with her latest escapades. There was also Robert L. Carter. He had joined the Fund early and was already deeply involved in the school desegregation cases when I came to know and admire him greatly. Later, both Carter and Motley became judges in the federal district court in New York.

Another energetic and deeply committed lawyer was a young white man, Jack Greenberg, who had already decided to cast his lot with the causes espoused by the Fund and who soon became a valued assistant to Thurgood Marshall. When Marshall left the Fund in 1961 to become a judge on the United States Court of Appeals, he nominated Greenberg to succeed him, and the board elected him to the position of director-counsel.

Greenberg was all over the place in those early years, working simultaneously on cases involving the admission of African American students to graduate and professional schools; black men alleged to have raped white women; racial discrimination in the armed forces; and, of course, the school desegregation cases as they moved toward their climax in the 1950s. With no background or experience as a victim of racial discrimination, but with a strong family background of commitment to fairness and justice, Greenberg had no difficulty in becoming a vigorous advocate for racial justice. While he did not take advantage of his race in seeking out and prosecuting racial bigots, as Walter White, the African American executive director of the NAACP, had used his fair skin and blue eyes to witness and report lynchings, Greenberg did not hesitate to use his race when there was an opportunity to advance the cause of eradicating racial segregation and discrimination.

While there have been numerous works dealing with the civil rights movement, with countless references to the remarkable contributions of LDF, Greenberg's book, to my knowledge, provides the first insider's account of the work of LDF. This makes it not only valuable but unique. The vignettes of Franklin Williams, who had left before I arrived, of Connie Motley, Bob Carter, and many others, are so important in understanding the human component that was, after all, crucial to the success of the Fund.

There is, of course, the close-up of Thurgood Marshall, who was, in the eyes of Greenberg, a legal giant as well as a wonderfully decent human being.

Perhaps even more important than Greenberg's "insider" view of his colleagues are his accounts of the Fund's response to the attempts by the foes of desegregation and racial equality to destroy the organization. For the first time, moreover, Greenberg reveals the state-by-state strategies the LDF developed to counter the opposition to school desegregation. Much has been written of "Black Monday" (May 17, 1954) and "Massive Resistance," but the struggle that the Fund was carrying forward, dramatically portrayed here by Greenberg, can best be described as heroic. Between May 1954 and April 1955, LDF had eight college and junior college cases in various stages of adjudication in Texas, Oklahoma, and Louisiana. During the same period it had a half-dozen recreation cases, while Greenberg himself had at least as many criminal cases under way.

When the civil rights movement reached its zenith in the 1960s, LDF had so many cases involving the right to march, picket, boycott, and protest in other ways that it was difficult for the New York office to keep up with them. There were, moreover, new frontiers that LDF was exploring, such as death penalty cases, poverty law, and racial discrimination in housing—to name but a few—and many wondered where the Fund would strike next.

Regardless of the area of litigation, LDF was compelled to fight the same battle from one state to another and, in some instances, from one county to another. Like Churchill's strategy for defeating the Germans in the Second World War, LDF did not "flag or fail." It fought the enemy in the county courts, in the state legislatures, in the Congress, and before the United States Supreme Court. It would carry on the struggle until, as Churchill would say, "in God's good time" a new democracy "with all its power and might steps forth to the rescue and liberation of the old." Even during its young life, the NAACP Legal Defense and Educational Fund possessed the courage, the human and sometimes financial resources, and the staying power to reshape American society. The descriptions of the inner life of LDF, including the doubts and apprehensions, the fears and insecurities, and the difficulties in seeing the end of the road, are vividly set forth in this truly important and unique account of its history.

—*John Hope Franklin*

PREFACE

In 1939, Thurgood Marshall, a little-known attorney working for the National Association for the Advancement of Colored People (NAACP), the most widely known civil rights organization of its time, sat down and in his own hand wrote out the charter for a new organization to be spun off from the NAACP. The new organization's charter stated that it was incorporated:

(a) To render legal aid gratuitously to such Negroes as may appear to be worthy thereof, who are suffering legal injustices by reason of race or color . . . and
(b) To seek and promote the educational facilities for Negroes who are denied the same by reason of race or color.

The official name given this new organization was the N.A.A.C.P. Legal Defense and Educational Fund, Inc., but it quickly came to be known as the Inc. Fund, and later as LDF. From that point on, the NAACP confided the legal assault on Jim Crow to its new offspring, under its special counsel, later titled director-counsel, Thurgood Marshall, while the Association continued to concentrate on politics, lobbying, propaganda, and encouraging its members to turn to the courts.

Ten years later, at the ripe old age of twenty-four and just out of Columbia Law School, I joined LDF as a staff attorney. For the next twelve years I observed, learned, and eventually helped litigate some of the most important cases to be argued in the civil rights struggle. Then, in 1961, seven years after the Fund had won the case for which it is most widely known, *Brown v. Board of Education*, President John F. Kennedy appointed Thurgood Marshall, who had been chief counsel in that case, to the court of appeals. Marshall was only the second black American to sit on a United

States Court of Appeals (the first had been William H. Hastie). Thurgood and the LDF board of directors selected me to take over my mentor's position as director-counsel.

For thirty-five years I remained with the Fund, the first twelve working under Thurgood and the remaining twenty-three directing its civil rights strategies in the courts. During that period I personally argued forty cases in the United States Supreme Court and hundreds in lower courts, all at the cutting edge of civil rights law, yet these cases represent only a relatively small proportion of the cases handled by the LDF staff and cooperating lawyers. In 1984 I resigned from LDF to join the faculty at Columbia Law School and this book, more or less, stops at that point.

This is a history of LDF and, for the years I was there, a memoir as well. I have tried to place our legal struggles and accomplishments in their social, political, and economic contexts, but this is far from a chronicle of the entire civil rights movement. In my writing, of course, I have had to supplement my own recollections with a variety of other materials. Among the most important collections I consulted were those at the Kennedy and Johnson libraries; the Schomburg Center for Research in Black Culture; the files of the NAACP; materials from my heavily censored FBI file, which I obtained only after five years of administrative appeals and litigation; and, most important, of course, the files of LDF itself. These last constitute records of almost a thousand reported cases that the Fund handled (according to a count by Lexis and Westlaw, the legal data bases) as well as the circumstances surrounding these cases. Many unreported cases didn't end up in lawbooks because they were decided in lower courts that didn't publish opinions, were settled, or were, to some, not important enough to publish even though they meant a great deal to those who were involved.

I have reviewed other activities of the Fund, including major LDF scholarship and internship programs, fund-raising activities, internal operations, internal and external rivalries, and a variety of other matters.

While I have mined much of this material in depth, a book of this kind cannot include an examination of every case we argued, every issue we discussed, every person we dealt with and still be readable. I regret that I have been forced to omit or treat very briefly some significant cases and activities that are illustrative of issues and programs discussed in the text; some of these I have expanded upon in the notes, which consist of documentation and elaboration of the text. But choices had to be made and I hope that the reader won't mind treating the notes as an appendix of sorts, to be turned to for further particulars, if desired. I think, however, that I have covered most matters of importance, if not in the text, then in the notes. I have tried to keep in mind the concerns of the legal scholar and historian while making LDF accomplishments intelligible to lay persons, all in a volume of manageable size. In walking this fine line I risk leaving both groups dissatisfied.

In writing this memoir, I have tried to re-create what it was like to be part of the organization that played a major role—often the leading role and, at some times, the only role—in the legal struggle to obtain for black Americans their full civil rights as citizens. I hope to convey a feeling for the issues we engaged, the positions we stood for, the obstacles we faced, the good people whose minds we changed and whose hearts we converted, the entrenched opponents we antagonized, and the many, many friends who played a part in helping us do what we were able to do for American justice. I have written more about myself than I would have preferred simply because it is from my own personal involvement that I best know the work of the LDF, and the reader deserves to know the perspective of the author. At the same time I have written less about myself than some might want because this isn't a book about me.

Some LDF cases or groups of cases I have written about have been the subjects of many books: the White Primary Cases (1944), which ended exclusion of black people from the Democratic party in the South; the Restrictive Covenant Cases (1948), which held unconstitutional the enforcement of covenants prohibiting the sale of property to blacks; the higher education cases (1950), which prohibited Southern graduate and professional schools from excluding blacks; the Little Rock case, which gained nine black children admittance to a white high school under military guard (1959); the trial of Martin Luther King, Jr., arising out of the Birmingham demonstrations (1963); and the capital punishment cases (1972), which held capital punishment unconstitutional as it was then enforced. There have been two books on the *Meredith* case (1962), which ordered the University of Mississippi to admit its first black student, a decision that had to be enforced by military action; and a book is in progress on *Griggs v. Duke Power Company* (1970), which held illegal the denial of a job on the basis of a test that cannot be shown to measure ability to do the work. There is a superb book, *Simple Justice:* Brown v. Board of Education *and Black America's Struggle for Equality*, by Richard Kluger, about the School Segregation Cases, or *Brown v. Board of Education* (1954), which ended all state-enforced racial segregation in public schooling. A new biography of Thurgood Marshall deals with cases leading up to *Brown*, as well as *Brown* itself. There are scholarly and popular articles too numerous to mention that deal with LDF cases.

Some of these books and articles, written by historians or legal scholars, bring the detached analysis of the scholar to the events they chronicle; some present the more involved viewpoint of actual plaintiffs. I have written, inevitably, from my own perspective, that of a lawyer who is not as detached as a historian nor as engaged as the plaintiffs themselves. While I would not claim to have written impartially, I do hope I have been fair. I have tried to be accurate. Some readers will find some of what I write controversial. Surely, other witnesses to these same events, calling on different memories, will write different histories.

ACKNOWLEDGMENTS

F irst, of course, I owe an immeasurable debt to LDF, which provided for me the best job a lawyer, indeed, anyone, could have. Thurgood Marshall, with whom I experienced a great deal of what appears in these pages, and whom I visited a number of times during the writing to refresh my memory and seek his insights, deserves the accolades that history has bestowed on him. He was a complex man, much more so than usually has been described. I hope I have done him justice. The LDF leadership, Julius Chambers and then Elaine Jones, and staff have helped me in every way I have asked in the research and writing. Columbia University, under President Mike Sovern, and Columbia Law School, under Dean Barbara Black, provided a congenial environment and a willingness to assist that were all a faculty member could ask. When I returned to the law school after having been dean of Columbia College, Dean Lance Liebman and Vice Dean Vivian Berger extended equal hospitality. The Ford Foundation funded expenses involved in exploring LDF archives and other research. The Rockefeller Foundation provided a home for a highly agreeable month at Villa Serbelloni at Bellagio, Italy, where I wrote a great deal and had the opportunity to talk about my work with scholars in related fields. Two friends, Christine and Raymond Vulliez, extended their most comfortable hospitality while I edited the final version of the manuscript.

Two research assistants deserve special mention: Daniel Halberstam, while still my student at Columbia College and during the year following his graduation (and before going on to law school), did all one might hope for from a law student or lawyer in his assembling of legal materials. Aaron Brenner, a graduate student in history, found everything I asked for and more, drafted the notes from materials that he found or I furnished, and offered wise commentary on much that I wrote. Many others helped as well, including Kerry Candaele, Gail Javitt, David Spievack, Enid Sterling, and Michael West. I interviewed current and past LDF staff members and others involved in the civil rights movement with whom LDF worked and who are too numerous to mention here, but whose names appear in the text and notes. Many read passages about events with which they were most familiar and offered useful comments and corrections. One deserves special mention, Jim Nabrit III, who was not only a comrade in the struggle, but who is a dear personal friend.

David Vladeck of Public Citizen, and Pat Carome, Tonya Brito, and Martha Aaron, all with the law firm of Wilmer, Cutler and Pickering, represented me tirelessly and excellently in extracting from the FBI such parts of my file as I have been able to obtain. Marvin Frankel, Linda Kerber, and Eben Moglen read the manuscript and offered a great many useful suggestions. Marvin Chirelstein, Jackie Farber, Eric Foner, Jerome Skolnick, and Jay Topkis also were helpful with editorial advice.

For whatever in these pages is wrong the fault is mine.

My life at LDF was one of dedication and work in a cause. But, like others on the staff, as the reader may discern from a part of the story touched only in passing, most of us integrated work into personal lives of family, friends, fun, and, certainly for Thurgood and me, food and drink. Since I haven't wanted to write an autobiography, I've told only enough of that aspect to enable the reader to know of its existence. Surely, however, it requires a word of acknowledgment to my children, Josiah, David, Sarah, Ezra, Suzanne, and Billy, as well as my grandchildren, Jessica, Sam, and Julia, that my life with them has been as important, or more important, than my life with LDF. As I traveled and immersed myself in work, they may sometimes have doubted it. And Debby, who has read these pages and offered informed counsel on this book and everything else that matters, has meant more to me than I can express in these pages.

Finally, a word of thanks to my editor, Susan Rabiner, who helped me immeasurably in reshaping massive materials, which were often complex and confusing and which dealt with many events that went on at the same time. At LDF we frequently handled many school, employment, criminal, demonstration, and other cases simultaneously, usually at all levels of the judicial system, while raising funds, fending off critics, and planning for the future. Often it wasn't easy to sort it all out for presentation in an intelligible manner. If the story is accessible to the nonspecialist reader, she deserves much of the credit.

PART I

PREPARING THE GROUND

1

PROLOGUE: THE MOSES OF THE JOURNEY

He guided us through the legal wilderness of second-class citizenship. He was truly the Moses of that journey. He lived to see us close to the promised land of full equality under the law, closer than even he dared hope when he set out on that journey and so much closer than would have been possible without his genius and his leadership.

—William H. Hastie, speaking at the funeral of
Charles Hamilton Houston

I met him only once, and my only memory of the man is like a fleeting twenty-frame image of a famous but long-gone relative caught in an old family movie. Thurgood Marshall was walking Charles Hamilton Houston back to his own office, past mine, and he stopped for a moment to introduce me. They went into Thurgood's office and closed the door. That's all.

I recall high cheek bones, receding hairline, wide eyes, a broad, generous face that suggested—maybe reading what I knew of the man into what I was seeing—compassion and pain. I saw in that face everything I'd heard about this special man during the brief time I had been at the NAACP Legal Defense and Educational Fund (LDF). At Houston's funeral in 1950, Thurgood simply repeated what he had been saying to those of us at the Fund all along: "We wouldn't have been anyplace if Charlie hadn't laid the groundwork for it."

Though I had met him for only that one brief moment, I became immensely curious about the life of this singular man, for though he was only peripherally involved with the work at the Fund during my time there, his shadow was across everything we did. He was taken from us early, at the age of fifty-five, and I have sometimes wondered how different things might have turned out had he lived longer. His greatest contribution lay in conceiving a grand strategic framework and in educating his students at Howard University Law School to do legal battle for racial equality, and in his continuing guidance of his protégés. And so, at the time of his death, untimely though it was, the struggle was left not leaderless, but with an entire generation of talented people who had been well trained to continue the fight.

While working at LDF, before I resolved all doubts about whether I could spend my career as a civil rights lawyer, I took evening courses at Columbia University on the way, I hoped at the time, to an eventual Ph.D. in political science. Perhaps someday I would be a college professor. As things turned out, a heavy litigation schedule prevented me from keeping up with the course work. After leaving LDF many years later, and still without the Ph.D., I did become a professor at Columbia Law School and in 1989 dean of Columbia College, where I also taught before returning to the law school— a long way around.

During the time I was still working toward a doctoral degree, I planned to write my dissertation on Houston's life, and in connection with this project interviewed Houston's father, who survived his son and was still at the firm once known as Houston, Houston, Hastie and Waddy. The Washington office I went to was small and not at all elegant. Charles Houston and William H. Hastie were no longer there. The firm specialized in representing black railroad workers and their unions. William Houston spoke proudly of his son's academic honors and his achievements as a lawyer and as a human being passionately devoted to justice.

By then I knew quite a bit about the remarkable reputation of Charles Houston: a towering intellectual; a law dean on a magnificent scale, one who almost single-handedly changed the education, and so the expectations, of America's black law students; a legal and social architect who conceived the legal campaign that developed into the work of the LDF, which in turn helped change American law and the way it was practiced. But from his father I learned of a living, breathing, struggling advocate for justice, often disappointed but never despondent, always hopeful that the future could be better than the present.

He had done his undergraduate work at Amherst College, where he was elected to Phi Beta Kappa. When the United States entered the First World War, he became an officer in this democracy's Jim Crow army and reacted angrily to the racial injustice he witnessed during those years. After the war, at Harvard Law School, he was the first black elected to the *Harvard Law Review*. He graduated in the top 5 percent of his class in 1922. After receiving his law degree, Houston stayed on at Harvard to continue his studies with Felix Frankfurter, becoming one of the few lawyers of his time to earn a doctor of juridical science. He won the law school's Sheldon Traveling Fellowship and used the stipend that came with it to study in Europe, earning a doctor of civil law at the University of Madrid.

In 1924, Houston went into practice with his father in Washington, while teaching part-time at Howard Law School. In 1929, the president of Howard University, Mordecai Johnson, stung by the comment of Supreme Court Justice Louis Brandeis that blacks' legal education had to be improved because he could "tell most of the time when I'm reading a brief by a Negro attorney," decided to do an overhaul of Howard Law School top to bottom. For the job he chose Houston, who in six energy-filled years transformed it from a law school with a part-time faculty and student body into an accredited institution that became a West Point of civil rights, producing an annual crop of lawyers rigorously trained to do battle for equal justice.

All who knew him personally report that Houston was a hard taskmaster. A favorite aphorism of his, often quoted by Thurgood, was "No tea for the feeble, no crepe for the dead." Students sometimes called him "iron pants" or "cement shoes." Thurgood was his student, and in time they worked together on the case that won the first admission of a black applicant to a white Southern law school, the University of Maryland. Houston became part-time counsel of the National Association for the Advancement of Colored People (NAACP) in 1934, and its special counsel in 1935, traveling indefatigably, covering all the Southern states by automobile on a per diem of five dollars, which was not always paid promptly. He was a constant publicist, writing a weekly column, "Along the Highway," for the Baltimore *Afro American*, a leading black newspaper, and regularly for *The Crisis*, the magazine of the NAACP, as well as for the *Journal of Negro Education*. As a journalist, his aim was to educate the white populace about the injustice of racial segregation and to arouse the black populace to oppose it.

He conceived of the notion of the litigation campaign. Using it first to launch a broad-based attack on discrimination in the selection of juries, he drafted legal papers that could be used as a model by black lawyers preparing attacks on such discrimination all over the South. He planned and began an effort to equalize the salaries of black teachers. Southern school boards until then unashamedly maintained two salary scales, one for white teachers, another for blacks, thereby mocking their own self-professed belief in the concept of separate-but-equal.

Houston's most important conception may have been the step-by-step assault on segregation in education, which he began in the mid-1930s with a series of cases against all-white professional schools. After a false start with a case against a school of pharmacology in North Carolina, he focused on states that had no law school offering admission to blacks. He reasoned, first, that judges might start out somewhat receptive to a young man's desire to avail himself of the good legal education being offered right in his home state, even if the young man's skin were dark. And, second, because there were few women among law students, he hoped to make a temporary end run around the ultimate bugbear of white Southerners of the time—the fear that black males would be sitting in classrooms alongside white females.

In 1936 Houston was working in New York as staff counsel to the NAACP and brought one of his star pupils at Howard, Thurgood Marshall, north to work with him. In 1938, he left Thurgood in charge and returned to Washington to go back into private practice with his father. When Houston left he told Thurgood, "Shock troops don't occupy towns." By 1950, under Thurgood's leadership, and by winning some of the first cases on which I worked after coming to the Fund, LDF had succeeded in the graduate and professional school campaign that Houston had begun fifteen years earlier. Tragically, in April 1950, before Houston could rejoice in these hard-won victories, he died of a heart attack. He had been working at the time on the precursor to the District of Columbia case that became one of five cases later known as the School Segregation Cases or *Brown v. Board of Education*, decided by the Supreme Court in 1954.

IF HOUSTON HAD LIVED

I have often wondered about the joy, anguish, and disappointment Charles Houston would have experienced if his life had been as long as his father's and he had lived until 1978, or even a half-dozen years more, until 1984, the year I left LDF. He would have lived to see a long series of civil rights victories, in all of which the LDF played a leading part. Following the Supreme Court's 1950 ruling ordering Southern states to admit blacks to their graduate and professional schools came the landmark 1954 victory in the School Segregation Cases, which extended the concept of equal educational access to all public schools and in doing so erased the fifty-eight-year-old stain of separate-but-equal as a viable precedent in American constitutional law. But he would also have seen a furious Southern racist counterattack, called "massive resistance," that was launched against the NAACP, the LDF, and civil rights advocates generally, one that included efforts to enjoin us from functioning and, even at times, to disbar our lawyers for being too good advocates of their cause. What would he have thought of 101 Southern representatives and senators signing a congressional manifesto denouncing the Supreme Court, or twentieth-century Southern states resurrecting and re-adopting pre–Civil War declarations of interposition and nullification and establishing state sovereignty commissions, all in almost comic efforts to deny the power of the national government to enforce constitutional rights extended to all citizens nearly a hundred years before? He would have seen Congress come within a single vote of stripping the Court of large parts of its jurisdiction and heard respected pillars of many communities calling angrily for the impeachment of Chief Justice Earl Warren. What would he have thought of those white citizens councils that tried to inflict economic damage on any who dared go on record for equality and sanity in race relations, while the Ku Klux Klan and its sort regularly threatened and often took the lives of these same people, while broadly read journalists like James J. Kilpatrick ground out columns that purported to explain how the Supreme Court had overreached in extending the equal protection of the law to all its citizens?

But Houston would also have seen us triumph and his prize student appointed first to the Court of Appeals for the Second Circuit, only the second black so appointed, and then to the United States Supreme Court, the very first black ever to sit on the Court. It was upon Thurgood's appointment to the court of appeals that the LDF board selected me to succeed him. The selection came as a shock to me. Over the years, Thurgood had given me more and more responsibility and had put me in charge of the office during the time he was in London advising the Kenyan delegation during the Lancaster House conference that negotiated that country's independence from Britain. But I had certainly never politicked for the job nor, until the day Thurgood called me into his office to tell me what the board's decision would be, had I ever dreamed of getting it.

Thurgood had discussed his successor with the board of directors, he told me that day, and they had decided that I should be the new chief counsel. Virtually all the members of the board, which included a broad spectrum of black leadership—among them Bill Hastie, who, with Thurgood, probably had been closest to Houston—attended the meeting at the Roosevelt Hotel, where they took the formal vote. Those who didn't attend wrote or called to express agreement. I have always believed I had good reason to hope that Houston would have joined with them.

On the other hand, the NAACP, from which Thurgood had years earlier decisively declared the Fund's independence, objected to LDF making its own decision about its new chief counsel, and probably would have made a different choice. The rift reflected a preexisting conflict that has dogged relations between the Association and LDF until this day. These days, when black–white tension is so much in the news, it may seem astonishing that a black leadership group selected a white as its head. Though it would be naive to say that my race did not come up, the black press and lawyers with whom we worked in those days endorsed the choice, probably because the goal of the LDF had always been to secure equal opportunity for all, regardless of race. Moreover, they all knew me well.

Still, Dorothy Rosenman, a board member, the wife of Sam Rosenman, who had been counsel to Presidents Roosevelt and Truman, told me that when Thurgood consulted her, she asked, "Won't they say the Jews are running everything?" Thurgood did not hesitate. "Anyone who would say that," he told her, "would say it no matter who was selected." When in 1992 my successor, Julius Chambers, decided to retire after eight years as director-counsel, he prepared a list of possible successors that included black, white (including Jewish), and Asian candidates. LDF was then and is now genuinely interracial in staff and board.

As Thurgood was leaving LDF, he repeated to me Houston's statement: "Shock troops don't occupy towns." But the job that fell to me was no more one of occupation than the job Thurgood inherited when he assumed the leadership. If anything, my years at LDF, spanning the birth and rise to national attention of what came to be called the civil rights movement, were often more tumultuous than anything that had occurred in the past.

If Houston had lived through my tenure as head of LDF, he would have seen a broadly based civil rights movement emerge, flourish, and achieve many of the advances he had called for so long ago. He would have seen the LDF grow from five lawyers with a budget of about half a million dollars to twenty-five lawyers and a $6.5 million budget by the time I resigned in 1984.

Even in the 1930s Charles Houston had had clients who, in sporadic acts of courage or anger, defied Jim Crow by refusing to sit in the back of the bus. By 1960, that courage and anger had caught fire all over the South. He would have been gratified to see thousands of young men and women, black and white, of all faiths, joining in the movement—marching, picketing, expressing their commitment to racial justice in every way they knew—while a new generation of lawyers stood trained and ready to defend them when they came under attack by entrenched forces. When a great leader of the mass movement, Martin Luther King, Jr., emerged, LDF was his lawyer. Through the 1960s, usually in company with local black lawyers, some of whom had been Houston's students, the LDF defended the movement, student sit-in demonstrators, Freedom Riders, as well as movement leaders such as Dr. King, Ralph Abernathy, John Lewis, and Hosea Williams, and won virtually all of the thousands of cases it tried. As the sit-ins spread, a new president, John F. Kennedy, coupled the usual presidential calls for respect for the law with references to the right to petition for the redress of grievances. In 1964, after Kennedy had been assassinated, Lyndon Johnson, a Southerner nobody could have predicted would become the courageous civil rights pioneer he became, signed the first comprehensive civil rights legislation since Reconstruction, consisting of many measures Houston had long ago advocated, for example, fair employment and public accommodations acts and a prohibition on spending federal funds on discriminatory activities. Then Johnson did something even Houston might have had a hard time imagining. If Houston were to return to earth today I would recommend that he be seated before being told that Thurgood Marshall had been appointed to the United States Supreme Court, and that the former citadel of reactionary intransigence, the United States Senate, had confirmed him.

Houston would have witnessed the LDF moving on to mobilize its skill and experience to breathe the life of judicial sanction into the many provisions of the civil rights legislation, an effort that continues even today. In the late 1960s, the 1970s, and beyond, our cases enforced the new law requiring those offering public accommodations to serve everyone; gave substance to the Equal Employment Opportunities Act; succeeded in establishing the right of fair treatment for prisoners; and created certain basic rights for poor people in the administration of justice, like the right to a hearing before a creditor could attach their wages. Employing Houston's paradigm of a litigation campaign, we tried and failed to invalidate capital punishment as racially discriminatory (actually, we won cases holding it unconstitutional as administered in 1972, but in 1976 lost others upholding procedures that had been newly crafted to avoid proscription under the 1972 decision); our efforts did at least introduce a modicum of procedural fairness into the barbaric process of capital punishment.

We were more successful in persuading the Supreme Court, in 1977, to outlaw capital punishment for rape, a sentence that had been more consistently and more blatantly racist in application than any other in American law. We made Southern schools the most desegregated in the country, at the same time fighting school segregation in many cities, north and south, by extending the controversial concept of busing. We took a leading role in defending affirmative action. LDF played a large part in enforcing and amending the 1965 Voting Rights Act.

Black lawyers now sit on the supreme courts of Alabama, Arkansas, Mississippi, Florida, and other Southern states; black federal judges are on the bench all over the South. At the Association of the Bar of the City of New York, a recent meeting for minority lawyers interested in becoming judges attracted so large an audience that it filled the enormous Great Hall of the association. As a result, in part, of LDF work over the years, a large black middle class has emerged.

Houston's experience of segregation as an officer in the First World War had grated badly, and all of his life he had campaigned continuously to secure integration of the armed forces. As staggering as Thurgood's appointment to the Supreme Court would have been for Houston, he might perhaps have been even more astonished by Colin Powell's appointment as chairman of the joint chiefs of staff in 1989.

THE PROMISED LAND IN REALITY

But no promised land ever turns out to be as true to its promise as we hope it will be when we view it from afar. If, to employ Hastie's metaphor, we are now in the promised land of "full equality under the law," or even of *nearly* full equality under the law, it is also true that many other gross inequalities based on race remain firmly in place. The now-substantial black middle class has moved from the inner cities, leaving behind drug-ravaged ghettoes. Social and economic problems associated with race seem in many ways even more intractable than the legal barriers Houston faced. But we can console ourselves by recalling that as refractory as the present difficulties seem to be, the prospects for victory seemed equally remote in the days of that earlier struggle for legal equality. There is no guarantee that we will triumph over the present tragic situation, but the fact that victory is not in sight and that the way to achieve it is in dispute doesn't mean that improvement and success won't come. The first prerequisite for progress is to want to achieve it and to determine to work at it.

Some tend to look back on history as a chain of events, each new event, on cue, jumping into place to allow itself to be forged onto the chain. Such is not the case, of course. Only in retrospect do certain historic milestones appear to have been part of an inevitable progression. For example, the victory against the University of Maryland, the first decision ensuring the right of blacks to attend a graduate school with whites in a border state, and the *Brown* decision, ending segregation in all state-supported education, may appear from today's perspective to have been firmly linked by historical determinism. Yet two decades had to pass between these important decisions, and through that long period there were none of us who saw ourselves as riding, stop to stop, along railroad tracks that history had laid down for us. We were acutely aware that making the wrong choices—presenting inadequate evidence or arguing unpersuasive theories—as well as choices made by others, could bring our progress to a halt, or even, our worst fear, bring about a regression in racial justice similar to the one that had gripped the country in the last quarter of the nineteenth century.

For many of their earlier years in the conflict, Thurgood Marshall and Charles Houston were lonely warriors: The American Bar Association reflected and validated the widespread prejudice within the practicing bar by excluding blacks from membership. Virtually no Southern white lawyer would represent a civil rights litigant. No major foundation would support the LDF until the late 1960s. Southern leaders and the Southern press called us Communists so often that many Americans came to believe that where there was smoke there must be fire. Klansmen and their ilk threatened Thurgood's life and mine. During the Autherine Lucy case in 1956, in which a black woman whom we represented was driven from the University of Alabama campus by rioting whites, an Alabama politician called Thurgood a Communist. Informed of this by a reporter, Thurgood replied, "So is his mother." We spent an anxious and amused night waiting to see whether the press would carry the quote, hoping it would and hoping it wouldn't. It didn't.

At most difficult moments those carrying the struggle did not have the world at their shoulder telling them that the way they were going about it was just right. At the outset of the campaign against school segregation in the mid-1930s some black spokespeople, including W. E. B. Du Bois, counseled against it. On the eve of *Brown*, Marjorie McKenzie, a leading black journalist, opposed our efforts. White liberals, like Harry Ashmore, editor of the *Arkansas Gazette*, argued that there was so much opposition to desegregating schools that the Supreme Court would rule against us. James William Fulbright, whose fellowships added luster to his name and made him a darling of the academy, filed a brief against us in the Supreme Court when we opposed Arkansas Governor Orville Faubus's attempt to suspend integration in Little Rock in 1958. President Dwight Eisenhower's decision to strip Faubus of his power by nationalizing the Arkansas Guard, and then to post troops to Little Rock to enforce the court order, was criticized by some of the national press as too provocative, too draconian a measure, taken too early in the negotiations—a general's solution, some said, to a political problem. It is not surprising, then, that when we tried to bring about the court-ordered admission of James Meredith to the University of Mississippi in 1962, John F. Kennedy waffled, attempting to negotiate with the racists who had promised to block Meredith's way. Finally, unable to bribe, placate, or win over the state's governor, Ross Barnett, he belatedly directed federal marshals to enforce the court order we had won, by force if necessary, and Meredith entered the university through tear gas and gunfire that cost several lives.

Alas, even among people similarly committed to good causes there will be conflict and struggle. Thurgood had insisted on our independence from the NAACP, which I maintained. The Association fought the separation, and this led to conflict between us. We defended the newer soldiers in the struggle for equal rights, including Martin Luther King, Jr.'s Southern Christian Leadership Conference (SCLC) and the Congress of Racial Equality (CORE); sadly, this moved us farther from the Association, which resented our support for those it saw as its parvenu rivals. The Association mistakenly accused LDF of having received funds it felt it deserved, arguing— wrongly—that the funds had come to us because of the close association of our two organizations in the minds of most contributors. In 1980 the NAACP sued us to make us change our name, and lost.

Internal conflict tore LDF apart over my refusal to represent Angela Davis when California indicted her in the kidnapping and murder of a judge. Black students at Harvard picketed Julius Chambers and me when we taught a course at the law school, because they objected to a white professor teaching a civil rights course, even, apparently, in conjunction with a black professor. Some black college presidents protested because they thought LDF was trying to put them out of business by seeking to integrate higher education. We fought the Nixon and Reagan administrations when they tried to roll back advances of the previous decades. The struggle was hard then. It is hard now. If it seems harder now, or easier, it is only because it is different.

MY COUNTERFACTUAL NOVEL

At one time I thought of writing a novel about an America in which the NAACP Legal Defense and Educational Fund had never existed, in which Charles Houston had never envisioned the concept of the legal campaign and Thurgood Marshall had never directed the organization that carried it out. The great victories—the 1944 White Primary Cases, which enabled blacks to participate meaningfully in Southern politics; the Restrictive Covenant Cases (1948), which prohibited courts from enforcing agreements to exclude blacks from housing; and the 1954 decision in *Brown v. Board of Education*, which signaled the end of legal segregation—would not have occurred in my fictional world. The civil rights movement of the 1960s, inspired by those victories, might not have been born, at least not at that time and quite likely not as a nonviolent movement. If by some chance it had been born, it could not have long survived without effective legal defense. Without a forceful movement, the Civil Rights Acts would not have been adopted. If by happenstance some similar measures were adopted, they might not have survived the baptism of fire that court challenges exposed them to, and might never have developed into effective instruments for social justice.

In my novel, a few border states—Arkansas, Delaware, eastern Tennessee, Kentucky, Maryland, and West Virginia—would slowly open lunch counters, theaters, department stores, and other public accommodations to blacks on an equal basis, though only within a few major cities; only a token number of blacks would be admitted to the white world of higher education. It is hard to believe that in the absence of that great effort known as *Brown v. Board of Education*, the lower grades would never have undergone systemic desegregation in the South, but some private elementary and high schools in those areas might have admitted a handful of black students. If so, great controversy would have surrounded even these small breaches, and the white South would have fought to remain true to the beliefs it cherished during the Civil War and for nearly a century thereafter. In this very different America, black elementary and high schools remained racially segregated and inferior, with hand-me-down textbooks from white schools and rundown schoolhouses.

The novel continues: Without recourse to the courts and unable to vote, Southern blacks would turn to peaceful sit-ins, Freedom Rides, picketing, and demonstrations. As in the 1960s, they would be beaten, arrested, and jailed. Virtually no white lawyers would defend them, and the few black lawyers willing to try to handle the huge volume of cases would be largely unschooled in sophisticated constitutional litigation and without sufficient resources. No national legal organization would exist to back them. In the Deep South the protests were suppressed, as they were in the real story by Chief of Police Bull Connor and his police dogs and fire hoses in Birmingham, when Martin Luther King, Jr., tried to march on Good Friday, and by

Sheriff Jim Clark and his tear gas–equipped mounted posse at the Edmund Pettus Bridge, when demonstrators first attempted to walk from Selma to Montgomery.

Frustrated in their attempts to protest nonviolently, blacks in my novel would finally accept the lesson that Bull Connor was trying to teach them: Only might makes right. The movement would start to develop its skill at underground tactics. Terrorism, bombings, shootings, general strikes, disruption of government and the courts would become the order of the day. Northern ghettoes, which in real life have rioted under more benign circumstances, would join the rebellion. Troops would occupy key points to prevent violence. The nation would begin to resemble Northern Ireland, only worse, perhaps South Africa under apartheid or Peru facing the Shining Path. Many in the North and a few liberals in the South would be torn between acknowledging the clear justice of the ends of the freedom fighters and deploring their tactics. White Southern congressional committee chairs, who had achieved seniority by being elected again and again in the one-party South by a Democratic party that had never been prevented from excluding blacks, would block efforts to enact civil rights laws. Efforts to bypass committees and bring bills to the floor would be defeated by filibusters.

Once the novelist's mind has taken the country this far, what can be done to reverse the damage and restore American democratic institutions to vitality? A second Civil War? Repeated truces, followed by arrangements that would falter without success? Endless struggle, as in Northern Ireland? A police state struggling to keep blacks in their place, like South Africa before global condemnation and internal resistance forced some sense upon the country's rulers?

I never did figure out the end to my novel. Maybe once I had taken the country so far down this path, I realized that there was no longer a good end to the story.

Happily, the America of real life followed a different course. Fortunate for the country, there was an LDF with the vision, resources, courage, and intellect to move America ahead on the path of racial justice. I was lucky, too, to have been a part of that noble effort.

2

SOWING SEEDS

THE ASSOCIATION

Before lawyers can win cases there have to be clients willing to stand up for their rights. The American blacks who proved willing to fight segregation and discrimination were organized for the most part by the National Association for the Advancement of Colored People (NAACP), in an environment hostile to change in the kind of justice afforded blacks. The NAACP was created in 1909, in reaction to a lynching in Springfield, Illinois, the home of Abraham Lincoln. The new group's object was to seek "equal rights and opportunities for all." William English Walling, a white Southerner, and W. E. B. Du Bois, the great black scholar and social activist, members of an earlier group, the Niagara movement, were among the NAACP founders.

Du Bois has written, "We had on our board of directors many incongruous elements. . . . philanthropists like Oswald Villard; social workers like Florence Kelley; liberal Christians like John Haynes Holmes and liberal Jews like the Spingarns; spiritual descendants of the Abolitionists like Mary Ovington and radical Negroes." It was run by a staff selected by a board of directors, elected by members in many branches across the country. It, therefore, expressed the values that informed a wide sampling of the black communities across the country, and in turn was able to influence those values.

Headquartered from the beginning in New York City, by 1940 the NAACP had more than 350 branches and 50,000 members. By 1945 NAACP income had grown to $401,000, and by 1947 its membership was 369,000. The war apparently brought hope that if blacks participated in the fight to save democracy, they would be allowed to participate fully in the democracy of their native land, a hope that quickly proved hollow. By the time I joined LDF in 1949, the Association was in a steep decline, with membership falling to 149,000 in 1950 and income to $260,000.

Though Association branches existed across the country, most members were in the South, where the overwhelming number of black Americans then lived. That fact, along with the reality that lawsuits were more effective against virulent Southern racism and state-sanctioned segregation laws than against the often covert Northern variety of each, led lawyers to focus the legal attack in the South.

The organization, though fully secular, was made up mostly of members of those Protestant denominations that dominated the South. Gloster Current, the Association's director of branches for almost thirty years, estimates that perhaps 55 percent of the members were Baptists and close to 40 percent Methodists of one sort or another. Almost always they attended black churches. A few, like Thurgood, were Episcopalians; there were some Presbyterians, members of the United Church of Christ, and other denominations where the congregations were somewhat more likely to be integrated. The black church was a vital ally; in the South most meetings were held in churches. When I spoke to NAACP branches in the South, which I did often, it was occasionally at the black YMCA or YWCA, at a black college, or at a black union local, but most often it was in a church.

The NAACP was essentially a political action organization, consisting of a branch department that sold and recorded memberships, a labor secretary, a church secretary, a public relations office, and *The Crisis* magazine, once a journal of considerable intellectual reputation, particularly when edited by W. E. B. Du Bois, but later a practical house organ that kept the membership informed about the Association and the issues in which it was interested.

For most of this century, the NAACP was the only civil rights organization that made a difference. The Urban League existed through much of this time (it was founded in 1910), but in its early life had none of the influence later gained under Whitney Young, who from 1961 to 1971 transformed it into an effective national force, or under Vernon Jordan, who succeeded him and also achieved national leadership. In pre–Whitney Young days, the Urban League was sometimes derisively referred to as "the colored employment agency," where one looked to hire someone black or where a black person went to find a job, too often without success. In 1949, Martin Luther King, Jr., had not yet graduated from the seminary; the Southern Christian Leadership Conference did not yet exist and wouldn't become a force until the early 1960s. The Congress of Racial Equality (CORE), a small interracial organization originally interested in promoting pacifism that later developed a program in civil rights, was born in Chicago in 1942, but did not attain national prominence until its sponsorship in 1961 of the "freedom rides," attempts by integrated groups to end segregation on interstate buses by riding them, seated in sections from which blacks were banned. The student movement that would develop out of the sit-ins of 1960 and give birth to the Student Nonviolent Coordinating Committee (SNCC) was not yet imaginable.

The dominant figures at the NAACP of the time were Walter White, who was the secretary (the highest executive officer), and Roy Wilkins, the assistant secretary. White was an anomaly, black by legal and sociological definition (in Georgia, where he came from, a black was by statute someone with "any ascertainable drop of Negro blood"), but he looked and dressed like a tweedy English country squire and had blue eyes, pale white skin, pink cheeks, silky white (once blond) hair, and a white mustache. He sniffled a lot as he spoke, his speech carrying a bit of an English accent. His flair for the dramatic and considerable personal courage (in 1918 he investigated a lynching in Georgia, pretending he was white) made him exceptionally useful to the cause. A few national political figures opposed racial discrimination, and White worked closely with them. He published many books and articles. He was generations ahead of his time in recognizing the international dimensions of human rights, pleading for anticolonialism and racial equality worldwide. At a time when it was important that the country and the world understand the true conditions of American blacks, he was a superb publicist.

Politically, he achieved miracles in the face of black people's insuperable political disability—near total exclusion from the ballot box in the area where most of them lived, the South, and Southern domination of congressional politics. The South was a one-party region, electing only Democrats, where the Republican party still suffered from the taint of having been the party of Lincoln and of Reconstruction. As a one-party region, it returned the same people to the U.S. House and Senate year after year, allowing Southerners to become the most senior members of Congress, and to use this seniority to acquire and hold indefinitely most important committee chairs. In this way, the South was able to dominate Congress. To make sure that this disproportionate national influence would be used in the cause of white Southerners only, and not for the advancement of the region generally, the Democratic party in the South—by law, party regulation, chicanery, and thuggery—kept blacks from voting in its primaries, the only elections that mattered in the area.

When representatives of other sections of the country tried to bypass the committee structure in order to enact civil rights legislation, Southern delegations blocked such enactments by endless filibusters, which could be broken only by supermajorities, a condition imposed and sustained by the Southern control of the organizational machinery of the Senate. Southern representatives spoke around the clock and were reputed to have urinated into hot water bottles so that they wouldn't have to leave the chamber and yield the floor. Back home, such conduct made them heroes to their white electorate. With minor exceptions, until the civil rights movement of the mid-1960s, the South was able to frustrate any national effort to make a dent in America's apartheid. In this climate, it was not even possible to pass so basic an expression of a national commitment to justice as an antilynching bill.

The NAACP fought for such a law. Walter White was a confidant of Eleanor Roosevelt and, through her, gained access to Franklin D. Roosevelt. In 1935, FDR tried to explain to White why he had chosen to sacrifice the rights of black Americans to the economic needs of the country as a whole: "I've got to get legislation passed by Congress to save America. The southerners by reason of the seniority rule in Congress are chairmen or occupy strategic places on most of the Senate and House committees. If I come out for the anti-lynching bill now, they will block every bill I ask Congress to pass to keep America from collapsing." By 1940, there had been almost 3,500 lynchings in the country, mostly in the small towns and rural areas of the South. Between V-J Day, the end of the war against Japan, and June 1947, less than two years later, there were twenty-six lynchings of blacks.

Politically, blacks had been Republicans until Roosevelt came onto the national scene. Indeed, Clarence Mitchell, the NAACP Washington lobbyist, and James M. Nabrit, Jr., who fought the District of Columbia school segregation case, remained among the many black Republicans until the 1960s. Although FDR maintained an intransigence on civil rights throughout his presidency, his economic policies, designed as they were to help the very poorest of Americans, offered many blacks an important helping hand in really hard times, and by 1940, 82 percent of black voters supported him and the Democratic party. In the multisided presidential election of 1948—Democrat Harry S Truman; Republican Thomas E. Dewey; Henry Wallace of the Progressive party, a splinter of the left wing of the Democratic party; and Strom Thurmond of the Dixiecrats, a party made up of Southern Democrats, along with the perennial Socialist candidate, Norman Thomas—70 percent of the vote in black areas went to Truman, a former senator and vice president from a border state. While Wallace conducted a campaign that focused on issues that should have been of enormous interest to blacks, the black vote for Wallace was negligible other than in New York and Los Angeles.

The NAACP was nominally nonpolitical and, indeed, had a rule prohibiting its officers from participating in partisan politics. But, while neither Walter White nor Roy Wilkins hesitated to criticize the Democrats for not doing enough and for submitting to Southern domination of its national platform, NAACP leadership approved highly of Truman. Hastie, who held no staff position with the Association (although he served as a member of the board) but was one of its inner circle, campaigned tirelessly for him. Truman's civil rights programs later became crucial for the advancement of black people and, indeed, his committee on civil rights fashioned the agenda for the civil rights developments of the next twenty years.

White was a maverick in other matters as well. While the NAACP was committed to integration in the public realm, there was resentment among many members when White divorced his wife, Gladys, who was black, to marry to Poppy Cannon, a well-known white journalist with an East Side townhouse, which at the time I first saw it was the most elegant residence I'd ever been in. Roy Wilkins found the delegates at the 1949 Los Angeles NAACP convention divided: "Half . . . wanted to lynch Walter for leaving Gladys, and the other half wanted to string him up for marrying a white woman."

A year later, even though White had been on leave for most of the preceding year, the issue was still causing trouble. In 1950, Elizabeth Waring, the wife of J. Waties Waring, the courageous South Carolina judge who had struck down segregation in several cases, sent a telegram to the Association convention, condemning the widespread rejection of Poppy White within the Association:

DISCOVERED MY FRIEND MRS. WALTER WHITE NOT ASKED TO YOUR N.A.A.C.P. TEA REPRESENTED AS BEING GIVEN IN MY HONOR, THEN I AM INFORMED DIVORCED WIFE OF WALTER WHITE ATTENDING YOUR TEA. . . . AN INSULT TO YOUR ASSOCIATES WHO ESTEEM WALTER WHITE AS THEIR LEADER AND . . . AN INSULT TO OUR FRIENDS THE WALTER WHITES AND HENCE I REFUSE TO ATTEND.

Thus it was not surprising that when White returned from his leave of absence after his marriage, the board diluted his authority by making him, Roy Wilkins, Thurgood, and Henry Lee Moon, the director of public relations, coequal in running the organization. Five years later, in 1955, not long after the decision in the School Segregation Cases, White passed away, but by then, at least, many of the changes he had worked for had come to pass.

Roy Wilkins succeeded Walter White as secretary. He was a very different person and provided very different leadership. Born in 1901, he grew up in St. Paul, Minnesota, in a racially integrated neighborhood, and went to the University of Minnesota. He knew the evils of racism, at the time widespread even in Minnesota. In 1920, while Wilkins was in college, three black men were lynched in St. Paul, hung from a light pole after having been accused of raping a white girl. In 1923 Roy became editor of the *Kansas City Call*, a black paper, and remained there for eight years, during which he built the paper's circulation and reputation. In 1931 he moved to New York to join the Association as assistant secretary. He was one of the most urbane, literate people I ever knew. He spoke in a quiet, cool manner, rarely displaying emotion or using hyperbole, in perfect sentences and paragraphs, which if transcribed would not have needed a touch of editing. Roy's rationality dominated everything he did.

His attitudes about religion and racial integration were perhaps best exemplified by his funeral service. It took place at the Unitarian-Universalist church, a denomination that holds no particular profession of faith, doctrine, or creed, in midtown Manhattan. Some blacks openly demonstrated across the street because they believed that the service should have been conducted at a black church in Harlem and with a black funeral director.

CREATING THE NAACP LEGAL DEFENSE
AND EDUCATIONAL FUND

Because the NAACP engaged in propaganda and lobbying, it did not qualify for the tax status that permits contributors to deduct contributions in determining income or estate taxes. Walter White pointed out at a board meeting that John D. Rockefeller, Jr., had refused to renew a $750 contribution because the Association was not tax-exempt. The solution was simple: Set up a separate charitable organization to perform the Association's non-propaganda, nonlobbying activities. As it turned out, after we got tax exemption the Rockefellers didn't contribute anyway—at least not for twenty years. In the 1960s several members of the family began giving, some regularly and substantially.

On March 20, 1940, the NAACP created the NAACP Legal Defense and Educational Fund, Inc. Thurgood drafted the corporate charter on a yellow pad in his own hand. Because the new organization was located in New York, and the word "educational" was in its title, it needed the approval of the New York State Education Department. It also needed permission from the state supreme court because it intended to practice law. Until the LDF was incorporated, permission had been granted to an organization of this sort on only one other occasion. We take for granted today advocacy associations working in the courts, but they were virtually unheard of before 1940. LDF was the first to show how effective such organizations could be.

As part of the procedure admitting the LDF to practice before the Court, the bar associations were asked whether they objected. Arthur Spingarn, an early member of the NAACP who had been involved in most of its Supreme Court cases as a volunteer and who became president of LDF, used his personal influence with the leadership of the Association of the Bar of the City of New York to assure that no one would object. But even with that he had to argue with the presiding justice for eight months before approval was given.

Over this long period, Spingarn almost gave up. Herman Zand, Spingarn's law partner, carried the incorporation papers to the office of the Department of State of the state of New York for filing, but the clerk refused them, because the name included "NAACP," which belonged to the Association. Zand had to go back to the NAACP, which then passed a resolution giving LDF permission to use the initials. The original directors of

the new corporation, which first met March 27, 1940, were all members of
the board of the Association, including William H. Hastie; Herbert H.
Lehman, the governor of New York; Arthur Spingarn; Hubert T. Delany,
who later would become a New York City domestic relations court judge;
Charles E. Toney, a municipal court judge; Mary White Ovington, a founder
of the NAACP; and William A. Neilsen, president of Smith College. Like
the NAACP board, it was interracial: Hastie, Toney, and Delany were
black, the others white. Soon, seven more directors joined, including three
more members of the Association's board. The LDF board was self-perpetu-
ating: The directors, the only members, elected and reelected themselves.
Unlike those of the Association, which had a more or less democratically
elected board, LDF policies, program, and personnel would depend ultimately on the wisdom of the board members themselves. Though the ultimate power remained with them, they soon turned over matters almost
entirely to Thurgood Marshall, their chief counsel, who was closely attuned
to the needs and aspirations of black America. Thurgood was personal
friends with most members of the board. (Arthur Spingarn spoke of Thurgood as a son and, indeed, at his death left small bequests to Thurgood's
two sons, the only ones he made to individuals outside his own family.
Thurgood vacationed at the Spingarn home in Amenia, New York, site of
early, historic NAACP conferences. He later bought the house and then
sold it back to the Spingarn family.)

The Association's influence on the LDF board assured indirect control
over the operations of LDF. Walter White became secretary of LDF, a title
he simultaneously held at the NAACP, and chief executive officer. Soon
the issue of control would come to the surface. It remained a source of
struggle until LDF separated from the Association, and even later as the
NAACP claimed the right to exercise control on the grounds that it had
founded LDF, which continued to maintain the name of its founding body.

White's extroverted personality, which made him so effective, also provoked resentment. He mixed into everyone's business, including the
lawyers', and often they objected. In September 1946, Bob Carter, who during an absence of Thurgood's was acting head of the legal department (and,
for all practical purposes, of LDF), excoriated White in a memorandum sent
"under seal," which presumably meant it was confidential. Bob was
"exceedingly astounded . . . to find that legal decisions are being made without my knowledge or consultation." White had permitted a client to be
interviewed by FBI agents despite Bob's "strenuous objections." As to
another matter, Bob wrote that "I cannot follow your . . . directive that stories, whether potentially libelous or not . . . be referred to non-legal members of the staff in whose judgment in legal matters, I now assume, you
place more reliance than the legal staff as presently constituted." He added
that "I have learned further that you had a lengthy conference with a

Branch representative concerning restrictive covenants. It is indeed strange that such information did not come directly from you but that I have to learn it as an item of idle gossip." He objected also to having heard "for the first time at a Board meeting your recommendation that LaFollette be retained as our attorney to handle our fight to unseat Bilbo [a racist Mississippi senator]," which, Bob wrote, "crystallized your apparent attitude that presently the legal staff is only nominally charged with the making of legal decisions but that you and others are more capable than we in carrying out the Association's legal programs." He admonished Walter that "I am and will be acting head of the Legal Department until Mr. Marshall's return."

These incidents were only part of a generally uneasy relationship between White and the lawyers who were the legal arm of the Association, but at the same time the staff of the increasingly independent LDF. In 1944, White made a tour of military bases in the Pacific. Either because non-lawyers could represent defendants in courts-martial or because he thought White's several honorary doctor of laws degrees qualified him, a judge advocate on Guam suggested that he represent black servicemen there. White publicized that representation. Some of the lawyers made fun of it. Worse, during Supreme Court arguments he would sit within the rail, a section closer to the justices but reserved for members of the Supreme Court bar only. One day, Thurgood told me, he whispered to a marshal, "See that fellow over there. I don't think he's a member of the bar." The marshal politely asked White if he was a member of the Supreme Court bar, and when White answered that he wasn't, directed him to the spectators' section in the rear. Subsequently, White sat in a section of the courtroom reserved for guests of the Justices, courtesy of Justice Hugo Black.

Not surprisingly, when Roy Wilkins took over, relations between the Association and the Fund improved.

FUNDING

The first LDF budget, for 1941, was $13,910, and it grew steadily. In 1945 it was $75,657; in 1946, $82,012; in 1947, $106,805; in 1949, $121,251. The 1950 budget, $390,000, was overly ambitious—in fact the Fund raised only $144,759 that year, still up considerably from the year before.

The Fund grew over these years because it was enormously successful in court and because it had teamed up with a great fund-raiser, Harold Oram. Oram, a former football player at the University of Miami with the frame and demeanor of a middleweight prizefighter, talked tough, his head always cocked to one side. He had been involved in raising money for the Spanish Refugee Relief Campaign during the Spanish Civil War; helped found and raise money for the International Rescue Committee, which aided intellectuals and Socialists in escaping from the Nazis during the Second World

War; and raised funds for National Sharecroppers Week. In these projects he accumulated a list of fifty thousand names of people disposed to support liberal causes to whom LDF could appeal.

In June 1943 a race riot exploded in Detroit arising out of a wildcat strike at the Packard engine plant in protesting the upgrading of three black workers. Thirty-four people were killed, more than six hundred injured. Harold organized a committee of prominent citizens for the NAACP that called upon the public to associate itself with a statement decrying the riots and to contribute to the "establishment of a vitally necessary Defense Fund. . . . We need immediately to raise $25,000 to make possible the legal protection of the American Negro community. . . . Our first job is legal aid for more than 1,200 victims of the Detroit riots. . . . Our fund will be administered by the Legal Defense Department of the National Association for the Advancement of Colored People. Your gift will be tax exempt." One hundred and six well-known Americans signed the statement, including Roger Baldwin, a founder of the American Civil Liberties Union; Edward Bernays, the creator of modern public relations; Mary McLeod Bethune, a leader of the National Council of Negro Women; Mrs. Louis D. Brandeis; Van Wyck Brooks, author and critic; Henry Sloane Coffin, president of the Union Theological Seminary; James Bryant Conant, president of Harvard; Jo Davidson, the sculptor; John Dewey; Albert Einstein; Dorothy Canfield Fisher, a prominent author; Harry Emerson Fosdick, pastor of Riverside Church; Frank P. Graham, president of the University of North Carolina; John Haynes Holmes, pastor of the Community Church; Sidney Hook; Alvin Johnson, director of the New School; Helen Keller; Alfred M. Landon; Archibald MacLeish; Karl A. Menninger; Reinhold Niebuhr; Adam Clayton Powell, Jr.; A. Philip Randolph; Rabbi Abba Hillel Silver; Raymond Gram Swing, a leading radio commentator; Norman Thomas, many-time Socialist candidate for president; Dorothy Thompson, perhaps the first woman syndicated columnist; William Allen White, a best-selling author; and Rabbi Stephen S. Wise. Most of these names need no further description today.

Harold's genius was in recognizing that these names, as well as others on the list who were as well known in their day, would lend credibility to an effort to muster support for civil rights. These days, the power in such a list is apparent, because we know so much more about the value of endorsements. In those days it must have seemed to some like a lot of work for little return to get commitments from all those busy people. The mailing was a great success and when the committee's work was done Harold felt that it would be a pity to disband it. He proposed making it the core of a "committee of one hundred" to be set up for the purpose of raising funds for LDF. The committee, he urged, "should include only the top flight liberals and the neo-liberals like Conant, [Robert M.] Hutchins, [Seth] Milliken, bank presidents, etc. . . . I would include great Negro artists such as Marian

Anderson, Paul Robeson, Roland Hays, etc., as well as a sprinkling of the leading Negro educators and professionals of the country.... I would tie them up with one burning issue in each case, timely and dramatic. Nothing like housing but much about lynching," he wrote to an associate while still in the army.

In 1943 Harold Oram and Company entered into a contract with the Fund and set up the Committee of 100 as a group that would appeal to the public to support LDF. Its first chair was William Alan Neilsen, president of Smith College, who was on the LDF board and Harold's father-in-law. The Committee of 100 did mass mailings, which Harold wrote, over Neilsen's signature; arranged parties to which potential big givers were invited to meet top LDF lawyers; and held dinners, benefits, and other events. In later years Harold was in the forefront of raising funds for other groups that have become important national institutions, including Planned Parenthood and the Natural Resources Defense Council.

One of Harold's vice presidents, Anna Caples Frank, became, for all practical purposes, an LDF staff member and took immediate charge of its fundraising. Anna was a slim, very attractive young woman, unaccountably shy and self-effacing, but enormously effective and enthusiastic. She came from Norfolk, Virginia, and had gone to Vassar, where she became involved in Socialist party activities. She went to Prague in 1935–36, when she was in her twenties, with Karl Frank, a German Socialist, whom she later married. Reinhold Niebuhr performed the ceremony. Using her precious American passport she entered Germany a number of times to help endangered Socialists. Lillian Hellman, without attribution, modeled her heroic character Julia, who risked her life in similar exploits, on Muriel Buttinger, Anna's close friend and collaborator in these adventures.

It is almost impossible to disentangle Committee of 100 income from that of LDF generally, because the committee indirectly stimulated contributions directly to the Fund. A fair estimate is that the Committee of 100 raised $15,000 in 1943, $59,000 in 1944, $63,000 in 1945, $93,000 in 1946, $79,000 in 1947, $124,000 in 1948, $107,000 in 1949, and $121,000 in 1950, all in rather small contributions; a big contribution was $100, and $1,000 was a tremendous gift. The typical giver was, as Harold put it, "a New England abolitionist type." Not until the late 1960s and early 1970s—after the civil rights movement exploded—did any of the great foundations contribute, having completely defaulted until then in their professed mission of pioneering where government dared not tread. A few smaller foundations like Field and New York and, soon, Norman contributed as early as the 1950s. These were relatively small family foundations that typically made grants not much larger than $5,000 or $10,000 in those days.

SUPPORT—AND LACK OF IT—FROM THE BAR

In 1941, the NAACP board reconstituted its National Legal Committee, chaired by Bill Hastie, consisting of outstanding black and white lawyers and scholars. None were what might have been called "leaders of the bar," for example, president of the American Bar Association, or a state or local bar association, or senior partner in a national firm that represented major corporations or persons of great wealth, though one of the whites, Francis Biddle, a member of the bar establishment, became attorney general of the United States that year, and could not continue on the committee. Moorfield Storey, a former president of the American Bar Association, who was a volunteer for the NAACP in the Supreme Court in the 1920s and 1930s, was an anomaly as a member of the establishment bar in openly supporting civil rights for blacks.

At that time, major law firms almost never hired blacks or Jews—most of the whites on the National Legal Committee were Jews—and the American Bar Association, which rejected Hastie's application for membership in 1939 because of race, did not admit blacks. While the committee was effective and influential, it was on, or maybe even outside, the fringes of the legal establishment. Nevertheless, that Biddle had been involved, and Felix Frankfurter had been a member of an NAACP advisory lawyers committee until his appointment to the Supreme Court in 1939, marked the group of lawyers who advised the Association as powerful.

Harold's Committee of 100 created a sort of *Good Housekeeping* stamp of approval for the uninformed and timid who might wonder whether the Fund was really respectable. While that wasn't its main function, the National Legal Committee served the same purpose for the NAACP. Most of the lawyers on both committees worked with LDF in one way or another, and some, like Hastie, W. Robert Ming, and Benjamin Kaplan, consulted a great deal. But the committee never met as a group; it had no power to decide or demand courses of action.

While LDF and Association staff had different tasks, leading at times to some conflicts, socially we mixed together as a single entity. There was probably no more friction than exists in most organizations. We were united in fighting discrimination. Every Friday afternoon someone got a bottle of bourbon or Scotch and a poker game would ensue, with both LDF and Association people playing. I didn't play because I discovered in the navy that I almost always lost. Connie Motley, another assistant counsel with whom I shared an office, didn't play either; no women played.

There was a lot of racial, but not racist, banter at these social gatherings. Those who today are concerned about politically correct language would have been jolted. But it was no different from how other groups who have been victimized—Hispanics, Jews, gays and lesbians, for example—refer to each other when they are in a party mood and among friends. One NAACP staff member was as dark as the darkest African. Some referred to him as

"Little Boy Blue," and sometimes when he entered a room someone would call out "Who turned out the lights?" At first I thought it cruel, but nobody, including the person who was the butt of the remarks, seemed concerned.

There also was a certain locker room kind of bragging, perhaps half in jest, about who was the "HNIC" (Head Nigger in Charge), or simply "HN." There was no doubt who Thurgood thought was "HN."

The mood always was exciting and upbeat, but we were plunging ahead into the unknown. I have friends who were once South African exiles, but who are now back in South Africa. Whenever I asked them when they thought apartheid would come to an end, they'd say they didn't know. One, Albie Sachs, responded, "Ten years ago I said it would be in five years." I have visited them, after their return, in Johannesburg and Cape Town— where I have stayed at Albie Sachs's house—and the transition seems as though it was inevitable. It was the same with us. Our generally upbeat attitudes told us that legal apartheid in America would end. We knew we were helping to end it. But for a long time we never knew how close we were to that end or even if we were yet on the right road through the maze.

3

FREEDOM HOUSE, 1949

I n September 1949, when I came to work at the NAACP Legal Defense and Educational Fund, its offices were on the fourth floor of Freedom House at 20 West Fortieth Street, just west of Fifth Avenue, in New York City. Early in the century, the seven-storied red brick and granite structure had been a German-American clubhouse. It was later subdivided into offices, its sculpted interior decorations painted over many times, its lovely fireplaces sealed, the original flooring covered with linoleum tiles. The basement, which had once been a beer cellar, was our conference room. A little of the building's history lingered. Once I reached under a radiator to retrieve a coin I'd dropped and found a dust-encrusted microphone. Thurgood called the police, thinking that we were being bugged, but the police had trouble identifying the microphone, a really old piece of business, as any model then in use. Eventually it was decided that it must have been under that radiator for decades. In *The Zimmerman Telegram*, Barbara Tuchman writes of the bugging of another German-American club in New York during the First World War, and upon reading her book, I later thought that our ancient microphone might have been part of a similar attempt by American intelligence to eavesdrop on our German-American club. Anyway, its discovery provided a day of excitement.

Three of us—Constance Baker Motley, Franklin H. Williams, and I—all assistant counsel, worked in a large, high-ceilinged office with big windows facing north, overlooking Fortieth Street, the monumental New York Public Library, and the green lawn and shrubbery of Bryant Park. To our left, also facing Fortieth Street and separated from us by a small office for two secretaries, Thurgood Marshall occupied another office; his desk was at the far end of the room from us. Annette Peyser, a sociologist, sat at a table on the opposite wall, her back to him when she faced her work. At right angles to their room, Robert L. Carter, Thurgood's first assistant counsel, had his own small office. That was the entire staff in those days of the NAACP

Legal Defense and Educational Fund, Inc., the organization directing a legal revolution for American blacks, which, by 1949, was already well advanced.

Thurgood Marshall was not only the boss, he was the commanding presence. I first met him in 1947, while working as a law student on a project for LDF. It was the first time I had ever met anyone who had argued a Supreme Court case; it was also the first time I had spoken to a black lawyer. I remember from that meeting only that he drummed his fingers on the glass top of his desk. In 1949 he interviewed me for a job with LDF. The interview was brief. After all, Walter Gellhorn, his good friend and some-time collaborator, had been my teacher for four semesters, and probably told him more about me than he could have learned in a dozen long interviews.

Walter's word was apparently good enough for Thurgood. I would be assistant counsel at a salary of $3,600 per year. Then Thurgood introduced me to Bob Carter, the senior lawyer who worked under him. With the kind of deference he often gave staff members, he told me that Bob really ran the office and that I would take orders from him. But, in fact, Thurgood made all the important decisions, making many of them impulsively or instinctively. If he got a phone call from a cooperating lawyer or civil rights figure who needed help, he would simply ask someone to jump on a plane or train. When John McCray, a black publisher, called Thurgood for help in a criminal libel case, I was sent to Columbia, South Carolina, to represent him. When a case against the all-white University of Delaware arose, I was sent because my in-laws lived there (which meant that I would have a place to stay). I was also sent to Baltimore for a case against the park system, which segregated blacks from whites. Connie Motley got cases in Connecticut, because that's where her family was. I did a little of everything: research for a friend-of-the-court brief on a suit brought by Thurgood's friend Loren Miller in the federal courts in California against American Legionnaires who had roughed up a political meeting; a memorandum on whether we had used the right procedure in a case against the University of Oklahoma graduate school of education; and sundry other research or writing tasks to help out my colleagues.

Juanita Mitchell, a fiery Baltimore civil rights lawyer, whose mother, Lilly, was for decades president of the NAACP Baltimore branch and whose husband, Clarence, was the longtime NAACP Washington lobbyist, has told, in generous terms, of how I was introduced to active litigation in Maryland. She called Thurgood and he said: "Now, Juanita, what is it now?" She asked that Bob Carter be assigned to a case in Maryland, but he replied that Bob was overworked. Juanita reports the conversation between herself and Thurgood:

> "Well, I tell you, Juanita, there's a young Jewish fellow, he's a graduate of . . . Columbia University Law School, very brilliant fellow, and

he says he wants to give his life to this effort. . . . Do you think he can work with the Baltimore branch?" Now, the Baltimore branch, there was some anti-Semitism because the merchants on Pennsylvania Avenue, who are mainly Jewish, stopped our "buy where you can work" campaign by going to a local law firm and getting an injunction. . . . I said, my mother said, "Oh no! Send anybody. We'll welcome Jack." And Jack came down and began to work with us. . . . And he was just, he was like Charlie Houston. He was humble and very brilliant. . . . And Jack Greenberg became one of the stalwarts in the struggle. . . . He came on into the segregated hotels with us and lived with us. And he, he just, we became brothers.

Thurgood had a large network of friends. He was on the phone all the time with law professors in Chicago and in Cambridge, Massachusetts; with cooperating lawyers in Richmond and Dallas; with NAACP officials in Charlotte and Memphis; with Masonic leaders in New Orleans and Tulsa; and with lawyers, political figures, and others on Wall Street. He readily called Averell Harriman and Nelson Rockefeller. He had frequent conferences with legal scholars and cooperating lawyers.

Courts and court officials had confidence in him. When representing a defendant on the eve of execution, he went to the Supreme Court clerk's office to file an application for a stay that had to be signed by a justice. It was late and the last day before the man would be put to death. The clerk took him to the home of Chief Justice Vinson in the Wardman Park Hotel. As Thurgood approached the door of Vinson's apartment, he noticed men in dark suits on either side of the door, which seemed strange. Inside, Vinson was playing poker with Tom Clark, whom Truman had chosen as his attorney general and then appointed to the Supreme Court, and Truman himself. Vinson looked the papers over and said, "I think I'll have to submit these to the Court." He gave them to the "Court," consisting of Truman and Clark, who looked at them, and then he signed the stay. Here was a testament to the confidence that those in power had in Thurgood's responsibility and discretion. I doubt that any other lawyer would have been ushered into that inner sanctum.

Sometimes I thought he called the most improbable people. During the Korean War, Thurgood decided to go to Korea to represent black soldiers accused of failing to have performed their duty. Korea was a war zone and he had to apply for permission to travel there, but it never came. Thurgood was on good terms with J. Edgar Hoover and decided to exploit the relationship. After all, who could help more than J. Edgar Hoover in getting permission to do something that involved national security? I sat in Thurgood's office as his secretary placed the call. He lifted the receiver when she reached her party. Thurgood explained what he was trying to do and asked Hoover's help in getting approval to enter Korea. After listening a moment or two, he expressed a few words of apology and hung up, shaking his head incredulously. The person to whom he was speaking had said, "I wish I could help you Mr. Marshall but I haven't been in government for almost twenty years and don't have any influence in matters of this sort." Only then did he discover that his secretary had put the call through to Herbert Hoover, then living in the Waldorf Towers in New York City! Thurgood finally got the approval—whether with the assistance of J. Edgar Hoover, I don't know—and went to Japan and Korea in December, 1950, for a five-week visit.

After victories in court he called conferences with branch leaders to inform them about what opportunities had been opened up. Like most good leaders, he did more listening than talking, but out of all he heard and absorbed he selected information from which he defined a position. He spoke regularly at NAACP meetings and was more in demand as a speaker than anyone in the Association. In a mass meeting he could bring an audience to its feet, clapping and stomping. In court, he was conversational and usually lectured as a professor might, although sometimes there were emotional riffs full of vivid imagery.

After I had been on the job for a week I received a surprise. Thurgood hadn't talked salary with the board before he interviewed me, and when he did, it authorized only $3,200 per year, instead of the $3,600 he had mentioned to me. Since $3,200 was still a pretty good salary, I wasn't too upset. It wasn't a highly structured place, and pay was not a high priority to anyone there. The board gave him trouble over salaries. Often he gave raises, promising the board it was the last time. It never was. He justified raises to Jim Nabrit III and Derrick Bell on the ground that they had gone to court although he had hired them only to do research.

When I joined the staff Thurgood was only forty-one years old, but he was already a legal giant. Over six feet tall, slender, handsome, with a Levantine nose, narrow, triangular mustache, and thick, wavy black hair combed straight back (one writer described him as resembling a Sikh warrior), he had an accent and manner that he could shift from refined Southern diction to Southern country style—pronouncing "ask" as "axe," "et cetera" as "excetra," "substantial" as "substantual," with lots of double negatives and "ain'ts" filling up his folksy stories. He didn't talk like a choirboy, but neither did he sprinkle his language with "fucking" this and "fucking" that, as one writer has reported. On this, his oldest friends and family agree.

He looked somewhat like Adam Clayton Powell, the fabled New York congressman-preacher, and now and then he was mistaken for Powell. I recall a time shortly after blacks were permitted into Washington's white restaurants when we were waiting in a line that reached out into the street for a table at Harvey's, a wonderful old seafood establishment with large tables, ample tablecloths, and aproned black waiters. One of them, spying

Thurgood near the end of the line, pulled us out of the line and seated us promptly, asking, "Congressman Powell, what would you like to drink?" Thurgood, grateful for small favors, never let on who he really was. Once a hotel elevator operator mistook him for Powell and said, "Reverend Powell, I hope you enjoyed your stay." Thurgood replied, as preacher and politician, "Bless you son, vote for me every time." Oliver Hill and Spottswood Robinson, old friends, sometimes called him "Turkey," but at the office we called him Thurgood or, more often, T. M. He liked to play with names: He often called me "Green bug" or "Jackson" and when Norman Amaker, a young Columbia law graduate, came on the staff in 1960, he sometimes referred to him as "Amaguku." As an affectionate rebuke he might call anyone "knucklehead." His personality immediately dominated any group.

Between 1933 and 1937 Thurgood had been an attorney in private practice in Baltimore, the city where he grew up, his mother a schoolteacher, his father a steward at an establishment men's club. From the beginning of his legal career, he represented civil rights claimants and in 1936, with Charles Houston, won the case in the Maryland Court of Appeals that ordered the first black admitted to a white Southern law school. That year the NAACP national office in New York hired him as assistant special counsel and, in 1938, promoted him to special counsel. With the creation of the NAACP Legal Defense and Educational Fund in 1939, Thurgood was appointed its special counsel as well, and he held both titles simultaneously. In 1944 he and William Hastie won the White Primary Cases, which gained for blacks the right to vote in Southern primary elections. In 1948 the Supreme Court ruled that Oklahoma couldn't exclude Thurgood's client, Ada Lois Sipuel, from an all-white law school during the time it would take to create one just for blacks. That year he and his colleagues also won the Restrictive Covenant Cases, which ended the practice of putting agreements (or covenants) in deeds preventing a piece of property, in perpetuity, from being sold to a black. Any of these landmark victories would have made a lifetime reputation for most lawyers. Thurgood's greatest accomplishments lay ahead of him.

He had graduated from Lincoln University, the only black men's college in the North, not far from Philadelphia, in 1930. (Carter, Williams, and many other black leaders went to Lincoln; it gave me an honorary LL.D. in 1977.) In 1933 he graduated from Howard Law School first in his class, under Dean Charles Houston. Thurgood helped get himself through school by waiting tables in railway dining cars. One of his encounters with reality in this school of hard knocks occurred when he objected that the white uniform trousers that the steward gave him were too short. The steward replied that he could get a new "boy" more readily than a new pair of pants. After graduation in 1933, he started his own practice in Baltimore, keeping his hand in civil rights through his connection with the Baltimore branch of the NAACP, and with Houston, who worked with the NAACP national office.

From his private practice, his work on the railroads, and probably the influence of his father, who in his work at the elite white businessmen's club observed their frailties at close quarters, Thurgood developed a healthy skepticism. He was always alert to fakery and fraud. For instance, he took no sworn statement at face value; he recalled Baltimore's "affidavit men," who loitered on the courthouse steps ready, for a fee, to sign any affidavit.

Early in my days at LDF a black woman visited the office and told me that her son had been sentenced to ten years in prison in Richmond, Virginia, for stealing a bag of peanuts. Shocked, I went to Thurgood's office to urge that we take the case. He picked up the phone and called Martin A. Martin, a Richmond lawyer, and asked him to check out the situation. Martin reported back that the bag of peanuts was one of those enormous burlap bags, the size of a flatbed truck, and that the defendant had hijacked the truck along with it. Thurgood's reply to my request consisted of Martin's report to him, pursed lips, and a raised eyebrow.

He enjoyed telling of a Baltimorean who was a celebrated philanderer and the only black man in town to own a yellow LaSalle automobile, a sort of junior Cadillac. One day the man's wife came upon the car parked on the street in an area where she hadn't expected to find it. As she paused to examine the car, the man came down one of those high stoops typical of Baltimore houses, the home of a woman friend he had been visiting. His wife approached him to ask for an explanation, but never got past uttering his name, "George?" Looking right at her, he replied, "I beg your pardon, madam," walked past her, got into the LaSalle, and drove away. So much for the probative value of the smoking gun.

Thurgood's skepticism contributed to a fundamental caution. While he was committed completely to the distant, ideal goal of ending segregation, he was not always too sure about particular steps or cases on the road to getting there. Sometimes, as we shall see, he restrained colleagues who wanted to dash ahead. Often, he preferred a tentative, brief advance to "going for the gold" all at once. This generated conflict and grumbling about how much caution could be accommodated within a proper commitment.

When he traveled in the South Thurgood never confronted Jim Crow head on, that is, by sitting in sections of railway stations or at lunch counters reserved for whites. Sometimes, with no hotel to stay in, he and Charlie Houston typed legal papers on a portable typewriter while sitting in their car. As he put it, "I wrapped my civil rights in cellophane and put them in my pocket." Sometimes he quipped, "I have a big yellow streak running down my back." Nevertheless, in forays south he could not always avoid personal danger. In 1946 in Columbia, Tennessee, Thurgood, along with the other defense counsel, drove two hundred miles round-trip daily from Nashville—there was no safe place for a black lawyer to stay in Columbia—to the trial arising out of charges lodged against twenty-six black men for assault with intent to commit murder. At one point police picked him up, took him off alone in their car, and charged him with drunk driving. Carl Rowan has written in detail of how they tried to lead Thurgood to the banks of a nearby river where a lynch mob had a rope hanging from a tree, ready for him. Brave, armed black citizens came to his rescue. Fortunately, a courageous magistrate smelled his breath and proclaimed him sober and he was able to return to Nashville.

Thurgood first moved to New York to a tiny two-room apartment on 149th Street and Bradhurst Avenue, north of City College, but as he advanced in the world, relocated to 409 Edgecombe Avenue in Harlem, a building where many black leaders, including Walter White, Roy Wilkins, and W. E. B. Du Bois, resided at various times. Before the pathologies of the ghetto afflicted the neighborhood it was an attractive area, not far from the Harlem River and near Giants' Stadium at the Polo Grounds. But despite its distinctive roster of residents and former residents, the building must at times have been like a fraternity house. Thurgood tells of the night Joe Louis, who lived nearby, chased Tallulah Bankhead screaming through the hallways. Thurgood lived there with his first wife, Vivian, who was called "Buster." She died of cancer in 1955.

Every civil rights leader and lawyer I knew around that time lived in Harlem. Frank Williams, Connie Motley, and Bob Carter lived at Riverton, a red brick series of apartment buildings, a black project that the Metropolitan Life Insurance Company built at 135th Street as a counterpart to its all-white Stuyvesant Town downtown. Today, hardly any of the black lawyers and leaders I know live in Harlem.

Frank Williams, a New Yorker from Flushing, Queens, who with Connie Motley made up the assistant counsel staff, was thirty-two at the time I came aboard. After graduating from Lincoln University in 1941, he finished Fordham Law School in 1945. He spent a year in the army as a private, repeatedly clashing with superiors over segregation, and was soon discharged with a 10 percent disability pension. He may have been the most gifted speaker I ever heard—his admirers use the term "silver-tongued," but even that didn't seem adequate to describe his oratorical skills. Those who didn't like him called him glib. In 1949 Frank went to the Supreme Court with Thurgood to argue *Watts v. Indiana*, a case testing whether a coerced confession could be used against a defendant. Frank, who died in 1990, gave to the Schomburg Center for Research in Black Culture, along with his other memorabilia, a series of notes passed on the occasion between Felix Frankfurter and his law clerk Bill Coleman: "Bill, take a few minutes off to listen to Franklin Williams (do you know him?)." Bill replied, "He is now Mr. Marshall's assistant. . . . I think he studied his law at Howard and comes very highly recommended." Frankfurter returned the note to Bill, striking out "Howard," inserting "Fordham" (Frankfurter had checked Frank's file), and adding "Excellent!"

Frank was tall and thin, had handsome features, and wore suits in the Brooks Brothers style (he couldn't afford the real thing). His incredible energy and independence at times put him in conflict with Thurgood's cautious, conservative, traditional lawyerly approach. Frank bridled at the limitations Thurgood placed on him and relations between them were often tense. When the *Watts* case had first come to the office, the Indianapolis branch of the NAACP opposed taking it, objecting to being associated with a defendant who had been convicted of criminal assault and murder. Frank recalls that Thurgood, likely on the recommendation of the branch, didn't want to represent Watts. Frank fought to take the case, as he tells it, ultimately prevailing on others to persuade Thurgood. Then Thurgood refused to permit Frank to argue the case in the Supreme Court, relenting only at the last minute. When Frank was in Thurgood's office behind a closed door, we sometimes heard angry shouting.

At great personal risk, Frank represented three black youths accused of having raped a white farm housewife in Groveland, in central Florida, in what became known as the Little Scottsboro case. When the case reached the Supreme Court, Frank once more had to fight to be allowed to make the oral argument, Thurgood ultimately allowing him to share the assignment with Bob Carter. Frank also asserts that there were differences with Thurgood over whether to move ahead with the Restrictive Covenant Cases, Frank urging speed and Thurgood caution. When at one time the Association's magazine, *The Crisis*, inadvertently referred to Frank as "special counsel," Thurgood sent him a memo, humorous in tone, but not in import, which said that "all pretenders to the throne may use any . . . exit[s] to the building without picking up any past due salary." It concluded, "Please acknowledge receipt."

Discussing these differences in recent years I suggested to Frank that perhaps Thurgood was under pressure to accommodate the branches, whose support he needed for the overall program (some were more conservative, some more radical), that he had to think twice before allowing a younger lawyer to appear in the Supreme Court, and that he feared bringing cases prematurely because they might make lasting unfavorable precedents. Frank conceded all this might have been true. But it was no surprise when in 1950 he accepted a job in San Francisco as West Coast director and regional counsel of the NAACP, where, he told me, he could give full scope to his energies, be as autonomous as anyone in an organization could be, and provide a better education for his children. Still, he confided to others that he felt he was being exiled. It was his ambition, never realized, someday to return as chief of the NAACP. In the Kennedy administration he got a position in the Peace Corps and was appointed ambassador to Ghana. Following his stint in Ghana he headed the Phelps-Stokes Foundation, which specializes in educational and African programs.

Constance Baker Motley, the third in our group, brought her own special brand of tenaciousness to the cause. When she arrived she was twenty-eight years old, the daughter of immigrants from Nevis, British West Indies (where she recently built a home). She was one of twelve children, three of whom died in infancy. Her father was a cook at Yale and at hotels and restaurants in the New Haven area. While in high school, she was discovered by Clarence Blakesley, a wealthy builder who had constructed the Yale Bowl. He was impressed by her suggestion that the reason blacks did not use a community center he had built was that no blacks were on its board. He helped finance her college education through Fisk and New York Universities. She graduated from Columbia Law School in 1946. While a law student she worked as a clerk at the LDF and continued in that capacity until 1949, when she was promoted to assistant counsel, the same position to which I was appointed. She was married to Joel Motley, a gracious, soft-spoken insurance broker, who was also a law school graduate. Connie was regal in appearance, deliberate in manner and speech, with somewhat of a nasal voice. She was a dogged opponent of Southern segregationists, who found her tougher than Grant at Vicksburg. She dug in to a position and wouldn't let go in the face of all kinds of threats, evasion, obfuscation, and delay.

Long before the days of political correctness, Connie taught me the importance of language, when as a naive young white lawyer I committed the faux pas of saying "Negress," a term then in common use. Connie said that it was like "tigress" or "lioness" and was offensive to black women. Others might have heard me and said nothing or borne a grudge. I learned something. Connie was a straight shooter, always candid.

Slightly above Frank, Connie, and me was thirty-two-year-old Bob Carter, Thurgood's first assistant counsel. Like Thurgood, he was a Lincoln (1937) and Howard law (1940) graduate with an LL.M. from Columbia in 1941. A careful lawyer, he displayed none of the pyrotechnics of Frank Williams or the folksy charm of Thurgood. William H. Hastie, one of his law school teachers, wrote, "Carter has a penetrating mind . . . and independence in thinking which helps him draw his own conclusions without undue deference to the thinking of others." His manner, quiet, even diffident at times, concealed a fierce dedication to his beliefs, perhaps best exemplified by his experience as an army lieutenant during World War II. He encountered vicious racism, but wouldn't submit to it—hardly an easy position to maintain during wartime, when the armed forces were segregated and there was no immediate possibility of changing the policy. He pressed charges against two white enlisted men who had made racial remarks to him and refused orders to live off base, as all other blacks did. The commanding officer transferred him.

In defending a black soldier accused of raping a white woman, Carter proved that she was a prostitute, apparently to establish a defense of consent. In retaliation, a major brought charges against him and he received an administrative discharge, which was neither honorable nor dishonorable and left him subject to the draft. Hastie represented him in a petition to the discharge review board, which changed his discharge to honorable.

Also working at our offices was Annette Peyser, surely the only sociologist to sign Supreme Court briefs with "Research Consultant" after her name. She had graduated from New York University, was very pretty, twenty-eight years old, white, with olive skin and long black hair. In 1946, one of her teachers at NYU, the celebrated political scientist Harold Lasswell, had recommended her for the job of propaganda analyst at the NAACP, where she prepared summaries of press reports and did other research. After Thurgood saw a study of educational inequality she had written, he thought she would be more useful working in his office. There she edited research material on housing and education for use in briefs, gathered expert witnesses, wrote speeches, assisted with law review articles, and worked with other organizations. Once, after she had furnished material for *Inside U.S.A.*, the author, John Gunther, thinking her black, sent her a note of thanks, remarking that she was a "credit to her race."

The staff worked together closely and aspired to be on the cutting edge of the law. Each of us was assigned several law reviews to read regularly. Everyone read advance sheets, early reports of decided cases, so that we'd be prepared for the many informal seminars held by the staff, often in the evenings, sometimes at Bob Carter's apartment. A great deal of work had to be done outside regular office hours, and everyone was on warning not to permit the meetings to degenerate into "bull sessions."

Finally, one other staff member would play a critical role: Spottswood (Spott or Spotts) W. Robinson III was southeastern regional counsel and remained in private practice in Richmond, Virginia. Spotts had studied law at Howard and in 1960 completed the cycle by resigning from LDF to become dean of the law school there, later becoming a judge of the United States Court of Appeals for the District of Columbia. He was pencil-thin, resembling a Modigliani portrait, with small mouth, thin lips, and slicked-back hair. He spoke with a pronounced Southern accent in a high-pitched nasal voice, but his most distinctive quality was meticulousness. When not handling civil rights cases he was mainly a property lawyer, following in his father's footsteps. All the care of the persnickety English conveyancer that he employed in his practice was mirrored in his hobby, woodworking. When I first met him he had a large stack of wood stored in his father's basement, left there under benign conditions of heat and humidity, to season properly. From that wood he eventually built a boat, each plank mitred on both sides and assembled without a single nail, fifteen hundred brass screws holding it all together. To this day he remains proud that the boat has never leaked. He is the only person I know on whom coffee has the opposite of its intended effect—it puts him to sleep.

Guiding all of us, directly and later in spirit, were Charles Hamilton Houston and William H. Hastie. I have written about Houston; more should be said about Bill Hastie. Born in 1904 in Washington, D.C., he also went to Amherst, where he won prizes in Latin, English, and mathematics, graduated Phi Beta Kappa, and was valedictorian, then to Harvard Law School, from which he graduated in 1930. As an editor of the *Harvard Law Review*, he became, like Houston, a protégé of Felix Frankfurter. The NAACP immediately involved him in its work. He also began teaching at Howard and practicing in the Houston firm. In 1937 President Roosevelt appointed Hastie a district judge in the Virgin Islands. He resigned to become dean of Howard Law School in 1939, leaving in 1940 to become a civilian aide to the secretary of war. He quickly began to attack racial discrimination in the armed forces, but the administration had no desire to take on the Southern political establishment when the always Democratic Solid South was that party's reliable support in presidential politics. In protest Hastie resigned in 1943 and returned to Howard. In 1944 President Truman appointed him governor of the Virgin Islands.

Truman's strategy for the 1948 election included seeking the black vote, and he enlisted Hastie to campaign for him. Hastie crisscrossed the country to convince black voters to vote for Truman rather than Henry Wallace, who had made a special effort to win black votes. This was the election, fabled as the archetypical example of how wrong political pundits and pollsters can be, in which Truman upset all predictions by beating Dewey, with surprising support from blacks in key states. Following the election, Truman in 1949 nominated Hastie to the United States Court of Appeals for the Third Circuit in Philadelphia, making him the first black to sit as a lifetime federal judge outside the Virgin Islands. He was not confirmed until July 1950, after bitter opposition by Southern senators that included race- and red-baiting.

Hastie argued and advised on many LDF cases. Before the canons of judicial conduct prohibited judges from serving on boards of litigating organizations, he served on the LDF board, continuing after Thurgood left and I succeeded him. Thurgood found his counsel indispensable, as did I. A tall, straight, handsome man, he was the very embodiment of judicial temperament—soft-spoken, thoughtful, balanced. He died in 1976.

LDF lawyers, frontline lawyers in the South, the Association, and our few friends existed in a racist, segregated environment. The social, economic, and political status of blacks was appalling. Everyday life was a constant affront. After Connie Motley joined the Association of the Bar of the City of New York in 1946, the doorman wouldn't take her word that she belonged and made her wait while he checked the membership list; he allowed her in with "Constance, right this way." She corrected him: "My name is Mrs. Motley." Not until the mid-1960s, when the country was torn by the civil rights movement, did the American Bar Association set up a section on civil rights to parallel its sections on criminal law, corporations, copyright law, and so forth. Not wanting to be misunderstood, it named it the Section on Individual Rights and Responsibilities. If blacks were to have rights they would have to be responsible!

During the Second World War, America shipped prisoners of war back to the states to be confined in prisoner-of-war camps. When Wiley Branton, the black lawyer who later handled the Little Rock case with us, was in the army and escorted Italian prisoners to their camps, the prisoners lunched at Southern white counters while he had to wait outside. Until 1953, when the Supreme Court resurrected a Reconstruction civil rights law, I could not have a meal anywhere in Washington with a black friend except at Union Station or the YWCA. (There was always occasion for amusement: The day after Harvey's began serving blacks, Thurgood and I went there for lunch. James A. Cobb, one of the earliest black judges in the District, was at an adjoining table. The waiter asked, "And what will you have today, Judge Cobb?" He replied, "The usual.")

Blacks were so far out of the economic mainstream that until the early 1960s, when I saw a black in an airport, chances were I knew him (rarely her). This seems so far-fetched that I have checked this memory with Andy Young, Vernon Jordan, and others, who confirm it. Although there were some marginal places, virtually no decent black hotels or restaurants existed in the South, except Paschal's in Atlanta, which opened in 1947, and Dooky Chase (nowadays a tourist attraction) in New Orleans, which opened in 1941. In Washington, D.C., there was the scarcely tolerable Charles Hotel, on R Street, which cost about $3.50 a night. One night, while we were there for a Supreme Court case, someone threw a bureau down the stairs. In Atlanta at the Negro Butler Street Y, only one room had a shower, which had to be booked far in advance and was almost impossible to reserve during conventions. Once, for an NAACP convention, I got the sought-after room, but then had to fend off a drunk who tried to break in all night. So blacks virtually always stayed with friends. I stayed with local lawyers, NAACP members, in a black college guest house, or with others in the black community. Occasionally discrimination limited whites: Herbert Hill, the white NAACP labor secretary, got into a black taxi in the Atlanta airport that refused to take him because he was white. Hill replied (straining to achieve credibility), "Man, I'm just as much a spook as you are." The driver drove him to his destination.

THE BLACK BAR AT MID-CENTURY

We five—Thurgood, Bob, Frank, Connie, and I—could have done nothing without the lawyers on the frontlines in the South. Long ago in England knowledge of the law consisted largely in knowing which form of writ to use for which kind of action. There developed an old English lawyers' saying, "No writ, no right"—without a procedure to pursue a legal claim, it might as well not exist. Similarly, "No lawyer, no law."

Southern white law schools excluded blacks and there were virtually no black law schools. Because the prospects for a black lawyer trying to earn a living practicing in the South were so dim, there was little incentive and less reason to spend money traveling North for a legal education. As a consequence, many of the black lawyers in the South had managed to get their legal educations in poor schools with part-time faculties, such as Howard Law School had been before Charles Houston turned it into a competitive, fully reputable, and accredited law school. Some took correspondence courses. Others apprenticed themselves to lawyers to learn law. Still, black lawyers operating at the local level were essential to civil rights claimants. Only a couple of Southern white lawyers handled integration cases before the mid-1960s. The Department of Justice had no effective civil rights jurisdiction and was politically shackled.

When black people asked each other how many lawyers (or doctors or undertakers) could be found in such and such a town or county, they were asking in effect how many *black* lawyers (or doctors or undertakers) could be found there. Usually in the South, often in the North, the answer would be one or two, or none. Even in New York City there were only a handful in active civil rights practice. Black lawyers in the South especially had a tough existence in those days. Instead of practicing law a few went into business, several started insurance companies, and some of those who continued to practice did so part-time. A few worked in the post office or as teachers or Pullman porters or wherever they could get a job to feed their families while they struggled to build a practice in a society where the only people who would hire them could not pay a great deal. The few blacks who could afford to hire lawyers often wouldn't hire black lawyers because they anticipated that the courts wouldn't treat them fairly; some may have come to accept white stereotypes of black incompetence. I knew and worked with every black civil rights practitioner in the South after I came to LDF and will be writing about many of them in the pages that follow.

As late as 1965, Mississippi had only three black lawyers in civil rights, R. Jess Brown, Jack Young, and Carsie Hall, plus Marian Wright (later Marian Wright Edelman), whom LDF placed there. Young and Hall became lawyers by reading, that is, studying with a practicing lawyer, Sidney Redmond, in St. Louis. Young was admitted to the bar in 1951. Hall joined the bar in 1954, but didn't always practice full-time. When we retained him in 1956 he was working in the post office. We paid him $5,000 per year, taking into account that his wife, a schoolteacher, was earning $280 per month and expected to be fired as soon as his retainer became known. Brown studied with the La Salle Institute by correspondence and also went to Texas Southern, the Jim Crow school set up in 1947 in response to LDF integration suits. He was admitted to the bar in 1953.

Connie Motley was the first black woman lawyer to appear in a Mississippi court when she tried a teachers' salary case in the 1950s with local lawyer James A. Burnes, then in his eighties. The judge addressed her as "*Mrs.* Motley," causing a stir; her opponents wouldn't use the title of courtesy. The press called her "that Motley woman."

Maryland had about thirty black lawyers around 1950, though only about half that number were in active practice. Five or six did civil rights work, and only Tucker Dearing, Lynwood Koger, Juanita Mitchell, and Robert Watts were particularly active.

In Delaware, Louis Redding, who had gone to Harvard Law School, was admitted to the bar in 1929 and was the only black lawyer in that state until 1956.

Around 1950, Virginia had three black lawyers in Richmond, Spottswood W. Robinson III, Oliver Hill, and Martin A. Martin, who had gone to Howard, and Samuel Tucker, who read law, in Emporia.

In North Carolina from 1932 to the early 1950s there were about a dozen; perhaps three, Conrad O. Pearson, William A. Marsh, and Floyd McKissick, regularly practiced civil rights law. C. C. Spaulding founded a black life insurance company, North Carolina Mutual, in Durham. John Wheeler was president of Mechanics and Farmers Bank in the same city. Reuben Dailey took some civil rights cases in Asheville. Some of North Carolina's black lawyers graduated from North Carolina College for Negroes Law School, established in 1939, taught by faculty from Duke and the University of North Carolina, but not accredited until 1950.

South Carolina in the early 1950s probably had a single black lawyer, Harold Boulware, in Columbia. Certainly he was the only one in civil rights.

Georgia between 1911 and 1950 had only one black lawyer working significantly in civil rights, A. T. "Colonel" Walden, a graduate of the University of Michigan Law School, and only a dozen others, all in Atlanta during this period.

From 1937 to 1947 Alabama had but one black lawyer, Arthur Shores, who studied through the La Salle correspondence course. He was joined by Oscar Adams, Peter Hall, and Orzell Billingsley by the early 1950s.

Florida in the late 1940s had three or four black lawyers, but no practicing black lawyer in Miami until 1952.

From 1927 to 1937 there were three black lawyers in Louisiana, but from 1937 to 1950 only one, A. P. Tureaud; between 1950 and 1952 a couple joined him, of whom only A. M. "Mutt" Trudeau remained in practice there. In 1954, Ernest Morial and Robert Collins, the first blacks graduated from Louisiana State University under court order, joined the bar.

James M. Nabrit, Jr., first in his class at Northwestern, practiced in Texas with partners J. Alston Atkins and Carter Wesley; but Wesley was mostly a newspaper publisher and Atkins handled only an occasional civil rights matter. Nabrit took Texas civil rights cases from the early 1930s, but moved to Washington in 1936 to teach at Howard, where he developed the nation's first civil rights course. W. J. Durham, in Dallas, who had read law, did a great deal of civil rights work and also owned an insurance company.

Kentucky had a couple of black civil rights lawyers, J. Earl Dearing and James Crumlin, who was the more active of the two.

There was a single black lawyer in civil rights in Nashville, Z. Alexander Looby, a Columbia graduate, joined in 1950 by Avon Williams, who had gone to Howard. Carl Cowan was the lone black lawyer in Knoxville.

Arkansas had a couple of black lawyers around 1950, Harold Flowers and George Howard, who handled some civil rights cases, and perhaps a few others, none of whom did any noticeable civil rights work.

There probably were some others whom I haven't mentioned, but they were so invisible that they made virtually no difference. With only a few exceptions, this small band of pioneers, who heroically represented victims of discrimination, had otherwise mundane practices of minor criminal matters, title closings, divorces, and negligence suits. Typically they had walk-up or storefront offices in the black part of town, worked with a single secretary, rarely had partners or associates or had at most only one or two, and had to cover large parts of their state by automobile, because there were not usually any black lawyers outside the state's largest cities. In case a black lawyer might get past these hurdles, each new success brought new threats to his own safety and the safety of his family. Arthur Shores's home in Birmingham was bombed repeatedly from the 1950s through the 1960s, and Julius Chambers's office in Charlotte was burned down almost a decade later, his car and home bombed.

When visiting LDF lawyers finished a controversial case, they got on a plane or train and went home. The local lawyers remained to take the heat from an enraged redneck population. Many faced efforts to disbar them. Judges, prosecutors, and clerks regularly humiliated them, requiring that their clients and their families sit in Jim Crow sections of courtrooms. Judges, clerks, and white lawyers persisted in calling black lawyers by their first names, not out of friendship or familiarity, but to remind them and everyone else in the courtroom of their inferior status. Not until the mid-1960s did the Supreme Court, in one of our cases, *Hamilton v. Alabama*, declare it unconstitutional to punish a black witness for refusing to respond when addressed by his or her first name—Earl Warren called *Hamilton* one of the Court's most important decisions. Many early black lawyers in the South used initials rather than first names—C. O. Pearson (North Carolina), A. T. Walden (Georgia), A. P. Tureaud and A. M. Trudeau (Louisiana), W. J. Durham and C. B. Bunkley (Texas), G. E. Graves (Florida), and many others—specifically to avoid being addressed by their first names.

Virtually all of these lawyers had unimaginable equanimity. They were amused by their racist adversaries and would joke about them, out of their presence, of course. One would have expected bitterness and hostility, but unrelenting anger would have killed them off prematurely. Lawyers too demonstrative in expressing their frustration or outrage at the absurdities they had to argue against often accomplished less. Thurgood sometimes would speak about the lawyer with a reputation for acting loudly and obstructively in the courtroom: As the client was dragged off to jail he would exclaim, "My lawyer sure gave them hell." He would repeat Charlie Houston's admonition: "Lose your head, lose your case." For Thurgood, this viewpoint was part of a more profound respect he had for judges. You never heard as many "Yes, sirs" and "May it please the courts" as when he argued a case.

That was part of a broader attitude of respect for senior people and institutions. Nothing illustrates that better than what occurred in connection with his proposed autobiography. Near the end of his tenure on the Supreme Court, he contracted to coauthor his biography and received an advance of $250,000. But he soon understood that he was expected to write about the inner workings of the Court and to reveal confidences about the Court and the justices. He refused to do so, returned the advance, and withdrew from the deal, declining to write a book that, he said, would be characterized as "Nigger judge tells all." He asserted that signing the $250,000 check that returned the advance really hurt. The book finally appeared as an "unauthorized biography."

Thurgood was a faithful Mason. Indeed, in his only non-NAACP or -LDF matter after he left Baltimore, he took a leave from LDF to represent the Supreme Council of the Masons when they asked him to.

Without this group of trailblazing Southern black lawyers, who had to temper their resentment with humor and too often swallowed their bitterness altogether, we never could have accomplished what we did.

4

WHY ME?

I have often been asked how a white lawyer from the Bronx came to a career devoted to the rights of black people, a career where he would work mostly with black lawyers and leaders. There is one simple answer and another, deeper one.

The simple answer involves going to college, serving in the Second World War, entering law school, and being steered toward civil rights by one of my professors. After graduating from Columbia College in 1945 (in absentia, while at sea), and before law school, I was a naval officer, lieutenant junior grade. I also attended Cornell for a year in the Navy V-12 program. V-12 students enlisted in the naval reserve and were permitted to finish their college education; they then went to officer's training school before going on active duty.

I served in the Pacific for over a year, mostly aboard a landing ship tank (LST 715) as deck officer, commanding the ship during one or two watches a day, and participated in the invasion of Iwo Jima, where we launched the first wave onto the black, volcanic sand beach under cover of shelling, rocket, and napalm attacks. We spent days on the beach unloading, shuttling back to receive more cargo from bigger ships, and serving as sanctuary to marines who came on board to rest and shower. Officers got fresh water showers, enlisted men saltwater. We were beached not far from Mount Surabachi. I have my own photo of the famous flag that was raised on it, taken with my small Kodak. It has none of the grace and movement of the famous Joe Rosenthal photograph, the subject of which has been reproduced in bronze at Arlington National Cemetery. In my photo the flagpole and flag, only a tiny sliver, appear atop the ugly, black, bare mountain.

From Iwo we sailed to pick up troops and munitions on Saipan and proceeded to Okinawa, where we landed about a week after the initial invasion, though the fighting remained fierce. In Okinawa Harbor we fought off kamikaze attacks, one of which blew up a cruiser. Only a twenty-year-old with an unthinking belief in his own immortality would have left the relative safety of his beached ship and wandered closer to the front lines to get a better view of what was happening. One memory of Iwo: a body blown apart, the flesh over the ribs marbled with fat, as in a butcher shop; a former human being, maybe a former comrade, and it stank. A memory of Okinawa: wandering into a shattered schoolhouse and picking up schoolbooks scattered on the floor.

Finally, we invaded Iheya Shima, the island closest to Japan and the last island hopped before the end of the war. Most people wrongly think I am referring to Ie Shima, where journalist Ernie Pyle was killed. At Iheya Shima, I commanded a small boat (LCVP), transported aboard the LST, that led amphibious tanks toward the beach. Another officer had volunteered for the job, but when his rudder failed and his boat began describing large circles, the captain ordered me to lower a second boat and proceed to the front of the column. Armed with only a fifty-caliber machine gun and displaying a flag atop a long pole so that the vehicles behind us could follow (the flag making us visible also to defenders on shore), my rectangular, flat boat led the procession very slowly. As I headed through choppy whitecaps toward land and the palm trees beyond, not certain whether I was aimed at the right point (a cleft between two hills, I had been told, but looking at the island, it turned out there were several similar-looking hills), the other boat's crew repaired its rudder and insisted on retaking the lead. Deprived of my moment of glory, I returned to the LST. In a comic-opera finish, the first troops ashore discovered that the Japanese had left the island shortly before we arrived.

We were on our way back to Hawaii to pick up troops for the invasion of Japan when the United States dropped the atomic bombs, ending the war. The captain celebrated by distributing one can of beer to every enlisted man and two to each officer—in violation of rules against alcohol at sea. Awaiting demobilization, I lived in Hawaii for about six months, applied to Columbia Law School, and in the fall of 1946 began my legal education.

During my second semester at Columbia I saw on the bulletin board in the lobby of Kent Hall, the law school building, announcement of a seminar, Legal Survey, to be taught by Walter Gellhorn. It offered a half-point credit and satisfaction of a writing requirement, but called for more work than one ordinarily would put in for a half-point credit. Students in the course worked for civil liberties and civil rights organizations, writing memoranda, complaints, briefs, gathering facts, and so forth. This was clinical legal education of a sort, perhaps a generation before such courses became common.

I ran up the two flights of stairs to Professor Gellhorn's office and, out of breath, signed on. Gellhorn, now in his late eighties, has been a great scholar, the creator of modern administrative law. He was also a person to put his beliefs to the test, and to ask his students to do the same. In 1949, he would testify in one case that the black plaintiff never could receive an equal education in the Oklahoma Jim Crow school set up for her. In 1950 he signed, with other law teachers, a friend-of-the-court brief in a case in which it was argued that Jim Crow legal education was unconstitutional, because the nature of legal education was such that when black students were separated from whites they could never receive an equal education. Gellhorn's Legal Survey seminar enabled law students to act upon their convictions and, maybe, pointed them into legal careers in which they might do more than make money.

Why call it "Legal Survey"? This was a time of virulent anticommunism, just before Senator Joseph McCarthy of Wisconsin came on the national scene to exploit the nation's fears. In this climate, it became convenient for those who opposed an extension of civil liberties to label civil rights activities as Communist-inspired. This led in the end to the absurdity of ascribing greater concern for individual rights to those who paid homage to a totalitarian state than to those who believed in democracy. But a poorly thought-out anticommunism was part of the reality we had to live with at the time. By giving his seminar a name that communicated nothing about the subject of the course, Gellhorn deprived critics, including other members of the faculty, of a convenient target.

I took the course for four semesters and for the last two was its chairman, visiting agencies that had requested our help, collecting projects and offering them to other members of the seminar, and acting as intermediary between the seminar and our clients. We worked on cases and projects for the American Civil Liberties Union, American Jewish Congress, American Jewish Committee, Japanese American Citizens League, NAACP, and other groups. I wrote one memorandum for the Japanese American Citizens League that argued that Japanese-American relocation-camp prisoners who had renounced their American citizenship had been coerced into doing so by their imprisonment. Therefore, the renunciations were invalid and, as their cases involved common questions of law and fact, they should be allowed to file a class action reclaiming citizenship for the individual plaintiffs and others similarly situated. Later, a court adopted this view, whether influenced by my memorandum or not, I don't know. In the course of my work for Legal Survey I visited the offices of LDF, met Thurgood briefly, and collected projects from Marian Perry Yankauer, a lawyer on the staff.

Following graduation in October 1948—the first postwar classes went to law school through the summers—I got a job with the New York State Law Revision Commission in Ithaca, New York, located in Cornell Law School. The commission drafted legislation, mostly of a noncontroversial sort, and tried to iron out anomalies that developed in laws with the passage of time. Some of the work was important—I drafted a bill giving life prisoners who had been paroled, and served the remainder of their sentences out of prison in that status, the right to marry, which they had previously been denied because under an ancient doctrine they were deemed "civilly dead" and, therefore, unable to enter into contracts. Some of my work was relatively inconsequential, such as a bill prescribing whether to count Sunday when it turns out to be the last of a prescribed number of days.

As I pondered what to do next, I got a note from Walter Gellhorn. Thurgood had asked him to recommend someone to replace Marian Yankauer, who was leaving because her husband's job required their moving to another city. Would I be interested? I was very interested. I had a vague notion I wanted to be a civil rights lawyer. I was, of course, aware of Jim Crow in the South. I had followed recent highly publicized cases, like those of Isaac Woodard, Willie Earle, and Rosa Lee Ingram, all of which, as it turned out, had been NAACP and Inc. Fund cases. Woodard had been blinded by a South Carolina policeman in a dispute arising out of an argument with a white bus driver; Earle, charged with stabbing a white taxi driver, had been taken from prison and lynched by a South Carolina mob; Ingram and her two teenage sons had been sentenced to death for killing a white farmer who pressured her to submit to him sexually.

The racial problem was the most urgent domestic issue facing postwar America. But jobs where a lawyer might work on this problem were virtually nonexistent. There were two or three positions at LDF; the ACLU dealt with civil liberties, mostly freedom of expression, with a single staff lawyer; the American Jewish Congress and Committee, which sometimes addressed civil rights issues, had a job or two; there were a handful or two of state government jobs, and that was about it.

I developed an amorphous notion that I'd like to be someone like Arthur Garfield Hays, whom I'd never met and about whom I knew next to nothing except that his name appeared in the paper frequently, that he represented the American Civil Liberties Union, and that he had something to do with the NAACP—as it was, he was on its National Legal Committee. He wasn't on the staff or payroll of a civil rights organization, but apparently made enough of a living in his private practice that he could afford to take civil liberties cases.

I had actually formulated a game plan, as it now might be called, of doing the same: going into private practice, making a lot of money—how, I wasn't quite sure—and using it to support myself while practicing civil rights law. Oddly, the making money part was the easiest part in those days. The years of my early legal practice were days in which prosperous careers developed, especially in the professions, and more than a few of my law school classmates became wealthier than they ever dreamed of becoming.

Now with the job opportunity at LDF came a chance to leapfrog the private practice stage and start doing the work I dreamed of immediately. I worried a bit about whether I could make a living working at LDF and what it might lead to when I ultimately moved on. One of the few lawyers I knew, Lee Epstein, my cousin's husband, advised that there was no way of knowing what anything would lead to. If I wanted to do it, I should. The woman I was planning to marry, Sema Tanzer, had been a member of the NAACP in her home state of Delaware, and she was all for it. I accepted the job.

That's the superficial answer to why I became a civil rights lawyer at LDF. It took a long while for me to realize that it is only a very partial answer. There were, after all, six or seven hundred students in the law school and only a dozen signed on for Legal Survey. I was the only one who enrolled for four semesters. And there were not scores of students trying to break down the doors of LDF and the few other civil rights organizations, as there are today. That suggests digging farther back.

My parents weren't involved in civil rights or even passionate about politics, but they did help me develop confidence in my ability to choose my own way, and I grew up prepared to rely on my own feelings to tell me whether or not what I was about to do was right, or even right for me. I couldn't have cared less when others criticized positions I took. Such an attitude was one that would be helpful in civil rights work, though as it turned out, classmates and friends engaged in more conventional jobs didn't criticize me at all. Perhaps that's a measure of the friends I made. One, who worked with banking clients for a prominent law firm, may have summed up the attitude of others when he once said to me, "I wish I had a case where I really cared how it came out."

I was only amused when a Florida newspaper called me a "Bolshevik" and the neo-Nazi press regularly denounced me as "the Jew Jack Greenberg." I wasn't set too far back when black students picketed me at Harvard thirty-five years later because they objected to a white man, even one who had spent an entire career preparing and arguing civil rights cases, teaching a civil rights course. Going through the picket line, I told myself, was nothing compared to Iwo Jima. How my parents managed to put this inner-directed tendency in me (some have called it insensitivity, or even arrogance—I hope it is neither), I cannot be sure.

My mother, Bertha Rosenberg, who died in 1983, came to America from an area in Romania, near Czernowitz, called Bukovina. She had little education herself, but valued it highly. From the day I was born she saved fifty cents a week at the Metropolitan Life Insurance Company so that I would have tuition to go to Columbia, the only school she ever considered. Sometimes she would have me carry the fifty-cent piece to the second-story office up the hill on 204th Street, a few blocks from where we lived. I once wondered whether there wasn't a lesson intended for me in that.

Our area of the upper central Bronx had only recently become urbanized: The street had been paved for the first time only a few years before we moved there. No blacks lived anywhere nearby; residents were mainly Jews in apartment houses and Irish civil servants in private homes, and some Italians. I walked a few blocks to PS 56 and later to DeWitt Clinton High

School, perhaps a mile away. This was a time when Ivy League schools had quotas for Jews, but I always assumed I would be admitted to Columbia.

Certainly my mother's praise, love, and support had a lot do with my self-assurance. I was expelled from a sixth-grade class because the teacher accused me of having called him an unmentionable name, which he refused to repeat. His name was Schwarzreich and he had heard me shout, in the excitement of a schoolyard punchball game, "Schwarzie's mad" when another boy hit a ball into the school garden, which was off limits to students. Apparently he didn't like that nickname. My mother persuaded Miss Hollahan, the principal, that I had been treated unfairly, but the teacher adamantly refused to take me back in his class. The principal explained that she thought Schwarzreich was wrong, but it was like being married, you had to put up with some things. There was no other sixth-grade class; I was effectively out of the school. The principal, therefore, personally tutored me for the balance of the year, and I was a sort of assistant to her. So, in a way, I came out ahead. I also learned something about bureaucratic intransigence.

My parents inculcated in me an abiding concern for those who are disadvantaged, which I later focused on the race issue. Once, as a five- or six-year-old, I recoiled from a shabby man (I can't remember whether he was black or white) who sat next to us on a lacquered wooden bench of a Brooklyn trolley car. My mother patiently explained why I was wrong to shun him. Sometimes my mother sent me out to knock on neighbors' doors to collect food for poor friends—specific individuals in hard times, not charity generally—perhaps a forerunner of my fund-raising for LDF and Columbia. I went through our apartment house, floor to floor, door to door, with a large brown paper bag, soliciting canned goods, flour, rice, and other items, which we would bring to Coney Island, where the recipients lived. Perhaps it was here that I learned not to hesitate to ask on behalf of others.

I never told my parents that on the way to first grade I joined other kids in throwing stones into a laundry because the owner was Chinese. We shouted gibberish, which someone told us was Chinese obscenities, at the owner, who chased us. I did it because the other kids did it. Ever since, I have felt shame for what I did. I also learned that kids follow the crowd.

My father, Max Greenberg, who died in 1974, was born in Lowicz, Poland, near Warsaw. With his grandfather, who had been a Russian *feldscher* (something like a paramedic), he lived in England and attended school there in his early years, returning to Poland before emigrating to America through Canada when he was about sixteen. I took unwarranted pride in the fact that he spoke English without the East European Yiddish accent all my friends' fathers had, because he had learned his English in London. I was even prouder that he had won a prize in grade school, a penknife awarded by the king, for being the brightest boy in the class. Although he picked up bits and pieces of education where he could, he never graduated from college. But he studied enough accounting and other subjects at City College to become a certified public accountant. I am amazed at how well-educated he was, how knowledgeable about literature, science, history, music. He was always reading at least two books, had a decent record collection, and was an excellent chess player.

Recently, on a human rights mission to Warsaw to observe the trial of the Polish dissidents Adam Michnik and Jacek Kuron (Lech Walesa and I were blocked at the courthouse door), I visited the town where he grew up. My uncle, his younger brother, had given me the address. As we wandered in the area a resident remembered my uncle's visit some years earlier and took us to the second-floor apartment in which the family had lived. Surprisingly, the area appeared to be middle class, garden apartments facing a green square. From across the street I could see flowers growing in the window box outside the apartment. I had assumed that he lived in a hut of some sort with a mud floor.

When I was old enough, my father took me to his office on Saturdays, where I helped by arranging canceled checks in sequence so that he could reconcile accounts. Then he would take me out to lunch. I had great fun on these occasions and remember being shocked when he confessed that he didn't like his work. That confession may have encouraged me to seek a career I cared about. My father was a debunker, skeptical about official action and explanations; he thought that all prizefights and, probably, most other sporting events were fixed; he didn't endorse the status quo.

We lived in a neighborhood where Communists were numerous; one of our neighbors went to prison for violating the Smith Act. My father was among the few adults among neighbors I knew who was anti-Communist, taking the Communists to task for the Hitler–Stalin pact of 1939 and the crimes of Stalin, far from widely acknowledged in those days. Of course, I sided with him. He was a model of someone opposed to the "system." In fact, he was suspicious of all received wisdom, but just suspicious, not so opposed as to reject any part of it entirely without close examination.

Perhaps it mattered that when my father went to synagogue, as he did infrequently with the rest of his family, he spent most of his time outside, on the steps, signifying that while he was part of the group, he was just part of its outer fringes; he did not seem to care to be identified with those at the very center of things. Could this moderate iconoclasm be a model for someone who would not break with the society, but stay just within its boundaries as a lawyer fighting some of its deeply entrenched institutions? I wonder whether my studying Chinese while in college, becoming a civil rights lawyer in 1949, becoming involved in international human rights in the early 1960s before almost anyone else, were not all expressions of a need to find myself of a piece with my father's outsider–insider stance, to stand on the pale. Founding the Mexican American Legal Defense and Education Fund, trying but failing to start a similar organization for Native Americans, and creating the first private national poverty law program (National

Office for the Rights of the Indigent) seem to me all to have something in common, which may be traced to those basic forces that had shaped my personality, not merely my adult social outlook. Perhaps the career of my brother, Daniel—the first journalist to specialize in the politics of science as an independent critic of its establishment—expresses that same inner impulse to go to the very frontier between insider and outsider.

Columbia College's core curriculum opened my mind to Western civilization, its philosophy and literature, particularly the concepts of the Enlightenment. I had entered Columbia with the goal of becoming an accountant, like my father, and a lawyer as well. I abandoned that notion almost immediately, taking off into Chinese in my second semester, but unable to continue with it after being called to active duty in the navy at the end of my junior year. The navy sent me to Cornell, where there was no course in Chinese. The great books of the Columbia core curriculum (still taught today) did not explicitly address contemporary American race relations. But all the values and issues relevant to them were explored through the works of the ancient Greeks, Romans, and Europeans who were our philosophical progenitors. Teachers played a role, too. At Columbia, Burdette Kinne, Raymond Weaver, and Irwin Edman taught me to read and think critically. At Cornell (while in the Navy V-12 program), Robert Cushman, my undergraduate constitutional law teacher, intrigued me by predicting, rightly, that a recent decision foretold the well-deserved doom of the white primary by holding that prosecution for vote stealing in a Democratic primary fell under federal jurisidiction and was not just private associational activity, which would not have been a federal crime. And Walter Gellhorn, who lived the life he believed in—committed to advancing civil rights, although not that alone—without regard to accumulating the money his talent in the law could have earned him, also earned my admiration.

While at Columbia I commuted from the Bronx, daily walking through Harlem up and down Morningside Heights. Father Ford, the Catholic chaplain at Columbia, was friendly with Father Divine, leader of a black cult that recognized him as God. Ford brought Columbia students to Father Divine banquets near the Polo Grounds and I went with him, my first introduction to Harlem. Father Divine blessed the heaps of food piled on large plates and we passed it around, careful not to let the food touch the table, which seemed to be a religious taboo.

In the all-white neighborhoods where I lived in Brooklyn, later in the Bronx, the Italians were the "others" with whom I would be likely to have a fight. On one ludicrous occasion two Jewish kids pummelled one another rolling around on the sidewalk in front of Hebrew school, one calling the other "you lousy Italian." I had no black friends until I got to college. There were only two blacks in my class (one was from Haiti), no Asians as far as I knew, and the category "Hispanic" didn't even exist yet. (Now Columbia is about 20 percent Asian and 20 percent black and Hispanic.) James Baldwin was at DeWitt Clinton High School when I attended, but I was unaware of his existence then. In the navy I was startled to be redirected to the front of a New Orleans streetcar after I had unwittingly taken a seat in the back, which was for blacks only. Perhaps the most unsettling racial situation I had to deal with was, as an officer, having black steward mates as my personal servants, serving my meals, cleaning my room, taking care of my clothing, and so forth, especially since, in combat, some of them manned guns. During my time at sea, somewhat more than a year, there had been five or six blacks on the ship, but only one had openly complained of his menial job. Two of the blacks serving on board were illiterate and I set up sessions to teach them to read and write, though I had little success. I really wasn't an elementary school teacher and we met only sporadically over relatively short periods of time.

I certainly wasn't the ship's rebel in my time in the navy, but I was often disquieted. Once I did approach the line the other side of which was court-martial: The captain confined a sailor to the brig, which on this ship was the locker where the anchor chain was stored, on bread and water, without a trial, for some trivial wrongdoing. The captain wouldn't release the prisoner nor would he give him a trial. I went to the captain's cabin and asked that he release the man. We had a shouting match. He threatened me with a court-martial; I said I would inform his superior. I was so tense that when I left his cabin I cried. To my surprise the captain backed down and released the sailor.

One question I have frequently been asked is whether being Jewish had anything to do with steering me toward my career. Of course it did, but other Jews went in other, quite different, directions. All sorts of evidence, including voting patterns in local and national elections, indicate that Jews have long tended to be more liberal than other whites on most social issues. A substantial number of the white lawyers involved in the earliest days of LDF were Jewish. Charles Black likes to point out that of the half-dozen white lawyers who signed the brief in *Brown v. Board of Education* he was the only non-Jew.

But while Jews have been among financial contributors to civil rights, this role has been exaggerated. The largest contributors to LDF, in amounts totaling millions, have been some of the biggest foundations, like Ford, Carnegie, Rockefeller, and major corporations, among which the influence of Jews is negligible. The largest individual contributors, those who have given at least hundreds of thousands of dollars, were almost entirely non-Jewish—Chauncey Waddell, William Scheide, Grenville Clark, Esther Johnson, and Hans Huber. Scheide has given millions and has been the largest contributor to the funds used to purchase the LDF condominium office and recently to an endowment fund. Among Jews, the J. M. Kaplan Foundation, a family foundation, headed by Joan Davidson, and Helen Buttenwieser have been among the largest contributors. Of the sixteen other largest regular givers in recent years, that is, those who gave between $10,000 and $30,000 per year, probably six are Jewish.

The myth of dominant Jewish financial support for civil rights probably comes from the 1960s when Jewish celebrities gave to SNCC (Student Non-violent Coordinating Committee) and CORE and Martin Luther King, Jr. But they scarcely gave in similar amounts to mainstream organizations like LDF, the NAACP, and the Urban League. When the movement dissolved, high-profile celebrities stopped giving. Nevertheless, while it would be unfair to call Jews the financial mainstay of the civil rights movement, as some have said, in proportion to population they have been overrepresented among the financial supporters of civil rights.

The problem with focusing on Jewish support is that it ignores Jewish opposition or apathy. Being Jewish can lead a person in any direction. The smaller national Jewish organizations supported affirmative action; the major ones initially opposed it. In time, some that opposed later supported. Moreover, those opposed to affirmative action would argue that they supported civil rights groups on other matters. Being Jewish influenced the vast majority of Jewish lawyers who did nothing about civil rights and the small number who were the Fund's opponents, like Sylvan Garfunkel, who, representing Savannah in a prosecution of blacks for playing basketball in a white park, argued that he was an Orthodox Jew and that there would be "a tremendous reaction in a truly orthodox synagogue" if a woman were to sit in a "section reserved exclusively for men." Earl Warren, visibly irritated, replied, "You think if an Irish policeman came in there and said, Get out of here . . . they would not have a right to say by what authority?" One of the leaders of Georgia's resistance to civil rights was a Jewish lawyer, Charles Bloch, and Jewish lawyers were among defenders of segregation in most of the Southern states.

There had to be something more that caused me to extract from my background the elements that made me a civil rights lawyer, rather than moving me in the direction of, say, Bloch or Garfunkel. I recall nothing in Jewish education that had that effect, although there is enough in the Old Testament that advocates racial equality (and in the New Testament as well). In any event, my own Jewish education was very diluted. I attended a series of afternoon and Sunday Hebrew or Yiddish schools some of which I quit; others asked me to leave for misbehavior or lack of attention. My parents said they went through the motions of a Hebrew education to satisfy my grandfather. I was bar mitzvahed, but my brother, who wasn't thirteen until after my grandfather's death, wasn't.

Maybe it was important that as a high school student I once was turned down for a summer job as a bank messenger because they weren't hiring Jews. I took it as a matter of course, though at some level it must have affected me—I still remember it. But that episode couldn't be the answer, either: Many Jews of my generation had similar experiences and ended up professionally at all points on the civil rights spectrum, from active aid to token support to full apathy to sub rosa resistance to active opposition.

My guess is that it wasn't Judaism per se that provided the religious or cultural impetus, but the Eastern European, Socialist-Zionist culture that my father, like many of his contemporaries, brought with him when he emigrated from Poland before the First World War. His family, my father being the exception, was deeply involved in Zionism. His sister, Masha, married the head of the Farband, an American labor Zionist organization. Two of her sons emigrated to Palestine to fight in the Haganah for the independence of Israel, but then returned to the United States. I would hear talk at home condemning Vladimir Jabotinsky and Menachem Begin, who led the terrorist Irgun in Palestine, which opposed Haganah. Not that my father was an active proponent of Zionism. But, through him, the rest of the family, and friends, I was surrounded by that value system, which I took as a call for justice, equality, and fairness for all people. I first heard the aphorism "From each according to his abilities, to each according to his needs" from my father and it was a revelation, not a cliché. (The first time I voted for president it was for Norman Thomas, the Socialist candidate.)

While many of the Socialist-Zionist immigrants were not sophisticated ideologues, even the least sophisticated or ideological among them deeply believed that discrimination and persecution were evils and that blacks, like Jews in Eastern Europe, suffered from a deep, economically based, and racially motivated hatred that had to be opposed. The idea of an alliance between Jews and blacks was a central tenet of all left-wing and liberal American Jews. In the early 1920s the Yiddish press regularly condemned American racism as it affected blacks. Jews then could not have helped identifying what America did to blacks with what Europe, and to considerable extent America, was doing to Jews. But as the decades progressed many of the old Socialists and Socialist-Zionists abandoned this belief along with many of the ideals of their youth, some perhaps because of fear of violence that they perceived as coming from blacks. Sometimes, their children became more conservative. Moreover, Orthodox Jews, Michael Stanislawski has reminded me, believed that the freedoms of the liberal and left agendas would, if achieved, adversely affect traditional Jewish society and values. He recounts a perhaps apocryphal story: When Napoleon attacked Russia, the then Lubavitcher rebbe is supposed to have said, "If Napoleon wins, the Jews will be free and economically successful, but Judaism will suffer and decline; if Tsar Alexander wins, the Jews will be poor and oppressed, but Judaism will flourish."

At the same time some Northern Jews tried to become Yankees, and some Southern Jews tried to become Southerners, taking on many of the views of the upper classes among whom they lived. Anti-Semitism was virulent in parts of the South, synagogues were bombed, and racists regularly blamed Jews for promoting racial equality. It was not surprising, therefore, that some Jewish lawyers in the South, who privately expressed supportive sentiments to me, did nothing openly, realizing that they would be ruined if they publicly supported racial equality.

Still, it might be facile to attribute too much to the Socialist-Zionist milieu in which I grew up; of all those many Americans who came out of that background, few took up careers in civil rights. It also doesn't account for those German Jews who came out of a very different background yet still supported civil rights, those like Herbert Lehman, an NAACP board member, and his niece Helen Buttenwieser, an LDF board member; Arthur Spingarn, president of the NAACP; and anti-Zionist Lessing Rosenwald, an early LDF contributor who was a major supporter of education for blacks. Rosenwald-built schools for blacks dotted the South. That pro–civil rights sentiment spanned German and Eastern European Jews suggests the power of the shared experience of anti-Semitism and its resemblance to the black experience.

Taken together with the influence of parents and teachers and other aspects of my background, however, perhaps a mosaic (if that word is permissible in this context) of factors that formed my attitudes may be discerned. But all this is speculation—none of it was in my consciousness as I made those choices committing me to the life of a civil rights lawyer. I knew as I went along only that I was on a path that would lead to my devoting the greatest part of my professional life to the fight for racial justice, and that I was happy I had done so.

5

THE GROUND IS HARD

MY FIRST DAYS

I went to work my first day at LDF not knowing what I would be asked to do, only vaguely aware of the cases in the office, hardly knowing the people. That first morning Thurgood called me in and asked me to do research for a friend-of-the-court brief in a case that was not an LDF case at all. His friend Loren Miller, a civil rights pioneer in California, who was involved in a range of dissident causes, represented members of the Progressive party who had been beaten up by a group of men wearing the caps of American Legionnaires. They sued, claiming that their assailants had deprived them of their constitutional rights. I was asked to make an argument in their support. I holed up in the bar association library for a week and produced a memorandum that, although it greatly pleased Loren, didn't help: He lost the case. Then Thurgood asked me to prepare a presentation to a conference dealing with why the New York State Commission Against Discrimination was ineffective. I asked around and studied and researched and concluded, like others before me, that mainly it was lack of political will combined with lack of real power. Very nervous, I delivered my conclusions to a group at a nearby hotel. Though I told them nothing new the exercise was part of an ongoing struggle to pressure the commission to act more effectively.

My work became a little more exciting. In January 1950 Thurgood assigned me to represent John McCray, the publisher of the Columbia, South Carolina, *Lighthouse and Informer,* the only black newspaper in the state. A black defendant was awaiting execution for the rape of a white girl, the daughter of the county solicitor, and in October 1949, McCray printed the man's story, including his contention that the girl and her boyfriend had asked him to find some whiskey for them and then invited him to have intercourse with her in their car. Harold Boulware, the first black lawyer ever to appear in that county, had represented the defendant, who refused to testify about the consensual sex, possibly because he thought he would be treated leniently if he kept quiet about what had actually happened. He was convicted, refused to appeal, and was electrocuted. For publishing his story with the allegation that a white female had had consensual sex with a black male, McCray was charged with criminal libel—a crime unheard of today, when the First Amendment is understood to protect against such prosecutions.

I traveled back and forth to Columbia and came up with a few defenses but never was able to put them to the test because in June McCray pleaded guilty to avoid jail and paid a fine. If the case had come to trial, this being the early 1950s, I almost surely would not have succeeded. In fact, the atmosphere was so hostile that a white lawyer in Columbia, who covertly helped us, asked us to enter his house at night through the back door. He would have been ruined if his involvement became known.

The court sentenced McCray to three years' probation, during which he was not permitted to leave the state, although his parole officer explained that he might take short trips for business purposes. But, in August 1951, the court revoked his probation, because he had gone briefly out of state on two occasions, and sentenced him to two months on the chain gang. The real reason for the court's anger with him was likely his newspaper's support for the School Segregation Cases, then being argued in South Carolina. McCray suspected that such an order must have come directly from South Carolina Governor James Byrnes, for many years a power in the Democratic party, a former associate justice of the Supreme Court, war effort organizer under Franklin Roosevelt, and secretary of state under Truman.

Because McCray had already pleaded guilty, the only legal issue became whether the parole had been properly revoked, and on that there was no second-guessing the state courts. Today, none of this could have occurred. The death penalty for rape is prohibited as cruel and unusual punishment, and a conviction for criminal libel for printing the defendant's statement of innocence would be inconceivable.

I soon got an assignment working on cases involving the integration of the University of Texas Law School and the University of Oklahoma Graduate School of Education, both about to be argued in the Supreme Court. Though the cases involved heady constitutional issues, my role was not at the level of great intellectual challenge. It was becoming apparent that being a good civil rights lawyer meant first being a good lawyer, which required doing many things that were not terribly exciting or important. But I knew also that there *were* great issues being debated, if not in the work I was doing, certainly in the work of the other lawyers, whose work was supported by my own.

I slowly became immersed in the core of LDF work as I attended staff meetings, the frequent conferences that Thurgood called with law professors and "visiting firemen" to deal with higher education cases, and after-hours bull sessions in the office, the 440 Club down the street, and colleagues' homes. I also knew there was a master plan guiding what seemed to be an endless stream of diverse cases.

Thurgood often referred to something he called the "Margold Report," so I got it out of the files, a blue-backed lawyer's document, and read it during my first few weeks at the Fund. The report was the product of a small committee, directed by Nathan Margold, a protégé of Felix Frankfurter, set up for the NAACP in 1930 to outline the direction it should take in the courts. The report was made possible by $20,000 provided by the American Fund for Public Service, a foundation set up by a young man, Charles Garland, who had inherited funds he declined to spend on himself. The committee's recommendations were remarkably bold and prescient, setting the direction we traveled, although with frequent deviation.

In 1930, when Margold was drawing up his plan, there were basically only a few important Supreme Court cases dealing directly, or even by implication, with discrimination based on race. One might have thought that the Fourteenth Amendment's equal protection clause, adopted after the Civil War, would have given blacks first-class citizenship. And, indeed, not long after the amendment was adopted the Court seemed to be following that course. *Strauder v. West Virginia*, decided in 1880, held that excluding blacks from juries was "practically a brand upon them, affixed by the law: an assertion of their inferiority, and a stimulant to that race prejudice . . . an impediment to . . . equal justice." But around that time the Court began to waver. The Civil Rights Cases (1883) held that in enforcing the Fourteenth Amendment, which provided that no "state shall deny to any person . . . the equal protection of the laws," the federal government had no power to pass laws prohibiting *individuals* from discriminating. Individuals were not the "state." They could keep blacks out of privately owned restaurants, opera houses, ferryboats, and other places, immune from the federal civil rights statutes that were enacted to prevent such discrimination. This decision gave rise to what became known as the "state action" doctrine and later stimulated discursive debates over what is the state and what is state action, all of which warmed the hearts of political scientists, but contributed little to racial justice. This issue was reprised in the sit-in cases of the 1960s, when demonstrators sat in at private establishments to force change in racial policies followed universally within certain states, and rigorously enforced by police and judges of those states. Were the policies being protested examples of private or state-imposed discrimination?

Civil rights did not always lose in that period. *Yick Wo v. Hopkins*, decided in 1886, held unconstitutional a San Francisco ordinance that had a discriminatory impact on Chinese by banning laundries in wooden buildings, which is where the Chinese typically located their businesses. The

Court said that the law was employed with "an evil eye and an unequal hand" and denied the Chinese their constitutional rights. Perhaps it is important in understanding this decision to recall that *Yick Wo* involved San Francisco and not the American South and did not involve blacks, the racial group singled out for disparate treatment more often than any other.

In 1896 the Supreme Court, in what became the dominant decision governing the lives of blacks for almost sixty years, repudiated the principal purpose of the Fourteenth Amendment in the infamous case of *Plessy v. Ferguson*, which ruled that states had the power to *require* segregation. *Plessy*, in upholding a Louisiana law that segregated railroad cars, said that "in the nature of things" the Fourteenth Amendment could not have been intended "to abolish distinctions based upon color, or to enforce social, as distinguished from political, equality, or a coming together of the two races upon terms unsatisfactory to either." It opined that if segregation made blacks feel inferior it was because they chose "to put that construction on it"; if the roles were reversed whites would never feel that way. Law could not change "racial instincts." The decision created the legal doctrine of "separate-but-equal," under which excluding blacks from opportunities and conveniences enjoyed by whites was okay as long as blacks were offered equal accommodations. Though it would seem to any fair-minded person that separate-but-equal could never obtain in the real world, the decision set a new obstacle in the way of civil rights lawyers, an obligation to prove to the satisfaction of a court that the separate accommodations were not in fact equal.

The Supreme Court had no evidence before it upon which to base its assertions about inferiority and instincts. These supposedly were statements about facts, but told more about the Court's values. Years later, in *Brown v. Board of Education*, the Court would confront issues about a sense of inferiority once more, this time after plaintiffs had indeed presented evidence on the subject. Based upon this evidence, or perhaps expressing contemporary values, it came to a contrary conclusion, which provoked a firestorm of criticism directed at what was called inadequate evidence.

Plessy had one saving grace. Justice John Marshall Harlan dissented, writing that "our constitution is color-blind, and neither knows nor tolerates classes among its citizens. In respect of civil rights, all citizens are equal before the law."

Following *Plessy*, not only were individuals allowed to discriminate against fellow citizens, free of federal prohibition, but the states could now require and enforce such discrimination. Predictably, with the power of the state now behind it, rigid Jim Crow segregation soon defined all aspects of Southern society.

Why the switch from a pro- to an anti-egalitarian interpretation of the Constitution? C. Vann Woodward has written that the 1877 presidential election between Republican Rutherford B. Hayes and Democrat Samuel J. Tilden was so close that a few electors could have decided it. Hayes offered a deal to Southern Democrats: withdrawal of Northern troops from the South, abandonment of blacks, and federal support of economic development in return for the votes of the white South needed to assure victory. They accepted; the bargain became known as the Compromise of 1877. It gave a free hand to Southerners to return blacks to a condition as close to slavery as could be achieved. The law can be a great teacher. It is also sometimes an obedient pupil, and in the years after 1877 the law began to reflect the new social and political reality.

Plessy metastasized, infecting more than half a century of constitutional law. As late as 1927, a unanimous Court, on which Holmes, Brandeis, and Stone sat, applied *Plessy* to schools, in a case that permitted Mississippi to require a Chinese girl to attend black schools, *Gong Lum v. Rice.* But Harlan's *Plessy* dissent continued to loom, as Charles Evans Hughes once described some dissents, like "an appeal to the brooding spirit of the law, to the intelligence of a future day."

There were some cracks in the united front. *Strauder,* the case proscribing discrimination in the selection of juries, never was overruled, merely distinguished as being applicable solely to the deprivation of "political" rights, a term never defined precisely. Therefore, its doctrine of prohibiting the state from imposing a stigma on blacks remained latent, available for use in later years. Twenty years after *Plessy, Buchanan v. Warley,* a 1917 NAACP case, held unconstitutional a Louisville law barring blacks from living in certain parts of town, a residential apartheid resembling that in South Africa. The case pointed out that *Plessy* dealt only with rail travel, and rejected the argument that the state's action in establishing residential segregation was necessary to prevent violence and intermarriage. *Yick Wo,* the Chinese laundry case, remained available to challenge rules that were written to appear evenhanded but that were clearly intended to discriminate.

A STRATEGY EMERGES

Faced with this state of the law, Margold first considered whether the NAACP should acquiesce in the *Plessy* framework and bring suits to force school districts to maintain completely equal, though separate, schools. There had been an earlier proposal to file such cases in South Carolina, Georgia, Mississippi, Louisiana, Florida, Alabama, and Arkansas in order to make separate schools so expensive that segregation would have to be abolished, a theme to be heard almost until the *Brown* decision. But, Margold argued, few districts would be equalized, soon they would slip back into inequality, and the struggle would have to start all over again. He concluded that:

it would be a great mistake to fritter away our limited funds on sporadic attempts to force making of equal divisions of school funds in
the few instances where such attempts might be expected to succeed.
Such an effort would eliminate only a minor part of discrimination
and only temporarily. It would not establish new principles or have
any general effect. . . . *We should be leaving wholly untouched the
very essence of the existing evils.* If we boldly challenge the constitutional validity of segregation if and when accompanied irremediably
by discrimination, we can strike directly at the most prolific sources
of discrimination.

He proposed exploiting the concept of *Yick Wo*, which condemned discrimination administered "with an evil eye and an unequal hand," as central to
his legal theory. The idea was that if wherever there was segregation there
also was inequality, which was invariably the case, segregation, therefore,
was unconstitutional.

An equally prescient aspect of Margold's report was that the litigation
effort would "stir . . . the spirit of revolt among blacks" and cause whites to
view them with more respect. Indeed, that turned out to be the case.

At the conclusion of his report, Margold wrote, curiously, that we "are
not trying to deprive southern states of their acknowledged privilege of providing separate accommodations for the two races. We are trying only to
force them to comply with their equally acknowledged duty to provide
'equal if separate' accommodations in white and colored schools." He urged
publicity to avert the danger of alienating "enlightened public opinion,"
perhaps a sop to those who feared stirring adverse public reaction. Maybe
the passage was put in by a conservative member of the committee.

During the same period black leaders conducted a similar debate over
equalization versus integration. W. E. B. Du Bois, a towering black scholar,
a founder of the NAACP, and editor of *The Crisis* until 1934, was forced to
resign for having written an editorial that stated that "thinking colored people of the United States must stop being stampeded by the word segregation. . . . It is the race conscious black man co-operating together in his own
institutions and movements who will eventually emancipate the colored
race." Bill Hastie, ordinarily a man of measured tones, attacked Du Bois in
language uncharacteristically harsh: "For fifty years prejudiced white men
and abject boot-licking, gut-lacking, knee-bending, favor-seeking Negroes
have been insulting our intelligence with a tale that goes like this: Segregation is not an evil. Negroes are better off by themselves . . . in theory there
can be segregation without unequal . . . treatment." Hastie unequivocally
rejected that view.

In a major debate in 1935 Du Bois argued that there was nothing wrong
with integration in theory, but he opposed sending black children to white

schools where they would be received with hostility and lack of understanding. Charles Thompson, dean of the Howard University Graduate
School of Education, replied that black children could be treated equally
only in an integrated system. Black schools did not always educate black
children more sympathetically. Members of both races could learn mutual
respect only if educated together. The NAACP, and LDF when it came into
being, held the Thompson view. The Du Bois view remains very much alive
today, although among nearly all of those within the civil rights leadership,
Martin Luther King, Jr.'s dream of a fully integrated society remains the driving force.

As NAACP lawyers faced a thoroughly segregated South on the eve of
the Second World War, they could find possibly effective legal tools in the
constitutional melange of the previous half-century or so, and could turn
them in a direction proposed by the Margold plan. In this, they were fortified by the values articulated by black integrationist civil rights lawyers and
educators, like Bill Hastie and Charles Thompson.

Around the same time the law began taking a more favorable turn and
fresh legal doctrines became available. In 1938, in one of the most influential passages in American constitutional history, Chief Justice Harlan F.
Stone, in a footnote, expressed a philosophy that gave primacy to constitutional rights protecting participation in the political process. One part of
that footnote asserted:

> It is unnecessary to consider now whether legislation which restricts
> those political processes which can ordinarily be expected to bring
> about repeal of undesirable legislation, is to be subjected to more
> exacting judicial scrutiny under the general prohibitions of the Four-
> teenth Amendment than are most other types of legislation. . . . [and]
> whether prejudice against discrete and insular minorities may be a
> special condition, which tends seriously to curtail the operation of
> those political processes ordinarily to be relied upon to protect minori-
> ties, and which may call for a correspondingly more searching judicial
> inquiry.

As America entered the Second World War, Supreme Court doctrine took a
further egalitarian turn, although the practical outcome of the cases sometimes was otherwise. In 1943, in a case involving wartime curfews of
Japanese-Americans, the Court upheld the restrictions on the basis of
wartime necessity, but asserted that "distinctions between citizens solely
because of their ancestry are by their very nature odious to a free people
whose institutions are founded upon the doctrine of equality." A 1944 case
involving Japanese removal from the West Coast during the war decided
that "all legal restrictions which curtail the civil rights of a single racial

group are immediately suspect. That is not to say that all such restrictions are unconstitutional. It is to say that courts must subject them to the most rigid scrutiny."

The Court also began making inroads into the state action doctrine, or how much private individuals might act free of constitutional restraint. In 1946 it reversed trespass convictions of Jehovah's Witnesses for proselytizing in a company town, holding that "the more an owner, for his advantage, opens up his property for use by the public in general, the more do his rights become circumscribed by the statutory and constitutional rights of those who use it."

Our job was to exploit the favorable decisions and use them to overwhelm the unfavorable ones.

NATIONAL AND INTERNATIONAL ATTITUDES EVOLVE

As LDF probed how far and fast it might go, a national political consensus began to emerge. In September 1946 Walter White, as head of a National Emergency Committee Against Mob Violence, visited the White House to ask that President Truman call a special session of Congress and undertake a study of American race relations. In response, the president, in December 1946, appointed the President's Committee on Civil Rights. Its mandate was broad: "To inquire into and to determine whether and in what respect current law-enforcement measures and the authority and means possessed by Federal, State, and local governments may be strengthened and improved to safeguard the civil rights of the people." The committee included Morris Ernst, of the LDF National Legal Committee, and Channing Tobias, chairman of the NAACP board. Thurgood testified before the committee urging a wide range of legislation and LDF filed a brief arguing the legal basis for federal protection of civil rights.

Like all presidents, Truman appointed a committee to propose what he wanted to do; he was not disappointed. Its historic 1947 report, *To Secure These Rights,* called for reforms that, within twenty-one years, were adopted in toto by the Congress and the Supreme Court. The report was a catalyst, regularly cited in briefs and before congressional committees. The President's Committee on Civil Rights recommended:

> The elimination of segregation, based on race, color, creed, or national origin.

> The conditioning by Congress of all . . . federal assistance to public or private agencies for any purpose on the absence of discrimination and segregation.

The enactment by Congress of a law stating that discrimination and segregation, based on race, color, creed, or national origin, in the rendering of all public services by the national government is contrary to public policy.

The enactment by Congress of a law prohibiting discrimination or segregation . . . in interstate transportation. . . .

Prohibition of discrimination and segregation . . . in all public or publicly supported hospitals, parks, recreational facilities, housing projects, welfare agencies, penal institutions, and concessions on public property.

The establishment of a fair educational practice program . . . in the admission of students to private educational institutions.

The establishment of a fair health practice program forbidding discrimination and segregation by public or private agencies. . . .

The outlawing of restrictive covenants.

Granting equal access to places of public accommodation.

On October 30, 1947, the day following issuance of the report of the president's committee, Truman's solicitor general, Philip Perlman, filed a friend-of-the-court brief in the Restrictive Covenant Cases supporting the LDF position that court enforcement of restrictive covenants was unconstitutional. Earlier, Truman addressed the NAACP annual convention and called for progress in civil rights.

MOVING AHEAD IN HIGHER EDUCATION: MARYLAND, MISSOURI, OKLAHOMA

The nation and the Court clearly seemed primed to move ahead on civil rights, but the question was *how* primed. NAACP and LDF lawyers proceeded principally with a campaign against segregation in higher education, not exactly following Margold, who had aimed at elementary and high schools, or his primary legal theory, which rested on *Yick Wo*. They also found it impossible to confine their efforts to schools only, tackling teachers' salaries, voting, housing, transportation, criminal cases, and other subjects. But the Margold Report had established the importance of a long-range goal and a plan for reaching it, lessons the LDF followed even as it adjusted the plan and occasionally substituted short-range goals.

In 1936 Thurgood and Charles Houston won *Pearson v. Murray* in the Maryland courts, requiring the state to admit Donald Murray, a black applicant who didn't want to go out of state, to Maryland's white law school because it didn't have a black one. The state didn't appeal to the United States Supreme Court and so no nationally binding precedent was established. Murray entered the University of Maryland Law School, graduated, and went into practice. (I knew him as a quiet, cheerful legal aid lawyer when I traveled to Baltimore. He showed up at NAACP events, but never participated in civil rights cases.)

Then in 1938 Houston, with Thurgood, Leon Ransom, and Sidney Redmond, early associates whose participation waned in later years, won a case against the University of Missouri on the same grounds as in the Maryland case, this time in the United States Supreme Court. That should have made clear that, at least when there was no comparable black institution, blacks had to be admitted to the white school. The Missouri plaintiff, Lloyd Gaines, disappeared, however, and, unlike Donald Murray, never did enjoy the fruits of his victory. Rumors flew about foul play, that he couldn't take the pressure and had run off to Mexico, and so forth. But no one ever discovered anything. Missouri opened a black law school, so that if the issue were to arise again, it wouldn't have to admit blacks to its white universities. So far as the South was concerned, the Maryland and Missouri cases had never been decided. No other Southern state admitted black students because of their precedent. Then there were no further Supreme Court decisions in higher education until the late 1940s, probably because the war made it difficult to find plaintiffs. The Association's efforts during the war and early postwar years focused on the White Primary Cases.

In a cautious approach, the NAACP, as late as 1945, though committed to ending segregation, nevertheless resolved to implement the earlier victories by stressing inequality rather than attacking segregation itself. A 1945 legal department report stated:

> The NAACP still believes that segregation in public education is unconstitutional. However, in view of the present decisions of the United States Supreme Court, it is believed that an affirmative campaign to compel the southern states to give absolute equality in its segregated schools will not only give Negro children equal educational facilities but the tremendous cost of maintaining an equal dual school system will eventually destroy segregation.

Higher education remained the model case of inequality: Whites had graduate and professional schools and blacks had virtually nothing. Admission to the white institution would be the appropriate relief. In 1946 Thurgood and Amos Hall of Tulsa, Ada Lois Sipuel's LDF lawyers, sought a court order requiring Oklahoma to admit her to its all-white law school. Oklahoma, too, had no law school for blacks, but defended on the ground that there weren't enough black applicants to make opening one worthwhile. Hall had invited Thurgood to enter the case because his office was the fount of expertise on segregation issues. I knew Hall principally as a Prince Hall Mason, the black Masonic group to which Thurgood also belonged, and they bonded together closely in that relationship and its rituals.

Around the same time another law school applicant appeared in Texas. Heman Marion Sweatt's LDF lawyers, Thurgood, W. J. Durham, and James M. Nabrit, Jr.—who taught the first civil rights course in America at Howard—applied for a court order admitting him to the University of Texas Law School. Texas didn't have a black law school either. Here we were all over again—virtually a decade later—still fighting over the same issues.

The Oklahoma Supreme Court ruled against Sipuel saying that she should have asked for a separate black law school and that also she could have had a scholarship to attend school out of state. The Texas courts took a different tack, giving the university six months to offer legal instruction "substantially equivalent" to that at the University of Texas. Texas then announced it would establish a law school for blacks that would be equal to the University of Texas Law School. It would be in the basement of a petroleum company building in downtown Austin, and consist of three medium-sized rooms, one smaller room, and a toilet, which had been leased for $125 per month. There would be no library, but students might use the library in the state capitol; the faculty would be three University of Texas professors who would teach part-time. There were no other students, moot court, legal aid clinic, law review, honorary societies, or scholarship fund. Charles T. McCormick, dean of the University of Texas, was made dean also of the new black school. He was a celebrated legal scholar, author of leading texts on evidence and damages. Demonstrating that one's status as a scholar was no guarantee that one would issue only intelligent utterings, McCormick testified that the two law schools were equal. If the thought of testifying honestly had crossed his mind he would have had to consider that the state legislature would retaliate with devastating disapproval.

Then in May 1947 Thurgood, Durham, and Nabrit conducted a full-scale trial to prove the obvious—the two Texas schools weren't equal and never could be. They built on an approach developed by Bob Carter in a 1946 friend-of-the-court brief that attacked segregation of Mexican Americans in California by documenting the psychological consequences of segregation. Social science materials had been used before, but not a great deal. Louis D. Brandeis had in 1908 written a pioneering brief that marshaled social scientific data in support of a law that limited the number of hours women might work. He showed that the law had a reasonable basis and argued that it was, therefore, constitutional. But, in the higher education cases, LDF lawyers went beyond published materials. They commissioned research and called sociologists, psychologists, psychiatrists, educators, and others as expert witnesses. Unlike Brandeis, who argued in support of a law, they used social scientific evidence to strike one down.

The evidence concerning library, faculty, classrooms, and other facilities was what one might have expected. But more important was social scientific testimony about intangible aspects of education presented by Robert Redfield, chairman of the department of anthropology at the University of Chicago, who also was a lawyer, and Earl Harrison, dean of the University of Pennsylvania Law School. They testified that race is not relevant to ability to learn and that segregation interferes with law school education. Charles Thompson, dean of Howard University's Graduate School of Education, testified that wherever segregation existed, black schools were vastly inferior to white ones in measurable respects. As was probably expected, it all went for naught in the Texas courts, which ruled that the schools were equal. To play it safe Texas moved to upgrade the black law school. Thurgood and Durham headed for the Supreme Court.

As *Sweatt* was pending, Thurgood took *Sipuel* to the Supreme Court also, arguing it one week before the argument in the Restrictive Covenant Cases. Two such arguments in a week is pretty much like the iron-man feat of pitching a doubleheader. After *Gaines*, *Sipuel* should have been a piece of cake, and it was. The Court held that "the State must provide [legal education] to her in conformity with the equal protection clause of the Fourteenth Amendment and provide it *as soon as* it does for applicants of any other group." Arguments concluded on January 8, 1948. The Court announced its decision in record time on January 12. It meant *"as soon as"* quite emphatically.

Though the *"as soon as"* language seemed to rule out any attempts to circumvent the decision by promising Miss Sipuel her own law school, Oklahoma did not accept Miss Sipuel graciously. The local court ordered that "unless and until the separate school of law for Negroes . . . is established and ready to function" authorities were required to enroll her in the University of Oklahoma *or* "not enroll any applicant of any group in said class until said separate school is established and ready to function." Oklahoma then set up a separate law school for Miss Sipuel by roping off a portion of the state capitol, and calling it a law school for colored students.

Thurgood went back to the Supreme Court and asked for an order requiring Oklahoma to admit her. Now he unequivocally asked for an end to segregation per se. He argued that a legal education, like any good education, is *collegial*, in that students often learn as much from frank discussion with each other as they learn from their professors, and that, moreover, segregation brands blacks with a "badge of inferiority." But rather than react with indignation at Oklahoma's response to its earlier ruling, the Supreme Court backed off. Maybe the justices had hoped that their first decision would cause segregation to crumble, and, that not having been the case, now found themselves unwilling to provoke a direct challenge to the authority of the Court by the politically formidable South. In February 1948, over a vigorous dissent by Justice Rutledge and a milder one by Justice Murphy, the Court said that it never had ordered Oklahoma to admit Miss Sipuel, only not to treat her unequally.

Further hearings in lower courts would be needed to determine whether the new school was unequal and whether requiring Miss Sipuel to go to a segregated school was unconstitutional. The experience taught that going for an end to segregation, and that alone, presented a big risk. After the second *Sipuel* argument, all of our school litigation rested on two legs, a demand for an end to segregation as such and a claim that it should be abolished because black and white offerings were unequal, in a physical sense obviously, but also unequal because of the educational and psychological effects of segregation itself.

Thurgood and his colleagues returned to the trial court and presented virtually the same evidence on the effects of segregation that they had offered in May 1947 in the Texas case, with a few more witnesses, including Erwin Griswold, dean of Harvard Law School, and Walter Gellhorn. They lost again in the Oklahoma courts in August 1948.

That month LDF lawyers commenced another higher education case, *McLaurin v. Oklahoma*, using a procedure they had never tried before—filing in a three-judge United States District Court. McLaurin, then in his sixties, had applied in early 1948 to the University of Oklahoma's Graduate School of Education. (His wife had applied and been rejected on racial grounds in 1923!) But more than litigation was going on. The state also was under pressure from its own citizens. In January 1948 one thousand of the university's twelve thousand students protested segregation by cremating a copy of the Fourteenth Amendment and sending the ashes to President Truman.

In October 1948 the three-judge court held that Oklahoma was violating the Constitution by excluding McLaurin because it had no graduate instruction for him at a black school—the word was getting around, at last. But the court refrained from issuing an order because the governor, in a letter to the court, promised to propose legislation to permit blacks to attend white universities. The rights of blacks could wait—a common official reaction, which persisted through the *Brown* case. Before the new law was passed, however, the university admitted McLaurin, and introduced a new twist, which might seem cruelly comic today, but which could only frustrate and humiliate him. They would teach him a lesson! He would not be permitted to sit in the classroom with white students; instead, he was assigned to an anteroom from which he looked into the classroom occupied by whites. As the desegregation controversy swirled, the Oklahoma legislature, in June 1949, amended its laws to permit blacks to attend white graduate and professional programs, where such programs were not given in black schools, *but on a segregated basis only.* Around the same time the university admitted Ada Lois Sipuel under the new law, but didn't segregate her and her case dissolved. Maybe a black female was seen as less threatening than a black male, even one in his sixties.

McLaurin's segregated status, however, continued to present a real issue, and Thurgood wanted to pursue his case. But he reported to the LDF board that there was a problem with Amos Hall, which he didn't describe, who like some other black lawyers at that time was not eager to attack segregation. My guess is that Hall and others like him were afraid to rock the boat, believing that pushing too hard, too fast would be counterproductive. McLaurin, however, wanted to push on, which was the decisive factor and determined that LDF lawyers would appeal. After all, McLaurin's wife had been waiting since 1923 for things to change. Thurgood and Hall went back to the district court seeking an order prohibiting segregation. McLaurin testified about sitting in the antechamber, saying it was "quite strange and humiliating to be placed out in that position, and it handicaps me in doing effective work."

But the district court again said no. LDF lawyers appealed and, when *McLaurin* reached the Supreme Court, the university's confining McLaurin to the anteroom seemed so ludicrous that he was admitted into the classroom—but, once inside, he was limited to a seat for blacks only. In the cafeteria and library, too, he was confined to blacks-only chairs and tables. The case had begun with exclusion, moved to the anteroom, then to Jim Crow seats in the classroom, library, and cafeteria. So in the Supreme Court the case increasingly looked like one of segregation per se.

As the 1940s came to a close, *Sweatt* and *McLaurin* were in the Supreme Court. Sipuel was attending the University of Oklahoma Law School without having established any sweeping principle. *Gaines* had long before established that where the state had no black law school, blacks had to be admitted to the white law school. LDF lawyers filed a few more higher education cases in Louisiana and South Carolina. In North Carolina, Texas, and Virginia they began campaigns against discrimination in elementary and high schools in which the complaints ambiguously attacked inequality and segregation, leaving them free to proceed on either basis.

At the same time other LDF cases across the entire South were equalizing black and white teachers' salaries. None of those cases ever was decided by the Supreme Court. After some stonewalling by school boards and one firing of a teacher (later reversed in court) most cases were settled and school systems began paying black teachers equally—sometimes phasing in equality because boards couldn't afford it all at once. Thurgood was involved in almost all the cases personally, while bringing the monumental voting, travel, restrictive covenant, and education cases.

THE WORLD AROUND THEM

In this environment, international and political developments inspired hope. The more than 900,000 black soldiers who risked their lives for the four freedoms laid a powerful claim to the right to enjoy them. Also, service in the armed forces developed in many Americans a more spacious and less xenophobic view of the world: Different peoples, cultures, colors became more familiar, less strange. Whites could not ignore that blacks' blood had been shed in defense of their country. Everyone felt more sensitively the opprobrium with which other countries viewed American apartheid. Hitler had given scientific racism a bad name and the country's "National Origins" immigration policy increasingly became an embarrassment. Articles about Africans clad in tribal robes, served in Southern restaurants or seated in white Pullman cars, while American blacks were Jim Crowed, became almost commonplace. Sometimes American blacks faked being African diplomats and were served in places where they would have been excluded in mufti. When they revealed who they were there would be a lot of publicity ridiculing racism. White journalists, disguised as blacks, traveled in the South and wrote about the experience. The Soviet Union missed few opportunities to denounce the United States for its racial practices. And while we decried European colonialism, it was difficult to demand that Europeans cease ruling countries inhabited by darker races while we persisted in similar practices. In a South Carolina voting case, Judge J. Waties Waring wrote, "When this country is taking the lead in maintaining the democratic process and attempting to show to the world that the American government and the American way of life is the fairest and best that has yet been suggested, it is time for us to take stock of our internal affairs."

The NAACP regularly capitalized on the international criticism of America. Harold Oram's first appeal concerning the Detroit race riot asserted: "The shock was all the greater because our country is now in the midst of a struggle of life and death with the Axis powers, whose avowed object is the destruction of democracy and the enthronement of dictatorships run on the 'master race' theory. . . . The Detroit race riot embodied many of the practices which have been associated with Nazi Germany and her partner, the Japanese empire. Here race was pitted against race."

Supreme Court Justice Benjamin Cardozo, discussing how law develops, once wrote that "the final cause of law is the welfare of society. The rule that misses its aim cannot permanently justify its existence." The rule of law was beginning to move toward its proper mark.

6

LAW SCHOOLS IN
THE SUPREME COURT

SWEATT AND McLAURIN

My role in both *Sweatt* and *McLaurin* was slight. In *Sweatt* I did such low-level things as spend day and night in the library researching cases, constitutional history, social science literature, and reading proof at the printer. Having taken *McLaurin* to the Supreme Court, Thurgood then questioned whether we'd followed the proper procedure for three-judge courts—a little late, but everything was not programmed neatly. Three-judge courts were established in the twenties to hear cases in which a plaintiff wanted to enjoin operation of a state statute. The idea was that so serious a decision should not be left to a single, perhaps idiosyncratic judge. Three-judge courts had some advantages, a great one being that the case was heard promptly and went immediately to the Supreme Court, swiftly bypassing the court of appeals. Besides, as the three-judge law was written, the Supreme Court was obliged to hear a case, which went up under a mandatory jurisdiction called *appeal*, and could not slough it off as it usually did under its discretionary jurisdiction, called *certiorari*. Of course, if the Court wanted to avoid deciding a case, it often found a way. The three-judge court jurisdiction was fairly untried and I was supposed to become expert in it to anticipate any tricky questions that might arise during argument. I researched the law to a fare-thee-well and finally concluded that I was wrestling with a phantom question; by the time I was through everyone was satisfied that the three-judge court presented no difficulty, and it didn't. No problems involving the question arose during Bob Carter's argument, but in the process I think I came to know as much about three-judge courts as anyone in the country and we used that knowledge effectively over the years at LDF. The procedure became so popular in later years that it became a burden on the courts, taking the time of three judges when one might do, and it was repealed not long ago.

The *Sweatt* brief, filed in February 1950, flatly attacked the constitutionality of segregation. Yet, it made arguments that could bring victory while allowing decision on grounds short of overruling *Plessy*. First, it asserted, *Plessy* was a railroad car case and inapplicable to schools; it also urged that equal protection prohibits segregation in education because it cannot be justified on any ground, including keeping the peace or alleged intellectual differences between the races; and it said that segregation invidiously penalizes blacks, demoralizes whites, and disrupts democratic institutions. Here the brief elaborated on psychological, sociological, and anthropological material offered by witnesses at the *Sweatt* and *Sipuel* trials. Second, it argued that earlier cases assumed the validity of segregation in education, but didn't decide it.

Finally, however, if *Plessy* applied to education, it should be overruled, the *Sweatt* brief claimed, because the framers of the Fourteenth Amendment rejected separate-but-equal and because segregation inevitably resulted in inequality. The brief showed the tangible ways in which blacks' higher education in Texas was inferior to whites'. White plant was valued at more than $72,000,000, black at $4,000,000; per capita black investment was one-quarter of that for whites. Whites had 106 fields of specialization, blacks only 49, including mattress making, auto mechanics, carpeting, laundering, and dry cleaning. Whites could get graduate degrees in 40 fields, blacks in 13. Texas gave whites 212 doctorates between 1940 and 1945; no black institution qualified to grant a doctorate. The University of Texas library had more than 750,000 volumes; the black school about 82,000.

The brief then turned to the law schools. The University of Texas library had 65,000 volumes, the black school none of its own. The university had sixteen full-time faculty, the black school none, other than three of the white school's faculty who were supposed to teach at the black school. The university had 850 students; if Sweatt had gone to the black school he would have been alone. The university had a moot court, legal aid clinic, law review, honor society, and scholarship fund. The black school had none of these. This litany supported two arguments: Sweatt should be admitted because of the tangible inequalities. Those inequalities also could support an argument based on *Yick Wo v. Hopkins* suggested by Margold: The law prohibiting laundries in wooden buildings was unconstitutional because *in operation* it discriminated against Chinese; similarly, the law placing blacks in separate schools, which always were unequal, was unconstitutional because *in operation* it inevitably treated blacks unequally. The brief also pushed hard the social and psychological consequences of segregation, from which it argued that segregation per se was unconstitutional.

The *Sweatt* approach, arguing from inequality and segregation per se, wasn't viable in *McLaurin* where everything tangible was equal: McLaurin was in the same classroom, had the same teachers at the same time, used the same library and cafeteria. *McLaurin* was an attractive case because, on the one hand, it offered the Court no escape (we thought) from deciding the issue of segregation; it was dangerous because it allowed no victory on grounds short of overruling *Plessy*, which the Court might be reluctant to do. The *McLaurin* brief argued that "to admit appellant and then single him out solely because of his race and to require him to sit outside the regular classroom could be for no purpose other than to humiliate and degrade him—to place a badge of inferiority upon him." There was a secondary argument to the effect that *Plessy*, which dealt with travel, shouldn't govern education.

I learned that merely writing and printing our briefs was not enough. LDF lawyers urged other interest groups to file briefs to inform the Court of the broader implications of LDF cases. Thurgood lobbied the solicitor general (who represents the government in the Supreme Court), the attorney general, and even the president to get the government on our side in cases. We polished, edited, and reedited everything. The briefs and legal papers looked good because we proofread everything carefully, reading aloud to one another. There were no erasures, no strikeovers, no smudges, no wrinkles. When Thurgood was in law school he once carried some legal papers to court for a black practitioner. They were messy. The clerk looked them over and commented, "A nigger brief." Thurgood vowed we never would file "nigger briefs."

There was no doubt about the ultimate objective. Despite the hedging arguments aimed at winning on grounds short of overthrowing segregation, Thurgood focused on the end of Jim Crow. In 1950, in acerbic correspondence with Carter Wesley, a Texas lawyer-publisher, Thurgood wrote: "A segregated school can never be the equal of any school which has all other racial and ethnic groups in it ... even if the two schools were practically identical as to plant, library, curriculum, and faculty."

STANDING UP BEFORE THE COURT

Sweatt and *McLaurin* introduced me to how to prepare a Supreme Court argument, a skill at which Thurgood excelled. He dictated an argument not to read in court, but as a base from which to speak extemporaneously and to which he might return if distracted by questions. Standing before the Court he might, however, sometimes read the portions of the written argument that dealt with particularly sensitive issues. He would also craft in writing answers to questions that a justice might ask and turn to that text if necessary. One explosive issue was interracial sex: Would overruling *Plessy* mean invalidating interracial sex laws, sometimes referred to as miscegenation and cohabitation statutes? The white South was insane on the issue—

Northern attitudes weren't very rational either—contributing to the large number of capital sentences imposed on black men convicted of raping white women. White mobs lynched blacks who dated or had personal relationships with white women. The attorneys general of eleven Southern states filed a brief in *Sweatt* that raised high the sex issue: "Negro men do not want their daughters, wives, and sweethearts dancing, dating, and playing with white men any more than white men want their women folk in intimate social contact with Negro men. 'White trash' is the hated name which Southern Negroes apply to white men who keep the company of their women folk. Worse names are applied to Negro men who 'cross the line.'"

To assert that laws prohibiting miscegenation or interracial sex were unconstitutional would bring down a firestorm of criticism and possibly intimidate the Court or some of its justices. But to deny that those laws were unconstitutional would be wrong and lack credibility. Moreover, some blacks would view such a position as craven. The thing to do would be to duck, artfully, if possible. Answers were prepared in the nature of "that's not this case," "the considerations which govern the two situations are very different," and so forth. In *Sweatt* and *McLaurin* the justices, as it turned out, were not interested in exacerbating the issue, so the prepared formulations never had to be used.

Thurgood would also prepare a notebook of summaries of all the pertinent cases for quick reference; the summaries were later replaced by edited photocopies. He thoroughly indexed the record with tabs—and kept the case summaries and index at his side during argument for quick reference.

There was also the "dry run." We were perhaps the first to have dry runs before Supreme Court arguments—at least on a regular basis. LDF never had a Supreme Court argument in those days that was not first argued at Howard Law School before a panel of lawyers and professors who asked every imaginable question they thought might come from the Court. Most focused on what Justice Frankfurter might ask—he was the most prolific questioner on the bench. I did a count of his questioning during the School Segregation Cases: He asked more questions—punctuated by rocking and swiveling back and forth and all around in his chair—than all the other justices combined, and that was typical of him. Neither I nor any LDF lawyer was ever asked a question in actual argument that had not first been asked at the dry run—until Warren Burger became chief justice. Some of his questions were so idiosyncratic that no one could predict them. Whereas a Supreme Court argument used to take an hour, dry runs kept you on your feet for two or three hours; I sometimes quit with a sore back.

And, finally, like a boxer going into training, for the period of preparation—about a week before argument—Thurgood would limit himself to one glass of wine at dinnertime, usually sherry, and no other alcohol.

The Court heard *Sweatt* and *McLaurin* with a third case, *Henderson v.*

United States, which arose out of a Southern railway practice of refusing to serve black passengers in dining cars, except during a brief period when blacks might be served behind a curtain. (*Henderson* was the only important civil rights case that was not an LDF case until at least a decade after I got to the Fund.) The railroad installed curtains to separate the two tables nearest the kitchen from adjoining tables, drawing them into position before mealtime and placing "reserved" cards on them. Should all other seats be taken before any black passenger entered the diner, the curtain would be pushed back, the cards removed, and white passengers would be served at those tables. Should a colored passenger appear he would be served behind drawn curtains as soon as the end tables were vacated. Elmer Henderson, a black field representative of the President's Committee on Fair Employment Practices, filed a complaint against this practice in 1942 and, as in *McLaurin*, the railway squirmed to substitute something it thought more acceptable, but made things worse, if that were possible. It put up a permanent partition in one diner behind which was a table always set aside for blacks and had begun reconstructing all its dining cars by the time *Henderson* got to the Supreme Court.

Perhaps most important about Henderson's case was that the United States government intervened on his side—peculiar, in that it was attacking the Interstate Commerce Commission, part of the government. In any event, the government argued not merely that the regulation was illegal, but that if it were justified by *Plessy v. Ferguson*, *Plessy* should be overruled. The brief alluded to Communist efforts to infiltrate black groups; quoted Dean Acheson, then secretary of state, as testifying "that the existence of discriminations against minority groups in the United States is a handicap in our relations with other countries"; cited the United Nations Charter and its human rights provisions; and quoted Soviet attacks on American racial practices. It concluded, "It is neither reasonable nor right that colored citizens of the United States should be subjected to the humiliation of being segregated by law, on the pretense that they are being treated as equals."

In *Sweatt* and *McLaurin* the government filed another, more concise amicus brief, concluding that "the 'separate-but-equal' theory of *Plessy v. Ferguson* is wrong as a matter of law, history, and policy." Most persuasive was that the United States came out four-square against segregation. That political act reflected the inexorable movement toward racial equality manifested in the 1947 report of the President's Committee on Civil Rights and the influence of black voters in the 1948 election.

Well aware that in the Supreme Court law intersects with politics, Southern segregationists enlisted Sam Hobbs, a member of the House Judiciary Committee (which could propose laws determining the Court's jurisdiction and set its budget), to argue as a friend of the court for segregation aboard railways.

On April 3 and 4, 1950, Thurgood argued *Sweatt* and Bob argued *McLaurin* along with Belford Lawson and Jawn Sandifer, private lawyers who argued *Henderson*. The marble four-storied Supreme Court building, which resembles a Greek temple, occupies a square block and is set back from the street, its second-floor entrance atop a lengthy staircase, nearly a hundred feet wide. On its pediment is inscribed "Equal Justice Under Law," a maxim later adopted by LDF as the name of its newsletter and, often, as the title of its annual convocations, which review recent civil rights events. Inside, the courtroom is forty feet high, and about eighty feet wide by ninety feet long. Some have ridiculed as overdone and un-American its classic grandeur, massive columns inside and out, coffered and rosetted ceiling, rich dark woods and deep red velvet fabrics, and sculpture of scenes and personalities representing themes of law and justice. But from the beginning I was awed, as I still am when the marshal, who sits to the right of the bench, calls court to order with "Oyez, oyez, oyez," which is Old French for "hear, hear, hear," ending with "God save the United States and this honorable Court" and a rap of the gavel. The clerk, whose management of many aspects of the Court's business makes his a powerful position, sits at a desk to the left of the bench. Upon first entering the building I felt a nakedness on my head, as if I were in a synagogue and not wearing a skullcap.

A mahogany rail separated members of the Supreme Court bar from others; inside the rail perhaps a hundred lawyers who had come to hear the arguments sat on straight-backed chairs with padded leather seats; in front of them were tables, one on each side of the courtroom, each with two capacious armchairs for lawyers in the next case. Further toward the front were two long tables, together extending almost the length of the justices' bench, where the lawyers who were arguing sat. Goose quill pens, which now sell in the Court's gift shop for seventy-five dollars, with which no one possibly could write, were placed in front of counsel. Lawyers brought them home as souvenirs. An associate or two might be seated at counsel table because he (in those days, rarely, she) might be helpful, or, not infrequently, as a gesture to accord recognition for assistance rendered in the case. A lectern, which lawyers could raise and lower, separated the two sets of opponents. There were two lights on the lectern, a red and a white one. The white light was to warn that the allotted time for argument would soon expire. Before argument the advocate was supposed to tell the marshal how many minutes should be saved for rebuttal and how far in advance the white light should be turned on. The illuminated red light meant time was up. At that point, it was said, you were supposed to stop in the middle of the word "if." Thurgood loved telling of Francis Biddle who once, in arguing a case, was being particularly hard-pressed. As the red light lit up, instead of answering, he placed one foot on the other and exclaimed, "Red light!" as if saying "Safe!"

On the right side of the courtroom was a section for the justices' guests—back in those days, most often their wives. The press sat on chairs between the counsel table and the bench. Reporters would write notes, place them in cylinders, and drop them into pneumatic tubes that sucked them to the press room. Behind the rail were seats for perhaps three hundred members of the general public, some reserved for guests of lawyers who were arguing cases. The others were for the public at large, frequently groups of school children visiting Washington, who were seated in batches, permitted to listen for ten or fifteen minutes, and then quietly ushered out to make room for the next bunch. Throughout the courthouse and courtroom were marshals in blue serge suits who quietly and efficiently kept order, directing people to where they ought to go and keeping them out of where they shouldn't be. To the right of the counsel table and a little forward of it sat the marshal, who calls the Court to order.

The raised bench at which the justices sat, and on which they placed their papers, overlooked all this. The bench was a long mahogany desk that ran the length of nine high-backed leather swivel chairs, each individually crafted for a particular justice. Behind the chairs were the red velvet drapes from which the justices emerged when the marshal rapped his gavel and called the Court to order. Today it is all virtually the same, although Chief Justice Burger introduced innovations. The justices' bench is no longer straight. It is in three sections, with a right and left wing jutting into the courtroom, connected at shallow angles to the center section, three justices sitting at each section. The press, with whom Burger had a tense relationship, no longer sit directly in front of the bench, having been moved to the left side of the courtroom. Burger also gave each justice a silver cup in place of their ordinary drinking glasses. Some skeptics made the irreverent suggestion that it was to conceal what they were drinking. Burger didn't like the activity of note taking, and preferred to isolate it; he wouldn't allow lawyers to take notes if they weren't seated at counsel table. Jack McKenzie of the *New York Times,* who was a Supreme Court reporter at the time of the change, did not get along well with Burger and often criticized him. McKenzie tells that Burger explained to the press that he was moving them to the new area and that perhaps it would be enclosed in glass. McKenzie asked, "Will there be oxygen?" eliciting a look of strong disapproval. Burger always was rearranging and refurbishing the courthouse. One day, while Thurgood was a justice, he ambled down a corridor, his law clerks trailing behind him, muttering, "Warren Burger sure knows how to pick good carpets."

At the argument there were no surprises and no fireworks. Attorney General J. Howard McGrath argued that segregation was unconstitutional, calling it "ceremonial," an imposition of legally enforced caste status; few things could be more humiliating than to be publicly labeled as inferior; unless segregation were ended the United States would suffer seriously in world affairs. He pointed out that the Court's decision could reinforce segregation or undermine it and bring it into disrepute. Solicitor General Philip

Perlman mainly fenced with Justice Frankfurter over whether the Court had to decide the constitutional question in *Henderson* if it could dispose of the case by the Interstate Commerce Act's requirement that passengers should be treated without prejudice.

Bob Carter, in *McLaurin*, argued that *Plessy* was inapplicable—it dealt only with travel—and had been wrongly decided. Thurgood, in *Sweatt*, also attacked segregation: "They can build an exact duplicate but if it is segregated, it is unequal." His rhetoric was concrete and tinged with irony: Texas had argued, he said, that the black law school in a basement in Austin was better than the University of Texas, but then it built a new black school in Houston. Now, didn't the white students have cause for complaint? But, carefully, one step at a time, he said that this case would not decide the fate of elementary and high schools or swimming pools, only law schools. And he was not looking for a remedy against personal prejudice: "We want to remove governmental restriction—if they want to, they can keep their prejudices."

The memory of that argument that survives is of how ordinary, conversational, and undramatic the presentations and exchanges were—as, I came to learn, most courtroom arguments are. Sidney Poitier, playing Thurgood in the television play *Separate But Equal*, had it all wrong when he declaimed loudly, shouted, waved his arms, and made faces. Thurgood never did any of that; good lawyers never do. Bob Carter was quiet and occasionally hesitant. But there is such a thing as being too low key. Perlman seemed inarticulate. Only Thurgood, evoking tangible images of building exact duplicates—basement law schools, swimming pools—and of groups "covenanting together," employed a rhetoric with persuasive force beyond its basic ideas.

Some of the byplay of argument as it then was has disappeared in recent years, a victim of efficiency. In 1950 opponents lunched together. Checking into the clerk's office in the morning, the lawyers who were scheduled to argue and a few close associates would indicate their orders on a menu. At lunch break a marshal would usher them down a restricted back staircase to a private dining room on the ground floor where lunch would be delivered on a wheeled cart and served by Court attendants, who were always black. There wasn't an express rule that we had to eat together, but if it weren't required, hard-bitten segregationists never would have dined with us, as they regularly did until much later when Burger introduced new lunching arrangements—now a marshal takes lawyers to the head of the cafeteria line. Blacks and whites dining together was high on the list of racist taboos; we took special delight at being seated at the same table as Southern attorneys general who before and after lunch would rail at the social disruption we were trying to create. But at the table they were never unpleasant, occasionally they were affable, although mostly each side talked only among themselves. If there is an index of social discomfort generated by being forced to dine with unwilling partners, it peaked when Jim Nabrit III and I invited Dick Gregory to join us at lunch in the Supreme Court in the early 1960s. We had run into him in the elevator of the Statler-Hilton the night before I had an argument and suggested that he come to the Court and listen. At the lunch break he approached us and I impulsively took him along to lunch. As he dined with us and our uncomfortable opponents he said loudly, "Them cats in the white robes are trying to take it away from us, Jack, but the guys in the black robes are going to give it back."

On June 5, 1950, the Court decided *Sweatt, McLaurin,* and *Henderson.* In *Sweatt,* after reciting that the black law school was inferior in building, library, and faculty, the Court turned to "qualities that are incapable of objective measurement" in which the black school also was inferior. These included "reputation of the faculty, experience of the administration, position and influence of the alumni, standing in the community, traditions and prestige." The Court went on to state that

> the law school in which Texas is willing to admit petitioner excludes from its student body members of the racial groups which number 85% of the population of the State and include most of the lawyers, witnesses, jurors, judges and other officials with whom petitioner will inevitably be dealing when he becomes a member of the Texas Bar. With such a substantial and significant segment of society excluded, we cannot conclude that the education offered petitioner is substantially equal."

In the *McLaurin* decision the Court held that confining McLaurin to certain seats in the classroom, library, and cafeteria "handicapped [him] in his pursuit of effective graduate instruction. Such restrictions impair and inhibit his ability to study, to engage in discussions and exchange views with other students, and, in general, to learn his profession."

The most intriguing aspect of *McLaurin* was the observation that treating black teachers in an inferior manner would hurt black pupils: "[As our] society grows increasingly complex ... our need for trained leaders increases correspondingly. . . . Those who will come under his guidance and influence must be directly affected by the education he receives. Their own education and development will necessarily suffer to the extent that his training is unequal."

Henderson was decided simply on the grounds that the railroad had violated the Interstate Commerce Act: "The curtains, partitions and signs emphasize the artificiality of a difference in treatment which serves only to call attention to a racial classification of passengers holding identical tickets and using the same public dining facility."

A clean sweep! But while *Sweatt* had appeared to offer a way of winning without ruling on the constitutionality of segregation, *McLaurin* had seemed to present the issue of segregation and nothing else. Nevertheless, saying that McLaurin was being treated unequally was not the same as deciding the issue of segregation. Of course, that might mean that all segregation amounted to inequality, which the Court carefully avoided saying. That afternoon I attended the victory party in the office at 20 West Fortieth Street. There was lots of Scotch and bourbon, clouds of cigarette smoke, lots of laughter and noise and bragging, jokes about race and racial banter, and the almost obligatory poker game. Bobbie Branch, the office manager, an ample woman who resembled Bloody Mary in *South Pacific,* swaggered around, swearing like a marine with great glee. Everyone stayed late, visitors came by, the press was on the phone. The euphoria went on and on. I was elated and swept up in the partying, a new experience. After the party was all over, it seemed that the victory had been so easy, although it really hadn't been. We had researched the law, written briefs, put our coin into the machine, and the right answer came out. And we had a great time doing it. Everyone was psyched up for the next great adventure, the assault on elementary and high schools that *Sweatt* and *McLaurin* invited. We knew also that the work at higher levels of education was far from done.

The Court's reasoning suggested how next to attack segregated education at elementary, high school, and undergraduate levels—go after the intangibles.

THE WORLD THE DECISIONS CONFRONTED

In theory blacks could now go to state-operated, but not private, white graduate and professional schools in the South, although no one anticipated how many more cases would be needed to implement the decision at other schools in Texas and Oklahoma, to say nothing of other Southern states. It would turn out to be even harder than filing and trying more cases, because we hadn't thought about how badly lower levels of Southern education had impoverished black students. Sweatt failed to graduate from the University of Texas Law School. The university built up the all-black school it created for him and it attracted more black students than the University of Texas. Ironically, Texas's predominantly black Thurgood Marshall Law School in Houston is its descendant.

Higher education for blacks continued to be difficult to achieve. Even after the higher education victories, 80 percent of black Americans lived in the South, which continued to take the position that separate-but-equal was still the law of the land. White colleges and universities continued to deny admission to blacks, and we had to continue to litigate in every single state. The deficit that black Americans faced in higher education was so enormous that it would not yield readily—indeed it has not yet been entirely overcome. Of the 1,685 institutions of higher education in the United States in 1945, only 106 were black. In 1947, only about 74,173 of 2,330,000 persons enrolled in colleges and universities were blacks who attended those black institutions. Fewer than fifty blacks in only three Southern states and the District of Columbia attended white institutions. Of the black college and professional school graduates, 90 to 95 percent had gone to black colleges and universities. The disparities were compounded by a gap in curricula and degrees. In the South whites had fifteen medical schools, sixteen law schools, and seventeen schools of engineering; blacks had two medical schools, one accredited law school in Washington, D.C., and no engineering schools. No Southern state, except Maryland (which had been forced by court action), admitted blacks to its white law school. In the arts and sciences, education, commerce, agriculture, home economics, engineering, architecture, and the trades, offerings in white schools far outdistanced those for blacks. Not a single black institution provided work leading to the Ph.D. In engineering and architecture, blacks could not even earn a master's degree. In sum, though blacks were 10 percent of the population, they received only slightly more than 1 percent of the advanced degrees earned in the United States during 1947, none above the master's level except for eight of 3,375 doctoral degrees awarded by nonsegregated institutions.

Some states claimed that they compensated by scholarships to study out of state. In 1954, about 125 black students left Alabama to attend Columbia, Cornell, Harvard, Michigan, Penn, and other elite Northern schools to study medicine, dentistry, law, pharmacology, and to pursue graduate work across the arts and sciences; others scattered to less well-known schools. The overwhelming number went to black institutions like Atlanta University, Howard, and Meharry. Among that year's holders of Alabama out-of-state scholarships was Coretta Scott King, who went to the New England Conservatory of Music. Out-of-state scholarship programs were no more adequately funded than those of in-state black colleges and universities. A black Texan attending Teachers College of Columbia University in New York would have to spend $508 more than he or she would to attend college in Texas. The Texas grant allowed only $235 for tuition and travel.

Lest one think this is ancient history, it is worth remembering that today's blacks who are in mid-career are the near descendants of a generation that was, for all practical purposes, shut out of higher education.

KOREA

To the extent that integration in higher education depended on LDF, as it did for many years, that effort was limited by other demands upon us, some obvious, some unanticipated, like discrimination against black servicemen in the Korean War.

In June 1950 North Korean troops invaded South Korea, and the United States, under the aegis of the United Nations, came to its defense—mobilizing a racially segregated army. At the outset North Korean troops overran both black and white regiments. In September, the military court-martialed a black officer, Lt. Leon Gilbert, a World War II veteran with five battle stars and a record of exceptional bravery, for violation of the 75th Article of War (misbehavior before the enemy) and sentenced him to death. Altogether, two white servicemen had been convicted of that crime, but sixty blacks were charged with it and twenty-three convicted. The whites received five- and three-year sentences; fifteen of the blacks received life terms.

The clamor among the NAACP members and the black public demanded action. Thurgood decided to go to Korea to represent the black soldiers and to strike a blow against segregation in the armed forces. Following his return he wrote and spoke widely about his Korean experience, raised some funds, and attacked the trials as having been conducted in an atmosphere that, rooted in the army's Jim Crow policies, made justice impossible. Specifically, he blamed General MacArthur for having failed to implement the president's order requiring elimination of segregation from the armed services. Thurgood's indictment had its effect. The *New York Times* published an editorial calling for an end to armed forces segregation.[16] A *Pittsburgh Courier* columnist wrote: "While Negroes are fighting Communists in Korea, their people at home are battling anti-Communists. . . . The simple truth is that the Negro has less incentive to fight for America than a but-yesterday-arrived alien with a pale skin."

Thurgood turned over defense of black soldiers in Korea to me and Frank Reeves, who was then in Washington, D.C., but urged exercise of care in deciding which cases to take. In one case he wrote to a local NAACP branch: "There is absolutely no evidence that I can see of injustice to him because of race." In another he wrote that the soldier "is just a bad egg and is using the race question as a cover up for his misdoings." His father had taught him that a black snake and a white snake are the same, a metaphor he was fond of using.

In July 1951 the Department of the Army announced plans to complete integration of Negro personnel in all combat and service units of the Far East command over a period of about six months. In 1952 I wrote a memo stating that we no longer could take cases on the ground that segregation had contributed to a serviceman's plight or that our representation would hasten the abolition of segregation. I proposed that we take only cases in which racial discrimination played a role and limit ourselves to assisting government-appointed appellate defense counsel on matters they could not cover adequately. Thurgood agreed, and we reduced our involvement in military cases.

INTO THE 1950s

The NAACP Legal Department's 1951 annual report (which was still reporting on LDF activities as its own) reported that staff lawyers that year had traveled 72,000 miles. It described seventy-seven court cases and more than seven hundred other matters, many of which were courts-martial or applications for change of military discharge, referrals to the Department of Justice, administrative proceedings, and informal advice in response to letters or walk-ins. We referred most walk-ins to the New York branch of the NAACP. Every now and then an escaped prisoner from a Southern chain gang came in. Thurgood required us to tell them we could not even talk to them, because that might constitute the crime of harboring an escaped felon, but that if they ever were arrested, or turned themselves in to the authorities, they might contact us for help. Some were arrested and we fought their extradition, in a few instances to the Supreme Court, without success. In some cases we persuaded governors not to sign extradition papers, having argued that the convict was innocent or that the chain gang was cruel and unusual punishment. Some walk-ins were obviously paranoid and complained that someone was spying on them (by means of a TV transmitter imbedded in one complainant's back) or trying to poison them (by contaminating paint or piping gas through the floor).

But our eyes never left the prize. By year's end, 1951, we had twenty elementary and high school cases, a dozen higher education cases, five in housing—against segregated public housing projects in Detroit and Schenectady; against Birmingham, Alabama's racial zoning ordinance; one against Levittown, on Long Island, New York, which openly refused to sell to blacks (we lost *Levittown*, because there was no state action)—five against railway and bus companies; a half-dozen in recreation (several involved golf courses on which black doctors and dentists wanted to play); one voting case; a couple of teachers' salary cases; a great many courts-martial; and a variety of miscellaneous matters. Among eleven major criminal cases those with a sex factor loomed large, partly because of the death penalty for rape. Southern irrationality about interracial sex made all such charges suspect.

Still, segregation was at the root of the racial injustices in our society. We had argued, and we believed, that the race excluded from mainstream life comes to be perceived, often by its own members as well as by those of the majority race, as having somehow earned this exclusion, and to be entitled to less than the full protection of the law, even in the meting out of justice.

We had won our graduate and professional school cases. Now it was onward—toward an end to all segregation—and downward—to colleges, high schools, and grade schools.

PART II

EDGING TOWARD
A SHOWDOWN:
BROWN V. BOARD OF
EDUCATION

7

AN END TO SEGREGATION—
NOTHING ELSE

THE NEW STRATEGY

The Association and its lawyers, who at that time for all practical purposes constituted LDF, edged toward a decision to file only cases that asked for an end to segregation. The turning point was 1950. That year, following *Sweatt* and *McLaurin*, they convinced the Association's national convention, held in Boston, to adopt such a resolution. That year, too, I headed irrevocably down the path of a lifetime civil rights career, which I had started upon a year earlier.

In a memorandum to the convention, Thurgood and the legal staff, citing the two recent victories (*Henderson*, as will be recalled, was another victory won by lawyers not affiliated with us and, at any rate, was decided on the very narrow basis that the railroad had violated the Interstate Commerce Act), assigned priorities for the assault on Jim Crow in the following order: public education; transportation with emphasis on local street cars and buses; health, housing, and recreational facilities; public gatherings; places of public accommodation. A tall order for the South, which was totally segregated in all these aspects.

What this decision to attack Jim Crow head on meant in practical terms, however, was not entirely clear. We were, in our aggressive program to end segregation, out in front of many members of the black community. Among the reasons was that school integration would create problems for black teachers, who reasonably anticipated that whites would fight against their teaching white children; we didn't fully appreciate how serious this problem would become. In response, rather than allowing the teachers to be kept hostage by segregationists, we vowed to research how to deal with that problem, though we didn't really know what could be done about it that would be effective. Even so, Thurgood knew that the black population might not be ready. He told a board meeting that "some of the lawyers are ready to fight through the college level but are not ready through the high school and elementary level. They will accept a good Jim Crow school. Many desire to leave it up to the local community and to go as far as they want to go." The board response was recorded as "we can't back out at this time but must try and educate the people."

In January 1951 the board refused to assist the Athens, Georgia, NAACP branch in bringing a school case based on the separate-but-equal theory: "We cannot waive our rule in this case." But they decided to ask Walter White, then scheduled to be in Atlanta, to meet with the branch to try to convince it of the "desirability and necessity of filing an anti-segregation suit."

In Memphis, in 1950, the NAACP branch complained about having access to the zoo on Thursdays only, the rest of the week being reserved for whites. They didn't object to segregation, but protested that on the Thursday that was Thanksgiving the zoo had been turned over to whites. They asked not for an end to the segregation, but for days "proportionate to population and citizenship." This was an occasion on which, as Thurgood sometimes would say, "the easy part of the job is fighting the white folks."

At the same time, even among ourselves, the decision to seek an end to segregaton in all cases left open the question of whether we would attack only *Plessy* or also point out the inequality of buildings, books, and expenditures as reasons why a court should end segregation, either as a remedy for particular situations or as recognition that *Plessy* never had and never could secure even tangible equality. Implicit in the latter strategy was that the inequality might be remedied and Jim Crow retained. To ask for integration because a school was physically inferior *and* segregation was unconstitutional was viewed by some as cowardly and unprincipled. Jim Nabrit, Jr., for example, rejected this approach and attacked only segregation per se in the District of Columbia school case. He would have nothing to do with anything that faintly suggested that if schools were equalized segregation might be acceptable.

But Thurgood was a conservative on this question. Up to the very end of the struggle, he wanted to give judges an opportunity to rule with us on the basis of physical inequalities, whether or not they shared our moral outrage. In the meantime we continued work as we had before, case by case, one day at a time.

As for me, in 1950 I not only got my first real cases but I was asked to participate in matters that were critical to the main work of the Fund.

Though *Sweatt* and *McLaurin* dealt only with graduate and professional education they clearly implied that all higher education had to desegregate, down to the undergraduate level. But no white Southern public undergraduate college made a move to admit blacks. Not even the not very Southern, former slaveholding state of Delaware was ready to comply. I was delighted when Thurgood called me in one day and said that Louis Redding, the sole black lawyer in Delaware, needed our help to attack segregation at the undergraduate college of the University of Delaware—the first case challenging segregated college education. Delaware had black and white schools of higher education—the University of Delaware (white) and unaccredited Delaware State College (black). He picked me because my in-laws lived in Delaware, not a bad reason and an expression of the personal, free-form way Thurgood ran the office. The case was mine.

MY FIRST BIG CASE: THE FIRST TO INTEGRATE A COLLEGE

In 1929 Redding had become the only black lawyer in Delaware, a solitary role that he filled for almost three decades. He had gone to Brown and Harvard Law School and returned home at the urging of his father, a Howard graduate who was a letter carrier and wanted Louis to become the first black lawyer in the state. Lou's brother, Jay Saunders Redding, became a professor of English at Cornell and wrote books on black history and culture. Lou spoke in cultured tones, slowly, considering every word. He was of medium height, with close-cropped hair and a trim mustache, and was always impeccably dressed. He wore Brooks Brothers and J. Press suits, button-down shirts, silk rep or paisley neckties, and usually carried or let dangle from his lips an unlit cigarette, filter end outward. Lou did not suffer fools lightly. Some called him an arrogant snob. His first wife, Ruth, told of the time at a wedding when a man from the congregation offered a long prayer that she said had affected her emotionally. Lou responded, "The grammar was terrible." A so-called white liberal said, "If that man was white I could learn to hate him." But I loved Lou for many reasons, in part, perhaps, because I saw in his manner, which was admittedly more reserved than mine, something resembling my own taciturnity and intolerance of nonsense.

Lou's office was one flight up in a walk-up building in downtown Wilmington, where he shared the second floor with a photographer. He knew the landlord, who rented to him though he was the only black in the neighborhood. He practiced alone, with a secretary, and handled a wide variety of matters throughout Delaware, like title closings, mortgages, divorces, wills, major and minor criminal cases. On the long automobile trip from Wilmington to the state capital in Dover, where his practice regularly took him, there was only one place where blacks could stop for a cup of coffee. In Wilmington, the only places he and I could lunch together were at the railroad station and the Negro Y. Early in his career court officials tried to segregate him in the courtroom, but he wouldn't submit. He fought the policy of segregating black plaintiffs, defendants, witnesses, and spectators. He wouldn't live in Delaware, but resided at first in New Jersey and later in

Pennsylvania in a wonderful eighteenth-century farmhouse, and commuted to Wilmington to minimize his contact with segregation. He regularly did his research on weekends in New York at the County Lawyers Association or the Association of the Bar of the City of New York. In 1992, when Lou was ninety, the city of Wilmington named the city-county building after him and dedicated a bronze statue of him. It took them a long time to recognize the greatness of one who, while insulted by the dominant powers in his home state, had returned to be close to his family and origins, and to make it better for everyone.

We prepared the college case by digging through records and visiting faculty of the black school at night in their homes. They feared reprisals and knew that if we succeeded their school might be closed and they might lose their jobs, but they spoke to us anyway. I tracked down educational experts to testify on the differences between the schools and the inequality created by segregation per se. We visited the president of the University of Delaware, who was the defendant. Segregation was so pervasive that we had no way of knowing his attitude until we actually interviewed him. To our surprise he cooperated and wished us well. He was embarrassed that he had to segregate. I did a lot of legal research to demonstrate the obvious, that the university was a state institution—it was founded and funded by the state—which its lawyers denied. The university's lawyers denied the obvious up and down the line. How embarrassed *they* were, if at all, at having to utter such nonsense, I never learned.

The state court judge, Collins J. Seitz, who had the ancient English title of vice-chancellor, had been elected by the state legislature and would have to think twice about whether he would be reelected, promoted, or forced to return to private practice before ruling in our favor. During the trial he decided to see for himself and drove to both schools at breakneck speed, our car in pursuit, to inspect them. Among my witnesses was Charles Thompson, who helped launch the campaign against segregated education and had clashed with W. E. B. Du Bois in the celebrated 1935 *Journal of Negro Education* issue that reported the debate of black leadership over whether to go down the road of equalization or integration. Thompson demonstrated that the college was inferior to the university. He offered the opinion that separate-but-equal education is impractical, uneconomical, and theoretically impossible. He cited the dire effects of segregation on the personalities of black boys and girls and on whites as well. He referred also to the U.S. struggle with the Soviet Union for the allegiance of the colored peoples of the world. One might wonder at the legal relevance, but he wanted to say it anyway. Admitted into evidence or not, factors like those influenced legal development.

Besides the argument that the University of Delaware was not a state institution, lawyers for the university claimed that it provided no better an education than that offered at the unaccredited black school. They apparently had no shame, for this was another blatantly ridiculous argument. In curricula, faculty, buildings and grounds, library, money, and every other imaginable respect the university, situated on a beautiful campus, was vastly better than the shabby, decrepit college. We pursued the dual approach: integrate because the schools are unequal (and promises to equalize do nothing to alleviate that inequality); integrate because segregation is unconstitutional. An argument that bracketed both approaches was that segregation affects black students adversely and that inherent inequality necessarily invalidates segregation, the basis of *Sweatt* and *McLaurin*.

Of course, we most wanted a decision that segregation was unconstitutional. But Vice-Chancellor Seitz, despite his political vulnerability, exercised courage not often seen even in federal judges with lifetime appointments. He ruled that, while he had no authority to hold segregation unconstitutional, bound as he was by Supreme Court precedent, the schools, if separate, were required to be equal, and they were grossly unequal. He ordered the university to admit blacks. No order to go and equalize. Delaware had had its chance. To our delight Lou and I won the first case requiring an undergraduate school to admit blacks—heady stuff for a twenty-five-year-old lawyer.

LDF was waging the battle on a broad front. In Tennessee, the state adopted a grade-a-year plan for higher education, the case went to the Supreme Court on procedural nonsense, and we finally won on the merits in the court of appeals, with one judge dissenting. But Tennessee for a time required one case per university. Texas required more cases for schools other than the University of Texas—they wouldn't follow *Sweatt* without court orders directed precisely at each.

We fought Virgil Hawkins's case to enter the University of Florida Law School until he gave up in 1959 and went to Boston University to get a degree in public relations. Then, from 1961 to 1965, Hawkins went to New England School of Law, from which he graduated at the age of fifty-eight. But because the school was not accredited, he could not be admitted to the Florida bar. In 1976, when Hawkins was seventy, the Florida Supreme Court admitted him to practice, waiving the requirement that he take the bar examination, relying on a precedent in which the state attorney general's brother had been admitted even though he had flunked the bar exam four times. In 1983, when Hawkins was seventy-seven, the Florida bar disciplined him for alleged unprofessional conduct and that year the state legislature established ten law fellowships at the University of Florida and Florida State University in his name.

When *Sweatt* came down, we had a case in Maryland to admit Esther McCready to the School of Nursing. Because Southern states couldn't afford to duplicate white facilities, they created a regional compact with the Board of Control for Southern Regional Education to maintain cooperatively a few schools for blacks from all over the South, pressing Congress to ratify the compact, thinking it might thereby become immune to litigation. Thurgood testified against the proposal and Congress refused the board's request. Nevertheless, Maryland directed McCready to Meharry School of Nursing in Nashville, which had places for three Maryland students. The trial court approved, but the state court of appeals reversed. Maryland went to the Supreme Court and lost.

In Louisiana, Thurgood and A. P. Tureaud sued the state university to admit Roy Wilson to law school. After winning in the Supreme Court in 1951, Wilson withdrew because someone discovered that he had received a less than honorable discharge from the armed forces. But Robert Collins and Ernest Morial did enroll that year and were graduated in 1954. (In 1978, Collins became the first black federal judge in Louisiana and Morial the first black mayor of New Orleans.)

Bob Carter sued the University of North Carolina in late 1950 for excluding Floyd McKissick, later to become president of CORE, from law school. The trial court held that the black law school at North Carolina College for Negroes was equal to the white state school. The court of appeals reversed; the university petitioned the Supreme Court, which in 1951 refused to hear the case. McKissick later transferred to the state's black law school.

Georgia fought back doggedly, successfully keeping out Horace Ward, who decided to go to Northwestern rather than waste time in a lengthy lawsuit. (He is now Georgia's first black federal district judge.) Like Louisiana, Georgia required a certificate signed by two alumni for admittance to a state institution of higher learning. The University of Virginia Law School folded after a brief hearing. Only Arkansas, among Southern states, integrated higher education without an LDF lawsuit, though they were threatened by one.

As early as 1952 a score of private Southern universities, including Johns Hopkins and St. Johns in Maryland, Washington University in St. Louis, and American University in Washington, D.C., taking their cue from the courts, began admitting blacks for the first time.

But now social and educational factors, some promoted by the South, came into play to maintain segregation or as much of it as possible. We hadn't foreseen how they would keep down the flow of blacks into newly integrated institutions. The atmosphere was inhospitable at the white schools, while black schools were receptive and had experience in educating underprepared students. Black elementary and high school education remained essentially segregated until 1970, and its quality was terrible, equipping few black youngsters to enter white institutions on an equal footing with whites. Also, the white colleges and graduate schools were more expensive than the black schools. Finally, somewhat out of shame, but also as a last-ditch attempt to stave off desegregation, the states began to build up black colleges and universities. Where white schools had programs like nursing or accounting that black ones lacked, states set up duplicates in black schools to entice black students. Some black educators began developing vested interests in keeping the all-black schools as institutions of choice for black students.

I COMMIT MYSELF TO STAY AT LDF

While I had no thought of looking for a job with a private firm, a very tempting offer came along, and I turned it down, not even weighing the financial consequences, which someone else who was recently married and thinking of starting a family and had a more practical mind would have done. Not long after the Delaware decision, Milton Handler, the country's leading authority on antitrust law, who was one of my law school teachers, and for whom I had been a student research assistant, invited me to join his law firm, now known as Kaye, Scholer, Fierman, Hays and Handler. The firm then had a handful of lawyers, although now it has more than four hundred. The offer was attractive. I liked Milton. I was interested in antitrust law, though my sympathies were not with the defendants, whom he usually represented. I was not so sure about the rest of my career. Was there a future for me in civil rights? Could I earn a decent living? Although it hadn't so far, would being white handicap me in an organization run by blacks? I said to the partner who extended the offer that I had just won the first case ordering blacks admitted to a white college. It would probably be appealed to the Delaware Supreme Court later in the year and I would argue the appeal with Louis Redding. Would it be possible for me to come to work for the firm after the appeal? He replied that I would be no more valuable to the firm for having argued that appeal. I went home and mulled it over. I had just won the first case to gain admission for blacks to a white college. And he didn't think I would be any more valuable for having argued the appeal! I might have asked Milton for the extra time, but I turned down the offer. Maybe I wouldn't be more valuable, but I didn't want to work at a place like that. In fact, the state later decided not to appeal.

This decision was key for the rest of my career. The fact is that I might not have been very successful at the firm. I have to care about what I do. It's hard to tell how that would have played out. I wouldn't have cared too much about most of the kinds of clients I would get, although I might have identified with some of them. There was also the professionalism and craftsmanship of legal practice that I might bring to bear on cases of those with whom I might have no particular personal sympathy. It very well might not have worked out. But, in any event, it couldn't compare to the excitement of coming to grips with Jim Crow, the major evil of the America into which I had been born.

I toyed with the idea of leaving LDF only one time, not long after this, when Rutgers Law School offered me a teaching job. But by then I had the action and thrill of actual combat in a cause I cared about and wasn't ready to turn to the more tranquil, reflective life of the academy. Oliver Wendell Holmes, Jr., once wrote, "It is required of a man that he should share the passion and action of his time at peril of being judged not to have lived." LDF was my best opportunity to do just that.

8

GROVELAND

RACE, RAPE, RIOTS, MURDER

I would get more than my fill of action and passion in the next big case I handled, *Groveland*, the single most influential experience persuading me to launch the LDF capital punishment program in the late 1960s and one that continues to influence the operation of LDF. It led to our getting the Supreme Court in 1972 to decide that all capital punishment as then administered was unconstitutional; in 1976 to uphold the death penalty only under certain procedures, in a case that continues to be the law today; and in 1977, to outlaw the death penalty for rape.

The events that led to what became the *Groveland* case began on the night of July 16, 1949, when Willie Padgett, a twenty-three-year-old white farmer from Lake County in central Florida, was on a date with his wife, Norma, seventeen, from whom he was separated. As Willie told it, they left a dance about 1:00 A.M. to go to the town of Okahumpka for something to eat. En route their car stalled and a car with four blacks in it stopped to help. A fight developed, Willie was knocked unconscious, and the blacks drove off with Norma in their car. In what one newspaper characterized as a sort of game of musical chairs they took turns raping her and then put her out alongside the road. She said she could recognize them by the light of the dashboard. Willie came to, got his car started, drove to a gas station, called the sheriff, and they went looking for the assailants.

As Willie and the sheriff drove around they passed a car parked in front of a black home in Groveland. Willie believed this was the car the attackers had used. When confronted, the man at the wheel called to Samuel Shepherd and Walter Irvin, two young men who had been driving the car the night before, to come out of the house and, when Willie identified them as two of the four who had beaten him, the sheriff arrested them. Then Willie went looking for Norma; at the same time she was looking for him. They found each other, and together drove to Groveland, where, as she put it, "They had a nigger." She identified him, Charles Greenlee, as a third assailant, although, at first, Willie disagreed.

The first two people arrested, Shepherd and Irvin, described their movements that night totally differently: They had gone to the movies, a café, and a club. Neither of them knew Greenlee. The sixteen-year-old Greenlee and Ernest Thomas, the fourth suspect, had just met in Gainesville and had hitchhiked together to Groveland to get work picking oranges. Greenlee had decided to go with Thomas to Groveland because his three-year-old sister had been killed by a train just three weeks after another sister, fourteen, also had been killed by a train, and his mother cried so much he could no longer stand it. Once at Groveland, Greenlee waited alone at a freight depot while Thomas went off to get clean clothes into which Greenlee might change before visiting Thomas's family. While waiting for Thomas to return, Greenlee fell asleep. A night watchman discovered him and called the police, who arrested him for having Ernest Thomas's gun in his possession. He was being held in the jail when Norma came and identified him.

Right after the sheriff arrested Shepherd and Irvin, officers took them into the country on a clay road and beat them for half an hour with fists and billy clubs. Then they took them to the jail in Tavares, handcuffed Shepherd to a water pipe that ran across the ceiling, dropped his pants, and whipped him with a rubber hose and billy across the face, head, and all over his body, until he confessed. Officers beat Greenlee, too: "I first told him no; and then the other one started helping him to whip me—both at the same time. Everything they say then, I say 'Yeah.' They hit me across my back and legs and face. I was bleeding all over, my arms, face and all was bloody." They beat Irvin just as mercilessly, but he was tougher and refused to confess.

Three weeks later, when Frank Williams got a doctor in to see the defendants, they still were badly bruised, depigmented in various areas, swollen, tender, scarred, and abraded. Shepherd had broken teeth.

This was not a situation in which the defendants all came out of abject poverty. Samuel Shepherd's father, Henry Shepherd, was a controversial figure and local legend. Uneducated, handsome, with high cheekbones, hollow cheeks, one eye, and an empty socket where the other should have been, he had cleared thirty acres of woods near Groveland in 1943 and built his house himself. White neighbors continually harassed him, letting their cows into his crops, tearing down his fences. He called the sheriff, who offered no help. He wouldn't allow his daughter to work for a white man who had tried to rape her. But he prospered. His son Sammy was a veteran and, his father said, "They didn't like no veteran's attitude." There would be no sympathy in the community for the likes of Sammy Shepherd.

Word of the confessions swept the area and mobs formed around the jail. Angry men tried to seize the prisoners, but local officials moved them to the state penitentiary at Raiford, a hundred miles away. The Orlando *Sentinel Star* reported the opinion of many citizens as, "We will wait and see what the law does, and if the law doesn't do right then we will do it." But some members of the mob could not wait to see how the legal proceedings might come out and immediately turned on the black community. Armed with shotguns and rifles and throwing gasoline bombs they burned to the ground Henry Shepherd's house, as well as houses owned by a prosperous black gambler who dealt in "boleta" (locally pronounced "bleeder"), a numbers game in which the winning number was radioed from Cuba; attacked a café, the Blue Flame, owned by Ernest Thomas's parents; and drove through the black section of town, firing at random into homes. A committee of the "better" white people rounded up blacks in trucks and evacuated them to Orlando, where army cots were set up; the Salvation Army served food prepared by an American Legion auxiliary.

Back at Groveland, the sheriff tried to disperse the mobs with tear gas, but failed; the governor called up the National Guard, and armed troops in full battle dress patrolled the streets. A line of cars drove through Groveland tossing Ku Klux Klan pamphlets from the windows. The following night new mobs gathered and on Tuesday, the 19th, the governor called out more troops, including the 116th Field Artillery from Tampa, which occupied Clermont, Groveland, and Mascotte until the end of the week.

The press ran one inflammatory headline after another, topping them with a front-page editorial cartoon in the *Sentinel Star* that depicted four electric chairs with straps at the ankles and seats, and hoods on goosenecks, resembling vultures, rising from the backs. Bold letters on the seats proclaimed "The Supreme Penalty." The headline read "No Compromise." An editorial admonished, "A few smart lawyers who are agents of different organizations, seek to hamper justice through the employment of legal technicalities. They may bring suffering to many innocent Negroes."

The grand jury indicted Shepherd, Irvin, and Greenlee. The police continued to look for Ernest Thomas. On July 26, a posse led by three sheriffs and six bloodhounds found him asleep in a wood forty miles from Groveland. They shot and killed him, claiming that he had threatened them with a loaded pistol. A coroner's jury found that he was unlawfully armed and attempted to shoot his pursuers, but did not release the testimony it had heard. The local NAACP called on the New York national office for help.

On July 29, almost two weeks after the alleged rape, Thurgood sent Frank Williams to Florida. Working in temperatures of 105 degrees and higher, he saw the defendants, took their statements, became convinced of their innocence, and looked for a black lawyer to represent them. L. E. Thomas was in Miami, too far away, and in bad health. William Fordham, a member of the bar for only three months, was in Tampa, not close, but closer than Miami. There were no black lawyers in central Florida. Finally, Frank worked out an arrangement with a white lawyer, Alex Akerman, Jr., of Orlando, who was enough of a maverick to be a Florida Republican in 1949 and to be handling Virgil Hawkins's case for admission to the University of Florida. Akerman agreed to take the case if no other Florida lawyer would. Eleven other white lawyers turned Frank down, two because they couldn't get the fee they wanted, in one case $10,000 and another $25,000. Akerman agreed to accept $2,500. Frank did, however, get Horace Hill of Daytona Beach, a black lawyer who recently had begun practice, to help.

Handicapped by failure to file certain motions in time because they had entered the case late, by the thirty-mile distance between Akerman's office and the courthouse in Tavares, and by hurricanes, Frank and Akerman moved on August 25 to attack the racial composition of the pool from which jurors were selected as unconstitutional because blacks had been excluded. They also moved for a change of venue from this area, where white mobs had hunted down blacks to the point that black residents who had had nothing to do with the crime had to be evacuated in trucks and sheltered in Orlando. Akerman put into evidence scores of clippings to establish the public hysteria dominating the area. Witnesses whom the prosecution called to contradict the claim of mob psychology were so locked into the dominant mindset about such matters that they actually corroborated the claim. A bank president testified, "You could not expect any other situation," when asked about the rioting and home burning. The bank's vice president testified that if a defendant were acquitted and walked out of the courtroom, "it might be a good idea to keep on walking." The mayor testified that the "Ku Klux Klan have their place. If they want to have it there, it is perfectly all right. I might even join it myself, sometime." The prosecutor called a black insurance man who swore that race relations in nearby Leesburg were "the best in the State of Florida."

No black had served on a grand jury in twenty-one years and the prosecution had no explanation for that. Nevertheless, the chair of the Board of County Commissioners testified that "colored and white people" were in the pool from which jurors were selected "in proportion as the colored people were to the total registration in the county." This was so improbable that it should have undermined the prosecution's credibility, and indeed would later prove its undoing. The trial judge denied both motions—for change of venue and attacking the composition of the jury—and set the trial for September 1, just one week off. He announced rules to assure strict security in the courthouse, limiting the number of spectators permitted inside, providing for weapons searches, prohibiting any "bag, basket, bottle, jar, jug, bucket," or other such items in the courthouse, and requiring inspection of "crutches, canes, walking sticks, and other aids to locomotion."

The trial commenced on September 2 and was relatively simple. Akerman objected to admitting Willie Padgett's statement that his wife had reported to him that she had been raped, because it wasn't a "fresh complaint," an exception to the hearsay evidence rule. She had spoken to someone else at a restaurant earlier. The court allowed the evidence in. Deputy Sheriff James L. Yates testified that he made plaster casts of footprints and tire tracks at the scene of the crime that matched the tires of Shepherd's car and the prints of Irvin's shoes. The defense objected that the shoes had been taken by an illegal search and seizure because Yates got Irvin's shoes from his mother without a warrant and without Irvin's permission. The judge overruled the objection. Even though Norma had been examined by a doctor, the state put on no medical testimony to prove that rape had taken place, as, for example, evidence of abrasions or about the presence of semen in the vagina, evidence one would expect the prosecution to make a great deal of in any rape case where there had been a medical examination. Further, the judge refused to make the results of the medical examination available to defense counsel, preventing the defense from learning what finding during the examination might have led the prosecution to omit the medical testimony.

Even though Shepherd and Greenlee had confessed, the prosecution didn't put the confessions into evidence, mute proof that it knew they could be attacked on the ground that the police had beaten them out of the defendants. But the newspapers had trumpeted news of the confessions all over the area and the jury had to have heard and read all about them anyway. This left the prosecution in the position of being able to reap all the benefits of the confessions and yet not have to meet the burden of having to demonstrate that they had been offered voluntarily.

The defendants took the stand and described their whereabouts that night. They testified that they had been nowhere near the scene of the crime. But, having been rushed to trial, defense counsel had no opportunity to find alibi witnesses—people who had seen Shepherd and Irvin in the cafés they'd visited the night of the crime, a police officer who sold them gas at a gas station that night—or to find and bring in the first person Norma Padgett saw after the alleged assault, to whom Norma said nothing of rape. There was no time for scientific examination of the plaster casts of footprints and tire tracks that, if left unchallenged, would certainly be persuasive with a jury.

The jury was out for two hours and returned with three guilty verdicts, the death penalty for Shepherd and Irvin and life imprisonment for Greenlee, possibly because he was only sixteen.

The night the trial ended, Frank Williams left the courthouse with Horace Hill and a couple of black newspaper reporters. As they pulled away they were pursued by what one of the reporters described as a "motorized mob." Three cars they noticed parked at the side of the road as they drove toward Orlando began pursuing them in a chase that reached speeds of ninety miles per hour. As they entered the town of Apopka, a pickup truck crossed the road behind them and cut off their pursuers, who then gave up the chase.

We took Shepherd and Irvin's case to the Florida Supreme Court, where we lost, and then to the United States Supreme Court. Charles Greenlee declined to appeal. He feared that if he were to win a new trial, the jury might sentence him to death. Nowadays he would not have to face that grim choice. The Supreme Court in a 1981 case, in which LDF assisted defense counsel, held that the possibility of getting the death penalty the second time around discouraged appeal and thereby deterred the assertion of constitutional rights. But at that time, Greenlee's decision was prudent.

Thurgood gave me the job of writing the petition for writ of certiorari to ask the Supreme Court to hear the case, and I consulted some of my former law school professors, other academics, lawyers, and Bill Hastie. Not long after the trial, but before the case was decided in the Florida Supreme Court, the United States Supreme Court decided *Cassell v. Texas*, which held that racial proportional representation in the selection of prospective jurors—which is what the chair of the county commissioners claimed they had done in the *Groveland* case—was unconstitutional. But the Florida Supreme Court chose to ignore *Cassell*. I thought that the United States Supreme Court would not be likely to treat its own precedent so cavalierly and made it the first point of the petition we filed on September 30, 1950. We argued also that the defense should have had more time to prepare, and that mob violence and hysteria dominated the trial, denying the defendants' rights to due process of law. These constitutional arguments were possible only because Williams and Akerman had made a record at the trial of how the jury was selected and of the atmosphere in which the trial had been conducted. They raised their objections with the trial judge, even though they fully expected him to deny their motions, and made sure to frame their arguments on the motions so that they were based explicitly on constitutional grounds. Good lawyering. Far too often lawyers raise their constitutional objections for the first time at an appellate level, where they are rejected as having been raised too late.

On November 27, the Supreme Court agreed to hear the case, and Thurgood assigned me the job of writing the brief. On February 12, 1951, we filed the brief, which essentially argued the points we had made in the *cert* petition. In addition to Supreme Court precedents, I threw in a number of old English cases from the 1700s on change of venue, because Justice Frankfurter liked English precedents. Poking through crumbling pages of dusty old English volumes in the bar association library stacks to find them had given me sneezing fits. On March 9, 1951, Frank and Bob Carter argued the case superbly. Exactly a month later we won, but the opinion was not at all discursive and so there was no language that could be quoted in arguing future cases. It said merely, "Reversed. *Cassell v. Texas*." This meant that the reversal had been limited to the issue of racial proportional representation in the selection of prospective jurors, which the state of Florida admitted—indeed claimed—had been followed.

Justice Jackson, however, wrote a blistering concurring opinion in which Frankfurter joined. Jackson referred to "prejudicial influences outside the courtroom becoming all too typical of a highly publicized trial" that were "brought to bear on this jury with such force that the conclusion is inescapable that these defendants were prejudged as guilty and the trial was but a legal gesture to register a verdict already dictated by the press and the public opinion which it generated." He recounted the press hysteria, the widespread reporting of confessions that were never introduced in evidence, the mob violence, calling out the troops, special rules to prevent violence at the trial, and wrote approvingly of Frank Williams and Alex Akerman's motions for change of venue or postponement of the trial until passions cooled. He thought that the case should be controlled by *Moore v. Dempsey* (1923), one of the earliest NAACP cases, which was filed to invalidate a conviction obtained while a mob dominated an Arkansas trial, and concluded, "The case presents one of the best examples of one of the worst menaces to American justice." Jackson's opinion was a precursor of modern, widely accepted doctrine: Defendants have the constitutional right to be tried in an atmosphere free of prejudice against them.

The prosecution in *Groveland* moved for a second trial and set arraignment for August 15, 1951. By then Frank Williams had moved to the West Coast. Bob Carter was deep into preparing the School Segregation Cases. I, too, was involved in early phases of two of the cases, but Bob's responsibility in these was greater. When Thurgood asked for help with the second trial, I volunteered.

LITTLE SCOTTSBORO

LDF took on *Groveland* as part of a tradition of trying to assure fairness to blacks in the criminal process. Indeed, much of the current state of the law assuring fairness in criminal cases has roots in early NAACP and LDF cases. *Moore v. Dempsey,* to which Justice Jackson referred, first announced a right to federal habeas corpus to review state court convictions for constitutional violations in trials dominated by mob violence. In 1940 the NAACP had won *Chambers v. Florida*, in which the police had for five days repeatedly questioned young, ignorant, black tenant farmers in an atmosphere charged with fear of mob violence. They confessed to the murder of an elderly white farmer and were sentenced to death. The opinion of Justice Hugo Black is often quoted today: "Under our constitutional system, courts stand against any winds that blow as havens of refuge for those who might otherwise suffer because they are helpless, weak, outnumbered, or because they are non-conforming victims of prejudice and public excitement."

In the mid-1940s Thurgood lost and won other confession and jury discrimination cases. One rape case turned on the obscure question of federal jurisdiction over crimes committed on military bases.

Groveland was known also as Little Scottsboro, which tells volumes
about the deeply imbedded racial attitudes *Groveland* exposed. The famous
Scottsboro case—which captured the attention of the world through much
of the 1930s and 1940s—brought to center stage the virulent passion for violence whenever interracial sexual transgression was alleged. These were
both rape cases, but the prospect of consensual sex between a white female
and a black male was apparently so disquieting that many Southerners simply presumed that any such contact had to have been forced by brutal
means. W. J. Cash, in his classic, *The Mind of the South*, has written that
while the likelihood of a Southern white woman being raped by a Negro was
much lower than her chance of being struck by lightning, such rapes did
occur and there "was real fear, and in some districts even terror, on the part
of the white women themselves. And there were neurotic old maids and
wives, hysterical young girls, to react to all this in a fashion well enough
understood now, but understood by almost nobody then." Cash added:

> In their concern for the taboo on the white woman, there was a final
> concern for the right of their sons in the legitimate line, through all
> the generations to come, to be born to the great heritage of white
> men. . . . Such I think, was the ultimate content of the Southerners'
> rape complex. Such is the explanation of the fact that, from the begin-
> ning, they justified—and sincerely justified—violence toward the
> Negro as demanded in defense of woman, and though the offenses of
> by far the greater number of the victims had nothing immediately to
> do with sex.

Scottsboro arose in 1931 out of the charge that nine young black men
had raped two white women in a freight car as it traveled through Alabama.
Within less than three weeks they were indicted and convicted, and all but
one got the death penalty. The NAACP defended them. A Communist
party front organization, the International Labor Defense (ILD), attacked the
defense provided by the NAACP as inept and sent a telegram to the judge
stating that he would be "personally responsible unless the defendants were
immediately released," an empty threat, but one sure to appeal to people
who had for so long been powerless. While appeals were pending, the ILD
persuaded the defendants' parents to retain its counsel and fire the NAACP
lawyers. It accompanied the defense with an immense worldwide propaganda campaign of mass meetings and picketing of American embassies,
letters and telegrams to the president, the governor of Alabama, and the
judge. This was during the deepest part of the worldwide Depression and
the Communist party was at the height of its credibility. They used the
case to raise large sums of money, much of which probably was diverted to
other Communist party purposes. But their campaign exposed Southern
injustice more effectively than ever before.

Later, in 1935, following a new party line of cooperating with non-Communist groups, the ILD entered into a *Scottsboro* defense committee, including the NAACP, the ACLU, the League for Industrial Democracy, and others, which saved the defendants' lives and freed most of them. *Scottsboro* was close enough in time to my coming to the Fund that I saw one of the defendants visit the office regularly for money, which the Association doled out, a pitiful five or ten dollars at a time, when he needed it. An editorial in *The Crisis* magazine asserted: "It is not a question of whether the Communists have done a good job in exposing and fighting the evils under which Negroes live. They have. The question is: did they have the right to use the lives of nine youths who . . . did not know what it was all about to make a propaganda battle in behalf of the Negro race or the theories of Communism? *The Crisis* does not believe they had that right." *The Crisis* editorial didn't gainsay the fact that the Communists had publicized and internationalized civil rights and had exposed violations in a way and to a degree never before accomplished.

Scottsboro and *Groveland* weren't isolated episodes. Such cases kept coming up all the time, sometimes in outlandish form. In the summer of 1951, North Carolina prosecuted Mack Ingram in Yanceyville for assault with intent to rape for looking at a seventeen-year-old white girl in a "leering" manner from seventy feet away. The charge was subsequently changed to attempted assault. Thurgood characterized the crime as "highway looking and attempting to want." Bob Carter, and cooperating lawyers Conrad Pearson and Martin A. Martin, represented Ingram, and somewhat unusually had as cocounsel a couple of white North Carolina lawyers. The prosecutor claimed that Ingram "undressed this lovely little lady with his eyes." The jury couldn't agree, because two black jurors wouldn't vote for conviction. The state then reindicted Ingram. As might have been expected, reporters from all over the world attended the trials. The local solicitor reported that an official of the State Department called him, "concerned over the interest shown by the Communists in the trial." Finally, in November 1952, Ingram was convicted of "assault with intent to commit rape by leering" and sentenced to six months' suspended sentence and five years' probation. In an unprecedented move, the North Carolina attorney general asked the state supreme court to review the case because blacks had been excluded from the jury. The North Carolina Supreme Court reversed because "the facts in the evidence are insufficient to make out a case of assault."

From the beginning the Communists attempted to compete with us for control of *Groveland*. The Civil Rights Congress, dominated by Communists, charged that Frank Williams had falsely accused it of trying to steal the case. As late as 1952, an NAACP field secretary wired from Los Angeles: "Wire immediately information status Walter Lee Irvin Case. . . . Left wing now raising funds here for our case." While struggling to keep them out, we played the Communist card by appealing for justice for *Groveland* defendant Walter Irvin on the ground that he faced "death, giving the worldwide Communist propaganda apparatus the chance to assert that Justice in the United States turns its face from the Negro."

Such cases also provided branch-building and fund-raising vehicles. Roy Wilkins urged the branch department to send the father of Samuel Shepherd, another *Groveland* defendant, on a speaking tour to help pull the branches out of a "rut." Shortly after the case began, Frank Williams raised $4,600, then a big amount, on a speaking tour that featured *Groveland*. Frank also urged Gloster Current to make better use of *Groveland*: "We have provably innocent sons of fine, decent Negro-American families in the old tradition (as over against unattached railroad tramps [*Scottsboro*] or suspect individuals [*McGee*] . . .). We have burnings. Mob action. . . . A whole community of peace loving Negro workers scattered . . . lawyer intimidation, etc."

Race–sex cases evoked a conflicted response. Thurgood did not want to see this one kind of case, controversial in its own special way, crowd out other important work. He expressed his feelings in writing to an Alabama civil rights leader who wanted us to take the case of a black man facing prosecution for miscegenation: "I am, however, more and more worried about our having so many cases involving sex offenses. [But I am] perfectly willing to recommend we go along, provided it has the approval of the State Conference of Alabama."

In time LDF developed criteria for which criminal cases to enter, which to turn down. For LDF to accept a case it had to be determined that "redress of the denial of constitutional rights [in a criminal case] is likely to be of benefit to a large number of people," or "build up the morale in [a] branch," and all of the following three factors had to exist: (1) an injustice based on race, (2) an experienced lawyer believed that the client was innocent in light of the entire record and other available information, and (3) there was a possibility of establishing a precedent that would advance the due process or equal protection rights of black people. We weren't a general legal aid society. Merely defending the accused, who are entitled to counsel in all cases, wasn't our aim, rather we had an agenda: to demolish Jim Crow. But, as with other standards, we dealt with these pragmatically and indeed later took cases that involved important constitutional principles—right to counsel, to jury selection free of racial discrimination, to protection against cruel and unusual punishment—without thinking very much about guilt or innocence.

THE ASSOCIATION AND THE COMMUNISTS

As the foregoing shows, *Scottsboro* and other interracial crime cases had a lot to do with the relationship between the NAACP and communism, which deserves examination here, because it came up again and again during my years at LDF. That blacks never were drawn in any numbers to communism, in fact, much less drawn to it than whites, has long been of special interest to some students of race relations. Though I will leave a full discussion of the subject to others, one major factor that helped decide the issue was the role of religion in black society. Another was that Communist doctrine was, in the main, irrelevant to black concerns. In the late 1920s the Communist party proclaimed a policy of "self-determination in the black belt," derived from Stalinist doctrines about Soviet racial and cultural minorities that defined the Soviet republics, each with its own ethnic character. Self-determination in America would lead to independent Negro republics wherever blacks were a majority in the South. Though some American Communists considered the doctrine unrealistic, they went along. Most American blacks, however, especially those in the South, finding the party's solution destructive of the vision of America dominant among black leaders, including those within the NAACP, showed virtually no interest in such a plan that would be impossible to achieve, to say nothing of its divisive force.

In the North the party pursued a more sensible program of interracial activity in labor organization, partly through a front organization, the International Labor Defense (ILD), and did attract a number of but not many, blacks to the party. The ILD attacked the NAACP, W. E. B. Du Bois (who later embraced communism), and Walter White for "bowing and scraping" in the "ante-rooms of the mighty," and scored its most forceful blows against the NAACP over the *Scottsboro* case.

Less than a year after I had joined LDF, in 1950, I attended my first NAACP convention in Boston; the tension was particularly high. Within the NAACP, probably most of the Communists were white, so when I appeared on the floor, the new kid on the block and unknown to the delegates, several people tried to chase me off on the assumption that I was a Communist. Gloster Current, director of branches, referred to that convention as the "Commie Convention." As at the previous one, a faction pushed a resolution to denounce the Marshall Plan for the economic revival of Western Europe, which the Soviet Union opposed energetically. Their argument should have been appealing to American blacks: Western European powers were colonialists and America should not support nations that dominated colored peoples in Africa and Asia. Nevertheless, the leaders of the Association opposed the resolution as having nothing to do with the program of the NAACP and needlessly bringing it into conflict with its friends in the Democratic party over foreign policy.

Many in the Truman administration were very concerned about Communist efforts to influence the NAACP. Thurgood told me that at the Boston convention the FBI was "all over the place. Even Lou Nichols [one of J. Edgar Hoover's top assistants] was there." The resolution opposing the

Marshall Plan was defeated. Afterward, an apocryphal story—maybe it was a joke—spread that some delegates had voted against the resolution opposing the Marshall Plan because they thought it opposed Thurgood Marshall, but clearly the vote was a rejection of communism. FBI files reported that the convention "voted 6 to 1 in favor of appointing a special board for purpose of uprooting Communist infiltration." A later FBI memorandum described Roy and Thurgood as having "been associated with CP front organizations in 1940s but now appear to be strongly anti-Communist." I found the story about Thurgood's association with Communist party front organizations incredible because Thurgood has always been among the most outspoken of anti-Communists, and Roy had the same attitude.

The NAACP expressed its position even more clearly in another resolution to which an FBI memorandum referred: The Association's board of directors was authorized to suspend any branch that fell under Communist or other political domination. In December 1950 the board suspended the San Francisco branch because "a known member of the Communist party had become chairman of the Nominating Committee." Board meetings regularly dealt with expulsions and suspensions on grounds of Communist party membership.

LDF had a special problem with the House Select Committee on Foundations, which searched for Communists in tax-exempt organizations. In November 1952 Thurgood filed a lengthy report with the committee, listing the names of all staff members (mine included) and our largest contributors, asserting that the organization and its officers "have complete and unqualified support for our government," that "there has never been any problem of infiltration by subversive persons," and adding, "we are, however, alert to such a possibility."

The NAACP was not alone in dealing with this problem. In the motion picture industry, advertising, radio, television, the bar, labor unions, academe, and elsewhere scenes of this struggle were being played out. The Truman administration, as well as congressional and Senate committees, summoned Communists, ex-Communists, and suspected Communists to tell all about the party, under threat of contempt. Some went to prison for refusing to testify about their own or friends' present or past associations with the Communist party or other groups that expressed sympathy or solidarity with Communists.

Anti-Communist fervor ran so high that a charge of Communist sympathy was often enough to deprive an individual of his reputation and an organization of its support within the general population. It thus became convenient, or perhaps a reflexive reaction to the strange and new, for segregationists to accuse the Association of being Communist-controlled, even though the Association's goals were clearly an extension to black Americans of American constitutional rights, rights that were denied in Communist countries. Sometimes, indeed, they used the term "Bolshevik," a harsh, sinister-sounding term that was in reality originally coined to distinguish the majority group of a precursor to the Russian Communist party from the minority group, the Mensheviks. Certainly, part of the Association's anti-Communist activity was intended to blunt the damage such wild charges could cause.

But if there was strong feeling that the Association should do everything possible to avoid being lumped with Communists, there was also strong feeling among some that a civil rights group should play a role in resisting the worst abuses of the anti-Communist crusade. Among civil rights lawyers there was concern over the curtailment of civil liberties that was often a part of the hunt for Communists. On the one hand, Thurgood believed that the Smith Act denied First Amendment rights, and he asked, unsuccessfully, for permission to file a friend-of-the-court brief in the Supreme Court on behalf of the Communist defendants in *Dennis v. United States*, a prosecution under the Smith Act that, for all practical purposes, made it a crime to belong to the party. On the other, Roy ordered branches to "not cooperate in any movement whatsoever" concerning the Smith Act and prosecutions brought under it. He directed that "members and officers of the N.A.A.C.P. . . . may not use the N.A.A.C.P. . . . not even 'for identification purposes only'" in expressing themselves about the issue.

Not a small part of the determination to stay out of this issue was the growing reality that the Supreme Court was a friend to the civil rights cause and promised in the future to be an even more committed friend. As Bob Carter put it: "Although the Supreme Court record in the field of civil liberties of late has not been good, we certainly have no cause to complain about their handling of civil rights cases involving the question of racial discrimination." Walter White replied: "I thoroughly agree."

Just how strongly White felt about the need to distance the NAACP from any person or organization with Communist sympathies was made clear as early as 1947 when he solicited an encomium from J. Edgar Hoover on the Association's anti-Communist position. Hoover replied: "It is indeed a pleasure to submit the following statement for inclusion in your proposed pamphlet: Equality, freedom, and tolerance are essential in a democratic government. The National Association for the Advancement of Colored People has done much to preserve these principles and to perpetuate the desires of our founding fathers."

To those who recall Hoover's lack of interest in pursuing those who committed violence against blacks, the FBI's lily-white hiring policies, and the vigor with which he persecuted Martin Luther King, Jr., this praise must ring phoney. The Association and Hoover were using each other.

In summary, the Association's and later the Fund's strong anti-Communist stance arose from a combination of factors: blacks' religious beliefs; Communists' insistence on advocating the divisive and unattainable goal of "self-determination in the black belt"; competition over turf and Communist diversion to other uses of funds that had been contributed to aid in the defense of black defendants; a disinclination to fight battles that would aid a group of which we disapproved, even though the liberties of many Americans were under attack in the often mad hunt for Communists; a satisfactory series of decisions by the Supreme Court we didn't want to undermine; and a desire to show that we were not Communists or Communist sympathizers, despite the frequency with which such charges were made about us and others who opposed segregation. And, of course, we could turn anti-Communist fervor against our adversaries: As Hoover's endorsement indicated, one way to fight communism was to support racial equality by supporting us.

9

PREPARING FOR BATTLE

The traditional legal model is that of lawyer representing a client, doing the client's bidding and representing only the client's interests, irrespective of the needs of society or groups within it. LDF, however, practiced an early version of what has come to be known as public interest law, which is these days in some ways as much a part of government as the legislature but which at that time was still a novelty. Generations later, some critics attacked our kind of legal practice as not responsive to the needs of constituencies who might be affected by the cases we brought and the precedents we helped make, and not fully focused on the special needs of individual clients. LDF rejects those charges now and would have rejected them then, but that debate had not developed at a time when going to court offered the only avenue of reform with any real prospect for success.

THE FUND'S LITIGATION STYLE DEVELOPS

As I became an integral part of the LDF team I assimilated myself into a style of legal practice that had marked the LDF approach to litigation from the beginning up through the School Segregation Cases and beyond. In three groups of cases, Charles Houston, Bill Hastie, and Thurgood defeated the white primary, enforcement of restrictive convenants (a legal term for agreements among white property owners not to sell to blacks), and segregation in interstate travel, demonstrating in their wisdom a tactically cautious, yet strategically bold technique that came to mark LDF legal efforts. As it turned out, it suited my personal temperament very well. I should look back a bit here, as I did in my research at that time, to review those cases before getting on with discussing the School Segregation Cases.

THE WHITE PRIMARY CASES

Blacks were grossly underrepresented in every branch of government. They constituted 10 percent of the United States population in 1945, but William L. Dawson (Chicago) and Adam Clayton Powell, Jr. (New York), were the only black members of Congress. In 1935, the Supreme Court rejected a challenge to the longstanding Southern practice of excluding blacks from Democratic primary elections, then the only meaningful elections in the South. For all practical purposes this cut blacks out of effective representation in that region. In 1940 less than 1 percent of eligible blacks in Alabama, Louisiana, Mississippi, and South Carolina were registered to vote; the highest percentage in the states of the old Confederacy was in Arkansas, 8.1 percent. Conservative Southern Democrats, a seemingly invincible segregationist bloc in Congress, were repeatedly reelected, giving them the enormous national power that goes with congressional seniority.

The legal theory that protected this situation was based on a claim that the Democratic party was private, and thus immune to the Fourteenth and Fifteenth Amendments, which prohibited only discriminatory state action. Thurgood and Bill Hastie tried to fashion a case to demonstrate that the primaries were action of the state because they were integral to the electoral process. Moreover, the Democratic primary was the only election that counted in the South; excluding blacks from Democratic primaries in effect denied them their right to participate meaningfully in elections.

As Thurgood and Hastie struggled with a pending suit, involving a Texas primary election for state office, the Supreme Court handed down *United States v. Classic,* a federal prosecution for falsifying returns in a Louisiana primary election for Congress. The charge was conspiring to injure a citizen in the exercise of a right secured by the Constitution. The legal issue was whether the right to vote in a primary election was secured by the Constitution. The Court held that it was, implicitly contradicting the 1935 decision that had decided that the Democratic party was nothing more than a private club. Chief Justice Harlan Fiske Stone's opinion held that "primary elections . . . are a step in the exercise by the people of their choice of representatives in Congress," and "we cannot close our eyes to the fact . . . that the practical influence of the choice of candidate at the primary may be so great as to affect profoundly the choice at the general election." No small reason for the shift was that seven of the nine justices who had sat on the 1935 case were no longer there to decide *Classic.* Because *Classic* differed in important ways from their pending case, which involved a primary for state office, Thurgood and Bill dropped the pending case and started a new one, *Smith v. Allwright.* Now known as the White Primary Case, it dealt with excluding blacks from a primary election for senator and representative. The shift angered their clients, some accusing Thurgood of "messing up." One Texan warned Marshall that he "had better win the next case or not return to Texas."

Thurgood and W. J. Durham made a record that showed that, with two exceptions, only winners of the Democratic primary had been elected in Texas general elections since 1859. While blacks could vote in those elections, they faced a fait accompli when offered only the option of voting for the primary winner or the Republican, who was bound to lose. Thurgood visited my former teacher and present colleague Herbert Wechsler, then in the Justice Department, who had handled *Classic,* to persuade him to back us as a friend of the court. But Wechsler declined on the grounds that *Classic* dealt with voters who already were in the Democratic party, pointing out also that Southerners dominated the Senate Judiciary Committee, which had considerable influence over the Justice Department and the jurisdiction of the federal courts. Thurgood and Bill Hastie argued *Smith v. Allwright* twice. The result was that the Court decided to overrule its earlier ruling that had held that the control of primaries was a private and not a state matter, a major triumph for the LDF. Chief Justice Stone first assigned Justice Frankfurter to write the opinion. But Justice Jackson wrote a memo pointing out that Frankfurter "in the first place, is a Jew. In the second place, he is from New England, the seat of the abolition movement. In the third place, he has not been thought of as a person particularly sympathetic with the Democratic party in the past." Justice Stanley Reed, a Democrat from Kentucky, got the assignment. His opinion held that: "The privilege of membership in a party may be . . . no concern of a State. But when, as here, that privilege is also the essential qualification for voting in a primary to select nominees for a general election, the State makes the action of the party the action of the State."

What about precedent? Hadn't the Court only recently decided just the opposite? "In reaching this conclusion we are not unmindful of the desirability of continuity of decision in constitutional questions. However, when convinced of former error, this Court has never felt constrained to follow precedent. In constitutional questions, where correction depends upon amendment and not upon legislative action this Court throughout its history has freely exercised its power to reexamine the basis of its constitutional decisions."

All Supreme Court victories were celebrated at the office by big parties. By all accounts, the party that celebrated *Smith v. Allwright* was a whopper. Thurgood had phone calls to him referred from one secretary to another. Justice Frank Murphy, who called to congratulate him and invite him to lunch, couldn't get through until the next day.

TRANSPORTATION

Railroads put Negroes in separate cars and put screens around them when they ate in the diner, bus drivers sent them to the back of the bus. The strategic problem for Thurgood and his colleagues was whether to attack

Southern travel segregation laws as a violation of the equal protection clause of the Fourteenth Amendment—*Plessy* revisited—or as an interference with the free flow of passengers throughout the country and, therefore, a violation of the Commerce Clause of the Constitution. But while a favorable decision based on Commerce Clause grounds would strike an important blow against segregation, its effect on the larger campaign would be limited—most segregation did not take place in interstate commerce. If, on the other hand, a direct attack on segregation under the equal protection clause proved premature and failed, we would risk imbedding *Plessy* even deeper in American law.

When Virginia prosecuted Irene Morgan in 1946 for refusing to go to the back of a bus while on a Maryland–Virginia trip, Thurgood and Bill Hastie decided that the time was not yet ripe to attack travel segregation under the equal protection clause. They argued only that Morgan deserved redress under the Commerce Clause, that the state had usurped federal power when it tried to impose regulations on interstate travel. During oral argument, Justice Wiley Rutledge asked Hastie whether the case was controlled by the Fourteenth Amendment. "I pretended not to hear him," Hastie later said. When Rutledge repeated the question Hastie replied with fifteen minutes of "irrelevancies." The rhetoric of the written brief, however, did go a step beyond sometimes recondite Commerce Clause jurisprudence, asserting, "Today we are just emerging from a war in which all of the people of the United States were joined in a death struggle against the apostles of racism."

They won *Morgan* on the limited grounds that the Virginia law violated the Commerce Clause. But segregation took a big hit below the water line.

THE RESTRICTIVE COVENANT CASES

Even blacks who could afford better housing were walled into the ghetto by legal devices, the most effective of which was the restrictive covenant. Two or more white property owners, sometimes scores or hundreds, would agree among themselves never to sell to blacks, and frequently Jews, Asians, and other groups (some excluded Mongolians, Turks, Indians). Any signer could get a court order to force violators to obey. The discrimination was obvious, but was the covenant, or the court order enforcing it, state action? The Fourteenth Amendment says that the *state* may not deny equal protection. No one could claim for a moment that the state isn't *involved* in creating or enforcing a restrictive covenant. We own property and enforce agreements only because the state recognizes our interests and provides the ways we can establish and enforce them by deeds, contracts, wills, trespass laws, and legal enforcement of various sorts. There are no legal rights in organized society without state action. But this proves too much, because it erases much of the distinction between public and private conduct and, as Bob

Ming, one of our closest advisers, once said about the private rules that had been adopted to evade *Morgan,* "Any time you are denied the power of the government to enforce your rights it is anarchy." If all state involvement were state action in a Fourteenth Amendment sense, most private disputes could be turned into constitutional issues—an unacceptable result.

And yet, and yet . . . this dispute over where one draws the line is a bit excessive in dealing with the simple proposition that courts ought not to enforce private agreements that result in widespread residential racial segregation.

In 1926 the Supreme Court held that the covenants were simply agreements among private property owners with no state action involved, and therefore were not unconstitutional. Not until 1945 did NAACP lawyers meet, in Chicago, to plan an offensive against covenants, this time deciding not to attack their constitutionality per se, but the constitutionality of enforcing them. Three cases began progressing upward, two led by Thurgood and Charles Houston, the third by a St. Louis lawyer, George Vaughn, who had been born in the 1880s, the son of parents who once had been slaves. Thurgood and Houston had ideas very different from Vaughn's. In the cautious mode of the White Primary Cases and *Morgan* they wanted to move slowly, hoping to win a lower court victory that might encourage the Supreme Court to rule with them. Moreover, they wanted to amass an overwhelming body of socioeconomic material to impress the Court that it faced an urgent social problem. Vaughn, on the other hand, raced ahead with a relatively simple legal approach. Acting alone, he filed a petition asking the Supreme Court to hear his case, *Shelley v. Kraemer,* in April 1947. Having no alternative other than to suffer the issue being decided in Vaughn's case, about which they had fears, the NAACP lawyers filed their cases in the Supreme Court promptly. But Houston's case was so far behind the others that they would not ordinarily be heard together and so Houston asked Vaughn "if the court should grant certiorari in the *Hodge v. Hurd* . . . case [Houston's case], should we ask that these cases be argued simultaneously?" Vaughn dodged: "Because of my clients, I cannot make a definite statement about a delay at the present time." In fact, the Court granted review in Houston's case, and Houston sped ahead of the regular timetable to file his brief along with the others.

All the cases were presented together. The NAACP briefs were outlined and coordinated at a New York conference on September 6, 1947, attended by all the lawyers in all the pending covenant cases, and by law professors and lawyers from other organizations. A secondary purpose of the conference seems to have been to bring Vaughn into line with NAACP theory. Everyone paid great deference to him, but to no avail. Thurgood and Houston's briefs, while arguing that what courts do is state action, made abundant use of social science materials, imparting extra bite by showing the effect that restrictive covenants had on society. But Vaughn relied mainly on a Reconstruction statute enacted to implement the Thirteenth Amendment that provided that "all citizens of the United States shall have the same right ... as is enjoyed by white citizens thereof to ... purchase ... real and personal property." The statute didn't speak of state action and the Thirteenth Amendment had no state action requirement. It just abolished slavery. Implementing statutes, including, arguably, those that prohibited racial stigmatization, might deal with private action. This perhaps suggests that Vaughn had a novel and brilliant idea about how to approach the case, one that somehow had eluded LDF lawyers. The problem, however, was that some of the early interpretations of the statute indicated that it was, indeed, subject to a state action requirement. Marshall and Houston probably were correct in fearing disaster if Vaughn were to get to the Supreme Court alone where he was betting all on his narrow, then-idiosyncratic argument.

And still the argument best remembered is that of George Vaughn. Vaughn appeared to be ancient—actually he was sixty-two—and obviously not accustomed to arguing in that rarefied atmosphere. It did not appear that his seemingly simplistic demand that the Court start and end with reading the words of the Reconstruction statute as he understood them would be taken seriously. He also argued that as covenants became more widely used, blacks could end up excluded from entire cities and counties, and might even be denied the right to be citizens of the state of their choice, an argument sophisticated members of the Supreme Court bar must have found ridiculous. Yet Vaughn worked a kind of magic. None of the justices asked a question. He concluded with a stunning peroration. As Thurgood put it, he reared back and shouted that as the Negro knocks at America's door, he cries—and here Vaughn orated as loud as he could—"Let me come in and sit by the fire. I helped build the house."

On May 3, 1948, the Supreme Court decided that courts may not enforce racially restrictive covenants; to do so would violate the Fourteenth Amendment. The Court ruled that the prohibited state action was court enforcement—but did not rule that the covenants were invalid.

A BLACK SUMMIT ASSESSES THE OPTIONS

In April 1952, under the sponsorship of the *Journal of Negro Education,* Charles Thompson assembled at Howard University a group of scholars, lawyers, journalists, organizational leaders, and others, black and white, from North and South, advocates of extreme gradualism and those who demanded an immediate end to segregation. Charlie was not staging an academic exercise. He was aggressively gathering support for our campaign, while trying to defuse the opposition—not that of segregationists, most of whom were hopelessly intransigent, but of some blacks and white liberals who held their own strong views about what ought to be done next. At one extreme, Harry Ashmore, editor of the *Arkansas Gazette*, was opposed to segregation in principle, but hardly in favor of attacking it. He predicted, quite wrongly

> that the Court will not in the near future render a final verdict upon segregation in the public schools of the United States. . . . The elemental fact is that the majority of the people in the South are white, and the majority of the whites are opposed to dropping the color bar. This means that in any test at the ballot box this majority opinion would prevail and would therefore be supported by existing political processes at every level of state and local government. I doubt if court action could prevail against it.

Marjorie McKenzie, a black lawyer and columnist for the *Pittsburgh Courier*, had written columns criticizing an all-out attack on segregation because she too thought we would lose. She argued that we should present the cases the same way we argued *Sweatt* and *McLaurin*. Of course, we felt that this was precisely what we were doing. She charged that the lawyers had allowed "too much distance to come between them and their plans, and the people to be affected," and advocated putting pressure "on the Executive and on the Legislative branches as well." It was hard to fathom what she would have had us do. The cases, of course, had arisen out of local demands for some sort of redress. The plaintiffs knew that we wanted to seek integration, not equalization. And her advice about legislative and executive action didn't address the question of how we were to get past the Southern stranglehold on Congress and the presidency. I can't help but think that she was influenced by the fact that she was married to Belford Lawson, the lawyer who handled *Henderson* and earlier District of Columbia school cases, and who was a competitor of the NAACP and had a standoffish relationship with us. John Frank, a Yale law professor and former clerk to Justice Hugo Black, counseled us not to structure the cases so as to preclude the possibility of gradual change:

> It would be a mistake to press the attack on "separate but equal" education so exclusively that the courts are precluded from deciding, even if they desire to do so, that particular separate school systems are in fact unequal. More specifically, it would be error to concede by stipulation that white and colored school systems are in fact equal in every respect except for the discrimination inherent in segregation itself.

He advised against pushing the cases to decision before the November 1952 elections, fearing adverse political effects.

In between, Thurgood and others offered a tempered view of what the courts were likely to do and how the country might react. Thurgood observed:

If anybody thinks you are going to get the Supreme Court, in any decision in the foreseeable future, to say that all segregation under any circumstances on any ground is unconstitutional, you are crazy. The most that anyone asks the Supreme Court to rule is in so far as segregation is applied to this phase of what we are talking about, that it is unconstitutional. . . . If the Supreme Court says everything we ask them to say, it will only be that the segregation statutes as applied to elementary and high schools are unconstitutional. It will not touch transportation; it will not touch assembly; it will not touch barber shops; it will not touch bulldogs . . . ["bulldog" was the metaphor Thurgood used when others might have said "whatever"]. I believe quite firmly that we will have to go from county to county and from state to state even after we get it, whichever kind of decision we get. Bear in mind in Georgia you have two hundred and some counties. So I still say there is no short-cut to it.

Spotts Robinson added that lawyers' ability to influence events was constrained:

[It is] an improper assumption . . . that we, the lawyers, had a full freedom of choice. . . . For a period of more than two and a half years we even tried to substantially solve the problem without making a head-on, direct attack on segregation.

We had four cases. . . . In each of the four cases . . . we had to go back to court because the injunctions—equalization injunctions, mind you—were not abided by. . . . Contempt was not the answer. . . . To get the problem solved we must go back and this time seek further relief which involves a direct attack on segregation itself.

Our situation [in Virginia] . . . was a consequence of a decision which was forced upon us, not by people in New England or New York; not by people outside the State of Virginia, but indeed by Virginians themselves. . . . Negroes would never in Virginia have waited the length of time it would have taken for us to see tangible progress in the public schools so long as we had confined ourselves within the boundaries of the separate-but-equal doctrine.

Jim Nabrit, Jr., advocated an all-out attack on segregation per se. Jim was medium height, slim, with a reddish, freckled complexion and slightly reddish curly hair (some called him "Red"). He almost always carried immense, excellent cigars, which he chain-smoked. He spoke with a deep accent exuding his Georgia roots overlaid with seven years of Texas, where he lived before coming to Washington. He spoke as if with lots of exclamation marks sprinkled throughout and at the end of sentences: "I believe that the Constitution gives the Negro the fundamental right to enjoy *now* all benefits offered by the state, without any limitations based on race. Since that is our right, why disguise our fight for it? Why try to sneak up on it? Why not make a bold assault for it? The attack should be waged with the most devastating forces at hand."

Mordecai Johnson, president of Howard University, summed up:

> Now is the time to attack. Now is the time to proceed. Now is the time to precipitate the decisive combat. And let us be aware that if we are to prevail, we must pray that the God who enabled us to overcome the slave system will give our members of the Supreme Court and our national leadership the wisdom to see that the decision on segregation *must* come now—or else, the Communists may not need to *take* the world, we may have folded it in a nice piece of paper, wrapped it up, put an Easter ribbon around it, and handed it to them.

Out of all this deeply held, but often conflicting, advice came the style of attack as the school cases moved from trial courts to the Supreme Court: a clear eye on the goal, cautious probing, with a simultaneous willingness to retreat a bit or accept only modest gains rather than risk a total setback. The legal leadership of the LDF, while always idealists, were never ideologues.

One romantic notion has the heroic leader charging into battle, sword held high, ready to smite the enemy, whomever it turns out to be, entertaining no possibility of adjusting the pace or temporarily moderating the goal. But these were of a different breed of heroes.

10

JIM CROW AND THE VOICE
OF GOD IN KANSAS

Statistics alone can't depict the stigma so often imposed by black children's tarpaper shack schools, outhouses, and hand-me-down books. But some numbers offer a shorthand summary. In 1940 the average south-wide annual educational expenditure on black children was less than half that on whites, $21.54 per black school child compared to $50.14 per white child. By 1952 the average Southern state was spending $115.08 per black child and $164.83 per white child, still almost 50 percent more for whites. In 1940 capital outlays for black schools were 23 percent of those for white schools. While by 1952 the black share had risen, it was still only 82 percent of the per capita expenditure for white schools. The number of books in school libraries was another damning indicator. Five states kept such statistics: Georgia, Louisiana, North Carolina, South Carolina, and Texas. In 1940 the average white child in those states had 3.3 library books, the average black, 0.8 books; by 1952 whites had 4.7 books per child and blacks 1.8.

If there is one civil rights case, perhaps one Supreme Court case, whose name most people recognize it is *Brown v. Board of Education*. Indeed, as I speak to high school and college students I never have to explain that it was the decision that outlawed legalized segregation in the United States. It is described in high school social studies texts and has been the subject of at least two TV documentaries.

Nominally, the Court's only legal directive in *Brown* was that states might no longer segregate the races in schools. But in fact the decision destroyed the edifice of legitimacy upon which *Plessy* had placed segregation, laid the foundation for the civil rights movement, and revolutionized the notions of what courts, lawyers, and the law might do to expand racial justice. And much more, including setting in motion consequences for other minorities and disadvantaged groups besides blacks, as well as suggesting how the law might be used to advance and secure human rights in other countries.

The School Segregation Cases became known as *Brown* only by accident. Brown was the surname of one plaintiff, Oliver Brown (the father of Linda Brown), who had been listed near the end of a score of plaintiffs in one of the cases, the one coming out of Topeka, Kansas, before the list was alphabetized. Actually, another plaintiff family, that of Darlene Brown, should have appeared before Oliver Brown. But, in what today would be seen as an irony, Oliver was listed first because he was a man. Originally, among five cases, from four states and the District of Columbia, that we (and in the District, James M. Nabrit, Jr.) had in trial courts around the same time and that the Supreme Court combined for argument and decision, the Topeka case was listed second, because it was the second to be appealed. Had nothing changed, the School Segregation Cases might have been known as *Briggs v. Elliott* (from South Carolina), the name of the first case to be appealed. But the Supreme Court sent *Briggs* back to the trial court for further hearings, and *Brown* moved up to number one. Among ourselves we called them the "school cases," rather than by one name. A recent TV film on the cases shows Earl Warren deciding to name them *Brown*, suggesting that he did so to indicate that they dealt with the rights of brown-skinned people. But the Court had it listed as the lead case in 1953 even before Earl Warren's appointment as chief justice.

The cases, as they finally were decided under that single name, actually were:

No. 1

Oliver Brown, et al. v. Board of Education of Topeka, Shawnee County, Kansas, et al.

No. 2

Harry Briggs, Jr., et al. v. R. W. Elliott, et al. (the South Carolina case)

No. 4

Dorothy E. Davis, et al. v. County School Board of Prince Edward County, Virginia, et al.

No. 8

Spottswood Thomas Bolling, et al. v. C. Melvin Sharpe, et al. (the District of Columbia case)

No. 10

Francis B. Gebhart, et al. v. Ethel Louise Belton, et al. (the Delaware case)

Bolling was not an LDF case. A District of Columbia parents' group, at first represented by Charlie Houston, sponsored it. He had been preparing a school equalization suit for them when he was stricken with a heart attack and sent the group's leader, Gardner Bishop, to Jim Nabrit, Jr., to ask him to take over. "Big Jim" (whose son James M. Nabrit III became my dear friend and indispensable colleague) refused to argue for equalization but assented to represent the group if it would attack segregation. He was teaching full-time at Howard and not in practice and, therefore, brought in George E. C. Hayes, also a Howard law professor and one of Washington's leading black practitioners. *Bolling* differed from the LDF cases in one other way: The Fourteenth Amendment said "no state" might discriminate. The District of Columbia is not a state and the Washington lawyers had to look to other arguments.

But the old dilemma reappeared: to fight for equalization or for an end to segregation? The attitude of the black community, or at least that part with which we came in contact, shows how exquisitely well-timed was the June 1950 decision to make desegregation, not equalization, the focus of all future cases. In some of the school cases, plaintiffs and the local NAACP had come to us because they wanted to integrate. In others, the impetus stemmed from a desire to equalize badly inferior buildings or get transportation where whites rode to nearby schools and blacks walked or were bused past the white school to far-off black schools. It should be remembered that at the very time of Jim Nabrit's taking over the District of Columbia case even Charlie Houston was preparing to ask a court for equalization. Other lawyers were divided as well. Most of the black lawyers with whom we worked willingly, or even eagerly, filed cases against segregation, while a few resisted. For example, in Richmond, Spotts Robinson had become convinced that desegregation was the only effective remedy, while Martin A. Martin and Oliver Hill for some time disagreed and at first preferred to proceed down the equalization route.

In any event, when we counseled desegregation, plaintiffs and their lawyers, if not already convinced, went along. Bob Carter has written of the period: "I believe that the majority sentiment in the black community was a desire to secure for blacks all of the educational nurturing available to whites. If ending school segregation was the way to that objective, fine; if, on the other hand, securing equal facilities was the way, that too was fine."

At an executive committee meeting in 1951, Thurgood reported that "we need non-lawyers on the staff to educate the public concerning the importance of our school cases." He referred to a program of North Carolina branches to bring a number of separate-but-equal cases and said, "They must be educated to our way and start to listen to us." He hired two staff members "to work with our branches in an attempt to educate the public about the evils of segregation and to insure community support for our cases." Good leadership consists of not lagging behind one's constituency but not being so far ahead that they won't follow. We were ahead of some, but close enough for them to accept our lead, and they did.

Several years earlier the Clarendon County, South Carolina, plaintiffs who spearheaded *Briggs*, the first case to be filed, hadn't been asking for desegregation. They had begun by trying only to obtain busing; white children were bused, blacks walked. Harold Boulware represented them with remote backup from our office, but they lost their first case on a technicality—the only plaintiff lived just over the district line. How could Boulware make such a mistake? He practiced alone, had limited experience in complex cases, and mostly handled marginal matters. Once I accompanied him to a judge's chambers in a divorce case. I was shocked when he took out a bottle of whiskey he had brought along and offered it to the judge as a token of good will. I was slightly startled, but the judge took it without a word and put it in a bottom drawer of his desk. I later observed the same gesture in an Indian village court in Chiapas, Mexico, a ragged peasant propitiating the judge who was considering his case. Not classy, but sometimes the best the powerless can do in nearly impossible circumstances. Boulware knew more about rural justice than I did.

Black schools remained so intolerable that the parents in the dismissed case regrouped and once more asked for help. In March 1949, Thurgood went to South Carolina and advised a black community meeting that they should attack inequality in all its aspects. But, by November 1950, when the complaint was filed in *Briggs v. Elliot*, the new standard applied—we would ask only for desegregation.

Soon many of Clarendon County's black leadership, their families, and other blacks were fired from jobs, denied credit, forced to pay up on longstanding debts, refused renewal of leases on farmland, had trouble getting their cotton ginned, were sued for slander, threatened by the Klan, and one black person was beaten to death. They stuck it out. Anyone must wonder where they found the courage to persist in the face of such terrorism with all the power of society—financial, political, law enforcement—on the side of criminal elements prepared to maim and kill if necessary to deny them justice.

In the second case to be filed, in March 1951, *Brown v. Board of Education of Topeka*, the plaintiffs and the black community had for several years been trying to get their schools desegregated. Teachers' salaries, teacher training, teacher load for black and white schools were about the same. The precipitating factor in filing the suit was that some black children were bused to remote schools, while their white neighbors walked to nearby schools. Much later, when school busing to end segregation became a national debate, many blacks wondered why opponents of busing hadn't objected when it had been so widely used to *insure* segregation. But the goal of the Kansas NAACP at the time was not merely a black school in every black neighborhood. Indeed, the pro–separate-but-equal president of the Coffeyville, Kansas, NAACP branch was overwhelmingly voted down when he objected to integration because he expected, accurately, that it would cause black teachers to lose their jobs.

The third of the five School Segregation Cases, filed in May 1951, *Davis v. County School Board*, came out of Prince Edward County, Virginia, where, as in South Carolina, intolerable conditions precipitated the suit. The white community didn't want to spend the money it would require to upgrade black schools, so the situation dragged on until it erupted into a two-week student strike.

The students at first wanted a new high school and wrote for help to Spottswood Robinson and Oliver Hill in Richmond. But Spotts and Oliver, although dubious about a desegregation suit in rural, heavily black Prince Edward County, explained that in keeping with NAACP policy it would have to be that or nothing. The students and parents agreed.

In Delaware, suburban Claymont had no black high school. Blacks had to commute to Howard High School in Wilmington, eighteen miles away. The plaintiff, who had no interest in having a black school built, wanted integration—to go to Claymont High School. On the other hand, the Hockessin elementary school case began with a mother's effort just to get equal bus transportation because it was inconvenient to drive her child to school. Louis Redding told her that we would file only a desegregation case. She readily agreed; he filed the fourth case, *Gebhart v. Belton*, in July 1951.

We began with all the available theories:

1. That separate schools never were equal anywhere in America, that the systems in our cases weren't equal either;

2. That the inequalities stigmatized black children;

3. Moreover, severe and persistent inequalities amounted to law administered with an evil eye and an unequal hand—Margold's original theory based on the *Yick Wo* Chinese laundry case;

4. Segregation was unconstitutional because, as in cases involving Japanese Americans subjected to curfews and sent to relocation camps, "distinctions between citizens solely because of their ancestry are by their very nature odious to a free people whose institutions are founded upon the doctrine of equality" and "all legal restrictions which curtail the civil rights of a single racial group are immediately suspect . . . [and] courts must subject them to the most rigid scrutiny";

5. Standard equal protection doctrine, developed in economic regulation cases, held that a classification violates equal protection if based upon differences not reasonably related to a proper legislative objective.

We also would follow *Sweatt* and *McLaurin*: Certain aspects of education can never be equal under segregation, for example, the ability to exchange ideas with white fellow students. Related arguments drew upon studies that showed that segregation does psychological harm to children.

Much of this could be characterized as common sense, based on perceptions so widely held that it was not necessary to prove them. Indeed, in *Plessy v. Ferguson* there had been no evidence for the Court's conclusion that segregation does *no* harm. No one had proved in *Strauder* that excluding blacks from juries inflicts a stigma. These were views of the world, not derived from evidence, such as when a court concludes that an automobile did pass a red light. But we felt that, as in *Sweatt* and *McLaurin*, where we had presented evidence or materials in briefs on the effects of segregation, we should give the Court all the information about educated attitudes on the subject we could get. The Supreme Court heard this evidence and took judicial notice of it, leading to charges after our victory that the school cases rested on social science, not law.

BRIGGS V. ELLIOTT

Bob Carter enlisted a group of social scientists to testify in *Briggs v. Elliott*, the Clarendon County, South Carolina, case. The federal district court judge, J. Waties Waring, had shown that he would hear claims of racial discrimination sympathetically. In the early 1940s he had ruled with black plaintiffs in a teachers' salary case as well as in a pre-*Sweatt* law school case that concluded with setting up separate-but-(allegedly) equal legal education—an advanced view for that period. In 1947 he held the South Carolina white primary unconstitutional. He had prohibited the use of race in jury selection and segregated seating of spectators in his court, and appointed the only black bailiff in any Southern federal court.

Briggs, the case that Thurgood and Harold Boulware filed in his court, could have been framed two ways: It could have asked for an injunction to prohibit enforcement of the South Carolina school segregation *statutes* as unconstitutional or merely could have claimed that segregation and inequality were unconstitutional—with no mention of the statutes. If the former, the case would be heard by three judges—as *McLaurin* was. The other two judges probably would be John J. Parker, chief judge of the Court of Appeals for the Fourth Circuit, who would be unsympathetic to ending segregation, and George Bell Timmerman, an outspoken racist. If the case did not seek to enjoin enforcement of the statute, it would be heard by Waring alone.

A lawyer attacking segregation would presumably prefer to be before Waring alone. But there was a problem. Any attack on segregation would run into a defense that it was required by the statute and so, whether you liked it or not, the statute would be put in issue and three judges might be summoned. Even if Waring agreed to try the case alone, an appellate court might overrule him and order a three-judge hearing. On the other hand, the three-judge statute had been construed very technically, and by a close reading of its *language* might not cover a case where the plaintiff did not literally ask to enjoin enforcing a statute—so it was worth a shot. The complaint, therefore, claimed that the plaintiffs were denied equal protection by the "policy, custom, usage, and practice of the defendants in maintaining public schools for Negro children because of their race and color which are in every respect inferior to those maintained for white children." Thurgood and Bob planned then to introduce the social science evidence and make legal arguments, as in the past, that segregation per se was unconstitutional.

But Waring had another agenda. He had grown increasingly estranged from the Charleston white community, ideologically and personally. Whites there criticized his race decisions and also his recent divorce and remarriage to a Northerner, a woman from Detroit. He was the object of personal abuse, including physical harassment. He was in contact with Hubert Delany and John Hammond, NAACP board members, who thought Thurgood was not militant enough and told Waring so. (Delany was an influential black lawyer and political figure whose membership in the left-wing National Lawyers Guild set him apart from Thurgood politically. Hammond, a talent scout and record producer, has been described as "the most influential non-performing" individual in the field of jazz.)

Waring scheduled a pretrial hearing for November 17, 1950. At that time, because the three-judge court statute very well may have prohibited him from hearing the case alone, but more because he wanted to confront segregation head on, he refused to hear the case alone. He suggested that Thurgood withdraw the complaint and file a new one attacking South Carolina's school segregation laws. Thurgood, having no choice, filed a new case, asking for an injunction against South Carolina's segregation statutes; it came to trial May 28, 1951. But Waring's efforts to push Thurgood to measures he didn't want to take, his backdoor dealings with Walter White and NAACP board members (he urged Walter to enlist other organizations to file amicus briefs in the school cases), and efforts to instruct Thurgood about strategy and argument irritated Thurgood and made him a bit uncomfortable about the propriety of being in that court. If Waring's extrajudicial communications became public, it could cause trouble nobody needed. Thurgood dealt with Waring circumspectly then and later, after Waring retired and moved to New York. Indeed, Waring complained that when Thurgood called him about a dinner planned in Waring's honor in April 1952, it was the first communication from him in nine months.

The May 28 trial commenced before Waring, Parker, and Timmerman and produced several memorable exchanges. Herbert Hoover had nominated Parker to the Supreme Court, but the Senate rejected him, responding to opposition from the NAACP and organized labor. Thurgood, while believing that Parker would decide for the state, thought that he would act decently, follow the law—which, of course, was against us—but employ fair procedure and find facts accurately. Indeed, he had thought so well of Parker that, when a possibility arose again that he might be nominated to the Court, Thurgood promised that if the NAACP were to oppose him once more, Thurgood would support him. But Harold Burton got the appointment and the matter never arose. Counsel for the defendants, Robert McC. Figg, Jr., put up no defense for the disgraceful condition of the black schools and commenced with the best tactic when confronted with an overwhelming argument: Give away what your opponent can take away. He conceded that the black schools were inferior, justifying the inferiority on the ground that education in rural districts had not kept pace with urban ones and that the inequality wasn't intentional. Moreover, the state had just passed a 3 percent sales tax, to take effect in July, to raise $75,000,000 for education and to equalize the schools. He did not oppose an order requiring equalization and asked for "a reasonable time to formulate a plan for ending such inequalities and for bringing about equality of educational opportunity."

Thurgood insisted on presenting details of the inequalities and put on witnesses who described them in detail. Beyond that, one of our expert witnesses, Horace McNally, professor of education at Teachers College of Columbia University, testified in support of our main theme in the school cases: "There is basically implied in the separation . . . that there is some difference in the two groups which does not make it feasible for them to be educated together, which I would hold to be untrue. Furthermore, by separating the two groups, there is implied a stigma on at least one of them." Ellis Knox, a professor of education at Howard, testified similarly: "When children are segregated . . . segregation cannot exist without discrimination, disadvantages to the minority group, and that the children in the Negro schools very definitely are not prepared for the same type of American citizenship as the children in the white schools."

Our main witness was Kenneth B. Clark, then a young assistant professor of psychology at City College of New York, who would become one of America's foremost social scientists. Bob Carter recruited him through Otto Klineberg, a professor of social psychology at Columbia, indeed a creator of modern social psychology, who had been Kenneth's professor and had supervised his Ph.D. dissertation. He and his wife, Mamie Phipps Clark, who also had a Ph.D. in psychology, had done pathbreaking work to ascertain the psychological effects of segregation on the self-image and self-esteem of black children. We brought him to Clarendon County to repeat this research on black children there.

In what are called projective tests, the Clarks placed in front of children dolls that were identical except for skin color, one white, the other brown, and asked questions such as, "Show me the doll that you like best or that you'd like to play with," "Show me the doll that is the 'nice' doll," "Show

me the doll that looks 'bad,'" and "Give me the doll that looks like you."
Kenneth gave these tests to sixteen black elementary school children in
Clarendon County between the ages of six and nine. As he later described
it, some of the children responded with statements like "I'm a nigger, that's
a nigger." He viewed the tests not as making a precise statement on *school*
segregation, but rather as describing the effect of societal discrimination, of
which school segregation was a part.

The Clarendon County results were consistent with tests Kenneth previously had given to more than three hundred children. In Clarendon County
ten of the sixteen black children liked the white doll better and thought it
was nice. Eleven picked the brown doll as looking "bad," while more than
half identified themselves with the "bad" doll. Seven of the black children,
when asked to pick the doll that looked most like themselves, picked the
white doll, all of which he interpreted to mean that the "Negro child
accepts as early as six, seven or eight the negative stereotypes about his
own group," and that a "fundamental effect of segregation is basic confusion in the individuals and their concepts about themselves conflicting in
their self images." He concluded that "children in Clarendon County, like
other human beings who are subjected to an obviously inferior status in the
society in which they live, have been definitely harmed in the development
of their personalities." It was the kind of injury that would endure or last as
long as the situation endured, changing only in its form and in the way it
manifested itself.

He described also "confusion in the child's concept of his own self
esteem—basic feelings of inferiority, conflict, confusion in his self image,
resentment, hostility towards himself, hostility toward whites, intensifica-
tion of sometimes a desire to resolve his basic conflict by sometimes escaping or withdrawing." Later the doll tests were attacked as having been based
on faulty research. Not all of us were in favor of using Kenneth's testimony.
Bob Ming and Bill Coleman opposed the doll test evidence because they did-
n't believe in it. But Thurgood wanted to use eveything he could. I was a bit
skeptical myself, but certainly believed that Dr. Clark's conclusions were
right. We didn't have the luxury of time to do further testing and answer
every doubt the evidence might raise, as if we were writing a Ph.D thesis. If
the decision had been mine alone I would have used the evidence.

With one witness Bob stepped over the sometimes not terribly clear line
between social science and policy. He asked Louis Kesselman, associate
professor of political science at the University of Louisville, whether a segregated public school system "would have adverse effects in operation
among the individuals."

Figg objected: "I don't think that this witness has been qualified. . . . "
Bob replied: "He is a person who has studied the science of government."
Parker turned to Thurgood, in whom he apparently had as much confidence
as Thurgood had in him:

PARKER: Do you seriously contend he is qualified to testify as an educational expert? What do you say about that, Mr. Marshall?

THURGOOD (evasively): We have been trying to . . . present as many experts in the field with as many different reasons why we consider that segregation in and of itself is injurious. . . .

PARKER: Are you going to offer any more witnesses along this line?

THURGOOD: No, sir. The other witnesses are REAL scientists. [Here the court reporter used capital letters, seeking to indicate Thurgood's emphasis].

Kesselman then testified: "Segregation . . . prevents them from gaining an understanding of the needs and interests of both groups . . . breeds suspicion and distrust . . . and . . . enforced by law, it may even breed distrust to the point of conflict."

Thurgood cross-examined one witness in surgical strokes that bared South Carolina's adamant opposition to integration. E. R. Crow, director of the State Educational Finance Commission, testified that recent legislation would soon provide much more money to Clarendon County schools. (Outside of court, his name, although not "*Jim* Crow," was occasion for joking; during the Supreme Court argument Thurgood poked fun at it.) Crow testified that to abolish segregation "would eliminate public schools in most, if not all of the communities in the State." He was "sure" that there would be "a probability of violent emotional reaction." Thurgood questioned him:

Q.: About what is the percentage of Negro population to white population in South Carolina?

A.: . . . About forty percent, or forty-five.

Q.: . . . Are there any Negroes on your Commission?

A.: No.

Q.: Would the fact that Negroes have been admitted to public schools in Indiana for the first time within the last year, change your opinion [that if schools were mixed the public schools of the state would be abandoned]?

A.: No. . . . We have in South Carolina a different ratio of the two races. . . .

Q.: Mr. Crow, assuming that in Clarendon County, specially in School District No. 22, the population was 95% white and 5% Negro, would that change your opinion?

A.: No.

Thurgood read into the record the testimony in *Sweatt* of Robert Redfield, the University of Chicago law teacher, that "differences in intellectual capacity or inability to learn have not been shown to exist as between negroes and whites."

And that was the end of the first trial. Less than a month later, on June 23, 1951, the Court ruled against us. Parker (Timmerman joined him) held that the district had to equalize the schools and report in six months what it had done. He refused to hold segregation unconstitutional. In summary, his opinion said: States had power to legislate about safety, morals, health, and general welfare; *Plessy* held that they have authority to segregate schools; *Sweatt* and *McLaurin* expressly refused to overrule *Plessy*; *McLaurin* "involved humiliating and embarrassing treatment of a Negro law student [actually a graduate student] to which no one should have been required to submit"; "if public education is to have the support of the people through their legislatures, it must not go contrary to what they deem [to be in] the best interests of their children." How about the testimony of the social scientists? They had presented issues to be resolved by the legislatures. Seventeen states and Congress (for the District of Columbia) for three-quarters of a century had required segregated schools.

Judge Waring, in a long and passionate opinion, concluded that "all of the legal guideposts, expert testimony, common sense and reason point unerringly to the conclusion that the system of segregation in education adopted and practiced in the State of South Carolina must go and must go now. *Segregation is per se inequality*." He couldn't resist taking a swipe at the "witness, significantly named Crow."

BROWN V. BOARD OF EDUCATION

Two days later, on June 25, Bob Carter and I, along with the brothers John and Charles Scott, our lawyers in Topeka, began the Topeka trial, *Brown v. Board of Education*. As early as September 1948, Isabel Lurie, a Topeka NAACP branch member, had visited our office, asking for help in filing a lawsuit attacking school segregation. Under the state's segregation law only the lower grades were segregated, children transferring to integrated schools in seventh grade. In 1948, however, neither *Sweatt* nor *McLaurin* had been decided and LDF bided its time. The local branch got nowhere in continuous negotiations with the school board. In September 1950 McKinley Burnett, the branch president, wrote to Walter White that the school board had referred the branch to the state legislature to seek repeal of the school segregation law. "Words will not express the humiliation and disrespect in this matter," he added. Shortly afterward, Connie Motley sent Burnett a model complaint used in Virginia equalization cases, adding (in view of the June 1950 mandate that all school cases should ask for an end to segregation), "It will be necessary . . . to add in the prayer for relief a specific *prayer for the admission of Negro children to the white schools*." Between October and December 1950 Bob Carter and Charles Bledsoe of Topeka corresponded, Bob urging him to sign up a large number of plaintiffs and discussing whether the case should be in a one- or three-judge court.

In November the Topeka lawyers had sent us a list of twenty children as plaintiffs; the twentieth entry on the list was "Linda Carol Brown, Father: Oliver Brown." But when they drafted the complaint, because Brown was first in alphabetical order, they captioned the case *"Oliver Brown, et al. v. Board of Education of Topeka, Shawnee County, Kansas,"* bestowing immortality on a family that was neither more nor less involved than any of the other nineteen. I redrafted the complaint to request a three-judge court and an injunction against the school segregation law as unconstitutional. *Brown v. Board of Education* was ready to go. Bledsoe filed it on February 28, 1951.

In March, at the suggestion of the Kansas City director of the Community Relations Bureau of the American Jewish Committee, who had been enlisted by its New York headquarters, I recruited Hugh Speer, head of the Department of Education of the University of Kansas City, to survey the Topeka schools. On May 29 he sent me a telegram: "PRELIMINARY EVIDENCE REVEALS NO SIGNIFICANT DISCRIMINATION ON TEACHER PREPARATION SALARY OR CROWDED CONDITIONS PROBABLY SOME INFERIORITY IN BUILDINGS TRANSPORTATION SPECIAL TEACHERS AND CURRICULUM SUGGEST EMPHASIS ON SOCIAL AND PSYCHOLOGICAL HANDICAPS OF SEGREGATION PER SE."

By the end of May, I was looking for social scientists for the Kansas case, scheduled for trial at the end of June, and the Delaware cases, which would be filed in August. I telephoned and wrote to the sociologist Robert S. Lynd at Columbia, author of the great Middletown study, because I knew him slightly. Once, while on leave in the navy, I had visited him, seeking suggestions about what to read. Among his recommendations was his own book *Knowledge for What*, a powerful argument that scholars should devote their energies to addressing social problems about which they might make a difference. But Lynd said he couldn't help us. Karl Menninger (a member of the original Committee of 100), of the famed psychiatric clinic located in Topeka bearing his name, was opposed to segregation; Hugh Speer solicited his testimony but received no reply. Some speculated that he preferred not to have a collision with authorities in Topeka, but, later, Menninger said he had not been asked. After the lower court decision, however, he helped raise funds to pay for the case. I was particularly interested in recruiting social scientists from the Midwest, to keep travel expenses down, so I wrote to a long list, including another eminent scholar, Arnold Rose, a professor at the University of Minnesota and a collaborator with Gunnar Myrdal on the *American Dilemma*. Rose at first agreed but then couldn't appear, although he offered to write an affidavit. He suggested various names, including Louisa Holt of the University of Kansas, who happened to live in Topeka. With the trial scheduled for June 25, I worked out the appearance of eight experts from Midwestern universities, making arrangements with some less than a week before trial.

On June 13, Bob sent Thurgood a memorandum stressing that the case might be important because we might win: "Our possibilities for winning here seem much better than they are in South Carolina, particularly in view of the fact that the statutes involved in this case are permissive and give cities of certain size in Kansas the right to enforce segregation, if they so desire. Thus, the pressure for the maintenance of the segregated system is not as great as it would be in southern communities." He pointed out that the Topeka case would go to the Supreme Court with South Carolina.

Topeka was a Jim Crow city, but some public accommodations took in blacks who came properly recommended. A local lawyer offered to arrange for Bob and me to stay at the Jayhawk, the best hotel in town and ordinarily for whites only, but we wouldn't become exceptions to the general rule. Another suggestion was that I stay in a white hotel and Bob stay in a black one. I declined. So, I flew out four days before trial, on a particularly bumpy Lockheed Constellation, to join Bob and went to a black hotel. Shortly after checking in, I went to the bathroom, a sort of enclosure down the hall, lath showing through the crumbling plaster of its walls, which did not quite reach the ceiling, and pulled the light cord, which brought down a large chunk of ceiling. That was enough. We moved to a private home where we stayed for the duration of the case. The night before the trial we all went to Louisa Holt's house and discussed each witness's testimony.

Walter A. Huxman of the Court of Appeals for the Tenth Circuit and two district judges, Arthur J. Mellott and Delmas C. Hill, presided at the trial. Bob and I were joined by our local counsel, John and Charles Scott, of the firm of Scott, Scott and Scott. The third Scott was their father, Elisha, a legendary black lawyer who began practicing at a time when black lawyers were even scarcer than in the early 1950s. He was said to be so good that white racketeers sought him out as counsel.

The trial first developed that black and white schools were unequal and that black children who lived near white schools had to travel considerable distances to black ones, often waiting for buses in the rain and cold, unable to come home for lunch as the white children did. One of the black parents whom John Scott examined on such matters gave us a fright. Silas Fleming testified that his children took the city bus past white schools, at some expense, because the school bus stopped more than six blocks from his home.

Then suddenly he said: "I would ask this [sic] for a few minutes to explain why I got into the suit whole soul and body."

After some initial confusion, Judge Huxman asked, "Didn't you consent to be a plaintiff in this case?"

Fleming responded, "That's right."

Now, it would have been more than an embarrassment if Fleming testified that he had not voluntarily brought the suit, or that he had been pressured into suing; it could have caused real trouble. It was then a crime and grounds for disbarment to engage in "champerty," "maintenance," "running and capping," and, colloquially, "ambulance chasing." Even after solicitation came to be held legal in civil rights cases, there was no right to file suit for someone who hadn't given permission. The colloquy between witness and judge was for a while confused:

JUDGE HUXMAN: You did not?
JUDGE MELLOTT: He said he did, but he wants to tell the reason why.
THE WITNESS: I want to tell the cause.
JUDGE HUXMAN: You want to tell the Court why you joined this lawsuit?
THE WITNESS: That's right.
JUDGE HUXMAN: All right, go ahead and tell it.
THE WITNESS: Well, it wasn't for the sake of hot dogs. It wasn't to cast any insinuations that our teachers are not capable of teaching our children because they are supreme, extremely intelligent and are capable of teaching my kids or white or black kids. But my point was that not only I and my children are craving light, the entire colored race is craving light, and the only way to reach the light is to start our children together in their infancy and they come up together.
JUDGE HUXMAN: All right, now you have answered and given us your reason.

We breathed sighs of relief. But more than that, Fleming inspired us and, maybe, the judges.

I examined Hugh Speer, who described respects in which the black schools were inferior to the white ones, like buildings, sites, books, staffs, and so forth. The differences weren't enormous but they certainly existed. Then, suddenly, during defense counsel Lester Goodell's cross-examination of Speer, Elisha Scott, the senior Scott, who until then had nothing to do with the case, appeared.

MR. SCOTT: I object to that.
JUDGE HUXMAN: Mr. Scott, are you entered here as an attorney of record?
MR. SCOTT: I am supposed to be.
JUDGE HUXMAN: Go ahead.
MR. SCOTT: I object to that because he is invading the rights, and he is answering a question not based upon the evidence adduced or could be adduced.
MR. GOODELL: You just got here; you wouldn't know.
MR. SCOTT: Yes I do know.
JUDGE HUXMAN: Objection will be overruled.

Elisha Scott, unhappily, was drunk. But the judges knew him well and didn't react unkindly. The court declared a brief recess, he was hustled out of the courtroom, and the trial resumed.

We had a half-dozen social scientific witnesses, three white women, the others men, and had decided that Bob Carter should take the testimony of the white women, while I would examine the men, simply because we thought that would irritate the other side. If any single social scientist had more impact than the others in the Topeka case it was Louisa Holt. After describing her credentials (bachelor's, master's, and Ph.D. degrees in the Department of Social Relations at Radcliffe) and teaching and research positions, including her current teaching post at the University of Kansas, she answered Bob's questions:

Q.: Mrs. Holt, are you at all familiar with the school system in Topeka?
A.: Yes; I have one child who entered that system this last year and another who enters next September.
Q.: Based upon your experience and your knowledge, taking the segregated factor alone in the school system in Topeka, in your opinion does enforced legal separation have any adverse effect upon the personality development of the Negro child?
A.: The fact that it is enforced, that it is legal I think, has more importance than the mere fact of segregation by itself does because this gives legal and offical sanction to a policy which inevitably is interpreted both by white people and by Negroes as denoting the inferiority of the Negro group. Were it not for the sense that one group is inferior to the other, there would be no basis, and I am not granting that this is a rational basis, for such segregation.

A sense of inferiority must always affect one's motivation for learning since it affects the feeling one has of one's self as a person, as a personality or a self or an ego identity, as Erik Erickson has recently expressed it. That sense of ego identity is built up on the basis of attitudes that are expressed toward a person by others who are important. First the parents and then the teachers, other people in the community, whether they are older or one's own peers. It is other people's reactions to one's self which most basically affects the conception of one's self that one has. If these attitudes that are reflected back and then internalized or projected, are unfavorable ones, then one develops a sense of one's self as an inferior being. That may not be deleterious necessarily from the standpoint of educational motivation. I believe in some cases it can lead to stronger motivation to achieve well in academic pursuits, to strive to disprove to the world that one is inferior since the world feels that one is inferior. In other cases, of course, the reaction may be the opposite and apathetic acceptance, fatalistic submission to the feeling others have expressed that one is inferior and therefore any efforts to prove otherwise would be doomed to failure

On August 3, 1951, the court handed down its decision. We lost, but in that loss were the seeds of ultimate victory. The court held that it was bound by *Plessy*. Judge Huxman's opinion recognized that *Sweatt* and *McLaurin* had made inroads into that doctrine. In fact, unlike Judge Parker, who wrote that there were meaningful differences between higher and lower schools that justified a difference in outcome between the Clarendon County case and the graduate and professional school cases, Huxman wrote that

> if segregation within a school as in the *McLaurin* case is a denial of due process [actually it was equal protection], it is difficult to see why segregation in separate schools would not result in the same denial. Or if the denial of the right to commingle with the majority group in higher institutions of learning as in the *Sweatt* case and gain the educational advantages resulting therefrom, is lack of due process, it is difficult to see why such denial would not result in the same lack of due process if practiced in the lower grades.[34]

Nevertheless, he made two important findings, first, that schools for blacks and whites in Topeka were equal (although in fact they weren't—there were real, though slight, differences), possibly to highlight the second key finding: No matter how equal the facilities, segregation injures the black child. Adopting almost verbatim Louisa Holt's testimony, he concluded:

> Segregation of white and colored children in public schools has a detrimental effect upon the colored children. The impact is greater when it has the sanction of the law; for the policy of separating the races is usually interpreted as denoting the inferiority of the negro group. A sense of inferiority affects the motivation of a child to learn. Segregation with the sanction of law, therefore, has a tendency to retard the educational and mental development of negro children and to deprive them of some of the benefits they would receive in a racially integrated school system.

Louisa's words, which found their way into Huxman's findings, later were adopted by the Supreme Court in critical passages of *Brown v. Board of Education*. Huxman, in finding the schools equal in all respects, except for the fact of segregation, was trying to box in the Supreme Court. In 1967, he told Hugh Speer, one of our experts, "I tried to wrap it up in such a way that they could not duck it. They had whittled away at it long enough."

After the trial the school placed Louisa's daughter in the slowest first-grade reading group, which she felt was a retaliation for her testimony. In Berkeley, California, where they moved shortly afterwards, her daughter placed in the highest group.

I sent thank you letters to all the witnesses. In looking over the correspondence as I prepared to write these pages, I blanched as I read my letter to Louisa Holt. After expressing appreciation, I added: "It is rare that an expert witness combines the qualities of scholarship, residence in the community about which she is testifying, two children in the school system and the irrefutable authority of being exceedingly attractive." Those last words today would be viewed as not politically correct. At that time, however, nothing of the sort would have occurred to me. Recently I spoke with Louisa (now Louisa Howe) about her recollections. She reminded me that she had not expected to testify until several days later and was unprepared when we called her as a witness. While she is not religious, she felt that a God-given eloquence had descended upon her. I asked about the letter. She laughed, "I guess I was reasonably O.K. looking those days."

Appeal from a three-judge court went directly to the Supreme Court of the United States. But, in the meantime, there still was *Groveland.*

11

GROVELAND, DELAWARE, AND DANCERS DRESSED IN FEATHERS

TO FLORIDA

The state of Florida planned to retry Sammy Shepherd and Walter Irvin for the rape of Norma Padgett, a charge that had set off rioting and pillaging and had caused the governor to summon the National Guard. The arraignment was scheduled for August 15, 1951, and the trial for November 7.

That summer, while working on Topeka and Delaware, I had started traveling to Florida to prepare *Groveland*. I usually went by train, sometimes alone, sometimes with Thurgood. Air travel wasn't much faster than taking the train in those days and the train had the additional advantage of affording time to work and confer. We rode great trains with wonderful names like East Coast Champion, Silver Meteor, and Orange Blossom. On one trip we made together, I asked Thurgood if he wanted me to arrange for a double bedroom or separate rooms. He replied, "I don't sleep with nobody who don't wear lacy drawers," so I got him a bedroom and a roomette for myself. During waking hours we worked in Thurgood's room.

At dinner we were often the object of stares. *Henderson* had been decided only the year before and white travelers were not yet accustomed to seeing blacks in dining cars. The porters and waiters, however, loved us. They knew that Thurgood, now a celebrity, had been one of them while working his way through school. We got treats like the outside cut of the roast beef, which the chef usually saved for himself, and bar service in our rooms on Sundays—when serving alcohol was prohibited—even in dry states. One day I found a large fly in my salad and pointed it out to the waiter. He started to remove the plate, but Thurgood placed his hand on the waiter's arm, told him to bring a new salad and then remove my plate. When the waiter was gone, Thurgood explained. As a former dining car waiter himself, he knew what would happen in the kitchen—the waiter would remove the fly and return with the same salad.

More than forty years after these trips, after the old Confederacy had begun to modify its racial attitudes, the region was regenerated as the Sun Belt, an area of booming growth. But, in 1951, our train travel took us through a poverty-stricken Dixie that time had left behind—endless miles of pine forests; unpainted wooden shacks; old, deserted, and uncared for railroad stations; an occasional coffin waiting to be shipped home; sometimes cardboard crates of cut flowers to be sent north.

Thurgood knew the route and I would ask him to identify places along the way. In Georgia I asked him what river we were crossing and he quickly answered, the Rappahannock, pronouncing it Rrrrrappahannock. But I knew that the Rappahannock was in Virginia and that this had to be some other river. He then told me of an old porter who, whenever asked by a passenger what river they might be passing, immediately, and confidently, identified it as the Rrrrrappahannock. Thurgood didn't know the name of the river we had just crossed.

I never stayed in white hotels, but for this case I broke the rule—feelings generated by the *Groveland* case still ran so high that no black family wanted me to be seen entering or leaving their house. Alex Akerman had a friend who owned the San Juan, a hotel in Orlando; he put me up and allowed Thurgood and Paul Perkins, a black lawyer just graduated from Howard who had set up practice in Orlando and joined the defense team, to come to my room so that we could confer and take our meals together. (Rights wrapped in cellophane, which is what Thurgood said he did with his rights when he went south.) We lived with battlefield tension, but not battlefield conditions, occasionally enjoying a dinner of grilled Florida lobster in my room.

Our investigations went well. We found witnesses who hadn't been found for the first trial because there hadn't been time. We found a black woman, a waitress who had seen Shepherd and Irvin at Club Eaton the night of the crime at an hour that made it impossible for them to have been at the scene of the crime. She agreed to testify; we sent her a check for her expenses. Through friends in the Pentagon with whom we worked on courts-martial we located Lawrence Burtoft, the first person Norma Padgett saw after the alleged rape, and to whom she said nothing about being raped. Burtoft, who had since gone into the army, agreed to testify if we subpoenaed him. We found the doctor who had examined Norma Padgett, but he wouldn't talk to us. That left us with the question of whether to subpoena him—most likely he feared the consequences for his personal safety and his medical practice of testifying on behalf of a black man, and therefore might give testimony that would hurt us.

A private detective friend of Thurgood's, Buck Owens, referred us to a detective in Miami who agreed to evaluate the plaster casts of tire tracks and footprints, the most important pieces of hard evidence the prosecution had. Despite Thurgood's admonition that private detectives report only "progress," we had to plan what we would do about that part of the prosecution's case and pressed him for his findings. We were lucky. He came to the sensational, irrefutable conclusion that the plaster casts had been faked.

To establish whether we could get a fair trial in Lake County we commissioned a rudimentary public opinion poll to be conducted by four clergymen led by Paul Moore, then a parish priest on New York's Lower East Side and later Episcopal bishop of New York. (Since 1965 Paul has been chair of the Committee of 100.) The poll reported that white residents thought the first trial was fair; that blacks and whites agreed it would be impossible to find twelve white people who had not already made up their minds about the case; that there was widespread fear among whites of being identified as a nigger-lover; and that the community generally trusted the sheriff, the prosecutor, and the trial judge.

With Paul Perkins I visited the Irvins to ask about the circumstances in which the sheriff had taken Walter's shoes and trousers. The Irvin home was an unpainted, weather-beaten, tin-roofed shack, its muddy front yard teeming with shoeless children, listless dogs, and chickens. Indoors the hot, humid cabin reeked of a kerosene heater. Walter's mother, a somber, quiet women, showed us his room, which had a lock on the door, and told us that he paid rent, thereby supporting our argument that his mother had no legal authority to give away his clothing and our claim that the police had conducted an illegal search and seizure.

Our case seemed to be in pretty decent shape, but no matter how much the facts might support him, a black man accused of rape by a white woman in the Deep South was always convicted, and no doubt this would also be the case in Lake County. Aware of the unlikelihood of a verdict of innocence, we hoped to get Shepherd and Irvin sentences of life imprisonment rather than execution. Even this much would be a major victory. Unhappily, there wasn't too much time to spend on *Groveland* in advance of the trial, which was scheduled for early November. There were, among other pressing matters, the Delaware school segregation cases.

THE DELAWARE CASES

The University of Delaware case Lou Redding and I had won had been heard by Vice-Chancellor Collins J. Seitz, so it would have made good sense to file the elementary and high school cases in his court, but Seitz was up for promotion to chancellor. Segregationists in Delaware, of whom there were plenty, hated Seitz, and downstate legislators were already lining up in opposition. We hardly wanted to reward his courage by costing him the votes he needed for promotion. So we filed two cases, *Wilson v. Beebe* and *Johnson v. Beebe*, in federal court on June 2, 1951.

The state, however, moved that the federal court do nothing until the state court had first had an opportunity to construe the segregation statute. There is a doctrine called abstention, which allows state courts first to interpret their statutes to have a meaning that would be constitutional, obviating the possibility that federal courts will declare them unconstitutional. The argument was ridiculous in this case, because it could hardly be contended that state law permitted integration. In the meantime, however, the legislature confirmed Seitz as chancellor. Now without any reason to fight the abstention motion, in July and August we filed *Belton v. Gebhart* and *Bulah v. Gebhart* in state court, and these ultimately became the Delaware school segregation cases in the United States Supreme Court. When Lou told the federal court that we would proceed in state court, the judges seemed so clearly sympathetic that we wondered whether we shouldn't have tried to stay there.

Early in August I began assembling a group of expert witnesses. As in Topeka and South Carolina, we needed someone to survey the schools, and once more there were the social scientists. I put together a great crew, including some distinguished scholars who had never testified before. Kenneth Clark agreed to test some of the Wilmington children. Among the new witnesses were Jerome Bruner, who has since become one of the world's foremost social scientists; Otto Klineberg, one of the founders of social psychology, who later became a good friend; and Fredric Wertham, a famous psychiatrist who ran a mental health clinic for black youngsters in Harlem and who cared deeply about discrimination.

Wertham and I agreed that it would be best if he were to spend time speaking with some of the children from Delaware. I arranged to bring batches of kids to New York to be interviewed at the Lafargue Clinic, Wertham's facility at St. Philip's Episcopal Church in Harlem. The clinic had a staff of thirty professionals and was open two nights a week. A member of the Wilmington NAACP accompanied a small group of black and white children to New York City (a two-hour train trip) on three or four occasions. I met them at Pennsylvania Station, took them to the clinic, and, after their interviews, back to the Station for the trip home.

The first time they came up I thought I would treat them to dinner in a Chinese restaurant, a new experience for all of them. That turned out to be a big mistake; as they went about sampling all the strange and exotic dishes they had never seen before, I began to wonder whether or not I'd have enough money to pay the bill.

Wertham was of an imperious nature and quite temperamental, and everything had to be precisely as he wanted it. He insisted on testifying first, ahead of the other experts, offering the reason that by the time the trial began he would have examined the children and his testimony would be the most detailed, and he didn't want to face the burden of defending the testimony of preceding witnesses. He had an injured knee and until almost the last minute I couldn't be sure that he would show up. One point of tension was Wertham's view that comic books, particularly those that depicted sadism, violence, and racism, had a very harmful influence on children. As we discussed his testimony Wertham kept veering off into denouncing the malignant influence of comic books, and I kept trying to steer him back to the case at hand, thinking the comic book issue irrelevant and distracting.

The trial began on October 22, 1951. It went much like the Clarendon County and Topeka cases. Stephen Wright, dean of Hampton Institute, and Ellis Knox and Paul Lawrence, professors of education at Howard, testified about material aspects of the schools. In a delicious twist, Louis Redding called as a witness Maurice Thomasson, acting president of Delaware State College, to which black students had been restricted until our case of the previous year integrated the University of Delaware. In light of how some whites, as well as some blacks, might react, it took courage for Thomasson to testify. He offered the opinion that the white schools were materially better than the black ones and that segregation per se indicated a belief that "the persons designated for [the separate] school[s] are not quite fit to go to the regular schools."

Kenneth Clark's social scientific testimony was about the same as at the Clarendon County trials: Segregation impaired the self-esteem of black children and confused their sense of identity. Otto Klineberg testified that there are no racial differences in intelligence, referring to some of his great original studies of the subject as well as other research. In the earliest of these Klineberg had studied blacks as they moved from the South to the North and demonstrated that as their environment changed their IQs went up.

Only Wertham's testimony was different than expected—he captivated the courtroom. The Viennese accent helped, but the impact came from what he had to say. He responded to my questions:

> It is my opinion that the State . . . injures the child's health. . . . I hold the scientific opinion that if a rosebush should produce twelve roses and if only one rose grows, it is not a healthy rosebush. . . .
>
> Now, the fact of segregation in public and high school creates in the mind of the child an unsolvable conflict. . . .
>
> One way to overcome such a conflict is to have a realistic understanding of why it is that one group of children to which one belongs is excluded and another group of children to which one does not belong is included. . . . I have found that the children cannot find such a realistic rationalization for the simple reason that the adults don't give it to them and . . . the State . . . cannot give an understandable explanation. . . .
>
> If the State of Delaware would employ Professor Einstein to teach Physics in marble halls to these children, I would still say everything I

have said goes: It is the fact of segregation in general and the problems that come out of it that to my mind is antieducational, by which I mean that education in the larger sense is interfered with.

Now, of course these facts that I have mentioned are not caused only by the school segregation, but the school segregation is important, of paramount importance. . . .

In the first place, it is absolutely clear cut.

Secondly, the State does it.

Thirdly, it is not just the discrimination—it is discrimination of very long duration. . . .

Fourth, it is bound up with the whole educational process.

He was very powerful, and, up to this point, he hadn't got into the comic books. I was hoping he wouldn't get the chance. But then he told of a child he had interviewed who had had with him a copy of Jumbo Comics. I stood powerless as Wertham turned to the chancellor:

THE WITNESS [WERTHAM]: I would like to show a picture which shows a cage up in a tree, and there are colored people in there, clearly understood by these children as being Negroes, and it says, quote: Helpless natives left to starve or to be prey to any prowling beast.

There is a white girl underneath looking upward (indicating). Can I show this to you?
THE COURT: You will have to introduce it through your counsel.

I tried to be casual:

MR. GREENBERG: May I introduce this in evidence? It is a photostat of a comic book from one of the children whom Dr. Wertham examined.
THE WITNESS: And this one is a close-up (indicating). And in this one there are Negroes tied to a tree and being beaten.

The attorney general started asking questions about the original documents. I had no way out and introduced the photocopies of the comic book into evidence, as well as the comic book itself, as if I had planned to do so all along. I tried to link the comic books to school segregation with a few questions and Wertham helped a bit:

The children read that, and they are there indoctrinated with the fact that you can do all kinds of things to colored races. Now, the school problem partly, as you say, reinforces that, but it is very much more, because after all these commercial people who sell these things to children do so to make money. The State does it as acting morally. . . . So that the State really stabs very much deeper than these things do.

Wertham's summary was the best part of his testimony:

> Segregation in schools legally decreed by statute, as in the State of Delaware, interferes with the healthy development of children. It doesn't necessarily cause an emotional disorder in every child. I compare that with the disease of tuberculosis. In New York thousands of people have the tubercle bacilli in their lungs—hundreds of thousands—and they don't get tuberculosis. But they do have the germ of illness in them at one time or another, and the fact that hundreds of them don't develop tuberculosis doesn't make me say, "never mind the tubercle bacillus; it doesn't harm people, so let it go."

Lou and I wrote briefs and waited for the decision. In the meantime, *Groveland* came alive, and I got caught up in a cause célèbre that exploded in New York City and was compounded by Walter White's penchant for playing lawyer.

JOSEPHINE BAKER

Josephine Baker, a famous black dancer and actress who was born in the United States but lived in France, and who was a friend of White's, was performing in New York at the Roxy Theatre. On October 16, 1951, she went with friends to the Stork Club, a nightclub on East Fifty-third Street owned by Sherman Billingsley and frequented by celebrities. A wide range of politicians and notables—the Duke and Duchess of Windsor; Joseph P. Kennedy, Sr.; J. Edgar Hoover; Andrey Gromyko; Grace Kelly; John Steinbeck; and Senator Joseph McCarthy—patronized it. Baker ordered a seafood cocktail (some reports say crabmeat, others shrimp), steak, and a bottle of wine, and waited to be served. An hour later a waiter told her the restaurant was out of steak and seafood and that he couldn't find the wine. One of Baker's companions said he would call the police if Baker was not served. She was then served a steak, but was too upset to eat and left. It seemed clear to Baker that she had been maltreated because she was black, and she complained to the police and the NAACP.

Walter Winchell, a newspaper columnist and TV and radio commentator, broadcast regularly from the Stork Club, which brought it a great deal of publicity. His radio program had the country's top ratings; he was extremely influential in the entertainment industry, and, in fact, had given Baker's show a great review. (Sometimes I would hear the program, which began, staccatolike, with "Good evening Mr. and Mrs. America and all the ships at sea.") Winchell was in the club during part of the episode involving Baker, but said he had no idea of what was going on.

Walter White demanded that Winchell repudiate the discriminatory practices of the Stork Club by refusing to broadcast any longer from the club. Winchell, however, resentful at being dragged into a dispute that he felt did not involve him, denounced Baker on the radio and in his column, saying she had supported Mussolini's invasion of Ethiopia, that she wouldn't shop at Negro-owned stores, and that the Immigration and Naturalization Service was investigating her. He charged that there were Communists in the NAACP picket line that began marching in front of the Stork Club to protest the episode. Because Winchell was a confidant of J. Edgar Hoover some took these charges seriously. On the other hand, some editorials asserted that Baker's treatment played into the hands of the Communists. All sorts of politicians, from City Hall to the White House, got involved. All the Paris newspapers reported the episode.

Thurgood was out of town. White called me to his office and directed me to sue Winchell for libel. Somewhat puzzled about what a lawyer could do in these circumstances, I got a yellow pad and some pencils and went to the Roxy Theatre to gather the facts. Backstage, jostled and distracted by the corps of dancing girls clad in almost nothing but feathers, I interviewed Josephine Baker and got the details of her story. I concluded that, while it was theoretically feasible to persuade the district attorney to prosecute Billingsley for violation of the antidiscrimination laws, to bring suit ourselves on the same grounds, or to try to get the Stork Club's liquor license lifted, none of these possibilities was actually very promising. It would have been difficult to prove with certainty that Baker had been a victim of racial discrimination. A libel suit made no sense legally or practically.

Then Thurgood returned and was furious that White had directed one of *his* lawyers to do anything at all. Thurgood put a stop to all my activity in the matter, and he and White fired nasty memoranda back and forth until the matter was forgotten. Later, Baker, employing other lawyers, including Arthur Garfield Hays, sued Winchell for libel, seeking $400,000 in damages, but eventually dropped the case. The State Liquor Authority and the district attorney declined to act. Reviewing this episode with Thurgood years later, he chuckled, "She *was* a commie."

This Felliniesque episode illustrated a deeper problem that continued to recur: Was it a higher priority to work on cases that might make important legal precedent, as I had been doing when White coopted me, or on high visibility cases, like Baker's, which by publicizing discrimination against celebrities might focus attention on the racial discrimination in public accommodations all black Americans had to endure almost daily? Equally important, who should make that decision, the director of the organization or the chief lawyer? As some phrased the question at the time, who was the HNIC?

GROVELAND—THE TRIAL IS SCHEDULED TO BEGIN

On November 6 I was in Orlando for the *Groveland* trial, which would begin the next day. Thurgood hadn't come down yet, leaving the preliminary motions to Alex Akerman, Paul Perkins, and me. After dark, a procession of cars and trucks, horns tooting, confederate flags flying, some carrying blazing torches, drove round and round the San Juan Hotel, where I was staying. A white-hooded, sheeted figure sat on the outsized hood of a Nash Ambassador, waving as it drove by. Before I went to sleep, I took the vain precaution of putting a night table against the door—at least I would be awakened if anyone tried to enter.

My 7:00 A.M. wake-up call roused me and I pulled the night table aside to get the newspaper that had been shoved under the door. On the front page of the Orlando *Sentinel Star* I saw the blazing headline: "Lake County Sheriff Shoots Two Negroes. Officer Kills Suspect in Attack Case. Pair Enroute to Hearing Try Escape." The story told that Sheriff Willis McCall had been transporting Irvin and Shepherd to the Tavares courthouse for the hearing when he had a flat tire. He got out and started repairing it and the pair jumped him. He drew his revolver, killed Shepherd and wounded Irvin. Surgeons removed blood clots and a bullet from Irvin's lung and left a bullet in his kidney, but he was not expected to survive. McCall entered the hospital for shock and a heart condition.

A national and international firestorm burst out. Andrei Vishinsky, the Soviet foreign minister, said, "This is what human rights means in the United States of America." Walter Reuther at the CIO (later merged into the AFL-CIO) convention being held in New York denounced the shooting as fuel for Communist propaganda. United States Attorney General J. Howard McGrath sent in the FBI to determine whether federal statutes had been violated.

That morning Perkins, Akerman, and I drove to the hospital to see Irvin. He was propped up on a pillow, wearing a white hospital gown, with a tube taped to his cheek that went into a nostril and a heavily bandaged neck, the white tape and bandages particularly stark against his dark skin. As he began talking to us, Deputy Sheriff James L. Yates, who had the build of a blocking back, entered and directed us to leave the room, saying he had orders not to let anyone talk to Irvin without permission from the judge and Irvin's doctor. Yates kept going back and forth from Irvin's room to Sheriff McCall's down the corridor for instructions. We phoned for permission and went for a walk around the block, waiting for a response. As we walked, Yates kept us under surveillance from a hospital window.

Later that afternoon Thurgood arrived. But not until the next day, November 8, were we, in the company of a representative of the governor's office and a stenographer, able to visit Walter again. Gasping for breath, he told us that after dark he and Sammy Shepherd left the prison with McCall and Yates on their way to the courthouse; they went in McCall's car, handcuffed to one another. En route, they stopped and Yates got into his own car; Shepherd and Irvin stayed with McCall in the front seat, still handcuffed together. McCall stopped a couple of times to check a shimmy and then said, "You SOB's get out and let me get a tire and fix my car." Irvin continued:

Shepherd, he takes his foot and put it out of the car, and was getting out, and I can't say just how quick it was, but he shot him . . . and then right quick he shot me right here [pointing to the right side of his chest] . . . he snatched both of us and threw both of us on the ground. Then I didn't say anything, I didn't say nothing. So after later he snatched us, he shot me again, in the shoulder. And still I didn't say anything at all, all that time. And I knew I was not dead, and I heard him say, "I got rid of them, I killed the sons of bitches." He ran around the car, and called the Deputy Sheriff on the radio, and I heard him say, "Pull around here right quick. These sons . . . tried to jump me and I did a damn good job on them." In about ten minutes the Deputy Sheriff was there. . . .

The deputy he shined the light in my face, and he said to the Sheriff, "That son of a bitch is not dead" and then he said "Let's kill him." The Deputy Sheriff then pointed the pistol on me, and pulled the trigger, and the gun did not shoot. . . . So he turned it on me again, and pulled it and that time it fired. It went through here [pointing to his neck] and then I began to bleed and bleed, out of my mouth and nose.

We left the room. Thurgood announced on the hospital steps: "The good people of Lake County should have time to take action, but if they don't the N.A.A.C.P. will"—a gesture toward Southern resentment of Northern interference. A sensitive recognition of "lose your head, lose your case." Thurgood called for the governor to replace the sheriff's deputies with state troopers to guard Irvin. A coroner's inquest cleared the sheriff and deputy, finding that they acted in the line of duty and in self-defense. The court had rescheduled the November 7 motions for December 6. We amended our motion for change of venue to allege that Walter Irvin couldn't get a fair trial because McCall and Yates had tried to murder him and Lake County had taken no steps to punish them. The court also scheduled for that day our motion to remove the state's attorney from the case because he was not impartial, and a motion to suppress as evidence Walter Irvin's shoes and trousers, which had been taken by an illegal search and seizure.

At the December 6 hearing Truman G. Futch was the judge, as in the first trial. A pinched-faced man with a wrinkled brow, he presided over a small wood-paneled courtroom, with a balcony upstairs for black spectators. On the bench was a pile of cedar sticks, each the dimension of a pencil, stacked up to form a rectangular box. As the hearing went on, Futch removed them one by one, whittled each to a fine point, then started on the next, as a pile of shavings accumulated around the bench.

Alex Akerman started off routinely by moving the admission of the out-of-state lawyers, Thurgood Marshall and Jack Greenberg. The prosecutor, Jess Hunter, who looked like a somewhat taller version of Barry Fitzgerald, balding, with a protruding lower lip, and a day's growth of white stubble, shuffled up to the bench and in a gargley voice offered an objection, which the judge agreed to without a further word.

Akerman, therefore, proceeded with the motions himself, as we sat and looked on. Actually, we harbored a bit of secret satisfaction, because keeping us out might be the basis of reversal on appeal. Judge Futch denied the motion to disqualify Hunter and deferred the motion to prohibit introducing Walter's shoes into evidence until the trial. Hunter then, to our amazement, filed a paper that said that although the case could be tried fairly in Lake County, "because of the slanderous and libelous matters which have been published by the N.A.A.C.P. and other radicals over this country," he suggested the venue be changed. The judge then issued an order, obviously prepared in advance, moving the case to adjacent Marion County, in the same judicial circuit, with the same prosecutor, and the same judge, Futch himself. He postponed motions again to January 9 and trial to January 14, 1952.

In Marion County the change of venue issue would be harder, although prejudice there against Irvin would not be very different. I got the idea that we should conduct a public opinion poll to prove community attitudes. Nowadays such polls are common but this would be the first public opinion poll on a change of venue motion anyone had conducted. Bob Carter had a friend, Louis Harris, who worked for Elmo Roper, and through him we were able to get the Roper agency to conduct our poll at cost. Julian Woodward, a Roper executive and past president of the American Association for Public Opinion Research, directed the poll with twelve regular Roper interviewers, all Southerners. Lou Harris tells of being followed by Sheriff McCall and other law enforcment officers wherever he went and being questioned by them. On one occasion he and a car full of interviewers were chased out of the county at ninety miles an hour.

The poll results in Lake County (where the first trial took place) were that 63 percent of those polled were sure that the defendants were guilty and 14 percent only thought they were, and in Marion County (where the new trial would take place) 43 percent were sure of guilt and 20 percent thought they probably were guilty. But, of the blacks in Marion County, 69 percent were sure the defendants weren't guilty and 20 percent thought they weren't. A change of venue from Marion, however, would place the trial in a more neutral atmosphere: In fairly distant Jackson County only 17 percent of those polled were sure of the defendants' guilt and 13 percent thought them guilty. Moreover, in Jackson County, 42 percent of those questioned never heard of the case or refused to answer and 26 percent didn't know whether the defendants were guilty or innocent. So to obtain an impartial jury and hold trial in as impartial an environment as possible, it would have made sense to move the trial farther away from Lake County.

On Christmas night, 1951, shortly before trial, a bomb went off under the house of Harry T. Moore, the Florida NAACP state secretary, killing him and his wife. Another national outcry arose. Once more the attorney general said the FBI would investigate, but once more nothing came of it.

Badly battered by publicity, Florida's governor, Fuller Warren, sent a representative who offered us a deal: If Irvin would plead guilty he would get life imprisonment. Thurgood and I put the proposition to Walter and told him that the alternative was a trial and appeals, which almost surely would end in his execution. We left it up to him, but clearly implied that we hoped he would accept the deal. We didn't want him to go to a certain death; if he lived, something might turn up someday to win his freedom. But Walter Irvin, who wouldn't confess after brutal beatings, and who wouldn't die after having been shot three times, looked at us without expression. His right hand and side were dead to sensation; the fingers on his left hand were numb; he showed no emotion when he said that we made him feel he had no choice. But, he insisted, *we* would have to say it for him. He was not guilty and, he said, "won't say it on myself." That, however, was impossible. The judge always asks the defendant whether the guilty plea is his. We had to go to trial.

At the courthouse in Ocala in Marion County, to which the trial had been removed, Judge Futch once more was on the bench, whittling the pile of cedar sticks beside him. On the walls hung portraits of judges of years past, all with elaborate beards and mustaches. Blacks, including Walter Irvin's and Sammy Shepherd's families, climbed up to the Jim Crow section. Once more Akerman moved our admission and Hunter objected. But this time Judge Futch allowed us to participate, giving as a reason, which made no sense, that conditions in Marion County were different from those in Lake. We were glad to be in the case but sorry to lose a basis for appeal.

Thurgood put Julian Woodward on the stand to get the public opinion poll into evidence. Hunter ridiculed it, alluding to the polls' prediction that Dewey would beat Truman in the 1948 election. The judge excluded the poll from evidence, ruling that the evidence was hearsay. Today, however, courts commonly admit public opinion polls into evidence.

In response, Hunter put a number of witnesses, including blacks, on the stand who testified that Irvin could get a fair trial in Marion County. A black dentist told the court that Marion County was so fair that, indeed, there was once a Negro city councilman, county treasurer, and deputy sheriff in the county. Thurgood was incensed. He cross-examined:

Q.: Now, Dr. Hampton, when were these Negroes, Mayors, City Commissioners like you have testified?

A.: Well, it's so far back that I can hardly remember.

Q.: About how far back was it?

A.: Well, it was something like sixty years ago.

Q.: Then, what you mean to say is that there were Negroes who held those kind of offices back immediately after the Civil War, don't you?

A.: Well, it was a long time ago.

Another black witness, the head of the black American Legion post, testified about how good race relations were. Thurgood, quietly seething, asked him:

Q.: Are there any white members of your American Legion Post?
A.: No, sir, there aren't, we have our own post, we are all colored people, we have our own post to ourselves, because that is the way we want it, it could be the other way if we wanted to I think, the only reason is we have one to ourselves like we have always wanted to have, and I am head of our post, and what else do you want to know about it?

Later that week a black newspaper ran a cartoon of this witness, which condemned him as a turncoat, referring to him as "big, fat, greasy."

Futch, all the while whittling cedar sticks, denied the motion for change of venue, as he did the motion to exclude from evidence Irvin's shoes and trousers, which we claimed were taken in an illegal search. Nowadays, if the trial court did not exclude such evidence, a federal court very well might invalidate the conviction. But this was before the Supreme Court, in 1961, in *Mapp v. Ohio*, interpreted the Fourteenth Amendment to require excluding evidence taken without a warrant.

Seven blacks were on the panel from which the jury was selected. Four did not believe in capital punishment and, therefore, were disqualified. The state then struck the other three blacks by peremptory challenges, probably grounds for reversal today.

Norma Padgett, dressed for a party, testified that she was a third-generation Floridian and that her family originated in Georgia. As at the first trial, she told of having been out on a date with her husband (from whom she was separated), of a fight between him and four black men, and described the rape. She testified that after they left her by the side of the road she met a young man, whom she knew, but to whom she said nothing about an attack. This was Lawrence Burtoft, whom we had located at his army base and who at that very moment was flying in a chartered plane to Ocala.

He arrived after the lunch recess, still in uniform, and testified that Padgett had told him of the attack on her husband, but said nothing about having been raped, nor could she identify the blacks who attacked her husband. All in all, the testimony was not terribly powerful, but it did raise serious questions about whether or not Padgett had been raped. On cross-examination Burtoft testified that Padgett did not appear to have been hurt, except that she said that her feet hurt from walking, that "she looked in pretty calm condition for her husband to be lying down dead beside the road," and that he had previously told all of this to Hunter.

Hunter dealt with him by asking whether he had "a great deal of animosity" and if he was "still trying to get even with the State of Florida." Why

Burtoft might harbor animosity toward Florida, Hunter never said. All this Burtoft denied. Hunter put some of Burtoft's neighbors on the stand, and they testified that he hadn't much of a reputation for telling the truth.

Irvin testified that he and Sammy Shepherd had visited a couple of clubs the night of the crime. But the waitress who corroborated his story to us, and to whom we had sent expense money to testify, never showed up. We were told that she hoped to become a school teacher and feared reprisals.

Our star witness was the private detective Herman Bennett. He demonstrated that the plaster casts of footprints at the scene of the crime, which the prosecution matched with Walter's shoes, had been faked. He explained that in normal walking a shoe leaves a concave impression in soft earth, as if a rocker on a rocking chair had been rocked from rear to front. But the impression that Irvin's shoes matched were convex, an impression that could have been made only if an empty shoe, held in someone's hands, had been pressed into the ground by heel and toe, not by normal walking. To us there was no doubt about it. But Hunter ridiculed the testimony.

Q.: Do you mean that every man that walks in his shoes leaves the same kind of impression, is that correct?
A.: Yes, unless he is deformed.
Q.: You mean that all footprints are alike?
A.: No, I mean that every person walks in the same way and will leave the same type of impression unless he is deformed.
Q.: Then you mean that everybody wears their shoes out in the same way?
A.: That's right.
Q.: Then, how do you account for the fact that some people wear the soles or the heels out quicker than they do their heels and vice versa?

Bennett answered that perhaps some people have suffered injuries, not a satisfactory answer. Probably he didn't understand the question or its implications. Hunter attacked again by eliciting that Bennett's fee would be seven or eight hundred dollars for four or five days work, a huge sum for farmers in Marion County. Giggles and murmurs swept the courtroom.

Any doubt about Bennett's testimony would vanish in 1962, after another case in which we represented two blacks, Jerry Chatman and Robert Shuler, accused of rape in Lake County. Once more James L. Yates was the law enforcement officer. Once more conviction was obtained by means of plaster casts of footprints that matched the defendants' shoes. Shortly before Chatman and Shuler were to be executed, two former Lake County deputies accused Yates and another deputy, Lucius G. Clark, of having falsified the footprints. The FBI conducted an investigation and found soil from Clark's backyard in the plaster casts, and concluded that the footprints had been made by empty shoes. Yates and Clark were indicted and suspended, but the indictment was dismissed by a state judge as barred by the statute of limitations. They were reinstated with back pay. We did, however, save Shuler's and Chatman's lives.

During a couple of evenings Jess Hunter came over to my table in the dining room of the Ocala hotel where all the white participants stayed. He ordered corn bread and milk—he couldn't chew anything substantial—and it dripped down his shirt as he ate. He told me of a college commencement he had attended up north, the graduation of a nephew I think, and how the young people were embarrassed to be seen eating with him. Then, for no apparent reason, he added, "McCall's a brute."

Alex Akerman's closing argument summarized and analyzed the evidence. Thurgood played a different role; he appealed to the jury's sense of fairness: "Now, in cases of this type, we are all of us up against a pretty tough proposition. . . . When the crime of rape involves a white lady and a colored man, there is a great amount of ill feeling and ill will against the alleged defendant." Nevertheless, he went on in conversational tones:

> Every American citizen is guaranteed a fair and impartial trial, no matter whether or not he is white, black or yellow, and our Government is the finest Government in the world, and the basic principle of our Government is justice under the law for every man, and that no citizen is going to get more or going to get less than his fellow citizens will get, regardless of race, creed, or color. . . .
>
> Most of the laws that have been written into law in this country came from the basic precepts set down by God himself in Heaven, and those laws have been written lovingly and painstakingly, through the hundreds of years, until such time as they now have evolved down to the point where we have the best Government in the world. . . .
>
> To make this government work and assure a fair trial is why you twelve men have been called from your homes and your work to come to this Court Room to come and sit on this jury . . . and your purpose is to give this Defendant, Walter Irvin, a fair and impartial trial . . . and you are going to decide this case solely from the evidence that you have heard from this stand.

The lunch break followed Thurgood's argument. I was seated near the jury box and heard one juror say to another as they filed out to lunch, "Damn, that nigger was good. Sure looks like it'll be close."

Following lunch Hunter delivered his reply: "Now, Gentlemen, I agree with part of what Mr. Marshall said this morning, in that I believe that every man, white or black, should have a fair trial, and furthermore I believe that any Negro can get a fair trial in Marion County, if the outside world would just leave us alone." He attacked Walter Irvin's credibility and Burtoft's reputation for telling the truth and then lit into Bennett:

> He struck me as being afraid that [J. Edgar] Hoover was going to call him up to take over Hoover's job . . . and it reminds me of a story about two colored men walking down the street, and heard a politician talking on the street corner, and one of them says, "Jake, who is that fellow?" And the other colored fellow said, "I don't know, but he shore do recommend himself." Now, Gentlemen, there was a great United States judge, one of the greatest judges who ever sat on the bench, and he described three different types of liars; one of them was a common liar, the other one was a damn liar, and the other one was an expert witness. Now, Gentlemen, here came a man with a great theory, to put against facts in this case, and he begins to tell you a lot of rot about how a man puts his foot down, and he wanted you to try this case on that kind of stuff, and it was so remarkable to me that I could not believe it, and so I was careful to write it down.

Hunter went on, this time about Norma Padgett, "an honest old cracker girl, born and raised up in Lake County, Florida."

> I want to tell you gentlemen that in a case of this kind, every sacred tradition of your life and of my life, and of our civilization is at stake, in cases of this kind, because many thousands of years ago, woman was nothing but a chattel, and you can read the history books about that, and when those tribes warred, when the battle was over, then the women were captured and the women became the spoils of war and went to the victors, but now time has passed, and woman has come into her own, and a woman's chastity is the greatest thing on earth to her, and nothing else in the world compares to it. In the olden days, one of the old English kings killed his wife because after she had been criminally ravished, he said that he could not know whether or not it was his child or the other man's so he had her destroyed. Now, Gentlemen, you have a right to sit on this jury for the protection of your women folk, and I would like to tell you this example, on one historical occasion, there was a good woman, from a good family, on the eve of her wedding, and she was caught in the back yard and savagely raped, and she walked over to the edge of the cliff and hurled herself into eternity, rather than sacrifice that to which to her was dearer than life itself. That Gentlemen, was her chastity.

Now, Gentlemen, Norma Padgett, this simple little country girl, chose to live, and she has suffered the greatest tragedy that can befall any woman, and she will suffer for it the rest of her life, she has lived to tell the story, and don't you gentlemen forget that that thing, that horrible thing, will never be erased from her mind.

W. J. Cash, whose *Mind of the South* detailed Southern whites' obsession with black–white sex, would have loved it. Hunter spellbound the courtroom and then he capped it all by telling the jurors that he suffered from a fatal disease—leukemia.

I don't want to meet the Almighty with any innocent man's blood on my soul, and Gentlemen, I don't believe that I will ever do so, but I do want to leave this County in such condition, that you and your wives and your daughters and your sisters and your sweethearts can walk and ride the streets of this County and this State in perfect safety, as you should do. I want to leave this County and this State in such a condition that no bunch of men can come in and snatch up your wives or your daughter and carry her out in the woods and rape her.

After an hour and twenty-three minutes the jury returned a verdict of guilty without recommendation of mercy. There was nowhere to go but the supreme court of Florida, and, if that failed, to the United States Supreme Court. Once more we started down that road. But at the same time the school cases were going on.

THE VIRGINIA CASE

The trial of *Davis v. County School Board of Prince Edward County, Virginia,* ran from February 25 to 29, 1952. It went pretty much like the other cases: Witnesses described the material differences between black and white schools. Our social scientists, including Kenneth Clark, testified. Virginia differed from the others in two respects: defense counsel was openly racist and for the first time the state called its own expert witnesses. The chief defense counsel, Justin Moore, acting like the Nazi heavy in an old war movie, behaved like the racist he was, asking our social science witness Isadore Chein, "What kind of name is that? What sort of racial background does that indicate?"; "Are you one hundred percent Jewish?"; and "Were your parents native born in the United States?"[10] He asked Kenneth Clark where he was born (Panama), and then, "What percentage, as near as you can tell us, are you white and what percentage some other?"

For the first time defendants called their own social scientists and educators as witnesses. But one, William H. Kelly, a child psychiatrist, conceded that racial segregation "is adverse to the personality." In response to Bob Carter's question on cross-examination, "Do you feel that racial segregation has an adverse effect on a healthy personality development?" the psychologist John Nelson Buck admitted that, "As an abstract statement—as a generality, let us put it that way—I should say yes." Henry Garrett, the state's star social scientist, who had been Kenneth Clark's teacher at Columbia, attacked Kenneth's testimony and that of the plaintiffs' other social scientists. But he, too, had to admit on cross-examination that, "Wherever a person is cut off from the main body of society or a group, if he is put in a position that stigmatizes him and makes him feel inferior, I would say yes, it is detrimental and deleterious to him."

On March 7, 1952, the court entered a decree declaring that there was inequality in buildings, facilities, curricula, and "conveyances." It ordered the school board to immediately equalize curricula and transportation, and to pursue with "diligence and dispatch their present program, now afoot and progressing," to equalize buildings and equipment. But it refused to hold segregation unconstitutional: "So ingrained and wrought in the texture of their life is the principle of separate schools, that the president of the University of Virginia expressed to the Court his judgment that its involuntary elimination would severely lessen the interest of the people of the State in the public schools, lessen the financial support, and so injure both races."

THE DELAWARE CASES DECIDED

On April 1, 1952, Lou Redding and I won the first case ever to order black children admitted to white schools. The chancellor held that the black and white schools were unequal in material respects and that black children should be admitted to the white schools. "Such a plaintiff is entitled to relief immediately, in the only way it is available, namely, by admission to the school with the superior facilities. To postpone such relief is to deny relief." But he went a step farther than simply ruling that the only way to bring about equality in a timely way was to end segregation. He expressed approval of our testimony on the psychological effects of segregation irrespective of whether or not the segregated facilities were equal. Referring to Wertham as "one of America's foremost psychiatrists," he accepted his testimony that "State enforced segregation is important, because it is 'clear cut' and gives legal sanction to the differences, and is of continuous duration."

The judge concluded, "From the testimony . . . in our Delaware society, State-imposed segregation in education itself results in the Negro children, as a class, receiving educational opportunities which are substantially inferior." He refused to hold segregation unconstitutional, however, because it had been upheld by the Supreme Court. Now we had to hope that the state would appeal, because Delaware would be a great case to take to the Supreme Court.

Thurgood had called the Delaware school case "our best case." True, it was a border state, and thus more moderate on racial issues, but a court had ordered what, until then, would have been unthinkable to many. It was an entering wedge that might persuade the Supreme Court that it could do likewise. It's always easier to undertake a difficult task when you see that someone else has done it successfully.

12

THE SCHOOL SEGREGATION CASES AND BULLDOGS

LDF GROWS UP AND MOVES OUT

From the time of its creation, LDF (or as it was then commonly called, the Inc. Fund) had been referred to as the "legal department" of the NAACP. But as we achieved more and more success over the years, we developed a separate identity. While earlier summaries of the year's work had been called the "Legal Department Annual Report," in 1952 we published the "Annual Report: NAACP Legal Defense and Educational Fund, Inc." As early as 1950, in discussing fund-raising, Thurgood had placed conspicuously in the minutes: "Mr. Marshall made it clear with this Board that NAACP can do nothing concerning this outfit." Like some other statements in the minutes, this was not merely a record, but scored a point in organizational politics.

Money exacerbated the differences between the two groups. When the LDF executive committee considered paying its secretaries more than those at the Association, one LDF board member who was also on the Association board objected. But another member of both boards, John Hammond, replied, "These are entirely two different corporations. . . . The Legal Defense Fund has money and the N.A.A.C.P. does not." On another occasion, when the LDF awarded salary increases, Roy Wilkins wrote a long letter objecting that they were too large. This was a period during which Connie Motley's salary and mine had been raised from $3,600 to $4,200 and Bob Carter was making $7,200 per year, all still somewhat less than the salaries private firms paid for similar legal talent and experience.

By 1952 LDF income had gone up to $215,000. We were moving into a new level of giving and benefited by the tax deductibility of LDF. Marshall Field had just anonymously pledged $200,000 to be paid over a period of four years. Howard Seitz, a partner at Paul, Weiss, came to the office one day and announced the pledge. He didn't know anyone at the Fund and the receptionist directed him to me. After finding out why Seitz had come, Thurgood being away, I sent him to Walter White. Such large donations were the exception, however, and donations in the thousands were ordinarily the best we hoped for: Lessing Rosenwald gave $10,000; James Ryan, $5,000; Louis Rabinowitz and Godfrey Cabot, $2,000 each; and a few others contributed over $1,000, as did some NAACP branches and black organizations.

Thurgood's success and charisma also attracted funds. The Prince Hall Masons (the black Masonic order) began giving $20,000 per year to a Prince Hall Masons Research Fund created at LDF (the contributions continue to this day), not only to support civil rights, but because Thurgood was an active and dedicated Mason. He always wore a gold thirty-third degree Masonic ring; when the Shriners, a higher level of the Masonic order, visited to make their annual contribution, he would put on his red Shriner's fez.

Through this same period there was a time when the Association's income took a sharp dip. In 1945 it had taken in $401,000, but by 1950 it was down to $260,000. A staff analysis attributed the decline in donations to job insecurity, a rise in the cost of living, crop failures, unfavorable public opinion, the recent doubling of annual dues to two dollars, and competition from other groups. Whatever the causes, the hard-pressed Association could not avoid comparing its situation with that of its more fortunate progeny.

In time, however, NAACP fortunes started to move upward again. In 1951 income increased to $309,000 and in 1952 it reached $347,000. By 1953 it was back up again to $393,000, double that of LDF, but with a vastly larger establishment to maintain. Because we were tax-exempt we were not permitted to transfer funds to the non–tax-exempt Association. We helped, however, by adding some of their clerical workers to our payroll when they might otherwise have been laid off.

We occasionally lent money to various NAACP branches for legal cases and paid independent lawyers to handle cases for them. Consequently, the branches and lawyers began to perceive us as an organization to which they might turn when they were in need of funds. The nominal arrangement with the branches was that they would pay the expenses of cases. But usually they didn't, at least not in full. In the School Segregation Cases only the South Carolina branches paid entirely for their case. For the Kansas case Bob Carter dunned branches all over Kansas and Missouri with only partial success.

One minor, yet irritating, matter demonstrated the interaction of personality conflict, money, and tax exemption. An anonymous contributor wanted to give LDF $4,800 (tax deductible, of course), to enable Walter White to expand articles he had written for the *Saturday Review* into a book. But the arrangement required the agreement of LDF. The executive committee referred the matter to the full board, a bit of a run-around. Not long thereafter, at a specially called meeting, the executive committee agreed to accept the money after all, with a variety of stringent conditions. One can imagine the politicking that went on between the first meeting and the agreement to accept. The arrangement could have been worked out administratively, without executive committee action, and the process needlessly humiliated Walter by turning him into a supplicant.

Other stirrings revealed the two organizations' growing sense of separate identity. In April 1952, twelve years after its creation, the LDF executive committee resolved for the first time that the building directory at Freedom House should list our name separately. If the matter weren't contentious it just would have been done—without a resolution. Thurgood scored a major internal political victory at that same meeting when the executive committee changed his title to director-counsel, indicating that he, not Walter White, was the boss of LDF, and decided that the "Executive Staff consist[s] of a Director-Counsel, Assistant Counsel, Fund Raiser and Field Secretaries." Walter White and Roy Wilkins, the secretary and assistant secretary of the NAACP, were "designated as Secretary and Assistant Secretary respectively" of the LDF, but they were not part of the executive staff. LDF hired its own public relations officer.

A critical step in the split occurred at the end of 1952, when we moved out of Freedom House to a decrepit building at 107 West Forty-third Street, in the Times Square area, only three blocks north of Freedom House, but psychologically much farther. We had the space divided to our specifications, but couldn't afford central air conditioning. Some lawyers had window units and a big electric fan carried cool air from their offices to the windowless library–conference room in the rear, where long pine bookshelves sagged under the weight of Lawyers Edition Supreme Court reports. Bums occasionally urinated in the rickety elevator and we had a couple of burglaries, but we also had more space than at Freedom House, one reason we had moved.

LDF and the NAACP remained intertwined. A majority of our board members were members of the Association board: Nominally, they controlled us as a subsidiary corporation. Thurgood went to their board meetings and Walter White and Roy Wilkins attended ours. Virtually all our cases arose out of NAACP branch activity and if they didn't, like the Delaware and Virginia school segregation cases, the branches soon became involved. We were the only lawyers to whom the branches could turn; the NAACP was the only organization that could generate our cases.

Nevertheless, we retained freedom of action and wouldn't undertake a case just because an NAACP branch asked us to. When a Connecticut branch asked us to handle a rape case, *Higgs v. Connecticut*, the executive committee resolved that "as a matter of policy we should make decisions in regard to cases solely on the basis of the merits of the case and without regard to pressure and insistence by any other organizations or individuals."

Having had our say, we undertook the defense, and with Connecticut lawyer Peter Marcuse I won the case in the Connecticut Supreme Court, establishing the important precedent that a defendant's lawyer has the right to question potential jurors about racial bias.

However, our press releases, captioned with the LDF name, more often than not referred to our cases as NAACP cases. Also linking us together were many personal friendships among members of both groups. But as the civil rights movement of the 1960s emerged, rival organizations entered the scene, new strains appeared, and those conditions began to change, as, once more, did our relationship with the NAACP.

FIRST PASS AT THE SUPREME COURT

In July 1951 Spotts Robinson, Bob Carter, and Thurgood appealed the South Carolina case *Briggs v. Elliott*. On October 1 Bob, Thurgood, and I, along with the Kansas lawyers, appealed *Brown v. Board of Education*, the Kansas decision. In December Clarendon County filed a report that told of progress in equalizing facilities, which the district court forwarded to the Supreme Court. The Supreme Court, in turn, sent the report back to the district court for appropriate action. Physical improvements had nothing to do with segregation, and Justices Black and Douglas dissented on the grounds that any additional facts were "wholly irrelevant to the constitutional questions."

Back in the district court in March 1952, Thurgood once more pushed for a decision on the unconstitutionality of segregation. J. Waties Waring had retired and, although Judge Parker invited him to take part, he declined to do so. Robert Figg, the school board's lawyer, reported that the board had made great progress and that although equality had not been achieved there soon would be "a modern and complete public school system for all alike." Thurgood conceded, "They are proceeding to lay the plans for the buildings which will eventually furnish equal facilities." The colloquy turned testy:

JUDGE PARKER: Well, none of us can build a building overnight. . . .

MR. MARSHALL: I might say, sir, that every day they are not equal, these plaintiffs are losing rights, for which they cannot be adequately compensated.

JUDGE DOBIE [who had replaced Waring]: Well, what can we do about that? . . . They can't do any more at this stage, can they?

MR. MARSHALL: No, sir, they cannot physically do more. It is impossible for them to build those schools overnight.

JUDGE TIMMERMAN: Well, do you want us to put them in jail for not doing something that you know they can't do?

MR. MARSHALL: It is something they can do, sir. They could break down the
   segregation.
JUDGE DOBIE: Let that alone.

Thurgood hadn't been overly ambitious in the district court. He said he
was "not saying to strike it down on the basis of segregation per se, but on
the basis that the facilities that are being offered the Negroes are not equal
as of today"—the basis of the decision soon to be handed down in the
Delaware cases. But, of course, the South Carolina trial court would have
none of it, approved what the school district was doing, and on March 13,
1952, denied further relief. Observing Thurgood, Bob, and Spotts's
chortling, thigh-slapping, and mimicking when they recounted what had
occurred after the hearing, one might not have guessed that we had lost.
They took particular delight in imitating Dobie's "Let that alone." Of
course they had never hoped to win the case in the district court, but just to
build a useful record for our day at the United States Supreme Court.

On May 10, 1952, Thurgood and his cocounsel appealed to the Supreme
Court in *Briggs v. Elliott* for the second time. In June the Court agreed to
hear *Briggs* and *Brown*, scheduling argument for October 13. That left three
cases in lower courts: Delaware, Washington, D.C. (Jim Nabrit, Jr.'s case),
and Virginia. A few days earlier, on March 7, the Virginia court had ruled
against us, in *Davis*, and on July 12 Thurgood and associates appealed and
suggested that it be heard with South Carolina and Kansas.

On April 1, 1952, we won the Delaware cases. The state attorney general
appealed immediately. Lou Redding and I argued the appeal in the tiny colonial Delaware Supreme Court courthouse in Dover, downstate Delaware,
before the three-judge supreme court. At the end of August, we won again—
the Delaware Supreme Court affirmed the chancellor's order that required
admitting the black plaintiffs because the schools were unequal. Now we
had to hope that Delaware would appeal. The Supreme Court finds it easier
to affirm lower court decisions than to overturn them and to follow a precedent rather than break new ground. One winning case before the Court
would improve the chances of all the cases. Ego was involved, too: We
wanted *our* case up there. The Delaware attorney general, of course, wasn't
interested in our needs or feelings and did nothing, possibly hoping to have
the issue decided first in cases from the Deep South, where, presumably,
the Court might be less inclined to abolish segregation.

Just before the arguments in South Carolina and Kansas were due to
begin on October 13, the Court postponed them until December and
agreed to hear *Davis* from Virginia at the same time. The Court clerk also
called Jim Nabrit, at the direction of Chief Justice Vinson, and requested
that he file a petition in the D.C. case, even though it had not yet been
decided in the court of appeals. It was like the navy, where a request from
an officer is the equivalent of a command. The Court also entered an order

stating that the "Court will entertain a petition for certiorari in the case of *Bolling v. Sharpe*, which if presented and granted will" be heard with the other cases. Jim did as he was told, and then the Court, in a rarely employed procedure, certiorari before judgment in the court of appeals, granted the petition.

We were startled in the Kansas case, where the district court had held the schools to be equal and segregation constitutional, when a newly elected school board majority decided it would no longer defend the case. The state attorney general took the position that it was a local question, and that if the local board was willing to go along with whatever the Supreme Court might decide, he was not going to Washington to argue the case. The Supreme Court, however, as demonstrated in *Bolling*, wanted a comprehensive picture of school segregation throughout the country. At the end of November it requested, which again amounted to requiring, the Kansas attorney general to appear on behalf of the state, and he complied.

Toward the end of November, as the ninety-day filing period was running out, the Delaware attorney general broke the suspense and filed a petition for writ of certiorari; apparently, if he couldn't have the Deep South cases decided first he wasn't going to forfeit his right to Supreme Court review. Lou and I immediately filed a response, two-thirds of a page long, which said, "Respondents waive the right to file a brief in opposition . . . and urge that if petitioners' petition . . . is granted this Court schedule the above-entitled cases for argument immediately following argument in Nos. 8 [Kansas], 101 [South Carolina], and 191 [Virginia], for the reason that the issues involved are closely related." We passed up the opportunity to file a cross-petition claiming that segregation was unconstitutional. If we had, the state would have thirty days to answer our brief and the case might not be heard with the others. That waiver would later prompt argumentative questions when, at oral argument, I challenged the constitutionality of segregation—why hadn't I cross-petitioned? Eleven days after Delaware's petition the Supreme Court granted *cert*, and set all five cases down for argument together. Delaware was allowed until three weeks *after* argument to file its brief, following which we might reply. But we wanted the Court to understand the case fully as it heard oral argument so we rushed and filed our brief before argument.

The chancellor refused to stay his desegregation order. The Delaware attorney general appealed the stay denial to the state supreme court and it, too, denied a stay. Black children immediately began attending school in Claymont and Hockessin on a nonsegregated basis.

IN THE MEANTIME

During 1952, while we devoted first priority to the School Segregation Cases, we were doing a great deal more on a broad front and finding some success, especially outside the Deep South. We worked with Nashville lawyers in a case that sought integration, not on the basis of segregation's being unconstitutional, which was the argument around which all LDF cases were now being framed, and not even on the basis of black and white schools being unequal. Black children were being bused thirty three miles from Clinton to Knoxville because there was no black school in the county, and a suit had been brought to end the practice of busing by admitting black children to the nearby white schools. Such long-distance busing of black children because there was no black school in town was not unusual.

We brought a case in Cairo, Illinois, for black children who wanted to attend white grammar schools. June Shagaloff, our field worker, and an NAACP staff member were arrested for conspiring to "endanger the health and life of certain children," but charges were dismissed after the grand jury refused to indict. June's efforts, along with those of our other field worker, Dan Byrd, inspired a suit against Alton, Illinois. Alton then integrated, and integration, without suit, followed in the southern Illinois towns of Sparta, Ullin, and Tamms. Branch activity integrated some junior colleges in Texas and suits continued against Kentucky and other Texas junior colleges.

In other areas, little was changing. We took *Groveland* to the Florida Supreme Court; Mack Ingram's "highway looking and attempting to want" case concluded its third trial and was on appeal; and the New Jersey Supreme Court reversed the Trenton Six case. Spotts Robinson lost the case of Albert Jackson, who was executed for the rape of a white woman, once more failing in the argument that the death penalty for rape was used in a discriminatory manner and, therefore, was unconstitutional, an argument that would not prevail until 1977 in our case of *Coker v. Georgia*, which I discuss later in this volume.

As the options in *Groveland* wound down, we focused not only on the remaining legal moves that might still save Irvin's life, but on the case's fund-raising and organizing potential. Down the road there would be similar cases of injustice; we would need organization, funds, and support to save future victims.

In January 1952 the Louisville park case showed, as little else could, the convoluted legal labyrinths civil rights lawyers had to navigate. Blacks wanted to attend the musical comedy *Blossom Time* in the amphitheater, play on the municipal golf course, and fish in a city-owned lake. We lost the amphitheater case because, while it was city owned, it had been leased to a private company to operate (supposedly making the operation not state action and therefore not governed by the Fourteenth Amendment); won the golf case because there was no black golf course; and lost the fishing case because there was a separate-but-equal lake (maybe we should have counted the number of fish in each). We appealed the amphitheater case, but the plaintiff in the fishing case didn't want to pursue it.

For the second time the Supreme Court declined to review the Florida

Supreme Court's refusal to desegregate a Miami golf course, for the reason that the decision rested on state law grounds. The Supreme Court will reverse a state court only if it was wrong on some federal question. Kansas City appealed its swimming pool case in which it had been ordered to stop excluding blacks. We filed suit to open a golf course in Charlotte, a park in Baltimore, and a playground in the District of Columbia.

In May 1951 the United States Supreme Court had denied the Atlantic Coast Line Railroad's petition to review rulings that the railroad had burdened interstate commerce when it removed a black high school principal from a white car in Virginia during a trip from Philadelphia to Parmelee, North Carolina. Then there was a trial on damages, and the railroad appealed the verdict to the court of appeals and the Supreme Court, which in November 1952 once more refused to review. Segregationists did not give up easily.

As usual there were a great many military cases. Bob took a case to the Supreme Court on the question of federal court power to review courts-martial. Thurgood petitioned the president to free Lt. Leon A. Gilbert immediately. He was the army officer who had been sentenced to death for misbehavior in the face of the enemy, while whites convicted of similar offenses had received three- to five-year terms.

GETTING READY FOR THE SUPREME COURT

The Court now had before it a range of school cases—two from the Deep South, two from border states, and one from the District of Columbia—presenting a great variety of factors to be considered. Back then the Court required that briefs and petitions be printed, rather than typed and reproduced by some photocopying process. When not working on other cases—I was doing *Groveland* at the time—we spent all day and virtually every night at the office, at the Association of the Bar library on Forty-fourth Street, and at the printer way downtown. There we read proof aloud to one another and edited on ink-stained tables, sometimes until dawn, surrounded by clattering hot-lead Linotype machines and clanging presses. I lived in Bensonhurst, Brooklyn, at the time and often took the subway home in the early hours of the morning, a ride of over an hour.

Apart from the excitement of the work, the pleasure in this regimen was found in frequent dinners with Thurgood, other staff members, and out-of-town lawyers at the Blue Ribbon, a German restaurant on Forty-third Street. In what once was a townhouse, with heavy wooden furniture, leaded-glass windows, and small, dark paneled dining rooms hung with autographed pictures of stars of the opera and theater, the Blue Ribbon served great dark Munich beer on tap, black bread, various wursts, and one of Thurgood's favorites, pigs' knuckles. He made a ceremony of ordering the dish and, indeed, enjoyed talking about food, about his own she-crab soup, which was delicious, and about his Aunt Meenie's "sad cake." As soon as it started rising she'd open the oven and slap it down; as it tried to rise again, she'd spank it gently until it succumbed and lay almost flat until baked through.

Sometimes we lunched at the Algonquin, where visiting lawyers stayed and some staff lawyers stayed overnight when they worked into the wee hours. When we lunched there Thurgood focused on scrambled eggs, brought to him by the maitre d', Raul, with whom he had a relationship of bonhomie.

Brief writing was aided by frequent conferences among the staff, local counsel, and professional and academic friends. We consulted most often with Bob Ming, Louis Pollak, Bill Coleman, Charlie Black, and Jack Weinstein. William R. (Bob) Ming, Jr., a brilliant lawyer who taught at the University of Chicago, was the first black appointed to the faculty of a major white law school. He had great imagination and, in addition to his teaching, developed a successful practice in Chicago, representing, among others, the leading Polish Roman Catholic organization in the city. Bob spoke proudly of this, asserting that one would hardly have expected the organization to hire a black lawyer. He had the habit of pacing around a lot in a semi-crouch, not unlike Groucho Marx in his Captain Spaulding routine, as he thought and talked.

Louis H. (Lou) Pollak had gone to Yale Law School, been clerk to Supreme Court Justice Wiley Rutledge, worked for the State Department, and then had taken a job in New York in the legal department at the Amalgamated Clothing Workers Union. There was no question that he would employ his considerable talents at something other than getting rich. Tall, thin, ascetic looking, but rarely without a smile, he came to civil rights not only by conviction, but by descent and marriage. Lou's father, Walter Pollak, had argued one of the Scottsboro cases in the Supreme Court. His wife, Cathy, was the daughter of Louis Weiss, one of the leading liberal lawyers in New York, a founder of the firm Paul Weiss Wharton and Garrison and later chairman of the LDF National Legal Committee.

One day as we worked together on an early phase of the school cases, Lou and I met at the Columbia law library and took a walk outside and speculated about how we hoped to spend our careers. We agreed that we would be happy if we could work at matters we cared about so long as we could earn five or six thousand dollars a year. Not long thereafter, he was appointed to the Yale faculty and later became dean of the law school there. Years later he became dean of the University of Pennsylvania Law School and then a United States District Court judge.

William T. (Bill) Coleman had been first in his class at Harvard Law School, and law clerk to Justice Frankfurter, the first black to become a Supreme Court law clerk. No Philadelphia firm would give him a job because he was black, and so he tried New York and found work at Paul, Weiss, where he shared an office with Lou Pollak for a time. Bill continued to live in Philadelphia, making the more than two-hour commute to and from New York. Ultimately Bill was offered a job at one of Philadelphia's leading firms, the Dilworth firm, where he became a partner. He was later the secretary of transportation in the Ford administration. After that he became a top partner at O'Melveny & Myers, one of the country's largest and most prestigious law firms, as well as a member of the boards of Pan Am, Chase Bank, IBM, and other corporations, and chairman of the LDF board.

Bill was of medium height and quite stocky, not unlike Winston Churchill in general physique. He rarely dressed in anything other than a three-button Brooks Brothers suit, with a vest and a gold watch chain across his waist, from which dangled his Phi Beta Kappa key. He loved a good meal—at our frequent breakfast meetings he usually ordered eggs with beurre noire, which sometimes flummoxed the waiter to whom he would explain that the chef had to burn the butter. Bill was quite unusual among our friends and colleagues in that he was a Republican, although later, in the Nixon, Reagan, and Bush administrations, he never hesitated to disagree publicly with the party's policies on racial issues. He had come to Republicanism because of an affinity for Fiorello La Guardia's politics and his belief in the role of business as a beneficent force in American society.

Charles L. (Charlie) Black was a Texan, with a pronounced drawl, whom we met when he taught at Columbia. He soon moved to Yale to become the Henry Luce professor of law. His twin legal specialties were constitutional law and admiralty. A thorough intellectual, who sometimes quoted the classics in Latin, Charlie always followed his heart. He plays the trumpet and harmonica, paints, and has published poetry, is a great teacher and prolific scholar. In the 1960s he stopped off in Iceland for a brief look and fell in love with the country, learned its language, and has returned there often, even lecturing on American constitutional law in Icelandic.

Charlie tells of when he was sixteen having heard Louis Armstrong play in Austin. Armstrong was in "the dazzlingly inventive small-band period of the Hot Five and Hot Seven, and the first period of improvisation around popular melodies—Stardust, Chinatown, When Your Lover Has Gone. . . . It is impossible to overstate the significance of a sixteen-year-old Southern boy's seeing genius, for the first time, in a black. We literally never saw a black then, in any but a servant's capacity." A good old boy from Charlie's high school had "pronounced judgment of the time and place: 'After all, he's nothing but a God damn nigger!'" Charlie further observes that "it was just then that I started walking toward the *Brown* case, where I belonged." When some scholars theorized abstractly about the constitutionality of segregation, arguing that though it treated blacks and whites separately, it treated them equally, Charlie responded with a healthy dose of reality. He *knew* the purposes and effects of segregation firsthand.

Jack B. Weinstein was my law school classmate. His stamina was boundless and his encyclopedic knowledge of procedural law and evidence later was embodied in the leading treatises and encyclopedias. Not long after Jack began working with us he joined the Columbia law faculty. He was so energetic that while going to law school he built an apartment in his father's basement. He later became chief judge of the United States District Court in the Eastern District of New York and has become widely recognized as the most creative judge on the federal bench, pioneering in many areas of the law, including the mass tort litigation of the asbestos and Agent Orange cases. Jack may be best known to the general public as the federal judge who declines to preside over his court in a black robe, not always sitting on the raised bench, preferring the more egalitarian practice of dressing in suits and joining counsel and defendants at courtroom level.

The Bensonhurst apartment I lived in at this time was only a few blocks from where I had lived with my parents when I was a child, before we moved to the Bronx. The trip from Manhattan on the West End BMT line took about an hour, but the rent was only $65 a month, much less than I would have had to pay for a similar apartment in Manhattan. Riding the subway late at night in those days involved no danger. Once I fell asleep, awoke in the caryards at Coney Island, and had to find another train home. In May 1952 I was shuttling North to South on cases, but I was lucky to be home when Sema gave birth to our first child, Josiah.

13

IN THE HOUSE OF THE LAW

COUNCILS OF WAR

We worked in a conference room in the basement of Freedom House or, after we moved to Forty-third Street, in the library in the rear of the office. Thurgood's way of presiding was to listen a lot and challenge virtually everything everyone said, often fiercely. If someone suggested that a certain course of action *had* to be taken, he'd often respond: "There's only two things I have to do: stay black and die." Or to one who argued that "we" should do this or that, he might say, quoting an old song of Bert Williams, "I may be mistakin', but I think that you're makin', that 'weeeeeee' too long." We all researched and discussed and wrote, and out of all the give and take Thurgood ultimately would come to a decision, one whose wisdom almost always came to be borne out by time and events.

The briefs in each of the five cases that we were scheduled to bring before the Court in December 1952 were tailored to the circumstances of each, but as organized they all more or less took an approach to constitutional litigation that had been the hallmark of NAACP and LDF style from the beginning: fact specificity—the circumstances of each case spelled out in detail; presentation of the issues in broader context, with reference to the social consequences of educational segregation; and restraint in limiting constitutional claims to the issue at hand—asking for an end to segregation in education, not public accommodations, employment, housing, marriage laws, or anything else. We offered options: We would take a decision in our favor on any grounds, including a finding of inequality of schools or facilities.

I did the first draft of the *Brown* brief, for Kansas, and sent it to Bob Carter, who was on vacation on Martha's Vineyard. Such differences in the briefs as there were came about because of the different factual circumstances of each case, or were adventitious, not the result of a planned strategy of different emphases for different cases. But whatever their differences, each brief called for an end to segregation in education.

The briefs for each case cited pure legal doctrine. For example, the claim that "the State of Kansas has no power . . . to use race as a factor in affording educational opportunities" called for applying *Sweatt* and *McLaurin* to lower schools, and argued that where there was physical inequality the trial courts "should have enjoined enforcement of the segregation laws." As to *Plessy*, the briefs argued that it had no relevance to education; the governing authority was *Sweatt* and *McLaurin*, both of which had treated education. The briefs were short, citing little constitutional history and giving slight attention to how desegregation might be accomplished.

We filed an innovative appendix to the Kansas, South Carolina, and Virginia cases (Delaware had not yet arrived in the Court and Jim Nabrit, Jr., for the District of Columbia case, made a pure legal attack), signed by many of the country's leading social scientists and entitled: "The Effects of Segregation and the Consequences of Desegregation: A Social Science Statement." Its preface stated that it had been "drafted and signed by some of the foremost authorities in sociology, anthropology, psychology and psychiatry who have worked in the area of race relations." The appendix asserted that segregation imposes on individuals a distorted sense of social reality; leads to blockage of communication, which increases mutual suspicion, distrust, and hostility; perpetuates rigid stereotypes and reinforces negative attitudes; and leads to violent outbreaks of racial tensions. It drew heavily on the report of the Midcentury White House Conference on Children, for which Kenneth Clark had done a report on race.

The appendix was modest in its claim to scientific precision. It might accurately be characterized as a compilation of the views of enlightened scholars who had studied racial issues as deeply as existing resources permitted, and was not based on previous studies such as a report in the physical sciences would be. But this made the appendix no less valuable for a Court that, after all, had to make a decision based on the best information available.

The line of attack spurned the warnings of the liberal white supporter and *Arkansas Gazette* editor Harry Ashmore, who thought we couldn't win an attack on segregation per se, and of the black columnist-lawyer Marjorie McKenzie who, as best as she could be understood, seemed to urge pursuing a political solution, but also shied away from the daring of Jim Nabrit's purely legal assault. We gave the Court whatever we thought it might find useful in striking down segregated schooling.

As in other major civil rights cases, Truman's solicitor general filed an amicus brief. It began, as all amicus briefs do, with a statement of interest: "Racial discrimination imposed by law . . . inevitably tends to undermine the foundations of a society dedicated to freedom, justice, and equality." It turned to the conflict with the Soviet Union: "It is in the context of the present world struggle between freedom and tyranny that the problem of racial discrimination must be viewed." The brief quoted Dean Acheson, the secretary of state, extensively, referring to Soviet attacks on the United States for our racial practices and to the hostile reaction among otherwise friendly peoples to how America treated its black citizens.

The amicus argument urged, as we did, that the physical inequalities in South Carolina, Virginia, and Delaware, as well as the psychological harm done by segregation irrespective of the equality question, as found by the court in Kansas, warranted prohibiting segregation in the defendant school systems. But then the brief went even farther, arguing that the Court should reach the conclusion that "compulsory racial segregation is itself, without more [that is, even in the absence of tangible inequalities], an unconstitutional discrimination." It quoted extensively from *Strauder* and other cases in which racial distinctions were held unconstitutional. As to social scientific considerations: "The facts of every-day life confirm the finding of the district court in the Kansas case that segregation has a 'detrimental effect' on colored children; that it affects their motivation to learn; and that it has a tendency to retard their educational and mental development and to deprive them of benefits they would receive in an integrated school system."

The government's most significant innovation was uncoupling the question of whether segregation was unconstitutional from the practical question of how desegregation might be accomplished. The strategy, of course, was to allay fears some justices might have about provoking hostility and about issuing orders that might be disobeyed, thereby undermining the authority of the Court, which might constitute a constitutional crisis. The headnote of the final section of the amicus brief advised: "If in any of these cases the Court should hold that a system of 'separate but equal' public schools is unconstitutional, it should remand the case to the district court with directions to devise and execute such program for relief as appears most likely to achieve orderly and expeditious transition to a non-segregated system."

The brief "recognized that racial segregation in public schools has been in effect in many states for a long time," asserting that "the practical difficulties which may be met in making progressive adjustment to a non-segregated system cannot be ignored or minimized." It called, however, for expeditious settlement of problems by district courts within a "specified period." It did reveal a willingness in effect to sacrifice some black children's access to nonsegregated education throughout the remainder of their educational careers by proposing the possibility of "integration on a grade basis, i.e., to integrate the first grades immediately, and to continue such integration until completed as to all grades in the elementary schools," or to "integrate on a school-by-school basis."

John W. Davis represented the state of South Carolina and was the leading advocate for the other side. Davis was seventy-nine, had been Democratic candidate for president of the United States in 1924, and headed one of the largest, most prestigious law firms in the country. He had been solicitor general and had argued hundreds of cases in the Supreme Court. He was an active practitioner and by all accounts had lost none of his prowess as an advocate. The other school districts had their own counsel, but everyone looked to Davis as the spokesman for the segregationist side.

The states' briefs boiled down to reliance on precedent; the concept of federalism, which, under the Constitution, arguably allocated control of internal matters to state authority, so that education and the running of schools was in the power of individual states, not in the federal government; and separation of powers, in support of the contention that school segregation was an issue for legislatures, not courts. They attacked our social science evidence as inconsistent and unpersuasive. They stressed that the defendants had already equalized schools or were in the very process of doing so. They did not mention that the states had taken this action only under the gun of litigation.

Washington, D.C., had begun to relax a few segregation barriers in 1952, although there was no meaningful desegregation until the Supreme Court, in 1953, decided the *Thompson* case, which resurrected two Reconstruction public accommodations laws for the District and made it a crime to discriminate in certain public accommodations. While it had been possible to stay at the Statler or the Wardman Park over the previous year or two, rooms often weren't available (we had to wonder whether we were being told the truth or if the hotel preferred not to admit blacks) and most of us often stayed at the black hotel, the Charles. But now, for the first time while arguing before the Supreme Court, we stayed at the Statler. Unfortunately, over the years, the exercise of this choice, replicated many times over by others who had formerly stayed at black-only hotels, spelled doom for marginal black enterprises. In later years, blacks set up a few hotels and other businesses in the District of Columbia and elsewhere. LDF lawyers made a pass or two at patronizing them, but for a variety of reasons we, like other black groups, continued to use the big downtown hotels.

Before the argument, as we did prior to all Supreme Court cases, we conducted a "dry run" in a classroom at Howard Law School, which was then housed in the basement of the university's Founders' Library.

On Monday, December 8, 1952, Thurgood moved my admission to the bar of the Supreme Court. The brief ceremony, which takes place most days before arguments commence, lasts less than a minute, and consists of the sponsor reading a couple of sentences from a script that the clerk's office has prepared: "I move the admission of ——, a member of the bar of the State of ——. I am satisfied that (he) (she) has the necessary qualifications." The chief justice then announces that the motion is granted and extends a word of welcome to each applicant. The standard was simply that a lawyer must have been a member of the bar for three years. Almost none of the lawyers who are admitted ever actually argue in the Court. Nevertheless, while nowadays it is possible to be admitted by mail, with no personal appearance, many lawyers travel to Washington to be admitted in person because the moment before the Court is highly prized.

Following my admission ceremony, we lined up in the clerk's office to pay the $25 admission fee and provide information for the certificate we would receive—an impressive engraved diploma at the crest of which is seated blindfolded Justice, holding scales in one hand and a sword in the other, to her left an angel, a shining sun over its head, holds a document entitled "Constitution of the U.S.," and to her right an eagle confronts a stack of lawbooks. A lawyer admitted with me asked which of his several offices to list as his address on the certificate. The clerk replied, "Whichever will allow you to charge your clients higher fees."

Every once in a while a sponsor strays from the script and waxes eloquent about the candidate, usually in moving the admission of a son or daughter; veteran Supreme Court lawyers cringe and make little jokes. According to tradition, it is considered a "class act" when one moves the admission of one's own child and makes no mention of the relationship. I couldn't wait to move the admission of my son Josiah in 1987, when Thurgood was sitting on the Court. After the ceremony, in Thurgood's chambers, we joked knowingly about my insider's "sophistication" in not mentioning that Josiah was my son. When Thurgood moved the admission of his own son, Thurgood, Jr. (Goodie), while the Court was in session, he stepped down from the bench, removed his robe, went to the podium, and made the motion in the prescribed terms for Goodie and Goodie's wife, Colleen.

Well before we appeared in court, we anticipated that *Brown* might be a historic case. We weren't alone in this perception. Long lines of spectators formed far in advance, some arriving in front of the courthouse as early as 5:30 A.M. and standing in line for admission as if for a rock concert. The crowds attested that many sensed that the Court might be ready to write *finis* to an institution that had existed in parts of the country since soon after the end of the Civil War. None of us recalls that any of the plaintiffs in the cases from the states were in court, possibly because of the expense of travel, although some from the District of Columbia were present.

We knew that if we won there would be momentous changes in the lives of black people, indeed of all Americans. On the other hand, we also knew that if *Plessy* were specifically upheld, we would have spent our best chance and would face a long, dismal future of quibbling over the equality of school buildings, books, libraries, gyms, playgrounds.

There were no animated discussions about hopes or fears or possibilities. We were there to do the best we could, and that's all we could think about.

Reaching back and using the only analogy I can find out of my own experience, I recall that as my ship approached the battles of Iwo Jima and Okinawa, turning points in the Second World War, no one talked very much about what might happen if we succeeded or if we failed. We had undertaken a job, set out to do it, and focused on doing what we had been trained to do.

Court officers allowed spectators to observe the arguments for about twenty minutes, then ushered the group out and seated another batch. A privileged few, guests of the lawyers presenting argument, were permitted to sit through the entire day. But if they left to go to the bathroom or to the cafeteria, they would forfeit their seats. Jim Nabrit, Jr., gave his son, Jim Nabrit III, then a law student, one of the precious all-day passes. He sat next to Mordecai Johnson, president of Howard University, who surreptitiously munched peanuts while Jim watched enviously, racked with hunger pangs. Every seat was filled.

Arguments began at noon, went on to 2:00 P.M., with a half-hour break for lunch, and then continued from 2:30 to 4:30. At the beginning of the session the marshal rapped his gavel, cried his "Oyez, oyez," and the justices emerged from behind the maroon drapes almost simultaneously.

ORAL ARGUMENT NUMBER ONE

Arguments in the School Segregation Cases commenced at 1:35 P.M. The conventional wisdom is that oral argument makes little difference for the outcome of most cases, particularly those of great importance, which are largely shaped by the times and by what lawyers have done before they find themselves standing before the Court. Once, after I had lost by a vote of five to four the appeal of Martin Luther King, Jr.'s conviction of contempt for having marched in Birmingham on a Good Friday to protest that city's racial policies in violation of a court order, I met Justice Douglas at a reception. "What did I do wrong?" I asked. "Nothing," he replied. "Once the case reaches us the record is made and we look at it and decide what to do." Still, lawyers do not, should not, and had better not approach oral argument with the mindset that it doesn't matter. Argument is an opportunity to answer questions, large and small, that the submitted papers may not have answered for one or more of the justices. It also offers a chance to smoke out their concerns, which then may be addressed. Some of the justices may be unsure about what story the facts of the case really tell, and argument may tip them one way or the other. In the school cases perhaps oral argument also served to build confidence in us as partners in a venture into uncharted waters.

Any description of the oral arguments must make clear how dull they often are, relieved only rarely by a probing question or two and marked even more rarely by one of those conflicts of personality dramatic writers love to introduce into the retelling of legal proceedings. Bob Carter led off in Topeka in a style typical of mainstream appellate argument—conversational, not terribly loud, not very aggressive, perhaps even a little softer than ordinary. He did not leave any doubt that we were going all the way: "Here we abandon any claim, in pressing our attack on the unconstitutionality of this statute—we abandon any claim—of any constitutional inequality which comes from anything other than the act of segregation itself."

Not far into the arguments, Justice Burton asked Paul Wilson, assistant attorney general of Kansas, the key question: "Don't you recognize it as possible, that within seventy-five years the social and economic conditions and the personal relations of the nation may have changed so that what may have been a valid interpretation of them seventy-five years ago would not be a valid interpretation of them constitutionally today?"

Wilson recognized the possibility, but denied that conditions had changed.

During Bob's rebuttal Justice Black turned to the Kansas District Court's findings, which were based on our social scientific evidence: "Do you think that there should be a different holding here with reference to the question involved, according to the place where the segregation might occur, and if not . . . why do you say that it depends on the findings of fact at all?" Justice Black challenged the social science evidence from another viewpoint: Was it specific to Topeka alone? Bob, not very responsive, replied that the trial court merely had used the same approach that the Supreme Court had used in *Sweatt* and *McLaurin*.

Thurgood was next up to argue *Briggs v. Elliott*. He hovered imposingly over the lectern as he addressed the justices familiarly, but respectfully. He had been before the Court many times and the justices knew him well and trusted him. Some had had dealings with him over the years in political or professional roles, and some may well have considered this appearance a continuation of dialogues they had had over the years. While the case was specifically *Briggs v. Elliott*, the subject was a long-standing one between Thurgood and the Court—the status of blacks and the role of the Constitution in defining, perhaps advancing, that status to one of full equality. Thurgood spoke slowly, for him, on this occasion, making sure to articulate his words in an educated Southern way, rather than in the country style he often used.

Justice Frankfurter showed great interest in how a decree would be implemented if we were to win: "What would happen if this Court reverses and the case goes back to the district court for the entry of a decree?"

After a bit of give and take Thurgood replied that the details would have to be worked out by the district court, which might allow some time:

It would be my position that the important thing is to get the principle established, and if a decree were entered saying that facilities are declared to be unequal [note, again, not giving up victory based on unequal facilities] and that the appellants are entitled to an injunction, and then the District Court issues the injunction, it would seem to me that it would go without saying that the local school board had the time to do it. But obviously it could not do it overnight, and it might take six months to do it one place and two months to do it another place.

Just before Thurgood sat down, Justice Jackson turned to whether his argument would affect American Indians, a number of whom lived in upstate New York, Jackson's home. Thurgood replied that he thought that it would, but that Indians had not had the "judgment or wherewithal to bring lawsuits." In a bantering exchange, Jackson suggested, "Maybe you should bring some up," to which Marshall responded, "I have a full load now, Mr. Justice."

The colloquy was important because, in its casual good-naturedness, it showed a kind of rapport and confidence that might well have predisposed some justices in Thurgood's favor. Thurgood later told me that during the argument he flashed the Masonic secret distress signal to Jackson, who signaled back.

The legendary John W. Davis arose to reply. Of medium height, with white hair, thoroughly at home in the Court, having argued there more than any living lawyer, he came dressed in a club coat, exciting a fair amount of comment. (The things lawyers talk about even when matters of such high moment are at issue!) Many years before, lawyers who argued in the Court wore cutaways, also called morning coats, though the Court sat only in the afternoons, and striped trousers. In modern times, however, while lawyers from the solicitor general's office continued to wear cutaways, private attorneys, with the rarest of exceptions, have worn conservative business suits. Davis split the difference. The club coat, something none of us had heard of before, was a black suit jacket, which Davis wore with striped trousers.

Though styles of dress have changed to some extent, a certain code of formality continues. Lawyers who argue, and all others within the rail, must wear a vest or keep their jackets buttoned; if they don't, the marshal will tap them on the shoulder and request that they button up. A recent TV show about the *Brown* case depicted Thurgood arguing with his hands in his pockets. Unthinkable.

The justices had interrupted Thurgood's argument scores of times. Davis at first argued almost without interruption, commencing on Tuesday afternoon and arguing until 4:30 when the Court adjourned, resuming on Wednesday, December 10, shortly after noon. The schools were now equalized, he said. As to the Fourteenth Amendment and school segregation, Judge Parker, who had heard and decided the case in South Carolina, was right. Moreover, the same Congress that adopted the amendment voted for separate schools in the District of Columbia, "and from that good day to this, Congress has not wavered in that policy."

But Davis ran into heavy weather when Justice Burton asked the question he had earlier asked Wilson of Kansas, about whether constitutional standards might change over time: "What is your answer, Mr. Davis, to the suggestion mentioned yesterday that at that time the conditions and relations between the two races were such that what might have been constitutional then would not be constitutional now?"

Davis answered that "changed conditions cannot broaden the terminology of the Constitution." He agreed, however, that "many things have been found to be interstate commerce which at the time of the writing of the Constitution were not contemplated at all. Many of them did not even exist."

Justice Frankfurter then jumped in: "Mr. Davis, do you think that 'equal' is a less fluid term than 'commerce between the states'?"

Davis replied, "I have not compared the two on the point of fluidity."

Frankfurter rejoined, "Suppose you do it now."

Davis fenced a bit and then responded: "I should not philosophize about it. But the effort in which I am now engaged is to show how those who submitted this amendment and those who adopted it conceded it to be, and what their conduct by way of interpretation has been since its ratification in 1868."

When Frankfurter asked whether Davis meant that "history puts a gloss upon 'equal' which does not permit . . . admixture of white and colored in this aspect to be introduced," Davis agreed.

In rebuttal, Thurgood responded to Justice Reed's question as to whether the legislature might consider the disadvantages of segregation to blacks against the advantages of maintaining law and order. It might, although "I know of no Negro legislator in any of these states." He added that, while some might say it was and is necessary, "it is not necessary now because people have grown up and understand each other."

They are fighting together and living together . . . in other places. As a result of the ruling of this Court, they are going together on the higher level. . . . I know in the South where I spend most of my time, you will see white and colored kids going down the road together to school. They separate and go to different schools, and they come out and they play together. I do not see why there would necessarily be any trouble if they went to school together.

Spotts Robinson was up next. He argued *Davis*, the Virginia case, with the careful, literal precision of the real property lawyer that he was. He attacked segregation, but argued also that the Virginia plaintiffs should have been admitted to white schools under the reasoning of *Gaines*: If the state did not have equal accommodations to offer the blacks, then they must be admitted to the better white schools. Of course, once they were admitted, he argued, they couldn't thereafter be resegregated should physical equality be attained—another example of the conservative yet ambitious advocacy. As part of the response to Spotts, one of Virginia's lawyers, Justin Moore, a partner in Richmond's leading law firm, disparaged the social scientific material we had presented, declaring, "You might as well be talking about the Sermon on the Mount or something like that." To which Frankfurter replied, "It is supposed to be a good document." Jackson, in a series of questions, suggested that perhaps Congress, not the Court, should solve the problem—an outlook we had feared he held.

George Hayes and Jim Nabrit argued the District of Columbia case. They would have none of our modulated, less than all-or-nothing approaches. They argued that segregation was impermissible as a matter of constitutional principle, without regard to physical or psychological evidence. George argued too that Congress never had explicitly required segregation and, therefore, it was prohibited. But while Congress never had used the language of Southern segregation laws, its understanding seemed quite clear: It was prepared to accept it in the District of Columbia, an area under its own control. It regularly appropriated money for separate black and white schools that functioned in plain view of the Capitol, as some of the justices pointed out.

Justice Frankfurter brought up the "M" word (miscegenation): "Would [you] say, right off from your analysis of the Constitution, that marriage laws relating to race are ipso facto on the face of things, unconstitutional?"

George replied that "legislation based upon race is immediately suspect." To which Frankfurter replied, with satisfaction: "Well, that is a very candid and logical answer. That simply means that it can be valid. It is not an absolute prohibition, that good cause must be shown or great cause must be shown for the rule."

Jim Nabrit's argument began on Wednesday afternoon, was interrupted by the 4:30 recess, and resumed on Thursday. He largely devoted his time to trying to show that Congress had never required school segregation in the District of Columbia. But it appeared that he convinced nobody. He then, briefly, turned to the Constitution: School segregation in Washington was unconstitutional, he urged, because it violated the due process clause of the Fifth Amendment. Then Jim brought up the subject of bills of attainder, the legislative pronouncement that a convicted felon has forfeited all of his property and civil rights. Such bills often included a corruption of blood, meaning the felon's heirs would inherit his guilt. Bills of attainder are specifically proscribed by the Constitution. If the statutes were interpreted to require segregation, he said, "They have done it without a trial . . . merely because for some undisclosed crime, some status, some position, some matter of birth . . . or something else in the past, these Negroes are unfit to associate with whites, and under the definition of a bill of attainder . . . there would be another danger that these acts would be unconstitutional."

It was an innovative but too imaginative argument. Everyone knew that attainder referred to a specific historical practice. No justice was interested enough to ask a question.

Milton Korman, assistant corporation counsel for the District of Columbia, had a big belly, wore a morning coat, and made an incredibly bad argument. Everything he said was overshadowed by his startling quotation from the *Dred Scott* case, an infamous decision that had helped precipitate the Civil War by requiring the return of a runaway slave and declaring that a black man had no rights that whites were bound to respect. Korman's point was that constitutional interpretation should be immune from changes in public opinion. But *Dred Scott* was best known for having said that blacks were "beings of an inferior order, and altogether unfit to associate with the white race, either in social or political relations," an interpretation of the Constitution surely no longer held in any quarter, not even by the most ignorant. Heads shook in wonderment.

Jim Nabrit arose for rebuttal. In a peroration that he had prepared the night before, he wrapped himself in the flag, as he had promised he would:

The Negro should not be viewed as anybody's burden. He is a citizen. He is performing his duties in peace and in war, and today, on the bloody hills of Korea, he is serving in an unsegregated war. . . .

In the heart of the nation's capital, in the capital of democracy, in the capital of the free world, there is no place for a segregated school system. This country cannot afford it, and the Constitution does not permit it, and the statutes of Congress do not authorize it.

His stirring words mesmerized the courtroom.

The Delaware cases began at 1:27 on Thursday afternoon. From the beginning they were different. The Court is generally reluctant to overturn state court judgments and for once we had one in our favor. The Delaware attorney general, H. Albert Young, was trying to reverse his own Delaware Supreme Court and he had a rough time. He attacked the relief the courts ordered, integration rather than equalization. But several of the justices asked him whether the relief wasn't something to be left to the discretion of the judge. Justice Frankfurter responded to Young's assertion that the chancellor misunderstood the governing law: "If I may say so, a chancellor who shows as much competence as this opinion shows, probably can read the opinions of this Court with understanding."

Lou Redding got into a series of exchanges with Justice Frankfurter, who asked whether the Court might not simply affirm and leave the case alone:

"If we just affirmed this decree below without an opinion, that would be an end of the matter, and the plaintiffs in this case would get all they asked, would they not?" Lou replied that the attorney general had threatened that "the moment he has shown to the court that facilities are equalized they [the black students] would then be ejected from the schools."

I concluded the argument in the Delaware case, which was also the end of the arguments for all five cases. I was eleven days short of my twenty-eighth birthday. Was I nervous? Strangely, I wasn't. I knew the case inside out and had a detailed notebook on the lectern in front of me, which contained my argument, with marginal notes to guide me back if I lost my way. I had been in the trial and appeal and had done a dry run. I had listened to other LDF lawyers argue before the Court over two days and then heard Lou. I felt as well prepared as possible. Even if I did terribly the others already had made many of the points I planned to present.

The questions focused on two issues: Was the chancellor right in ordering *immediate* integration; and how should the Supreme Court treat the social science evidence? I argued that if the state had presented evidence warranting delay, then the courts below might have considered it. But, in fact, "the decree of the Supreme Court of Delaware came down, I believe on August the 28, at which time both counsel for the respondents were on vacation, and before we could even return from vacation, the children who had read about the decree in the newspaper had applied to the school and had been admitted, and there was no more administrative problem involved than admitting anybody else."

Justices Black and Frankfurter explored whether the social science testimony was significant only for Delaware. I replied that a great deal had been presented by social scientists from Delaware, but that segregation generally was unconstitutional. Frankfurter observed that "if a man says three yards, and I have measured it, and it is three yards, there it is. But if a man tells you the inside of your brain and mine, and how we function, that is not a measurement, and there you are."

I argued that the testimony was uncontradicted and that the chancellor had been persuaded and then I concluded, "We urge that this Court affirm the judgment below, and assure that the respondents' stay in the schools to which they have been admitted and which they are now attending will be one unharassed by future litigation and attempts to segregate them once more."

With that the arguments ended. Each day, after the arguments, we would return to the hotel, dead tired, and try to read the tea leaves of the questions asked by the justices. Since Justice Frankfurter asked more questions than all the others combined, and Bill Coleman had been his law clerk, everyone hoped that Bill might shed some light on Frankfurter's mind and perhaps that of the other justices as well. But he was of little help.

After the last day, we just scattered. Neither following *Brown*, nor after other cases, did we hold post-mortems. About the only surprise questions from the bench had been those that Justice Jackson put to Thurgood about the education of Indians. No one had been prepared for that, but it didn't matter. Our side had ranged across all the possible styles of advocacy, from Spotts's meticulous, dry, complete coverage of the issues to Thurgood's vivid imagery about children playing together and then separating to go to school—everyone presented our arguments well.

I felt that I was particularly favorably situated in a case that we already won in the Delaware courts, because our plaintiffs actually were in the formerly white schools, and I could argue that there was no reason to postpone desegregation; it had already occurred without incident. John W. Davis had said all there was to be said in favor of keeping the status quo. He certainly had a cool, commanding presence, but the most persuasive factor in his favor was not the legal argument, but rather the fear in the minds of the justices about what might happen if the law were to change.

BLUEPRINT FOR LEGAL ACTION, STRUGGLE ON OTHER FRONTS

We didn't wait for the Court's decision before preparing a forty-four-page "Blueprint for Legal Action" and a fifty-five-page "Civil Rights Handbook" for the NAACP national convention in March 1953. These documents urged an attack on segregation in education, housing, travel, employment, voting, and public accommodations and proposed how to go about it. What stands out is that the "state action" doctrine cramped our proposals to go after privately operated businesses. Not until Congress passed the civil rights legislation of the mid-1960s did that become possible.

At the same time, we continued to file higher education cases and odds and ends of suits against parks, swimming pools, beaches. For a case in Baltimore I got a professor of recreation, Roscoe Brown, to swim offshore at segregated beaches, wearing fins and a snorkel mask to inspect the bottom. He found potentially dangerous sharp rocks on the ocean floor at the black beach and smooth sand at the white beach. We won the case. Maryland invested $60,000 to equalize the beaches and the judge resegregated them.

Thurgood, on another front, complained to the Justice Department that a Mississippi registrar was asking black voters, "How many bubbles in a bar of soap?" The registrar stopped, but resorted to other techniques—registrars had a bottomless bag of tricks ranging from violence to switching dates and times of opening and closing—designed to achieve the same end.

Having failed to win a ruling that would require the Public Housing Authority to desegregate nationally, Connie Motley pursued public housing cases across the country. A half-dozen bills to end segregation in interstate travel were submitted to Congress but got nowhere. Bob Carter pursued the issue against eleven Southern railroads before the Interstate Commerce Commission.

We won a dubious victory against the Nashville Board of Park Commissioners requiring it to permit blacks to play on the white golf course every Wednesday and alternate Saturdays and Sundays, during which whites would be excluded, until a new golf course, then under construction, would be completed. It sounded suspiciously as if the old course then would be given to blacks.

And so we pushed ahead, while the Supreme Court debated the most important set of cases we, perhaps anyone, ever had brought before it.

14

BACK TO THE DRAWING BOARD

FIVE QUESTIONS

All we could do was wait. In controversial cases the Court tended to delay deciding until near the very end of the term. At an April 1953 executive committee meeting Thurgood reported that he thought we would win at least three of the school cases—which three he didn't say. This suggested the victories might come on grounds short of holding segregation unconstitutional—perhaps finding physical inequalities in some of the cases, as in Delaware, and upholding segregation where the bricks, mortar, and books were equal, or maybe, ducking deciding the others.

We were all astonished when, on June 8, 1953, the Supreme Court ordered that the cases be reargued, setting reargument for October 12, but later postponing it to December. The Court asked both sides to answer five questions.

First, what was the understanding of the Congress that adopted, and the state legislatures that ratified, the Fourteenth Amendment as to whether it would proscribe segregation in public schools?

Second, if neither Congress nor the states understood that the Fourteenth Amendment would require immediate abolition of school segregation, did they nevertheless understand that Congress in the future might have the power to abolish it or that the Court in construing the amendment might abolish it in the light of future conditions? The latter part of this question was, of course, like the one pressed on John W. Davis during argument, about the effect of changing conditions on interpretations of what might constitute equality before the law.

The third question addressed whether, without regard to the understanding of the framers, it was within the power of the Court to construe the amendment to abolish school segregation?

The final two questions suggested to the South that it had better start thinking the unthinkable, for they addressed how desegregation should be brought about, no longer merely whether or not segregation was constitutional. Question four asked, "Assuming it is decided that segregation in public schools violates the Fourteenth Amendment, would a decree necessarily follow that, within limits set by normal geographic school districting, Negro children should forthwith be admitted to schools of their choice," or might the Court permit an "effective gradual adjustment"?

The final question assumed that gradual change might be permitted and inquired who should work out the transition—the Supreme Court, a special master, or the district courts? The United States attorney general was invited to submit a brief and participate in the oral argument.

Materials made public subsequent to the *Brown* decision indicate that following the first argument the Court was divided, perhaps with our side getting five, six, or maybe even seven justices voting with us if the vote had been taken at that time. The only certain, or near certain, dissenters seem to have been Reed and Vinson, with Jackson and Clark open to persuasion to join the majority. Justice Frankfurter, however, feeling that unanimity would be highly important in so emotionally and politically controversial a decision, wanted to hold off deciding the cases for a year. He drafted the five questions and persuaded the Court to issue them along with its call for reargument. Among his reasons in proposing the questions about remedy was that "it is not undesirable that an adjustment be made in the public mind to such a possibility." He offered his belief that "the ultimate crucial factor in the problem presented by these cases is psychological—the adjustment of men's minds and actions to the unfamiliar, the unpleasant."

I took the five questions as a favorable omen, as did some of the other lawyers, including Spotts and Oliver. Why, after all, would the Court have put questions about remedy if it weren't seriously contemplating ordering a remedy? Bill Coleman was sure we would win—everyone suspected that he had an inside line to Frankfurter, but he didn't. Jack Weinstein also was sure we would win. Putting all the legal issues aside, he believed that following the Second World War and all the horrors that had come out of Nazi racial doctrines and laws the Court would have no alternative but to come down on the side of full equality for all citizens. Bob Carter, on the other hand, remembered being less optimistic, recalling that the Court's questions "shook us—not completely—but they shook us. Where we had been 75 percent confident, we now were down to 50 or 55 percent confident."

LOGISTICS

After the brief was filed, Arnold De Mille, who handled our public relations, issued a press release on November 11, 1953, in which he got somewhat carried away. While everything in the release, in any public relations release, should not be taken entirely at face value, De Mille did convey to the general public, with some exaggeration, the spirit of what the previous twenty-two weeks had been like for us:

> By midsummer, some staff workers were going two and three days without sleep, taking time out only to eat. [I doubt it.] By the end of October, no one was getting more than three or four hours sleep at a time. [No one? Hardly.]
>
> Enough coffee was consumed by the workers in the Legal Defense office to supply a regiment for a full week. [How much coffee does a regiment drink in a week?] . . .
>
> The secretaries and volunteers put in shifts of fifteen to twenty hours a day, seven days a week, without requesting extra pay. [Almost true.]
>
> All members of the NAACP legal staff gave up their vacation time. [True.]
>
> The staff has used 1,000,600 sheets of copy paper, 6,000,225 sheets of manifold, 2,700 stencils, more than twelve million sheets of mimeographing paper and 115,000 sheets of carbon paper. [I didn't count, but almost 20,000,000 sheets of paper? I can't believe it.]. . .
>
> Some 325,000 miles were covered by lawyers who shuttled back and forth across the nation. [Probably true.]

We also had to engage in serious fund-raising. The Fund's income, at best, covered only ordinary expenses, but we estimated that the reargument would cost an additional $39,000 (remember, this was in 1953 dollars). Today any one of a number of large foundations and a handful of wealthy individuals would readily make such a contribution. Then, $39,000 was not so easy to come by. Marshall Field had given $75,000 of his $200,000 anonymous pledge in 1952, but in 1953, he gave only $50,000. The Field Foundation gave $15,000, but no other really big gifts were in the offing. In any event, those large gifts were budgeted to cover only the ongoing program, which did not count unanticipated expenses for the reargument.

The black press started a campaign that produced $14,000. The *Pittsburgh Courier* called it "EE" (Equality in Education), the *Afro American* named it "Dollar or more will open the door," and the *Birmingham World* labeled it "Put up or shut up." In September Walter Reuther of the CIO contributed $2,500, and the black American Teachers' Association (Southern black teachers weren't permitted in the National Education Association, the national teachers' guild) gave $5,000. Charles Buchanan, a black impresario who owned the Savoy Ballroom in Harlem, gave $500 for law books (over the years he supported our library generously). Churches (the Second Baptist Church of Los Angeles gave $1,500), black businesses (Rose Morgan, who owned a large beauty salon raised $5,000), and others gave amounts of similar magnitude. The Prince Hall Masons continued to contribute about

$20,000 per year in gifts ranging from $100 to several thousand dollars from lodges all over the country. The South Carolina and Virginia state conferences of branches of the NAACP contributed $5,000 in September and $5,100 in December, respectively.

To bring in such income Thurgood or some other staff member often would have to go out and speak to the potential donors. We appeared at branches, universities, and churches, before fraternal associations, veterans' groups, labor unions, professional associations, and other organizations. Rarely did we appear at fewer than ten meetings in a month and often we spoke at well over twenty, with Thurgood speaking far more often than anyone else. Besides being greatly in demand, Thurgood was the only staff member permitted into the Masons' inner sanctums. So a heavy travel schedule burdened everyone's, but especially Thurgood's, ability to do other work.

I frequently spoke about *Groveland* at these fund-raising meetings. Merely reading Walter Irvin's statement, made as he lay wounded in a hospital bed, describing how sheriffs McCall and Yates had shot him, drew gasps and cries from the audience and could be the most effective part of a speech, putting some emotion into my not terribly inspiring style. One night as I spoke in a Richmond, Virginia, church before an audience of perhaps fifteen hundred, I turned the pages of Irvin's statement and to my horror discovered a page missing. I took a deep breath and winged it, paraphrasing as best I could—a lesson to check out whatever you hope to read from before going to the podium, something I now do every time.

By September Thurgood reported that we were still $25,000 short in paying for the extra expenses generated by the reargument, although "many of the research people are working just for carfare and lunch money." But before the brief was filed in November, the $39,000 shortfall was in hand, 70 percent of it raised from black people of no great means.

On July 13 Thurgood reported preparations for the reargument to the National Legal Committee. He had assembled a team and placed the historical research under John A. Davis, a political scientist at Lincoln University, his alma mater, assisted by Mabel Smythe, another political scientist, who later would teach at Brooklyn College and in 1977 became American Ambassador to the United Republic of Cameroon. With Davis, Thurgood had recruited Howard Jay Graham, law librarian of the Los Angeles County Bar Association Library, an authority on the history of the Fourteenth Amendment, and Horace Mann Bond, president of Lincoln and a historian of early education for blacks. They later enlisted C. Vann Woodward, of Johns Hopkins, and John Hope Franklin, of Howard, both of whom had studied and written extensively on Reconstruction. Davis asked social scientists and educators, including Kenneth Clark, Otto Klineberg, and Dean William O. Penrose of the University of Delaware—situated near the newly integrated Delaware schools—as well as staff member June Shagaloff, to study those and other recently desegregated schools "with the idea of devising an administratively sound plan under which integration can be accomplished without undue delay."

Connie Motley was given the task of researching the power of Congress to outlaw segregated schools under Section 5 of the Fourteenth Amendment; Bob Carter was asked to study cases in which the Court had overruled prior decisions; staff member Elwood Chisolm to study the debates and early cases concerning the contemporary understanding of the terms *civil, political,* and *social* (words used in *Plessy* to distinguish matters controlled by the Fourteenth Amendment from those left untouched by it); staff lawyer Dave Pinsky to analyze cases where constitutional rights were defined as immediate, in contrast to antitrust cases where gradual adjustment sometimes was ordered; and Spotts Robinson to study cases where special masters had been appointed by the Supreme Court. I got the task of defining the equity powers of federal courts (and Delaware state courts) and was asked particularly to study and report on the reluctance of federal courts to supervise the performance of state administrative functions.

Other scholars joined our effort, including Alfred H. Kelly of Wayne State University in Detroit, who had written a book on constitutional history, and who came to play a large part in the final drafting of the historical argument. And some scholars refused to participate. The noted historian Henry Steele Commager declined because he thought that our position on the history was wrong. He wrote: "The framers of the amendment did not, as far as we now know, intend that it should be used to end segregation in schools. . . . I strongly urge that you consider dropping this particular argument as I think it tends to weaken your case."

Bill Coleman recruited friends from law school and former Supreme Court clerks to research ratification of the Fourteenth Amendment in thirty-six states. He requested information about states immediately preceding submission of the Fourteenth Amendment for ratification and also at the time of submission: Whether there were provisions referring to segregation in the state constitutions that the secessionist states were required to submit to Congress after the Civil War before they could be readmitted to the Union; whether schools were unsegregated in those states between 1865 and 1877; and what the legislative history of segregation laws was after adoption of the Fourteenth Amendment.

Some of Bill's friends in the Deep South helped him with his researches at considerable personal risk to themselves. Truman Hobbs in Montgomery, Alabama, son of the congressman who had argued to retain segregation in dining cars in the *Henderson* case, researched Alabama, and James Wilson of Atlanta researched Georgia. Hobbs is now a federal judge in Alabama and Wilson a partner in one of Georgia's leading firms; if their roles had been known then their careers most assuredly would have been ruined.

This foray into original intent posed seemingly unanswerable questions. How do you allocate weight to the differing expressions of different framers, to those who voted proposals up or down and the many members of the many ratifying state legislatures across the country? Most had said nothing about schools; a few had occasionally, but hardly systematically. Some may have changed their positions between the time of a recorded statement and the vote. Expressions about formal education were particularly sparse, because it didn't play the role it does today. But the most important factor in examining "intent" is the level of generality at which one chooses to address the question. If the question were "What did the Congress and the ratifying legislatures intend specifically with regard to schools as they then existed?" there might be one answer. This might be called the micro level of inquiry. But if the question were taken to be "What did the framers and ratifiers intend with regard to activities essential to full citizenship?" an inquiry, so to speak, at the macro level, the question of intent might elicit another answer. For, in the mid-twentieth century, a list of prerequisites essential to full citizenship certainly had to include equal access to good education.

Justices Burton and Frankfurter's questions to John W. Davis posed this dichotomy. As advocates, however, we felt we had to answer both versions of the question.

As we went about our labors, on September 8, Chief Justice Vinson died. President Eisenhower appointed Earl Warren to succeed him at the commencement of the new term. The change had no discernible effect on our work; I can't recall any speculation about what difference the new chief justice would make. If we had reflected, we would not have been encouraged, for we would have remembered that Warren had been a prosecutor in his native state of California and that he had played a supporting role in the relocation of Japanese Americans from the West Coast during the Second World War. Philip Elman has written, however, that Felix Frankfurter remarked at Vinson's death, "This is the first indication I have ever had that there is a God."

The briefs of both sides and the government's amicus brief on the historical questions combined totaled more than one thousand pages. We filed individual briefs for our four cases, a 235-page joint brief of the history, plus a forty-page reply brief; a government appendix was almost 400-pages long.

Our massive effort culminated in a meeting of more than one hundred participants at the Overseas Press Club on West Fortieth Street in September. It divided into seminars to consider all the major problems and made recommendations for the final product. Then, in October, Thurgood, Bob, Connie, Spotts, Lou Redding, Bob Ming, and I met with Alfred Kelly over a period of five days to struggle with the history, which concluded in a drafting session between Ming and Kelly. Finally, that draft was redone in November by Kelly and John Frank.

Our battle over the history of the Fourteenth Amendment was finished and nothing would be gained by rehearsing the contending positions. While we came up with a highly persuasive argument at the level of the general purposes of the amendment, when we got down to specifics about education there were difficulties. For that reason our brief led off with the answer to the third question, the one in which the Court asked whether, without regard to the understanding of the framers, it was within the power of the Court to construe the amendment to abolish school segregation? We pointed out that "normal exercise of the judicial function calls for a declaration that the state is without power to enforce distinctions based upon race or color in affording educational opportunities in the public schools," and set forth the arguments that had worked so well for us in *Sweatt* and *McLaurin*.

On the history, one difficulty was that the same Congress that had enacted the Fourteenth Amendment appropriated funds specifically for segregated schools in the District of Columbia (indeed, as did all Congresses after that one), suggesting at the very least that it wasn't hell bent on ending segregated education. As to this uncomfortable circumstance, a Committee on Historical Development, which included John Frank, Horace Mann Bond, Mabel Smythe, and Buell Gallagher, wrote:

> We feel that here we are at the heart of one of our most important difficulties. It is imperative that we so analyze the District of Columbia material as to show that this is not indicative of a belief that the Constitution condones segregation. We believe that the material can be analyzed to show the exact opposite. To show a widespread expanse of the conviction that segregation was incompatible with equal protection.

The way to do this, the memorandum suggested, would be to point out that the Thirty-ninth Congress inherited an "institutionalized system of segregation in the District, which was begun immediately upon the termination of slavery in the District," and that "early action came from a background of separate and discriminatory treatment of free Negroes in the District in the late 1850's." The congressional legislation was "permissive only" with regard to segregation and did not compel it. At the same time, the "Freedmen's Bureau was running non-segregated education in the District, and . . . private organizations were also running non-segregated education. . . . Sometimes colored students were, in fact, introduced into the white schools by action of the District of Columbia School Board."

The memorandum proposed taking the position that failure to eliminate segregation in the District was "not . . . a matter of constitutional judgment" but a "yielding to financial and political pressure which in no wise reflects a constitutional judgment." It included the following caveat: *"It is the firm consensus of the group that we shall not attempt to make too much of the foregoing lest it may boomerang."*

Indeed, the brief heeded the caveat so well that it did not discuss education in the District of Columbia at all. But when the segregating states' briefs made much of school segregation in the District of Columbia, we proceeded down the line of the memorandum, and in our reply responded that "the 39th Congress considered the District of Columbia school situation perfunctorily, as routine business, with little debate and practically no discussion of note. There is nothing in any of the debates on these measures to indicate that Congress contemplated or understood that the Fourteenth Amendment did not prohibit segregated schools."

The history of the Civil Rights Act of 1866 presented an equally prickly problem. An earlier version of the bill commanded "no discrimination in civil rights or immunities . . . on account of race, color, or previous condition of servitude." The "no discrimination" clause became immensely controversial; some opponents claimed that it would confer equality with regard to real property, punishment for crime, and require the abolition of separate schools, all of which they regarded as unthinkable. Others contended that Congress had no authority under the Constitution to adopt such legislation. As enacted, however, the 1866 act omitted the "no discrimination" clause. That would be bad enough for our position, but the excision was made on the motion of John Bingham, the very person who later drafted the Fourteenth Amendment. He advocated the amendment for the purpose, at least in part, of placing the 1866 act beyond the possibility of congressional amendment or repeal, should conservatives gain control of the Congress. This lent support to an argument that the framer of the Fourteenth Amendment had no intention that the act, and, inferentially, the amendment, would prohibit school segregation.

We decided to deal with the problem by arguing that Bingham's amendment to the Civil Rights Act of 1866, which removed the "no discrimination in civil rights" clause, was adopted "simply because a majority of the members of the House believed that so sweeping a measure could not be justified under the Constitution as it stood. They accepted Bingham's argument that the proper remedy for removing racial distinctions and classifications in the states was a new amendment to the Constitution."

It was also arguable that Bingham, who moved to remove the sweeping "no discrimination" clause from the 1866 act, saw the Constitution as not yet ready to support it, and that he saw the Fourteenth Amendment as curing this defect. Though this was not something we could prove with certainty, it did beat saying nothing on the point.

We were able to argue even more forcefully that proponents of the Civil Rights Act of 1875, among whom were many supporters of the Fourteenth Amendment, understood that it would prohibit segregated schools.

(Recently, Michael W. McConnell, in an exhaustive examination of the legislative history of the amendment and the 1875 act, has concluded that "a very substantial portion of the Congress, including leading framers of the Amendment, subscribed—often passionately—to the view that school segregation violates the Fourteenth Amendment." Bills prohibiting school segregation failed because of "procedural obstacles, including supermajority vote requirements and filibuster tactics.")

The principal difficulty in researching the question of what went into the ratification debates was that virtually none of the state legislatures kept records of them, although something about intentions might have appeared in the newspapers and could be inferred from contemporaneous actions. But the researchers also found much better stuff than we ever expected. Nevertheless, we had to recognize that school segregation was widespread even in the North. On October 5, Horace Mann Bond, still in the midst of his research, wrote to Mabel Smythe:

> NOW THE WONDERFUL THING ABOUT THESE TWELVE STATES—NEBRASKA [which, while not a secessionist state, was admitted to the Union during the life of the Thirty-ninth Congress, which prepared the Fourteenth Amendment], TENNESSEE, ALABAMA, ARKANSAS, FLORIDA, LOUISIANA, NORTH CAROLINA, SOUTH CAROLINA, MISSISSIPPI, TEXAS, VIRGINIA, GEORGIA IS THAT NOT A SINGLE ONE WAS ADMITTED, OR READMITTED, TO THE UNION, WITH ANY PHRASE IN THE CONSTITUTIONS (CONSTITUTIONS DRAWN AND REDRAWN TO MEET THE SCRUTINY OF THE 39 AND SUCCESSIVE CONGRESSES, AND TO BE IN CONFORMITY WITH THE CONSTITUTION AND WITH THE FOURTEENTH AMENDMENT)—*that sanctioned segregation, or mentioned race, in connection with the public school system. I do not know at this time what the Statutes, on final check, and recheck would show; but I think the rule is perfectly unanimous.*
>
> The point was that these States *knew*, that if they put anything defining or restricting rights of any kind, into their constitutions and statutes, in terms of race, *prior* to readmission, that they would not be readmitted.
>
> What better proof do you want, of the intent of the 39th Congress, or of the contemplation or understanding of the ratifying States?

The segregating states' eventual response to this argument was that prior to readmission to the Union these states' legislatures were controlled by blacks and carpetbaggers; following admission and return to conservative white control eight of these states instituted school segregation, which, the states argued, would not have been done if they had understood it to be prohibited.

Other memos were not so encouraging. A preliminary memorandum from a New York team concluded: "It is apparent that New York's official position was that segregation was still legal as long as 'equal' facilities were furnished to Negroes." But, as the memorandum pointed out, white school appropriations were about three times more per capita than those for blacks during that period. California had segregated schools both before and after adoption of the Fourteenth Amendment. Connecticut, and other New England states, did prohibit segregation, either before or shortly after ratification, and other states, sometimes within a decade or more following ratification, prohibited school segregation. It was impossible to tie what the states did conclusively to the Fourteenth Amendment, but surely we were able to make a lawyerlike case concerning ratification. Lawyerlike, yes, but far from airtight. In our reply brief we printed elaborate pull-out charts detailing states' laws and practices before and after readmission and before and after ratification.

But if our argument at the micro level was difficult, at the macro level, that is, concerning the overall ambition of the framers of the Fourteenth Amendment, we were in wonderful shape. Howard Jay Graham wrote a ninety-eight-page paper, which we distilled into a thirty-six-page appendix and used elsewhere. His paper began:

> The Thirteenth and Fourteenth Amendments are fully intelligible and can be correctly understood only in the broad perspective of the antislavery movement of which they were the consummation. . . .
>
> Ethical and religious opinions were here molding and remolding constitutional doctrine. Moral premises were being translated into legal and constitutional premises—i.e., *enforceable rights*. This was being done, if you please, by a "due processing" and "equal protecting" of the law of nature. . . .
>
> In short, the Fourteenth Amendment, in Professor ten Broek's phrase, marked a "reconsummation" of the antislavery movement, and of that movement's broad purpose to root out the "badges and incidents" of slavery. It was drafted by the Joint Committee of Fifteen on Reconstruction. Ten members of that Committee are known to have grown up in states where they were exposed for years to the old antislavery constitutional theory.

But the question then arose: How account for later interpretations of the Fourteenth Amendment that not only ignored these origins but condoned the opposite in, for example, *Plessy v. Ferguson?*

We turned to a paper C. Vann Woodward had written for us, "The Background of the Abandonment of Reconstruction" (a distillation of his great work, *Reunion and Reaction*), which described how Rutherford B. Hayes acceded to the presidency in 1877 even though "Tilden received over a quarter of million votes more than Hayes." Congress created an electoral commission to rule on disputed vote counts in several states and to assign electoral votes. Woodward's paper demonstrated that a deal was struck and that in exchange for a promise to take certain economic steps beneficial to the white South, Hayes gained enough disputed electoral votes to be elected. As Woodward wrote:

> The Reconstruction policy was quickly abandoned, radicalism was renounced, Federal troops were withdrawn from South Carolina and Louisiana, future use of force was disavowed, and the conservative governments that replaced the Carpetbaggers were publicly informed that responsibility for the disposition of the freedman's status was thenceforth in their hands. Acquiescence in the abandonment of Reconstruction and the adoption of the new policy of laissez faire accumulated in the form of endorsements by the press, by public opinion, by administrative rulings, and eventually by decisions of the courts.

We distilled Woodward's twenty-seven-page paper into a part of the brief concerning early decisions that treated the Fourteenth Amendment in strongly egalitarian terms, like *Strauder v. West Virginia*, the Slaughter House Cases, and, of course, Justice Harlan's dissent in *Plessy*.

In our Summary of Argument, we encapsulated the historical argument in a couple of sentences:

> The Fourteenth Amendment was actually the culmination of the determined efforts of the Radical Republican majority in Congress to incorporate into our fundamental law the well-defined equalitarian principle of complete equality for all without regard to race or color. The debates in the 39th Congress and succeeding Congresses clearly reveal the intention that the Fourteenth Amendment would work a revolutionary change in our state–federal relationship by denying to the states the power to distinguish on the basis of race.

The government's brief took essentially the same position.

The segregating states hit hard on school segregation in the District of Columbia, the amendment to the Civil Rights Bill of 1866, and the retention of school segregation in many of the ratifying states.

The stubborn problem remaining at the end of the historical exercise was how the justices would reconcile the two versions. One told of the framers embracing abolitionist idealism, committing generally to full equality, and, in debates on the 1875 act, expressing the belief that the amendment prohibited school segregation; the other presented examples of less than full commitment to complete equality—amending the 1866 bill and sustaining segregated schools in the District, for example. When there was original intent of several different sorts the choice of which intent to follow came down to the values of the justices, and on that count we felt vastly stronger than the other side.

Alfred Kelly, one of our principal consultants on the Fourteenth Amendment, addressed the American Historical Association in 1961 and angered some of the lawyers who had been with us in *Brown* by saying he had faced a "deadly opposition between [his] professional integrity as a historian and [his] wishes and hopes with respect to a contemporary question of values." He referred to "bearing down on facts, sliding off facts, quietly ignoring facts and, above all, interpreting facts in a way" that would "get by" the justices. He would have preferred a scholar's paper that set forth "on the one hand" and "on the other hand," without marshaling facts to support a particular conclusion. He seemed to be unaware of the nature of legal advocacy, in which the other side is given both the opportunity and responsibility for presenting the conflicting view, and for pointing out errors, omissions, and misinterpretations, if any, in the first side's presentation. Ultimately, he conceded that while the conclusions we had offered to the Court had not been, in his view, "hammered out with . . . historical truth as our [only] objective, [they] nonetheless contain[ed] an essential measure of historical truth."

Kenneth Clark's research team had the assignment of suggesting how desegregation might be best achieved. It conducted a massive study, not merely in education, but across American society, of churches, the armed forces, housing, interstate transportation, public accommodations, organized sports, employment, politics, higher education, prep schools, and elementary and secondary public schools. It considered instances where desegregation had been brought about by population changes, the pressure of public opinion, referendums, community action, legislation, and lawsuits. It concluded that to desegregate with a minimum of social disturbance there should be:

A.   A clear and unequivocal statement of policy by leaders with prestige. . . .

B.   Firm enforcement . . . and persistence. . . .

C.   A willingness to deal with violations . . . by . . . strong enforcement action. . . .

D.   A refusal of the authorities to . . . tolerate subterfuges. . . .

E.   An appeal . . . in terms of . . . religious principles . . . and . . . acceptance of the American traditions of fair play and equal justice.

The *Journal of Social Issues* published the study in full.

But in our 1953 brief we made no reference to the study or its underlying materials. (However, in 1954, in a brief dealing with implementation only, we made considerable use of it.) As for time to comply, we hung tough and in a handful of pages set forth the straight legal proposition that the children should be admitted to integrated schools "forthwith." We agreed that time might be taken to make administrative changes, but not to deal with threats of violence, to fire black teachers, or to close public schools. We attacked the United States' last brief's grade-a-year and school-by-school plans as "intolerable": Many plaintiffs would never obtain relief. Defendants should offer reasons for delay; we would respond and the courts could decide.

Before the brief was put in final form Thurgood sent the Summary of Argument to lawyers outside the staff for comment and editing, including to Lou Pollak, who was then in the State Department. Thurgood had taught that the Summary of Argument was the most important part of a brief; most justices read it first, some don't read beyond it. Lou thought it wasn't clear and didn't argue forcefully enough. Lou, who writes beautifully and with great precision, self-deprecatingly recalls that he painstakingly rewrote the section and brought it down the hall for a secretary to type. When she returned it she asked whether she might ask a question: "Mr. Pollak, the brief was so interesting. I really enjoyed typing it," she said. "It was clear and well written. But, I have one question. Do you want the little colored children to go to school with the little white children, or don't you?"

The states' briefs argued that courts might allow time for transition. The United States agreed on the need for a transition period, but backtracked from its first brief by not repeating suggestions about grade-a-year and school-by-school, arguing that there should not be delay of more than a year, although a school district might ask for more time.

REARGUMENT

The first reargument began December 7, 1953, a year after the original argument. Thurgood and Spotts decided it would be best to assign to Spotts the historical presentation and to Thurgood the argument about judicial power, obviating the need to repeat each argument about the history, particularly, in each case. Virginia, South Carolina, and the Court agreed; those cases were combined. From the beginning, these arguments were different from last year's. Spotts led off with a meticulous, dull, historical presentation and spoke for perhaps forty minutes before he was asked a question by, of course, Justice Frankfurter, about the weight to be given individual utterances by congressmen or senators. Not a terribly important issue, and a question to which everyone knew the answer. Justice Reed asked several questions about the power of Congress, and that was all. Had they made up their minds? Didn't they care about the history? I wondered and others did too.

Thurgood's presentation was equally uninspiring, eliciting unedifying questions about the basis of decision in *McLaurin*: Had it been decided under separate-but-equal or was it a tacit rejection of segregation per se?

Law professors' questions. Of course, the decision in *McLaurin* could be described either way. Thurgood was thrown a bit off base when he got questions about the history, for which Spotts had specially prepared, but segued back to his prepared presentation. Thurgood made clear that we rejected segregation in any shape, manner, or form.

John W. Davis argued for close to an hour, also with only a couple of questions. His peroration survives as one of the grand rhetorical errors of advocacy.

> I am reminded—and I hope it won't be treated as a reflection on any-body—of Aesop's fable of the dog and the meat: The dog, with a fine piece of meat in his mouth, crossed a bridge and saw the shadow in the stream and plunged for it and lost both substance and shadow.
>
> Here is equal education, not promised, not prophesied, but present. Shall it be thrown away on some fancied question of racial prestige? . . .
>
> I entreat them to remember the age-old motto that the best is often the enemy of the good.

As he closed, tears ran down his cheeks. I later expressed my surprise to my classmate Marvin Frankel, who was in Court that day, having argued a case for the government just prior to ours. He said that one of his colleagues had whispered, "That sonofabitch cries in every case he argues."

Justin Moore for Virginia received the same largely silent treatment as Spotts. A hint of things to come emerged when he suggested that Virginia might desegregate by setting up three sets of schools: black, white, and non-segregated.

Thurgood's rebuttal was his best argument ever. First he picked up on John W. Davis's reference to "prestige":

> As Mr. Davis said yesterday, the only thing the Negroes are trying to get is prestige.
>
> Exactly correct. Ever since the Emancipation Proclamation, the Negro has been trying to get what was recognized in *Strauder v. West Virginia*, which is the same status as anybody else regardless of race.

And, building on an argument he made the year before, Thurgood concluded with passion:

> I got the feeling on hearing the discussion yesterday that when you put a white child in a school with a whole lot of colored children, the child would fall apart or something. Everybody knows that is not true. Those same kids in Virginia and South Carolina—and I have seen them do it—they play in the streets together, they play on their farms

together, they go down the road together, they separate to go to school, they come out of school and play ball together. They have to be separated in school.

There is some magic to it. You can have them voting together, you can have them not restricted because of law in the houses they live in. You can have them going to the same state university and the same college, but if they go to elementary and high school, the world will fall apart. And it is the exact same argument that has been made to this Court over and over again, and we submit that when they charge us with making a legislative argument, it is in truth they who are making the legislative argument.

They can't take race out of this case. From the day this case was filed until this moment, nobody has in any form or fashion, despite the fact I made it clear in the opening argument that I was relying on it, done anything to distinguish this statute from the Black Codes, which they must admit, because nobody can dispute, say anything anybody wants to say, one way or the other, the Fourteenth Amendment was intended to deprive the states of power to enforce Black Codes or anything else like it. . . .

The only thing can be is an inherent determination that the people who were formerly in slavery, regardless of anything else, shall be kept as near that stage as possible, and now is the time, we submit, that this Court should make it clear that that is not what our Constitution stands for.

Assistant Attorney General J. Lee Rankin, a dry, uninspiring Nebraskan, whose presentation, nevertheless, perhaps for that reason, was highly effective, argued for the United States and after a few minutes of clear sailing it was questions every inch of the way. The Court had invited the United States to participate. The government's brief for the first argument (a Truman administration product) attacked segregation head on. This time (under Eisenhower), it was a bit vague; although called a "supplemental brief," it only implicitly embraced the earlier position. Justice Douglas pushed Rankin, asking what was the position of the government. Rankin replied, "It is the position of the Department of Justice that segregation in public schools cannot be maintained under the Fourteenth Amendment." We breathed sighs of relief.

On implementation, Rankin introduced "handling the matter with deliberate speed." On another occasion he said "diligent speed." He urged sending the cases to the lower courts and placing the burden on the defendants as to how much time they would need to adjust, suggesting a year for presentation and consideration of plans. Nothing more specific was offered.

The argument on the District of Columbia case was punctuated with many questions about its segregation policy. A majority of the school board now consisted of new members who were opposed to segregation. A number of the justices wanted to know whether there still was a lawsuit or whether the District had capitulated. (By this time Delaware had integrated somewhat, and Topeka was no longer resisting integration.)

Justice Black asked Milton Korman: "Will you let us know in the morning, when the case comes up, whether the Board wants you to defend this case?"

The next day, in a rather confused set of exchanges, Korman took the position that the school board had not *officially* changed its position and he was permitted to continue.

Jim Nabrit, Jr., once more made a patriotic appeal, with tremendous effect:

> America is a great country in which we can come before the Court and express to the Court the great concern which we have, where our great government is dealing with us, and we are not in the position that the animals were in George Orwell's satirical novel, *Animal Farm*, where after the revolution the dictatorship was set up and the sign set up there that all animals were equal, was changed to read "but some are more equal than others."
>
> Our Constitution has no provision across it that all men are equal but that white men are more equal than others.
>
> Under this statute and under this country, under this Constitution, and under the protection of this Court, we believe that we, too, are equal.

Bob Carter, whose argument preceded Jim's, and I, following Jim, ran into similar problems for similar reasons: We were arguing that defendants should integrate the Topeka and Wilmington schools, but in each case integration was under way. In Topeka, the school board had abandoned its policy of segregation; in Wilmington, the chancellor's decree was being implemented. Justice Frankfurter badgered Bob with the proposition that since his clients were getting what they had asked for, he no longer had any case. Bob, after perhaps ten minutes, said, "I certainly have no real desire to proceed with an argument," and sat down.

In my own argument I tried to raise the point that the Delaware case remained alive because defendants claimed the right to resegregate once blacks got equal schools. But Frankfurter pounced on me with the assertion that I should have cross-appealed if I wanted a ruling on the constitutionality of segregation. Of course, we hadn't cross-appealed, because we wanted our case to be heard right away, along with the others. A cross-appeal would have had to await the other side's answer, defeating our purpose in waiving response. I argued that the Court should affirm the chancellor, not on the grounds he gave—desegregate because the black schools were physically inferior—but because segregation was unconstitutional. (That's what the Court ultimately did.)

But I felt that I was in a cul-de-sac and couldn't get off that issue into anything else I wanted to talk about. At the mid-afternoon break we hastily conferred and agreed that Thurgood could use the balance of my time more profitably by concluding the Delaware argument and folding all the cases together. He rushed to the clerk's office to ask permission to change the batting order. The clerk, Harold Willey, who had been in the bathroom, came running out, his suspenders dangling, and hastened to convey word to the justices that Thurgood would wrap up.

It all seemed rather curious. They had turned our world upside down with a demand for the most exhaustive historical research ever conducted for a Supreme Court case, and with inordinately difficult questions about implementation. Then they gave most of their attention to whether we had live lawsuits or issues. Even if they were to get rid of Topeka, Wilmington, and the District on mootness grounds, South Carolina and Virginia would continue to stare them in the face. Did they, perhaps, not care about the history? Or were the questions at oral argument just a game justices play?

Most of us assumed that we would win, but with the exception of Spotts Robinson and Jim Nabrit, who spent a long evening analyzing the Court, none of us concluded that we would win unanimously. The rest of us vacillated in our predicted outcomes from five to four, to six to three, to seven to two. The general view was that Justice Jackson was opposed to segregation (not least because he just had returned from prosecuting the Nazis at Nuremburg), but was leaning toward deciding that Congress should end it, not the Court. Douglas and Black in many ways had shown that they were on our side—they had opposed sending the South Carolina case back for findings about equalization as not relevant—and would be safe votes. As to Frankfurter, we followed Bill Coleman's intuition. Frankfurter had hired him as the first black law clerk on the Supreme Court. He always voted right in civil rights cases involving blacks, with the arguable exception of not having joined the dissenters in the second *Sipuel* case, going along with calling for a further hearing. He had been on the NAACP National Legal Committee. Bill thought he would vote with us. Tom Clark, although a Texan, had always voted right in civil rights matters. Thurgood knew him personally and felt good about his vote. But personal relationships were not always good predictors of how a justice might come down.

A case in point had been Oliver Hill's optimism about Vinson, who had written the opinions favoring us in *Sweatt* and other cases. Oliver's wife's brother, Armistead Walker, had been Vinson's chauffeur, and when Vinson moved from the Senate to the Supreme Court, he made Armistead his bailiff there. Armistead was so close to the Vinson family that Oliver, his wife, and son became friendly with them too. So much so that Oliver once seated his son Oliver, Jr. (Dukey), in the chief justice's chair in the Supreme

Court, hoping that some day he would attain that position on his own. When, much later, records of the Court's conferences revealed that before his death Vinson had been against us, Oliver was dismayed—personal friendship and official positions about blacks were not necessarily related.

There were no clear views about Minton, who was perceived as possibly negative, or Burton, who seemed to be a possible favorable vote. Reed was counted by everyone as pretty much against us. There was general optimism that we would win by some margin, however, because we were on a roll. Until then we hadn't lost any case, although at times the victory had been empty, as in *Sipuel*, where the Court ducked facing up to Oklahoma's refusal to integrate.

At Davis, Polk, John W. Davis's law firm, the lawyers saw things differently. Davis assigned two young lawyers to the case, Sydnor Thompson, a 1950 Harvard Law School graduate, who sat next to him at the oral argument, and William C. Meagher, as well as Taggart Whipple, who supervised the younger lawyers. Nothing at all like the immense army we assembled. Thompson, who came from Lynchburg, Virginia, recently recalled that he spent 322 hours, 15 minutes, on the case, writing the principal part of the brief, including the history of the Fourteenth Amendment, which Davis touched up. Meagher wrote the part dealing with the history of ratification in the states. Thompson's researchers absolutely convinced him that Congress had no concept of abolishing school segregation. When he read our brief he couldn't see how we could have reached the opposite conclusion.

As Davis and his colleagues counted the votes, they believed they had Reed and Jackson on their side at the very least. They had reason to be optimistic about Frankfurter, because they thought he wouldn't want the courts to become involved in administering school desegregation. There was chance at Clark and maybe, out there, another vote or two to make a majority for their side. Davis did not contemplate the possibility that they could lose unanimously. But once, when Thompson was in the library, another young associate pointed a finger at him, looked him in the eye, and asked, "Do you ever think you're on the wrong side?"

PART III

BROWN DECIDED:

EYES ON THE FUTURE

15

A HISTORIC TURN

VICTORY

Thurgood got a tip that the School Segregation Cases would be decided on May 17, 1954, the last day of the Court's term, and went to Washington to hear Earl Warren read the opinion in *Brown v. Board of Education*, a name now instantly recognized by almost every American. In what may well have been the most important Supreme Court decision of the century, maybe ever, we won unanimously. Though the opinion itself was relatively brief and simple (there was a separate and even shorter one for the District of Columbia), it touched on all the stubborn points that had bedeviled civil rights lawyers over the years: the history, the precedents, and harm done by segregation. The historical sources "at best . . . are inconclusive," the Court held. Moreover, because public education was rudimentary at the end of the Civil War, "it is not surprising that there should be so little in the history of the Fourteenth Amendment relating to its intended effect on public education." We had fought the opposition to a draw on the history.

The history, however, deserves an additional word. While the Court could not conclude that the amendment or its framers and ratifiers "intended" that there be either segregated or nonsegregated schools, in effect it accepted our way of looking at the question of intent, embracing the view that there was a clear intent to prohibit state discrimination that might stigmatize black people as inferior. It did not matter whether or not the framers had been thinking of education at the time. This was the moral and religious notion of equality that, we had argued, the Fourteenth Amendment constitutionalized.

The precedents? The Court adopted our view again: *Plessy* was a travel case and didn't pertain to education; other school cases based on *Plessy* were irrelevant. *Sweatt* and *McLaurin* found inequality in the fact that segregation inhibited the plaintiffs' "ability to study, to engage in discussions and exchange views with other students, and, in general, to learn [their] profession," and that "such considerations apply with added force to children in grade and high schools."

Quoting the Kansas District Court, which had adopted the God-given eloquence of Louisa Holt, the psychologist who testified for us, the Supreme Court cited the harm that segregation inflicts on black children—that it denotes a sense of inferiority and retards their educational and mental development. *Plessy*, it will be recalled, had made a contrary social scientific assertion that "the underlying fallacy" of the plaintiff's argument was the assumption that segregation "stamps the colored race with a badge of inferiority," but if so, it would be "solely because the colored race chooses to put that construction upon it." To this, the Supreme Court replied: "Whatever may have been the extent of psychological knowledge at the time of *Plessy v. Ferguson*, [the finding that segregation is harmful] is amply supported by modern authority. Any language in *Plessy v. Ferguson* contrary to this finding is rejected."

Here the Court placed a footnote, footnote 11 at the bottom of the page, citing works by Kenneth Clark, other social scientists, and Gunnar Myrdal's *An American Dilemma*. The footnote became tremendously controversial, giving rise to charges that *Brown* was based on social science, not law. But, of course, *Plessy*'s contention that no real harm comes about from the stigma of forced segregation was based on the then current understanding of social science factors.

The questions the decision did not address were those dealing with relief, making no determination about how segregation might be dismantled. It scheduled the cases for another argument on the last two of its five questions, in which it had asked for comments and ideas on how the change might be brought about if the Court were to decide as it eventually did.

There remained the District of Columbia case. Because the Fourteenth Amendment applies only to the states, and the District of Columbia is not a state, it is governed by the Fifth Amendment's provision, which prohibits the United States from denying life, liberty, or property without due process of law. Liberty, the Court held, "extends to the full range of conduct which the individual is free to pursue. . . . In view of our decision that the Constitution prohibits the states from maintaining racially segregated public schools, it would be unthinkable that the same Constitution would impose a lesser duty on the Federal Government."

That the *Brown* decision was unanimous is universally attributed to Earl Warren's political skills in bringing along some of the doubters, including Jackson and Reed, likely the strongest dissenter. Bill Coleman says that Frankfurter also worked on Reed, telling him that a dissent is written for the future, but that there was no future for segregation.

Thurgood rushed to a telephone and called me with the news. I immediately called Roy Wilkins and Walter White. Thurgood also called Kenneth

Clark, who was teaching a class, which he left to receive the news. The switchboards at the Association and LDF began lighting up. Walter called a press conference, which he dominated while Thurgood sat quietly. After every other Supreme Court victory we had celebrated with a raucous, boozy party. But after *Brown* there was quiet. It was all so awesome. We still didn't know what it meant or where it would lead. Besides, if the decision were not to become merely a moral victory, we had to prepare for the argument on the relief questions.

Two days after the decision we had a dinner for the lawyers and leading witnesses at the Roosevelt Hotel. Kenneth Clark recalls that Thurgood asked Bill Coleman and Bob Ming to bow down to him and admit they were wrong.

Sydnor Thompson, the lawyer who wrote South Carolina's brief in *Brown*, today practices in Charlotte, North Carolina, where he is a friend of Julius Chambers, who succeeded me as head of LDF. Back then he had had difficulty understanding Stuart Marks, a young associate who challenged him about his role in the case. But now he says, "I thank God every day we lost the case. It was an idea whose time had come." John W. Davis refused to take a fee from the state of South Carolina and in lieu of payment, Governor Byrnes sent him a silver tea service, which was displayed in the law firm's library. On it was an inscription stating that it was a gift from the people of South Carolina. Stuart Marks notes that despite the donor identification, the gift givers did not likely include the black people of South Carolina.

FIRST REACTIONS

A week later, the Court summarily vacated, for reconsideration in light of *Brown*, judgments in two university cases and a junior college case. The order said, in effect, that now that we were into the next step, desegregation at elementary and high school levels, the Court would tolerate no more fooling around in higher education. Significantly, in the Louisville City Amphitheatre case, which presented the state action question of whether a lessee of the city could exclude blacks, the Court vacated the judgment of the court of appeals "for consideration in the light of the Segregation Cases . . . and conditions that now prevail." While *Brown* may have seemed to have nothing to do with that issue, the order illustrated that its power reached beyond the question of segregation in schools.

In February 1955, to prepare for the second reargument, June Shagaloff wrote a memorandum detailing desegregation since May 17, 1954. Some parochial schools and public and private colleges and universities, inspired by *Brown*, had desegregated. June's memorandum detailed the experiences in Southern black children in formerly all-white schools.

But those who had come up with an assortment of foot-dragging schemes

to frustrate the intent of the Court in the higher education cases now out-
did themselves in attempting to deny black children the fruits of the victory
they had won in the nation's highest court. Florida enacted a complex procedural scheme, known as "pupil placement," soon adopted across the
South. Districts assigned black children to black schools and required them
to apply for transfer, virtually always finding a basis to turn them down.
Criteria included the effect of admitting children upon "orderly and effi-
cient administration," "effective instruction," and "health, safety, education and general welfare." Louisiana made its contribution to legal anarchy
by adopting a constitutional amendment, soon copied elsewhere, that provided that "all public elementary and secondary schools in the State of
Louisiana shall be operated separately for white and colored children."

Equally disturbing, mobs took their cue from their political leaders and a
movement of massive resistance was born. In September 1954, to protest
enrollment of eleven black high school freshmen in downstate Delaware
Milford High School, fifteen hundred whites met at the American Legion
hall. The superintendent closed the schools. The state board ordered them
reopened with the black children in attendance, and criticized the local
board for not having consulted the state before taking action. The local
board resigned and the state took over. Four thousand whites then rallied at
an airport meeting led by Bryant Bowles, president of the National Association for the Advancement of White People. Schools reopened, surrounded
by reporters, cameramen, and hundreds of white protestors. Police escorted
the black children into school, but a new local board expelled them. I went
with Lou Redding to the edge of the demonstration, observing the mobs.
We drew up a complaint and won a court order requiring that the black kids
be readmitted.

H. Albert Young, the state attorney general, a Republican, backed us,
saying that the court order would be enforced even if it takes "the governor
of Delaware and our two United States senators to lead these Negro children by the hand back into the Milford school." But he was immediately
repudiated by Republican Senator John J. Williams and Delaware's other
senator, a Democrat. The state supreme court stayed the chancellor's order
and the black children remained out.

Lou lost the appeal, the court holding that although segregation was
unconstitutional, the local school board had not followed proper procedure
in admitting the blacks. It would have taken no great ingenuity to uphold
the admission of the black children, simply a declaration that whatever the
procedural defect, the constitutional rights of black children were more
important. The Milford outcome presaged how many state courts would
treat school segregation issues in the following years: uphold *Brown* rhetorically, but frustrate it by allowing the imposition of justice-mocking procedural obstacles.

Defiance of the spirit of the law did not immediately establish itself in all areas that had formerly segregated. In West Virginia partial integration took place in over half the state's districts. But Milford was followed by similar demonstrations in White Sulphur Springs, West Virginia, in Washington, D.C., and in Baltimore. Milford led to smashing Republican defeats in Delaware elections and destroyed Young's political career—he had hoped to run for senator. The lessons were clear for demagogues and politicians alike: Violent opposition could intimidate courts and political disaster might attend support for the law.

One consequence was that blacks, who continued to be assigned initially to black schools, became reluctant to apply to attend school with whites. Though there was little that lawsuits could do about violence and intimidation, or the fear it engendered in black parents for the safety of their young children, we tried to deal with it. Connie Motley, after a trip to Florida where she met with NAACP branches, wrote that we must convince "Negroes that there is much more to be gained than lost under an integrated set up." Dan Byrd helped prepare ten Louisiana undergraduate and trade school cases and fifteen elementary and secondary school cases for filing, and accompanied black students to the schools. Byrd exhorted the black community to vote and to demand integrated education across Mississippi. June Shagaloff organized black families in Northern communities. Bill Hastie proposed that we create a "flying squadron," consisting mostly of whites of significant reputation, to speak out publicly, and another group with knowledge and experience in community education to "work on teachers and children" to muster support for school integration.

The Philip Murray Foundation, named after the late president of the CIO, gave us $75,000. We put half into educational materials, including a film, the other half into field work. We hired three new workers to assist June Shagaloff and Dan Byrd in urging the black community to seek desegregation and advising how best to accomplish it. Thurgood hired Dr. John W. Davis, a great black educator, once president of West Virginia State College, formerly an all-black school, which he led toward integration even before *Sweatt*, and at that time head of United States aid missions in West Africa, to head up a department of Teacher Information and Security to protect black teachers.

But as whites in great numbers across the South defied the law, egged on by political leaders who pledged defiance forever, blacks balked at relying for their children's safety on the protection of nine black-robed men in Washington. They needed evidence that white officials were prepared to enforce the law, and this assurance was not forthcoming from those in charge of law enforcement. Though progress was made here and there, real changes in attitudes, among blacks and whites, would not come about until the civil rights movement arrived in 1960 with the sit-ins. Although our cases had paved the way for some of what was to come, we would not get to see the concrete results of our work until others had reinforced our courtroom victories in the streets.

Joining the backlash against our victory, the Internal Revenue Service threatened our tax exemption. In September 1954 Thurgood distributed to the executive committee a Treasury Department letter requesting information about our activities between 1951 and the first half of 1954, for the purpose of determining whether we would continue to be tax exempt. At a later meeting he reported, "There is a strong possibility that our tax-exempt status might be taken away. . . . One of the rumored regulations would prohibit participation in any social reform program of a controversial nature."

We retained Adrian W. (Bill) DeWind, the tax partner at Paul, Weiss, who waived any fee and represented us. Bill reported that the Treasury officials told him frankly that they needed a result that would satisfy Southern congressmen and senators.

CHANGES

As we prepared for the second reargument Walter White died; Roy Wilkins succeeded him as secretary of the NAACP. Old conflicts surfaced for the last time when—because we had no pension or insurance plan—the LDF board voted to make gifts of $1,200 to Poppy Cannon, Walter's wife at the time of his death, and $2,400 to Gladys, whom he had divorced a few years earlier.

In February 1955 Vivian (Buster) Marshall died of cancer, Thurgood having been at her bedside, almost without interruption, for months. During this period he lost so much weight that he became cadaverous in appearance. In March the board voted to "make available [to him] the sum of $600 . . . for the purpose of a short cruise at the expense of the Corporation during this interval between now and the argument of the school cases . . . as a necessary precaution to preserve Mr. Marshall's health as a result of the great strain he has been under both personally and with respect to his official duties."

In fact, Thurgood went to Mexico, where he visited with my cousin in Mexico City and stayed at a spa in San Jose Purua. At the end of the year he married Cecilia (Cissy) Suyat, who had been a secretary at the Association, at St. Philip's Episcopal Church on 134th Street. Shelton Hale Bishop, St. Philip's rector, performed the ceremony. Later there was a party at the Roosevelt Hotel, where we had often held board meetings.

THE IMPLEMENTATION BRIEF

The urgent task at hand was to prepare a brief on how to implement *Brown*. In June the executive committee resolved: "While recognizing the need for administrative adjustments from a segregated to a desegregated school system in any community, we are opposed to any time beyond the actual time needed for such administrative adjustment."

Our opening brief was short and pointed: In the normal course of events, the decision would be put into effect "forthwith" or by September 1955. Should the states desire postponement, "the affirmative burden must be on them" to state what they propose and to justify it, in light of the fact that black children were suffering serious injury. The brief reviewed data that Kenneth Clark had gathered on experience with desegregation and asserted that "gradualism, far from facilitating the process, may actually make it more difficult. . . . This, like many wrongs, can be easiest and best undone, not by 'tapering off' but by forthright action." The brief argued that the local conditions that might be taken into account should include only "variations in administrative organization, physical facilities, school population and pupil redistribution," and should not include "need for community preparation" and "threats of racial hostility and violence." It suggested that whatever "the reasons for gradualism . . . if the Court decides to grant further time . . . September, 1956 [should be] the outside date by which desegregation must be accomplished."

In another brief filed after argument, we submitted two forms of district court decree: (1) declaring segregation unconstitutional, and ordering schools to "cease using race as a basis of determining admission . . . in public schools . . . so that no later than . . . September, 1955, plaintiffs . . . will be attending schools on a basis not involving race"; (2) allowing that if defendants could show, by August 15, 1955, that "administrative factors . . . would cause serious and substantial dislocation" and submitted a plan to "eliminate as soon as feasible but in no event later than September 1, 1956, racial segregation" and provided for commencement of transition in 1955, the district court might allow them one more year to achieve integration.

While briefs often are a joint effort and a particular writer's product often is unknowable, the conclusion to our reply brief displays Charlie Black's unmistakable style:

> Appellants recognize that the problems confronting this Court as it turns to the implementation of its decision in these cases are of primary magnitude. Their high seriousness is enhanced by the fact that sovereign states are in effect, though not formally, at the bar and the evil to which the Court's decree must be directed is no transitory wrong but is of the essence of the social structure of a great section of our nation.
>
> Yet, it should be borne in mind that the very magnitude of these problems exists because of the assumption, tacitly indulged up to now, that the Constitution is not to be applied in its full force and scope to all sections of this country alike, but rather that its guarantees are to be enjoyed, in one part of our nation, only as molded and

modified by the desire and customs of the dominant component of the sectional population. Such a view, however expressed, ignores the minimum requirement for a truly national constitution. It ignores also a vast part of the reality of the sectional interest involved, for that interest must be composed of the legitimate aspirations of Negroes as well as whites.

The government's position in many respects was unexceptionable: Time might be allowed for administrative, procedural, fiscal, regulatory, and related changes. We wouldn't deny that. It also maintained that "general community hostility cannot serve as justification for avoiding or postponing compliance." Our position, too. But the government adopted a yielding tone that delivered a message encouraging accommodation, not resolve. One passage, said to have been drafted by President Eisenhower himself, counseled:

> The Court's decision in these cases has outlawed a social institution which has existed for a long time in many areas throughout the country—an institution, it may be noted, which during its existence not only has had the sanction of decisions of this Court but has been fervently supported by great numbers of people as justifiable on legal and moral grounds. The Court's holding in the present cases that segregation is a denial of constitutional rights involved an express recognition of the importance of psychological and emotional factors. . . . In similar fashion, psychological and emotional factors are involved—and must be met with understanding and good will—in the alterations that must now take place in order to bring about compliance with the Court's decision.

The defendants, along with the six other Southern states, filed briefs offering grounds for delay: "sustained hostility," withdrawal of white children from public schools, racial tensions, violence, loss of jobs for black teachers, the loss of legislative support for or even the destruction of the school systems. Virginia argued that blacks scored far lower on IQ tests than whites and had higher levels of tuberculosis, venereal disease, and illegitimacy than whites. North Carolina argued that in some counties one-third of the black children were retarded, and to integrate them would create "more numerous and more serious administrative and instructional difficulties" than it would to integrate in counties with few black children.

THE SECOND REARGUMENT

The second reargument took four days, beginning April 11, 1955. The Court invited every state with school segregation laws to submit briefs and argue.

Topeka, Delaware, and the District of Columbia purported to have desegregated, or to be well on the way. Yet each allowed transfers or grandfather clauses that permitted both black and white children to attend schools where their own race was in the majority, continuing a large measure of segregation. The Deep Southern states were downright defiant. I. Beverly Lake, one of the leaders of the resistance in North Carolina, told the Court that his state had appointed a commission that concluded: "The mixing of the races forthwith in the public schools throughout the state cannot be accomplished and should not be attempted."

Lake argued that the state, by forcing integration, "could abolish the public school system." When Justice Frankfurter countered, "It could bring up its children in ignorance if it wanted to," Lake responded, "It could do that also."

John W. Davis had died since the May 17 decision and the local school board lawyer, S. E. Rogers, argued for South Carolina. He told the Court: "I am frank to tell you, right now in our district I do not think that we will send—the white people of the district will send their children to the Negro schools."

Earl Warren asked, "You are not willing to say here that there would be an honest attempt to conform to this decree, if we did leave it to the district court?"

Rogers replied, "No, I am not. Let us get the word 'honest' out of there."

Warren, restraining his fury, responded, "No, leave it in."

But Rogers persisted, "No, because I would have to tell you that right now we would not conform—we would not send our white children to the Negro schools."

THE ATLANTA DECLARATION

Less than a week later the NAACP met in Atlanta and announced in the "Atlanta Declaration" that "we approach the future with the utmost confidence." It proposed to "resist the use of any tactics contrived for the sole purpose of delaying desegregation," and to "accelerate our community action program to win public acceptance." It insisted that there be no discrimination against teachers. At the annual convention in June the Association called on Southern branches to get "signatures of as many parents of children in public schools [as possible] on petitions," and to "engage local counsel immediately."

Nothing could better illustrate the gap between successful litigation to secure rights and the actual enjoyment of those rights than the difficulties that beset our office messenger shortly after *Brown II*. Two police officers came to the office and arrested him on a charge of grand larceny. Everyone was astonished—he was such a nice young man. One of the lawyers who knew his mother called her. She seemed to know what it was all about, but wanted nothing to do with it. We reached our young messenger by phone at the police precinct, but he politely declined our assistance. The next morning he returned to work as if nothing had happened. A legal aid lawyer had arranged his release. The charges had been lodged by his former girlfriend, to whom he had given a ring. When he took the ring back she reported it to the police as a larceny, although it was a run-of-the-mill lover's quarrel. I said, "Ronnie, I don't understand. Here, you've been working with us for years. We are the lawyers who won *Brown v. Board of Education* and all sorts of other cases in the Supreme Court. Yet, instead of allowing us to help, you turned to the Legal Aid Society." He replied, "Mr. Greenberg, I didn't want to go to the Supreme Court. I just wanted to get out."

"WITH ALL DELIBERATE SPEED"

On May 31, 1955, in a virtually unprecedented opinion, the Court sent the School Segregation Cases back to the district courts. Having decided in 1954 that blacks had constitutional rights, it then paradoxically announced that they might continue to be denied the exercise of those rights for an indeterminate time. For how long? The Court spoke with forked tongue: under one interpretation, hardly any time at all, under another, perhaps indefinitely. At the outset the Court made clear that "constitutional principles cannot be allowed to yield simply because of disagreement with them." It required that school districts "make a prompt and reasonable start toward full compliance" with the Court's ruling. It then allowed more time to comply—but "at the earliest practicable date." To warrant allowance of additional time courts might take into account problems related to "administration, arising from physical condition of the school plant, the school transportation system, personnel, revision of school districts and attendance areas into compact units to achieve a system of determining admission to the public schools on a nonracial basis, and revision of local laws and regulations which may be necessary in solving the foregoing problems."

It would be difficult to argue that systems shouldn't be allowed time to accomplish such major changes. What nullified any sense that desegregation should proceed with dispatch, with only brief delays for administrative adjustments, was the final paragraph of the Court's opinion, which called for district courts to "enter such orders and decrees consistent with this opinion as are necessary and proper to admit to public schools on a racially nondiscriminatory basis *with all deliberate speed* the parties to these cases."

ELSEWHERE

As the law changed and there was not much we could do to desegregate schools promptly, black migration from South to North accelerated. As a consequence, the number of blacks affected by a decision prohibiting segregation required by statute (in the South) continued to diminish, while the number of black school children increased in the North, where racial concentrations, created by school board or administrative practices, not statutes, could not then be touched by the courts. Moreover, the growing number of urban blacks who were forced into ghettoes created or gave rise to new pathologies that would create further resistance to desegregation. Nevertheless, general measures of black education improved over this period.

College- and secondary-level school cases continued in lower courts. Connie Motley's housing docket could have kept a small law firm busy. We had a half-dozen recreation cases. After Judge Thomsen ruled in Baltimore that the beaches had been equalized and might be resegregated, I argued that the School Cases required integrating the beaches, but Thomsen decided that *Brown* covered schools only. Bob Carter argued the appeal and the Fourth Circuit promptly reversed. The Supreme Court affirmed in November 1955. I came to despise Thomsen's sanctimonious manner; he seemed to me to be devoid of any sense of justice.

In Bob's case before the Interstate Commerce Commission, the examiner recommended that segregation be prohibited aboard trains and in terminals, but permitted in terminal restaurants leased to private operators.

While the *Brown* decision provided new impetus to the idea that racial justice was part of America's wave of the future, there was no immediate and wholesale transformation of American racial practices.

CRIMINAL CASES

I worked also on a half-dozen criminal cases during this period, including that of seventeen-year-old Jeremiah Reeves, who had an eighth-grade education and was mentally unstable. The Birmingham, Alabama, police held him incommunicado for two days, questioning him in the presence of the electric chair about a series of rapes, to which he confessed. The state indicted him in six cases, three of them capital. Birmingham was 43.6 percent black, but the jury "box," from which jurors were chosen, was only 8 percent black. The judge closed the trial to the public and press. One juror was chief of the reserve police. After all, he said, "I am a member of the Naval Reserve and that doesn't enter into my qualifications." I argued the appeal in the Supreme Court in mid-November 1954 and won three weeks later on the grounds that Reeves's confession had been coerced. The Court's order relied on two earlier NAACP/LDF cases. In criminal law, as elsewhere, we developed the jurisprudence—of confessions, right to counsel, jury discrimination—on which further LDF cases, and those of the rest of the country, depended. But it turned out to be another hollow victory; following the undoing of the first conviction Reeves was tried again and executed.

We received a steady stream of requests to oppose extradition of escaped prisoners from the South who sought asylum in the North. Southern prison conditions were intolerable; the chain gang was notorious. But, while a governor might refuse to extradite, courts had no power to prevent extradition. Some cases suggested that if no relief from abuse were available in the state from which a prisoner had fled, perhaps a court in the state to which he escaped might prohibit extradition. Other cases made something of the fact that the state that wanted the prisoner returned hadn't been represented in the habeas corpus proceeding in which the escapee tried to prevent extradition. Perhaps if the state from which the prisoner escaped had its day in court and lost that would have been the end of it.

In one case I tried to prevent the extradition of Jesse Dukes, who, at the age of twelve, was tried in Georgia, without counsel, and sentenced to fifteen to twenty-five years on the chain gang for the theft of five automobiles. He was beaten, placed in a sweat box for twelve days, and forced to wear iron picks on his legs. Dukes couldn't read or write; he couldn't drive, either. He escaped to New Jersey, where his sister lived, was caught and returned to Georgia. After twelve years he escaped again to New Jersey and was picked up on a Georgia warrant. Mendon Morrill, later to become a federal judge, was Dukes's New Jersey lawyer.

In my petition to the Supreme Court I tried to fit Dukes's case within the possible narrow exceptions of a defendant who couldn't get a fair hearing in the state to which he was being returned. But the Supreme Court denied review. We then tried to persuade the governor not to send him back. Fredric Wertham examined him and concluded that with proper treatment he could be rehabilitated. But New Jersey's governor returned him to Georgia, in part because Dukes kept getting in trouble in prison in New Jersey. Paul Moore, then a priest in Jersey City, took a particular interest in Dukes. He reported that "Dukes is really a pretty sick fellow mentally, but there doesn't seem to be anything that can be done about it now."

A Philadelphia lawyer asked us to fight extradition of Edward Brown, another Georgia chain gang escapee. Guards had beaten him, forced liniment into his rectum, placed him repeatedly in a sweat box, and fed him only bread and water, once a day. Witnesses corroborated his allegations. Using a study prepared by a University of Pennsylvania law professor, I showed that in the past decade no Georgia prisoner had filed an application for habeas corpus; this tended to support the argument that Georgia prisoners had no access to the courts. Moreover, Georgia lawyers had appeared at the extradition hearing in Pennsylvania, and therefore couldn't claim that the state didn't have its day in court. But the Supreme Court denied review.

In January 1954 the United States Supreme Court refused to hear Walter Irvin's appeal in the Groveland, Florida, rape case. I prepared a petition for federal habeas corpus—asking the federal courts to undo what the state courts had done—and a clemency application.

LDF GROWS AND CUTS THE UMBILICAL CORD

The LDF budget continued to grow—to $361,842 by the end of 1959. We got our first big bequest in 1959, about $140,000. We hired new lawyers, including James M. Nabrit III, Jim Nabrit, Jr.'s son, occasionally called "Little Jim" to distinguish him from his father, "Big Jim." Little Jim was, in fact, more than a head taller than his old man. A graduate of Bates College and Yale Law School, he began working as a cooperating lawyer for LDF in Frank Reeves's law firm in Washington and likes to trace his LDF contact back even further, to attending Bill Coleman's parents' summer camp, where Bill was his counselor.

Jim was an intense hobbyist. Not long after moving to New York he became an accomplished amateur magician, hanging out in magic supply shops, going to demonstrations, and putting on performances himself. He provided the entertainment at my son Josiah's bar mitzvah. Later he switched to horse racing, betting daily at New York Off Track Betting parlors, through his telephone account or at the track, where he used a powerful hand-held computer to take advantage of shifts in betting odds. He actually made money. He would take parties to the Belmont Stakes and other big races. Jim III put on, for the staff and visitors, what became his celebrated Kentucky Derby seminars. Held on the eve of the Derby, Jim would handicap the contenders while, of course, serving authentic mint juleps. Outsiders begged to be invited.

Jim also became an inveterate scuba diver and underwater photographer, taking annual trips to Bonaire—almost the only place he has gone on vacation for decades. Jim has visited Bonaire so regularly that he is acquainted with particular fish. Before the personal computer became widely known, he owned an Apple, which predated disk drives and ran on audio tape, and regaled his friends with computer games. Early on he began computerizing LDF.

In court Jim was highly persuasive, having prepared his cases with exceeding thoroughness, the same diligence he applied to his hobbies. He was particularly good with highly technical expert testimony and superb in patiently counseling younger lawyers, explaining how to analyze problems and marshal evidence. A great lawyer, his highest virtue was superb judgment, which I would consult unfailingly, even if I didn't always follow his advice. I may have been more willing than he to take chances, but when I acted contrary to his advice I took some comfort in the fact that at least I now better understood the risks.

By 1960 the board included leading black and white professional and business figures from all over the country, although as a sign of the times, the talented, effective women on the board enjoyed their status mainly through husbands or fathers—far from the situation at the LDF today.

The status of blacks in the law was exemplified by another board member, Francis Rivers. Born in Alabama, he had entered Yale in 1911, where the dean had requested that he move from the dormitory because whites objected to the presence of a black, despite his pink and white complexion and blue eyes. A graduate of Columbia Law School, early in his career Rivers rose as high as a black then could. He was elected to the state assembly in 1930, becoming the first black judge on the city court in 1943, then the highest judicial position held by a black in the country and the best paid position of any black in public office. Later, he became a judge of the civil court. In 1944 Rivers was the second black to become a member of the American Bar Association (Judge Jonah J. Goldstein, who sponsored Rivers, submitted his resignation when the rules for admission were changed to keep Rivers out and his application was delayed for more than five months); in the early forties Rivers became the first black member of the Association of the Bar of the City of New York. He conducted himself as one might imagine British nobility would, certainly in the manner of his daily lunch ritual of ordering a "martini, made with Tanqueray gin, up, with a twist."

Rivers's standing in the legal community served LDF well. Once, a young staff member, Fred Wallace, couldn't be admitted to the bar because he had been convicted in Virginia of assault on a sheriff during a voting rights demonstration. Rivers took me to visit Lowell Wadmond, a partner in a New York law firm, who chaired the bar's committee on character and fitness. Wadmond asked whether I would submit a statement that in my opinion Fred's conviction was illegal. I did, and Fred was admitted.

On another occasion, when New York State, uncomfortable with the proliferation of public interest law firms, enacted a law requiring that they register with the courts and furnish information about their operation, we were uncertain about how to comply and whether we could secure exceptions to certain provisions. Some organizations brought suit against the law. The NAACP claimed that the law didn't apply to it. I felt we were too busy defending the movement and pressing civil rights cases to take either course, risk noncompliance or bring suit. Judge Rivers took me to visit a judge of the appellate division. He waved off my questions with: "Oh, do anything reasonable, you're not the guys we're after." Not the way we liked to see the law work, but we submitted a registration form and went about more important business.

Some of the members increased access to funding and persons of influence, but we hardly rolled in money. Lois Jessup chaired theater benefits that might bring in a profit of $11,000 on $17,000 worth of ticket sales. Dorothy Rosenman had parties in her home at which well-to-do contributors might give a total of $10,000. Large dinners featuring Martin Luther King, Jr., George Meany, and other prominent figures brought in money.

The Committee of 100 mailed four or five appeals for donations each year. Smaller foundations, like Field, were faithful supporters at about $15,000 per year, but none of the great foundations supported us, although the Fund for the Republic, set up as an independent entity by the Ford Foundation to promote civil rights and liberties, gave $50,000 in October 1955. The Fund for the Republic later collapsed and was sometimes referred to as a "wholly disowned subsidiary of the Ford Foundation."

Our lease at 107 West Forty-third Street approached expiration; the offices were barely tolerable—the floors and walls were rickety, the elevator creaked and sometimes reeked of urine—and Thurgood asked me to find new space. I found a real estate broker who, after a great deal of trouble finding the right space for us, became convinced that landlords were refusing to rent to us because we were a black organization. He then began negotiations for space without disclosing his principal and found ideal offices in the brand-new Coliseum Building at 10 Columbus Circle. When he revealed who we were, the agent replied that there had been a mistake, the space in fact was rented.

The Coliseum office building was owned by the Triborough Bridge and Tunnel Authority. Hulan Jack, the first black borough president of Manhattan, was a member of the authority's board of directors and I suggested that Thurgood call him to enlist his help. Thurgood did. A few days later the rental agent told us that equivalent space was available on another floor. At the end of the year we moved to 3,050 square feet of space costing $17,000 per year. We were on the seventeenth floor, with wonderful views of the city, and everyone had small but comfortable offices. Thurgood had a somewhat larger one, with a desk topped by an enormous overhanging surface that I likened to the deck of an aircraft carrier, but his imposing presence made the size seem right. Secretaries were ranged outside lawyers' offices in a light, almost spacious hall and there was a decent library with a conference table. I fully appreciated how high up in the world we had come when I entered the aroma-free elevator and it sped upward.

16

THE SPIRIT OF BLACK REVOLT STIRS AND JIM CROW FIGHTS BACK

THE COMMUNITY MOBILIZES: THE MONTGOMERY BUS BOYCOTT

In the Margold Report Nathan Margold had argued in favor of the litigation campaign in part because "the psychological effect upon Negroes themselves will be that of stirring the spirit of revolt among them." How right he turned out to be. Soon after the decision in *Brown* was reported, in December 1955, Rosa Parks, who was secretary of the Montgomery, Alabama, branch of the NAACP, refused to move to the back of the bus when a white person demanded her seat. In many towns of the South there was a fixed partition line between the black and white sections, but in Montgomery whites filled seats from the front and blacks from the back. When there weren't enough seats for whites, blacks were supposed to give up their seats, whether or not there were empty seats for them farther back in the bus.

A dozen years earlier Rosa Parks had engaged in a similar act of defiance, which had been pretty much ignored, and she resumed obedience to the Jim Crow law. However, in the post-*Brown* South the reaction to her refusal to yield her seat was different. Her impulsive act of defiance was the impetus behind the 1955 Montgomery bus boycott led by Martin Luther King, Jr. The entire black community refused to patronize the buslines until they reformed their discriminatory seating practices. Dr. King was catapulted into world prominence.

Indicating how modest their demands were at that early stage of the movement, the Montgomery protestors didn't seek nonsegregated seating. At first they only wanted not to be forced to give up seats when there weren't enough for whites. What was most important about the boycott was that the community organized and stuck together. Car pools and ride-sharing plans were devised. An overwhelming majority of the black community participated in the boycott, so that businessmen who depended on the buses to bring them their black customers, as well as the buslines themselves, were financially hurt by the boycott.

Bob Carter, assisting Arthur Shores and two newly admitted lawyers, Fred Gray and Orzell Billingsley (the three were perhaps half the black bar of Alabama), defended Parks and King against prosecution for leading the boycott. Both were convicted, but lost the right to appeal because their Alabama lawyers filed their papers late. But, before Alabama could carry out their punishment, we won another case in the Supreme Court in November 1956 holding segregation on Montgomery buses unconstitutional—a rejection of *Plessy*, which also had been an intrastate transportation case. That ended the boycott; there was nothing left to boycott and there was no way to prosecute the former boycotters successfully.

Still, segregation on buses died hard. In 1958 we had to file another bus case in Memphis, which the district court dismissed because it was a test case. The Supreme Court reversed.

BACKLASH AND DEFAULT AT THE TOP

While the Montgomery boycott expressed a revitalized passion to put an end to the racial injustices, recognition of which had been at the heart of the Court's reasoning in *Brown*, the decision inspired the very opposite reaction among many whites who remained unaware of, or uncaring about, the damage systematic segregation inflicted upon American blacks. Among those who might have had some positive influence, President Dwight Eisenhower expressed his antipathy in refusing to endorse the Court's decision or to provide national leadership beyond saying that "I think it makes no difference whether or not I endorse it. The Constitution is as the Supreme Court interprets it; and I must conform to that and do my very best to see that it is carried out in this country." He also said, "It is difficult through law and through force to change a man's heart," which hardly encouraged compliance. Such statements by the president of the country, which could be read as a rejection of the wisdom in the Court's decision, surely encouraged some to express themselves in more extreme fashion.

But if the executive branch was derelict, Congress was downright antagonistic. In 1956, 101 congressmen—19 senators and 82 House members—all from states of the former Confederacy, signed the Southern Manifesto (among Southerners, only Lyndon Johnson, Estes Kefauver, and Albert Gore, Sr., refused to sign) denouncing *Brown* as having "substitute[d] naked power for established law."

Senators and representatives introduced numerous Court-bashing bills. Senator Strom Thurmond of South Carolina declared that the Court was "a great menace to this country" and called for the impeachment of justices who had voted to curtail the anticommunism campaigns of Congress. In

1958, prosegregationists, states rights advocates, and anti-Communists launched the most serious assault against the authority of *Brown*, the Jenner-Butler bill. It would have deprived the Supreme Court of jurisdiction over the practice of law in state courts (responding to a decision that prohibited disbarring an alleged Communist); over the conduct of congressional committees (to counteract a decision that had required a committee's questioning of a witness before it pass a "test of pertinency to legitimate legislative powers"); concerning executive employee loyalty–security programs; over state regulation of subversive activities; and with respect to school board regulations dealing with subversive activities among teachers. The proposals came quite close to passing. Only adroit parliamentary maneuvering, led by Lyndon Johnson, defeated the whole lot at the last minute.

The nation's legal and judicial establishments were hardly supportive of the supremacy of the Supreme Court in determining the law of the land. The Conference of State Chief Justices criticized the Supreme Court for decisions in cases involving subversion (the Communist issue) and the rights of defendants in criminal cases. A *U.S. News & World Report* survey of federal judges reported that a majority of those responding agreed with the state judges and believed that the Supreme Court "too often has tended to adopt the role of policymaker without proper judicial restraint." The National Association of State Attorneys General debated a resolution attacking the Court for decisions in cases involving the rights of criminal defendants. The resolution was defeated, but opponents used the opportunity to get off some serious criticisms of the High Court. The American Bar Association House of Delegates adopted resolutions recommending passage of legislation that would overturn recent Supreme Court decisions, especially those limiting the prosecution of Communists. The assault went beyond attacking the Court to assailing those who brought cases to it.

The federal government prosecuted Louis Redding for income tax evasion, but a Delaware jury acquitted him. I was a defense witness and knew, as was widely believed, that the prosecution really stemmed from his role in the School Cases. Virginia commenced disbarment proceedings against Sam Tucker, one of the state's few black lawyers, who had also been involved in the School Segregation Cases. But after a vigorous defense, charges were dropped.

Meanwhile, the John Birch Society splashed "Impeach Earl Warren" across billboards all over the country, attempting to foment a constitutional crisis at the very least, and national anarchy at the most. I saw pickets try to club Earl Warren with their signs as he entered the Association of the Bar of the City of New York for a meeting. While these were the acts of know-nothings and yahoos, often part of a calculated strategy to intimidate anyone who might want to implement *Brown*, they acquired a sort of respectability when highly regarded scholars and jurists expressed criticism of *Brown* in a more intellectual cast.

Learned Hand, then retired, but a man who had earned a special reputation as a federal appellate judge and legal scholar, gave a series of lectures that chastised the Court for having become a "third legislative chamber" and for having exceeded "its proper scope in some recent cases." Senator Albert Jenner used Hand's 1958 lecture series at Harvard Law School to promote his court-curbing bill. In a celebrated article, "Toward Neutral Principles of Constitutional Law," Herbert Wechsler, while personally opposed to segregation, took the Court to task for what he characterized as unprincipled decisions, mainly in civil rights, and *Brown* in particular. His most stinging charge was:

> If the freedom of association is denied by segregation, integration forces an association upon those for whom it is unpleasant or repugnant.... Where the state must practically choose between denying the association to those individuals who wish it or imposing it on those who would avoid it, is there a basis in neutral principles for holding that the Constitution demands that the claims for association should prevail? I should like to think there is, but I confess that I have not yet written the opinion.

Edmond Cahn, a highly regarded legal philosopher, in an article that expressed opposition to segregation, argued that *Brown* had come to the right result, agreed that segregation harms black children, asserted that the decision had not turned on the social scientific testimony and brief, but then excoriated Kenneth Clark and other social scientific witnesses, though he did so in polite language: "Merely translating a proposition of 'literary' psychology into the terms of technical jargon can scarcely make it a scientific finding."

Cahn refused to review my book *Race Relations and American Law* for the *New York Times* because, he told me, while he thought highly of the book, his review would be discredited by the fact that his son had married a black woman. That's how convoluted thinking became when race was the subject.

In Alabama, Georgia, Louisiana, Mississippi, North Carolina, South Carolina, and Virginia lopsided majorities in state referenda and constitutional ratification elections (in which blacks, still limited by violence, arbitrary officials, and all sorts of other strategies, had a hard time voting or couldn't vote at all) adopted laws and constitutional amendments that threatened to abolish public education whenever courts might require integration. These measures prohibited integration outright; required or permitted abolition of public schools; authorized sale of public schools to private groups (so that defendants could claim there was no state action); authorized public funds for segregated schools only; and made grants for private education. Related provisions in these states and in Arkansas repealed or modified compulsory school attendance laws. Alabama, Florida, Louisiana, North Carolina, and South Carolina changed teacher employment laws to frighten black teachers away from supporting desegregation and, they hoped, to enlist them in the effort to retain Jim Crow schools.

James Kilpatrick, editor of the Richmond *News Leader*, touted declarations of "interposition" and "nullification," in which eleven Southern states joined "to interpose their sovereignty between the Federal government and the object of its encroachments upon powers reserved to the States." If it weren't so serious, the orotund language would be grist for an H. L. Mencken–style lampoon of Southern pomposity. Most Southern states set up State Sovereignty Commissions or committees to study segregation that whipped up sentiment against desegregation. A Joint Legislative Committee for the Preservation of Segregation in the State of Louisiana placed an advertisement in the New York *Herald Tribune*, paid for from a public appropriation of $100,000, to attack segregation and defend the state's opposition to integration. When the NAACP protested, the *Tribune* asserted that it had published the advertisement in the "best tradition of a free press."

White citizens councils, states rights councils, the National Association for the Advancement of White People, and similar groups developed throughout the South. By mid-1957 they claimed as many as 80,000 members in Mississippi; 100,000 in Alabama; 40,000 in South Carolina; 20,000 in Texas; and 15,000 to 20,000 in North Carolina, Georgia, and Virginia. Membership included leading political figures, such as Senators Strom Thurmond of South Carolina; Herman Talmadge of Georgia, and James Eastland of Mississippi, and Governor Marvin Griffin of Georgia. These groups propagandized about school desegregation, intermarriage, and "mongrelization"; boycotted and harassed whites and Negroes who got out of line; and socially ostracized whites who seemed to be soft on segregation.

This broad-fronted resistance to the Court's authority fueled and validated uglier efforts, such as violence and threats of violence, bombings, and even murder. Ku Klux Klan activity and cross burnings erupted across the South. In Hoxie, Arkansas, white citizens councils tried to block the integration of twenty-five blacks into a school with one thousand whites. The school board, aided by the Justice Department, obtained a court order enjoining them. Behind the scenes we drafted the legal papers for the school board. In Clinton, Tennessee, a mob led by John Kasper of the white citizens council gathered at a school where twelve blacks had been admitted to a student body of more than eight hundred, picketed, and threw rocks and tomatoes. Though the governor called out the highway patrol and National Guard, a mob of fifty whites and adults chased black students and beat one of them. Members of the football team rescued the blacks, but attendance at the school dropped sharply. The principal, D. J. Brittain, Jr., brought suit against Kasper and, in a proceeding in which the Justice Department took part, the court sentenced him to one year in prison for contempt. In Texas, following a court order that Mansfield schools admit blacks, a mob of more than 250 persons threatened violence. Governor Allan Shivers announced that he would not "shoot down or intimidate Texas citizens who are making orderly protest against a situation instigated and agitated by the N.A.A.C.P. " When blacks registered to attend white schools in Clay and Sturgis, Kentucky, riots erupted that required calling in the National Guard. Similar mob scenes and boycotts developed in South Carolina, on the mere rumor that blacks would be admitted to a white school; Maryland; and Little Rock, Arkansas, in what developed into a national crisis. There were bombings and bomb threats in Tennessee, Alabama, Georgia, North Carolina, and elsewhere.

In April 1959, in Poplarville, Mississippi, whites broke into the local jail and lynched a black man, Mack Charles Parker, who was being held for trial on the charge of raping a white woman. The local paper saw the connection between the lynching and the broader attempt to intimidate blacks out of asserting their Court-won rights: "Reprehensible as the act of lynching is, it served to emphasize again the fact that force must not be used in pushing revolutionary change in social custom. Every action produces an equal and opposite reaction." As if they hadn't been lynching blacks before the Court upheld their rights!

SOUTHERN LEGAL EFFORTS TO DESTROY LDF

There was no doubt whom the South saw as the mastermind behind it all. In a coordinated effort, virtually every Southern state passed laws and started legislative investigations, criminal prosecutions, suits for injunction, and disbarment proceedings against lawyers to put the NAACP and LDF out of business. Neither the NAACP nor LDF had registered to "do business" outside New York, where they originally were incorporated, because they did not consider their activities to be "business." Nevertheless, under some interpretations, some states might have required them to so register.

On the weekend of June 10, 1956, Thurgood, Charlie Black, Bill Coleman, Spotts Robinson, Oliver Hill, Bob Ming, Lou Pollak, and I met at our office to shape a counterstrategy. We outlined model pleadings, focusing on denial of access to the courts, suppression of speech, the right of association, the right to assist in enforcing the law, the right to be free from self-incrimination, and other defenses. We also questioned whether the new laws had a reasonable relationship to purposes within the legislatures' power. As the cases unwound for over half a decade the defenses worked effectively.

In many Southern states the Association quickly registered; it sued for a declaratory judgment in North Carolina to determine whether it was required to register. But in 1956 Alabama got a temporary injunction in one of its state courts restraining the NAACP from doing business there, claiming it had not registered as a foreign (out-of-state) corporation, had refused to produce its membership list, had fomented the Montgomery bus boycott, and had paid Autherine Lucy to enroll at the University of Alabama.

When the Association tried to register, state courts prohibited it. The Association turned over much of the information Alabama requested, but withheld members' names to shield them from persecution, for which Alabama courts fined it $100,000. The case went to the United States Supreme Court four times, with Bob Carter representing the Association. The result was a complete victory, not only for the Association but for principles of freedom of speech and association. Alabama kept resisting through a series of shoddy procedural arguments until 1964; the NAACP was unable to function in the state for eight years.

Before the ultimate victory, a majority of the Association board resolved not to comply with the Alabama order to produce members' names even if it were ultimately required by the court to do so. Bill Hastie, however, counseled that they should obey:

> Certainly all members of the legal profession, and I would hope all responsible citizens, ought to consider very soberly whether there is justification for defying the authority of the duly constituted courts. . . . Certainly some of the extreme segregationists are completely honest in their misguided view that the Supreme Court's decision was arbitrary, unfair and contrary to their understanding of the Constitution. Our answer to them is that they must accept the authority of the courts whatever their personal views may be.

South Carolina enacted a law declaring that the NAACP had "as its major objective the fomenting and nurturing of a bitter feeling of unrest, unhappiness and resentment among members of the Negro race with their status in the social and economic structure of the south." (There was a certain amount of truth in this.) The law prohibited schools from employing Association members and authorized requiring from teachers "written oaths . . . regarding NAACP status." I filed a case for black teachers in Elloree, South Carolina, in which a three-judge court ruled against us. My main claim was that the law impaired freedom of association and speech because teachers who registered could expect reprisals. But John J. Parker, who had been chief judge of the three-judge court in *Briggs v. Elliott*, dissented on the ground that the law denied freedom of association. During the hearing he told the state's lawyer, "This goes to the roots of the republic." I appealed on April 22, 1957, but the next day South Carolina repealed the law, substituting one that required districts to demand that applicants list membership in associations. The Supreme Court rejected our appeal.

Arkansas, Florida, Georgia, Louisiana, North Carolina, Tennessee, Texas, and Virginia proceeded along similar lines. Florida went the route of having a state legislative committee investigate our activities; as part of the investigative process the committee demanded the NAACP member lists. When the Association refused to produce them, it was held in contempt. When the Association wouldn't produce names in Georgia, its courts imposed a $25,000 fine and sentenced Association officials to jail for contempt.

Virginia's assault ended in *NAACP v. Button*, which Bob won, holding that organizing for the purpose of bringing public interest litigation is a First Amendment right.

In the Texas case Thurgood, characteristically, took a pragmatic approach, deciding to settle for an outcome that would permit us to continue functioning, rather than risk the entire Texas operation in an attempt to get a decision holding the state's efforts unconstitutional. Many within the Association, however, wanted to resist to the end, even if it would mean being out of business in a state for years. In the end, Thurgood prevailed, but badly bruised feelings lingered.

The Texas case began in September 1956, when Texas Rangers swooped down on Association offices all over the state and seized records. At the same time a Texas assistant attorney general and an auditor appeared at the NAACP office in New York and demanded materials. After checking with LDF lawyers, staff members at the NAACP wouldn't give the Texans their membership files, but did give them other information. On September 21 the state sued the Association and LDF, and immediately got a temporary restraining order and later a longer-lasting injunction, prohibiting both organizations from doing business in Texas. In April 1957 the state went after a permanent injunction.

Attorney General Ben Shepperd tried the case himself, with eight assistants, three secretaries, and three auditors. Four TV cameras were set up in the courtroom. Thurgood, with W. J. Durham and C. B. Bunkley, represented the NAACP and LDF for months in out-of-the-way Tyler, Texas. In a touch worthy of a Hollywood script writer, the trial was broadcast daily on local radio, jointly sponsored, incredibly, by J. J. Jones, the Happy Undertaker, and the white citizens council. Shepperd, who may have been planning to run for the Senate, milked the situation for all it was worth.

In April 1957 the court permanently enjoined the Association from engaging in any activity in the state, including litigation and lobbying, but permitting "educational and charitable activities," which could, depending on how one looked at it, encompass most of what the Association did.

As to LDF, Thurgood and Durham worked out a compromise that permitted us to register and conduct all our normal activities, but prohibited solicitation of litigation, which we didn't do anyway. In other words, we could keep on doing what we had been doing, we just could no longer do what they had erroneously accused us of doing. I suspect that Durham, who was as influential as a black man then could be in Texas, had negotiated the "educational and charitable" and solicitation exceptions as part of a deal by which we would not appeal and Texas would not interfere with the Association and LDF activities.

Thurgood counseled against appeals: The exceptions would permit the Association to do what it had to do. As to LDF, it had always conducted itself carefully to avoid running afoul of solicitation laws. The trial had consumed enormous time, energy, and funds and when an opportunity for compromise presented itself Thurgood thought it better to get on with other matters. The alternative would be to risk a repeat of what had developed in Alabama, where the Association was out of business for the better part of a decade.

The problem was that some people on our side might see compromise as cowardice, and some on Texas's side might claim victory. Nevertheless, the LDF board went along with Thurgood and decided not to appeal. But the NAACP disagreed and, at a highly controversial meeting, ordered an appeal. Thurgood wrote to Bill Hastie:

> The board members were canvassed to come to the meeting for the specific purpose of voting against the recommendations of the lawyers. Typical of this is Gov. Lehman who had not been to a meeting for a few years. Roscoe Dunjee, ill with a bad heart, was also canvassed, and he had not been to a meeting for a longer period of time. As a result of that vote, we were in a terrific jam in Texas and thousands of dollars were spent on perfecting the appeal over the objections of the laywers.

Durham refused to appeal, withdrew from the case, and personally argued to the Association's board that appeal would be fruitless, that the existing decree would not inhibit the Association in any meaningful way, and that appeal might possibly lead to an even harsher decree. The board then changed its position and did not proceed with the appeal. The advice turned out to have been wise. The Association carried on normally in Texas, and LDF filed cases there, all without further harassment. But the abrasive internal disagreement, which took up parts of at least five NAACP board meetings over a year, left a toll in injured relationships, particularly between Thurgood and some NAACP board members.

Throughout all this we managed to go ahead with almost everything we would have done if the South had not undertaken to repress our activity. The Southern assault, however, imposed heavy losses on the NAACP.

Members and would-be members were intimidated. In 1955 the Deep South membership had been over 90,000; in 1956 it dropped to about 69,000 and in 1957 to about 40,000. Overall national membership remained flat during this period: 305,589 in 1955 and 312,277 in 1957, indicating growth in the North. However, in response to Southern attacks, NAACP income during this period went up, from $672,422 to $727,156.

By 1964 it became clear that the South's drive to crush the Association had failed. At the peak of the civil rights movement, membership was up to 455,839 and income was $1,143,426. Nevertheless, the NAACP paid a price. The partial vacuum created by its membership losses contributed to the growth of the Southern Christian Leadership Conference (SCLC), the Student Nonviolent Coordinating Committee (SNCC), and the Congress of Racial Equality (CORE) as alternative centers for civil rights activities.

The troubles the NAACP and LDF endured during this time should not obscure the real progress that was made during this post-*Brown* period. Despite the furor over the decision, some border states began to comply, though always haltingly. Within the Eisenhower administration Attorney General Herbert Brownell helped bring about passage of the Civil Rights Act of 1957, which created the Civil Rights Commission and the Civil Rights Division in the Justice Department, giving it a little more power to enforce voting rights. But a proposed provision that would have allowed the Justice Department to enforce school desegregation was deleted. Brownell did participate in the Hoxie, Clinton, and Little Rock cases on the side of law and order—instances not merely of school integration but of violent opposition to federally secured rights. Eisenhower did call for the immediate desegregation of the District of Columbia. Lyndon Johnson did oppose the Southern Manifesto and helped bring about passage of the 1957 act.

Even the campaign of vilification against Earl Warren failed to engender grassroots support anywhere but in the South. Following Eisenhower's heart attack in 1955, when there was some question as to whether or not he would stand for reelection, public opinion polls indicated that Earl Warren was so popular he could have beaten Adlai Stevenson in a presidential election. In the 1958 elections some of the senators who had led attacks on the Court—Jenner, Malone, and Bricker—were defeated. In the National Association of State Attorneys General and the ABA House of Delegates debates, many speakers supported the Court. Mail sent to the Supreme Court was evenly divided in support of and opposition to *Brown*. In many instances state and local officials started to do their duty and call out police and National Guard to put down violent opposition to desegregation.

Charlie Black and Lou Pollak, among others, wrote powerful articles defending *Brown* against attacks from the legal academy. Charlie responded to Herb Wechsler: "If a whole race of people finds itself confined within a system which is set up and continued for the very purpose of keeping it in an inferior station, and if the question is then solemnly propounded whether such a race is being treated 'equally,' I think we ought to exercise one of the sovereign prerogatives of philosophers—that of laughter."

Lou's article offered a proposed rewrite of *Brown* that addressed Wechsler's concern about freedom of association: "To the extent that implementation . . . forces racial mingling on school children . . . this consequence follows because the community through its political processes has chosen and may continue to choose compulsory education. . . . Parents . . . are presumably entitled to fulfill their educational responsibilities in other ways."

THE INTERNAL REVENUE SERVICE ATTACKS

The Internal Revenue Service's challenge to our tax exemption continued unabated. In March 1956 Thurgood met with the general counsel of the Bureau of Internal Revenue, who elaborated its dissatisfaction with our relationship with the Association. He complained, as Thurgood reported, that

> a great many things point to the interlocking of the two corporations. (1) The fact that we have NAACP before our name; (2) in the past we have given money to NAACP branches in law suits; (3) we were not operating as a legal aid society because we were helping people who could afford to pay their own legal fees. He further remarked that if these corporations are so separate why is it we are defending the NAACP in North Carolina and Louisiana [against efforts to compel it to register and to enjoin it from functioning]?

To defend the Association without risking our tax exemption Bob Carter took a leave of absence for the balance of the year, which later became permanent. Bob's leave enabled him to become the Association's lawyer at the Association's expense and to defend it against Southern efforts to put it out of business, so that LDF no longer subsidized the Association by providing free legal counsel. Thurgood resigned as special counsel of the NAACP. Later, in November, we adopted a resolution codifying our policy on taking cases, making clear that we decided *ourselves* which cases to take. The resolution said:

> [We will] give . . . legal aid only when requested to do so . . . by the party involved. . . .
> All members, officers, employees and employed and retained lawyers of this corporation are specifically prohibited from soliciting . . . anyone to be a party to litigation. . . .
> The relationship between the lawyer involved and the party in

interest continues to be controlled by the Canons of Ethics of the American Bar Association.

When requested by the N.A.A.C.P. or any other organization to act . . . we enter cases only when requested to do so by the parties in interest. . . . Each case is considered on its individual merits.

The resolution concluded with a reminder that we were not permitted to engage in political action or propaganda or to influence legislation.

The purpose was, of course, to protect us from charges that we stirred up litigation and that nonlawyers solicited our cases, which were then violations of law. It also answered IRS claims that we were a tool of the NAACP, making clear that we were not under its domination and not obligated to take cases it might refer to us.

A final gambit, with historic consequences, eliminated the interlock between our board and the Association's—cutting the umbilical cord. In May 1957, at a special meeting, following conferences of a committee consisting of members of both boards, the LDF board resolved that "no person should be a Board Member, officer or employee of this corporation who is also a Board Member, officer or employee of the NAACP." The board also considered eliminating the initials NAACP from our name, a measure that both organizations rejected. The NAACP dropped its National Legal Committee. Various other board members and officers resigned from one organization or the other. Thereafter, no one served both organizations, although Roy Wilkins remained on as the LDF secretary, though without a salary. The break was not at first absolute. Bob, as general counsel of the NAACP, continued to have an office on our premises and used our library and facilities.

Minutes of an executive committee meeting in December 1958, read with hindsight, suggest Thurgood's thoughts about my future: "[Mr. Marshall reported that] since Mr. Carter is no longer with the Fund, there has been no one in charge of the office when he has to be away. He stated that both Mr. Greenberg and Mrs. Motley had almost equal seniority with Greenberg slightly more. It was agreed that Mr. Greenberg would be in charge of the office in Mr. Marshall's absence."

During a brief period at the end of 1959 I actually ran the office while Thurgood spent about a month in London at the Lancaster House Conference, advising the Kenyan delegation in its negotiations for independence from Great Britain. I helped out by doing research on British Commonwealth constitutions, which I passed on to him.

In 1959 Senator Harry F. Byrd of Virginia, chairman of the Senate Finance Committee, wrote to the commissioner of Internal Revenue, once more protesting LDF's tax exemption. Thurgood reported that the IRS questioned Bob's presence in our office, and so Bob moved to the Association's offices full-time. Following these changes Thurgood met several times with the IRS. Although the IRS subjected us to a three-week-long audit in our offices in 1959, it never explicitly approved or disapproved what we had done. Ultimately, the separation from the NAACP became complete, except for our common interest in ridding America of Jim Crow, our representation of NAACP branch members, and, of course, our personal friendships.

Some Association board members believed that it was Thurgood's "idea of completely divorcing the two organizations so as to be relieved of the control from the N.A.A.C.P." While he had not initiated the process, this allegation was not far from the mark—he at least saw some benefit in the split. In his 1977 Columbia oral history Thurgood says, "The government did us a favor by separating the two organizations."

The formal changes in relationship between LDF and the Association were to have important consequences. The Association no longer could determine which cases we would handle. Conversely, while the Association once was limited in taking legal action by whether the LDF would pursue a case or not, it now had its own lawyer, and could go it alone. It soon would. While Thurgood thought Bob had been sent to the NAACP to handle its defense, not to pursue a civil rights program, Bob did not understand himself to be confined in that regard.

There was also the irritant of who gets the money. A dispute developed over who was entitled to the estate of Ruth Weinberg, an LDF board member, which she had bequeathed to the "NAACP for its legal defense fund." The NAACP board instructed Bob to file a pleading in court asserting its claim to the estate. Thurgood then sent a letter to the Association pointing to Weinberg's LDF board membership. There is no available record of how the matter was resolved.

Bob's meager resources as a solitary lawyer with a large docket in which the Association's life was at stake—by March 1958 he was having a hard time defending the Association all by himself—combined to keep the relationship, mainly although not entirely, as it had been in substance. We continued to provide legal support to the Association as Bob defended it against Southern assaults.

Between 1955 and 1960, in addition to my LDF work I found time—by getting up at 6:00 A.M. and working at night—to write two books and several law review articles. The first book, *Citizen's Guide to Desegregation* (with Herbert Hill, the NAACP labor secretary, now professor at the University of Wisconsin), published in 1955, analyzed the School Cases and answered commonly asked questions about them. I wrote that "it would be foolish to assume that all of the nation will be desegregated tomorrow, or even within the next few years: the unevenness of development will reflect countless local factors." In *Race Relations and American Law*, published in 1959, I wrote what was at the time the only comprehensive book treating every law and case relating to the subject of race. Today, a similar book would be many volumes long.

17

LUCY AND LITTLE ROCK:
WAR OF ALL MEN AGAINST ALL MEN

INCHING AHEAD

In June 1955 Thurgood acknowledged, referring to *Brown* and the subsequent "deliberate speed" decision, that "we may have to go from district to district but that was inevitable . . . and we knew that. . . . But the May 17th and May 31st decisions give us the tools with which we may secure compliance at the lower court level. . . . We would tackle the difficult states with one or two cases and then go to the more easy ones." That notion was soon frustrated by reality. Thurgood reported to an executive committee meeting almost a year later, "There appears to be a feeling taking root among the good people that we should not be pushing so hard in the Black Belt [loosely, black soil areas of South Carolina, Georgia, Alabama, and other states] Counties." By "good people," Thurgood meant Southern whites sympathetic to civil rights. Nevertheless, at the same time he proposed filing cases in Norfolk, Newport News, Charlottesville, and Arlington County, as well as farther south in Sumter, Charleston, and another town in South Carolina.

THE AUTHERINE LUCY CASE

A defining case of the period was not an elementary or high school suit. Rather it was Autherine Lucy's effort to enter the University of Alabama. After Connie, Thurgood, and Arthur Shores litigated up and down the courts for three years, they finally got a court order under which Lucy registered at the University of Alabama at Tuscaloosa in February 1956. (Her co-plaintiff, Polly Ann Myers, was rejected because of her "marital record.") Mobs surrounded and invaded the university, chanting "Where is the nigger?" "Keep 'Bama white," "Lynch her," and so forth. Those who were less uncouth (or, indeed, feigned a certain refinement) objected that she had arrived at the school in a Cadillac (in fact, it was a Buick), driven by an undertaker friend, paid her tuition in new $100 bills, and sat in the front row of her geography class. (A *New York Times* magazine piece expressed an understanding of the whites of Tuscaloosa citing Lucy's supposedly provocative behavior.)

The university expelled Lucy after three days of classes, allegedly in response to a statement in our pleadings that it had intentionally permitted an atmosphere of mob rule to develop. In February 1957, the judge who had ordered her admission held that the university was justified in expelling her because of our allegation. The stress of the situation proved too much for Lucy, and in March she dropped her effort to enroll.

In 1989 Lucy reported, "Recently the university wrote me a letter that said I'm no longer an expelled student. I can now enroll. . . . It's very late. Thirty-two years." That year she reenrolled at the same time that her daughter registered and both graduated in 1992, two of 1,755 blacks on a campus of more than eighteen thousand students.

The Lucy experience was traumatizing. While Thurgood reported the intention to file a motion for relief in another case, he raised the question of whether we should not be "reexamin[ing] strategy" with a view to revising it and considering "what we should do . . . *to prevent another Lucy case* so that we can arrive at the point that when the Court stated a plaintiff goes in she will be permitted to enter." But Roy Wilkins responded that while there was indeeed great resistance in the Black Belt, we had a moral obligation to proceed there. The meeting arrived at a "consensus": "Since we have the Supreme law of the land on our side we are obligated morally and legally."

Political and social circumstances more or less resolved this dilemma. While we did file in areas of high resistance, courts rarely ordered extensive desegregation in the face of physical resistance. In most of the worst places we did nothing because there were few, if any, plaintiffs prepared to face the very real risks involved. Carsie Hall, our lawyer in Mississippi, reported, "There is not one town ready for a school segregation case." Thurgood informed the board, "We must realize that as far as school cases are concerned, there will have to be a delay in Mississippi." Perhaps we might file a voting rights case, he suggested, against the Mississippi procedure of asking prospective voters questions like "How many bubbles in a bar of soap?" Another factor in favor of pursuing voting rights cases, according to Thurgood, was that if we won the cases and "nothing happens to the plaintiffs, it will show the people in Mississippi that they can go to court and nothing will happen to them. It will then give them the impetus to proceed on other cases."

FORCIBLE RESISTANCE: KENTUCKY

In 1956 when a handful of blacks registered, unnoticed, for admission to public schools in Clay and Sturgis, Kentucky, and arrived to attend class they found a mob of five hundred angry whites blocking their entry. Another mob ran newspapermen and photographers at the scene out of town. The governor, A. B. "Happy" Chandler, who had been the commissioner of major league baseball when Jackie Robinson broke the color barrier, called out the National Guard, which arrived at the school with tanks. Chandler said, "The tanks were taken along for the proper psychological effect. Some men won't let a soldier with a gun push them. No man is going to argue with a tank." Then, twenty-five hundred whites, including some white teachers, boycotted the schools. The Kentucky attorney general, who was opposed to the governor, issued an opinion that justified expelling the black children on the grounds that parents were not allowed to enroll children without school board approval. The board then removed the children and the mob went home.

Thurgood assigned me to work with James Crumlin to get the children back in school. Crumlin was a soft-spoken, jowly, black country lawyer, not at all a firebrand, who had just begun to practice in Louisville after having been graduated from Terrell Law School in Washington, D.C. Altogether there were about seven or eight black lawyers in Kentucky, of whom only two or three handled civil rights cases. Typically, they barely made a living. Someone had to pay them or they couldn't afford to file a case. Crumlin said of one of them, he "would sit in the white section of the bus station, but would not file civil rights cases. He was more interested in preaching."

In September 1956 we filed cases to integrate the Clay and Sturgis schools. As the cases proceeded, segregationists harassed the plaintiffs, fired on their homes, and cut off the water to one plaintiff's house. I traveled a half-dozen times to Kentucky for meetings with Crumlin, black parents, and the local NAACP, and for court hearings before Henry Brooks, a lanky, laconic federal judge. In December 1956 Brooks entered an order that required both school boards to file desegregation plans. The Clay plan, filed in January 1957, proposed complete desegregation commencing September 1957. Sturgis proposed desegregating the high school by 1959 and offered no plan regarding the elementary schools.

Neither plan, however, contemplated truly integrating the systems; they would merely allow blacks to enroll in white schools. The result would be a continuing dual system—of all black schools and formerly all-white schools attended by some blacks—rather than one in which students were assigned to schools without regard to race. Judge Brooks accepted Clay's plan, but rejected the too-long-deferred nature of the Sturgis plan. To our complaint that it did not include grade schools, he replied that our plaintiffs were high school students and grade schools were, therefore, not part of our case. A decade later courts would hold that a child in any grade could raise the issue of desegregating all the schools. The right was the right to be educated in an integrated system.

LITTLE ROCK

For a while it looked as if desegregation would develop peacefully in Arkansas. The university had desegregated its professional schools in February 1948, even before *Sipuel*, after Wiley Branton threatened suit. Following discharge from the army, Branton went to the University of Arkansas Law School, from which he graduated in 1953. By the time he began practicing in Pine Bluff, there were perhaps nine black lawyers in the state, not all with active practices and even fewer who handled civil rights. Following *Brown*, as state chairman of the Arkansas NAACP legal committee and an LDF cooperating lawyer, Wiley wrote to every school district in Arkansas with more than a few blacks, asking them to adopt integration plans. Some did.

Wiley was about five feet eight, with black wavy hair, and spoke with the Southern accent of the gentry of his hometown, Pine Bluff, Arkansas. His father was a small businessman who owned a taxi company, and the family was well to do. Wiley was sufficiently light complexioned to be mistaken for white, a circumstance he sometimes exploited. He delighted in telling and retelling of the time he drove from Arkansas to Florida with another black man to represent the son of a Pine Bluff woman who had been falsely accused of impregnating a woman. The defendant was the target of local ire because, according to the prosecutor, he was a "high steppin' nigger." The prosecutor got the notion, which Wiley did nothing to dispel, that Wiley was a "Colonel" Branton of Little Rock. When the prosecutor asked why the colonel would take the trouble to travel all the way to Florida, "hemmed up in a car with a nigger," for such a minor case, the "Colonel" swallowed his pride and improved the illusion by explaining that the defendant's mother worked for Wiley's family. The prosecutor added to the insult by attempting to bond with Wiley, offering the view that a "good nigger woman" was hard to find. Wiley won the release of his client by agreeing to compensate for the hospital costs of, as the prosecutor put it, birthing a "nigger baby." Paying the money to the prosecutor, Wiley bit his tongue, and as they drove back to Little Rock he and his newly freed client chortled over their Uncle Remus story, the racist, who thought he was colluding with a fellow white supremacist, undone by his racism.

One week before the 1955 *Brown* opinion the Little Rock school board approved a desegregation plan. Its first stage provided for desegregating grades ten through twelve, commencing in 1957, with completion by 1963. Wiley, with U. S. Tate, LDF Southwest regional counsel, sued in early 1956 because the plan was too slow and uncertain. But the courts, in April 1957, upheld the board, although they retained jurisdiction, perhaps to move things along faster later on. We decided not to go to the Supreme Court, fearful it might place its imprimatur on so gradual a scheme. As well, we thought it wise to let the plan begin in September and see what would happen, rather than risk stalling it for a year or more by a dragged-out lawsuit.

As the 1957 school year approached, Georgia's governor, Marvin Griffin, came to Arkansas and made a speech about how he would not tolerate school integration in Georgia. His remarks were so enthusiastically received that Arkansas Governor Orval Faubus apparently decided to reap some of the same political advantage for himself.

Faubus is a strange case in Southern segregation politics. Until the late 1950s he had been seen as somewhere between a moderate and a liberal, according to Wiley. Labor, blacks, and liberals assumed he shared their values. The white citizens council must have seen him the same way, for they attacked him. Faubus was midway through his second term in 1957, and ordinarily that would have been the end of it: The term for governor was only two years and only one person in the history of the state had ever been elected for a third term. It soon became clear that whenever Faubus attacked integration his support broadened and deepened. According to Wiley's analysis, this created too great a temptation for a governor facing imminent unemployment, and Faubus quickly made the desegregation issue the centerpiece of his stump speech. Time bore out his political judgment if not his moral rectitude: He ultimately served six terms.

Under the school board's plan, more than three hundred black children would have been eligible for admission to Little Rock's Central High School. The board first screened that number down to seventy-five, and ultimately approved only about twenty-five for admission. But even this small number would not be admitted without a fight. A white woman sued in late August to enjoin integrating the schools. The suit was probably brought at Faubus's instigation; he testified in her case that revolvers had been taken from Negro and white pupils. The local judge prohibited integrating the schools.

The school board then went to federal court and requested an order permitting it to proceed with the desegregation. Wiley, with LDF, joined the school board. The judge, Ronald N. Davies of Fargo, North Dakota, who happened to be sitting in Little Rock by special assignment, forbade the state court to interfere with the desegregation. However, on September 2, 1957, the day before school was to open, Faubus went on radio and television and announced that he had called out the Arkansas National Guard with instructions to block the admission of black children to Central High School because, if the black children were admitted, he said, "Blood will run in the streets."

In fact, there had been no evidence to support this fear of violence. The mayor and police believed they could cope with any problems that did arise and hadn't asked the governor for help. Nevertheless, the school board asked the black children not to attempt to enter the school.

On September 3, the board asked the federal district court for instructions. Judge Davies ordered it to proceed with the plan. But of the twenty-five children scheduled to enter Central, the parents of only nine agreed that their children would try to run the gauntlet of the civilian mob and the

National Guard who were trying to keep them out. The next day, September 4, Elizabeth Eckford and Terrence Roberts, proceeding alone, and seven other black children, accompanied by two white and two black ministers who had been enlisted by Daisy Bates, president of the local NAACP, tried to attend the school. Jostled and shoved by a growing mob of segregationists attracted by the publicity and the governor's fiery speeches, the children made their way to the line of National Guardsmen who, shoulder to shoulder, blocked their entrance. A captain announced that they would not be admitted, pursuant to Governor Faubus's orders. When informed of what had occurred, Judge Davies ordered the United States attorney to investigate and fix responsibility for interference with the desegregation order.

The school board decided to capitulate to Faubus and the mob, and on September 5 went into district court to ask Judge Davies to suspend the desegregation order. By now Thurgood was virtually in full-time residence in Little Rock. He and Wiley, with George Howard, another young black lawyer in Arkansas, today a United States district judge there, opposed the delay. Judge Davies refused to postpone desegregation. Now, as Thurgood said, there was a lot of "fast play around second base."

On September 9, Judge Davies requested the United States attorney general and the United States attorney in Little Rock to enter the case as "friends of the court." He directed that they file a petition seeking an injunction against the governor to prevent interference with the integration order. The very next day, September 10, the United States filed a petition. It asked that Faubus and the National Guard officers be made parties to our original case "in order to protect and preserve the integrity of the judicial process of the Courts of the United States and to maintain due and proper administration of justice." It asked also that they be enjoined from "obstructing or interfering with the carrying out and effectuation of" the court's orders in the case. The same day, Judge Davies made Faubus and the guard officers defendants in our case and set a hearing for September 20. Faubus responded by making a motion to disqualify Judge Davies as prejudiced against him. He obviously would have preferred a good old Little Rock judge.

The next day, though Davies had already done so, Thurgood and Wiley filed our own motion to make Faubus and the National Guard officers defendants and to enjoin them from interfering with the integration plan—we wanted to keep control and not concede the power of deciding how to proceed to the government. If we had not sued Faubus and justice had decided to withdraw or settle, we might have been without standing to urge a different position. There was also a real question of whether the United States had the authority to participate as a friend of the court and make motions, put on evidence, and otherwise act as a party to the dispute. Our motion would serve as a backup if it were held later that justice had overstepped its bounds.

Following the September 20 hearing, on that same day, Judge Davies enjoined Faubus and Arkansas National Guard officers from obstructing black children from attending Central High School. The order carefully preserved the governor's power to use the guard to maintain peace and order. But Faubus decided to withdraw the guard and leave the school at the mercy of the mob.

Although some police officers sympathized with the segregationists, the chief of police, who himself didn't favor desegregation, was devoted to upholding law and order. But the mob completely overran his forces, pulling black citizens from their cars near Central High School, and venting its wrath on Northern journalists, beating three members of the *Life* magazine staff, who, ironically, were then arrested for inciting a riot. Daisy Bates's husband, L. C., sat up nights with a shotgun cradled in his arms.

The Little Rock mayor, Woodrow Mann, and Harry Ashmore, editor of the Little Rock *Gazette,* and other influential people, called President Eisenhower, as well as senators and representatives who in turn called the White House, asking for federal troops. On September 23 President Eisenhower issued a proclamation entitled "Obstruction of Justice in the State of Arkansas" that "commanded all persons engaged in such obstruction of justice to cease and desist therefrom, and to disperse forthwith." The next day he issued another proclamation authorizing the secretary of defense to order the Arkansas National Guard "into the active military service of the United States . . . and to use such of the armed forces of the United States as he may deem necessary." The secretary federalized the National Guard and also sent to Little Rock one thousand paratroopers of the 101st Airborne Division from Fort Campbell, Kentucky.

Soldiers were on the Central High School campus every day to keep the peace, until November 27 when the Defense Department removed the army and left the federalized National Guard in charge.

For the first few months of that school year, the Little Rock Nine, as they became known, gathered at Daisy Bates's house every morning. From there National Guard troops escorted them to school.

On their first day they reported that some of the white pupils had been friendly and had even invited them to lunch, some were indifferent, and only a few showed open hostility. But soon a pattern developed in which groups of whites harassed, insulted, and attacked the Nine, not enough to force them from the school, but enough to make their lives unpleasant. The school suspended Minnijean Brown, one of the Nine, for six days, after she emptied her tray on the heads of two boys who shoved chairs in her path in the cafeteria. Afterwards, the boys said that they "didn't blame her for getting mad." On another occasion a white boy dumped soup on her head, following which the principal suspended Minnijean and the boy for the remainder of the term. Rather than fight the suspension, during which Minnijean most likely would have been out of school for months, she moved to

New York, where she lived with Kenneth Clark and his family, and attended private New Lincoln High School, from which she graduated in 1959.

During that school year Thurgood, Connie Motley, and I shuttled between New York and Little Rock, taking depositions, gathering facts, preparing further proceedings. Segregationists kept up their harassment of the children and continuously threatened Daisy and the parents and families of the Little Rock Nine. But on May 27, 1958, when the school year ended, Ernest Green became the first black graduate of Central High School.

On several occasions over the year school board lawyers approached us to ask whether we would put school integration on hold, pending an improvement in the political and racial climate in Arkansas. Of course, we said no: A "yes" would have invited violence elsewhere and would have forced us to go through the Little Rock experience all over again.

Judge Davies returned to North Dakota and was replaced by Harry J. Lemley, an Arkansan. In February 1958 the school board, unable to gain a postponement by agreement, tried the courts again. Citing "pupil unrest, teacher unrest, and parent unrest" the board alleged that

the principle of integration runs counter to the ingrained attitudes of many of the residents of the District. For more than eighty years its schools have been operated on a basis of segregation. . . . The transition involved in [the] gradual plan of integration has created deep-rooted and violent emotional disturbances. . . . The concept of "all deliberate speed" should be re-examined and clearly defined by the Federal Courts.

In May the board elaborated on its earlier plea and asked that desegregation be postponed until January 1961, that is for two and a half years. Judge Lemley then held a trial from June 3 to 5. School board witnesses testified to "chaos, bedlam and turmoil," racial incidents, and vandalism. On June 20, 1958, Judge Lemley granted the board's petition and suspended school integration in Little Rock until midsemester of the 1960–61 school year.

The fast play around second base got faster. On June 21 we filed a notice of appeal to the Eighth Circuit Court of Appeals and simultaneously asked Judge Lemley for a stay of his order suspending integration, which he promptly denied. The next day we asked the Eighth Circuit to stay the order and docketed the appeal there.

In the normal course of events the Eighth Circuit would have taken some months, maybe even more, to hear and decide the appeal. Whatever its decision, the case would go to the Supreme Court and, therefore, integration of the Little Rock schools could have been delayed at least for a semester, perhaps longer. The best course would be to skip the court of appeals and go the Supreme Court first—a technique we had encountered in *Bolling v. Sharpe*, the District of Columbia school segregation case. To move that fast, however, required some cooperation from court clerks, because cases can't be appealed to higher courts without having filed the records in the courts below, and ordinarily that takes time. Wiley loved to tell the story of how he moved the record rapidly from Little Rock to Washington:

> I talked with Thurgood and a decision was made that we would seek to bypass the Eighth Circuit and go straight to the Supreme Court of the United States. But Thurgood told me, he said Cullinan [E. P. Cullinan, chief deputy clerk of the United States Supreme Court] . . . had told him you've got to have a transcript certified as the record in that case before they could do anything at all. At that time, the Eighth Circuit had a very peculiar rule which I understand was different from the other circuits. They didn't want any records sent up to them, any transcripts sent up to them unless they requested it.
>
> So I had a problem there. I asked the clerk in Little Rock to certify it as the transcript and they said we can't do that because we're under instructions pursuant to Eighth Circuit rules not to send up any transcript unless the court requests it. And I didn't tell them what I wanted to do with it, I really wanted to bypass the Eighth Circuit, although Thurgood had told me that I had to come through there.
>
> And I said, "Well I need to take it up."
>
> And they said, "Well, you can't take it. When the Court sends for it, then we will send it up there."
>
> So I got on the phone and called Judge Lemley who was down in Hope, Arkansas. And he said, "What do you want, Wiley?"
>
> I said, "Well, Judge, I want to appeal your order."
>
> He said, "Oh, I knew you were going to do that. What's the problem?"
>
> I told him about this transcript and all and he said, "Oh, hell put the clerk on." And he said to the clerk, "Listen, give Wiley that transcript. I trust him quicker than I would the United States mail and if they don't want to take it up there at the Eighth Circuit, he'll just bring it back to you all. Fine."
>
> So I left there then, without any certification, and go to the Eighth Circuit and tell them I don't want to do anything in the Eighth Circuit, but I want to come through there and let them certify that at least they have seen it. And the Eighth Circuit was already on vacation.
>
> The clerk said, "Mr. Branton, if you give me that I'll have to file it and if you file it I cannot release it without a court order, and I don't know how soon you can get a court order." And he said, "Or I can give it back to you and you can do whatever you want to do." So it was

agreed that I would take it back. This was, I think, on a Monday morning. So I caught a plane then and came on to Washington with full knowledge that Cullinan wanted something that said, "this is the record."

So, I go there and we present it and Cullinan starts thumbing through it and he says, "Where is the certificate?" So I start telling him my problem and he said, "I can't do a damn thing without a certificate. I want a certificate either from the Eighth Circuit, but preferably from the District Court." And he said, "Today is really the last day, if I hope to get this Court back in any way at all." And he had somebody checking airline schedules to see if there was a plane going out to where I had to go and come back, and that was going to push it. He was willing to accept it even late at night. But, it didn't look like I'd get back until too late.

I think I went to Frank Reeves's law office. And I said let me try something else. I don't even remember the lady's name now but in the South it is customary to call women by their first name so long as you put Miss in front of it. I'll just call her Miss Ellen, who was the deputy in the clerk's office. So I tried to use my Southern charm and the conversation went something like this:

"Miss Ellen, this is Wiley Branton up here in Washington."

And here Wiley raised his voice half an octave to imitate Miss Ellen:

"In Washington, I thought you just left here going to St. Louis."

"Yes ma'am, but they couldn't take care of what I needed there so I came on up here to the Supreme Court of the United States. And guess what Miss Ellen, I got that transcript and they tell me that I should of had you put on a certificate on there coming to them that this is the record."

She said, "Well, that's what we put on it going to the Eighth Circuit, but we can't do that until the Court wants it."

I said, "Yeah, but they wouldn't take it up there. The Supreme Court wants it and they want that certificate on there, and they claim that we made an error down there in not putting it on there. I said I know ya'all know what ya'all are doing Miss Ellen. They just got things all screwed up. You know how technical they can be." So I got her on my side on that.

I said, "Now they tell me I got to get on a plane, come all the way back out there and get you to just stamp that thing, attach a certificate saying this is the transcript and record, and then bring it back to them." I said, "You know, I don't get up to a place like Washington very often and while I'm up here I sure would like to spend a couple of days. But I told them, shucks, ya'all don't know how we get along down there. I told them I don't need to get on no plane go all the way back down there. All I got to do is call down to Little Rock and they'll put the thing on a plane and send it up here to me."

"Well, you know we'll do that, Wiley."

I said, "Yes, ma'am." I said, "Here's where it needs to be sent to and here's what it needs to say."

She took all that down and she said, "Now, I got one little problem."

I said, "What's that?"

She said, "Well, everything we send out with franking privileges is just regular mail and we don't have any airmail postage on things like that." She said, "Even if we send it out it will be late." She said, "You really need to put it on the plane."

I said, "Yes, ma'am, that's what I was talking about."

Finally, she said, "I'll tell you what I'll do. I will advance the money out of my pocket and take it out to the airport."

And in those days you didn't have Federal Express and stuff like that; you'd go out and make arrangements with the people at the desk to put something on the plane as long as somebody met the plane and took it. So she paid for it out of her pocket and that's how we got the certificate in time to file a record.

In the meantime, Thurgood, Connie, Irma Feder, an LDF staff lawyer, and I worked day and night preparing a petition to file with the record requesting the Court to hear the case. Perhaps as much time had to be spent in printing the petition (with hot lead type), proofreading among rackety Linotype machines all through the night at the printshop in downtown Manhattan, and hand-carrying the petition to Washington, as in actually writing it. We filed it on June 26, only four days after docketing the appeal in the Eighth Circuit.

The petition focused on reasons why the Court grants review, the caption of the petition's main section stating, "The Decision Below Conflicts With Applicable Decisions of This Court." It cited two NAACP and LDF cases—*Buchanan v. Warley*, which held residential apartheid unconstitutional against the claim that it would promote public peace, and the School Segregation Cases, which held that "it should go without saying that the vitality of these constitutional principles cannot be allowed to yield simply because of disagreement with them." Less than a week after Lemley's decision, on June 30, 1958, the Supreme Court denied our petition but entered an order almost as good as granting it. It referred to our appeal in the Eighth Circuit and wrote, "That court is the regular court for reviewing orders of the District Court here concerned." It made clear to the Eighth Circuit that it should treat the case as an urgent matter: "We have no doubt that the Court of Appeals will recognize the vital importance of the time element in this litigation, and that it will act upon the application for a stay or the appeal in ample time to permit arrangements to be made for the next school year."

We had successfully impressed on the Court the urgency of the issue and primed it to hear the case again if necessary.

The court of appeals gathered in St. Louis en banc, that is with all of the seven judges of the Eighth Circuit sitting on the case, rather than the ordinary panel of three. On August 18 it reversed Judge Lemley, stating that "an affirmance of 'temporary delay' in Little Rock would amount to an open invitation to elements in other districts to overtly act out public opposition through violent and unlawful means."

And, in italics, the court emphasized that *the time has not yet come in these United States when an order of a Federal Court must be whittled away, watered down, or shamefully withdrawn in the face of violent and unlawful acts of individual citizens in opposition thereto.*"

But Archibald Gardner, the nearly ninety-year-old chief judge, dissented. He argued that

> for centuries there had been no intimate social relations between the white and colored races in the section referred to as the South. . . . It had become a way of life in that section of the country and it is not strange that this long-established, cherished practice could not suddenly be changed without resistance. Such changes, if successful, are usually accomplished by evolution rather than revolution, and time, patience, and forbearance are important elements in effecting all radical changes.

Then the court of appeals did something we found unintelligible as well as intolerable. On August 21, without allowing us the five days provided in the rules to reply to the board's application, it granted a stay of its own order reversing Judge Lemley, at least until the school board could file a petition in the Supreme Court. School was scheduled to open September 2, and although the board advanced the date several times to await the outcome of the legal wrangling, a stay would delay integration beyond the opening of school. The board won on procedural grounds what it had lost on constitutional grounds.

On August 23 we filed an application with the United States Supreme Court to vacate the Eighth Circuit stay and to stay Lemley's judgment. (The procedural nicety—addressing what had occurred in Lemley's court as well as in the court of appeals—stemmed from the fact that if the Supreme Court vacated only the Eighth Circuit stay, Lemley's judgment would remain in effect until the Eighth Circuit judgment could be transmitted to him, following which he would have to implement it—which would take time. Given his frame of mind, he could have stalled, dissembled, or refused to obey.)

Applications to vacate stays and other motions ordinarily are presented to a circuit justice, a member of the Supreme Court with responsibility for such matters in the region comprising his circuit. So we addressed our papers to a new Eisenhower appointee, Charles Evans Whittaker, who was attending the American Bar Association meeting in Los Angeles, with Chief Justice Warren and Justices Tom Clark and William J. Brennan. As often happens with important motions, Whittaker referred this one to the entire Court. Warren consulted with the justices who were with him in Los Angeles and, by telephone, with the others. On August 25 the Court scheduled a special term and set a hearing on the motions for August 28. In one of those judicial invitations that amount to a command, the Court requested that the government enter the case as a friend of the court. Warren, Clark, and Brennan took the train to Washington; Justice Douglas, vacationing in the state of Washington, drove to Portland, Oregon, and flew to Washington, D.C. Justice Burton was in Europe and wasn't expected to attend. The last special term had been in 1953 and dealt with the Rosenberg spy case. The one before that, in 1942, decided the fate of Nazi saboteurs who had been captured during the Second World War.

The political waters became even more turbulent. President Eisenhower disclosed at a press conference that at the time of the *Brown* decision he had told friends that he preferred "slower" progress toward integration. Roy Wilkins denounced the statement as "incredible," pointing out that seven states had not made "a single move" toward integration and only 770 school districts out of some 3,000 in the South had "done anything toward integration." On the other hand, notwithstanding his sentiments about school segregation, Eisenhower supported the courts. He believed that the law must be enforced and stated also that in the Little Rock case his views would not diverge materially from those of the Justice Department. His attorney general, William P. Rogers, in a major address to the American Bar Association meeting in Los Angeles, said that racial segregation in public schools, transportation, and recreation "must be considered a thing of the past." Senator Richard Russell of Georgia, one of the most powerful Senate Democrats, sent a telegram to Rogers, demanding that the Justice Department not "flaunt [sic]" the will of Congress. The Arkansas legislature passed its package of anti-integration, anti-NAACP legislation and Governor Faubus continued to excoriate the courts.

Arkansas Senator J. W. Fulbright's position indicates better than anything else the powerful hold that segregationist sentiment had on political figures who should have known better. Fulbright, whose name is honored in the academic community for the fellowships that bear his name, has written in his autobiography, published in 1989, that he disagreed with the

Southern Manifesto as originally written, but he swallowed his objections and demanded as a price for his signature that "we would oppose the *Brown* decision only by constitutional means." He felt, however, "that there were issues fundamental to this nation as a whole in foreign policy that I wanted to focus on." "In those days in Arkansas my constituents were not about to be persuaded on civil rights." He adds, "I avoided taking a stand." While he subordinated the rights of blacks to foreign policy considerations, he didn't seem to realize the foreign policy implications of America's racial policies.

In fact, however, he *did* take a stand. He entered the Little Rock case against us by filing a friend-of-the-court brief that argued that it was a grave error not to realize that there was a "Southern mind." He urged that the integration problem in Arkansas "is more likely to yield to the slow conversion of the human heart than to remedies of a more urgent nature."

On August 28 we filed a short brief in the Supreme Court that argued that the procedural device of granting or denying a stay cannot be employed where the result will be to delay or nullify the exercise of clearly determined rights. The same day the Justice Department filed a brief—now the government was four-square behind us. The issue was no longer segregation or desegregation, but the integrity of the courts and, indeed, as in the Civil War, when the status of blacks was also the focus, whether the Union would hang together. It called upon the Court not only to decide our application to vacate the stay, but to pass on the merits of the case, and, if the Court deemed it necessary, to require the school board to file a petition for review at once. It asserted that "there is no likelihood that the [school board] can prevail on the merits."

At oral argument that day all nine justices were present. Thurgood, described by Russell Baker in the *New York Times* as "having the hint of a scowl on his face, looking like Othello in a tan business suit," addressed the Court in his customary conversational manner, scarcely looking at his notes. He pushed the Court to decide the merits, not merely our application to vacate the stay. But the justices resisted because the board had not yet filed a petition for review. Richard Butler, a tall, soft-spoken Little Rock lawyer, argued in a quiet, controlled manner that integration at that time would "destroy the public school system of Little Rock." He asked that the two-and-a-half-year delay be affirmed to allow Arkansas citizens to learn "what the law is." In that time a "national policy could be established" and state laws designed to prevent integration could be "clarified," or tested in the courts.

From that point on the justices were all over him like "white-on rice," to use a Southern black colloquialism. Frankfurter asked, "Why aren't the two decisions of this court a national policy?" Warren said, "Suppose every other school board in the South said the same thing." When Butler began a sentence, "Mr. Chief Justice, you've been the Governor of a great state," Warren, with scarcely controlled anger, replied, "But I never tried to resolve any legal problem of this kind as Governor." He went on sternly, "I thought that was a matter for the courts and I abided by the decision of the courts." And when Butler brought up Faubus's views, Warren interjected, "I have never heard such an argument made in a court of justice before, and I have tried many a case through many a year. I never heard a lawyer say that the statement of a Governor as to what was legal or illegal should control the action of any court."

The most powerful argument of the day—because he spoke for the United States—was that of J. Lee Rankin, the solicitor general. About five feet six or seven inches in height, dressed in the traditional morning coat of the solicitor general's office, he spoke in the flat tones of his native Nebraska. In essence, his argument was that "no court of law in this land, state or Federal, can recognize that you can ever bow to force and violence. We have paid too great a price to come this far along the road of lawful action." But the major impact of his words was that he had discussed the government's position with President Eisenhower and had received his approval.

Russell Baker, reporting for the *New York Times*, described the scene in a remarkable passage: "The room momentarily looked like a crowded tableau in the rich deep colors of the Flemish masters—the justices in their black at the polished wooden bar, the deep maroon curtains draping the side walls, the lawyers and young assistant attorneys general in somber blues, grays and blacks and, here and there, a splash of bright color from the costumes of the women."

The Court recessed at about 3:30. The merits were on everyone's mind, but technically the only issue before the Court was whether to revoke the Eighth Circuit's stay. Following the rules meticulously, the Court declined to pass upon the merits at that time, but instead, at 5:00 P.M. the same day, entered an order that said that it agreed with the parties and the solicitor general that the Court had to consider the merits. In view of the fact that school was scheduled to open on September 15, and that Butler had said that he planned to file a petition for writ of certiorari, the Court ordered him to file by September 8. Both sides were required to file briefs on the merits by September 10. The Court set oral argument for September 11. To tie the loose ends up properly it deferred action on our application to vacate the court of appeals stay and to stay Lemley's order, pending disposition of the board's petition. In a case involving whether the law must be obeyed, the Court took pains to cut square corners.

On September 8, the school board filed a short petition seeking review. It pleaded "not to simply return the school district to the bedlam, turmoil and chaos which has been destroying the school district and has emasculated the educational program." It argued, rather incomprehensibly, that to refuse delay "would discourage any further voluntary compliance by school districts." The next day the school board filed its brief on the merits, which, in its main thrust, argued that it had "not pursue[d] a plan of desegregation through choice and it should not now be placed in the position of being duty bound to quell defiance."

During another hectic week I worked on our brief along with Thurgood, Wiley, Bill Coleman, Lou Pollak, and other staff members. There wasn't a lot of time and there also wasn't a great deal to be said. The issue was basically whether the Court would tolerate Faubus's rebellion. If it did in any way, the idea of a national government would be damaged severely, perhaps fatally. We took a short cut around the ordinarily lengthy statement of facts by referring to the court of appeals description. We led off our argument by pointing out that the case involved "the very survival of the Rule of Law," and cited the cases in which the Court had rejected claims that rights should be denied because of violent opposition, many of them NAACP or LDF cases. At that point in the brief I took particular pleasure in quoting one of the great books I had read in my Columbia College Contemporary Civilization course, Thomas Hobbes's *De Cive* (1651). The brief asserted that if transient emergencies were a ground for denying rights, "then we have returned to a state prior to civil society, when there was the Hobbesian state of a 'war of all men against all men.'" We concluded by arguing that to suspend the integration plan would subvert the fundamental objective of public education and quoted Rankin's August 28 argument: "If you teach these children . . . that as soon as you get some force and violence, the courts of law in this country are going to bow to it . . . I think that you destroy the whole educational process then and there."

On September 11 the Court met to hear oral argument. For me, the argument offered a small personal thrill—Thurgood asked me to sit at counsel table with him. Nominally, a colleague seated at the counsel table is there to help argue the case, but there is relatively little one can do, maybe hand up a citation or find a page in the record. Essentially, a seat at counsel table in the Supreme Court is a form of recognition.

The argument was basically a rehash of the August 28 argument. But the Court asked Thurgood and Rankin only a single question each. On the other hand, the justices raked Butler over the coals. Brennan distilled the essence of the questioning into his observation that the Constitution required every state official to take an oath "to support the Federal Constitution." He asked whether Butler was familiar with that. Butler said he was. Brennan went on to ask was it not curious that the board should ask delay because of action by the governor and legislature opposed to the Constitution in "every way that the state can contrive?"

The next day the Court unanimously affirmed the Eighth Circuit. Judge Lemley's two-and-a-half-year stay was held invalid. The justices wrote a short per curiam (by the Court) order, which stated that "in view of the imminent commencement of the new school year we deem it important to make prompt announcement of our judgment." President Eisenhower appealed for public support of the Supreme Court's decision. Governor Faubus retaliated by issuing a proclamation closing all four high schools in Little Rock. But from that point on the fantasy that violent resistance could succeed in undermining the law began to fade. On September 29 the Court issued a full opinion addressing more elaborately the issues in the case.

The opinion, at the outset, listed as its authors each justice by name, something which had not been done before or since. The Court described the case as raising "questions of the highest importance to the maintenance of our federal system of government." Citing *Buchanan*, the Court wrote, "Law and order are not here to be preserved by depriving the Negro children of their constitutional rights." The Court then answered "the premise of the actions of the Governor and Legislature that they are not bound by our holding in the *Brown* case." It cited Article VI of the Constitution, which makes the Constitution "the supreme Law of the Land," and quoted John Marshall's 1803 opinion in *Marbury v. Madison*, which "declared the basic principle that the federal judiciary is supreme in the exposition of the law of the Constitution." The Court's opinion concluded, therefore, that "the interpretation of the Fourteenth Amendment enunciated by this Court in the *Brown* case is the supreme law of the land."

The Court addressed another issue provoked by Faubus's actions—whether the state might turn public schools into private ones. Right after the Court's September 12 order to desegregate, Faubus closed the schools and, five days later, a group of Little Rock whites filed a private school charter. On September 23 the Little Rock school board asked the district court whether it might lease the public schools to the private group. The next day we were in court asking for an order restraining the school board from transferring school property to private corporations, and asking also that, if the transfer were permitted, that those schools be required to be nonsegregated. On the same day the attorney general filed a friend-of-the-court brief in support of our position. The Supreme Court's September 29 opinion demolished this attempt at evasion by stating, in passing, that segregation in schools was prohibited "where there is state participation through any arrangement, management, funds or property." This would include private schools that the state might subsidize.

The district court dismissed the board's petition inquiring about whether it might lease to private schools and on September 29 the board declared the public school properties surplus and authorized leasing them to the Little Rock Private School Corporation. We went to the court of appeals that same day and got an order prohibiting the leasing.

At the end of 1958 more than two thousand white and nine black students were attending Central High School; white Hall High School was closed and its 717 students had no school to attend; about thirteen hundred students were in private schools; and others were attending school outside the city or state, were out of school, or were being educated only part-time.

State courts upheld a student transfer aid law that sent state aid to schools attended by displaced students. Little Rock residents, refusing to see the writing on the wall, voted overwhelmingly against school integration in a special election.

In June 1959 we got a federal court to hold the school closing and student aid transfer laws unconstitutional. That case went to the United States Supreme Court, where we won once more. Then, under pupil assignment laws, which required black children to apply for transfer to white schools and permitted school boards to decide the merit of the applications according to vague criteria defining the suitability of children for transfer, the school board began registration in July for the 1959–60 school year. The school board granted only six of sixty applications from blacks who tried to transfer to white schools. Some white students attempted a protest walk-out, but the school board suspended them. The board permitted sixty-eight whites who refused to attend class with blacks to transfer to whites-only classes. The Little Rock Private School Corporation announced it was broke and went out of business.

At the same time the nearby community of Dollarway, so named because of the high cost of the highway that ran through it, began using the pupil assignment law in the same way. As we shall see, Dollarway led to serious conflict over turf between the NAACP and LDF.

By spring 1960, pupil assignment was working in Little Rock pretty much as elsewhere. Central had 1,510 whites and five blacks. Hall High School had 730 whites and three blacks. That month the Little Rock school board assigned eight more black students to the two high schools for the September term. From that point onwards, punctuated by violence, real bombs, and bomb threats, the Little Rock case took the form of litigation elsewhere: The board continued to hold the line against integration by means of pupil assignment laws, and LDF lawyers fought to overturn them, winning admission to white schools for a few students at a time.

The Little Rock convulsion made clear once and for all that the federal government would not tolerate rebellion against the *Brown* decision. Only twice more did the federal government have to call on troops to quell resistance to school integration: when James Meredith entered the University of Mississippi accompanied by gunfire; and when Alabama Governor George Wallace stood in the schoolhouse door flanked by troops—both incidents arose out of LDF cases. In each instance the outcome was preordained by Little Rock. Thereafter, violence and physical obstruction having failed, bureaucracy in the form of pupil assignment laws became the principal means of fighting integration.

What becomes of kids who have been through such an ordeal? In 1982, at its annual Civil Rights Institute, LDF celebrated the twenty-fifth anniversary of the Little Rock case. Seven of the Little Rock Nine attended the event. Ernest Green had been assistant secretary of labor in the Carter administration and was president of his own consulting firm, which dealt with employment and training. Minnijean Brown Trickey and her husband, a zoologist, and two children lived on an 880-acre farm in northern Ontario. She was active in antiwar, antinuclear, and conservation groups. Thelma Jean Mothershed Wair was a vocational counselor in the East St. Louis, Illinois, school system. Gloria Ray Kaarlmark was a manager at Philips Telecommunications Industries in Brussels, Belgium, and was founder and editor-in-chief of *Computers in Industry*, an international journal. Terrence J. Roberts, Ph.D., was director of Mental Health and Social Services at St. Helena Hospital and Health Center in Deer Park, California. Jefferson Thomas was in charge of employee training and contract reviews for the Defense Department in Los Angeles. Carlotta Walls LaNier was a real estate broker in Fresno, California.

Generalizations are always suspect, but examination of these seven veterans of the war in Little Rock, and what they made of themselves, seems to suggest that being a civil rights pioneer need not interfere with a child's chances for a normal, or perhaps better than normal, life.

18

TRENCH WARFARE

CONFLICT WITH THE ASSOCIATION

As the Little Rock case wound down, the Association branch in Dollarway, Arkansas, wanted to file a school case. Thurgood put it on hold; he didn't want a second case in Arkansas possibly harming the Little Rock case. When he thought the time appropriate for filing, he discovered that Bob Carter had already filed the case. He was angered because Little Rock might have been put at risk, but also because Bob, in filing without consulting Thurgood first, had displayed a view of his role as counsel for the Association that was radically different from Thurgood's. Thurgood assumed that, as general counsel to the NAACP, Bob's job was to defend the Association against Southern attacks against it, but Bob did not see his job as being so limited. By 1960 he had appeared in perhaps a dozen cases that did not involve assaults on the NAACP. Often we found out about these cases by reading press or legal reports, or from local counsel. Connie Motley sent Thurgood a memorandum describing a Miami contretemps:

> When the case was set for trial, you assigned me to handle the matter with Graves [a Miami lawyer]. The complaint . . . was prepared by Jack. . . . The trial was to take place on the same day on which the trial in the University of Florida case was to take place. . . . I, therefore, asked Jack if he could go to Miami and help Graves. . . . Graves . . . stated that Bob was planning to be at the trial. . . . Jack and I then talked to Bob by telephone . . . and . . . urged him to withdraw. . . . Bob advised . . . he could continue to handle any school case, etc., with which he had previously been identified, including but not limited to those on which his name had appeared. . . . Jack decided that he would not appear in order to avoid further confusion.

In a memorandum written to Bill Hastie around the same time, Thurgood referred to a Norfolk case filed by the "General Counsel of the N.A.A.C.P.": "If we are to have some school cases run by one group of lawyers and others run by other groups of lawyers, without consultation, the possibilities [for confusion] cannot be exaggerated."

Thurgood referred also to a personal dimension: "The real problem is not one which you or any one else can solve. That is, the ever present problem from one end of the country to another brought about by 'you said'; 'he said'; 'she said'; 'they said.' This type of foolishness does nothing except disturb the people who listen."

There was an issue over who would pay for Bob's former LDF cases. Father Gibson, president of the Miami branch, had promised Bob that he could handle all the cases in the Miami area, but the Association had no money for them. Connie "suggested . . . a compromise . . . allowing Bob to continue as counsel in the school case and . . . allowing Mr. Graves to be free to refer other cases to us in the future." Connie's compromise was accepted. To wrap up the financial problem LDF sent Graves $1,700.

On November 10, 1960, Thurgood wrote to Bill Hastie once more to illustrate that our uncoordinated efforts would be disadvantaged against a well-coordinated adversary:

> We are finding an ever increasing amount of evidence of the close cooperation among attorneys general and private counsel representing school boards, etc. . . . It is well known that lawyers in Arkansas, Louisiana and Georgia have visited Virginia and North Carolina to confer with the governors and attorneys general of those states. I imagine much more of this is going on. Along the same lines, the two school cases in Arkansas, Little Rock and Dollarway, are both being defended by the same lawyer, Herschel Friday. In Georgia, all of the cases are being defended by the same lawyer, "Buck" Murphy.

The organizational friction continued to be a leitmotif in school cases all over the South.

LOUISIANA

Integrating schools in Louisiana, where "segregation forever" translated into "litigation forever," involved a tough, lengthy struggle. It was played out in *Bush v. Orleans Parish School Board*, where, from early 1956 through late 1960, LDF fought an obstinate army of defendants' counsel, alone at first and later with the Justice Department at our side. Thurgood, with Connie Motley, Jim Nabrit III (who had joined us in 1959), and I virtually commuted to the New Orleans district court and the court of appeals, where our every appearance was greeted by hordes of reporters, pickets, and, at times, pushing, shoving, and screaming mobs.

We stayed at the home of Dan and Mildred Byrd. Mildred regularly prepared a wonderful gumbo for me. Dan, who usually chomped an unlit stub of a cigar in a rubber holder, was one of the small number of LDF field workers who organized the black community and assured black teachers that we would defend their jobs. Like Thurgood, he was a serious Mason. He would pick us up at the airport, take us to court, and then home. Hearings went on late into the night after the judges' staffs left for the day. One night, after the district judge, Skelly Wright, issued an order, and because his secretary had gone home, Jim Nabrit typed it out and the judge signed it.

Our lead lawyer in the New Orleans school case was A. P. Tureaud, at whose sparely equipped office we worked day and night. A. P. stood for Alexander Pierre, but everyone called him Tureaud. Like many other black lawyers, he never used his given names. He was rotund, the crown of his bald head ringed by gray hair, very soft-spoken in style, and always calm, even in trying situations. Indeed, he often seemed to be on the verge of chuckling, amused by the shenanigans of the opposition. He had graduated from Howard Law School in 1925, returned to New Orleans in 1927, and worked in the customs house, a job he got through political connections. Like many other Southern blacks of this period Tureaud was a Republican. He went into full-time practice in 1935.

For a while there had been two other black lawyers in town, graduates of Straight University in New Orleans, which had been set up as an integrated institution during Reconstruction, but which was defunct by the 1880s. Tureaud was the only black lawyer in New Orleans from 1937 to 1950, when he was joined by Earl J. Amadee, who did virtually no civil rights work. In 1952 or 1953 A. M. "Mutt" Trudeau (the similarity of names sometimes led to confusion) became the next black lawyer in New Orleans and devoted a great deal of his time to civil rights. In 1954 they were joined by Ernest Morial, who entered Tureaud's firm, and later became mayor, and by Robert Collins, the first black law graduate of Louisiana State University—the fruit of cases Tureaud and LDF had won.

Tureaud's office was in a modest walkup in the black section of town. Books, furniture, and office equipment were minimal. He also conducted a real estate business from the premises. These were the forces with which we confronted the assembled might of the state of Louisiana, its governor, mayors, legislature, treasury, corps of lawyers, and a hostile white population.

In early 1956, Tureaud, with "Mutt" Trudeau, Thurgood, and Bob (who dropped out of the case following his resignation from LDF), presented the New Orleans case to a three-judge court, which referred it to a single judge, Skelly Wright. Wright then presided over a litigation that by 1962 resulted in forty-one judicial opinions and many more trials and arguments. Wright had a straight back, held his head high, in a military manner, and spoke concisely, as if accustomed to giving commands.

Before he went on the bench, Wright was best known for having argued in the Supreme Court the case of Willie Francis, a black adolescent who had been sentenced to death for murder. The execution was bungled and the electric chair didn't kill Francis, though it burned and shocked him severely. Wright argued that to execute Francis at this point would amount to double jeopardy and cruel and unusual punishment, but in 1947 he lost five to four and the state was allowed to take a second shot at executing Francis, this one successful.

In 1948 Wright was among the few Louisiana Democrats who supported Truman, the majority having defected to Strom Thurmond's Dixiecrats. That, plus the fact that he had become a United States attorney and was reasonably well connected politically, got him the United States District Court judgeship in 1949.

For some time there were only two federal judges in New Orleans, Wright and Herbert W. Christenberry. While Christenberry was not a hard-line segregationist, his sympathies were not as much in tune with ours as were Wright's. At times, he permitted cases to linger interminably when we thought he should have ruled for us, so civil rights lawyers always preferred Wright. The method of assigning cases between Christenberry and Wright was for one to get the even-numbered cases, the other the odd-numbered ones. Those who preferred Wright would lie in wait near the clerk's desk. As soon as a case was assigned to Christenberry, a lawyer seeking Wright would step right up and file. It didn't take long for the clerk to catch on, and the system was changed.

Louisiana filed a slew of defenses: It had not consented to be sued; the court had not given permission to file a supplemental complaint; the newly appointed school superintendent should have been named in an amended complaint; plaintiffs had not stated a justiciable controversy and hadn't exhausted their administrative remedies. Wright entered a rather gentle temporary injunction. Segregation had to end "with all deliberate speed." He expressed sympathy for white Southerners: "It is a problem which will require the utmost patience and understanding, generosity and forbearance from all of us, of whatever race."

The defendants then began an interminable hegira of litigation from court to court that went on virtually daily for years. The bulwark of the Constitution in all of this became the United States Fifth Circuit Court of Appeals, the heroes of which were Richard T. Rives, Elbert P. Tuttle, John R. Brown, and John Minor Wisdom.

Rives, of Montgomery, belonged to the traditional Deep South culture of Alabama, but had developed a sympathy for the plight of Southern blacks. He had served as campaign manager for Hugo Black when he was elected to the United States Senate. Associates speculated that Rives's feelings derived from his son, who had been educated at Exeter and Harvard, served in the Second World War, and became committed to working against racial injustice. Rives had planned to practice with his son, but he was killed in an automobile accident while still in law school. One of the son's friends believed that "Rives wanted to live the new South his son talked to him about."

Tuttle had lived in Atlanta since 1923, but had grown up in Hawaii, where he had attended the elite, multiracial Punaho school, and went to college and law school at Cornell. Well over six feet tall, thin, with ramrod posture, he had been a war hero who engaged in bloody hand-to-hand combat with Japanese in the Pacific. He carried his military bearing while on the bench; lawyers felt they were in the presence of their superior officer.

John Minor Wisdom came from a traditional, well-connected New Orleans background, belonged to—and continued to after he went on the bench—the "right" clubs, even those that excluded blacks and Jews. He was outspoken, however, in his belief in absolute racial equality. One of his grandfathers, Wisdom proudly observed, came from "a Jewish, French background." Wisdom went to Tulane Law School and to Harvard as a graduate student. In the Second World War he worked in the office of legal procurement with a group of lawyers from all over the country who would later become part of the national legal elite. Wisdom returned to New Orleans to build a highly successful practice and developed a national, nonracial perspective. He was on the board of the New Orleans Urban League and the President's Committee on Government Contracts, which had been set up to prevent racial discrimination in letting of government business. This raised some questions with virulently racist Mississippi Senator Jim Eastland, who chaired the Judiciary Committee. But Wisdom's establishment connections assured Eastland that he was not a radical or liberal and he was confirmed.

John Brown grew up in Nebraska in a small town in which only one black person lived, a shoe shine man, with whom Brown was friendly. Abraham Lincoln was Brown's boyhood hero. He went to law school at the University of Michigan and then practiced with an admiralty firm in Galveston, Texas, where he became a partner. Southern traditions scarcely had touched him.

Tuttle, Brown, and Wisdom were Southern Republicans who had supported Eisenhower in 1952, indeed, helped assure his winning the Republican nomination. Like Skelly Wright, who was among the few Democrats who did not join the Dixiecrats, they were not part of the dominant segregationist Democratic oligarchy.

In the Fifth Circuit, which presided over the core racial issues of that time, the churning effect of the Second World War had weakened the sense of regional isolation and undermined many parochial perceptions about race. A growing number of people in the area began to view the racial status quo as neither right nor inevitable. This kind of reorientation came to a focus in the persons of Rives (through his son), Tuttle, Wisdom, and Brown. Through them the broader values of places like Harvard, Michigan, Cornell, Washington, Hawaii, and Nebraska, aided and abetted by perspectives born of other experiences outside the South, would find their way into Fifth Circuit decisions.

In the meantime, the Louisiana state legislature passed a mountain of ridiculous obstructionist legislation, and the schools continued to segregate, with the full encouragement of political leaders in all branches of Louisiana government. At one point the district court cited the state attorney general, Jack P. F. Gremillion, for contempt because he had called the district court "a den of iniquity" and a "kangaroo court." Gremillion defended, saying that he had been misunderstood: He really had said "a den of *inequity*." He got sixty days in the custody of the United States attorney general, probated to eighteen months if he remained on good behavior.

As the end approached in 1960, the legislature passed twenty-five more acts crafted to prevent desegregation. In the meantime school officials began screening 137 black applicants for transfer to white schools under seventeen pupil assignment standards, including psychological and ability testing. Officials decided that five black children were qualified to transfer to white schools. But, on November 13, 1960, the eve of desegregation under the district court's desegregation order, the state superintendent of education declared a school holiday.

Staying up all night to prepare the papers, Thurgood and Tureaud got an injunction against observing the holiday, and only then did the first, tiny step toward integration begin in Louisiana. The *New York Times* reported:

Federal deputy marshals escorted four black girls into two white elementary schools, while angry crowds hurled jeers and insults. Many white parents withdrew their children from school. Marching youths sang "Glory, glory segregation" to the tune of the "Battle Hymn of the Republic" and legislators filled the capitol at Baton Rouge with threats and a flood of oratory.

Norman Rockwell painted a *Saturday Evening Post* cover of the event in which one of the girls entered the school, depicting all the radiant beauty of innocence Rockwell had long found in the faces of his young white subjects.

Mobs gathered and police restrained them; there was no violence. Two days later, however, mobs "surged through New Orleans streets . . . in demonstrations against school integration that were marked by sporadic rioting, assaults and vandalism." Blacks retaliated by throwing rocks and bottles and prepared Molotov cocktails. The Louisiana Citizens Council gathered a mob of five thousand shouting segregationists. White students boycotted the schools the blacks had entered. The state legislature called for Judge Wright to step down. Louisiana Senator Russell B. Long said, "I would personally vote to impeach the entire Supreme Court if I thought my vote would do it. But we simply do not have the votes." The Louisiana House of Representatives passed a resolution accusing President Eisenhower and the federal courts of "making common cause with the Communist conspiracy."

Later in November, Judges Wright, Rives, and Christenberry authorized the United States attorney general to appear as amicus curiae in the case and, on November 30, 1960, held twenty-five new laws unconstitutional. The burden on us began easing a bit when the district court upheld the right of the United States to participate in the case. In two hearings in early 1961, in which the United States attorney appeared on our side, the district court knocked out some additional state laws.

The year 1961 marked the beginning of a new administration in Washington and, with it, a change in the composition of the federal judiciary in the South. Not long after desegregation began in Louisiana, John F. Kennedy named Skelly Wright to the United States Court of Appeals for the District of Columbia. Under any other circumstances Wright would have been promoted to the Fifth Circuit Court of Appeals. But sending him to the D.C. Circuit gave Wright a well-deserved promotion, while it served the segregationists in Louisiana as well, getting rid of a jurist who was dedicated to upholding the law in the face of all manner of challenges. Kennedy replaced Wright with Frank Ellis, his Louisiana campaign manager. While not as unfriendly to blacks as some other Kennedy-appointed Southern judges, Ellis went right to work cutting back on Wright's desegregation orders, limiting them to the first grade, and did little to enforce civil rights law.

VIRGINIA

Virginia's white public and politicians, though farther north, were right up there with those of Louisiana in the vanguard of the massive resisters of segregation. But the small group of black lawyers there, led mainly by Spotts Robinson, with Oliver Hill, Jim Nabrit III, Frank Reeves, and Otto Tucker, battered the state into some acquiescence, so that by mid-1960, 103 black children were in school with whites.

The courts had debilitated the practice of pupil assignment as it was being applied because race had been a criterion for assignment to a black or white school from which a student would have to apply for transfer. They struck down the administrative process of pupil assignment because it treated blacks and whites differently, and held the school closing law unconstitutional because it was only called into effect when white schools were forced to admit blacks. By 1960 Virginia was starting to face the fact that Jim Crow, while not yet shot down, was trailing smoke and in a steep descent.

PUPIL ASSIGNMENT: THE DEFENSE IN DEPTH

In the early years after *Brown*, only in Mississippi was the black community too intimidated to file even one case. Then, when across the South violence finally was beaten down, and outright defiance was subdued, blacks had to run the gauntlet of pupil assignment, which in the end became the South's most effective defense against desegregation. Pupil assignment statutes erected unknowable and insurmountable procedural barriers to desegregating and put a premium on lying; officials could exclude children because of race simply by giving false reasons for the exclusion, including adverse effects on health, welfare, and the effective administration of the schools.

The strategem had its origins in the South Carolina case that had gone to the Supreme Court as part of *Brown*. Less than six weeks after the Supreme Court's implementation decision returned *Briggs* to the district court, Judge Parker, while declaring the South Carolina school segregation laws "null and void," merely enjoined the defendants from excluding blacks after they made the necessary arrangements "for admission . . . on a non-discriminatory basis with all deliberate speed." He added:

> If the schools which [the state] maintains are open to children of all races, no violation of the Constitution is involved even though the children of different races voluntarily attend different schools, as they attend different churches. . . . *The Constitution, in other words, does not require integration. It merely forbids discrimination*. It does not forbid such segregation as occurs as the result of voluntary action.[15]

Parker's opinion imposed no deadline, invited school boards to do nothing, and placed the burden of change on blacks, enlisting black fear and white recalcitrance in the cause of the status quo. Finally, because children had the spurious opportunity to transfer to nonsegregated schools, boards might invoke the doctrine that requires a plaintiff to exhaust many time-consuming administrative procedures before going to court. Virtually every ostensibly race-neutral standard applied discriminatorily to exclude blacks could only be challenged with airtight proof of discrimination, for its honest intent and application were always presumed by those running the administrative appeal processes. Applicants might have to learn how whites were assigned, something about their residence, grades, and conduct, or what went on during deliberations of the board—among an almost infinite number of possibilities. A simple matter of applying to a school would become, literally and figuratively, a big federal case.

The Parker opinion encouraged widespread adoption of pupil placement laws. The people who drew up the North Carolina law were said to have been good friends of Parker. Thurgood said he had learned that Parker had privately offered the opinion to state officials that such laws would meet the requirements of *Brown*. In any event, Arkansas, Florida, Louisiana, Mississippi, North Carolina, South Carolina, Tennessee, Texas, and Virginia all adopted such laws. They typically required that children might transfer from one school to another according to vague criteria, such as (in North Carolina) "health, safety and general welfare." They authorized local school boards to adopt rules for transfers and set up appeal procedures. Transfer forms were distributed only on certain days and had to be picked up in person (usually during working hours), returned in person promptly, and notarized. Appeals had to be in person, not through counsel. Every state with such laws first placed black and white children in the "school the child normally would attend." It then was nearly impossible (in most places entirely impossible) for a black child to get out. Those few who did were anomalies: They surely weren't in integrated systems.

Within pupil assignment some systems adopted grade-a-year plans, admitting black children to the first grade during the first year of the plan, to the second during the second year, and so forth, under which plan it would take twelve years to integrate the system. The rationale was that younger children take to integration better. But other grade-a-year plans admitted blacks to white schools in the twelfth grade during the first year, to the eleventh during the second year, and so forth, on the theory that older children integrate better. The only point of concurrence seemed to be that slower was better than prompter when it came to integration.

Other districts enacted minority-to-majority transfer procedures, which made it sound as if they were dealing with both races equally: A white child assigned to a predominantly black school had the right to transfer, and a black child assigned to a predominantly white school also might transfer. Given the choice, virtually all members of both groups did transfer out of the school where they would be in the minority, usually effecting the transfer on paper before school began. The practical effect of such policy was that the education system remained totally segregated, or very nearly so.

We had to consider whether to attack pupil assignment head on as unconstitutional, or whether to build a record of how it worked, to demonstrate that it was, in fact, a means of perpetuating segregation. If we were able to attack it head on, or in its face, and it was upheld, it might then be viewed as presumptively valid in later challenges based on how it was applied—or so we thought. We believed that the Supreme Court, having struggled through three years of *Brown*, and having observed the Southern uprising against it, would be reluctant to confront school segregation so soon again. We decided to forego the head-on attack and to build a record instead.

The slow, yet continuing, growth of the black bar proved to be a mixed blessing. Other lawyers had ideas different from ours and chose to attack pupil assignment head on. Lawyers in North Carolina and Alabama launched attacks on pupil assignment by themselves. They didn't ask us and we had no input into their cases. They lost.

One of the early cases was in Asheville, North Carolina, the birthplace of novelist Thomas Wolfe. High in the Smoky Mountains—the area had once been a favorite summer resort of the Vanderbilts, whose red tile–roofed estates dominated the area—Asheville had a single black lawyer, Reuben Dailey. Its black population was small and those not engaged in agriculture worked in local mica mines, out in the "hollers" (hollows), as the locals called the area. Black kids had to make what was an eighty-mile round trip to the nearest black school.

I spent a lot of time in many hearings in Judge Wilson Warlick's court, watching him sentence moonshiners while I waited for my case to be heard and finally won a court order requiring the local school board to admit some plaintiffs to a white school. This was the first court order in North Carolina requiring any desegregation. But as we had learned elsewhere, such cases were rarely concluded all at once. Courtroom skirmishes continued into 1963.

I brought my sons Josiah and David, then aged eight and six, to Asheville. We stayed in Reuben Dailey's house, and the boys came to court with me the next day. Then, with Conrad Pearson, we traveled to a nearby Indian reservation where I bought them a peace pipe and had their pictures taken with Indians in full headdress. Their clearest recollections are of the enormous quantities of fried chicken they consumed and of Reuben feeding his dogs chicken bones, which was supposed to be death for dogs in the North; Reuben's dogs apparently thrived on them. They have no memories of the historic drama played out in the courtroom.

Much earlier, in November 1955, I had filed suit against Harford County, Maryland, and the school board there agreed to admit children without regard to race, beginning in September 1956. I therefore dropped the case, typing the order myself in the clerk's office, making clear that I was withdrawing the suit only because black children would be admitted to the white schools. But when four of the plaintiffs applied to the white schools, the board rejected them. Learning of this, I tried to reopen the case but the judge, Roszel Thomsen, held that we had to exhaust our administrative remedies before being allowed back in court, and then ordered the school board to reconsider the applications of only two of the four plaintiffs. I argued that the school board was bound by the representation on which I had dismissed the complaint. The Fourth Circuit upheld the judge. The school board then announced that it would admit black students in all grades by 1963.

We didn't have much luck with grade-a-year plans either. Shortly after *Brown II* Thurgood sued the Nashville, Tennessee, schools with local counsel—Avon Williams, Thurgood's cousin, who had graduated from Boston University Law School and begun practice in 1949, and Avon's partner, Z.

(Zephaniah) Alexander Looby, who had graduated from Columbia Law School in 1925. Looby, as Thurgood called him—Avon referred always to "Mr. Looby"—spoke with a West Indian accent, walked with a bad limp, and, remarkably, was elected to the Nashville city council in 1964. Looby and Williams were the only lawyers handling civil rights cases in Nashville and most of eastern Tennessee at that time. There was another black lawyer in Knoxville, Carl Cowan, and a couple in Memphis, right on the Mississippi border.

Not long after *Brown*, the board submitted a plan to permit blacks to attend white schools in the first grade, which the federal district court held was an acceptable start. But it was a struggle every inch of the way. It later held unconstitutional a state law allowing segregated schools to exist with nonsegregated ones, and rejected the school board's argument that we had to exhaust administrative remedies. In 1958 the court ordered the board to present a plan to desegregate the entire system.

In the meantime, John Kasper, a notorious segregationist, led riots to attack first-grade desegregation. A bomb destroyed a synagogue. Hattie Cotton School, where one black child was enrolled, was bombed. The school board then proposed that blacks be permitted to transfer to white schools one grade each year commencing in 1958, completing the process in 1968, actually a little faster than grade-a-year. The courts upheld the plan. We took the case to the Supreme Court, which refused to hear it. As with virtually all denials of certiorari, the Court never gave a reason, but we speculated, I think correctly, that the Court did not want to become embroiled in contentious school desegregation cases any more than absolutely necessary.

Pupil assignment, grade-a-year integration, and minority-to-majority transfer accommodated to the violence, the political remonstrances, and the threat of congressional retaliation. They allowed schools to claim they were desegregating, while actually doing nothing, or very little, and allowed courts to dismiss cases or enter minimal orders. The best remedy for this inertia would be a change in political climate.

THE EXTENT OF SCHOOL DESEGREGATION: 1960

By end of the 1950s LDF had commenced more than sixty elementary and high school cases, but only a few had been concluded. The issues under litigation included flat refusals to desegregate (Louisiana and Virginia), outright violence (Little Rock), lower courts' reluctance to enforce the law vigorously (Maryland, South Carolina, Texas, and Virginia), pupil placement rules (Maryland, North Carolina, and Tennessee), and other stratagems to subvert integration. Many cases involved a combination of resistance tactics. In June 1960, forty-six school cases were still pending in Arkansas, Delaware, Florida, Georgia, Kentucky, Louisiana, Maryland, North Carolina, South Carolina, Tennessee, Texas, Virginia, and West Virginia—virtually all LDF cases.

The LDF staff and board urged that something be done to spur blacks and whites to do more apart from litigation. Even before *Brown II*, June Shagaloff and Dan Byrd were already working with community groups. As early as January 1955 we had hired three educational specialists to work with NAACP branches, churches, labor groups, and school boards to bring about desegregation without legal action. We set up a committee of social scientists, including more than forty scholars, under the leadership of Alfred McClung Lee, a professor of education at Brooklyn College, and Kenneth Clark, to offer expert advice. Dr. John W. Davis, former president of West Virginia State College, set up a department of Teacher Information and Security at LDF to preserve jobs of black teachers. The idea was right. However, while the field workers and social scientists were able to promote desegregation in a few Northern and border areas, they were greatly underfunded and badly understaffed, which severely limited what they could accomplish.

What had all our efforts achieved? By June 1960, in five states of the Deep South—Alabama, Georgia, Louisiana, Mississippi, and South Carolina—not a single black child was in school with whites. In Arkansas, Florida, North Carolina, Tennessee, and Virginia the numbers of black children attending white schools ranged from 34 to 169. But in border areas the numbers were substantial: Delaware, 6,196; the District of Columbia, 73,290; Kentucky, estimated 12,000; Maryland, 28,072; Missouri, estimated 35,000; Oklahoma, estimated 10,000; Texas, estimated 3,300; and West Virginia, estimated 12,000. Little of this, however, was genuine integration, generally consisting instead of a few blacks in formerly white schools and not of whites in formerly black schools. Virtually no school districts were yet fully integrated, with all students assigned to schools on bases other than race.

States began improving the schools blacks attended. There were two basic motivations for this change. The first, of course, was that blacks might be less inclined to transfer from all-black schools if the schools available to them were of a higher quality. The states were, however, too late in coming to this understanding. The states' second reason for improving the conditions of black schools was that if any whites ended up having to go to black schools they would at least be decent schools. Of course, the prospect of lawsuits was no doubt the ultimate moving force.

Another important effect of the suits was that they kept the issue before the public: Blacks, especially, now knew they had rights that the majority population had an obligation to respect. This new awareness soon translated into the civil rights movement of the 1960s.

19

VIVID MEMORIES

From the beginning of my involvement in *Brown* and into the early 1960s, certain episodes stand out in memory, even though some of those better-remembered moments were no more important than many others I now have difficulty recalling.

THE FRESHLY CIRCUMCISED RAPIST
AND OTHER CRIMINAL CASES

I keep thinking that if I had done something different, I might have saved Ozzie Jones's life. In October 1952 he was sentenced to death for the rape of a white woman in Savannah. His parents hired a lawyer but were unable to pay him, and for that reason, he told the prosecutor, he wouldn't represent Jones. But, on the day of trial, when he happened to be in the courthouse, the judge ordered him to proceed.

The lawyer was totally unprepared and didn't even know the most important facts—that the victim was a white woman and that not long before the rape Jones had been circumcised. Jones's doctor had a photograph of Jones's stitched and swollen penis, taken after the circumcision; the photo certainly could have been used to demonstrate that it would have been impossible for Jones to have committed a rape when this rape occurred. Jones also could have proved that he was at a location from which it was very unlikely he could have reached the scene of the crime at the time it occurred. But the lawyer, who had only fifteen minutes to prepare, put on a flimsy defense. In April 1953 the Georgia Supreme Court affirmed the death sentence, with Jones still represented by the same reluctant lawyer.

The NAACP branch in Savannah engaged a local black lawyer who, with A. T. Walden of Atlanta, then in his seventies, drove hundreds of miles back and forth to interview Jones in the state prison at Reidsville. At the branch's request I prepared a petition for habeas corpus in the state courts and the local lawyer filed it. We lost in the state supreme court in December on the grounds that Jones had had his own lawyer at the trial and that the representation was not a "nullity." At that point I began preparing the case for the United States Supreme Court and filed a petition, which it denied in April 1954. The only course left was a petition for federal habeas corpus, which, in those days, was an extremely difficult remedy, and one most likely to lose.

I sent a draft petition for federal habeas corpus to our local lawyer in Savannah, asked him to file it and secure a stay of execution. He said that he would. For a long while I heard nothing, and, wondering what was going on, called him. The phone had been disconnected. I should have called earlier. I discovered now that he had left town. He had fallen into serious financial difficulties in a real estate business and fled, telling no one where he was going and dropping everything, including Ozzie Jones's case. There was no other black lawyer in Savannah and no white lawyer to whom we could turn.

I immediately called Walden in Atlanta, who discovered that Jones's execution was scheduled for the next day; he drove to Savannah to file for habeas corpus and get a stay of the execution. United States District Judge Frank M. Scarlett, who was adamantly hostile to blacks, turned him down. There was no time to prepare an appeal. Thurgood tried to get a stay over the telephone from one of the judges on the court of appeals, but it was impossible. Finally he called the Georgia attorney general, Eugene Cook, who had been opposite Thurgood in many lawsuits. I sat with Thurgood during the conversation; his face lit up at first, but quickly changed to a frown. After he hung up he said that Cook at first was willing to agree, but then recalled the case, asking, "Say, isn't that the nigger who raped a white girl over in Savannah? I can't go along on that."

Ozzie Jones was electrocuted for rape, a sentence that is now unconstitutional, for a crime he almost surely didn't commit. The disgrace to the legal profession is that he was executed as a consequence of a conviction obtained while he was without the effective assistance of counsel. I got word of the execution while at home. My immediate reaction was to slam my head against the wall.

This occurred during the Army–McCarthy hearings. When the U.S. Army failed to provide David Schine, a former assistant to Senator Joseph McCarthy, the special treatment the senator thought he should have received, the senator took it as a reflection of the army's lack of conviction in rooting out Communists and took off after the army. The army had its friends in the Senate, and soon hearings were convened to learn if indeed the senator had used undue pressure to obtain special treatment for his former aide. The hearings turned into that summer's favorite afternoon television fare.

For days I had no stomach for work. I sat in a bar around the corner from the office, following the hearings on TV. If I had been more diligent in checking with the Savannah lawyer we might have had a hearing in the federal courts, although federal habeas corpus didn't become meaningful until the 1960s. My belief in the unjustness of the death penalty for rape, and the racially discriminatory way it was used—executed in Ozzie Jones's case and barely avoided in the *Groveland* case—was the reason I started our campaign against capital punishment, which led to the Supreme Court's 1977 decision finding the death penalty unconstitutional in rape cases.

GROVELAND AGAIN

On January 4, 1954, the Supreme Court had refused to hear *Groveland*. I had thought we had a shot at winning on the search and seizure point—the taking of Walter Irvin's shoes without a warrant. But we couldn't overcome the fact that Irvin's mother had given consent. Worse, in 1949, the Supreme Court, in *Wolf v. Colorado*, had refused to exclude illegally seized evidence from consideration. There were other ways to encourage the police to behave legally in their collection of evidence, the Court suggested, like suits for damages against the police. Not until 1961, in *Mapp v. Ohio*, would the Court adopt the exclusionary rule, the principle that evidence obtained illegally could not be used to convict a defendant.

I prepared a petition for rehearing *Groveland*, which the Court promptly denied. As a last resort, we hired a private detective to find out what had really happened the night of the alleged rape. In the usual manner of private detectives, however, he reported only "progress" and we never received any useful information.

By the end of 1955 we had exhausted all possibilities of judicial relief, but the governor still had the power to commute the death penalty. Allan Knight Chalmers organized clergymen in Florida to stir up support for clemency. The *St. Petersburg Times* and the national press strongly supported commutation. The new governor, Leroy Collins, while far from a flaming liberal—he had opposed Virgil Hawkins's admission to the University of Florida—was decently disposed. Collins had been shocked by *Groveland*—particularly by the widespread violence the case provoked and by the conduct of Willis McCall, one of the sheriffs who had shot Irvin—and asked two private lawyers to conduct a confidential investigation. They reported that the plaster casts of footprints and tire prints were fake. Jess Hunter, the prosecutor who obtained Irvin's conviction, was dying of leukemia, and told Collins that he had doubts about Irvin's guilt.

In December 1955 Collins commuted the death sentence to life imprisonment; this caused him great political grief, even though Hunter supported him publicly. McCall and his supporters in Lake County fought

Collins, trotting out Norma Padgett at political rallies all dressed up in her Sunday best.

Years later, the state paroled Irvin on condition that he not return to Lake County. He got a job in Miami, where he had an exemplary work record. Subsequently, the parole commission gave him permission to visit his family in Lake County, but for a single day only. While sitting on the front porch, at the home of relatives, he suddenly dropped dead.

PIGTAILS, BEANS, AND THE LOLLAPALOOZA

While by the mid-1950s there were a few black lawyers in Durham, North Carolina, C. O. (Conrad) Pearson, Howard Law School class of 1932, was the first to do much civil rights work. A gentle, patient man with a general practice and a small office on the second floor of a walkup building in the black section of town, he and his wife, Mildred, lived in a farmhouse. I stayed with them when in Durham, and we all enjoyed great dinners of fried chicken and corn bread. Conrad helped me buy real North Carolina moonshine, which I once smuggled back to New York, fearful all the way that it would be discovered and bring my legal career to ruin. Although, as recommended, I placed a gauze-wrapped peach in the jar to absorb the virulent flavor, it tasted too yeasty, but not unlike Dutch genever gin. Conrad's ambition was to own racehorses and late in his career he bought several, including Mandace Brave and San Sun Set, who had a club foot. As far as I know, neither horse ever won anything. Conrad's young associates, Billy Marsh and Floyd McKissick, also took part as lawyers in the Durham school case.

McKissick, who had integrated the University of North Carolina Law School, later became national chairman of CORE and creator of Soul City, a black new town in the North Carolina countryside. But I never can remember him without recalling the "pigtails and beans." As the Durham case progressed, McKissick reported that he had acquired a client who, while eating a plate of pigtails and beans at a restaurant, discovered a mouse under the beans. He called over the manager who insisted that the object was a pigtail. The client then attempted to take the plate from the restaurant (to preserve the evidence). The manager restrained him, and a struggle ensued from which the client broke loose, carrying with him the plate with the pigtails, beans, and mouse, if that's what it was. He placed the plate in a freezer and retained McKissick, who sued for assault, breach of contract and warranty, negligence, and so forth. McKissick had visions of big money damages and a large fee. As the case progressed, the restaurant's lawyer interviewed the plaintiff and examined the disputed object. It turned out that the "mouse" was a white albino laboratory rat, just like ones caged in the hospital laboratory where the plaintiff worked, and very unlike the kind of mouse that might inhabit a restaurant kitchen. McKissick dropped the case. But the saga lasted for more than two years and talking about it took up almost as much of our time as the school case itself.

The Durham case began in 1955, right after *Brown*. Seven hundred and forty blacks petitioned the school board to prepare a desegregation plan and continued petitioning until 1959, when the board admitted McKissick's daughter to the white high school. That year 225 children applied under the pupil assignment law. The board admitted nine to high school and three to junior high school, but none to any white elementary school. Our appeal took place in the basement of a school building, the evening of September 21, 1959, eighteen days after school began, making any further transfers for that semester impossible.

At seven o'clock the six school board members, pillars of the society, filed in and sat at tables at the front of the room, solemn and inscrutable—like an egregious tribunal in a lithograph by Daumier, some members fat, some gaunt, all grave, none alert to do justice. The room was packed with black parents. The chairman called the roll. Conrad presented powers-of-attorney for parents of 165 children and written appeals requesting reassignments. The appeals argued only that the school system was segregated. The chairman called the roll of petitioners. Some were present and others absent.

At eight o'clock the board retired to deliberate. Soon they returned: The children of parents who were not present had failed to exhaust their administrative remedies, even though represented by counsel. All their appeals were denied. The appeals of all the other children—those whose parents were present—were also denied. The board gave no reasons.

I returned to New York and reported to Thurgood. He remarked that the only way a child could have transferred was to have been "neither here nor there." He sometimes told a story about a poker game that took place in a remote Alaskan village. With an enormous pot on the table, an out-of-towner turned over a royal flush, which should have beaten anything. But a local player threw down a three of clubs, four of diamonds, seven of hearts, ten of spades, and jack of clubs. "That's a lollapalooza," he said, "and under the rules in this town it beats even a royal flush." He raked in the money to the raised eyebrows of the out-of-towner. Later in the game the local player had a pair of tens. This time it was the visitor who miraculously turned over the five cards necessary for the lollapalooza. As he reached for the money, the fellow with the pair stopped him and said, "There's one thing about lollapaloozas I forgot to tell you. Only one allowed per night." And he raked in the money again.

So we filed our lawsuit, for the lead plaintiff, John Wheeler III, son of a black banker. For more than seven years Jim Nabrit, other staff lawyers, and I engaged in pretrial activity and nine lower court trials and appellate arguments. By 1966 we won an order allowing any child to transfer to any school; teachers were encouraged to teach where pupils were wholly or predominantly of a race other than their own; new teachers were to be employed regardless of race. But even this victory hardly constituted true integration, because most black children and very few, if any, white children would transfer. Encouraging teacher transfer, while a nice idea, would not, by itself, integrate the teaching corps.

Years later, John Wheeler, the high school student plaintiff, became an airline pilot and founded his own regional airline.

DESEGREGATING THE NATIONAL GUARD

I prepared a petition to the governor of Maryland asking him to desegregate the National Guard, arguing that while it was, according to the Universal Military Training and Service Act, supposed to be "an integral part of the first line defenses of this nation," a segregated National Guard could not be integral to nonsegregated armed forces. Integrated armed forces fought better, segregation weakened America in its relations with other nations, was unconstitutional, and caused black troops to be treated unequally. It was a little awesome to sit at the conference table with Governor Theodore Mc-Keldin, where Juanita Mitchell and I argued the case, I making legal and policy arguments, and Juanita urgently, stridently, emphatically, endlessly pounding away at the immorality and injustice of segregating those who would defend their country. That McKeldin would receive us was a sign of change in political climate. To our astonishment, he ruled with us and desegregated the guard.

COULD JOE LOUIS FIGHT MAX SCHMELING IN LOUISIANA?

Jim Nabrit III's first Supreme Court brief for LDF, in 1959, involved a Louisiana law prohibiting any "fistic combat match, boxing, sparring, or wrestling contest or exhibition between any person of the Caucasian or 'white' race and one of the African or 'negro' race." Under that law Joe Louis couldn't have fought many of his great fights, including the ones against Max Schmeling and Jimmy Braddock. A three-judge court held the law unconstitutional. Louisiana took the case to the Supreme Court, which upheld the lower court without argument.

THE CRUCIAL NECESSITY OF "STATE ACTION"

Hubert Eaton, a North Carolina doctor and the mentor of Althea Gibson, the great black tennis star who was Wimbeldon champion in 1957 and 1958, for years tried to practice medicine at the James Walker Memorial Hospital in Wilmington, North Carolina, but was excluded because he was black. Finally, a local lawyer sued and lost on the grounds that Memorial was a private hospital. Because there was no "state action," the Fourteenth Amendment's equal protection clause, which prohibits *states* from denying equal protection, did not apply. But he had failed to put in evidence that the city and federal governments had heavily supported the hospital. I prepared a petition to the United States Supreme Court, which made these important facts clear, although they had not been offered as evidence in the lower court, using the somewhat irregular procedure of simply "lodging" documents in the clerk office. The rules didn't provide for it, but I simply went to the Supreme Court clerk's office and handed in the papers. I failed to win a review. Three justices, Warren, Douglas, and Brennan, however, dissented from the denial of review, suggesting that there might be sentiment on the Court for relaxing the requirements for demonstrating state action. I set about preparing a new case.

It began to appear that where the courts saw some significant state involvement they would act. We desegregated the North Carolina state dental association, a private organization, on the grounds that it helped select the State Board of Dental Examiners, which approved the qualifications of dentists.

But another Durham case underscored once more how little the state action doctrine was understood by general practitioners. In the "ice cream case," the state convicted blacks of trespass for entering a whites-only ice cream parlor, where they preached Christian principles to the proprietor who would not serve them and refused to—a precursor of the sit-ins. A Durham ordinance prohibited service of whites and blacks together, and a police officer arrested them. The cooperating lawyers arguing the case proceeded with the argument that the conviction violated the Fourteenth Amendment, but didn't call the ordinance prohibiting service of blacks and whites to the court's attention. The ordinance would have provided crucial evidence of state action. [Conventional legal doctrine holds that the existence of a local ordinance has to be proven as a fact (unless state law permitted some other method); it couldn't be found in and cited out of the law books, like a state or federal statute.]

LDF took up the case after it had been lost in the North Carolina Supreme Court. I wrote a cert petition, which argued that it was unreasonable to ignore the ordinance; there was no doubt it existed. But the Supreme Court denied certiorari.

Other memories that stand out:

• After we won the New Orleans airport case: A. P. Tureaud's daughter skipping down a corridor of the New Orleans airport with an ice cream cone she wouldn't have been permitted to buy a week earlier.
• The Greenville, South Carolina, airport case: Court attendants carrying ancient Judge George Bell Timmerman up to the bench—he couldn't get up there himself without help—so he could rule against me on a dozen

grounds, including that the plaintiff hadn't proved that black facilities were unequal or even that he ever would return to the airport. The Fourth Circuit reversed promptly.

• The Greenville, South Carolina, city council trying to turn the municipal swimming pool into "a marina for seals, sea lions, exotic fish and herpatarium (snake house)" to become the sea lion capital of the world—this is true—rather than allowing blacks and whites to swim together.

• The name of the Atlanta airport case, *Coke v. City of Atlanta* (Atlanta is the home of the Coca-Cola Company), and the cheerful greetings that the white restaurant manager, a heavy-set, middle-aged woman, extended after we won. She was delighted to run the place on an integrated basis.

• Puzzling over why we had so many golf course cases in which plaintiffs were black dentists. Indeed, in civil rights cases generally, the number of dentist-plaintiffs was disproportionately large. Black professionals wanted to play golf, like their white counterparts. They were different from later militant leaders whose goal was radical economic reconstruction. Some said that dentists were socially active in order to gain status vis-à-vis doctors; others explained that their schedules were controllable and so they could set aside time for civil rights activities.

We debated whether to put resources into such cases, and decided we should. Dentists had rights too, every defeat of segregation contributed to its ultimate destruction, and last, but not least, these middle-class professionals were then the mainstay of the civil rights movement. Moreover, lots of people played golf, not just dentists and doctors.

• Thurgood the witness. Thurgood could be persuasive in a case even when he wasn't the lawyer. In the Virginia case, where a legislative committe demanded our contributors list, Jim Nabrit put Thurgood on the stand to testify that if we were to turn over our contributor lists our supporters might be intimidated. The state's lawyer objected that Thurgood's testimony was hearsay, to which Thurgood began to reply—this was Jim's job as counsel, not the witness's—with a learned disquisition on exceptions to the hearsay rule. The judge was fascinated by Thurgood and didn't seem to want to hear from Jim. Thurgood and the judge conducted their private discourse until the subject was exhausted. The Virginia Supreme Court upheld our argument that LDF was a controversial organization and was therefore protected against having to turn over the lists.

A CASE OF MISTAKEN IDENTITY

Oral argument in the Supreme Court begins with calling the number and name of the case, counsel for the appealing party rising and approaching the lectern, and the chief justice addressing him or her by name. For some reason, Earl Warren often, but not always, called me "Mr. Goldberg." I felt I shouldn't correct the chief justice of the United States and never did. I thought that perhaps someone else, another justice or law clerk, would help him get it straight. But he never did.

In 1954, not long after *Brown*, my son David was born and we moved to the Lower East Side of Manhattan to a cooperative project of the International Ladies Garment Workers. In 1958, twins, Ezra and Sarah, were born and we started worrying about more living space and schools. The price of houses was relatively low at that time, so the next year, with the help of a large mortgage, I bought a house in Great Neck for $29,000. To make the payments I earned a little extra money doing research for a New York State Bar Association committee, chaired by Milton Handler, writing reports on the New York antitrust and unfair competition laws and drafting an amended version of the state antitrust law. Great Neck was a middle-class community in which the schools were integrated, although there were relatively few blacks. This caused not a little soul searching, but I came down on the side of the best education I could find for my children. Thurgood and Connie had come to similar conclusions when they each enrolled their own children in Dalton, an elite private school on Manhattan's Upper East Side. We thought we wouldn't help anyone else by doing less than the best we could for our own children. But the answer wasn't clear-cut. While I lived in Great Neck I joined a group that tried to persuade the school board to invite black children from New York City to enroll in our schools, but the opposition was vigorous and we were defeated.

PART IV

THE MOVEMENT TAKES OFF

20

OUT OF THE COURTS AND INTO THE STREETS

THE END OF ONE ERA, BEGINNING OF ANOTHER

Although none of us knew it at the time, *Brown* marked the end of that phase of the civil rights struggle where all our important victories were won in court. By 1960, six years after *Brown*, the "spirit of revolt"—Margold's phrase—was a nationwide phenomenon. Whereas Rosa Parks's refusal to yield her bus seat was not quite an aberration, a new spirit was now taken up and widely shared by an army of young people who were formerly not active in civil rights. This new spirit led to the sit-ins; spread to the Freedom Rides; gave birth to the demand for full equality in all aspects of American life that in its nonviolent expression was personified by Martin Luther King, Jr.; and made inevitable the historic civil rights legislation of 1964 and beyond.

Until the sit-ins began in 1960, open opposition, apart from lawsuits, had usually been more or less compartmentalized, the work of isolated, brave individuals or groups, sometimes local NAACP branches, which might be backed up by lawyers connected with LDF. Charlie Houston had clients who had "sat in" in the 1940s, before that term became current. When I first came to LDF the Baltimore NAACP had been engaged in a "don't buy where you can't work" campaign. Mass dissidence had preceded the Prince Edward County school case; indeed, all of the School Segregation Cases began with some sort of expression of dissatisfaction, not necessarily a lawsuit, with the way things were.

On May 17, 1957, there was Martin Luther King, Jr.'s prayer pilgrimage, held to mark the third anniversary of the *Brown* decision. Association youth councils in Oklahoma City and Wichita sat in at lunch counters beginning in 1958. Of such localized protests, the 1955 Montgomery bus boycott captured national attention, though nothing else capable of achieving such prominence occurred for another five years. During these six years between 1954 and 1960, however, the broader implications of *Brown* were seeping into black consciousness.

Before the movement developed, nearly all advances in racial justice came through the courts. Only two important exceptions of national significance come to mind—the desegregation of the United States armed forces and the opening up of major league baseball to black Americans. Therefore, NAACP and LDF decisions about which cases to promote and which to decline—constrained by our limited resources and policy judgments—were crucial in setting the only national agenda in civil rights, and, as a consequence, in determining the direction that progress would take.

After *Brown*, and partly because of it, all that changed. It took five years to incubate, but beginning in 1960 the movement began a pervasive transformation of America with regard to race, not merely in constitutional law, but in the ways people treated each other, whether mandated by law or not. Black people, increasingly joined by whites, spoke up for racial equality in numbers so large and in protests so vigorous that they could not be gainsaid. They refused to put up with back-of-the-bus treatment, not just in buses but in any of the many places where they daily interacted with whites. They would no longer be denied the right to try on clothes in department stores. They wanted to be served at the lunch counters of the dime stores where they bought soap and toothpaste. They claimed a share of the jobs in offices and factories and universities where previously the presumption had been that such jobs were the exclusive preserve of whites. They pressed volubly and openly for the vote. They couldn't be made to go away by harassment or by the threat of arrest, or even by the actual arrest of a handful of their swelling number.

While much of the action was spontaneous and not centrally directed, national groups arose to help organize things. Joining the NAACP in trying to channel the discontent constructively were Martin Luther King, Jr.'s Southern Christian Leadership Conference (SCLC); the Congress of Racial Equality (CORE); the Student Nonviolent Coordinating Committee (SNCC); local groups like the Albany (Georgia) Movement and COFO (Council of Federated Organizations) in Mississippi; and paramilitary organizations like the Black Panthers.

The new associations did not at first think of courts and laws for redress of their grievances. They focused on direct nonviolent action taking, in the case of SCLC and CORE, Mahatma Gandhi's nonviolent resistance as their guide, and in the case of SNCC, even incorporating the message of nonviolence in their name. The Panthers, of course, rejected the nonviolent approach. In many cases the new groups took leadership away from the NAACP, or competed with it, and the Association sometimes resented them. But all of the groups usually turned to LDF for legal assistance, which we gave readily. In time, the groups would often make arrangements with us for representation in advance of their demonstrations, although during the first years of the movement we reacted as we went along. This role of ours further changed the shape of the movement and our relations with the Association.

It also changed the nature of our legal practice. Where previously we had taken the initiative, carefully choosing the issues and arenas we considered propitious, now we had to respond to situations the demonstrators had created. They made demands of society and when these demands went unmet, they invented and carried out forms of protest without much regard to whether or not their actions were defensible within the current state of the law, often conducting themselves in ways the law had never before addressed.

When the protesters were arrested, as they often were when the other side did not know how to respond to their new methods, they created moral, humanitarian, and practical levies on our resources. We had to create or reshape procedures to protect those who sat at lunch counters, paraded at statehouses, occupied forbidden spaces on buses, and, on the occasion of one world-famous event, to protect those who decided, at our suggestion, to escape the jurisdiction of a hostile federal judge by marching from Selma to Montgomery.

Sometimes LDF lawyers were the only nonthreatening human contact protesters had as they moldered in jails. Often our motions, injunctions, and bail applications secured their release from appalling prisons, which, for racial protesters, could be especially dangerous, even fatal. At the same time, we continued our earlier struggles, getting blacks into nonsegregated schools and universities that, a decade after *Sweatt* and *McLaurin*, were still refusing to treat their admission applications seriously. At the time, everything seemed chaotic. We had so many claims on our limited resources; so little time to do everything right; enormous pressure not to slip up on any detail that might provide the other side with relief, solace, or even just time. In retrospect, it seems remarkable that our efforts were so consistently successful.

BRUCE BOYNTON'S CUP OF TEA

In December 1958, Bruce Boynton, a Howard law student, set out on a Trailways bus from Washington, D.C., to Selma, Alabama, for Christmas vacation. His mother, Amelia Boynton, later became leader of a local voting rights movement, which in 1965 gave rise to the great Selma to Montgomery march. At the Richmond, Virginia, rest stop Boynton went to the black lunch counter, and, finding it crowded, went to the white restaurant, sat at the counter, and ordered a sandwich and a cup of tea. He was hardly a demonstrator—he had first sought service at the black counter.

According to the bus schedule, a limited time was allowed for the rest stop and skipping a meal marked the limit to how much Boynton would tolerate that day. The waitress in the white restaurant refused to serve him because he was black. Boynton persisted, and the police arrested him, took him away in a patrol wagon, and charged him with trespass. The police court convicted and fined him $10.

Martin A. Martin, our Richmond cooperating lawyer, represented him, claiming that Boynton had been convicted in violation of the Commerce Clause, the Interstate Commerce Act, and the due process and equal protection clauses of the Fourteenth Amendment—defenses that would become typical in sit-in cases several years later. The Interstate Commerce Act argument depended on a provision of the act that prohibited undue preferences and prejudices against travelers (not racial discrimination as such, but in the 1950 *Henderson* case the Court held racial discrimination to be within the prohibited conduct) in "facilities and property operated or controlled" by an interstate bus company, a limitation perhaps intended to exclude mom-and-pop rest stops, which often were in private homes along the bus route.

But while Boynton had surely suffered discrimination in the Richmond Trailways terminal, apparently owned by Trailways, Martin had made no effort to prove who operated or controlled the terminal—an omission that later raised big problems. Apart from that issue, all the others in the *Boynton* case would be front and center during the next half-decade of sit-in litigation. We took Boynton's case to the Supreme Court.

THE SIT-INS BEGIN

Among the many taboos devised to remind Southern blacks of their inferior station, eating with whites ranked high. This proscription even included the entirely impersonal seating together of blacks and whites at drugstore or bus terminal lunch counters. Such segregation was particularly galling, because it was enforced by bus lines that depended upon the patronage of black passengers, selling them tickets to everywhere, and by drugstores that coveted blacks' business, selling them bandages and shampoo, soap and cosmetics, but insulted them by denying them the simple comfort of a seat just because it might be adjacent to one occupied by a white person.

In some places or situations the color bar was required by state and local laws. But most often the segregation was dictated merely by custom, though violators of "custom" were treated like lawbreakers: When the custom was breached the local police called it trespass or breach of the peace or found some other convenient name that would allow them to arrest the violators, cart them off to jail like common criminals, and try them, so that they might be duly fined or imprisoned, or both, for their offense against local custom.

In the late 1950s the idea of nonviolent protest in the form of sit-ins began taking root at various points in the South—it had earlier appeared only sporadically. In 1959 in Nashville, James Lawson, a black theology student at Vanderbilt University, who had been to India and studied Gandhi's nonviolent movement and who had been a conscientious objector in the Korean War, began conducting a series of workshops on nonviolent protest against segregation in downtown restaurants. The Nashville students soon became active in the movement, but before they could act, on February 1, 1960, four black freshman at North Carolina Agricultural and Technical College, all members of the NAACP Youth Council, took the lead by demonstrating at Woolworth's in Greensboro.

Franklin McCain, one of the original Greensboro four (today a product development manager at Hoechst Celanese Corporation), recalls that his mother was concerned over his safety; she wanted him to withdraw from the demonstrations. His father, knowing that his son would continue on the road he had chosen even if told not to, said, "Do what you have to, but be careful." McCain says that there weren't many fathers like that. Parents of most of the other protesters wanted their sons to stop sitting in for fear they would be physically hurt. Their attitude was that they had sent their children off to college to get an education, not to protest. McCain recalls that *Brown* inspired these young students not as the vindication of a basic legal principle, but as an example of determined people setting out to accomplish something and succeeding. The synergy of law and social action was manifest. As one of the leaders of the Greensboro sit-in, Joe McNeil, put it: "I was particularly inspired by the people in Little Rock. . . . I was really impressed with the courage that those kids had and the leadership they displayed."

The four protesters entered the store, sat at the white lunch counter, and demanded service. They sat for an hour, until the store closed, but no one served them. Something about the quiet resolve of the four must have captured the imagination of the national press and television because the actionless event was reported nationally the next day; after that things changed. The following day more students sat in. The third day well over a hundred protesters turned out. That number soon multiplied to about a thousand. The students were orderly, well dressed, and nonviolent.

Suddenly, it was as if a spark had been struck in an oxygen-filled atmosphere. The sit-ins spontaneously spread to neighboring cities in North Carolina and within two weeks they were all over the South. Blacks began demanding nonsegregated service at lunch counters, department stores, bus terminals, and all the places from which they had been excluded or segregated; supporters joined them at branches of the offending chain stores in the North as well. But not everyone saw what was happening the same way: Harry Truman, who had been a courageous civil rights pioneer when he was president, thought that the demonstrations were Communist-led.

The sit-ins spread like wildfire to other Woolworth's stores and to such establishments as S. H. Kress, W. T. Grant, Liggett's, Sears Roebuck, Belk's, Ivey's, and other stores, national and local. Amazingly, the thousands of demonstrators, part of no organized group, seemed all to have spontaneously signed on to the nonviolent credo, for the demonstrators were nearly universally peaceful. Their massive presence had the desired effect of preventing the stores from doing their normal business.

Klansmen and others assaulted the demonstrators, tried to set them on fire, spat on them, poured ketchup on them, and abused them in other ways. Often the police stepped aside and permitted the violence. Officials arrested and prosecuted the protesters who often had been assaulted, charging them with breach of the peace, disturbing the peace, disorderly conduct, loitering, trespass, assault, and violation of segregation laws. Sometimes they were charged with conspiracy to interfere with commerce or violating fire regulations by blocking aisles. In Montgomery, black Alabama State College expelled students who had demonstrated at the lunchroom in the county courthouse.

There was no planned network, no prearranged signal. McCain reports that neither before nor immediately afterward did the Greensboro students communicate with others, anywhere. Diane Nash, one of the Nashville students, said that "we had no inkling that the movement would become as widespread as it did." The media made the big difference. Coordination did not begin until Easter recess, when many of the protesters assembled at Shaw University in Raleigh under the leadership of Ella Baker, SCLC executive director, who had been an NAACP organizer in the 1940s. Out of that gathering grew SNCC.

Before setting out the student protesters had not contemplated turning to LDF, or indeed to any lawyers. In fact, according to McCain, the Greensboro students at first resisted becoming involved with lawyers because they feared that some other organization would take over their movement. Very much like idealistic young generations of all colors and in all times they felt that the adults had "screwed up" and wanted to see what they could do on their own. Even though the original four were members of the NAACP Youth Council, they feared control by the NAACP, which they identified with adults; they didn't at that point know that LDF was a separate organization. (McCain, incidentally, as a successful businessman later became head of LDF's North Carolina fund-raising committee.)

When the sit-ins erupted, Thurgood was out of the country in connection with his work on the Kenyan constitution.

My instant reaction, like that of every other staff member, to the arrest of the protesters was a combination of admiration for their bravery and an instinctual desire to rush to the defense of those who were being abused by the law. We set out to defend the students immediately. From an organizational, rather than personal, standpoint, too, it seemed that something big was happening, something that LDF ought to be part of. If we didn't jump in, others would.

When Thurgood returned, his first reaction, as he might have put it, was to "woof." He raised all the problems that the cases would present. But we knew that was his style: He floated all possible objections and examined them thoroughly before going ahead. In fact, he already had argued *Boynton* and had presented to the Supreme Court many of the fundamental defenses the demonstrators would advance. He soon agreed that we should take on the students' defense.

This was in contrast to the NAACP attitude, which was to represent the students only through local branches. As their number grew, many protesters may have been suspicious of the Association, as McCain's group was, or may not have wanted to take the time and trouble to deal with an organization. The difference in the approaches of the NAACP and the LDF to this situation drove us farther apart.

Going to jail, being exposed to the indignities of that experience, and then coming out with a criminal record can never be an inviting prospect for a young person. Missing a semester or more would make problems with their schools. So, after their arrest, most students or their families or their ministers contacted local black lawyers, who almost always were our cooperating lawyers, with pleas to get these young people out of jail.

Even so, there was the question of whether some of the protesters (by now not everyone was a student) wanted to be defended or preferred to protest further by staying in jail. In Nashville, for example, lawyers and the ministers disagreed. The ministers had raised money to support the students, but advised them not to contest their prosecutions and to continue protesting by remaining in jail. Thurgood reported that he inquired of "the ministers if they are asking the students to stay in jail and are not paying the court costs or the lawyers, why were they raising funds?" Thurgood was told that "they plan to hold the money in the event it is needed." But our cooperating lawyer Z. Alexander Looby and other Nashville leaders explained to the students that if they served their jail terms they would not be able to appeal, and that if they spent thirty days in jail instead of attending classes they might lose a school year; the seniors might not graduate. The students decided to pay fines and appeal. (In this heated atmosphere, civil rights lawyers, who often were the object of attacks, faced greater risk. In April, Looby's house was destroyed by dynamite, but he and his wife escaped injury.)

Across the South the black civil rights lawyers with whom we had dealt on a daily basis for decades turned to us for help, and some black lawyers who until then had not been involved in civil rights did step forward and take demonstration cases. But it was a very rare Southern white lawyer who handled a demonstration case at that early phase of the movement, although more did later. A few white lawyers also assisted us secretly. Alvin Rubin, later a judge of the Fifth Circuit Court of Appeals, prepared materials to guide lawyers in defending Louisiana demonstration cases. But he kept the activity secret even from his own secretary.

For us, the legal issues weren't surprising. Over the years we had canvassed the problems that the sit-ins presented, that is, for example, whether the arrest and conviction of persons as trespassers would, where they had violated a rule requiring racial segregation, be state action prohibited by the Fourteenth Amendment. That question had been at the core of the Restrictive Covenant Cases, where the role of state courts in enforcing a private agreement among homeowners not to sell to blacks was held unconstitutional. While Boynton's action at the Trailways bus stop was not a deliberate sit-in, it presented similar issues, and we canvassed them all for our Supreme Court brief.

Jim Nabrit and I flew South immediately and continually, concentrating first on North Carolina, where the demonstrations had begun. I went to Alabama for the State College expulsions, and won reinstatement for the students. Thurgood went to Nashville and elsewhere.

As the sit-ins began, the Supreme Court had before it *Thompson v. City of Louisville*, which would affect the sit-in cases considerably—and the Court knew it. In this case, "Shuffling" Sam Thompson, a local character with a long series of convictions for minor offenses, was dancing by himself in a Louisville café where he hadn't bought anything. Even though no one objected, the police arrested him for loitering. Thompson then talked back to the police, for which they also charged him with disorderly conduct. The court convicted Thompson and fined him $10 on each charge. There was no appeal from so trivial a punishment. But Thompson's lawyer, Louis Lusky (later my colleague on the Columbia Law School faculty), an ardent civil libertarian and, indeed, a curmudgeon in the face of any official repression, got a stay of execution of the fine, which made possible the unusual feat of taking a case from a lower state court directly to the Supreme Court of the United States. That Court, on March 21, just six weeks after the sit-ins began, held: "We find no evidence whatever in the record to support these convictions. Just as 'Conviction upon a charge not made would be sheer denial of due process,' so is it a violation of due process to convict and punish a man without evidence of his guilt."

The decision strongly suggested that if shuffling feet was not the crime of loitering, and speaking back to a cop wasn't disorderly conduct, sitting at a lunch counter couldn't be a crime either. Local sheriffs and police, frustrated by the impertinent actions of students, could no longer run down a menu of misdemeanors and charge students without evidence that they had done anything wrong. While Shuffling Sam's case ostensibly had nothing to do with race or protests, at least some of the justices thought it did. Shortly after the decision, Justice Tom Clark saw Jim Nabrit, Jr., in Washington, where he was dean of Howard Law School, and said, "That takes care of your sit-in cases." To correct misapplications of the law wherever they occur, whether or not the victimized party is a sympathetic character—Sam, to many, was at least an annoyance—sometimes pays off in unanticipated, important ways.

On March 18, 1960, almost seven weeks after the sit-ins began, Thurgood called a lawyers conference at Howard to map out a strategy. Sixty-two lawyers attended; as at similar conferences, all those attending were friends. Jim Nabrit III recalls it as a meeting of "the gang." A spirit of camaraderie pervaded the proceedings as we went over issues that LDF lawyers had canvassed as far back as the *Morgan* case, which had prohibited segregation on interstate buses, and that had been probed intensively in the Restrictive Covenant Cases, which held unconstitutional court enforcement of agreements among property owners not to sell to blacks, Jews, and members of other groups, and for *Boynton*.

By this time more than a thousand protesters had been arrested. Thurgood announced at the end of the meeting that "every single lawyer who attended the conference unanimously agreed that we are obliged to defend those arrested in these demonstrations who call upon us for help."

We blocked out an array of defenses. First, the Shuffling Sam Thompson approach: It would violate due process to convict students charged with breach of the peace if they had been peaceful. Second, the invalidity of segregation laws: Convictions for violating those laws denied equal protection of the laws. Third, when demonstrators were convicted of trespass in places where segregation laws existed, the convictions were as invalid as those for violating segregation laws, because this was just another way of enforcing an illegal law. Fourth, convictions for sitting in state-owned facilities were invalid because the state certainly could not segregate. Where state control was not complete (for example, in facilities on government property leased to private persons), trespass convictions also violated equal protection for the same reason—a little state involvement was enough to bring the activity under the Fourteenth Amendment.

Jim Nabrit III lectured to the group about the law of vagueness, which might be a defense against some charges. As to interstate carriers, decisions that we had won earlier at the Interstate Commerce Commission and the *Morgan* case should invalidate convictions for sitting in restricted areas on buses, trains, and in terminals. (In bus cases, there was the additional matter of proving who operated and controlled the terminal.) We reached back into the recesses of the common law and discovered that innkeepers and vendors at fairs and markets in ancient England were obliged to serve all comers and extrapolated the argument—it was a long reach—that excluding blacks from large portions of the contemporary marketplace somehow violated the Constitution.

But one persistent question wouldn't go away. Where no law required segregation and a private person with no manifest connection to the state excluded blacks from a place of business, did a trespass conviction violate the Constitution? If a railroad or bus line discriminated did that violate the Commerce Clause? On the one hand, the state could convict anyone who remained in a prohibited area after having been told to leave for a nondiscriminatory reason. As for the enforcement making the private decision a state action, there were good arguments to support the need for such private decisions being enforced by the police; if they were not, we would be in the situation Bob Ming described during the 1946 conference following *Morgan*, one of anarchy, where the state couldn't enforce the private choices of private property owners, with the inevitable consequence that the disputing parties would take things into their own hands and resort to force.

On the other hand, to be realistic, weren't the police, courts, and prison systems in the sit-in cases enforcing private discrimination in the same way the courts did in the Restrictive Covenant Cases? The sit-ins posed the unanswered question put by those cases: Since private decisions cannot be enforced without an ultimate, although sometimes only implicit, state sanction, is everything we do "state action"? Do all personal decisions present constitutional questions? Where should the courts draw the line?

We decided to argue that state enforcement of private racial discrimination violated the equal protection clause, and we developed a number of detailed analyses. I got the job of preparing motions dealing with all types of arrest that we'd heard of or that seemed likely, which we distributed to cooperating lawyers all over the South. By April we had cases in Maryland, Virginia, five cities in North Carolina, three cities in South Carolina, two cities in Georgia, Montgomery, New Orleans, Nashville, and Memphis. Most were trespass prosecutions, but some involved loitering, violating fire regulations, and public demonstrations that were conducted without permits or in forbidden areas.

Over the next five years the motions and arguments I had prepared worked their way through the courts and ended up as the basis of one Supreme Court decision after another. One argument, however, that based on the English law of inns and fairs, which referred to exclusion from the "common market," raised a bit of confusion, if not ridicule, over whether we were making claims about the European Common Market. We quickly dropped it.

Our model was the campaign of *Gaines* to *Brown*, building case upon case. A hopeful starting point was the Restrictive Covenant Cases and another case, *Marsh v. Alabama*, in which the Supreme Court held unconstitutional, on First Amendment grounds, trespass convictions of Jehovah's Witnesses for proselytizing in Chickasaw, Alabama, a company town. Even though Chickasaw was private property the Court held it was a town and controlled by the state action doctrine. So, I reasoned, let's take to the Supreme Court a case in which demonstrators were arrested for trespass in a commercial establishment the size of Chickasaw, if we could find one. We ought to win that case on *Marsh* grounds. Then we would take up a prosecution for trespassing on smaller premises, which we should win on the basis of the previous case, and so on and so on, until ultimately we would win a case involving a dime store or corner drugstore.

Unlike the school cases, however, where we usually called the tune, the legal questions and sequence of cases were being determined by students and prosecutors. It was nearly impossible to make a plan that we could follow closely.

In some cases the arrests were clearly expressions of police pique at trivial acts. One of the earliest involved the unimaginative issue of whether three Johnson C. Smith University students in Charlotte, North Carolina, who were waiting in the aisles for service, had assaulted white patrons when they brushed against them. With cooperating lawyers Tom Wyche and Charles Bell, we showed that the touching was accidental. One student was acquitted and we appealed the convictions of the other two. Nothing far-reaching would come of that.

As luck would have it, we soon got the case of forty-three Shaw University and St. Augustine College students prosecuted for trespass in Cameron Village, an enormous shopping center in Raleigh, North Carolina. They had been denied service at Woolworth's and the next day returned to resume their sit-in, only to find the store closed to them. The police arrested them as they lined up outside. On March 14 and 28 they were convicted of trespass and fined $10 each. They were entitled to an appeal, which amounted to a new trial.

Jim Nabrit and I flew to Raleigh to represent them and, with our local lawyers, Sam Mitchell and George Greene, went out to Cameron Village. Our hearts jumped with joy when we saw how big it was. In fact, Cameron Village may have been bigger than Chickasaw. It had its own post office; public bus lines ran through it; roads, traffic signs, and sidewalks were indistinguishable from those elsewhere in Raleigh; the local police enforced the laws within it. It was called a *village*! It wouldn't be difficult to argue that Cameron Village was indeed a village. And if we won on that ground, then in the next case, involving a shopping center, for instance, we could argue that Cameron Village was only a shopping center.

On the day of the new trial, as we approached the courthouse, we saw hundreds of black people and some whites, student defendants, their friends and family, ordinary citizens of Raleigh, and others, in a line as long as one you might find outside a hit movie, waiting to enter the building. The entrance was jammed. The courtroom was on the second floor; we could hardly get up the staircase. We elbowed our way through the crowd, saying "lawyer in the case, lawyer in the case." We worked our way through the standing-room-only courtroom, where, ordinarily, misdemeanors like public drunkenness cases were tried, to counsel table, opened our briefcases, spread our papers out, and waited for the trial to begin. But within moments, out of nowhere, a couple of men in firemen's hats and boots stomped in, whispered a few words to the judge, and announced in booming voices that the mob in the courtroom constituted a fire hazard. The judge adjourned and rescheduled the trial to take place in the city auditorium the following week.

Jim and I headed to the Raleigh-Durham airport, but it was so badly fogged that the plane that was to carry us home zoomed down for a landing, couldn't make it, and went elsewhere. I went to a pay phone and discovered that there would be a train to New York early in the evening, but we didn't have enough cash to buy tickets, and the railroads then wouldn't take credit cards. I called one of the lawyers, Sam Mitchell, who came out to the airport to cash my check and invited us to attend a civil rights rally being held in a local church in support of the students.

We went to the rally and entered through a door that, unknown to us, opened onto the stage, and found ourselves being introduced to an audience of perhaps a thousand as the great lawyers from New York who had come to Raleigh to fight for freedom. Jim hates public speaking with a passion, but this was one of the few times he was forced into it. He was eloquent. After I said a few words we headed for the train station, but again were diverted.

Sam asked whether we wouldn't like to visit his club, where the members would like to meet the LDF lawyers from New York. We couldn't say no. There still seemed to be time, but we were getting a little nervous. There was a stop to pick up a bottle; the time grew shorter. As it began to rain and turn dark, we headed far into the countryside, turned into a Faulknerian forest and down a dirt road. The dirt turned to mud, the car slid and slithered, finally losing traction. The wheels spun and we didn't move. Train time grew closer and closer. Sam got out of the car and with a flashlight went down the road to the club in the rain to call a taxi. We sat for perhaps half an hour when another car pulled up behind us, making us not a little anxious—was it the Klan? But it was only the taxicab. The driver backed out of the woods, raced for the station, and we made the train, jumping aboard just as it was pulling out of the station. We unwound in our roomettes with a few drinks on the trip northward. As in the past, I marveled when Northern businessmen, white, of course, who had been at the Homestead in Hot Springs, Virginia, and the Greenbrier in White Sulphur Springs, West Virginia, boarded the train, white-coated black porters toting their golf bags, oblivious to our world.

We returned home to await what would happen. On April 22 the prosecutor dashed our grand scheme by admitting we were right. The court dismissed charges against the forty-three students and at the same time ruined our chances of making new and useful law. Our argument wasn't bad, but I have no doubt that growing black political strength in North Carolina—the only Southern state not to adopt anti-NAACP and -LDF laws—played a part. We were never presented with a similar opportunity and had, consequently, to turn to other theories.

By May we had cases in Maryland, which arose at Hecht's department store and ended when Baltimore stores agreed to desegregate; in Virginia, where forty defendants were being prosecuted for trespass in Thalheimer's department store (blacks couldn't get sit-down food service or try on clothes); in North Carolina in Durham, New Bern, Winston-Salem, Statesville, Henderson, Concord, Charlotte, Monroe, Raleigh, Greensboro, and Chapel Hill. In South Carolina we had cases in Rock Hill, Orangeburg, Charleston, Sumter, Florence, Greenville, Columbia, and Denmark. In Georgia, our cases were in Atlanta, Savannah, and Augusta. We defended demonstrators in Montgomery and Birmingham and Baton Rouge as well as in Nashville, Chattanooga, and Memphis, Tennessee; in Marshall, Texas, and in Lexington, Kentucky. We had a case involving sympathy demonstrators in Springfield, Massachusetts.

The issues in these cases ranged from trespass, assault and battery, loitering and loafing, disorderly conduct, conspiracy to obstruct commerce, contempt of court for singing in jail, violating fire regulations, and parading without a license. Special problems, arising because many defendants were students, included whether bond would be forfeited if trials came up while students were home for the summer; there were also the cases of suspension or expulsion from school to deal with.

One day, Kenneth Greenawalt, whose firm represented Woolworth's, invited Thurgood and me to lunch at Whyte's seafood restaurant in downtown Manhattan to explore whether there was some way that the cases might be settled and the demonstrations stopped. Greenawalt (father of my colleague at Columbia, Kent Greenawalt) was a distinguished civil liberties lawyer, who specialized in issues of religious freedom. He told us that Woolworth's would not seek arrests or prosecution and would, wherever feasible, abandon all segregation requirements. But, of course, he couldn't speak for other lunch counter owners or stores where segregation was required by law. And we had absolutely no control over the students. The movement continued.

There was no way our little staff could be present at all the cases. But the students were represented almost always by longtime cooperating lawyers. We conferred over the phone, shipped out model papers and briefs, personally attended cases that might have broader import, paid modest legal fees, and furnished some bail money. We stayed on top of the cases so that as they worked their way up to the appellate courts and the Supreme Court they would present the right issues and evidence. It is amazing how well we did. There were lapses, but not many.

BOYNTON V. VIRGINIA DECIDED IN THE SUPREME COURT

By the time Thurgood argued Boynton's case in October 1960, it had metamorphosed into something not imagined when he ordered his sandwich and tea in December 1958—a test of the legality of the sit-ins. *Boynton*, decided on December 5, 1960, ten long months into the sit-ins, capped the year's demonstration cases and signalled the Court's approach to those cases: The Court ruled with us, but on the narrowest possible grounds. Martin hadn't put into evidence information about who operated or controlled the Richmond Trailways bus terminal.

The Court, possibly seeking a way out of the case that would uphold plaintiff Boynton but avoid far-reaching implications, apparently was exploring the possibility of a decision that relied on Trailways' control of the terminal. If that were the case, we would win, but no new law would be made. The clerk wrote a highly unusual letter to Virginia's attorney general, inquiring whether "the intercorporate relationship between the Trailways Bus Company and the Trailways Bus Terminal, Inc., [was] set forth in any documents of which the Virginia courts can take judicial notice." If Virginia's courts could look at the documents so could the United States Supreme Court in an appeal from Virginia. But Virginia's attorney general stonewalled and said that the Virginia courts couldn't look at them. The Justice Department, however, filed Interstate Commerce Commission records that described the relationship: Trailways owned the terminal and leased space in it to the restaurant under a lease that tightly controlled its operation. That would be a weak reed if neither the Virginia courts nor the United States Supreme Court could not rely on the documents.

In light of this we decided to abandon the statutory argument, which depended on the intercorporate relationship, and to make only the constitutional argument that the Commerce Clause and the Fourteenth Amendment prohibited the state from using its police and courts to enforce discrimination by the restaurant management. In retrospect, that possibly wasn't the best strategy and raised the difficult state action issues.

Thurgood, other lawyers, and I went to Washington to prepare for the argument in early October, just as the Court's new session began. Bruce Boynton was especially interested, not merely as the defendant but as a law student, and visited during the preparations in Thurgood's room at one of the downtown hotels.

Boynton was thin, rangy, with a high voice and a talkative, insistent manner, and he had a few drinks. As we blocked out the arguments he got the idea that the case didn't sound too difficult and that as the defendant he had every right to represent himself. Lou Pollak and I tried to reason with and to mollify him. Thurgood was gruff and disagreeable. As we explained that the issues were too important to entrust to someone, even someone of his considerable ability, who never had argued a case in the Court before, he became more adamant.

What could we do? After all, he was the client and we were his lawyers, presumably his obedient servants in the sense that we were bound to serve his interests as he saw them. Suddenly, for no apparent reason he changed his mind. Angrily slamming down his fist on the table he said, "Okay, you all argue it. I got me a chick outside and I don't want to waste any more time here with you."

Boynton was the last case that Thurgood argued in the Supreme Court for LDF. Several justices asked him how a decision might affect small family-owned and -operated rest stops. Justice Frankfurter posed hypothetical questions about what our argument might be concerning a restaurant across the street from the terminal or a haberdashery shop in the terminal. The Court, however, resolved all the difficult problems by interpreting the statute in a way that the briefs hadn't argued and that Thurgood only had touched upon. We obtained a decision based upon a novel interpretation of the Interstate Commerce Act, which didn't require proof of who operated or controlled the terminal. Justice Black's opinion pointed out that the Motor Carriers Act prohibited "unjust discrimination" and that "should buses in transit decide to supply dining service," like the dining car in *Henderson*, they would have to furnish it, like all the other services they provided, on a nonsegregated basis. The opinion went on: "Whoever may have had technical title or immediate control . . . [passengers] had a right to expect that this essential transportation food service voluntarily provided for them under such circumstances would be rendered without discrimination. . . . Therefore, petitioner had a federal right to remain in the white portion of the restaurant."

Justice Black dealt with the mom-and-pop rest stop by writing that the decision did not cover every wholly independent roadside restaurant.

While *Boynton* meant something for interstate bus travel, it meant little for the demonstrators, except that the Court showed willingness to exercise some ingenuity to free someone like a sit-in defendant. It was not willing to decide that to arrest and prosecute a black who demanded service at a whites-only facility violated the equal protection clause.

Bruce Boynton later became a lawyer and practiced in Alabama and Tennessee, but had next to nothing to do with LDF.

KENNEDYS AND LDF ASSERT RIGHTS OF MARTIN LUTHER KING, JR.

As 1961 began John F. Kennedy was inaugurated. He had courted the black vote during the campaign, most dramatically by telephoning Martin Luther King, Jr.'s wife, Coretta, while King was in jail for a combination of traffic and demonstration offenses, in which LDF lawyers had been among those representing him for more than a year. King was by then a major national figure, principally because of the leadership of the Montgomery bus boycott. He was doubly important to Kennedy because his father was a leading Baptist preacher in Atlanta and had a large following.

King's troubles had begun in May 1960, when he was arrested for driving in Georgia with an Alabama driver's license, even though he was a Georgia resident. The real reason for King's arrest was that he had become a prominent figure in the civil rights movement, and because, on this particular occasion, he was in the car with Lillian Smith, the white Southern author of *Strange Fruit*, a powerful antiracist novel. The judge sentenced King to twelve months of labor, which he suspended, and a $25 fine.

In October King was jailed for demonstrating at an elegant Atlanta restaurant. For having committed that crime while under the suspension of the traffic offense sentence, he was locked up in the state's maximum-security prison at Reidsville. John F. Kennedy telephoned Coretta to express sympathy, scoring a great political coup in the presidential campaign. Robert Kennedy called the judge, who released King on $2,000 bond.

During all of this Donald Hollowell and Horace Ward represented King, and we worked with them every step of the way.

The legal issues involved matters far from our everyday fare. The judge released King because it was illegal under Georgia law to have combined, as punishment for the original offense, a maximum sentence of six months imprisonment and another of six months of labor, into a twelve-month suspended sentence. Don't ask about the underlying sense to it; that's just what the Georgia law was. Since the sentence was illegal, the probation of the sentence also was illegal and couldn't be revoked to jail King. No big constitutional principle. Students often ask how to prepare to become a civil rights or public interest lawyer. My answer is: First learn to become a good lawyer—the issues take every conceivable form.

CONNIE MOTLEY MARCHES THROUGH GEORGIA

On January 6, 1961, Judge William A. Bootle ordered the University of Georgia to admit two applicants to college, Charlayne Hunter, now co-anchor Charlayne Hunter-Gault of "The MacNeil/Lehrer NewsHour," and Hamilton Holmes, today a distinguished physician in Georgia. Even though *Sweatt* had been decided in 1950, and Connie Motley had filed suit for Hunter and Holmes in 1959, the university rejected both, interposing one spurious justification after another.

Vernon Jordan, who as one of Washington's great movers and shakers in 1992 headed President Clinton's transition team, was NAACP field secretary in Georgia in 1961 and took Hunter and Holmes to the registrar's office through a crowd of students shouting "Nigger go home." As they waited to register, a loud cheer arose from the crowd. Word had arrived that Judge Bootle had just granted the state's motion for a stay of his order and some white students looking in over the transom yelled, "The nigger lawyer ain't smiling no more."

But Georgia had not counted on Connie Motley's indomitability. Immediately, she raced to Atlanta to Judge Elbert Tuttle of the court of appeals, where she filed a petition to vacate Bootle's stay; he did—then and there. A newspaper headlined the story, "Tuttle Boots Bootle." The political uproar intensified. Attorney General Eugene Cook—who had refused Thurgood when he asked for a stay for Ozzie Jones, the "nigger convicted of raping a white woman"—went on television to announce that he would fly to Washington and petition the Supreme Court to reinstate Bootle's stay. Connie saw the broadcast, called me in New York—I had already gone home—and I called Jim Nabrit, who lived not too far away. He drove to my house and together we drafted a response to Cook's application.

There was, however, a problem: We had to prepare an answer to an application we had not seen. But we assumed that Cook would make the arguments one must, which would deal with the likelihood of success on appeal, and the relative harm that the parties would suffer if the stay were granted or denied. As to the first, certainly we would win on appeal. As to relative harm, Georgia could not demonstrate any legally cognizable injury to the university if Holmes and Hunter were to be allowed to enter while the appeal worked its way through the courts. Hunter and Holmes, on the other hand, would suffer considerable damage if their entry to college were delayed. As well, *Little Rock* had made clear that courts shouldn't bow to riots.

Late into the night Jim and I batted out the response. The next morning we flew to Washington on the earliest plane and arrived at the Supreme Court shortly after it opened. We went to the clerk's office to inspect Cook's petition, but Cook had not yet arrived. I asked E. P. Cullinan, the chief deputy clerk, whether he would take our response to papers that had not yet been filed, and he agreed. We left the papers and wandered around the corridors to kill time.

Later that morning Cook arrived, accompanied by assistant attorneys general, trailed by reporters and TV cameramen. As he strode down the hallways he issued pronouncements, which I could not hear clearly. Then he reached the clerk's office and, with a flourish, handed his papers to the clerk, announcing, "Here is the application of the State of Georgia for a stay." At which point Cullinan, deadpan, handed him my papers and replied, "And here is Mr. Greenberg's response." That day the Court denied Cook's application.

Hunter and Holmes entered the university. At the same time, Connie continued to press her attack. That day she filed an application for a temporary restraining order (TRO) to restrain the governor and other officials from enforcing a law cutting off funds to schools that integrated pursuant to a court order. The court immediately issued the TRO and set the case down for hearing on January 12 to decide whether to issue a preliminary injunction, which would remain in effect until a full trial could be held.

At the hearing Connie got the preliminary injunction, but rioting broke out at the university and state officials hustled Hunter and Holmes off the campus. Georgia obviously was hoping for a replay of the Autherine Lucy case; once Autherine was removed from the campus she never returned. That same day Connie brought the suspensions to Judge Bootle's attention, and he ordered that formal pleadings be filed the next day to enjoin them. Connie got the papers into court the next day. Bootle held a hearing, ordered that the suspensions be lifted and that Hunter and Holmes be re-admitted on January 16. They went back to school, Georgia appealed Bootle's orders, and the case bounced around the courts for a while.

I'm afraid I may be painting a picture of Connie as all grim devotion to the cause. That would be inaccurate, for she cared about some of the fun factors in life, about friends, family, and is recalled by many from those times for her more human side. Derrick Bell, who used to be an LDF lawyer, once said that if he ever were to write his memoirs about his days at LDF, half the book would consist of describing his trips to the drugstore to buy hair curlers and other articles for Connie.

Universities in Mississippi, Alabama, and South Carolina still held out, and we soon moved against them. On May 31 Connie filed *Meredith v. Fair*, for James Meredith, against the University of Mississippi; it would not come to a head for a good many months. Thurgood had pondered long and hard before ordering her to proceed. He feared bloodshed and didn't want to proceed without being certain that Meredith really wanted to go to Old Miss.

21

NEW CLIENTS, NEW CASES, NEW THEORIES

We at LDF had never thought of ourselves as practicing in an ivory tower, far removed from the stresses and strains of real life. But whatever accouterments of the legal academic life we may have enjoyed—conferring with scholars, probing research in depth, developing innovative theories—were quickly forgotten as the conveyor belt of the civil rights movement sped up exponentially with the advent of the 1960s. By 1961 we had seventeen hundred defendants—some in individual suits, others grouped in single cases—across the South. Old cases percolated upward to state appellate courts and the United States Supreme Court as new ones were added.

At the same time, demonstrations began taking a new shape, that of Freedom Rides, making new claims on our commitment to provide legal help to all those who found themselves under attack because of their civil rights activities.

THE FREEDOM RIDES BEGIN

As early as 1947, the Congress of Racial Equality (CORE), relying on the Supreme Court's 1946 decision in *Morgan v. Virginia*, which held segregated seating on North–South bus trips unconstitutional, planned a Journey of Reconciliation, with blacks and whites traveling together, each taking seats on buses reserved for members of the other race. CORE had evolved from the Fellowship of Reconciliation, a pacifist organization of blacks and whites, and became a relatively small but influential antisegregation group that fought for its principles by direct, nonviolent action, emulating Mahatma Gandhi and Henry David Thoreau.

Thurgood, fearful that in 1947 such forays into the Deep South would provoke violence, sought to dissuade CORE from extending the program into that area, stating that "a disobedience movement on the part of Negroes and their white allies, if employed in the [Deep] South, would result in wholesale slaughter with no good achieved." The main effect of the 1947 trip, which ventured only into the upper South, was that it planted a seed that would germinate in the early 1960s.

Despite the fact that we had won many cases in the 1940s, early 1950s, and in 1960 prohibiting segregation on interstate buses, in terminals, and in many terminal restaurants, bus companies and police continued to flout the law for a decade and a half. Following the victory in *Boynton*, the bus stop case in which the Court innovatively interpreted a statute that stood in the way of exonerating a defendant who only wanted a cup of tea on an interstate bus trip, CORE revived the Journey of Reconciliation on May 4, 1961. As in the first Journey, blacks would sit in the front of the bus, whites in the rear; together they would demand service at whites-only terminal lunch counters. In the very different political and social climate of the 1960s, the Freedom Rides joined the sit-ins to constitute the largest mass movement of blacks and whites for racial justice since the days of the abolition movement.

Brown v. Board of Education was at least a part of their inspiration, for the thirteen original Freedom Riders had planned to arrive in New Orleans on May 17, the seventh anniversary of *Brown*. But when they reached Anniston, Alabama, Klansmen firebombed their bus and brutally beat them. They barely escaped with their lives and completed their trip by flying from Birmingham to New Orleans. The Klan had prevented the completion of the trip, but, in terms of the Klan's own goals, their actions were completely counterproductive. Stories of the savage attack, accompanied by a photo of the flaming bus, appeared on front pages across the world, electrifying the country and inspiring others to join the crusade.

By May 17 a group of students, refusing to be intimidated by the firebombing and beatings that had befallen the first group of Freedom Riders, headed by bus from Nashville to Birmingham and Montgomery. Soon hundreds of others with no connection to CORE began their own Freedom Rides, and in a few weeks, the Southern Christian Leadership Conference (SCLC), including Martin Luther King, Jr., as well as an army of nonaffiliated students, chaplains, and professors at Ivy League universities, joined the effort. Sometimes they asserted their rights under *Boynton*, though neither waiters nor police seemed to have any idea of what they were talking about.

In response to cajoling and threats by the Justice Department and the White House, the states of Alabama and Mississippi furnished armed guards to riders traveling south to Jackson, Mississippi. The federal government mobilized a large force of federal employees somehow related to law enforcement to serve as marshals and protect the riders, if necessary.

On May 20 the Justice Department got a temporary restraining order in Montgomery against the Ku Klux Klan, prohibiting it from violently interfering with the freedom riders, and on June 2 an injunction against Montgomery law enforcement officials requiring them to protect the Freedom Riders was obtained. But Judge Frank Johnson, who issued the orders, also temporarily enjoined CORE, the SCLC, and other Freedom Riders from conducting any more rides.

Thurgood, Lou Pollak, and I immediately flew to Montgomery where we intervened in the Justice Department case on behalf of the Freedom Riders to lift the injunction against their proceeding with more rides. Johnson never decided our application, but implicitly acknowledged we were right when he allowed the prohibition against Freedom Riding to lapse. The Justice Department, in that same suit, could have requested, and probably would have obtained, an order to desegregate the buses and terminals based on *Henderson* and *Boynton*, to say nothing of *Morgan v. Virginia*, which the Supreme Court had decided fifteen years earlier. Instead, it decided to seek a declaration from the Interstate Commerce Commission that segregation violated the Interstate Commerce Act—a request whose answer had been clear for a long time but that the commission took months to respond to.

On May 25, with Fred Gray, we filed our own bus desegregation case. Gray had graduated from Western Reserve Law School, had been practicing in Montgomery since 1954, and right out of law school had been the local lawyer in the Montgomery bus boycott cases. Operating out of Fred's walk-up office in the black section of downtown Montgomery—like so many buildings of its sort, its walls covered with much painted over embossed metal—we prepared defenses for arrested Freedom Riders and assembled papers asking for desegregation of the buses and terminal that serviced Montgomery. The Justice Department joined us as a friend of the court. Sometimes the law didn't authorize Justice to file certain kinds of suits; sometimes it wasn't clear. Often, powerful Southern Democrats might object, or retaliate, if Justice were to file such a case. Often inhibited by such jurisdictional and political factors, in a pattern that continued through the Kennedy administration and beyond, Justice frequently piggybacked on our cases. Not until the civil rights movement brought about passage of new laws in the mid-1960s and Southern racists lost a large measure of their political power did that situation change appreciably.

The Kennedy administration, unhappy over the demonstrations that threatened its Southern political base and embarrassed its foreign policy, called for a cooling-off period, but the Freedom Rider leadership rejected the idea. The administration then came to an understanding with Southern political leaders, in which the Freedom Riders would be protected from violence but arrested, with the end of moving the demonstrations off the front pages and into the humdrum mill of police courts and lengthy appeals.

On May 25, the day we filed our bus desegregation suit, Ralph Abernathy, one of Martin Luther King, Jr.'s chief deputies, along with a group of New England academics and clerics, including Yale chaplain William

Sloane Coffin, Wesleyan professor of religion John Maguire (now president of the Claremont Graduate School), and several Yale law students (including George Smith, later an LDF staff lawyer and now a member of the New York Court of Appeals), arrived in Montgomery as Freedom Riders. Police arrested them, according to the new policy of arrest and prosecution in place of violent assault by angry citizens. Thurgood, Lou, and I, with Fred Gray, represented them; Lou later won the case in the Supreme Court.

Montgomery tried all its Freedom Riders in a single case, but Jackson, Mississippi, figured out how to impose a far more onerous burden on the demonstrators by trying each case individually and imposing heavy bail bond requirements. Although CORE had a lawyer, Carl Rachlin, and a few volunteers who were associated with him, it had no law office or legal program nor did it have the funds to start one. On June 10, I met with leaders of CORE, and we agreed to represent their Freedom Riders after they were found guilty in initial trials, following which they had the right to new trials in a higher trial court.

We prepared fill-in-the-blanks boilerplate pleadings, entitled Assignment of Error (the basis of our appeal) and Brief for Appellant, for the court in Jackson, and Motion for Reversal of Conviction, Assignment of Error, and Brief for Appellant for the state supreme court. As the cases moved along, the blanks were filled in with the number of each case, names of the defendant(s) and the arresting officer, date of the arrest, and page numbers in the records. We tried to have a staff lawyer in Jackson at all times during the cases. As local counsel, we hired R. Jess Brown, Carsie Hall, and Jack Young for a total of $1,200 per month.

By the end of the summer the state had mounted 315 separate prosecutions. All defendants were convicted and went to prison, where guards often beat them and jammed them into filthy, overcrowded, unsanitary cells. When the local jail couldn't hold any more, prison officials shipped the riders to the state's maximum-security prison at Parchman. In doing so, prison officials violated the basic principle that first-time, nonviolent offenders should not be mixed with hardened criminals—another illustration of the extent to which professional standards could be sacrificed in the interest of racism, as in the case of the celebrated law school dean who said that Sweatt's basement law school, which shared the state capital's law library, equaled the University of Texas.

If the defendants put up bail, they were released and later had to return for new trials. Mississippi demanded high bail, and bail bond companies refused to sell the riders bail bonds, which are essentially insurance policies to guarantee the defendant's return for trial. That meant that a lot of cash had to be put up, at the outset at least $100,000. CORE raised and borrowed a considerable amount of bail money, but soon exhausted its capacity. Thurgood told James Farmer, then national director of CORE, that we would put up bail money for their defendants.

BAIL BONDS

Grenville Clark—a pillar of the WASP establishment and retired partner of a Wall Street law firm, author of the Selective Service and Training Act of 1940, developer, with Louis Sohn, of the plan for World Peace Through World Law—took a particular interest in the Freedom Riders and the bail bond situation. In 1960, when he was seventy-eight years old, he wrote to Thurgood and Allan Knight Chalmers, proposing that we organize a group of at least one hundred contributors to give at least $1,000 a year for ten years, estimating that $100,000 per year would supply one-third of a minimum budget, assuming that we would attract considerable volunteer legal help. Clark foresaw a fifty-year—more likely one-hundred-year—struggle for full equality, but thought it impracticable to solicit for longer than ten years. He pledged $2,000 per year for ten years himself and offered to send to us a small list of "prospects."

We accepted with enthusiasm, never before having raised money at these stratospheric levels. Anna Frank and Harold Oram got to work, holding meetings and soliciting prospects. By June we had received $125,000 and had pledges for more. The Grenville Clark plan, as it came to be called, induced contributors to think bigger and introduced us to new donors.

Clark hired Louis Lusky, who had been his protégé at his law firm, to maintain a "watching brief," that is, to attend the Freedom Ride trials and report back to him. In this capacity, Lusky informed Clark that demonstrators, often from out of state, had to post bond as a guarantee that they would serve their sentences if they lost their cases. The alternative was not to post bond and serve a jail term of thirty to ninety days while the appeal proceeded. If a sentence were completed before the appeal was decided, the case would become moot and abort the appeal.

With arrests in the thousands, and bail ranging from $300 to $1,500, sometimes more, the cost of cash bail became enormous for a cash-poor organization like our own. In 315 Mississippi Freedom Rider cases, on appeals from police court to county court, bonds were $500. On further appeals to circuit court the bonds were $1,500, of which $500 was a guarantee to pay the costs of appeal and $1,000 was a bond to assure the defendant's appearance. Failure to make the cost bond would preclude appealing, except where defendants could swear that they were paupers; most could not. Failure to make the appearance bond would prevent a defendant from remaining at liberty pending appeal, which could take months or years. Furthermore, cases could go on and on, to the Mississippi Supreme Court and the United States Supreme Court, during which the bond money would be tied up.

CORE, after considerable difficulty, arranged with Resolute Insurance Company of Hartford, Connecticut, which was licensed to write surety bonds in Mississippi, to write the $1,500 cost and appearance bonds for a fee of 10 percent, with collateral in the amount of one-third of the bond liability—a rather profitable deal for the company. But before the first bond was executed, Resolute's top management, upon recommendation of its agent in Jackson, decided against the arrangement. At first, they admitted to political pressure, but then maintained that the decision was based solely on business reasons.

Lusky, CORE leaders, and I met with executives of the insurance company but could accomplish nothing. In October 1961 Grenville Clark offered to put up some bond money personally and to help us find another surety company. He gave me $10,000 for cash bonds, and others advanced $17,500, which I would return when it was no longer needed. In time, others gave more. Most did not want to contribute in this way because the tax consequences might be confused—a tax deduction in the year the money was handed over; then, when the money was returned to the lender, there would be the inconvenience and expense of paying back taxes. An outright contribution to LDF would provide a tax deduction but would preclude getting the money back.

In February 1962 the executive committee voted to set up an "informal trust account to which ten to fifteen people might make loans." I became the "trustee" of considerable sums, which I sent to Jack Young in Jackson to post as bond for the Freedom Riders. Ultimately, if the cases were won, the money would be returned. After a while it dawned on me that the arrangement was something to be nervous about. What if I were to die? Would there be a dispute, and how would the various relationships among the defendants, Jack Young, the donors, and my heirs be sorted out? "What would happen," I asked Bill DeWind, "if I were hit by a truck?" He tried to set my mind at ease: "If you were hit by a truck you wouldn't have to worry."

In October 1963 we finally found a bonding company that wrote bonds for a 2 percent premium, with one-third collateral. By then, however, most of the Mississippi cases were through the state court system. But bonds for demonstrations all over the country continued to be a preoccupation, and as late as January 1964 we still grappled with how to get enough bond money. Occasionally, there was a local black bail bondsman, but his resources, of course, would be limited. During Martin Luther King, Jr.'s Birmingham demonstrations, for instance, the local bondsman's collateral soon ran out, and there were no local resources for bailing hundreds of demonstrators out of jail, until several large labor unions, encouraged by the Kennedy administration produced, hundreds of thousands of dollars.

When finally we won the Mississippi Freedom Ride cases, the Mississippi courts returned our bond money, but kept one-half of 1 percent for circuit clerks as a processing charge. If anything, they should have paid us interest. But we had so much else to do that we didn't litigate it. At a meeting in the LDF library with those who had lent us the money, I passed out checks, paying off our lenders one hundred cents on the dollar. It felt pretty good.

THE REST OF THE DOCKET

By September 1961, apart from the demonstration cases, we had ninety-three active cases. In most of these, we sent materials to cooperating lawyers, consulted, and prepared appeals. School cases continued in most of the Southern states. We were busy in the Supreme Court defending a decision that integrated schools in New Rochelle, New York; reversing a ten-year sentence in Alabama where there had been discrimination in the choosing of jurors; upsetting a Louisiana voting law that required that candidates for office be identified by race at the polls. We persuaded the court of appeals to interpret federal jurisdictional law to enable a survivor of a murdered prisoner to bring suit for prison brutality. In these and other cases the courts interpreted the law to favor civil rights.

But in a case involving exclusion of blacks from a restaurant in a public garage in Wilmington, Delaware, we won by a divided vote, the Court signaling, as it had in *Boynton*, that it was not rushing boldly into broad pronouncements on issues of race, state action, and property.

THURGOOD LOSES HIS TEMPER

To be a civil rights lawyer in the 1960s was to be subjected to more than an occasional harangue by some racist judge. I can recall Thurgood Marshall's coming close to losing his temper in court only once, when Judge T. Whitfield Davidson of Texas delivered an opinion from the bench that must have lasted an hour. Davidson ranted on about warfare on the Syrian border even though, he said, Arabs and Hebrews are "descendants of a common father." In Haiti, he continued, integration was followed by one race destroying the other. But, in the Southern states, the former slave owner and the former slave retained racial integrity. "Is the Puerto Rican [a product of racial amalgamation]," he asked, "any better advanced than the Southern Negro?" He continued about planters who taught slaves to speak English and converted them to Christianity and about the mistress of the plantation who cared for slaves when they were sick.

But then, said Davidson, came "an interruption." Freedom. "Strong black people wept at the feet of their mistress, not because they were free but because they were parting from some one they loved." Carpetbaggers came for selfish reasons and "caused the Negro in so many ways to forget his God." It was at this point that Thurgood, who had been listening quietly, couldn't stand it any longer and threw his pencil down on the table, being as demonstrative as he could under the circumstances. After the court of appeals reversed, Davidson ordered a twelve-year desegregation plan, which also reserved the right of students to transfer out of the school to which they were assigned.

22

THE NEW CHIEF COUNSEL:
I SUCCEED THURGOOD

LDF TRANSFORMS

The sit-ins and Freedom Rides transformed LDF. Income for 1959 had been $361,000, but in 1960 it grew to over $500,000, and in 1961 we took in over $586,000. Many sent in unsolicited contributions—in some months doubling the receipts of comparable periods of years past—but the biggest category of growth came out of mailings to contributors, subscribers to liberal publications, and members of liberal organizations. By March 1961 we had 23,000 contributors. The Grenville Clark plan had supplied a major boost too.

We increased the size of our legal staff. Thurgood hired Derrick Bell, who had resigned from the Eisenhower Justice Department because it prohibited him from belonging to the NAACP. Years later Bell became a Harvard law professor, where he taught civil rights law, engaged in sit-ins and hunger strikes against the law school to challenge its hiring policies, and became a constant critic of LDF. For a time, he was dean of the University of Oregon Law School, from which he resigned because the school would not hire a minority woman whose candidacy he supported.

Bell disapproved of the Fund's school desegregation and other programs as well as of me personally, referring to LDF during the time I was its director-counsel as a "penthouse plantation," and writing that I "evidenced . . . intolerance based on a sense of hereditary superiority." He encouraged and counseled a black student boycott of me and Julius Chambers when we jointly taught a civil rights course at Harvard in January 1984. Bell later left the Harvard faculty in protest over its failure to appoint a black woman. But this all happened later, and during the time he was at LDF we were perfectly friendly, and Bell did his job well under Thurgood's leadership and mine. In those years I never had cause to doubt his commitment to promoting integration in public education and elsewhere.

During the early sixties we were not distracted by that sort of dissonance. We augmented our theater benefits with a series of annual concerts by Artur Rubinstein at Carnegie Hall. Dorothy and Sam Rosenman knew Sol Hurok, the impresario who represented Rubinstein, and Rubenstein's daughter Eva was married to Bill Coffin, the Yale chaplain whom LDF had represented in the Montgomery Freedom Rider case. After the concerts, Rubinstein came to parties for contributors at Dorothy and Sam's apartment—all of which lent glamour to being associated with LDF. Rubinstein liked LDF; in his marvelous Polish accent he called us a "push organization," with a gesture pushing his hands upward and outward.

In 1960 Spotts Robinson left law practice to become dean of Howard Law School. There he replaced "Big" Jim Nabrit, who became president of the university. We replaced Spotts, who had been our corporate agent in Virginia, with Lawrence Douglas Wilder, then a budding young lawyer, who in 1989 became Virginia's first black governor.

The NAACP responded to our success with concern. At its April 1960 board meeting the Association appointed a committee to meet with us because of a report that "some money being raised by NAACP branches is going to the Legal Defense Fund on behalf of the students in the South." (One branch did send us money once, and we sent it back.) There was dissatisfaction that LDF was representing student demonstrators, bypassing local branches. The NAACP board asked the committee to address the "question . . . of whether we want a fully-manned legal department, and if so for what purposes." It met several times with an LDF committee and both concluded that the organizations should cooperate, that LDF should encourage its clients to seek community support from the Association, and that Thurgood, Roy Wilkins, Bishop Stephen Spottswood (the Association's chairman), and Allan Knight Chalmers should visit each other's board meetings regularly.

At the Association resentment at the many new groups and individuals who had emerged to challenge its leadership grew. In July, Gloster Current, the NAACP director of branches, wrote to Roy Wilkins citing cases in Little Rock, Memphis, and in Monroe, North Carolina, where branches and local lawyers had disagreed about who should represent demonstrators, and where the lawyers followed LDF rather than NAACP advice. Current referred favorably to the Dollarway, Arkansas, case, which Bob Carter had filed against Thurgood's wishes, and complained that "branches are giving money to the Inc. Fund."

THURGOOD BECOMES A JUDGE—I SUCCEED HIM

In spring 1961 it appeared that President Kennedy was going to appoint a black judge to the federal bench. Early that year the press carried an article stating that he was prepared to name Bob Carter to the United States District Court in New York. For a long while nothing happened, and Bob's appointment did not come through. Then Thurgood hinted to me that the Kennedy people had suggested to him that he might be appointed to the district court. Thurgood said he had made clear that he was interested only in the court of appeals.

Nonetheless, Thurgood began to delegate to me more and more responsibility. He didn't attend the Fund's May 1961 annual meeting, and he didn't come to the June meeting either, turning the principal role at both meetings over to me. During a large part of the summer Thurgood absented himself and vacationed with his family at Arthur Spingarn's country home in Amenia, New York, where some of the most important early meetings of the NAACP had occurred many years before. Though Thurgood was not present to take charge at LDF, I spoke with him regularly by phone.

Every few days Thurgood would call to find out what was going on in the office and to offer advice. He told a story that parodied the role he was playing. When he was a dining car waiter, working his way through school, the chef put the assistant chef in full charge for a day and completely left him alone. That evening he returned to find the assistant frying steaks, baking cakes, preparing salads, everything in full swing. The chef sat down outside the kitchen, leaned back in his chair, and shouted through the door: "Assistant chef, what you doing now?" The reply: "Peelin' potatoes." "How many you got peeled?" "Peck and a half." "Take out six."

Midsummer, he told me that he was pretty certain that Kennedy would appoint him to the bench and that he wanted me to succeed him. I was astonished. As it had become more and more apparent that Thurgood probably would become a judge, I had begun to wonder what I would do when it happened. I had not the slightest idea who would succeed him.

In coming to his decision, Thurgood discussed with board members, including Bill Coleman, the fact that I was white and told Bill that race shouldn't be an issue—after all, that was what our fight was about, a country with no racial distinctions. He had a similar conversation with Dorothy Rosenman about my being Jewish. He spoke to cooperating lawyers. I had worked closely with almost all of them and many were good friends. Later, Juanita Mitchell, with whom Thurgood was close, articulated her understanding of the meaning of race for those who were conducting the struggle against Jim Crow: "It was white as well as black. The NAACP has always been that."

Thurgood also touched base with the editors of the principal black newspapers, with whom he was friendly, and they supported his choice. Bob Ming volunteered to take the job on a temporary basis, but Thurgood wasn't interested. As far as I know, the only counsel he got against my appointment was from some of the fund-raisers. They feared I wouldn't be good at raising money, which was not an unfair criticism, because I had no experience at fund-raising and no gift for it, being known for an ineptitude in making small talk. Moreover, my being white was not expected to be a plus with potential givers interested in giving to black causes.

Shortly after the announcement of his nomination to the United States Court of Appeals for the Second Circuit, Thurgood received a shock that confirmed his perception, reiterated most recently in a television interview not long before his death, that there was no city in America where he had to hold his hand up in front of his face to know that he was black. He returned from lunch one afternoon, called me into his office, and closed the door. As he was returning to the office a policeman had stopped him on the street and asked why he was following a woman who was walking ahead of him. The officer demanded identification, wrote down Thurgood's name and other information, and did nothing further.

Of course, Thurgood hadn't been following anybody, other than all those people who happened to be on the sidewalk in front of him as he returned to the office. But he was worried; if word of the episode got out it might affect his prospects for the judgeship. After all, politicians have never been famous for supporting nominees about whom there might develop even a whiff of scandal. We discussed whether to approach officials Thurgood knew in the police department, but decided to do nothing. Raising the issue might give it visibility. Doing nothing might allow the incident to die. In the end, this was the course he chose, and the event was never reported. I have wondered how history might have been changed if an eager reporter with an interest in politics had come across Thurgood's name in the policeman's report.

The LDF executive committee took up my appointment at its meeting of September 27, 1961. Allan Knight Chalmers read Thurgood's letter of resignation and reported that it was Thurgood's "hope that Jack Greenberg would be appointed to the position of General Counsel." On Chalmers's motion the executive committee voted to recommend to the full board of directors that I be promoted to general counsel at a salary of $20,000 per year, and that Connie Motley be promoted to associate counsel at a salary of $18,000.

The title would be general counsel, not Thurgood's director-counsel. The thought was that someone else would do the executive-administrative aspect of the job while I did the legal work. The executive committee put off the matter of an executive director, but did vote unanimously to promote me and Connie. It called an emergency meeting of the full board for the following week.

The full board met Wednesday, October 4, at the Roosevelt Hotel. Almost everyone attended. We had, as usual, a private meeting room where members had drinks and dinner before the meeting began. The Roosevelt was comfortable: We held board meetings there regularly and Thurgood and Cissy had had their wedding party there. Chalmers read Thurgood's letter of resignation. Bill Hastie read a resolution praising Thurgood's "technical legal skill, a sense of strategy in social struggle, and a feeling for people and an ability to work with them." Continuing to focus on Thurgood's efforts to combine legal and community work, Hastie added that he "has continued to rally and inspire broad community support for and participation in the work that has been his career." Then Connie and I were asked to leave the room as the board considered our futures.

Chalmers presented the recommendation of the executive committee concerning Connie and me, and the board adopted it unanimously. Several members who could not attend sent letters saying that they agreed. Chalmers proposed that he be appointed executive director, but the board rejected that motion, voting instead to compensate him, for the first time, in the amount of $15,000 per year for his work as president. I thought that separating the post of executive director from that of chief counsel was a bad idea, since virtually all of the important administrative decisions were tied up with legal judgments. But I surely wasn't going to confuse matters at that point. The board, however, understanding the intimate connection between the legal and administrative at LDF, independently came to the same conclusion and the administrative decisions became mine as well.

The NAACP did not participate directly in any of the decisions made at the meeting, but John Morsell (Roy Wilkins's chief assistant), Bishop Spottswood, chairman of the NAACP board, and Arthur Spingarn, its president, attended.

Someone called me in, Chalmers told me that I had been appointed, and the board asked me to speak. Feeling more than a little nervous, I told the board that LDF was in great shape, that we had a wonderful staff, a great tradition, a harmonious relationship with our cooperating lawyers. We had a demanding docket of cases, being somewhat overwhelmed with the demonstration cases, but we were managing to stay on top of them. For the future, I suggested that we had to become more active in issues of voting, housing, and employment. One of our greatest needs was to become more involved with the community, for it was there that the legal principles we won would have to be converted to reality. The biggest problem would be fund-raising, on which we depended for the resources to make the rest of the program work.

Present for my confirmation as general counsel were many old, good friends: Charles Buchanan, George Cannon, Bill Coleman, Bill DeWind, Walter Gellhorn, Amos Hall, John Lewis, Dr. John W. Davis (the latter three from the Masonic community), Bill Hastie, Shad Polier (chairman of the Commission on Law and Social Action of the American Jewish Congress), Dr. C. B. Powell (publisher of the *Amsterdam News*), Lois Cowles, Miriam Allen, Connie Lindau (the latter two members of the theater benefit committee), Dorothy Rosenman, and Catherine Waddell.

A *New York Times* headline the next day announced, "N.A.A.C.P.

Names a White Counsel." Rather than highlighting the fact that I had been one of Thurgood's senior assistants for several years, and had a long history with LDF programs and cases, the *Times* chose to focus on the least relevant aspect of my persona. Of course, the headline was also inaccurate, for though we had gone to great lengths to make clear our separate identity from the NAACP for many years, here was one more indication that the distinction would remain too subtle for some to handle.

The black press was almost unanimously supportive of my appointment. A *Pittsburgh Courier* article praised me and a week later wrote that "top officials of the organization said Mr. Greenberg, 37, had worked so long with the team that hardly anyone remembers that he is white." The *Afro American* quoted Thurgood: "As those who are fighting discrimination, we cannot afford to practice it." One column referred to my book *Race Relations and American Law* as "the authority in the field." A *Kansas City Call* editorial was headlined: "A Good Choice—and a Logical One."[10] The *Atlanta Inquirer* reported, "Atlanta civil rights leaders apparently found the choice a happy one." The article continued, quoting Donald L. Hollowell, the leading civil rights lawyer in Atlanta: "We were very happy to learn of Mr. Marshall's appointment. . . . Mr. Greenberg was the logical choice to succeed him." Evelyn Cunningham, a leading black columnist for the *New York Courier*, wrote concerning those who opposed me because of my race, "The whole dispute is rather sad—and dangerous. It is sad because Greenberg has got to take the rap for some time to come. . . . He's got to be something like Jackie Robinson."

There was, as Cunningham suggested, opposition, but not much. The chairman of the Jamaica, Long Island, NAACP branch, Lawrence R. Bailey, praised my ability but criticized the "image" projected by an LDF with a white chief counsel and white president, Allan Knight Chalmers. Jimmy Hicks, an *Amsterdam News* columnist, and a friend, wrote: "I think somebody goofed on this one. And although I'm going to tighten my belt and work like Hell side by side with Jack Greenberg, I'm still going to insist on my right to ask: 'Wha' Hoppen?'"

Some of the criticism, in which Bailey joined, was that my appointment was "arbitrary discrimination against Robert Carter and Constance Baker Motley." There was not the slightest evidence that Connie was displeased; we continued to work together effectively and have remained good friends to this day. Bob had a view of the appropriate LDF–NAACP relationship quite different from Thurgood's and mine, which I already have recounted and which affected our personal relationship.

Five days after my appointment, the Association board devoted a large part of a meeting to the complaint that they were not consulted in the choice of Thurgood's replacement. Roy Wilkins observed correctly, "The problem is one of structure rather than of personalities. It points up the fact that the Legal Defense Fund can act as it wishes irrespective of the wishes of the NAACP." Some members were unhappy that I had been given the title general counsel, the same as Bob's at NAACP. They were particularly bitter about erroneous press stories that "gave the impression that two names were going to be placed before the Board for consideration: that of Robert L. Carter and that of Jack Greenberg," although Bob was not a candidate for the post. "It became public feeling . . . that Mr. Carter had been voted upon and discarded." The board called for further meetings with LDF, which should find "an organizational set-up which will (a) prevent a recurrence [presumably of LDF making such decisions unilaterally] . . . and (b) clarify the titles of both men." They also suggested "that it may be necessary to solve our problem by setting up our own legal staff." The committees continued to meet. The LDF board satisfied one of their concerns by changing my title to director-counsel, which had been Thurgood's title and which I preferred, anyway.

As far as the NAACP was concerned, Roy Wilkins and I were good friends and our relationship was neither competitive nor compounded by racial factors, although he remained under pressure from some of his board members over having let my appointment go through without protest. Among others at the Association there was a diversity of attitudes about race, about me personally—many staff members remained good friends despite the years the two organizations had been apart—and about whether a white should head LDF. But the main problem was, as Roy had said, "one of structure," and my race had nothing to do with it.

President Kennedy made a recess appointment of Thurgood to the court of appeals: that is, Thurgood could sit as a judge until the end of the next term of Congress, awaiting confirmation. The confirmation process would take eight months of on-and-off hearings as Thurgood ran a gauntlet of racist Southern senators until he was confirmed.

When Thurgood left the Legal Defense Fund he quoted Charlie Houston, who, when he had left the NAACP earlier, had said: "Shock troops don't occupy towns." In fact, upon succeeding Houston, although he devoted much energy to consolidating gains Houston had achieved, Thurgood became as much one of the shock troops as Charlie had been. While I too devoted resources to solidifying gains Thurgood had won, as I became the chief counsel for those in the forefront of the movement, I found myself as much a member of the shock troops in the leading-edge issues of my time as Thurgood had been during his own tenure.

23

COMPLETING THE CIRCLE: FREEDOM FIGHTERS FREE THEMSELVES

THE COUNTRY FOLLOWS THE COURT

John F. Kennedy campaigned as a candidate of change. Even today we look back on vigor and freshness as the hallmarks of his brief presidency. While Eisenhower showed little public enthusiasm for the wisdom of the *Brown* decision, Kennedy endorsed it. He promised to prohibit Federal Housing Administration mortgage insurance and other governmental support for segregated housing. During his campaign for the presidency he called Coretta King, and Bobby Kennedy called the judge when Martin Luther King, Jr., was imprisoned for violating probation of his sentence for driving with an out-of-state license. Following his election Kennedy proposed the most comprehensive civil rights legislation in modern times—although it is not at all certain that, had he not been assassinated, he could have gotten it through the House and Senate. He appointed a head of the Civil Rights Division, Burke Marshall, who was committed to racial equality, and he appointed Thurgood to the court of appeals.

But Kennedy moderated his civil rights position to satisfy his Southern white racist constituency, and drafted his legislative proposals based on what he thought he could get through Congress; his civil rights bill did not contain a fair employment provision.

Through his attorney general, Bobby Kennedy, to satisfy some of his white Southern supporters, he appointed some of the worst, most egregiously racist Southern judges. When the Freedom Rides began, Bobby Kennedy tried to talk the demonstrators out of continuing with them. Instead of consistently pursuing civil rights aggressively in the courts he sometimes held back, referring segregation in interstate travel to the Interstate Commerce Commission, shilly-shallying in our case to get James Meredith into the University of Mississippi, trying to bargain for Southern assent, which, in the end, was not to be had.

In one of those gruesome twists history sometimes puts on things, the assassination of John F. Kennedy helped bring about the passage of the Civil Rights Act of 1964, which might not have passed had he survived to complete his term. His successor, Lyndon Johnson, a Southerner and a master politician and former Senate majority leader, was as skillful as anyone of his generation in moving Congress. It is well known that Johnson became a great civil rights president, but contrary to the perceptions of some, his commitment existed even before he inherited the presidency. Though coming from one of the states of the old Confederacy, he contrived while still in the Senate to bring about the defeat of legislation that would have limited the Supreme Court's jurisdiction in retaliation for *Brown* and other controversial decisions, and Johnson was one of but three Southern senators who refused to sign the congressional manifesto denouncing the *Brown* decision. As president, Johnson appointed Thurgood solicitor general and later to the Supreme Court. He pushed the Civil Rights Act of 1964 through Congress. Following Selma, he made a nationally televised address asking for passage of the bill that ended with the title of the movement anthem—"We Shall Overcome." He also got the Voting Rights Act of 1965 and the Fair Housing Act of 1968 through Congress, the latter enacted in a spasm of national guilt following the murder of Martin Luther King, Jr.

The 1964 act prohibited discrimination in public accommodations that "affected" interstate commerce, including, for all practical purposes, all restaurants, theaters, hotels, and establishments that offered services to the general public. It also prohibited employment discrimination (including that against women; this feature was introduced as a ploy by opponents who thought it would defeat the bill). In addition, it prohibited discrimination in any facility that receives federal funding, essentially subjecting all hospitals, school systems, and universities to federal administrative enforcement of antidiscrimination laws.

The Voting Rights Act went straight after the Southern chicanery that had defeated the intent of voting rights law from the time of Reconstruction. This act not only prohibited discrimination in voting, but by a formula that targeted Southern states and counties where discrimination had a long history, it discouraged end runs around the law by prohibiting changes in voting rules without the approval of a federal court in Washington, D.C. (not a local, possibly compliant, federal judge), or of the United States attorney general. It also provided for federal officials to take over administering the registration and voting process where local officials wouldn't treat blacks fairly.

The Fair Housing Act prohibited discrimination in sale and rental of housing. Relying also on congressional power to regulate activities that affect interstate commerce, it finessed the issue over which the Restrictive Covenant Cases were fought, that is, whether there was enough state action in housing transactions to justify applying the equal protection clause, which prohibits discrimination by states.

Interpreting and enforcing all those laws became a fresh battleground for LDF, but at least the foundation for further progress had been laid.

When the new laws came into effect one might have expected the government to be active in enforcing all the new provisions. It generally took an active role with regard to public accommodations and against the grossest sorts of voting discrimination, though we remained alone in giving meaning to the fair employment statute for many years. As Kennedy pursued a policy that was pro–civil rights and at the same time tried to accommodate the wishes of his Southern supporters, and later as Johnson pushed comprehensive civil rights laws through Congress, LDF continued to adapt to the new political environment. We learned that as in the past we had to proceed independently, not rely on the Justice Department, which, even in Kennedy—Johnson years, sometimes had an agenda different from ours. In many cases we took initiatives that Justice wouldn't; on some occasions it came to adopt our position, although on some issues we remained apart. When the Nixon administration came in with a program hostile to our aspirations, LDF litigation, independent of government enforcement of civil rights laws, became absolutely essential.

BOMBINGS, SHOOTINGS

As tense and bitter as were many of the political struggles, courtroom battles, and public demonstrations that marked civil rights progress, most of these conflicts tended to be played out within the constraints of civilized conflict. But there were also many who joined the crusade to maintain blacks in a subordinate status who were not part of that civilized process. Once they determined that the law might not continue to support their perception of an ideal society they searched about for other means to wage their fight. Some tried to marshal new political coalitions, but some turned to unrestrained violence to intimidate others into accepting the only outcome they would tolerate. Klansmen burnt Freedom Riders' buses. A bomb blew up Birmingham's Sixteenth Street Baptist Church, killing four black schoolgirls. The day after I had been working with NAACP field secretary Medgar Evers in Jackson, an assassin murdered him. Bull Connor, Birmingham's notorious chief of law enforcement, tried to suppress blacks who engaged in peaceful marches by turning police dogs and fire hoses on them. Sheriff Jim Clark's forces clubbed and brutalized marchers in Selma. Mobs beat St. Augustine demonstrators with clubs and whips. Klansmen fired into a car carrying people of both races, killing a white civil rights demonstrator, Viola Liuzzo, who had traveled from Detroit to participate in the historic march from Selma to Montgomery to secure voting rights. James

Chaney, from Meridian, Mississippi (who was black), and two New York-
ers, Andrew Goodman and Michael Schwerner (who were white), all three
in their early twenties, were murdered in Philadelphia, Mississippi, because
they were part of a great wave of idealistic young people who came together
to demonstrate for civil rights. When James Meredith entered the University of Mississippi, mobs rioted and gunfire killed a news photographer.
Troops were on the scene to restrain mobs when Vivian Malone and James
Hood tried to enter the University of Alabama.

LDF lawyers worked in the vortex and at the edges of all this violence,
but mostly came out unscathed. I can't think of a single instance of a
lawyer refusing to attend a case or meet with clients because of fear of violence, though we did our best to minimize the risks we might be exposed
to. Thurgood used to joke that he had a big yellow stripe down his back. We
followed his example.

Nevertheless, there were close calls. In Mississippi, Derrick Bell, arrested
for using a white telephone booth at the Jackson railroad station, was
released soon afterward. When he returned safely to the office, Thurgood
(who claimed he "wrapped his rights in cellophane" and stuck them in his
pocket when he went down South) told him sardonically, "Get yourself
shot and we'll raise a lot of money on your black ass." But Henry Aronson,
a staff lawyer in Jackson, who indeed was an exception in that he conducted
himself provocatively, was severely beaten in Grenada, Mississippi, while
there on a school segregation case, as police looked on. I worked with
Arthur Shores and visited his Birmingham house before and after racists
bombed it; on another occasion the Gaston Motel, where we all stayed
while in Birmingham, was bombed. In Birmingham I would sometimes,
standing off to the side unobserved, watch demonstrations and police
attacks on demonstrators with fire hoses and dogs. The *Thunderbolt* and
other neo-Nazi publications railed against the "Jew Jack Greenberg."

Only once did the threat of danger cause me to make special plans. In
May 1964 Burke Marshall, the assistant attorney general for civil rights,
called me to say that on May 17 an attempt might be made on my life in
Mobile, Alabama. J. L. LeFlore, president of the black longshoremen's
union, had invited me to speak at a tenth-anniversary celebration of
Brown v. Board of Education. My heavily censored FBI file refers to this
episode, based on information received from "a usually reliable informant."

PLOT TO ASSASSINATE MARTIN LUTHER KING AND JACK GREENBERG, ATTOR-
NEY NAACP, MOBILE, ALABAMA, FIVE SEVENTEEN, NINETEEN, SIXTY FOUR,
RACIAL MATTERS. . . . Information received [three lines blacked out]
Mobile has advised that there is to be freedom rally on 5/16–17/64, in
Mobile, to commemorate the Tenth Anniversary of the school deseg-

regation decision. Greenberg is slated to be the main speaker, however, there has been no mention made that King will be in this location on this date.

Another FBI document warned of armed men who would "use high powered rifles, carbines, and other weapons and have orders to kill KING and GREENBERG. Armed men are also to protect and assist each other to escape."

If I were to pull out because I had learned about a threat to myself I couldn't very well ask LDF lawyers to go South, where people involved in our cause faced similar risks daily. I told Burke I had to go and asked Gus Heningburg, a recently hired fund-raiser who had just been discharged from military intelligence, to check out the meeting hall. Gus conducted a professional security search, looking under every seat and in every nook and cranny of the longshoremen's auditorium.

About two hours before the speech, my Eastern Airlines flight landed and parked on the runway far from the terminal. A car pulled up to the stairway, a flight attendant whispered that the car was for me, and I descended. Two black Mobile police officers, maybe the only two, picked me up in a car at the bottom of the steps and drove me to the home of Vernon Crawford, our cooperating lawyer. As we left the airport, police cars blocked traffic behind us. On the ledge behind the back seat the police had stacked telephone books, which they told me were there to stop any bullets that might come through the rear window.

We sat around Crawford's house, having a drink or two, until a few minutes before speech time. Then the police drove me to the International Longshoremen's Association hall. Pickets of the National States Rights party, who were patrolling outside the building carrying anti-Semitic and white supremacist signs, left just before I arrived. Others had picketed the downtown Sheraton under the misapprehension that I was there. As I waited backstage, the Royal Ambassadors Choir of Mt. Olive Baptist Church sang and a local pastor offered the invocation. Vernon Crawford introduced me. I then stepped through a back door onto the stage and spoke before TV cameras to a packed hall of one thousand black people. I said that I was grateful to the pickets because they helped the audience find the place of the meeting (big laugh and applause), that "we must keep pressing hard for integration," and that "the very root of all our cases is the conception of human dignity." I concluded, after about half an hour, "What we demand is equal legal rights for all Americans." The applause was thunderous, but I didn't stay out there to enjoy it; I quickly returned backstage, where the police were waiting to drive me directly to the airport. No commercial flight was available: A chartered private plane flew me to Atlanta without incident, except for a tense time when its radio went out.

THE EVOLVING DOCKET

As LDF moved into the mid-1960s our work expanded rapidly.

• Two weeks after succeeding Thurgood I argued and won the first demonstration cases in the Supreme Court.

• By 1962 we had twenty-nine cases in the Supreme Court, more than any law office in the country, except the solicitor general's.

• By mid-decade our case load nearly tripled—ninety-nine cases grew to 281.

• Our client roster (with cooperating lawyers) included about 17,000 demonstrators. Among them: more than 300 Jackson Freedom Riders; 100 Selma demonstrators; and 1,500 Birmingham protesters. There were 743 defendants in Albany, Georgia, which became a focal point perhaps because it was the home of C. B. King, a courageous civil rights lawyer.

• By the late 1960s the Supreme Court had decided sixty or so demonstration cases. About forty were LDF cases. We vindicated virtually all the demonstrators, with one major loss: The Court upheld by a five-to-four vote Martin Luther King, Jr.'s contempt conviction for marching in Birmingham contrary to a state court injunction.

• The staff grew from five lawyers to seventeen.

• The budget grew from $500,000 to $1,700,000.

• We began enforcing the 1964 Civil Rights Act; by 1966 only thirty LDF protest cases remained, most awaiting dismissal. There were few public accommodations protests because we regularly won such cases and widespread compliance began.

• We fought the *Meredith* case to integrate the University of Mississippi and opened the University of Alabama—despite George Wallace's physically barring the door. With less strife we got Harvey Gantt into Clemson College (in 1990 he narrowly missed defeating Jesse Helms for a seat in the U.S. Senate) and we integrated Auburn University in Alabama, by which point every Southern state had some blacks in formerly all-white state universities.

• At the end of 1961 we had 46 school cases; as 1965 came to a close, 185. In Connie Motley's Memphis park case the Supreme Court warned that the time for "all deliberate speed" had passed. In the Atlanta school case, it repeated the admonition. I won the Knoxville case in the Supreme Court, striking down a rule allowing whites to transfer from formerly black schools, blacks from formerly white schools.

• We had a growing docket—fifteen cases—for black teachers who were fired during desegregation or assigned only to black schools.

• We started enforcing the equal employment sections of the 1964 Civil Rights Act, filing nearly a thousand complaints with the Equal Employment

Opportunity Commission in 1965, followed by sixteen lawsuits by early 1966.

• When the 1960s began, six cases involved Southern efforts to put us out of business, but by the mid-1960s, there were only two. Mississippi federal judge Harold Cox brought professional misconduct proceedings against R. Jess Brown, which, with Bob Ming, we defeated in the court of appeals.

• Lou Pollak and Bill Coleman argued *McLaughlin v. Florida*, persuading the Supreme Court to hold unconstitutional laws prohibiting interracial "cohabitation"—spelling the doom of antimiscegenation laws.

• I won a Fourth Circuit case that established a rule requiring desegregation of federally subsidized hospitals—the foundation for Title VI of the Civil Rights Act, which prohibits segregation in federally funded facilities. Soon after he came on the staff in 1961, I asked Mike Meltsner, a recent Yale Law School graduate, to launch a campaign against discrimination in hospitals. As part of this effort he sued a hospital in Newport News, Virginia, and another in Orangeburg, South Carolina; filed a case against the North Carolina Dental Association; and refiled the Wilmington, North Carolina, hospital case—we won them all. After the Civil Rights Act was passed in 1964 there was no longer any need for more suits against out and out exclusion. The Department of Health, Education, and Welfare (HEW) undertook that task.

• In a case that Earl Warren believed was among his most important, a black woman refused to respond when a prosecutor addressed her as "Mary." She insisted on "*Miss* Hamilton" and the Alabama trial judge held her in contempt. At her trial, Norman Amaker made the crucial constitutional objection to the court's demand that she respond even though she had been addressed in an insulting manner, and the Supreme Court later upheld him. During the *Brown* argument John W. Davis, for South Carolina, had argued that the plaintiffs were throwing away the possibility of having equal schools by insisting on the "prestige" of attending desegregated ones. Thurgood had responded that, indeed, blacks were arguing for "prestige." That is what Miss Hamilton was insisting on.

• Mike Meltsner prepared a case asking that the Congress be reapportioned to reduce Southern representation to the extent that blacks weren't permitted to vote. Section 2 of the Fourteenth Amendment prescribed that remedy, but no one had ever tried to enforce it. I lost in the District of Columbia Court of Appeals, which held out hope that a subsequent suit might prevail, but we never pursued the issue after the Voting Rights Act was passed in 1965.

• In the absence of a fair housing act, I put to work my fading knowledge of antitrust to win an injunction against Akron, Ohio, real estate brokers who wouldn't sell to blacks and filed a similar suit against Trenton, New Jersey, brokers who surrendered in a settlement.

• We started a national poverty law program, the National Office for the Rights of the Indigent (NORI).

• We launched a campaign against racial discrimination in capital punishment for rape, which developed into a broader-based attack on the constitutionality of capital punishment.

The calendar for eight days in May 1963 may help illustrate the pace of our lives. Between May 20 and 27, LDF, with Connie Motley as lead counsel, won the decision integrating Memphis parks, got a court order to admit two black students to the University of Alabama, secured a Fifth Circuit ruling reinstating 1,081 black Birmingham schoolchildren suspended for demonstrating; I won a group of sit-in cases in the Supreme Court.

THE SIT-IN CASES IN THE SUPREME COURT

The sit-in cases had top priority. If we won, the movement would continue on toward inevitable success. If we lost, the consequences would be unknowable. Things might slow down, but more likely there would be calls for changes in strategy and tactics, with nonviolence losing influence as the overall strategy of choice. At least some in the movement, frustrated in attempts to gain legitimate goals through peaceful protest, would start calling for violence. In a chaotic environment everyone would lose, most of all blacks. In any event, the influence of LDF would be sharply reduced.

The first three Supreme Court sit-in cases came to us from Johnnie Jones, a black Baton Rouge lawyer. He had been a letter carrier and in 1953, at age thirty-four, graduated from Southern University Law School, which the state had set up to thwart our efforts to integrate LSU. Jones was wiry, energetic, and rustic; one ordinarily would not think of a lawyer with his background capable of making constitutional objections that would command Supreme Court review. But he did. Moreover, one would not think that a small-town lawyer, suddenly having the almost unheard of opportunity to argue in the Supreme Court, would relinquish it. But for the good of the cause, this is just what he did.

Jones was a protégé of Tureaud, the dean of Louisiana black lawyers, who had brought him into the LDF circle. He was well-schooled in civil rights law; he received our materials, consulted, attended lawyers conferences, and was by all tests a member of the team. By 1972, in a new South, he was elected to the Louisiana legislature, but in the early 1960s he was lonely and beleaguered, a prophet with honor among blacks but not among whites in his hometown.

In the first case, on March 29, 1960, one group of students had gone to a local drugstore that served blacks, but did not serve them at the lunch counter. The students sat at the counter. The owner wouldn't serve them, but neither did he ask them to leave or call the police. He faced the dilemma of not wanting to offend blacks, who were "very good customers," or whites, who looked to business people to preserve segregation. A police officer, on his own, called a Captain Weiner, who arrested the students. In similar episodes, two other groups sought service at the Greyhound bus station and at S. H. Kress; the ever-ready Captain Weiner arrested both groups for "disturbing the peace," as he put it, "by the mere presence of their being there." The trial court convicted all three groups of disturbing the peace and sentenced them to thirty days in jail and a $100 fine or an additional ninety days. The Supreme Court decided to hear the three cases together.

Once more, we had to face the "state action" dragon. Thurgood and I submitted a brief, written with Charlie Black, Bill Coleman, Lou Pollak, and Jim Nabrit III, which led off with the argument that no matter who decreed widespread segregation, once police and courts enforced it, it became state action. To the response that the threat of court action hangs over many private disputes, we pointed out that this nominally private segregation really wasn't private because it obeyed a statewide custom long supported by state law and policy. Other private disputes resolved by law enforcement didn't have this background of widespread compliance with community and legally defined patterns of racial segregation.

Our strongest argument was that there was no evidence of a crime having been committed. "The mere presence of their being there," cited by Captain Weiner as evidence that the students had disturbed the peace, was in fact not evidence of any wrongdoing. Yet we placed this argument second, not up front where ordinarily the best argument would go, because, though we wanted the defendants exonerated, we were not looking for a very narrow decision that would apply to this issue only. We added as a third issue that the law was vague and that the demonstrators were engaged in freedom of speech. When the date of argument arrived, however, I felt discretion to be the better part of valor, pushed the no-evidence argument to the fore, and argued the pure state action doctrine second.

On Wednesday, October 18, 1961, I stood up before the Court in my first argument as chief counsel. If I were to win, no matter what the reasoning, the movement would interpret the win as vindication. The young demonstrators would be encouraged that there was some protection for them within the judicial system. LDF would be fortified in its role as counsel for the movement. I would be validated as the new chief counsel. Nothing succeeds like success; nothing fails like failure. My argument strategy, therefore, was to go for a win on any grounds, rather than try to hit a home run.

I started out by telling what had happened to the defendants in Baton Rouge—the statement of facts can be the most important part of an argument. To generate a bit of sympathy, I began by saying that the petitioners were "students, boys and girls, who attended Southern University." Justice Stewart got the idea that I was trying to make a different point: "Is their age at issue? . . . They should not have been dealt with as adults?" I explained, "There is no question of juvenile proceedings," and scrambled to return to my theme. From that point on, the justices, with Frankfurter as usual asking more questions than anyone else, were interested in the intricacies of whether the waitress asked the defendants to leave or merely to go to another counter, whether Louisiana had a trespass law, what state court interpretations of its disturbing the peace statute had been rendered, and so forth. By the time my argument ended, however, I had a sense of a friendly Court, looking for a way to vindicate my clients, though wary of making far-reaching doctrine.

My opponent had heavy weather all the way, not a single minute without questions. Justice Black pounded away at whether the state had a right to make it a crime to stay on premises if the owner had not ordered the defendant to leave. The focus was on property, not on race.

On December 11, 1961, the Court unanimously ruled in our favor. The majority opinion by Earl Warren concluded that there was no evidence of the students disturbing the peace. Frankfurter concurred, emphasizing that petitioners' "mere presence" had not been a crime and that there was no way of knowing whether their mere presence had threatened a disturbance. Douglas concurred, adopting our state action argument: "Segregation is basic to the structure of Louisiana as a community; the custom that maintains it is at least as powerful as any law." He went on to argue that there was state action in businesses affected with a public interest, like restaurants. Harlan concurred on the ground that the protesters were engaged in First Amendment–protected activity that the state could prohibit only under a narrowly drawn statute. This statute was too vague.

All of our arguments had been picked up by one or another of the justices, and we trumpeted the victory as a major triumph. But though it was a thorough rejection of the other side's position, the decision did not make new doctrine, or even stretch old doctrine. Rather it portended further legal battles every inch of the way, for the decision conveyed a wariness about establishing general principles that might broadly affect property and personal relationships in situations other than those closely resembling the cases at bar.

SIT-INS, ROUND TWO

In 1962 the Supreme Court heard sit-in cases from Birmingham, Durham, New Orleans, and Greenville, South Carolina; all were LDF cases, except the New Orleans case, and all were profoundly different from those we just had won. The Court also heard *Shuttlesworth v. City of Birmingham*, in which Fred Shuttlesworth had been convicted of urging students to sit in. Those five cases could not be decided, as the previous ones had been, on the grounds that there was no evidence of the crime charged having been committed. The students indeed were on someone else's premises without permission or invitation and save for the racial issue—if we were right—indeed would have been trespassers. Their only defense was that they had a constitutional right not to be convicted for demanding service by sitting in the restaurants, when the denial of service had been based on race.

Once again we had to face the state action bugaboos. Happily for our legal position, three of the cities had laws that required segregated dining—settling the question of state action. While New Orleans had no segregation ordinance, the mayor had proclaimed that "I have today directed the Superintendent of Police that no additional sit-in demonstrations . . . will be permitted." The state, therefore, not merely the private wishes of the proprietors, gave rise to the arrests. Along with those appeals, Joe Rauh, a superb Washington lawyer deeply involved in civil rights and liberal Democratic politics, argued a case in which a security guard, who also was deputized as a sheriff, ordered black teenagers to leave a suburban Washington amusement park. Was the guard/deputy a private person, which would present all the state action issues, or was he a cop? If he was a police officer, did his dual status of guard/sheriff make his conduct state action in the sense that the equal protection clause applied?

Lawyers who tried the Durham, North Carolina, case for us hadn't placed the Durham segregation law into evidence, although these same lawyers had lost a similar case in 1958 for that very failing. The Alabama Court of Appeals had written that the Birmingham segregation ordinance had likewise not been presented for decision, giving rise to the argument that the Supreme Court couldn't take it into account. Both of those cases were in jeopardy because of those procedural problems.

Joe Rauh and I lobbied the solicitor general, Archibald Cox, and Burke Marshall, head of the Justice Department's Civil Rights Division, to persuade the Justice Department to back us on the state action issue. Cox, a Harvard law professor, well over six feet tall, thin, ramrod straight, with a blond crew cut, was unquestionably pro–civil rights, but had serious intellectual problems with our position. He thought that if conviction for sitting-in were held to have denied equal protection, then conviction for crashing a private white garden party would have to be seen the same way. We argued that racial discrimination in a public setting was different from discrimination in a private place like a home and particularly different in a community where it was nurtured by state law and state-fostered custom. But Cox responded using the term *molliter manus imposuit,* a Latin phrase that I had to look up in the legal dictionary. The term in English law means "he gently laid hands upon" and is used in justifying physically moving the plaintiff to keep the peace, Cox's point being that if the proprietor could not call on the police for help, he might take it upon himself to throw the demonstrators out, leading to unpredictable levels of violence.

While Burke Marshall, head of the Civil Rights Division, agreed with us and was close to Attorney General Bobby Kennedy, no one would overrule Cox. I suggested that Cox's position was appropriate for a law review article, but that the solicitor general, the lawyer for the United States, was obliged to support us, even if personally he disagreed. But Cox stuck to his guns. While he agreed that we should win some of the cases on the basis of the city ordinances that supplied the state action we needed, if the government were on the other side on the pure state action issue in cases where ordinances couldn't be taken into acount, there was great risk that the Court would uphold the convictions. That would have been devastating to the movement.

His brief argued that our position would make it impossible for a homeowner to decide who might be excluded from his swimming pool:

> If a private landowner should invite all of his neighbors to use his swimming pool at will and then request one of the invitees to leave because of his race, creed or color, the decision would be private and, however unpraiseworthy, not unconstitutional. Furthermore, we take it that there would be no denial of equal protection if the State made its police and legal remedies available. . . . For, in a civilized community, where legal remedies have been substituted for force, private choice necessarily depends upon the support of sovereign sanctions. In such a case, the law would be color blind and it could not be fairly said, we think, that the State had denied anyone the equal protection of its laws.

The sit-in arguments took up almost the entire week of November 5, 1962. I led off in *Avent,* the Durham case, and did the rebuttal in all the cases, beginning with the emotionally charged fact that some defendants had been sentenced to thirty days in jail and others got fifteen to twenty days, quite a punishment for seeking service at a lunch counter. Then I argued that the state was deeply involved in segregation:

> There . . . exist[s] in North Carolina a state-wide custom of racial segregation . . . fostered and infused by a complex network of state segregation laws, including an ordinance of the City of Durham. . . . The premises . . . were extensively licensed and regulated by the state. . . .
>
> This case . . . does not involve state-enforced racial segregation in private homes, country clubs, nor does it involve discrimination against persons because they may be red-headed or personally disliked, personal enemies. . . .
>
> Such hypothetical cases would call into play countervailing constitutional considerations such as rights of privacy.

I never had an argument like that, before or since. The Court interrupted me 120 times.

Earl Warren wrote an opinion in the South Carolina case, reversing on the ground that the segregation was required by the ordinance. He wrote that the courts should not have to "separate the mental urges of the discriminators" in response to the argument that maybe the *owners*, apart from the ordinance, wanted to segregate. In the Birmingham case, the Court reversed, brushing aside Alabama's procedural objection that the Birmingham ordinance was not before the state court of appeals. Warren treated the New Orleans mayor's prohibition of sit-ins as a segregation ordinance. In the North Carolina case, he dealt with the absence of the Durham ordinance by sending the case back to the state supreme court to reconsider in light of the other decisions. The Court also got rid of five other demonstration cases from Virginia by sending them back to the state supreme court for reconsideration.

But Justice John Marshall Harlan, grandson of the dissenter in *Plessy v. Ferguson*, was uncomfortable. He wrote concurring and dissenting opinions that signaled trouble. Unlike Warren, he was ready to "separate the mental urges of the discriminators"—that is, whether they were motivated by the ordinances or their own prejudices. He extolled "freedom of the individual to choose his associates or his neighbors, to use and dispose of his property as he sees fit, to be irrational, arbitrary, capricious, even unjust in his personal relations. . . . This liberty would be overriden, in the name of equality, if the strictures of the [Fourteenth] Amendment were applied to governmental and private action without distinction."

Harlan's was a powerful and respected voice. Even though he dissented alone, he agreed with Cox, and there was trouble ahead. Another sign of heavy weather was the Maryland amusement park case, which the Court set down for reargument.

SIT-INS, ROUND THREE

On October 14 and 15, 1963, we had a fresh round of sit-ins to argue. Joe Rauh reargued the amusement park case. Connie, our Columbia, South Carolina, cooperating lawyer, Matthew Perry, and I argued another Columbia prosecution in which the charge was trespass and there was no segregation law. There also were a few other cases that didn't require confronting the state action issue. Connie Motley and Matthew Perry argued, and I did the rebuttal, in a South Carolina case, where the defense was that there was no evidence of breach of the peace. Alfred Hopkins, a Florida cooperating lawyer (one of the handful of Southern white lawyers then becoming involved in civil rights), and I presented a Florida case that involved a regulation requiring racially segregated toilets in restaurants.

The most difficult case was *Bell v. Maryland*. Here too there was no segregation law. The demonstration had occurred in a restaurant that did not serve blacks, not at the lunch counter of a store where blacks were otherwise welcome.

Charlie Black wrote a brilliant state action argument about conviction for seeking service in public places; state-engendered and -enforced segregation, which encouraged a general custom of segregating; and the difference between enforcing segregation in public and private life. I enlisted my old law school professor Richard R. B. Powell, then at Hastings Law School in San Francisco, where many retired professors taught. Powell had written the leading treatise on real property and was the reporter of the *Restatement of Property*, the legal profession's authoritative statement of the law.

I flew to San Francisco one morning, spent a few hours, mostly having lunch with Powell at the Poodle Dog restaurant, and flew back on the overnight red-eye, all in less than twenty-four hours. The essence of his section was that to reverse the convictions would do no violence to property rights: "Where, alas, has gone the 'liberty' of property owners to maintain and to operate structures which smell to high heaven, which are destructive of the lives, or health, or safety, or welfare of customers and workers? Just where it was bound to go! Into the limbo. By the curtailment of those 'liberties' there has been assured the larger liberty of society as a whole."

I asked Hans Smit, a Columbia professor of comparative law, who also was a member of the Netherlands bar, to write a section on how blacks would have been treated for similar conduct in other countries. In France, Italy, Belgium, the Netherlands, Norway, Germany, England, and the Commonwealth countries, they would not have been guilty of a crime. But neither opponents nor the justices responded to these fresh perspectives, except that Justice Black, from the bench, when the opinions were read, scoffed at the notion that the law of other countries mattered. The solicitor general argued only that the laws were unconstitutionally vague. On the big state action issue he was mum—he still didn't agree with us.

In *Bell*, I felt that I was arguing against the odds on the basic state action issue. At the outset I faced up to the uncomfortable fact that the plaintiffs had run past the hostess, seated themselves, and then "hedge-hopped," which they explained as fanning out to other tables. That didn't matter, I argued, "The choice of the proprietor was not an authentically private decision . . . but was influenced by the custom of the community" and "this choice of the community . . . was to some significant extent . . . influenced by the historic pattern of Maryland laws."

I had to face up to the fact that Maryland had, after the plaintiffs' demonstration, passed a civil rights law and now wasn't trying to enforce segregation; it merely was upholding the rule of law. I offered an analogy: "If one has poisoned a well and then later repented and sought to cleanse it—nevertheless some of the residue of the poison remains."

The Court had an extremely hard time deciding this round of cases and on November 18, by a five-to-four vote (Black, Clark, Harlan, and White dissented), invited the solicitor general to file a brief "expressing the views of the United States" on "the broader constitutional issues." There were four dissents on this innocuous matter of whether to extend the invitation, suggesting sharp disagreement among the justices. But now Cox no longer could avoid facing the issue.

Four days later, on November 22, John F. Kennedy was assassinated. As we waited for the decisions, Joe Rauh and I thought that we should try to convince the new Johnson administration to support our state action position. On Monday, December 9, we met with Lee White, Lyndon Johnson's assistant for civil rights, a position he had held with Kennedy as well, and laid out our legal position and the political implications. We argued that Cox was obliged to advocate the position of the United States, not his personal philosophy. After all, our analysis was endorsed by scholars as illustrious as he. Politically, if the demonstrators were to lose, the reaction among civil rights advocates would range from discouragement to outrage. The civil rights bill was pending in Congress; its prospects could be damaged severely. Our arguments, however, ran into the tradition that the solicitor general is allowed great latitude in deciding which positions to take. White said he would take the matter up with the president who no doubt would do whatever "Abe" advised—a reference to Abe Fortas. A week later White sent a memorandum to the president:

> Joe [Rauh], as well as the Counsel for the NAACP, are concerned that the Solicitor will not take a strong position. . . .
>
> I met with Joe and Jack Greenberg, head of the NAACP Legal Defense and Education Fund. There is some question of delicacy about pushing Archie Cox too hard on this point without his exploding and resigning. Yesterday Burke Marshall informed me that there was a very extensive conversation including the Attorney General, Nick Katzenbach, Marshall and Cox. He was satisfied that Cox would come out with a very satisfactory position for the government on the Constitutional questions and indicated that in his judgment no further representations were required. . . . Should the question arise, you might wish to indicate in a general way that we have assurances that the government will do a good job. Should you desire to go further in the sense of calling Cox or sending him a note, there is nothing to bar such action but it does raise the question of whether there would be any adverse results—and possibly without any corresponding benefits.

During the period preceding filing Cox's brief, Burke Marshall and Bobby Kennedy met with him regularly, usually when Cox, on his way to work in the morning, stopped by Burke's office. They, too, were urging that he change his position. Whatever the process of conversion, in January Cox did file a brief that generally followed our approach.

Maryland had been moving forward on civil rights. Following Bell's conviction, Baltimore prohibited discrimination in public accommodations, and in March 1963, Maryland adopted a similar law. Relying on this development in deciding *Bell*, Justice Brennan finessed the state action issue and sent the case back to the Maryland courts to determine whether under a doctrine known as "abatement" the new Maryland laws invalidated the earlier convictions. Until that time I had never heard of abatement and neither had any of our cocounsel. Under abatement doctrine the repeal of a criminal law while a case is pending terminates the prosecution. The Maryland trespass law hadn't exactly been repealed, but since Maryland no longer permitted discrimination, its court might decide that the application of trespass laws to such situations had been repealed. But while Brennan commanded a majority, most of the Court was unhappy with his opinion.

Douglas and Goldberg wrote that conviction to enforce a private property owner's discrimination is state action. Goldberg, Douglas, and the chief justice joined an opinion saying that the Fourteenth Amendment obligated a state to guarantee to all citizens access to public accommodations. Black, Harlan, and White dissented. The majority opinion, however, was written two weeks before enactment of the federal Civil Rights Act, undoubtedly with knowledge that it was coming. If the basis of Brennan's *Bell* opinion—that a civil rights law might abate convictions of demonstrators that occurred before the law was passed—were extended to that act, the Court might never have to decide the state action issue, which is what Brennan must have had in mind.

Following its pattern of reversing sit-in convictions on one ground or another, the Court also reversed six others from Virginia, North Carolina, South Carolina, and Maryland for reconsideration. We had a sweep. But the state courts would not play along. Maryland reaffirmed *Bell*.

However, where the legal issues were not so complex, the Court displayed a mood less and less tolerant of Southern shenanigans. In February 1964, I argued *Shuttlesworth v. City of Birmingham*, another in a series of cases in which Fred Shuttlesworth was prosecuted for civil rights activity in Birmingham; the Court decided the case less than two weeks later. Shuttlesworth was charged with resisting arrest while at the Birmingham bus terminal with Freedom Riders. There was no evidence of resisting arrest, so the Alabama Court of Appeals affirmed on the grounds that Shuttlesworth had committed a *different* crime, writing that he had assaulted the chief of police by blocking his path and had used words in "rudeness or in anger."

The Alabama Supreme Court refused to hear our appeal because our local lawyer hadn't filed it on transcript paper—large sheets, about 10 1/2 by 16 inches as required by the Alabama rules, having used ordinary legal size, 8 1/2 by 14 inches. If a state court dismisses on a state procedural ground the United States Supreme Court ordinarily won't hear the case. But if the state court doesn't apply its rule uniformly, the United States Supreme Court won't necessarily stay out of the matter. The legal research wasn't easy, because the indexes in the digests where the research had to be done don't refer to the size of paper. So, Jim Nabrit and Marian Wright paged through the Alabama Supreme Court reports at the City Bar Association one by one, while I went through cases in the office library, looking for a case where the Alabama Supreme Court decided the merits although the appeal was filed on the wrong-size paper. (Nowadays, with computers, research of this kind is much easier.)

We found four useful cases. The United States Supreme Court reversed, merely addressing two issues in the most summary fashion, indicating that Alabama had unconstitutionally upheld the conviction under one statute although the defendant had been charged under another, and holding that if a state court has discretion to decide a constitutional claim, even though it decides not to, that doesn't preclude the United States Supreme Court from exercising similar discretion.

SIT-INS, FINAL ROUND

On July 2, 1964, President Johnson signed the Civil Rights Act. Clarence Mitchell, the NAACP Washington lobbyist, was among the leading proponents who ushered through Congress the first major civil rights legislation since Reconstruction. As a political compromise, its public accommodations provision covered only places where food was sold (a department store, for example, with a lunch counter would be covered), theaters, and similar places. It did not cover bars, and litigation was needed to decide that it included such places as roller-skating rinks. In time, however, cases interpreting the law opened up all public facilities. Congress, empowered only to enact legislation authorized by the Constitution, finessed the state action issue and covered only places of public accommodation that affected interstate commerce and "discrimination or segregation carried on under color of any custom or usage required or enforced by officials of the State." This formula bypassed the Civil Rights Cases of 1883, which prohibited Congress from regulating private discrimination under the Fourteenth Amendment.

LDF brought the first case under the new law against the Pickrick Restaurant in Atlanta, where Lester Maddox, the owner, barred blacks by threatening them with a pick handle—hence the name "Pickrick." (He gave away or sold pick handles to glorify his position.) We won in the trial court on the ground that Maddox had violated the new law. The case never was decided by the Supreme Court.

Around the same time, Ollie's Barbecue in Birmingham sued the United States to enjoin enforcing the law. Continuing its standoffish position on state action, the government made "no contention that the discrimination at the restaurant was supported by the State." The Court decided the case on Commerce Clause grounds alone. Douglas and Goldberg, however, concurred on the basis of the Fourteenth Amendment. Maddox parlayed his flamboyant resistance into becoming governor of Georgia, an example of how much political advantage there was to be mined by resisting the law.

By March 1966 we had forty-four cases enforcing the public accommodations law, involving restaurants, coffee shops, truck stops, YMCAs, golf clubs, amusement parks, hotels, bowling alleys, ice cream counters, and bars. The cases were in Arkansas, Florida, Georgia, Louisiana, North Carolina, and Virginia. Some involved outright defiance, but others involved evasions, like pretending to be a private club although any white could join (at a Dallas hotel I received "club" membership for its bar upon checking in), or questions of whether the law applied, as in the cases of bars (which we won because they served food). One owner charged blacks five dollars for scrambled eggs, while charging whites much less.

Public accommodations desegregated quickly. Besides the threat of a burdensome lawsuit they were almost sure to lose, owners had an economic motivation to let go of the old ways—after all, blacks paid, and in the same currency whites used. Around the time the Civil Rights Act was adopted we had cases pending to desegregate South Carolina's state parks, which fell under doctrines established before the act passed and which we won.

The Civil Rights Act, however, left unsettled the fate of the demonstrators who had been prosecuted, some in jail, others on appeal, still others awaiting trial. *Bell v. Maryland* was our guide to argue, as Justice Brennan suggested, that the act abated all convictions that could not have been obtained once the act passed. Charlie Black wrote a brief for the last sit-in case, *Hamm v. City of Rock Hill*, which shone with his command of the language:

> If these petitioners are now to be punished notwithstanding [the public accommodations law] . . . it will be for having insisted upon something which the national conscience has now most decidedly declared they are entitled to insist upon, against a refusal which the national conscience has now declared affirmatively unlawful. Their punishment can serve no purpose . . . the only licit deterrence interest now runs the other way. Their punishment would afford the immoral spectacle of pointless revenge.

I argued *Hamm* on October 12, 1964, starting out by dangling the carrot of getting rid of three thousand sit-in cases then in the lower courts. If the new law abated them, that was the end of it. If not, the courts would continue to confront thousands of sit-in cases. We won, but only by a five-to-four vote. Justice Clark wrote the opinion, Harlan, Black, White, and Stewart dissented. When Charlie drafted the brief originally, half a dozen lawyers criticized it so severely that he changed the format to take the reader through a step-by-step analysis of "abatement" and related concepts necessary for the argument. Yet, when the Court wrote its opinion it analyzed the issues in a way that closely tracked Charlie's original draft. In the conference the chief justice spoke of "3,000 cases backed up." The carrot had not gone unnoticed. Justice Black, who dissented, replied that while he would prefer not to face those cases he could not agree with our argument.

In a poetic closing of the circle, the demonstrators, who had been convicted for seeking equality, brought into being a law that assured that equality and freed them of the convictions imposed on them in their quest.

24

JIM CROW CRUSHED IN MISSISSIPPI

JAMES MEREDITH WANTS TO ENTER OLE MISS

In 1958 Clennon King, a black professor at black Alcorn State University, applied to Ole Miss; the state locked him up in a mental hospital. Clyde Kennard applied to white Mississippi Southern College in 1959 and was prosecuted for a variety of criminal charges, culminating in a seven-year prison sentence for burglary for stealing chicken feed. R. Jess Brown twice took Kennard's case to the Supreme Court of Mississippi, which ruled against him, and then Thurgood and Connie petitioned the United States Supreme Court, which refused to hear the case. We went to the United States District Court in December 1962, where we lost. As we prepared an appeal, the governor, in January 1963, released Kennard, citing his ill health.

Around the time the sit-ins and Freedom Rides began, James Meredith, a black air force veteran from Kosciusko, Mississippi, was thinking of attending the University of Mississippi. Meredith wrote to the university in January 1961 for an application to transfer from Jackson State (a black school) and received a form asking for character references from five alumni and a picture. He completed the application, but because as a black man he did not know any Ole Miss alumni who would support his application (the idea behind the requirement), he included recommendations of five blacks and attached his picture. Ole Miss countered by saying it was overcrowded and wouldn't act on applications received after January 25—although the following semester it admitted more than three hundred more students than before, evidence that there was plenty of room. It then adopted a rule restricting transfer admissions to students from schools whose programs it approved.

Around this time Meredith wrote to us for legal assistance: "I am making this move in, what I consider, the interest of and for the benefit of: (1) my country, (2) my race, (3) my family, and (4) myself. I am familiar with the probable difficulties involved in such a move as I am undertaking, and I am fully prepared to pursue it all the way to a degree from the University of Mississippi."

Thurgood called Meredith and concluded that he was serious. But starting a case to integrate Ole Miss had to be viewed with trepidation. Nevertheless, there seemed to be no alternative. If we didn't take the case someone else might, and violence might occur anyway. Moreover, the case might, if taken by a lawyer or lawyers lacking the Fund's expertise, be botched legally, making future applications to Ole Miss even more difficult. Thurgood assigned the case to Connie, who just had won Charlayne Hunter and Hamilton Holmes's case against the University of Georgia. But, as racist as Georgia was, it was mild compared to Mississippi when it came to a capacity for violent response.

Mississippi rejected Meredith, citing a new rule: Students might transfer only from accredited institutions, and Jackson State wasn't accredited. With R. Jess Brown, Connie filed our complaint in United States District Court on May 31, asking for a preliminary injunction so Meredith could attend the June 8 summer session. From that point onward, Meredith's case was in the news, often on front pages and on national television.

R. Jess Brown was one of the three black Mississippi lawyers on whom we relied. Slight in stature, hawk faced, with sunken cheeks, he quietly and unassumingly made it possible for Connie to accomplish what had to be done. But while Connie was all business, and admired Brown's courage, she could not restrain herself from occasionally chiding him for wearing red socks, which he often did. He showed some little irritation with the criticism, but got on with the job.

Judge Sidney C. Mize set the hearing for June 12, after school was scheduled to open, and Connie made her first of more than twenty trips to Mississippi for Meredith. In mid-hearing, in the first of a series of delays and obfuscations, Mize suspended the proceedings and reset them for July 10, after the end of the first summer session. On July 10 he announced he couldn't hear the case that day after all and reset it for August 10, past the start of the second summer session. He held hearings August 10, 15, and 16. Fall registration ended September 28, but Mize didn't rule until December 12, when he denied a preliminary injunction. He found that Meredith had not been rejected because he was black.

By this time, Thurgood had left LDF to take his seat on the court of appeals, and I was in charge.

Connie sped to the court of appeals, which, a month later, ruled against Meredith in form, although it was a victory in substance for us. Judge John Minor Wisdom's opinion rejected Mississippi's incredible claim that it did not segregate, ridiculed Ole Miss's argument that we had to establish the genealogy of its students and alumni to prove that they all were white, and concluded, "We take judicial notice that the state of Mississippi maintains a policy of segregation in its schools and colleges." But the court realized it had a highly controversial case on its hands and cut the squarest of square corners. It ordered a fresh district court hearing at which Mize was required to allow Meredith to introduce evidence that previously had been excluded. Wisdom wrote, "A man should be able to find an education by taking the broad highway. He should not have to take by-roads through the woods and follow winding trails through sharp thickets, in constant tension because of pitfalls and traps, and, after years of effort, perhaps obtain the threshold of his goal when he is past caring about it." Wisdom ordered Mize to decide promptly, in view of the fact that a new school term was scheduled to begin on February 6, 1962.

Mize obeyed the instruction of the court of appeals but remained a petti-fogger. He promptly held another hearing and on February 3 concluded, "The evidence overwhelmingly showed that the Plaintiff was not denied admission because of his race. . . . The proof shows and I find as a fact, that the University is not a racially segregated institution." Connie went once more to the court of appeals in New Orleans for an injunction to order Meredith into Ole Miss immediately, while the appeal was going on. Once more, the court of appeals gave Mississippi more than its full measure of due process, this time by a vote of two to one. On February 12, Judges Rives and Wisdom wrote that the appeal should follow its regular course, but should be speeded up, so that if Meredith were to win he could be admitted before the beginning of the next term. The third member of the bench, Judge Tuttle, dissented, saying that enough was enough.

While the appeal was pending, on June 6 Mississippi arrested Meredith, because he had registered to vote in Jackson, where he attended Jackson State, although his residence was in Kosciusko. We then got an injunction from the court of appeals restraining the prosecutor and the state's attorney general from prosecuting.

On June 25 the court of appeals reversed Judge Mize's rehearing decision and, in a scathing opinion, demolished all of Ole Miss's and Mize's lies: Wisdom called the defense "a carefully calculated campaign of delay, harassment, and masterly inactivity. It was a defense designed to discourage and to defeat by evasive tactics which would have been a credit to Quintus Fabius Maximus." Maximus was a Roman army commander known as a master of attrition and described as famed for "conducting harassing operations while avoiding decisive conflicts." Wisdom concluded that "what everybody knows the court must know." Meredith had seen a psychiatrist while in the air force (one of Ole Miss's arguments for rejecting him), from which Wisdom concluded that his "record shows just about the type of Negro who might be expected to try to crack the racial barrier at the University of Mississippi: a man with a mission and with a nervous stomach."

Three weeks later, on July 17, in the normal course of events, the court's order went down to Judge Mize. The next day a new player entered the scene, prepared to break up the game rather than see his side lose. What followed was an unseemly challenge to the authority of the United States Court of Appeals by one of its own members. Judge Ben F. Cameron, a member of the court of appeals and a Mississippian, ordered a stay of the order his own bench had issued. It was nearly unheard of for a judge who was not one of those who decided a case to stay its mandate. The court of appeals could not have been pleased and on July 27 vacated Cameron's order and, pending Mize's action, entered its own order against Ole Miss, requiring it to admit Meredith.

The next day Cameron once more stayed the court's mandate. The same day the court vacated his order, and on July 31, Cameron entered yet another stay. On August 4 the court overruled Cameron once more. On August 6, Cameron reinstated his order. Apparently afraid they might be caught between conflicting court orders, or, more likely, to make matters more difficult for Meredith, Ole Miss's board of trustees adopted a rule that denied to university officials power "relating to action on the application of James Howard Meredith . . . and the same is reserved exclusively unto this Board of Trustees of Institutions of Higher Learning."

Ole Miss also petitioned the Supreme Court to hear the Meredith case. We waived the right to reply and, to put an end to Cameron's rebellion, asked Justice Black, who handled motions for the Fifth Circuit, to vacate Cameron's latest order. The Supreme Court's clerk asked the Justice Department for its views on Justice Black's power to vacate Cameron's orders. The department's brief argued that Black indeed had the power, that Cameron had acted improperly and that Ole Miss should be required to admit Meredith. On September 10, Justice Black announced that he had consulted all other members of the Court and that "there is very little likelihood that this Court will grant certiorari to review the judgment of the Court of Appeals which essentially involves only factual issues." He enjoined Ole Miss from "taking any steps to prevent enforcement of the Court of Appeals judgment and mandate."

Connie went back to Mize for an injunction to get Meredith into Ole Miss. Now sitting alongside Mize was Harold Cox, a new Kennedy appointee, and possibly the most racist judge ever to sit on the federal bench. Mize, at an age that permitted him to enjoy senior status (meaning he had the option of sitting only on those cases he might choose), would soon give up the Meredith case to Cox, and was acquainting him with the case. Cox began indicating that he would deny Connie's motion. But Mize at last knew that this battle had been lost. He placed his hand on Cox's arm and said, "It's all over, Judge Cox." On September 13, Mize ordered Ole Miss to admit Meredith.

The press, radio, television, and religious leaders began stirring racial emotions more than might have been anticipated even in Mississippi. Governor Ross Barnett, on September 13, went on statewide television and invoked the long-discredited and anarchy-inviting right of "interposition" under the Tenth Amendment, claiming it gave Mississippi the right to defy federal court orders. He issued a proclamation, full of "whereases" and "therefores" and "in witness whereofs," to which he "caused the great Seal of the State of Mississippi to be affixed, on this the 13th day of September in the Year of Our Lord, One Thousand Nine Hundred and Sixty-Two." Musical comedy material, but many of Mississippi's racists took it seriously.

The Justice Department began making preparations for trouble. Alerting federal marshals, corrections officers, and border patrolmen who might function as marshals to stand by, it moved to enter the case as a friend of the court. On September 18 Mize refused to allow the Justice Department to enter the case; Justice then went to the court of appeals, which granted the motion. On the 19th a state court enjoined Meredith, Ole Miss, and federal officials from "performing any act intending to enroll and register the Negro, James Meredith."

On the 20th, violating the June 12 federal court order, which prohibited prosecuting Meredith for false registration, Mississippi charged and convicted him of that offense. It also passed a law, Senate Bill (S.B.) 1501, prohibiting any person who has a "criminal charge of moral turpitude pending against him or her" from entering any state institution. The law excepted "any charge or conviction of traffic law violations, violation of the state conservation laws and state game and fish laws, or manslaughter as a result of driving while intoxicated." These exceptions covered thousands of Mississippians.

Back to the court of appeals: It gave us an order enjoining enforcement of S.B. 1501 and prohibiting "any steps to effectuate the conviction and sentence . . . of James Meredith for false registration." One can only imagine the effect this refusal of judges to obey superior courts had on the respect for law among young Mississippians.

Seeking to avoid responsibility, the university's board of trustees, on September 20, "invest[ed] Honorable Ross R. Barnett . . . with the full power . . . to act upon all matters pertaining to or concerned with the registration or non-registration, admission or non-admission and/or attendance or non-attendance of James H. Meredith." The orotund style suggested that they thought the words had a magical quality to absolve them of their responsibilities.

In the meantime, from the Justice Department, Bobby Kennedy, Burke Marshall, and John Doar called the governor, attorney general, and lawyer friends in the state in an effort to work out a way to get Meredith into Ole Miss peacefully. Before it was all over, the president would call the governor. But from the outset, Connie and I thought that the only way to get Meredith into Ole Miss was with so overwhelming a show of force that violence would be seen as futile. Mississippi had shown that it would go to unprecedented lengths to keep Meredith out, and the state's propensity for racially motivated violence was well established.

I told Justice Department lawyers—particularly John Doar and Burke Marshall—what we thought, but the administration was driven by political motives both lofty and base. On the one hand, a democracy should govern by persuasion and law, and in the first instance should try to act through moral persuasion, not brute strength. At the same time, President Kennedy, while holding pro–civil rights beliefs, and implementing them to some extent, had an important racist Southern constituency that he preferred not to alienate. He tried to satisfy all considerations at once; in the end he satisfied none.

On September 20 the Justice Department took Meredith from Millington Air Force Base in Memphis, on the Mississippi border, to the university campus in Oxford in a border patrol car. In the auditorium of the university's Continuation Center the registrar told Meredith that only the governor could register him. The governor then entered the room and denied Meredith's application, handing him the proclamation of September 13, the first of a series of rebuffs at the point of registration.

Meredith then returned to Memphis, and we went back into federal court. Connie and I drove to Meridian to Judge Mize's court and, with the Justice Department at our side, petitioned for an order holding the registrar and other university officials in contempt. But on the following day, September 21, Mize ruled that they were not guilty—the trustees had turned the matter over to Barnett and were powerless to act to admit Meredith.

Nothing succeeds like success, and as the governor seemed to have thumbed his nose at the federal government with impunity, segregationist passions rose. What the states of the old Confederacy had been unable to achieve a hundred years earlier, Mississippi would now attempt on its own. Daily newspapers in the state urged "bitter end defiance."

The Fifth Circuit Court of Appeals was in New Orleans, and we set up LDF headquarters at the Dillard University guest house—a nice two-story cottage, with a half-dozen bedrooms and a kitchen, an ample lawn and lovely trees—courtesy of its president, Albert Dent, father of Tom Dent, then our public information director. Meredith, Connie, other staff lawyers who came and went, secretaries, and I readied ourselves to take the case to the court of appeals. NAACP Mississippi field secretary Medgar Evers stayed with us too, since there was a good chance he would become involved in the aftermath of the case.

After a while the place began to resemble a fraternity house. We kept Meredith's presence secret to avoid the press and possible violence against him, but were deluged with so many phone calls that at times we pressed him into service as telephone operator. No one, however, recognized his voice. One night Meredith ventured out to a dance on the Dillard campus.

He later wrote that when the students learned who he was, "they literally swamped me for at least forty-five minutes to an hour. . . . I could not guess how many women must have offered themselves to me or asked me to go home with them."

Many of our meals consisted of takeout food from Levata's, a ramshackle seafood joint near the Dillard campus. Big bags containing boiled crabs, oyster rolls (fried oysters on a roll), lemon meringue pie, and Coca-Cola were brought in daily. This diet gave me a bad case of acne by the time the case ended. Sometimes we ate at Dooky Chase, the best black restaurant in town, nowadays a well-publicized tourist stop. We did our legal work out of A. P. Tureaud's office.

Flush with his success thus far, Barnett raised the stakes. On September 24 he issued another proclamation directing the summary arrest and jailing of any representative of the federal government who arrested or attempted to arrest, or who fined or attempted to fine, any state official in the performance of his official duties.

The same day, Connie and I and the Justice Department lawyers were back at the court of appeals. The issue was no longer just the question of one man's right to go to school at his state university. The authority of the federal judiciary had been called into question, and if its authority weren't established, the ability of one of the three branches of the United States government to fulfill the role given it by our Constitution would be seriously undermined. The court took the extraordinary step of gathering eight judges, not the ordinary panel of three—all the eligible judges, plus the highly respected, retired Joseph C. Hutcheson of Texas, a conservative law-and-order type, who had the right to sit but was not required to. Cameron alone didn't show up. Hutcheson was so old that he ascended the bench with great difficulty, but he was outraged and wanted to be there.

In a hearing that went from 11:30 A.M. to 6:32 P.M. the court heard testimony and received evidence, almost unheard of in appellate courts. Its attitude was exemplified by Hutcheson, when in referring to the trustees' order giving the governor control of Ole Miss, he asked the attorney general of Mississippi, "Did you advise them that this monkey business of coming around pretending to take over the school was legal?" Finally, during the hearing, the president of the Board of Trustees of Institutions of Higher Learning announced that the board was ready and willing to obey the court's orders. The registrar caved in too and agreed to be in Jackson not later than 1:00 P.M. on September 25 to register and admit Meredith. The court ordered the board to revoke its action of September 4, which relieved university officials of authority to register Meredith; to revoke appointment of Ross Barnett as the board's agent in matters pertaining to Meredith; and to instruct the registrar to register Meredith between 1:00 P.M. and 4:00 P.M. on September 25.

During all of this Meredith was curiously emotionless, at least in outward appearance. In court and back on campus, he spoke little and always in a soft voice. Sometimes he tapped a foot lightly a few times and prefaced what he had to say with a soft "mmmmmm." Often, while speaking, he smiled and shook his head a little. But, while he was not outwardly demonstrative, he certainly had great determination.

That should have been the end of it. Conservative judges, all of whom had long sat in the South, had expressed their anger at the disobedience of law and court orders. But reactions based on ignorance, goaded by demagogues, and emboldened by interim successes became difficult to control.

Robert Kennedy and Ross Barnett conferred by phone, but got nowhere. Kennedy told Barnett that the federal courts had ruled, and Barnett replied that the Mississippi courts had ruled to the contrary. Barnett would not agree to permit Meredith to register nor would he guarantee Meredith's safety.

At 8:30 A.M. on the morning of September 25 the court of appeals entered a temporary restraining order prohibiting Barnett, State Attorney General Patterson, and a raft of other officials from interfering with Meredith's registration by arresting, suing, injuring, harassing, or threatening him by force or otherwise. Barnett retaliated with another proclamation, which "denied to you, James H. Meredith, admission to the University of Mississippi."

During some of this time Meredith stayed in Memphis and at other times he stayed with us in New Orleans. He traveled by government plane to Mississippi to attempt to register. We drove from the Dillard guest house to the airport, where two identical aircraft, one carrying Meredith, the other a decoy, took off for the trip, a tactic designed to confuse any Mississippian who might try to end the matter by shooting down Meredith's plane—security people did not dismiss such an outrage as beyond infuriated Mississippians. I thought that if they'd shoot down one plane they'd shoot down two. As it turned out, the greatest peril to materialize appeared when the car taking us to the airport, traveling fast, hit a campus speed bump designed to slow traffic, and we bounced up, banging our heads sharply against the roof of the car.

At the state office building, Meredith, accompanied by John Doar and other Justice Department representatives, once more tried to register. Barnett, reading his latest proclamation, once more denied admission. Meredith turned back, passing through a jeering, threatening crowd, to try again another day.

The court of appeals slapped back an order that evening requiring the governor to appear in court in New Orleans at 10:00 A.M., September 28, "to show cause, if any he has, why he should not be held in civil contempt of the temporary restraining order entered by the Court this day." Justice officials, including Attorney General Kennedy and Burke Marshall, continued their telephone negotiations with the governor, state attorney general, lawyers for the university, and trustees, trying to work out a formula to get

Meredith into the university. But Mississippi continued to stonewall.

Although I knew nothing of the details of the negotiations, my own sense of the depth of the racism we were facing was different from that of administration officials. I objected that there was no way the Justice Department would ever persuade Mississippi other than by a show of more than sufficient force, such as Eisenhower had used in Little Rock.

Nevertheless, Justice officers took Meredith from Dillard to Oxford once more on Wednesday, September 26, to try again. This time Lieutenant Governor Paul Johnson turned him away. The *New York Times* reported that the Little Rock confrontation "seemed tonight to be just a shadow of the crisis developing in Mississippi. . . . Officials are in open defiance of Federal Law. Governor Barnett and his aides, evidently supported by state policemen, sheriffs and other law-enforcement officers numbering in the hundreds, are evidently prepared to offer physical resistance to Federal officers."

When mobs become intoxicated on their own rage, there is always someone willing to exploit it, even to raise it to insane levels. A state senator called for resistance "regardless of the cost in human life."

In the meantime Bobby Kennedy and Mississippi representatives were trying to work out a registration charade. They continued to keep Connie and me entirely in the dark, telling us nothing. Later, it was revealed that Mississippi had proposed that federal marshals should draw their guns, at which point Mississippi officials would step aside and, with a show of yielding to federal threats, would permit Meredith to enter the university. Kennedy countered that he preferred that only one marshal draw a gun, but that wasn't enough for Mississippi. Kennedy upped his offer: One marshal would draw a gun; the others would put their hands on their holsters. That still wasn't enough for Barnett, and so Kennedy gave in and agreed that all the marshals would draw their guns.

Kennedy and Mississippi officials having come to an agreement, Meredith's registration was once again attempted. But when a federal convoy carrying Meredith got within fifty miles of Oxford on Thursday the 27th, the mobs had grown so large and threatening that the convoy turned around and headed back. I issued a statement announcing that enough was enough:

> We have advised Mr. Meredith that we do not believe he should return to the University of Mississippi campus unless he is accompanied by sufficient force to assure his enrollment and continued attendance. He agrees with us. We have so informed the Department of Justice.
>
> A trip to the campus, which tentatively had been planned for today, with a force of marshals which may have been insufficient was not made after we asserted this position. Beyond question the United States possesses sufficient power to enforce the orders of its courts and assure the rights of its citizens, and we have no doubt that it will employ that power.

We filed motions, along with the Justice Department, in the court of appeals asking that Barnett be held in civil contempt. At each stage we made sure to file our own motions and be in court ourselves, refusing to allow Justice to conduct alone the case that they had treated with a mix of dither, politics, and principle.

On Friday, September 28, the scene shifted back to the court of appeals in New Orleans. Connie and I represented Meredith; Burke Marshall, John Doar, and St. John Barrett represented the Justice Department; and a team of defense lawyers represented the university, its trustees, and the state of Mississippi. But no one showed up for Governor Barnett. Mississippi's lawyer was John C. Satterfield of Yazoo City, the crown jewel of the Mississippi bar and the 1961–62 president of the American Bar Association, a position, as Satterfield soon showed, that reveals more about bar association politics than about professional skill or responsibility. Satterfield announced that he appeared for the state as a friend of the court and that no one in the courtroom represented Ross Barnett. Barnett was ducking service; Satterfield was claiming he was a friend of the court, not Barnett's counsel, in order to take the position that the court couldn't find Barnett in contempt because he hadn't been served and was not represented.

Looking like a praying mantis, Satterfield tiptoed around the courtroom as he addressed the court in elaborate, deferential tones and filed a motion to dismiss the complaint against Barnett. But the judges immediately caught on. Judge Tuttle replied: "All the Court has given the State of Mississippi the right to do, Mr. Satterfield, is to present the views of the State of Mississippi. The Court has thus far not authorized the State of Mississippi to file any pleadings on behalf of the Defendant . . . Barnett."

Tuttle conferred with the court and announced that Satterfield would not be allowed to proceed until the court determined whether Barnett had been served.

Satterfield asked whether he might make objections to evidence. Tuttle, visibly irritated, answered, "You can assume Counsel for Amicus Curiae has no right to object to any of the evidence." Satterfield replied, "To which we except," using a term that was formerly used to identify a ruling that could be appealed, but that was no longer employed in federal court. Tuttle riposted, "You also have no right to except, I might add." Satterfield, in drippingly deferential tones, responded, "Certainly. That is correct, sir. I am sorry." Tuttle, not letting go, added, "And you needn't do it anyway," pointing out Satterfield's ignorance of the Federal Rules, which had abolished the practice of oral exceptions as repetitive and time consuming.

The government then proved that Barnett had been served, in person, by mail, and by Western Union nightletter, with the court order requiring him to admit Meredith. A deputy marshal testified that he went twice to Barnett's office to serve the contempt citation and found it closed, with a piece of paper reading "office closed" affixed to the door. Attempting to serve the

citation for a third time that day, the marshal found a group of state police
at the door. They refused to state their names, refused to accept service, and
warned against leaving the papers on the floor. The marshal left. On a further attempt, the attorney general of Mississippi refused to receive service
for the governor. In another effort the marshal was turned away from the
governor's home.

Satterfield once more arose to say, "May I respectfully suggest to the
Court, it might be of benefit to the Court to have the credentials he exhibited introduced." Tuttle shut him up: "Mr. Satterfield, I do not think you
are in a position to make any suggestions." Satterfield, ever obsequious:
"Thank you, sir." Judge Rives, exasperated, went after Satterfield, and asked
whether he represented the governor. Satterfield said he did not.

Rives then asked, "What communication have you had with the Governor of Mississippi?"

Satterfield evaded, "Within what period of time?"

Rives said, "Since last Tuesday night."

Satterfield once more evaded, "I think it would take several hours to go
into that fully."

Rives, now becoming furious, continued the attack:

RIVES: Have you seen the Governor in person?

SATTERFIELD: Yes, of course.

RIVES: . . . Did you discuss this Order with the Governor?

SATTERFIELD: Do you care to have me sworn as a witness, may it please the
    Court?

RIVES: No, I am asking you as attorney.

SATTERFIELD: I thought I was not privileged to participate in the proceeding
    until later. I am sorry.

RIVES: You are an attorney and officer of the Court.

SATTERFIELD: Correct.

RIVES: And I ask you as an attorney and officer of the Court.

SATTERFIELD: May I respectfully object to being questioned by the Court
    unless I have the status of participating attorney, which I do not have.

RIVES: Yes, you may object, but I still want an answer.

Rives and Judge Brown then wrung from Satterfield that two days earlier
he had discussed with the governor the order to show cause and the time for
which it was scheduled to be heard, which Barnett had learned by reading
the newspapers, and that Barnett had obtained copies of the recently prepared court papers in the case. At that point Barnett was nailed and Satterfield's petty evasiveness exposed for what it was.

Nevertheless, further into the day Satterfield presented a motion to dismiss the contempt proceedings against Barnett. Tuttle at that point called a
brief recess to confer with the court. Satterfield asked for "the privilege of

presenting authorities" to the judges. Tuttle, expressing the annoyance of all the judges at Satterfield's temerity in continuing to speak up after he had been silenced, responded: "You don't know what I am talking about to the Court." When the Court finished conferring it lowered the boom on Satterfield. Tuttle announced, "The Court has unanimously voted to revoke its order permitting the State of Mississippi to appear as Amicus Curiae or in any other matter in the case. The Court will hear no further arguments on that. That is a final decision. I want to make it perfectly clear that the Court now revokes its order previously entered orally, permitting the State of Mississippi to appear in the case."

Satterfield tried to come back with another motion "with complete deference and respect." But Tuttle responded curtly, "The motion is denied."

Another Mississippi lawyer tried to pick up where Satterfield left off. Garner W. Green of Jackson challenged the court's jurisdiction and said that "the State of Mississippi is vitally affected by it and bloodshed may result from the continuation."

Tuttle jumped in with, "We have heard about the possibility of bloodshed for the last ten years."

Hutcheson intervened: "You are not threatening the Court with bloodshed, are you?"

Green retreated: "Oh, no, oh, no. I didn't say that at all, Your Honor." And he went on about how he wanted to have the issue resolved by legal proceedings.

Tuttle cut it all off: "Now we will not get into any further Socratic discussion of the case." Satterfield once more tried to participate, but once more was barred. Tuttle announced, "The Court has determined that there was adequate service of the citation."

Later that day the court entered its order holding Barnett in civil contempt, committing him to "the custody of the Attorney General of the United States and . . . [to] pay a fine to the United States of $10,000 per day unless on or before Tuesday, October 2nd, 1962 at 11 A.M.," he ceases resisting the orders of the courts. The order also required the governor to maintain law and order at Ole Miss "to the end that James H. Meredith be permitted to register and remain as a student."

On Saturday, September 29, the president tried his hand at persuading Barnett by phone. John Kennedy asked for obedience to the law. Barnett wanted delay. At one point the president made a deal with Barnett by which Meredith would register in Jackson, while Barnett and John Doar would pretend to be in Oxford for the purpose of registering him, thereby diverting mobs from the scene. But then Barnett changed his mind.[42]

In the meantime, the government's inaction left time for passions to rise even more. At the Saturday night Ole Miss football game, fans displayed what must have been the largest Confederate flag in the world. Governor Barnett spoke to the cheering crowd, affirming his allegiance to the cus-

toms of Mississippi. Retired Major General Edwin A. Walker, who had commanded federal troops in Little Rock, and later became a John Bircher,
called for volunteers to come to Mississippi to resist federal encroachment.

Finally, on September 30, at long last, President Kennedy issued a proclamation that directed all persons to cease and desist obstruction of justice
against court orders that required Meredith's admission. Later that day,
Kennedy issued an Executive Order that directed the secretary of defense to
take all appropriate steps to enforce orders of the courts in the Meredith
case. Yet, faced with a threat of violence that was by now much greater
than that faced at Little Rock, the administration amassed a potential military presence. A few hundred army troops and about five hundred marshals
gathered at the Millington Naval Air Station on the Mississippi border—
only a small fraction of the force mobilized by President Eisenhower—one
thousand airborne troops sent right to the scene and 9,936 National Guardsmen federalized and activated.

Late that afternoon, Meredith, with John Doar and the United States
marshal in charge, James J. McShane, flew from Millington to Oxford. They
drove from the airport to Baxter Hall, a campus dormitory. The Mississippi
Highway Patrol, federal marshals, and troops were already on campus.
Meredith went to a room that had been selected for him, a second-floor
counselor's apartment, and began reading a school assignment. To Meredith
it appeared that the campus was deserted—most of the students apparently
had gone to Jackson for the football game. In fact, they were beginning to
return and, by 7:00 P.M., they formed a mob that was becoming large and
nasty, taunting and threatening marshals. One member of the mob sprayed
a fire extinguisher in the face of an army truck driver. Soon the rioters
began throwing stones. To make things worse, Governor Barnett, or another
state official, ordered the highway patrol to leave the campus. Only strenuous efforts by Justice, including phone calls between Bobby Kennedy and
the governor, got that decision reversed.

The mob began to turn upon the press, attacking a TV cameraman,
reporters, and photographers. They beat a faculty member who attempted
to protect a camera that rioters were trying to smash. The crowd threw
rocks, bottles, bricks, lead pipes, Coke bottles filled with flaming gasoline,
and acid. Finally, the marshals fired tear gas at the mob and, incidentally, at
the Mississippi Highway Patrol.

At the same time President Kennedy went on radio and television. He
called for adherence to law and urged Mississippians to consider that they
had "a new opportunity to show that you are men of patriotism and
integrity." Just around that time an unknown person shot and killed an
Agence France-Presse photographer. More marshals came to the campus,
but rioters continued the fray. More racists began arriving on campus from
rural Mississippi. Gunfire against marshals erupted—by 10:00 P.M. four
marshals had been hit. Later a bystander was killed and others badly

wounded. State police pulled back and allowed events to take their course.

The riot had been going on for three hours and Justice officials still had not called in troops. Finally, the White House decided to permit the National Guard to act. By this time the mob was attacking the marshals and the guard with a bulldozer, a fire engine, and automobiles. They burned cars in the parking lot. As the battle escalated, the president, around midnight, called for troops at Millington to hurry to Oxford. Finally, sometime after 2:00 A.M., they arrived on campus to restore order. By dawn the campus was under control and, before 8:00 A.M., Meredith was driven to the registrar's office in a battered border patrol car, its sides riddled with bullet holes, its windows shot out, and registered.

I had a curious feeling. Along with Meredith we had launched this effort. We had sent him to the University of Mississippi armed with a court order. The courts had acted on our initiative—only after they entered their initial orders did they deal with the Justice Department. We dragged the government reluctantly into doing what it should have done. Indeed, there was an abrasive, sometimes adversarial relationship between us. We weren't sure we trusted them. They wondered what we would do next. But at the moment Meredith entered the university, the government was there, and we were helpless to do anything further to help him.

In 1990 John Doar, agreeing that Justice should have gathered more force sooner, said that it had handled the Meredith case badly: "Would the Justice Department of the United States government ever have done it that way again? No, they wouldn't have. . . . So when we went in with Vivian Malone to the University of Alabama in 1963, we went in in quite a different way. There was lots more military power."

Meredith began attending classes, but his was hardly the conventional life of a student. Other students harassed him and armed guards lived in his suite, but, after all we'd been through, Meredith had what I thought was an oddly relaxed attitude toward his studies. After all the pain and trouble, he didn't seem to take them very seriously. At the end of his first semester he announced that he would withdraw from the university and only just before classes resumed did he decide to return. When Connie and I told him that he hadn't done as well as we thought he could have, he responded that a black man had as much right to fail as a white man. Nevertheless, we arranged tutoring for him in Memphis on weekends. I flew there for the sessions to make sure that he took advantage of them, but he had other ideas and spent his time with a coterie of friends who clustered around him in admiration or at the bowling alley—anywhere but studying. Connie got him up to Yale for Christmas vacation, where she arranged for faculty to work with him on his courses. But Meredith was driven by forces we did not understand. He suddenly left and went to Chicago and then back to Mississippi. It was like trying to get one of your kids to study when he or she didn't want to.

Some years later, Meredith wrote, in a book about the case, "The decisions that I had to make were concerned primarily with the question of my Divine Responsibility. . . . My mission was clear. I had to devote my life to the cause of directing civilization toward a destiny of humaneness." Although we tried to keep him in school, the legal significance of the case dwindled, as did our involvement.

Apparently whatever Meredith lacked in dedication he made up in a natural talent as a student, for he was graduated from Ole Miss and then applied to Columbia Law School. Bill Warren, who was the dean at the time, called me and asked whether I thought the school should admit Meredith. I replied that I didn't know enough about his academic record to make a judgment. Meredith was admitted and graduated in 1968. Some faculty members have told me that he made useful and insightful contributions to classroom discussion. In recent years he has been an assistant to Senator Jesse Helms of North Carolina, and in 1991 announced his candidacy for the office of president of the United States.

The Barnett contempt case dribbled away. In 1964 the Supreme Court held that he was not entitled to a jury trial. The Fifth Circuit in 1965 then dismissed the contempt proceedings because, as to civil contempt, the purpose of the decree had been fulfilled: Meredith had been admitted. As to criminal contempt, while all the elements of the crime had been proved except intent, it could not be found fairly by the judges of the Fifth Circuit, because they had predetermined their own positions on the issue. The court also cited *Hamm v. City of Rock Hill*, the case that abated the sit-in prosecutions, to support a let-bygones-be-bygones decision. Judges Tuttle, Wisdom, and Brown dissented. But the case was all over.

Southern segregationists were flummoxed by Connie Motley, who beat them, not only in *Meredith*, but almost every time. Once, Attorney General Joe Patterson of Mississippi, possibly feeling that I would confide in him because I was white, asked me whether she really was black. I said I was sure that she was but that I would check with her; I relayed his question to Connie. She replied sardonically, "Tell him I'm an Indian."

In 1989 I visited Ole Miss to take part in a weekend conference celebrating the integration of the university. Connie Motley, John Doar, Burke Marshall, Judges Tuttle, Wisdom, and Brown, and other participants in the Meredith drama participated. Meredith was the only major actor who wasn't there. A bunch of neo-Nazi skinheads gathered outside, displaying racist banners and screaming racial epithets. A much larger integrated group of students gathered across the road and shouted them down. A band of black and white police officers kept order.

25

FREEDOM RIDES, FREEDOM SUMMER, FIGHTING AMONG FREEDOM FIGHTERS

FREEDOM RIDES

Right after I succeeded Thurgood, I tried to work out an arrangement with the Mississippi attorney general to avoid having to try more than three hundred separate Jackson Freedom Rider cases. I suggested that we agree that all the cases would be controlled by the outcome of a selected handful. He replied that the matter was local; he could do nothing. After sitting through a day of identical Freedom Rider trials in Jackson, I retired with the local prosecutor and Jack Young, our Mississippi lawyer, to a dimly lit, wood-paneled courtroom where oil portraits of bearded Confederate notables stared down. I explained to the prosecutor that my approach would save time and money and in no way affect the results. He was affable, one lawyer to another, but wanted me to understand that he had problems, too. He had been employed especially for these prosecutions. A Caribbean vacation he and his family had recently taken was paid for by these cases. Then, with a wink and a laugh, he confided, "Look man, I just got on this tit and you're trying to knock me off it." The man knew his economics even if he wasn't so strong on ethics.

The Mississippi courts denied our motions to consolidate. With our three Mississippi cooperating lawyers, we tried and appealed 328 separate Freedom Rider cases, from police court to county court to the Mississippi Supreme Court, the United States Supreme Court, and back down to the Mississippi courts. The Freedom Rider cases were decided, in effect, in December 1965, when the United States Supreme Court decided *Abernathy v. Alabama.* In October 1964 Lou Pollak, who had become dean of the Yale Law School and knew several of the justices as Yale alumni, masterfully argued the case, in conversational tones and with humor, before the Supreme Court. He orally re-created the Montgomery bus terminal and assigned imaginary places and roles to the justices: "They entered a rear door somewhat behind where Mr. Justice White's seat would be. . . . Inside the waiting room was a lunch counter. At this point if I may use your bench as that lunch counter . . . at the extreme wall . . . [it] ran along this way. . . . And back over there, somewhat to the rear of Mr. Justice Brennan was a ticket counter."

The Court reversed without opinion, merely citing *Boynton*. Three weeks later the Court reversed the first Mississippi Freedom Rider conviction to reach it, again with no opinion, citing only *Boynton* and *Abernathy*. That was the end of the Freedom Rider prosecutions, except for getting the bond money back.

MARTIN LUTHER KING, JR., IN BIRMINGHAM

In early April 1963 SCLC began a big push in Birmingham for desegregated public facilities, fair hiring, a biracial commission, and freeing jailed demonstrators. Protestors marched, picketed, sat in, and were arrested for parading without a permit, breach of the peace, loitering, resisting arrest, trespass, and so forth. Bull Connor's police dogs and fire hoses, used to attack and intimidate demonstrators, including many schoolchildren, became familiar images on the evening news and on front pages of the country's newspapers.

We set up headquarters in the Gaston Motel, with as many as a half-dozen lawyers and secretaries. One of the few hotels for blacks in the South and one of the very few that resembled white lodgings in comfort and convenience, Gaston's was swamped with civil rights activists, lawyers, black press, politicians, and hangers-on. Within the rooms sometimes Martin Luther King, Jr., Andrew Young, Ralph Abernathy, and others would let off steam by engaging in pillow fights. Elsewhere at Gaston's there was some heavy drinking and loud partying. Sometimes, in Martin's quarters, the conversation turned solemn and staff would discuss how to try to protect him during upcoming marches; no one seeming to doubt that someday he would be killed.

Birmingham had an ordinance requiring a permit, issued by the city commission, to hold a parade. Although it was clearly unconstitutional, setting forth as it did no standards for granting or denial, I counseled SCLC staff to play it safe and apply. I went to the local Western Union office myself on April 5 and wrote out an application for a permit, which I telegraphed to the notorious Bull Connor, a member of the city commission. He replied that the entire city commission had to act on a parade permit request. Connor had responded to another member of the movement who asked for a permit, "I will picket you over to the City Jail." As usual, special procedures had been devised for us; the city clerk, not the commission, routinely issued permits to applicants who were not black protesters.

As Good Friday and Easter Sunday approached, Martin announced that he would march on those symbolically important days. Without notice, the city promptly got a local court to issue a temporary restraining order, which the sheriff served on Martin and his aides at the Gaston Motel at 1:15 A.M., on April 11. The injunction prohibited marching without a permit and incorporated verbatim the local ordinance we believed was unconstitutional—six years later the Supreme Court held we were right in that belief. Later that day Martin issued a press release announcing that "in good conscience" he could not obey the injunction, "not out of any disrespect for the law but out of the highest respect for *the* law."

LDF staff lawyer Norman Amaker, a recent graduate of Columbia Law School, who was in Birmingham, stayed in touch with our New York office to formulate a response to the injunction. He and I discussed a number of Supreme Court cases governing labor disputes where unions had disobeyed injunctions and were charged with contempt. In one of these cases, involving John L. Lewis, former president of the United Mine Workers Union, the Supreme Court held that even an invalid injunction must be obeyed, although a more recent decision indicated a disposition among some justices to reconsider that finding. Of course, the mine workers case did not get into whether or not a blatantly unconstitutional ordinance administered in a discriminatory way had to be obeyed. Moreover, our case for disobedience was even stronger because of the symbolic importance of Good Friday and Easter Sunday, which would have passed, and with them a special opportunity, if Martin were to wait for a decision on the validity of the injunction. Amaker discussed the law as we saw it with Martin and his staff, concluding that they probably would be held in contempt, that we would do our best, and that the law offered some hope, but no certainty of reversal.

Martin was worried that injunctions had defeated the movement in Talladega, Alabama, and Albany, Georgia. He felt that he couldn't capitulate to the Birmingham order, because if he did the movement might collapse while we tried to get the injunction vacated. On the other hand, he had to remember that it was *we* who had been seeking greater respect for court orders. So greatly did we feel a need to support the rule of law that Bill Hastie counseled obedience to the Alabama court order that would require the NAACP to disclose members' names if it were to lose that case on appeal. In the end, Martin resolved that in this instance he could not obey the state court order; as promised, he marched on Good Friday, was arrested and carried off to jail, along with other protesters.

If I knew then what I know now, I would have somehow thrown together papers to file asking that the injunction be dissolved even before Martin marched. That, of course, would have been futile, because the courts, which took more than half a decade to decide the case, wouldn't have decided it in less than the forty-eight hours before Good Friday. Nevertheless, the Supreme Court would not have been able to take us to task for not having made that effort. Following Martin's arrest, Amaker and Birmingham lawyers filed motions to dissolve the injunction because it was unconstitutionally vague, violated First Amendment rights, enforced racial segregation, and incorporated an unconstitutional ordinance. The judge set the hearing for a week later, on April 22.

Connie Motley, Leroy Clark, Norman Amaker, Birmingham lawyer Arthur Shores, and I spent that week gathering evidence and researching the law. Meanwhile, Martin, in jail between the time of arrest and trial, was composing the magnificent *A Letter from Birmingham Jail*, which became a major document in moving the country toward racial equality.

On the 22nd we showed up in the nondescript courtroom of Judge William A. Jenkins, Jr., to defend Martin, Wyatt Tee Walker, and other movement leaders against the contempt charge. Any objective observer would have rated our chances as nil. Yet, as in so many other Southern courts, our local lawyers advised that the judge was "fair" and might rule with us. Two possible explanations: First, in disputes that were not predicated on racial issues many Southern judges indeed were fair, to black and white litigants. Second, the need to believe in equal justice under the law was so important in keeping these lawyers committed to the cause that they sometimes continued to believe that justice is blind against all evidence to the contrary. But this was one time we would all be quickly disabused of such idealistic notions.

Time and time again, Jenkins construed the law against us. I set out to prove, by questioning the city clerk, that the nominal permit procedure—filing an application with the city commission—was never required of others, my point being that the defendants should not be punished for violating a rule no one else had to follow. Jenkins sustained one objection after another. I was given an opportunity to proffer what I would have proved if permitted to do so, so that the Supreme Court would know what we intended to show, but it didn't carry the same force. Connie Motley and Arthur Shores demonstrated that the permit regulation was too vague to obey and was administered in a biased manner.

The trial ended on April 24. On Friday, April 26, 1963, Jenkins held the defendants in contempt and sentenced them to five days in jail and a fifty dollar fine, the maximum allowed under law.

The case did not reach the Supreme Court of the United States until 1967. Jim Nabrit and Tony Amsterdam, who together wrote most of the brief, were almost defeated by a power failure in Manhattan the day before it was due. They did their best by candlelight, then walked down twenty flights and over to Tony's father's East Side apartment, where they completed writing by pencil on yellow pads. The next day they returned to the office, where power had been restored, but not to the circuits that ran the electric typewriters. Most of the secretaries had forgotten how to use the few manual typewriters that remained, but frantic activity got the brief out in time.

I argued the case in March of that year. It was perhaps my most unsatisfactory experience in arguing a case; the Court showed no interest in the unfairness of the temporary restraining order, the biased way the permit ordinance had been administered, or its unconstitutionality. There was no outrage at how Martin had been treated, no sympathy for a leader who nonviolently had toppled Birmingham's regime of segregation and, indeed, had brought about passage of the 1964 Civil Rights Act.

Later that term, the Court upheld the convictions and Martin served five days in jail, almost unnoticed, and with no complaints. I apologized to him profusely, but he genuinely didn't seem to mind. Later it appeared that when the Court took its initial vote, Justice Harlan was inclined to vote for us on the issue of discriminatory enforcement; if he had, we would have won five to four. For unknown reasons he later joined the four who favored upholding the conviction, making a majority for affirmance.

Justice Stewart's majority opinion stressed that "no man can be judge in his own case."[14] He made much of the fact that we had not moved to dissolve the injunction between the time it was served at 1:00 A.M. on Thursday, April 12, and Good Friday, April 13. There was no reason to believe, he asserted, that the Alabama courts would not give us a prompt hearing. Indeed, he argued, Alabama provided for expedited review. The four years it took the case to reach decision in the Supreme Court should have been response enough to that statement. It would have been physically impossible to prepare, file, try, and decide, to say nothing of appealing, a motion to dissolve before Good Friday, a date that was integral to Martin's message. In retrospect, however, we should have tried to show that we had done everything possible. I don't think, however, that it would have made any difference.

In any event, in 1963, despite Martin's conviction, demonstrators continued to fill Birmingham's jails. LDF at one point represented 2,497 movement defendants, charged with the usual offenses. Across the country, movement supporters boycotted businesses with branches in Birmingham, causing the city's leaders serious concern about the damage that might be done to the city's reputation. Under this pressure, powerful whites in Birmingham and representatives of the Kennedy administration negotiated a settlement with SCLC calling for desegregating public facilities within ninety days, fair hiring, establishing a biracial commission, and freeing the demonstrators. The demonstrators were released on bail with funds furnished by the United Auto Workers Union and others. We came to an agreement with city lawyers that the cases would be governed by a test case in which the parading ordinance's constitutionality would be at issue.

In 1969, the Supreme Court decided that test case, reversing Fred Shuttlesworth's conviction for having marched on that same Good Friday in 1963, violating the ordinance that had been incorporated into the injunction against Martin Luther King. Shuttlesworth's victory disposed of the vast bulk of pending Birmingham cases. I argued Shuttlesworth's case as I had argued Martin's. Martin's conviction had been upheld; Shuttlesworth's was reversed. Why? One didn't have a better lawyer than the other. The Court thought there was an important difference between violating an ordinance and violating a court order.

By 1967 social turmoil had risen to a level the Court found frightening. Racial demonstrations appeared to be out of control. Ghetto riots devastated entire communities. Social confrontation was exacerbated by the Vietnam War. You could see the reaction particularly in Justice Black, probably the foremost proponent of First Amendment rights. Not only did his opinion become strident in the later demonstration cases, but his demeanor from the bench, in asking questions and reading opinions, was often angry. Moreover, the civil rights acts had been passed. The demonstrators' conduct no longer had the salutary purpose of advocating passage of that legislation.

While the Court was not willing to permit an unconstitutional ordinance to suppress free speech, there were five votes for upholding the local judge, whose on-the-spot judgment counseled a halt. The judge was treated like the captain of a ship. His word was law.

GEORGE WALLACE IN THE SCHOOLHOUSE DOOR

In May 1963 in the midst of the demonstration turmoil, two bright, attractive black applicants, Vivian Malone and Jimmy Hood, applied to the University of Alabama, were turned down, and came to us for legal help. By then, Alabama was the only state without a black student in its white university system. Rather than starting anew, Connie just added them as plaintiffs to the 1955 *Lucy* case, which still was pending. The registrar tried to squirm out by claiming that the decree bound only his predecessor. Judge Hobart Grooms, no integrationist—he had granted the stay that accompanied the *Lucy* riot—ruled that the new registrar was governed by the decree against his predecessor.

In the meantime, President Kennedy, not wanting a repetition of the *Meredith* case, was cultivating a political climate receptive to admitting the plaintiffs. On May 18, in a speech at Vanderbilt University in Nashville he said that the efforts of blacks to secure their rights were "in the highest traditions of American freedom." Just in case, he deployed three thousand federal troops to the Birmingham area (five hundred were later withdrawn).

On May 21, Judge Grooms ordered the university to admit Malone and Hood at the session beginning June 10. Almost immediately, George Wallace announced that he would keep them out and filed a case in the Supreme Court seeking to prohibit the president's deployment of troops. But the Court denied the application because the president's action merely was "preparatory."

Having learned its lesson in Mississippi, the Justice Department moved swiftly for an injunction prohibiting Wallace from interfering. On June 5, Judge Seybourne Lynne, from whom it was tough to get a desegregation order, granted the motion, but was distressed: "I love the people of Alabama. I know that many of both races are troubled and like Jonah of old are 'angry even unto death' as the result of distortions of affairs within this State, practiced in the name of sensationalism. My prayer is that all of our people, in keeping with our fine traditions, will join in the resolution that law and order will be maintained."

That night the National States Rights party held a rally on U.S. Highway 231, on the boundary line between Elmore and Montgomery counties. Edward R. Fields, its leader, made a fiery speech, calling on white people to stand up and fight and not be trampled into the ground any longer. He stated that the NAACP was headed by Jews, that they were "the real enemy," and that Jack Greenberg, a Jew, was the chief counsel for the NAACP, telling the assembled mob, "You are the law of the land." He counseled obeying the court order admitting blacks to the university, "but after Monday, it will be different," recalling the riot that drove Autherine Lucy off the campus after three days.

On June 11, President Kennedy issued a proclamation commanding the "Governor of Alabama and all other persons . . . to cease and desist" from unlawful obstructions of justice. At the same time he ordered the secretary of defense to take "all appropriate steps to enforce the laws of the United States" within Alabama, and to use such of the armed forces as he deemed necessary. Wallace replied with his own proclamation, which denounced Kennedy's action and said that he forbade "this illegal and unwarranted action by the Central Government."

While this was going on, I was in Birmingham dealing with the demonstrations, along with Connie, who also had her hands full with another case: expulsion of more than a thousand schoolchildren on May 20 from Birmingham's schools for having participated in demonstrations. On May 21, we filed suit to enjoin the expulsion, and asked for a temporary restraining order. Judge Clarence Allgood denied it writing that he could "not conceive of a Federal Court saying to the Board of Education . . . made up of dedicated courageous, honorable, men that they should take no action . . . and that the children who deliberately failed to attend school for some several days should not in any way be punished or penalized."

Connie went immediately to Judge Tuttle in Atlanta, who granted a temporary restraining order reinstating the children, holding that they had engaged in constitutionally protected activities. A month later the case came up before a panel of the Fifth Circuit, which reversed Algood, the court agreeing with Tuttle on the merits. The court also agreed with Connie's argument that allowing the board to go ahead and expel the children, which would have prevented their graduation on time, represented a final, not temporary, denial of relief and that, therefore, the case was appealable. Since then, the case has been more important as a procedural precedent about what is appealable than as a constitutional precedent. After all, the constitutional point should have been obvious from the outset.

June 11 was the first day of school at the University of Alabama and Jimmy Hood and Vivian Malone went to the campus in Tuscaloosa to register. I met with them before they went up; they were a bit apprehensive, but certainly not jittery. My only advice was simplistic—do your best—but it seemed to reassure them.

Governor Wallace was true to his word. He stood in the schoolhouse door flanked by more than five hundred federalized National Guardsmen. Nicholas Katzenbach, deputy attorney general, walked up to Wallace and, in a planned exchange, asked him to end his defiance. Wallace said he "refuse[d] to willingly submit to illegal usurpation of power by the Central Government." Katzenbach replied, "These students will remain on this campus. They will register today. They will go to school tomorrow." Katzenbach and Malone then walked to her dormitory, and Jimmy Hood and John Doar drove to Hood's dorm. Students greeted them in a friendly manner and later they joined others in the cafeteria without incident.

Wallace's opposition was real, but the incident in the schoolhouse door was strictly for public consumption. Wallace made it into a big media event, which advanced his national political ambitions. No reasonably well-informed person could have had any doubt about the outcome.

As with *Meredith*, I had the feeling that we had sent Vivian Malone and Jimmy Hood out into the struggle alone, with little more than our best wishes that it would all turn out all right. But this time our wishes proved accurate, and it was all right.

MISSISSIPPI FREEDOM SUMMER

The Mississippi Freedom Summer of 1964, directed by the Council of Federated Organizations (COFO), attracted around one thousand young people from all over the country. Large groups gathered first at Miami University in Oxford, Ohio, where I, and others, lectured about civil rights and tried to prepare the young people for a part of the country governed by traditions and laws that most of them hardly could imagine. They had no professional skills and often little knowledge of what they were heading into; they had only their passion and dedication. They dimly understood that they might be killed, as indeed some were.

Freedom Summer's political importance, short and long term, and that of similar projects in other parts of the South, cannot be overestimated. Idealistic young people, many of them black, but many of whom were middle-class whites, not all of whom were terribly well informed about racial justice, but all of whom were viscerally appalled at how black people were being treated, did the only thing they were capable of doing at their age: They put their physical beings on the line and involved themselves in fighting discrimination in ways large and small. Having helped transform the South's racial practices, many later became active in campus revolts and in the antiwar movement in the expectation that they could change society in other ways. They became catalysts that helped change the country politically. Often I meet people active in public life who tell me that they were in Mississippi during this period, or in other parts of the South, as activists, law students, or lawyers, and that those experiences still resonate in them today. Many say that those were the most important experiences of their lives.

In Mississippi, they established freedom schools; tried to register voters; organized the black community to fight for schools, streets, sewers, libraries, and better pay; attempted to integrate public accommodations; and got into lots of trouble with law enforcement officers who harassed them in every imaginable way.

Marian Wright (now Marian Wright Edelman) was one of the first two LDF interns (the other was Julius Chambers), under a program that I set up informally soon after succeeding Thurgood and expanded greatly after foundation funding became available. Born and raised in Bennettsville, South Carolina, Marian came to LDF at age twenty-four, a slim, beautiful Yale Law School graduate with a faintly Burmese appearance. She was no stranger to civil rights; while a student at Spelman College she helped organize the plaintiffs for a case I had in Atlanta that integrated the airport's Dobbs House restaurant. Much later she became chair of Spelman's board of trustees. Even as a law student, Marian's public-speaking ability, a talent inherited from her two grandfathers and her father, all Baptist ministers, was celebrated; she was addressing an LDF fund-raising dinner the night Yale chaplain Bill Coffin and a group of Yale Freedom Riders were arrested. Later on, she settled in Jackson, Mississippi, and became only the fourth black lawyer in the state.

Not yet a member of the Mississippi bar in 1964, Marian opened an office above a pool hall on Farish Street in Jackson and nominally clerked for three black Mississippi lawyers, Jack Young, R. Jess Brown, and Carsie Hall, who signed the papers she wrote until she became a member of the bar. At first she was alone with three law students: Lowell Johnston, later an LDF staff member; Ron Pollack, now head of Families USA; and Barrington D. (Danny) Parker, Jr., later a senior partner in Morrison and Foerster, one of the country's largest international law firms. Our Jackson office—with Marian, Young, Brown, Hall, staff lawyers, and Northern volunteers—handled more than 120 Freedom Summer–generated cases, some involving fifty to sixty defendants. We had more spurious traffic cases than any other kind. Many cases implicated classical free expression issues such as marching, leafleting, picketing. Still others dealt with demanding service at a lunch counter, or trying to buy a ticket at the white ticket window of a theater, or using the white entrance at a launderette—even after the 1964 Civil Rights Act was signed. There were many serious charges, too.

For many prosecutions it was easiest to negotiate a fine or settlement; sometimes upon the mere appearance of a lawyer the prosecutor dropped charges. We removed many cases to federal court, where they lingered until they expired, but appealed some in the state system. We sued for injunctions against public accommodations discrimination; against a proclamation of the mayor of Drew, Mississippi, who ordered civil rights workers to be taken into protective custody; against the refusal of the Mississippi Fair Commission to rent its coliseum for a folk festival; and to desegregate the state office buildings and capitol. Marian had some early equal employment cases and some seeking service at public accommodations, particularly against Dairy Queens, which for some reason were more resistant than other establishments to desegregating. Her office undertook many of these cases with volunteers; but after the volunteers went home the cases were hers and ours.

By the end of 1965 LDF lawyers were ranging over the South in all sorts of demonstration cases in which we worked out of the offices of cooperating lawyers, except in Mississippi (where Marian headed the official LDF office).

Henry Aronson, who was unlike any other LDF lawyer, soon joined Marian's staff. He had been working for the Aetna insurance company and went to Mississippi as a volunteer. I hired him scarcely knowing him; he was there, he was capable and more than dedicated to fighting Jim Crow. In Jackson he set up a shabby apartment, flies buzzing everywhere, furnished with articles from afar; he had a jazzy sports car purchased a thousand miles away, as well as a shoeshine machine with gears, and a "gentlemen's valet," a device for hanging his clothes. He wore boots, was a licensed pilot, and flew to cases across the state. His laconic manner reminded me a little of Humphrey Bogart, but he looked and acted like someone out of the old "Terry and the Pirates" comic. Aronson's chutzpah knew no bounds. Slight, intense, tilted forward, speaking with a deep voice and in clipped tones, pugnacious, he was the only LDF lawyer to be physically attacked; racists beat and machine-gunned him—missing him—in Grenada, Mississippi. When Selma sheriff Jim Clark hid out in the jail to avoid service of summons, Henry feigned a Southern accent, was let in to see him, and served the summons. The next day Henry went to Clark's office, but Clark wasn't in. Awaiting him, Henry sat in his chair and made a phone call, during which Clark arrived and, infuriated, bounced Henry off the wall a couple of times. Clark told Peter Hall, one of our Birmingham lawyers, "Bring him back here and I'll kill him." The last time I saw Henry, after he had left LDF, was in *Time* magazine: There was a picture of Henry taken in Vietnam, where he had gone to represent deserters during the war, riding in the back of a jeep, going God knows where.

Others, more gentle, brought the LDF macho index down. Anthony G. (Tony) Amsterdam, now a law professor at New York University, then at the University of Pennsylvania, became a virtual staff member. Having majored in art history at Haverford, Tony's academic record at Penn law school won him a clerkship with Felix Frankfurter, who until then had hired Harvard graduates only. I learned of Tony through an article he wrote as a law student on the constitutionality of vague statutes, perhaps still the leading treatment of the subject, and invited him, in 1962, to attend a lawyers training conference in New Orleans, at Dillard University. Tony is perhaps six feet two, emaciatingly thin. For many years he had a stepped-down version of a Dali mustache, which has recently evolved into mutton chops; then he was clean shaven. Stories of his genius and energy abound: He virtually commuted to Jackson by automobile from Philadelphia, where he taught at the University of Pennsylvania; he would drive from California to New York nonstop; if you gave him a brief for editing you would get it back, always, the next day or earlier, marked up with suggestions and insights; if you presented a problem, after a moment's reflection he would reply with exhaustive, documented analysis and authorities, including volume and page number. Once, arguing a case in the District of Columbia Court of Appeals, he cited a case. A dubious judge sent for the volume and told Tony the case wasn't where Tony said it was. Without examining the book, Tony replied that the volume must have been misbound. It was. Mel Zarr, a staff member, recalls long nights with Tony during hot Mississippi summers. Dressed only in their underwear to cope with the heat, writing briefs, they would work until they fell asleep and then wake up and get back to work.

Mark DeWolfe Howe, a Harvard law professor, also worked with Marian, as did Ed Koch, later mayor of New York City, as a volunteer. Everyone who was there seems to recall Koch, terrified, as Mississippi police followed him home at night, their headlights glaring through the back window of his car.

Paul Brest, recently out of Harvard Law School, and his wife, Iris, became part of this group in 1966. He, too, had a pilot's license and flew around the state on demonstration cases. Paul left to become clerk to Justice Harlan and was later dean of Stanford Law School. They were joined by Melvin Leventhal who began going to Mississippi as a law student in 1965, went into practice there in 1967, and remained until 1975. When Marian left Mississippi in 1968 to move to Washington, Mel and Alice Walker, to whom he was then married, bought her house. Fred Banks and Reuben Anderson, both Mississippians, worked for Marian as law students. Reuben became a justice on the Mississippi Supreme Court. Recently, when he stepped down, the governor appointed Fred to the same position.

Apart from offering front-line defense, the Mississippi lawyers won some decisions that went farther, creating rights that until then had not existed.

One held that a misdemeanor defendant who faced a substantial sentence had a right to a lawyer, extending the right to counsel established in *Gideon v. Wainwright*, which had been a felony case. They won another case holding it unconstitutional for justices of the peace to keep fines paid by defendants, a practice that persisted in many parts of the South, naturally creating an incentive to convict. After this decision the clerk's office in the Northern District of Mississippi gave Tony Amsterdam and Henry Aronson cheery good mornings whenever they arrived to file anything, the entire workforce swapping can-you-top-this horror stories about justices of the peace's cooking up parking and traffic fines.

Soon Marian became involved in bringing Head Start to Mississippi and fending off official attacks on it. It became clear to her that something more than lawsuits—namely community and political action—was needed to fight racism. Out of that early experience she developed the idea of and created the Children's Defense Fund.

LDF also had cases across Alabama—involving boycotts, failure to obey a police officer, demonstrating on or near school grounds, interfering with school operations, expulsion from school for having demonstrated, and delinquency. We removed over a score of Alabama cases from state to federal court. Defendants had been charged with crimes like attempting to destroy state property, vagrancy, and practicing medicine without a license. In Florida we had cases in St. Augustine arising from holding a public meeting in the old slave market, littering, and unlawful picketing. In Jacksonville we won more than three hundred sit-in cases; sued to desegregate the jails; and defended the SCLC and Hosea Williams (one of Martin Luther King, Jr.'s top assistants) in a damage suit arising out of a voter registration campaign in which children stayed out of school.

In Americus, Georgia, we defended black women who were prosecuted for standing in a white voters line; sued to set aside a justice of the peace election because of segregated procedures; and filed suit to enjoin police from interfering with demonstrations. We invalidated scores of Americus demonstration prosecutions in federal court and then got a federal court injunction against prosecuting civil rights workers for insurrection in Americus, an offense that carried the death penalty!

Some cases hung on after passage of the Civil Rights Act of 1964. In Atlanta we defended demonstrators who had sat in at Lebs restaurant. In Savannah we defended hundreds of sit-in demonstrators charged with trespass, getting writs of habeas corpus in federal court, extending the abatement doctrine of *Hamm v. City of Rock Hill* to win the release of demonstrators after the time to appeal expired. In Monroe, Georgia, we got an injunction against a curfew as unconstitutional. In Griffin, Georgia, we represented twenty black youths arrested for trying to desegregate a youth center and swimming pool. They had been convicted without counsel.

In Greenville, Mississippi, two black girls were convicted of breach of the peace for remaining in a white park after a white mob threatened their safety. To our astonishment we won in the Mississippi Supreme Court. In June 1963, blacks went swimming at a white Biloxi, Mississippi, beach that, while privately owned, was maintained with public funds. Mobs attacked them, the state prosecuted—the black bathers, not the assailants—and we defended them. In December 1966, we won the United States Supreme Court decision prohibiting segregation on the Biloxi beaches.

In the North, black anger erupted in the 1965 Watts riots in California, and we had to ponder whether there was a legal role for LDF to play. Blacks had rioted, burned, and looted businesses and property throughout Watts, the black section of Los Angeles. There was no way to justify the rioting or to defend the action of the rioters. But all defendants were entitled to a fair trial. Instead, innocent and guilty alike were being rushed to judgment without adequate representation. In October we filed an action in the California Supreme Court calling on it to appoint lawyers who would be adequately prepared and to nullify convictions obtained without adequate counsel. But the court ruled against us without even writing an opinion, merely sending us a postcard in response to perhaps a pound of legal arguments. The card tersely announced that our petition had been denied, and the case sank without a trace.

WHOM SHOULD WE REPRESENT?

Constitutional protections are owed as much to the most abrasive malcontent as to the mildest milquetoast. Unfortunately, judges, even the justices of the Supreme Court, are human beings with their own strong feelings about what constitutes proper behavior, and sometimes these feelings affect deliberations. Between 1961, when the demonstrations began, and the mid-1960s a pattern began to emerge: It became pretty clear that the Supreme Court wouldn't absolve demonstrators who exceeded certain limits of civility, even if they had adequate constitutional defenses.

In February 1964 Jim Nabrit argued a case for Dion Diamond, a student leader who had led demonstrations through the halls of Southern University in East Baton Rouge, Louisiana. Jim asserted persuasively that the law under which Diamond was convicted was unconstitutionally vague. But the Court obviously was turned off by Diamond's carryings on within the school. Four days later it dismissed the writ of certiorari as "improvidently granted"—it had made a mistake even agreeing to hear the case. In June 1964 it refused to hear another case that it pondered for a very long time (the petition had been filed in September 1962, almost two years earlier) where the defendant, who refused to sit in the rear of a church, ran down the aisle during a service. In December 1964 the Court refused to grant our petition in *Jones v. Georgia*, a similar church case. We hadn't been thrilled with these three cases, which looked like losers, but we believed in the movement and neither we nor anyone else could fine tune all its activities. The Court was less tolerant.

Drawing the line between cases we would handle and those we wouldn't wasn't easy. LDF board members, concerned by the increasingly violent or threatening turn some demonstrations had taken, wanted some expression of the principles that governed selection. In October 1964 I presented these propositions, which were approved, to the board:

> Many demonstrations . . . have been called civilly disobedient because they have . . . violated segregation laws, ordinances requiring permits to parade, and directives . . . banning meetings at certain places or times. But violating an unconstitutional requirement is not civil disobedience. . . . Segregation laws violate the Constitution: anyone who disobeys, violates no valid law. Some restrictive permit requirements or regulations . . . may be unconstitutional; or . . . vague, thereby breaching the constitutional command that laws . . . give fair warning . . . or may be enforced unevenly, exacting compliance from Negroes but not from whites. . . . Violating an invalid law is not civilly disobedient.
>
> Sometimes it may be unclear whether a law is valid. . . . Facts may be disputed. Such cases may fall in the well-recognized test case category. Demonstrators who have acted for moral ends and non-violently deserve representation in test cases. . . .
>
> There is . . . clear violation of law which no reasonably anticipated defense would protect. Genuine civil disobedience expresses a moral judgment that the protested evil is so great that violating the law . . . is warranted. Such civil disobedience while illegal . . . is not under all circumstances immoral or undesirable. Each of us can only make our own moral evaluation. Its moral validity must, however, be measured not only against the evil it attacks, but against alternative means . . . and against opposition which it may stimulate, that may even further imbed the wrong. . . . We would be extremely reluctant to defend civilly disobedient demonstrators. . . . We cannot in good conscience argue to a court of law that actions we cannot responsibly defend legally are valid under law. Indeed, participants in civil disobedience would not want us to. . . .
>
> In some cases civilly disobedient defendants may be prosecuted for crimes they did not commit. . . . They deserve representation with regard to [this and] . . . similar aspects of their involvement with the law. But the representation should be candid [and not offer] . . . defenses which deny the known facts or distort the law. . . .
>
> The riots, violence and looting which have erupted in a few places this summer . . . have no relation to civil rights except that the oppression and degradation of racial discrimination have contributed to cre-

Part of plaintiffs' legal team in *Brown v. Board*: John Scott, *James M. Nabrit, Jr., *Spottswood W. Robinson III, Frank D. Reeves, *Jack Greenberg, *Thurgood Marshall, *Louis L. Redding, U. Simpson Tate, and *George E. C. Hayes. Asterisks indicate those who argued before the Court. (*LDF*)

William H. Hastie, first black judge on the U.S. Court of Appeals, a founder of LDF, and close collaborator with Thurgood Marshall. (*UPI/Bettmann*)

Charles Hamilton Houston, "the Moses of that journey," vice dean of Howard Law School and pioneer of the legal strategy that led to *Brown v. Board. (C. H. Houston, Jr.)*

George W. McLaurin (foreground, with his back to camera), the first black person to attend graduate school at the University of Oklahoma, was forced to sit at a desk for blacks only while attending classes.
(*AP Wide World*)

Thurgood Marshall

Franklin H. Williams, former LDF assistant counsel. (*Shirley Williams*)

Charles L. Black, Jr., Sterling Professor Emeritus at Yale University Law School and now teaching at Columbia University Law School, who participated in many sit-in and capital punishment cases and in *Brown v. Board.* (*Barbara Black*)

William T. Coleman, Jr., chairman of LDF and former secretary of transportation under President Ford, worked with LDF in cases from *Brown v. Board* through *Bob Jones University.* (*W. T. Coleman, Jr.*)

Samuel Shepherd and Walter Irvin after being shot by Sheriff Willis McCall. (*AP Wide World*)

(Left to right) Paul Perkins, Jack Greenberg, Walter Irvin, and Thurgood Marshall at Irvin's trial. (*UPI/Bettmann*)

Roy Wilkins, Autherine Lucy, and Thurgood Marshall, after Lucy was driven from the University of Alabama campus by rioting students in 1956. (*LDF*)

Roy Wilkins, longtime secretary of the NAACP. (*NAACP*)

James Hood and Vivian Malone, the first two black students at the University of Alabama, in 1963, after Governor George Wallace stood in the schoolhouse door in an effort to exclude them. (*C. B. Motley*)

Thurgood Marshall with John W. Davis, who argued for the state of South Carolina in *Brown v. Board*. (*AP Wide World*)

Constance Baker Motley and Jack Greenberg on the steps of the United States Supreme Court. (*LDF*)

Dr. James M. Nabrit, Jr., former president of Howard University, who argued the District of Columbia school segregation case. (*LDF*)

Walter White, secretary of the NAACP in 1949 when I arrived at LDF. (*NAACP*)

Robert L. Carter, Thurgood Marshall's first assistant when I arrived at LDF. (*UPI/Bettmann*)

The civil rights leadership in the mid-1960s: (from left) Bayard Rustin, coordinator of the March on Washington; Jack Greenberg; Whitney M. Young, executive director, National Urban League; James Farmer, national director, CORE; Roy Wilkins, executive director, NAACP; Martin Luther King, Jr., president, Southern Christian Leadership Conference; John Lewis, chairman, Student Nonviolent Coordinating Committee; A. Philip Randolph, international president, Negro American Labor Council. (*NYT Pictures*)

Constance Baker Motley and James Meredith. Motley represented Meredith in his battle to enter the University of Mississippi. (*LDF*)

Marian Wright (later Marian Wright Edelman), one of LDF's first two interns and founder and president of the Children's Defense Fund. (*LDF*)

Martin Luther King, Jr., and Ralph Bunche at an LDF fund-raising dinner in the early 1960s. (*LDF*)

Grenville Clark, pillar of the WASP establishment, who started the Grenville Clark plan and
the Fund for Equal Justice which raised money for
LDF. (*LDF*)

Wiley A. Branton, LDF's cooperating lawyer in
the Little Rock school case. (*Lucille Branton*)

A. P. Turead, for years the only black lawyer in Louisiana and longtime LDF cooperating lawyer. (*C. B. Motley*)

Four LDF lawyers in 1964 (from left, clockwise): Jack Greenberg, Norman Amaker, Michael Meltsner, and James M. Nabrit III. (*LDF*)

Louis H. Pollak, former vice president of LDF, former dean of Yale University and the University of Pennsylvania law schools, and now U.S. District Judge in Philadelphia. Pollak worked on and argued many LDF cases. (*L. H. Pollak*)

Arthur Shores, for many years the only black lawyer in Alabama, and Constance Baker Motley examine the damage to Shores's Birmingham home after it was bombed during civil rights demonstrations in the early 1960s. (*LDF*)

Anthony G. Amsterdam, law professor who handled many LDF cases and led our campaign against capital punishment. (*A. Amsterdam*)

(Left to right) Jack Greenberg, Anna Caples Frank, longtime fundraiser for LDF, Conrad O. Pearson, an LDF cooperating lawyer, and John Wheeler, school case plaintiff in North Carolina.

Constance Baker Motley; Jack Greenberg; Dr. John W. Davis (directly behind Greenberg), LDF director of teacher information and security; and Shriners making their annual contribution to LDF. (*LDF*)

R. Jess Brown, one of three black lawyers in Mississippi in the early 1960s, was a cooperating lawyer in *Meredith*, the Freedom Ride cases, and many other demonstration cases. (*C. B. Motley*)

Jack Greenberg's retirement party in 1984 on the roof of LDF's headquarters (front: Julius Chambers, Jean Fairfax, and Jack Greenberg). (*D. H. Charles/NYT Pictures*)

Elaine Jones, first director of LDF's Washington, D.C., office and director-counsel of LDF since 1993. (*LDF*)

ating them. . . . We might defend such defendants as we might any defendant accused of a common crime—but only if the criminal proceeding is infected with fundamental unfairness or racial discrimination.

The principles were far from inexorable. Sometimes, under pressure from staff members or organizations, we took cases outside the guidelines where there was a credible defense. It was important sometimes to respect the staff's wishes to become involved in a case if I wanted to keep bright, energetic, idealistic lawyers working at LDF. We also had to maintain alliances with other organizations. It was a difficult line to walk.

MORE LAWYERS JOIN THE STRUGGLE

As the importance and glamour of civil rights caught public attention, Northern lawyers began going south to volunteer, some excellent, some nondescript, some ineffective. We found ourselves in some cases with lawyers whose help was indispensable; but there were others with whom we didn't get along or with whom we didn't agree on legal theory or approach to the courts. SCLC and other litigants would turn to us when volunteers went home, as almost all ultimately did. If we were to be the last resort, we needed control—where possible—over how demonstration law developed. We didn't want conflicting theories and unattractive facts before the courts. We, like the NAACP, became sensitive to the Johnny-come-lately syndrome. Where had the others been when the work was unglamorous and unrewarding? Where would they be tomorrow?

In early 1963, as the legal problems of the SCLC grew, I met with Martin Luther King, Jr., Andrew Young, and other SCLC staff in a Washington, D.C., church. SCLC had concluded that it couldn't function by relying only on a few friends and lawyers whom they would pick up as they went along, but it made no sense for them to set up a legal staff. They had limited funds and no expertise at running a legal program. LDF had represented Martin in the Montgomery bus boycott, during the Freedom Rides, and when he had been jailed for driving without a Georgia license, and it was natural for him to turn to us. But SCLC leadership was a mixed group, and some younger leaders were afraid that we were a bunch of establishment lawyers who would be telling them how to run the movement. Some identified us with the NAACP, which they viewed as unsympathetic. Our low-key approach, which kept lawyers out of demonstrations and avoided court-bashing pronouncements, lent credence to that view.

During the meeting Martin said little, essentially allowing his staff to talk its way through the problem. They were reassured when I made it clear that we were independent of the NAACP. We promised that we never would tell them what to do, only inform them of the likely legal consequences. Under these conditions it was easy for SCLC to agree that, wherever possible, LDF would handle all their cases and would have legal control of those cases. From then on SCLC was represented almost exclusively by LDF.

About 150 lawyers, singly or through groups—including the American Civil Liberties Union, American Jewish Congress, American Jewish Committee, and CORE—went south during Freedom Summer. Most worked under the umbrella of the Lawyers Constitutional Defense Committee (LCDC) consortium. American Bar Association (ABA) leaders Bernard Segal and Harrison Tweed set up outside the ABA—the rank and file of which either wasn't interested in or was hostile to civil rights—the Lawyers Committee for Civil Rights Under Law (the Lawyers Committee), which sent lawyers south. President Kennedy launched the Committee at a splashy White House event and it became known also as the President's Committee.

In Mississippi, where most of the volunteer lawyers went, federal judges Cox and Mize required out-of-state lawyers to appear with local counsel, although Judge Claude Clayton let in those who were admitted in other federal courts. The volunteers could appear in state court only with a Mississippi lawyer, requiring the cooperation of Mississippi lawyers, which many white lawyers would not give. There were only three black lawyers practicing in Mississippi at that time, Jack Young, Carsie Hall, and R. Jess Brown, with Marian arriving on the scene later. While the black lawyers cooperated with volunteers, there was a limit on how much time and attention they could spare.

Episodes of Cox's racism were legion. In a voting case he called blacks "chimpanzees." He wouldn't accept papers from Mel Leventhal, who was Jewish, unless "A.D." (*Anno Domini*, Latin for "in the year of the Lord") followed the date, but Cox required this of no one else. After he sentenced Mississippi law enforcement officers to prison for the civil rights law violation of having conspired to murder Schwerner, Goodman, and Chaney, the three young civil rights workers, Mel congratulated Cox, who confided: "Let me tell you something. It's one thing to beat them up, but another to kill them. That's going too far." When an out-of-state lawyer affiliated with a Mississippi firm appeared in Cox's court on a commercial matter, he waived the rule requiring membership in the Mississippi bar, saying it was just for "Jews and niggers from New York."

Ultimately, in September 1968 we got an order against Cox—Bill Coleman argued the case in the Fifth Circuit—which invalidated his restrictions on out-of-state lawyers. Under pressure from lawyers outside Mississippi (with whom they did business and had professional relationships), the Mississippi bar association adopted a rule calling on lawyers to represent demonstrators. But if any did it wasn't noticeable and the Mississippi bar president caught considerable criticism from Mississippi lawyers for his role in adopting the resolution.

I recommended to the board that, despite the problems presented by the involvement of the volunteer lawyers, we should cooperate with them, held training sessions for them at Columbia Law School, and assigned staff lawyers to work with them in Jackson. Perhaps the best part of their participation was that they returned home with incomparable stories of Southern life and justice, which had an important political effect and helped gain understanding of and eventually wider support for our efforts. The experience was also influential in creating a feeling among younger lawyers in private practice that they ought to devote at least some of their talents and energies to public service. For a time, major law firms had to promise, as an inducement to the brightest law graduates they were trying to hire, that they would allow them to do pro bono work while at the firm. To a considerable extent firms continue to promote pro bono activity among their partners and associates. In turn, young lawyers' interest and involvement in the movement reached back into the law schools and helped transform legal education to resemble more and more the model of Charlie Houston's academy for social engineers.

Some slight change in the involvement of Southern whites began to occur in Florida. Twelve white Florida lawyers, including Jerome Bornstein of Orlando, Howard Dixon of Miami, and Bernard Mandler and Irwin Block of St. Augustine, worked under the chairmanship of Earl Johnson, the LDF cooperating lawyer in Jacksonville, who was black. I established this relationship because, although it was important to involve whites, it also was important not to alienate blacks by creating the impression that whites were taking over. Tobias Simon of Miami was the most active of this group, and, in retaliation, the state filed disciplinary charges against him. I persuaded Cody Fowler, a former president of the American Bar Association and a Florida-based lawyer, to represent Toby, another sign of change; the charges were dismissed. Toby, in time, became one of our most important associates in Florida.

LDF AND THE NATIONAL LAWYERS GUILD

The National Lawyers Guild also sent lawyers to Jackson to represent Freedom Riders. The Guild had a well-deserved leftist political image, which came out of political positions at odds with the outlook of the NAACP and LDF. In the Guild's earliest days its membership defeated an effort of Jerome Frank (one of the early members of the jurisprudential school called "legal realism" and a great judge of the Second Circuit Court of Appeals), Morris Ernst (a pioneer of First Amendment law and a member of the committee that produced the Margold Report), and Adolf A. Berle, Jr. (my Columbia Law School professor and coauthor of the classic *The Modern Corporation and Private Property*), to persuade it to condemn communism and fascism alike. In 1948 the Guild's Committee on International Law and

Relations condemned the Marshall Plan, the plan for the economic recovery of Western Europe, which became a major factor in frustrating Stalin's effort to dominate the continent. The NAACP, on the other hand, rejected a similar call for condemnation of the Marshall Plan at the "Commie Convention" of 1950. Moreover, bitter memories of conflicts—in Scottsboro, Willie McGee, the Martinsville Seven, and the Trenton Six—with the International Labor Defense and the Civil Rights Congress, both in the same part of the political spectrum as the Guild, with considerable overlapping membership—resonated.

Still, the matter was not so simple. People were Guild members for various reasons. Some, like Bill Hastie, joined in part because, at the time, it was a nonracist alternative to the ABA. Being the man he was nobody was going to push Hastie into quitting when the Guild came under fire, although he hadn't been active in Guild affairs during the years I knew him. Louis Redding was a Guild member.

Thurgood resigned from the Guild around the time I came to LDF because, as he explained, it passed a resolution condemning Judge Harold Medina for his conduct of the Smith Act trial, in which eleven Communist party leaders were found guilty essentially of being members of the party. The resolution called for an investigation, but Thurgood believed that the Guild should have withheld judgment until the investigation that it called for was completed. Thurgood's reasoning may sound technical, but that was in reality a nonconfrontational way to leave the group, of which he disapproved politically. Later, as a judge, if a case had come to him involving the Guild's right to function, I am certain he surely would have upheld it. But in his personal and professional relationships, he was quite clear about wanting nothing to do with it, or indeed with any groups or individuals he knew to be Communists or who supported their positions. Thurgood showed this aversion in various ways. When the Guild's executive secretary Simon Schachter invited him to a celebration of the *Brown* decision in 1954 Thurgood declined. When a later executive secretary, Royal W. France, in 1956 invited him to discuss cooperation on various issues, Thurgood scrawled on the letter, "No reply." He said he "had a way of finding out who was a communist" and, to my astonishment, in 1990, identified lawyers whom he said were "commies."

The antipathy went back a long way. The NAACP board had refused to represent the Guild after the attorney general placed it on a list of subversive organizations in 1954 because, as the attorney general charged, it had "become more and more the legal mouthpiece for the Communist Party and its members." While the attorney general later dropped the case, the taint stuck. Thurgood was not swimming against a great tide in this. When the issue of representing the Guild arose, John Lewis, one of Thurgood's closest friends, wrote to Walter White, "I am firmly of the opinion that we should not connect ourselves with any matter in such a way that comfort could be given to reactionary elements in the southland at this critical stage in our fight for de-segregating education. . . . This, to my mind, would do us more injury than we could do the Lawyers Guild good."

While I worked with some lawyers who were Guild members, though not directly with the Guild as an organization, I too was worried about giving anyone any slim reason to attribute anything we did to advancing the party line.

This issue was part of a long-standing larger question of whether to get involved in civil liberties, as distinct from civil rights, cases. All of us were acutely aware of where things can lead once the courts allow themselves to be used as instruments of the majoritarian will, and many of us were disquieted by much of what was being done in the name of ridding the country of Communists. But the board resolved that "we should not go into civil liberties cases generally." It was like Thurgood's response to Justice Jackson about representing American Indians—"I have a full load right now."

Within weeks of the time I succeeded Thurgood, Victor Rabinowitz, a founding member of the Guild, invited me to lunch at Schrafft's on Fifty-seventh Street. Rabinowitz was a leading left-wing lawyer; many of his clients had been accused of being Communists or fellow travelers. He represented East Bloc countries and Castro's Cuba and, after the AFL-CIO purged itself of left-wing unions, he represented some of them. He asked whether now that Thurgood had left I would "work with" them. I told him no. So, when the question arose about whether to work with the Guild in Jackson, it had a long history, and I decided we shouldn't. This also was the view of the LDF board. Other organizatons were similarly wary of the Guild: The Guild wasn't invited to join LCDC; CORE and the NAACP wouldn't work with them. But SNCC went to any lawyer who would help it. And whatever problems associating with the Guild might cause for LDF would be compounded in the case of Southern cooperating lawyers who already were under attack for all sorts of other reasons. Lawyers like A. P. Tureaud and R. Jess Brown didn't need to fight charges arising out of working with the Guild. They might win, but had better things to do with their time. They also had families to support.

Our relations with the Guild have been described by some of its partisans as a conflict over legal tactics—the Guild being imaginative and daring and LDF being fuddy-duddy and plodding. An example they often gave was that Guild lawyers were committed to removing cases from state to federal courts, and LDF wasn't. The law provided that in certain circumstances state prosecutions might be "removed" to federal court, but how and when was poorly understood, as removal law virtually had been unused until then. Guild lawyers did little to unravel the complexities of removal. For example, when one group of Guild lawyers removed about 250 cases in Mississippi, they went back North, leaving LDF holding the bag, dealing with further litigation arising out of having used that dilatory tactic. Moreover, removal wasn't always desirable. No state judges were worse than some judges like Harold Cox, Daniel Thomas, Gordon West, or Robert Elliot. Nothing would be gained by removing a case to their courts. Indeed, apart from Tuttle, Wisdom, Brown, Johnson, and just a few others, Southern federal judges were indistinguishable from state judges in racial attitude.

I thought also that the law of removal didn't apply to most movement cases, although whether or not I was right wasn't clear. But Tony Amsterdam was of the same opinion and no one disagreed with him lightly. We turned out to be right, but just barely. In 1966, by a vote of five to four, the Supreme Court held that removal statutes covered only defendants prosecuted under a state law that denied equal rights (which, for example, would not cover prosecution for breach of the peace, which really was an attack on civil rights activity) or who were protected by a federal statute, like the Civil Rights Act in seeking service in a restaurant, for example. Defendants acting under the protection of a general constitutional provision like the First or Fourteenth Amendment could not remove. It was technical and arbitrary, but that was what the courts held the law of removal amounted to. But by that time virtually no movement people were being prosecuted under segregation laws. Prosecutions were for breach of the peace, parading without a permit, traffic offenses, trespass, and so forth. These were prosecutions for civil rights activity, but in the guise of general criminal law enforcement and, therefore, not removable.

As it became clear, after the Civil Rights Act was passed in mid-1964, that removal could be useful in demonstration cases involving public accommodations, where segregation was prohibited by the new act, we began using it in those limited circumstances. State prosecutors didn't know what to do with the cases—because the law was as much an enigma to them as it often was to us—and left most of them to languish forever. But that would not have been the best course with the many nonremovable cases that we won in the Supreme Court, like the early sit-in prosecutions, which invigorated the movement and enhanced its credibility.

Some claimed that while LDF refused to attack jury segregation, the Guild did. The facts do not bear out this position either. LDF pioneered in creating the law of jury discrimination and had more jury discrimination cases than anyone else. Another charge was that we had refused to work with an outspoken, highly publicized Virginia lawyer, Len Holt, who had been critical of our reluctance, as he saw it, to undertake anything but school integration cases or to challenge courtroom segregation at every criminal trial. But we thought he wasn't a very good lawyer or reliable. He had filed, for example, a case in Virginia directed simultaneously at discriminatory practices in the Danville school system, public housing, public buildings, nursing homes, cemeteries, parks and playgrounds, the city armory, technical institute, civil service, and the Danville Memorial Hospital—a case so big and complex it could not be litigated, a publicity stunt that got nowhere. Holt also said we told SNCC to be less aggressive because arrests had occurred that exceeded LDF's expectations and threatened its budget, but this was untrue. I told SNCC leaders only what I told Martin Luther King: I would never advise any course of action. If asked, I would offer my view of likely legal consequences.

I wouldn't take the same position on working with the Guild today. Its membership and policies have changed; it is an organization of activist lawyers and students concerned about many matters of public interest. The political issues of that time, which had made the Guild so controversial, no longer exist.

26

FROM SELMA TO MONTGOMERY

CREATING THE VOTING RIGHTS ACT

In early 1965 SCLC began a voter registration drive in Selma, Alabama, a black-belt community notorious for denying the ballot to blacks. Time and time again law enforcement officials, led by Sheriff Jim Clark, arrested and jailed would-be voters and demonstrators, including Martin Luther King, Jr. Moreover, Selma was within the jurisdiction of a hostile federal judge, Daniel Thomas. Judge Thomas wouldn't even enter an order enabling blacks to vote after he found that they had been denied registration illegally. Staff lawyers would file petitions with him, he would deny them, and off they would fly to New Orleans to appeal.

It wasn't an easy commute. Once, Chuck Jones and Henry Aronson had to charter a plane to file an appeal in the Fifth Circuit in New Orleans in time. The pilot refused to take them, but they started loudly discussing a lawsuit and the pilot had a change of mind—it might not have been very sensible for them to fly under such circumstances. But they did. En route bad weather jarred the plane so badly that a window popped open. Henry removed his belt and tied it around the window to hold it in place, but to no avail. The plane made a forced landing in Tuscaloosa, where they were able to join up with a plane being used by the Justice Department to complete the journey.

By the time the demonstrations ended that spring, LDF lawyers Chuck Jones, Leroy Clark, Norman Amaker, and Henry Aronson and cooperating lawyers from Birmingham and Montgomery had represented more than 3,400 defendants there. The Selma protests, which had gone on for three months, were getting nowhere. We knew, however, that the constitutional law protecting the right of the SCLC to protest could be enforced in not too distant Montgomery within the jurisdiction of federal district judge Frank Johnson. Johnson was fair and decent in enforcing the law, although he sometimes had his own idea of what should be done. At the time of the Freedom Rides he enjoined the Freedom Riders for a time, apparently to provide for a cooling-off period, not anywhere authorized by law. But in any event, when he finally decided the case he ruled with us, as he should have, for the law was on our side.

At the same time a consensus was developing within SCLC that its energies would be better applied elsewhere than in Selma. That place, it became clear, would be Montgomery, which had a bigger organizational base than Selma and, as the state capital, would attract more national attention. So the world-famous Selma-to-Montgomery march arose out of the decision, based on legal as well as organizational factors, to move the demonstrations to Montgomery, where the movement could marshal greater support and also could be protected in Frank Johnson's court. What better way to effect the transition than by a dramatic march from Selma to Montgomery?

This having been resolved, on March 5 Martin Luther King, Jr., met with President Johnson to discuss proposed voting rights legislation and inform him of the planned procession. At the outset there was confusion. SCLC leaders James Bevel and James Orange and others in the movement thought that the march was supposed to begin on Sunday, March 7. Martin understood that it would be later. When it appeared that marchers had gathered to set out on March 7, Martin was in Atlanta to conduct services at his church. Governor George Wallace entered an order prohibiting the march. Andy Young flew to Selma, but Martin urged that only he or Hosea Williams, another of Martin's chief deputies, not both, participate. Sheriff Jim Clark would put the protesters in jail and Martin wanted one of them to remain free to plan the subsequent march, in which he would take part.

On that Sunday, John Lewis, head of SNCC (today a congressman from Atlanta), and Hosea led more than five hundred demonstrators across the Edmund Pettus Bridge to begin the fifty-mile journey to Montgomery. A detachment of two hundred state troopers and volunteer possemen of the office of Dallas County sheriff James Clark faced them with guns, clubs, and nausea and tear gas. As the two groups approached each other, the officers attacked, launching tear gas and nausea bombs. Mounted possemen ran down marchers. Seventeen blacks went to the hospital, including Lewis, for a skull fracture; many others received emergency treatment. That Sunday the TV movie was *Judgment at Nuremberg*. A politically sensitive audience, steeped in Nazi atrocities, watched the mayhem on TV.

Martin's absence created the political problem for him of maintaining leadership of the more militant wing of the movement, particularly SNCC. On Monday, he announced that the march would resume the following day. Even before Monday arrived, Steve Ralston and Norman Amaker threw together a complaint and motion for a temporary restraining order against Governor Wallace and Selma's sheriff, Jim Clark, asking that they be prohibited from interfering with the procession. They flew to Montgomery where two of our Alabama lawyers presented it to Frank Johnson, getting Selma legal issues out of the clutches of Judge Daniel Thomas.

The law was absolutely clear: Wallace had not acted under a well-defined regulation controlling marching on the highway. He had made no effort to protect First Amendment rights; rather, state officials had brutalized the protesters. Unquestionably, we deserved an injunction, but Johnson denied it, giving as a reason that all defendants had not yet been served with our papers. Furthermore, he said, "There will be no irreparable harm if the plaintiffs will await a judicial determination of the matters involved." Then he did what he had done when we tried to enjoin interference with the Freedom Riders. Without any justification—indeed, without a request from any party—he prohibited the march, apparently to stabilize the situation and cool things off. Fred Gray, our Montgomery lawyer, reported that he really meant it. According to Fred, Johnson said he would "put Martin Luther King under the jail if he disobeyed the order."

Martin faced a terrible dilemma. If he disobeyed, Johnson would send him to jail. Moreover, Johnson had often ultimately upheld us, and as a consequence had suffered ostracism, vilification, and death threats. To flout his order might alienate him and cost us dearly in the future; I was sure that he would give us an injunction after a full hearing. On the other hand, if Martin did not march, he might be seen as a man who had been absent when John Lewis and Hosea Williams risked death and who was now buckling in the face of a white establishment court order.

Some time during that evening, Martin, Nicholas Katzenbach (who had become attorney general), and I had a conference call in which Katzenbach urged Martin to obey the court order. I told Martin what Fred Gray had told me—that Johnson would put Martin "under the jail," that he almost surely would rule with us, and that marching now in defiance of his order might alienate him. But I didn't tell him not to march. As with other advice, I felt he had to make his decision knowing the legal situation as fully as I could explain it. Martin ended the call by telling Katzenbach that he couldn't understand because he hadn't been a black man in America for the past three hundred years.

Former Florida Governor Leroy Collins, who had commuted Walter Irvin's death sentence and more recently had become head of the Federal Community Relations Service (CRS), became the *deus ex machina* in Selma. At the CRS it was his task to resolve hostile racial confrontations, and the Selma situation certainly had become that. He set out to persuade Martin to engage in a symbolic march, which would satisfy his followers but not alienate Judge Johnson or violate his order. Movement people were wary of Collins, but I knew him for his courageous decision to commute Walter Irvin's death sentence and felt that he could be helpful, even though he had opposed Virgil Hawkins's admission to the University of Florida. Collins worked out an understanding with Martin by which he would cross the bridge, face a cordon of law enforcement officers, and not attempt to continue to Montgomery. Whether the understanding was implicit or explicit was unclear to those who hadn't participated in the discussion. Collins had no doubt that he and Martin made a deal. Indeed, Collins gave Martin a hand-drawn map depicting the march route. Martin later said that he knew it would have been impossible to break through the troopers' lines.

In the early hours of March 9 I had a conference call with Martin and SCLC leaders and advisers Andy Young, Bayard Rustin, Harry Wachtel, and Clarence Jones (Wachtel and Jones were both lawyers close to Martin). The call has been described in my FBI file. We apparently were wiretapped, otherwise I don't know how the information could have been obtained. It was late at night and I lay in bed, not fully awake, in my nightshirt, offering blurred constitutional judgments with possibly historic consequences. A lot of movement business took place in the wee hours of the morning. Martin was terribly depressed and said there was a general feeling of depression in Selma, a feeling that "we are engaged in a kind of federal conspiracy, which in substance says . . . the robber can continue to rob for three more days and we will give you a hearing on whether the robbery was wrong." There was nothing in Johnson's order, he said, that was suggestive of moral principles.

By this time Martin had met with Collins and had agreed not to go beyond the bridge, but he said that his position had changed from what it had been earlier, at 6 P.M., because demonstrations were mounting all over the country. Roy Wilkins had called for federal troops to intervene. Martin apparently didn't want to inhibit the growth of support. Calling off the march might have that effect. Wachtel said that King would be stopped by the police anyway and that he need not fear that the record would show that he acted in contempt of a federal court order. I agreed that the injunction would be held invalid for "twenty different reasons." It became clear that King was going to march, but how far and what he should say about it never was resolved. Wachtel and I agreed to prepare legal documents stating why we thought the injunction against marching was illegal.

On Tuesday, March 9, without making public his arrangement with Collins (if, indeed, in his mind it remained in effect), Martin led fifteen hundred marchers to the bridge, halting briefly en route to hear a federal marshal read Johnson's order, and then crossed the bridge. At the far side, the police, instead of obstructing his path, moved to the roadsides, deliberately causing an embarrassment for Martin, who would not be able to claim that they had physically blocked his path. He was then without an excuse for not continuing the march, which would have placed him in contempt of Johnson's order. (It may be that Alabama police knew from our wiretapped conference call that Martin was counting on being stopped by them.) At the end of the bridge Martin kneeled in prayer, and then directed his followers to turn back. He announced, "We had the greatest demonstration for freedom today that we've ever had in the South." Danny (Barrington) Parker, who was far back in the procession, says no one in the crowd knew what was happening. They marched ahead, stopped, and turned back, baffled. Martin had hit upon a brilliant solution, for while it puzzled both followers and opponents, who had not expected the march to halt in the prayer, it focused world attention on Selma, avoided violence, and did not defy Johnson's injunction.

On Wednesday, March 10, the Justice Department filed papers by which it entered our case. The trial began the following day in Johnson's courtroom in Montgomery, where Johnson, his usual no-nonsense, businesslike self in his typical black suit, no judicial robes, presided over the courtroom sternly, with military crispness. It soon became clear that although we had filed the case in order to enjoin Wallace from preventing the march, for all practical purposes, Martin also was on trial for contempt. True, he hadn't marched from Selma to Montgomery, but had he crossed the bridge in disobedience of the order? Had he attempted to march to Montgomery and been thwarted in that intent by the police? Sheriff Clark and Al Lingo, director of the Alabama Highway Patrol, moved Judge Johnson to find King in contempt. Johnson replied, "Any contempt proceedings will be a matter between the court and the contemnor."

It seemed to me pretty clear that Martin had not been in contempt, but outside the courtroom his leadership was at stake. To avoid a contempt conviction he might have to admit that he had not intended to or had made an agreement not to march, having "betrayed" (a term some critics used) his followers, some of whom were expressing "open contempt" for him. To keep their allegiance he might have to proclaim he had intended to march, but was frustrated by the police. He couldn't slide past the issue. Someone was bound to ask him.

I opened the trial by calling Martin as our witness to elicit evidence about the proposed march. We thought that first he should put on the record what he meant by nonviolence. Martin testified: "One must have the inner determination to resist what conscience tells him is evil with all of the strength and courage and zeal that he can muster; at the same time he must not resort to violence or hatred in the process . . . never coming to the point of retaliating with violence." On cross-examination he said that "there are times that laws can be unjust and that a moral man has no alternative but to disobey that law, but he must be willing to do it openly, cheerfully, lovingly, civilly and not uncivilly, and with a willingness to accept the penalty."

Sheriff Clark's lawyer was so antagonistic to Martin that I objected that his manner was insulting. Johnson sustained the objection: "All witnesses in this court, regardless of who they are, are to be interrogated with common courtesy." The lawyer responded that he was trying and Johnson retorted, "Make a little better effort."

Still under cross-examination, Martin testified that Johnson's order distressed him, that the pent-up emotion of blacks was so intense that, had he not offered a constructive outlet, it would have erupted in violence. He testified that Collins had shown him a map of the area of the bridge with a line on it and had proposed that he not march beyond the line. Martin said Collins had said, "I think things will work out all right."

Judge Johnson then questioned Martin intensively. Martin walked a narrow line in his responses.

JOHNSON: Is it correct to say that when you started across the bridge, you knew at that time that you did not intend to march to Montgomery?

KING: Yes it is. There was a tacit agreement *at* [italics supplied] the bridge that we would go no further.

Nevertheless, this testimony left Martin's critics unsatisfied and some of his supporters unhappy. The next day I received a phone call from Clarence Jones, one of Martin's confidants. An FBI wiretap recorded it. Jones was distressed by the *New York Times* story "which gave the impression of an agreement more than anything else," that "while King was telling everyone that he was going to march he knew he was not and that the whole thing was staged." I told Jones that I had not elicited testimony on the subject, that it had been given on cross-examination, that I had objected to use of the term "agreement," that Martin "said definitely that there was no agreement, just . . . said what he was going to do and informed Collins of what he was going to do." I added that Martin was not unhappy about his testimony, and that he had done well.

Another wiretap, of David Lubell, a lawyer with some connection with Martin, reports that he called his wife to say that "Clarence [Jones] is very upset—because King testified wrongly—made it look like there was a deal with the Government—after Clarence had prepared him for his testimony—added that all Jack Greenberg was interested in was winning the case—thinks King did himself a lot of harm."

Further testimony detailed police violence against the marchers on the first effort to cross the bridge. Most telling were films of the event, which resembled a battle scene, with bombs, smoke, and widespread mayhem. One black witness testified that he had fled home to escape the violence, but that Sheriff Clark gave a deputy a tear gas bomb, which the deputy hurled through the window. At this point, a member of the state's team turned to Clark and could be overheard saying, "Damn, Jim that was my [rental] property."

For lawyers, a memorable exchange took place when a defense lawyer violated an axiom of cross-examination by asking a question to which he did not know the answer. He asked Hosea Williams what he meant by "police brutality." Williams launched into a long description of every wrong committed by authorities at the Edmund Pettus Bridge. To our astonishment, a recently appointed FBI agent testified that he thought Governor Wallace's ban was justified. John Doar, visibly disturbed, tried to get him to qualify what he had said. Johnson told Doar not to bother, he wasn't going to pay much attention to a "six months old FBI agent."

On Saturday, March 13, while the trial was going on, President Lyndon Johnson held a news conference at which he called for enacting a national voting rights law, and on Monday evening, March 15, he delivered an address to a joint session of Congress calling for its enactment, concluding his speech with "We shall overcome."

The state's case was that if King were to march from Selma to Montgomery, whites would attack the marchers and that the march would interfere with traffic. On Monday, Judge Johnson announced that he wanted to see a detailed plan of precisely what the marchers proposed to do, the numbers, the route, time of commencing and completion, where they would spend the nights, plans for food, sanitation, security, and so forth. Jim Nabrit and I undertook to write the plan. It wasn't easy. We had to consult the leaders, who hadn't thought it all through, hadn't made detailed arrangements, and were moving around so fast that they were hard to find.

Jim and I, holed up in my motel room, sat on the floor with a yellow pad, and began writing the plan. Regularly, we had to chase down Andy Young, John Lewis, Hosea Williams, or some other King deputy to fill in details. Others wandered in and out. We started by inquiring of Hosea, who was in charge of logistics. He replied, "I am the logician," but was of little help. I asked how many portable toilets he would need, but he really didn't respond, even after I quipped that he might be singing "We shall overflow." We mostly made it up, writing that the march would begin on Friday, March 19, and, not being entirely sure, added "or any day thereafter." We would in any event give notice before the march began. We proposed no limitation on the number of marchers within Selma and Montgomery, and along the four-lane highway, but where it narrowed to two lanes the number would be no more than three hundred. We set forth how many miles would be marched each day and that tents would be set up by professionals at night in designated fields. At night at the campground there might be singing. Marchers would walk along the shoulders, facing traffic, in groups of no more than fifty, each under a leader. We would provide food, truckborne washing and toilet equipment, litter and garbage pickup, and first aid.

Jim and I had set out to quantify things, but no one had much idea of numbers, so we used many generalities. At the completion of the march we would hold a mass meeting in front of the capitol. Not more than twenty persons would enter the capitol to seek an audience with the governor. When it was all over we would provide transportation away from the scene. We tried to be entirely reasonable. We even volunteered to keep off the grass in front of the capitol. We thought that was the kind of order Johnson wanted and it was fine with Martin and Andy. We finished in the early hours of the morning and took our draft over to Fred Gray's office to be typed.

Then, with a group of friends, I went to the noisy, smoke-filled Club Lagos, created in days when blacks couldn't go to white places of entertainment, for a couple of drinks, and took in an outrageously filthy show by Red Foxx. The morning of Tuesday, March 16, we submitted the plan to Johnson. The trial came to an end at lunchtime. Johnson, with his usual brisk efficiency, announced he would sign an order the next day. The *New York Times* wrote that if he were to incorporate the plan in his order, "the protest may take on the appearance of a Biblical wandering."

Wallace applied to Johnson for a stay—a futile gesture. Then he went to the court of appeals in New Orleans. He lost again. But we had to prepare opposition papers, and Jim and I flew to New Orleans to oppose Wallace's motions. We had so many cases in the Fifth Circuit that I was appearing there more often than any lawyer who lived in New Orleans.

LDF lawyers developed friendly working relationships with the staff of the clerk's office, invaluable when it came to filing, scheduling, getting in to see a judge, and so forth. The clerks kidded with us about the composition of the three-judge panels that ordinarily heard cases. The identity of the judges would never be revealed until the morning of argument. At that time we would ask anxiously who would be on the panel. Gil Ganucheau, chief deputy clerk, sometimes would respond by designating various combinations as the Red Team, the White Team, the Go Team, and the Chinese Bandits, names of LSU football squads. No one can recall which judges made up which squads, but it didn't matter.

President Johnson asked Governor Wallace to provide security for the marchers, but he refused, saying the state couldn't afford it. The president then nationalized the Alabama National Guard, and under its protection the march proceeded as we had planned.

Martin Luther King, Jr., led a glorious procession of people who had come from all over America, including ordinary citizens and national leaders. Celebrities of television, stage, and screen joined them. But nothing we did would have prevented Klansmen from murdering Viola Liuzzo as she drove to Montgomery after having participated in the march. She was one of those ordinary citizens, a mother who had come from Detroit just to join in affirming equal rights for all Americans, and her selfless act was answered by the ultimate act of violence, the taking of another's life.

In August, as a tangible response to the Selma march, President Johnson signed the Voting Rights Act of 1965. While it reiterated the prohibition of discrimination in voting, its innovative provisions were procedural: Ever since the Fourteenth and Fifteenth Amendments blacks had the right to vote, but it was difficult or impossible for them to take advantage of this right in the face of violence, evasion, frequent rule changes, and other artifices. Under the new law, federal registrars were empowered to register voters where local officials wouldn't. The Voting Rights Act opened the franchise to blacks in the South and some parts of the North (including some counties in New York, because they fell within a formula crafted to target most of the South). In districts where there had been a literacy test and registrations or voting had been low (indications of racial discrimination in voting) any changes in voting regulations had first to be approved by the attorney general of the United States or the federal district court in Washington, D.C. Even where it didn't apply or was not enforced, the act inspired and encouraged the black vote. In the years following the passage of the act, forty black members of Congress, black mayors in virtually every major city in the country, a black governor, and thousands of black elected officials have taken office and changed the face of Southern and national politics.

PART V

THE ERA OF THE CIVIL RIGHTS ACT

27

LDF GROWS AS AN INSTITUTION

THURGOOD BECOMES SOLICITOR GENERAL

When Thurgood was sitting on the Second Circuit Court of Appeals, he would sometimes come up to Columbus Circle for lunch. Jim Nabrit, Thurgood, and I would go to Whyte's on Fifty-seventh Street for seafood and then back to the office, where Thurgood would sit on a table in the library and regale the staff with war stories. Sometimes I would go downtown to see him at the courthouse at Foley Square, where the Second Circuit sat. We would shoot the breeze and then go out to lunch. On one such visit in July 1965, he told me that Lyndon Johnson had called him and asked if he would leave the court of appeals to become solicitor general. This posed a problem for someone with a family: He would be giving up life tenure on the court of appeals and taking a substantial cut in pay. But, the president had added, "This won't be the end of the road." The president wasn't promising anything, but still . . .

Thurgood accepted Johnson's offer. The solicitor general's job was to represent the government in the Supreme Court, and when we had LDF cases there we sometimes saw Thurgood argue cases in the traditional morning coat and striped trousers. The cases usually were of a conventional, non–civil rights variety, which could not be invested with the feeling and familiarity with which he used to argue our cases. He presented them in a more businesslike manner. President Johnson was true to his word—it wasn't the end of the road. In 1967 Johnson nominated Thurgood to the Supreme Court, where, after a bruising confirmation process, in which racism once more reared its ugly head, he began sitting that fall, the first black Supreme Court justice.

STAFF AND DOCKET ZOOM

Following the passage of the Civil Rights Acts, the LDF docket swelled and changed radically in content. Because the public accommodations part of the law was so effective, sit-in and related cases gradually phased out, as did defense of demonstrators, and within a decade there remained only one, involving a Mississippi doctor's office. About half of the new mix of cases involved schools. A major campaign to enforce Title VII, the equal employment sections of the 1964 act, soon became a major part of LDF work. There were smaller dockets of voting and housing cases.

Because it soon became apparent that black poverty was inextricably wound up with classic civil rights issues, we filed cases involving fairness and equality in welfare, issues of equalizing rich and poor parts of towns, and treatment of the poorest consumers by the law. In the criminal law side of that initiative we mounted the modern campaign against capital punishment. We handled cases of prisoners' rights, poor people who couldn't obtain bail, and jury discrimination. Many of the poverty issues were the same for groups other than blacks, and we began to represent Hispanics, Native Americans, and poor whites.

By the mid-1960s the LDF staff had grown to seventeen lawyers, who worked with about two hundred cooperating lawyers. We took additional space at 10 Columbus Circle. In 1964 Connie was elected to the New York State Senate and began spending a great deal of her time there. At the end of March 1965 the New York City Council elected Connie borough president of Manhattan, and she took a leave of absence. Connie never had a chance to return from that leave because, in 1966, Lyndon Johnson appointed her United States district judge for the Southern District of New York, where she later became chief judge. Jim Nabrit succeeded her as associate counsel of LDF.

Staff lawyers started at $7,200 per year; two years out of school they got $8,200, a salary that, in those days, constituted no great financial sacrifice at the outset of a legal career. But those who stayed in civil rights forfeited the big incomes many young lawyers looked forward to as they qualified for partnerships in private practice. My salary in 1964 was $27,500. LDF started a pension plan, a sign that we were in the struggle for the long pull.

As 1970 began, we had a total of twenty-eight staff lawyers, including interns, and, by 1975, our case load was over seven hundred. That wasn't as daunting as the number might indicate. Each case was handled with one or more cooperating lawyers and many school cases were only being monitored. In many capital cases we did little more than furnish prepared materials and consult with local counsel. Tony Amsterdam alone amounted to a corps of lawyers working on the death penalty. Legal research was shortcut because staff lawyers knew the law like the back of their hands. It was often easier to step into a colleague's office and ask where the law stood on some issue than to go to the library and look it up.

While the financial rewards for the bright men and women of LDF were not very lavish, the professional opportunities were a different matter. Lawyers one and two years out of school (sometimes even less) were trying cases and arguing in the courts of appeals. Those who were three years out (the minimum required by the rules) sometimes argued in the United States Supreme Court. Occasionally I made a motion for special admission for a lawyer who had not yet been a member of the bar for three years but who had handled a case from the very beginning or otherwise deserved the special recognition of arguing in the Supreme Court.

FINANCES ZOOM TOO

LDF income was $586,421 at the end of 1961, the year I became chief counsel, and grew to $636,000 in 1962, but the curve soon rose more rapidly. By August 1963, in less than two years, LDF income had almost doubled, to $925,000. In 1964 income was $1.5 million; in 1965, over $1.7 million, nearly tripling in five years. By 1970, annual income reached somewhat over $3 million.

Fund-raising events, held at large New York hotels on the anniversary of *Brown*, were regularly successful. On one occasion, with Earl Warren as the principal speaker, we attracted 2,500 guests. I treated myself to picking him up, introducing him, and delivering him back to the airport. On the ride into the city, he told my wife, Debby, and me that the thing he regretted most in his career was having taken part in the internment of the Japanese Americans during the Second World War when he was governor of California. Artur Rubinstein continued to give annual concerts to benefit LDF.

By the end of 1975, annual income was almost $4.3 million. As the 1970s ended, it continued to grow, reaching $6.3 million in 1980.

From the beginning, skillful fund-raising exploited the opportunities. In September 1962 Grenville Clark proposed setting up the Fund for Equal Justice Under Law to raise $2.5 million over a period of ten years (Clark himself pledged $500,000). Like the earlier Grenville Clark plan, his Fund for Equal Justice Under Law brought in new contributors and ratcheted up the level of giving. The Committee of 100 increased mailings, soliciting contributions for the most newsworthy cases. One LDF ad, appearing in the *New York Times* and prepared by the large advertising agency Doyle Dane Bernbach (Maxwell Dane was an enthusiastic LDF supporter) showed a black man throwing a Molotov cocktail and warned, prophetically, that if there were no racial justice, cities would burn. It brought in some money, but stirred immense controversy. In 1963 three ads in the *Times* cost $19,000, raised $33,000, and added many new names to our list. None of the other ads, including some in the black press, brought in very much. One, in *Esquire*, raised absolutely nothing. By 1965, the Committee of 100 had 45,000 individual contributors.

We got one bequest of over a million dollars, from Margaret Abel, whom none of us knew. From Alabama, with no immediate family and on the outs with those relatives she had, she originally left her estate to her dog, Peanuts. When her Wall Street law firm advised that the bequest might be upset by relatives, she left it to LDF. The family contested the will, but ultimately we settled, keeping almost all of the bequest.

We started fund-raising committees in Washington, D.C., Boston, Chicago, Los Angeles, and San Francisco. We tried to establish one in Detroit but failed because NAACP officials, including Walter Reuther, an Association board member and president of the United Auto Workers Union, urged a boycott of us. It was outrageous, but there was no point in fighting it, so we abandoned that effort. We organized a committee of black businessmen, headed by Asa Spaulding, a North Carolina banker, and Percy Julian, an Illinois scientist. We set up another group of black athletes— baseball player Maury Wills, basketball star Bill Russell, and football players Gayle Sayers and Buddy Young. Both committees were supposed to raise funds, but sputtered a while and died. Spaulding and Julian continued to contribute individually, as did a few others, including A. G. Gaston. I valued the contributions of black organizations above their monetary worth because the support of the black community showed that our program was on the right track.

FOUNDATIONS

LDF tried breaking into the foundation world, but the really big ones weren't interested. Right after succeeding Thurgood I visited Stephen Currier, who headed the Taconic Foundation, at their offices on Fifth Avenue, where Stephen brought his large white dog to work daily. Stephen was thirty-one years old, already balding, and somewhat resembling Adlai Stevenson, although with a thinner nose. His wife, Audrey, the daughter of David K. E. Bruce and Ailsa Mellon Bruce (whose father was Andrew W. Mellon), was an only child and heiress to one of America's greatest fortunes. Advised by Lloyd Garrison, Bill DeWind, and John Simon (Stephen's contemporary and friend and now a law professor at Yale), and by the Paul, Weiss law firm, Stephen and Audrey had, in 1958, formed the Taconic Foundation, which had some interest in child welfare and mental health, but which concentrated on civil rights.

In 1961 Taconic pledged LDF $75,000 to be paid over three years. Stephen promised that he would give more if we were to run a deficit, but we didn't. More important, in mid-1963, when an assassin murdered Medgar Evers in Jackson and bombs went off in Birmingham, Stephen held a fund-raising breakfast for the principal civil rights organizations at the Carlyle, one of New York's most elegant hotels, inviting people to whom we would not otherwise have had access. The event was attended by wealthy people we had never seen before, and others who represented corporations and foundations; the goal was to raise $1.5 million. Nothing of this sort ever had come out of the "establishment." Heads of civil rights organizations took turns at the podium and explained the situation of black people to a group who, until then, had been largely oblivious to the problems.

Soon afterward, with Stephen, we formed two organizations, the Council for United Civil Rights Leadership (CUCRL), to lobby and propagandize on civil rights issues, and the Committee for Welfare, Education, and Legal Defense (WELD), which would not lobby and, therefore, would be tax-exempt. The members groups included LDF, the NAACP, the National Urban League, the National Council of Negro Women, SCLC, CORE, the Southern Regional Council, the Voter Education Project, and SNCC—tax-exempt organizations in WELD and the others in CUCRL. Many viewed SNCC warily because it competed with them for membership and financial support, was irreverent, and often acted erratically. I was its main advocate, on the grounds that we had to embrace the students, who had always been one of the principal engines of activity in the South. Wiley Branton became the part-time executive director of the two new organizations and had an office in the LDF offices.

From the outset it was an uneasy alliance. The NAACP and the Urban League were in the consortium reluctantly, because they were loath to share their leadership with newcomers. Seemingly small things were irritating. For example, at an October 1961 NAACP board meeting devoted in large part to "Cooperation with Other Organizations," Roy Wilkins enunciated a list of problems with SCLC and SNCC: SCLC had published a leaflet that looked like one put out by the Association; set up an annual meeting program to resemble the NAACP annual conventions; used a membership envelope modeled on the Association's; published its constitution in a blue book, as did the NAACP; and in Mississippi SNCC "involve[d] our personnel, time and money on projects that we have not approved, discussed or agreed upon." SNCC had "little structure, no authority, no assets and no bank account. . . . They have no formal affiliation with the SCLC although they seem to be a working part of the SCLC. They have offices across the hall from the SCLC in the same building in Atlanta."

The Association also felt threatened by Taconic's proposal to foster cooperative voter registration efforts. Its minutes report that staff opinion objected to the "implication of equality of status of the NAACP with other groups, not one of which has anything which remotely approaches the voter-registration program of the Association."

At one CUCRL-WELD meeting, while SNCC's leader, James Forman, was out of the room, Roy asked, "Who are these people? . . . What are they doing? . . . What do they amount to?" At the same time, members and leaders of outfits like CORE, SCLC, and SNCC disparaged the NAACP as old-timers who did not expose themselves to personal danger and weighed consequences too carefully before acting. When Roy was arrested in May 1963 at a demonstration in Jackson, some of the others thought that it was his response to imputations of too-great caution. The clash of cultures was caricatured when Forman dumped a pile of laundry into the arms of Stephen's bewildered chauffeur, who had come to pick him up at the airport.

But, despite the infighting and politicking, the consortium did manage to get some important things done. On November 19, 1964, Dorothy Height, A. Philip Randolph, Roy, Whitney Young, and I met with Lyndon Johnson in the Oval Office to discuss civil rights appointments, regulations, legislation, and black participation in Democratic party affairs. As we left, Johnson asked whether I had any particular needs. I told him that we had real problems with Kennedy judicial appointments and that federal judges like Cox, West, Elliott, and Thomas stood in the way of achieving full civil rights. I suggested that before he made any judicial appointments in the South he ask for our views. He stepped close, gripped me firmly by the arms, and said that he would. And he did. Regularly the FBI would call and ask for my views on names under consideration for judicial appointment. I would check them out and report back. My name must have become inscribed on a list, because the practice continued for many years, into the Nixon administration and beyond.

In 1965 Hubert Humphrey invited the CUCRL-WELD group on a dinner cruise down the Potomac aboard the vice-presidential yacht. I went with Martin Luther King, Jr., Andy Young, Clarence Mitchell, Floyd McKissick, Whitney Young, Stephen Currier, Wiley Branton, who at the time had become Vice President Humphrey's assistant for civil rights, and several others. It was a lovely cruise with plenty to eat and drink and was, of course, intended to win the allegiance of the civil rights community. But it soon broke down terribly. The leaders began complaining about the slow pace of voting rights enforcement. Wiley tried to reassure the group. Clarence Mitchell exploded, referring to Wiley as an apologist for the administration. The evening disintegrated into loud recriminations.

An impasse loomed over how monies raised by the various members of the consortium would be divided. Finally, at the meeting where we made the first allocations, Whitney wrote some numbers on the back of an envelope, passed it around, and everyone agreed. The total for the WELD group was $200,000, half of which had been given by the Field Foundation. It gave LDF $60,000, the National Urban League $60,000, and the National Council of Negro Women $30,000. WELD never raised much more. CUCRL (to which the non–tax-exempt NAACP looked for its share) raised very little, although Martin Luther King, Jr., assigned to WELD royalties from his "I Have a Dream" recording. But the effort cannot be described as a failure because it introduced us to new audiences and raised the level of giving.

Tragedy struck the Curriers, who tried so hard to do so much for others less fortunate than themselves. In January 1967, a small plane carrying Stephen and Audrey between San Juan and St. Thomas disappeared. President Johnson called out the navy, which patrolled the area but found nothing. The Coast Guard concluded that the plane had been flying at about 800 to 900 feet above the water to save fuel, when unexpected tropical turbulence struck. The Currier's pilot probably was so badly battered that he became disoriented and hit the water, rupturing the plane's skin and causing it to sink without a trace.

ENTER THE FORD FOUNDATION

Around the beginning of 1963 Bill Pincus, a program officer at the Ford Foundation, called me. I didn't know him. He had come to Ford in 1957, a child of the Depression, as he described himself, and was dissatisfied with Ford's failure to contribute to social welfare causes, such as legal aid for the indigent. The foundation had given money earlier to the Fund for the Republic, which it established to advance social programs, but two Fords then on the foundation's board thought the Fund was too radical, and Henry Heald, the foundation's president, was determined to rid the foundation of that image. Heald directed the foundation's enormous annual giving mainly to universities, in the form of $5 million to $10 million block grants. I visited Pincus, who suggested that I call Heald, ask for an appointment, and bring with me other civil rights leaders. Heald was quite accessible and gave me an appointment. He told me not to bring a large group.

On February 6, 1963, in the company of three others—Martin Luther King, Jr., Leslie Dunbar, who was the director of the Southern Regional Council, and Wiley Branton, director of the Voter Education Project—I called on Heald. His first words were a bit startling: "I thought I told you not to come with a large delegation." I explained to Heald that I wanted him to understand the civil rights movement from a variety of perspectives. We discussed with him and two other Ford officers the situation of American blacks and why we needed help to make a peaceful transition from a segregated society. Martin was magnificent. As gifted an orator as he was before a mass audience, he was even more persuasive in conversation across a table. He employed none of the preacher's rhetoric, but marshaled facts and arguments in a rational and nonemotional manner that would have done an appellate lawyer proud.

We had some impact. Perhaps because of this meeting, Ford directed one of its university grants to Howard University; not exactly civil rights, but a step in the right direction. Subsequently, I met with Pincus and Ford staff members and began discussing creation of the National Office for the Rights of the Indigent (NORI) as an LDF subsidiary. NORI wouldn't have the image of a controversial, black civil rights organization. It would attempt to aid the poor in much the same way we were making law on behalf of blacks. If blacks benefited disproportionately from its programs, it would only be because blacks in America made up a disproportionate percentage of the poor, and Ford would be spared having to make grants to the contentious civil rights movement.

At the end of 1965, with staff lawyers, principally Leroy Clark, I developed a program for NORI. One of its main tasks would be to coordinate the work of government legal services offices, which were just then coming into being. It also would try to make law that would help poor people through the courts. But it took several years to get the Ford grant, because there was a conflict within Ford's staff. One group, led by Pincus, wanted to fund an LDF-type model, which would develop precedents. Others wanted to create a community service model, which would serve the interests of individuals, without regard to legal development. Ultimately the Pincus group won. But by the time Ford made the million-dollar grant, McGeorge Bundy had replaced Henry Heald as the Ford Foundation's president. The initial check was made out to LDF and later installments were supposed to be paid to NORI. However, with Heald's reluctance to fund civil rights organizations no longer a factor, we allowed NORI to fade away as a formal organization, and the entire grant went to LDF.

THE BOARD BECOMES MORE INFLUENTIAL

In January 1965 Allan Knight Chalmers resigned as president of LDF and chairman of the Committee of 100. The LDF board elected Francis Rivers president and Bill Coleman vice president. Paul Moore, a friend since the time of the *Groveland* case and by this time suffragan bishop of Washington, D.C., became chairman of the Committee of 100. The board continued to attract members of influence, including Cyrus Vance and Andrew Young, who would become Carter cabinet members; Bernard Segal, former president of the American Bar Association; and Charles Hamilton, a well-known political scientist. Even those less well known were nevertheless important and influential members of their communities. In 1971 Judge Rivers resigned as president, but stayed on the board; Bill Coleman became president and Lou Pollak vice president. When Gerald Ford appointed Bill as secretary of transportation in 1975 he resigned from LDF's presidency, although he remained on the board; Julius Chambers became president.

The board was effective and influential, many of the relationships became personal as well as organizational. But, on the other hand, I sometimes wondered how such an elite group, wherein the members were so similar to one another, could hope to determine the best interests of the black community. We hardly could be said to represent a cross-section of that population—no one set of interests could ever have been best for everyone in so large and diverse a community. Still, we couldn't hold a plebiscite, any more than Charles Houston and Thurgood did, or CORE or SNCC could. Ideally, the NAACP would have been our link to the black population at large, although it too may have represented only one part of the continuum of black opinion. It certainly did not represent separatists, nor many militants, and even within the Association there were divisions. But all this didn't matter, for the Association had distanced itself from us and we from it. There was no perfect answer. I tried to deal with the problem by forming the Division of Legal Information and Community Services, but in the end we had nothing to go on but our own best judgment on where right lay, assuming that where one racial group has been so badly deprived of equal justice, serving justice, even only as we saw it, would inevitably serve the interests of the entire group.

One way in which board members helped was to give dinners to raise funds, as Chauncey Waddell did in his elegant Beekman Place apartment overlooking the East River. He decided to cancel one event because the caterer's price was too high—$65 per person—and to give the cost of the dinner to famine relief in Bangladesh. He wouldn't hire a less expensive caterer because his housekeeper didn't allow any other in her kitchen. Rather than lose the funds we would have raised, I volunteered to cook the dinner, for which I prepared a New Orleans gumbo of chicken, sausage, shrimp, oysters, and crabmeat. Staff lawyers waited tables. It was a great success and we repeated the event for several years until the lawyers, not sharing my idea of what constituted a fun evening, revolted. Many had worked their way through college and law school waiting tables and some at least had promised themselves that once they passed the bar they'd never wait another table. The short-lived tradition of home-cooked fund-raising dinners came to an end.

BIG BUSINESS ENTERS THE SCENE

Corporate CEOs like Lee Iacocca, then at Ford Motor Company, and John Filer of Aetna, who had headed a national commission on philanthropy, used their board connections to lead fund-raising efforts; Robert Kutak, chair of an ABA commission on professional responsibility, helped raise funds for law school scholarships. Growing acceptance from this part of the world made me nervous about the ethics of possibly opposing a contributing corporation or lawyer, and I proposed that the board draw up guidelines to deal with conflicts of interest that might perhaps come up. It concluded, however, that we didn't need a general policy and decided to proceed case by case. The issue never arose.

Thousands of individuals contributed through the mail in modest amounts, and a fair number gave substantial sums, sometimes in response to personal solicitation. The Prince Hall Masons continued to give, as did the Shriners, who donated $35,000 in 1978, presenting checks on celebratory occasions, dressed up in red fezes as flashbulbs popped. Dr. C. B. Powell, a black physician and businessman, who owned the *Amsterdam News* and was a member of our board, left a $50,000 legacy to LDF upon his death.

One important new factor generating income after 1968 was the High Court decision in *Newman v. Piggie Park*. An owner of a drive-in restaurant had argued that the Civil Rights Act contravened the will of God and interfered with his freedom of religion. The South Carolina district judge hearing the case ruled with him on another ground, that the Civil Rights Act didn't cover drive-in restaurants. The court of appeals reversed, holding as well that under the 1964 Civil Rights Act the defendant should pay counsel fees to plaintiff's lawyers to the extent that its defenses had been advanced for purposes of delay and not in good faith. We thought that standard too permissive of frivolous defenses, petitioned for review, and got it.

Maurice Bessinger, Piggie Park's principal stockholder, announced that he personally would represent the defendant and argue the case, apparently believing that the publicity might get him elected governor of South Carolina, as Lester Maddox had been elected governor of Georgia after he used a pick handle in a vain attempt to keep the doors to his Pickrick restaurant in Atlanta closed to blacks and the twentieth century. The Court denied permission. Bessinger wasn't a lawyer and so was not entitled to argue before the Supreme Court. Further, he couldn't claim the right to be his own lawyer because the defendant was the restaurant corporation, not any of its stockholders.

Bessinger insisted that he was going to argue anyway and showed up in the spectator section in the courtroom. A blue serge–suited marshal stationed himself near Bessinger, poised like a defensive lineman, ready to charge, should Bessinger make a false move. Bessinger sat silently, and I argued alone. After the argument he held a press conference on the steps of the Court. The decision in *Piggie Park* held that civil rights plaintiffs who win a case "should ordinarily recover an attorney's fee unless special circumstances would render such an award unjust." Bessinger was never elected governor.

Counsel fees have grown to be about 20 percent of LDF's income, regularly exceeding a million dollars annually; they are now a substantial part of the income of other public interest organizations. That defendants would have to pay counsel fees provided incentive in settling cases and bringing about compliance. It also led to wrangles with a few cooperating lawyers about how to split up the money. It's funny, and dispiriting too, how a little cash on the table can excite differences between the best of friends. After a while we knew the handful of lawyers who would be difficult about dividing counsel fees. The best tactic usually was to wait a long while before coming to an agreement. When they needed the money badly their disposition to agree improved.

In 1980 we applied to enter the Combined Federal Campaign (CFC), a fund-raising arrangement in which government workers contribute to charities by agreeing to have money withheld from their paychecks. But CFC excluded us, mainly to preserve this lucrative charitable market for those already in it. We sued the government to open CFC to new groups like LDF and won the case in 1981, but, following protests by some groups in the CFC who were unhappy with admitting new organizations (objecting mainly to Planned Parenthood), new government regulations excluded us once more in 1983. We sued again, all the way to the Supreme Court, where we lost. After further litigation, however, Congress ultimately rescued us by passing a law, for which our Washington office lobbied, prohibiting the exclusionary regulations. Since 1981 LDF has raised over $5 million from the CFC.

THE EARL WARREN LEGAL TRAINING PROGRAM

In October 1962 I started the internship (later called fellowship) program to alleviate the shortage of Southern black lawyers with a Field Foundation grant of $25,000. Creating our own lawyer cadre provided a bonus by under-cutting early NAACP attempts to prohibit its branch-affiliated lawyers from associating with LDF. There never was any acquiescence to those out-rageous demands, but LDF interns/fellows developed a particular attach-ment to LDF and were deaf to pleas that they not work with us. Under the program we hired recent graduates to work for about a year in our office, following which they commenced practice in the South in areas where there weren't many black lawyers. For three years we paid a diminishing subsidy and about $1,000 (for books, typewriter, sometimes a rug or other office furnishings or equipment). We expected that the interns would be black but didn't exclude whites. Occasionally a black intern asked us to select a white who would join him or her and a few whites went into inte-grated firms in the South. Interns/fellows handled cases, became commu-nity leaders, and developed black business, political, and other institutions.

Many LDF interns turned out to be stars. Marian Wright and Julius Chambers were the first two. Chambers was the son of a North Carolina auto mechanic whose father had sent his older brother and sister to board-ing school, but couldn't make the tuition payment for Julius because a white trucker wouldn't pay his repair bill and Julius's father couldn't find a lawyer to bring suit. Julius went to black public schools near home, and vowed to become a lawyer who would provide services for blacks like his father. He went to college at black North Carolina Central in Durham. At the University of Michigan, where he got a master's degree in history, he wanted to enroll in the law school, but it accepted only one black per year and already had accepted one, Amalya Kearse (now a judge of the United States Court of Appeals for the Second Circuit). The admissions officer suggested Southern black schools, but Julius went home to the University of North Carolina. The dean, Henry Brandis, who became his good friend, advised that Julius should study, work hard, and stay out of social or political activities. Julius followed this advice and graduated in 1962 as editor-in-chief of the law review.

Walter Gellhorn heard about Julius, invited him to Columbia as a teaching associate and to get an LL.M. (a masters degree in the law), and brought him to my attention. I suggested that he join LDF as an intern and later return to North Carolina to practice. After a year at LDF Julius opened an office in Charlotte. We paid him $12,000 for the first year following his move south, $6,000 for the second, and $2,500 for the third.

Once, in reprisal for having sued to integrate a restaurant, the Klan bombed his car and the funeral home owned by one of his clients. Following his suit to compel the Shriners to include a black high school in a football tournament, his house was bombed. Because he was the lawyer for plaintiffs in the Charlotte school case, racists firebombed and destroyed his office. We raised funds to replace the office. Ultimately his firm, an integrated one, expanded to twelve lawyers. Julius became one of the leading lawyers in North Carolina and later a member of the state board of regents. In 1984, when I left LDF, he succeeded me as director-counsel.

The internship program evolved into the Earl Warren Legal Training Program (EWLTP), which we established in 1971 with $1.6 million in grants from the Carnegie and Rockefeller foundations, with indications that they would give another $400,000 later. EWLTP took the form of a separate educational arm created to attract money from those who would not give to support our abrasive litigation. I made sure that it had a staff and board identical to the LDF—I didn't want problems like those the NAACP had had with us. The money was for scholarships for blacks attending formerly white law schools in former Confederate states, a major expansion of the internship program (which we began to call the fellowship program), and lawyer training. Much of the organizing effort, including enlisting other foundations to contribute, was done by a Carnegie Corporation program officer, Eli Evans, originally from North Carolina, who developed EWLTP with Betty Stebman of the LDF fund-raising staff. For most of its years EWLTP was directed by Butler Henderson, a former teacher of economics and assistant to the president at Morehouse College in Atlanta.

We launched the EWLTP, with Earl Warren as our guest, at a Washington event. Because I didn't want to risk being late, instead of flying I took the train, slower but more reliable. Outside Wilmington the train caught fire and we sat motionless awaiting fire engines. Finally, they arrived and put out the blaze. I arrived at the meeting late, but still in time to thank Earl Warren for his support and to express my admiration.

The University of Maryland wasn't among the schools whose students would receive EWLTP scholarships. The dean of its law school called Eli to complain. Maryland, he said, was a Southern state, and deserved its share. Eli replied in his North Carolina drawl that during the Civil War Maryland hadn't seceded. And he added, "Where were y'all when we needed you?"

The fellowship program no longer exists. The number of black lawyers in the South has increased substantially. Although the shortage continues, the additional number we could afford to fund in comparison to need was no longer large enough to justify the effort and expenditure. But, while the program lasted, it produced almost one hundred fellows who served—and continue to serve—its purpose superbly. Among them are federal and state judges, congressional representatives, other elected officials, law professors, and deans and lawyers in all sorts of practice, many of whom are listed in the afterword to this book.

EWLTP has, however, continued to be a major source of scholarship funding for black law students.

LAW STUDENTS

As Thurgood had, I continued hiring law students during the summers, many of whom later achieved distinction. I helped establish the Law Students Civil Rights Research Council (LSCRRC), which was comprised of black and white law students who took time off from school or after graduation to work in civil rights, and gave it space in our office until it found its own. At the outset I gave LSCRRC a $5,000 start-up contribution and introduced its leaders to the Field and New World foundations, which gave it grants. I hired LSCRRC students at $30 per week to survey capital punishment sentencing patterns in rape cases. Bill Robinson, a black Columbia law student, who later joined our staff (after which he headed the Lawyers Committee for Civil Rights Under Law; he is now dean of the District of Columbia Law School), was an early leader of LSCRRC, as was Howard Slater, a white Yale law student. Hillary Rodham Clinton had a LSCRRC internship in which she worked for Marian Wright Edelman at the Children's Defense Fund (CDF). For many LSCRRC interns their experience was the beginning of a lifelong involvement in civil rights. Hillary Rodham Clinton retained her association with CDF throughout her legal career, ultimately becoming chair of its board.

THE CIVIL RIGHTS LAW INSTITUTES

After I took over, we set up a series of lawyers' conferences: one, dealing with demonstrations, at Howard; another, on Northern cases, at Columbia in March 1962; and a general program for more than eighty lawyers at Howard in February 1963. I asked Bob Ming and Marvin Frankel, my law school classmate and then a professor at Columbia, to establish regular sessions, which the New World and Stern foundations funded. Ming soon dropped out as a leader, busy with other matters. Marvin assembled a faculty that included Ming, Tony Amsterdam, Mark DeWolf Howe (of Harvard), Louis Henkin (of Penn and Columbia), Charles Black (Yale), Patricia Roberts Harris (Howard), and Michael Sovern (Columbia). In 1965 Marvin became a United States district judge and Mike Sovern, later dean of Columbia Law School, took over. When Mike became president of Columbia in 1980, Drew Days—who had been an LDF assistant counsel, head of the Justice Department Civil Rights Division in the Carter administration, and then professor of law at Yale—became director of the program. In the Clinton administration Days became solicitor general.

At first the Civil Rights Law Institute held its conferences in Atlanta, Dallas, New Orleans, and Washington, D.C. But in the early 1960s we discovered Airlie House in Warrenton, Virginia, one of the first national conference centers, which had just opened. Inexpensive, it had the added attraction of being the only unsegregated conference center in the South before 1964, apart from black college campuses. There was a certain forbidden pleasure for whites and blacks to confer and dine together in Dixie, served mostly by white waiters—crew-cut soldiers moonlighting from a nearby military base. When other groups or the NAACP tried to set up competing legal operations—as the NAACP did in the mid-1960s—the sense of being an LDF lawyer, in which the Civil Rights Law Institute conferences (simply, "Airlie" to many of the alums) played a powerful part, helped keep the team together.

THE HERBERT LEHMAN EDUCATION FUND

Although we had won cases requiring Southern states to admit blacks to white universities since 1950, and even earlier, relatively few blacks applied. White schools were more expensive and they were also often unfriendly. When Helen Buttenwieser, a member of our board and niece of New York senator and governor Herbert H. Lehman, asked about establishing a memorial to him with an initial gift of $50,000, Connie Motley and I suggested a scholarship fund to make it easier for blacks to attend formerly white segregated colleges; it became the Herbert Lehman Education Fund in 1964 and awarded fifteen scholarships in its first year. In 1965 the Lehman Fund began raising money through the mail and gave forty-six scholarships. Since the late 1970s it has awarded about two hundred each year—3,400 since it was founded—in amounts of $400 to $1,200, the typical grant being $1,000, a substantial part of state college tuition.

WHITHER?

Armed with *Brown* and the Civil Rights Acts, empowered by more money and a bigger staff, we developed a program for the years to come. Between

December 1964 and September 1965 I called a series of meetings with scholars and practicing civil rights lawyers, the classic Houston and Marshall technique. Sitting around the office, hotel rooms, restaurants, and law school classrooms, eating, drinking, joking, moving back and forth among the issues, in formal and informal sessions, we outlined new programs for the next decade, such as the attack on capital punishment, poverty law cases, municipal equalization suits, antitrust suits against realtors, health and welfare cases, civil suits to desegregate juries, and important criminal law initiatives. We continued also with classic cases involving school, voting, housing, and employment discrimination.

But there was a continuing sentiment among some staff members that we should become a general legal resource for militant activists facing criminal charges without regard to whether civil rights issues were involved in their cases. That feeling came to a head in the Angela Davis case. To address these concerns I held what we called the "Whither" conference on March 7 and 8, 1969.

A lot of revolutionary rhetoric filled the air. I thought the time had come to get a realistic consensus on what we should be doing and invited about twenty-five participants, some from the civil rights establishment, but also militants, academics, and foundation executives, and a general audience of others who might be interested to talk about the LDF agenda. The "Whither" conference met in the dark wood-paneled great hall of the Association of the Bar of the City of New York. The setting was grand, but the outcome not so dramatic. We concluded with decisions to set up legislative drafting and community counseling services as ways of addressing matters that lawsuits couldn't reach. LDF continued to evolve pretty much as before.

"Whither" also became a personal question. My marriage to Sema had been falling apart and in 1969 we were divorced. In 1970 I married Deborah Cole, whose husband had died in 1969 in an automobile crash. She had two small children, Billy and Suzanne, whom I adopted. Shad Polier of the LDF board insisted on being our lawyer in the adoption proceedings. Debby had graduated from Columbia Law School and gone to a Wall Street law firm, and I knew her from the Norman Foundation, which she directed and which was one of the earliest foundations to support civil rights causes. She continued at the foundation for several years until the Metropolitan Applied Research Council (MARC), run by Kenneth Clark, granted her a fellowship, which enabled her to retread and become a civil rights litigator at LDF, where she handled employment discrimination cases.

28

EDUCATION FOLLOWING THE DEFEAT
OF "ALL DELIBERATE SPEED"

The Civil Rights Act of 1964 and the Voting Rights Act of 1965 fulfilled almost all the recommendations of Harry Truman's 1947 Committee on Civil Rights; the Fair Housing Act of 1968 achieved its remaining goals. By prohibiting discrimination in public accommodations, travel, employment, and housing, the acts left the state action issue—which had tormented us in the Restrictive Covenant and sit-in cases—virtually meaningless for the lives of black people. Before these acts we had to prove that the state was somehow meaningfully involved in racial discrimination to establish a denial of equal protection of the laws. Afterward, we had to show only that a law had been broken. The Civil Rights Acts had to be interpreted and enforced, but that was different from the much more uncertain task of interpreting and applying the Constitution. Equally important, the new laws enlisted the federal bureaucracy for enforcement. The 1965 law secured voting rights against tactics that had denied them in the past. Discrimination was now prohibited in most spheres of life.

In the new role of putting flesh on the bones of the new laws and implementing them, LDF once more took the lead. Moreover, LDF cases continued to develop constitutional doctrine favorably, even while asking for compliance with new statutes. Some years later a judiciary heavily peopled by Reagan and Bush appointees headed in a different direction, and our task became to fight the efforts to reverse gains of the past.

As to education, in the ten years following *Brown II*, from 1955 to 1965, the number of black students attending school with whites throughout the South increased at the rate of about 1 percent per year. The importance of the federal role became manifest in 1965–66; in the first year of Title VI of the 1964 Civil Rights Act, mandating the Department of Health, Education and Welfare (HEW) to cut off federal funds from schools that discriminated, the percentage of black students in previously all-white schools jumped from 10.9 to 15.9 percent; in border states integrated black students rose to 68.9 percent of the black student population. Even in the states of the old Confederacy, we started to see some progress: Fewer than 1 percent of blacks attended school with whites as late as 1962–63, which rose to only 2.25 percent in 1964–65; in 1965–66 the percentage was 6.01. While there was some dispute about how precise these estimates were, and there was no doubt that area-wide statistics masked some local situations of severe racial imbalance, HEW, operating at wholesale, got more blacks into school with whites than our retail lawsuits. Our litigation, however, set standards that kept HEW honest and helped them resist political pressures to do less, especially after 1969, when Richard Nixon, with his Southern strategy, came on the scene.

A LAST CHANCE FOR FREE CHOICE

Pockets of resistance to the accomplished fact of *Brown* remained among some judges. In June 1963, Judge Frank M. Scarlett heard a group of witnesses in the Savannah school case, including professor emeritus Henry Garrett (who had been Kenneth Clark's professor) of Columbia and Ernest Van den Haag of New York University. At issue was whether *Brown* rested on a conclusion of law—that is, that segregated schools inherently were unequal—or a conclusion of fact—that in the cases before the Supreme Court there was inequality, but other segregated schools might be equal. During the *Brown* argument some of the justices several times asked whether the psychological effects of segregation might be different in districts that were not then before the Court.

Scarlett concluded that desegregation would psychologically harm children of both races in Savannah. Having found that fact, he distinguished his case from *Brown* and decided that segregation was constitutional in Savannah. Connie Motley immediately appealed to the court of appeals, which entered its own desegregation order. Jurisprudentially, this decision was important. It signified that *Brown* didn't rest on particular adjudicative facts, that is, social scientific findings in the group of cases then before the Court, which might or might not apply to other sets of facts in other districts. It rested on a rule of law based on what some legal writers have called "legislative facts," precisely like the facts on which *Plessy* rested when it held that segregation did not stigmatize blacks, and on which *Strauder* rested when it held that exclusion from juries did stigmatize a race of people.

Typically, however, resistance to segregation took the form of pupil placement laws and so-called "freedom of choice"; litigating forever—appealing, appealing, and appealing; requesting time to formulate plans and then time to comply with these plans, with stays of execution while the cases went on. As we fought such tactics in more than one hundred LDF cases through the mid-1960s, the courts began denying stays, requiring that desegregation proceed while the cases were being appealed.

First, courts struck down pupil assignment. When "freedom of choice" replaced it (students might choose any school, but various pressures caused blacks to choose black schools, whites to choose white schools), courts imposed stringent requirements on its exercise, even to the point of prescribing the forms that school boards had to use for transfer applications, times for filing the forms, and other minutiae to prevent onerous procedures from achieving bureaucratically what had been denied the districts legally. John Minor Wisdom of the Fifth Circuit declared, "These cases tax the patience of the Court," and that "the time has come for foot-dragging public school boards to move with celerity toward desegregation."

Wisdom gave free choice a last try in five Fifth Circuit cases from Alabama and Louisiana known as *Jefferson,* in which Jim Nabrit led the argument. Wisdom wrote, "The only school desegregation plan that meets constitutional standards is one that works," and spelled out every conceivable detail of a free choice plan that would make it work—if it ever could. These were among eleven LDF cases argued in eleven days. We immediately reopened school cases throughout the Fifth Circuit with *Jefferson* motions—twenty cases in Alabama, twenty-seven in Florida, six in Georgia, thirty-three in Louisiana, thirty in Mississippi, and five in Texas.

Some Supreme Court language began signaling impatience with the slow pace of desegregation, although the Court didn't order anyone to do anything faster.

THE DIVISION OF LEGAL INFORMATION AND COMMUNITY SERVICES

The cases couldn't happen by themselves. In 1964, we hired a staff member to help local NAACP branches sign up parents to transfer their children to white schools. Eighty parents in Albany, Georgia, fifty in Jackson, and one hundred in Richmond applied. Then, a remarkable new staff member, Jean Fairfax, created the LDF Division of Legal Information and Community Services, which conducted these kinds of projects, along with others across the range of civil rights. Jean came to LDF from the American Friends Service Committee (AFSC), for which she had been doing similar work in Mississippi. After she escorted Debra Lewis, the first black child to integrate the white elementary school in Leake County, I asked her to join LDF for six months; she stayed for two decades. Jean forged new links between LDF and the black community, organizing community groups to demand desegregated education and fair employment, and published influential pamphlets dealing with the school lunch program, busing, treatment of Native Americans, federal policies affecting elementary and high school education, and exclusion of women from private clubs. She became the most influential single staff member in determining the direction we took on such issues as integration of black colleges and which industries we should target in employment cases.

THE DEFEAT OF FREE CHOICE

We struck the final blow against free choice in three Supreme Court cases decided in 1968 that were simple models of why choice didn't work. In rural New Kent County, near Richmond, where one of the cases arose, more than seven hundred blacks and about six hundred whites distributed generally throughout the county attended two schools, one black, the other white. In 1964–65 under pupil placement, there was no desegregation. After we won two cases that knocked out Virginia's pupil placement, the state substituted freedom of choice. Thirty-five blacks began going to the formerly white school, but the black school remained all black and unequal; faculties remained segregated. Assigning students by drawing a line down the middle of the county would have integrated both schools.

In opposing our effort to do away with choice, my opponent's brief in one of the cases made much of the fact that I had written in 1959, in *Race Relations and American Law*, that if "there were complete freedom of choice, or geographical zoning, or any other nonracial standard, and all Negroes still ended up in certain schools, there would seem to be no constitutional objection." I had a reply prepared and at an opportune moment during oral argument delivered it: "I did not know then what I know now. And if I had . . . "

Justice Brennan interrupted with a twinkle in his eye: "You might not have written the book . . . "

I responded, "I would have written it differently."

Justice White went after me on whether to take race into account in drawing zone lines: "Even in a city where there are racial problems . . . you could draw school zone lines based on . . . so-called neutral factors."

I replied: "It is inconceivable to me [that] someone facing the situation to redraw the school zones [would] put the consideration of race out of his head. I have heard children play the game, 'Don't think of an elephant.' That is all they think of . . . an elephant."

The cases ended in a smashing victory in *Green v. New Kent County*. The Court charged school boards with the "affirmative duty" to "convert to a unitary system in which racial discrimination would be eliminated root and branch." Delay was "no longer tolerable."

We then immediately created a major conflict with the new Nixon administration by filing motions across the South calling for school boards promptly to eliminate segregation "root and branch." HEW also had to revise its guidelines to conform with *Green*. But Nixon didn't want to offend his Southern constituency. Leon Panetta, who was in charge of school desegregation at HEW and later became a California congressman and then President Clinton's head of the Office of Management and Budget, pushed to incorporate the latest Supreme Court standards into the HEW guidelines, while the Nixon staff tugged in the opposite direction. The Fifth Circuit then precipitated a crisis by holding that twenty-nine Mississippi districts had to prepare new desegregation plans in consultation with HEW, by August 11, and put them into effect by August 25.

On August 11, 1969, HEW filed plans to integrate thirty Mississippi districts. Senator John Stennis of Mississippi, chair of the Armed Services Committee, retaliated, announcing that constituents were protesting so much that he would have to absent himself from the Senate during consideration of the defense authorization bill. The secretary of HEW, Robert Finch, buckled under White House pressure to delay and wrote to Chief Judge John R. Brown of the Fifth Circuit that he was "gravely concerned that the time allowed for the development of these terminal plans has been much too short." Finch asked that the integration be delayed until December 1, 1969, and sent copies of the letter to the Mississippi district judges.

Nixon's Justice Department asked for the same delay. The Fifth Circuit sent the cases to the district court for hearing on the request. District judges Dan M. Russell, Jr., and Walter L. Nixon, Jr. (no relation to the president), granted the motions and recommended that the court of appeals grant Finch's request. On August 28, the court of appeals put off the requirement to file plans to integrate the Mississippi school districts until December 1. Pre-Nixon Justice Department lawyers revolted, some resigned, others signed protests.

DELIBERATE SPEED REPUDIATED

After the five-plus years of Lyndon Johnson's administration, powerful Southern senators and congressmen once again had a sympathetic ear in the White House. To make matters worse, the Fifth Circuit, until then a bastion of civil rights decency, had yielded to President Nixon. With this turn of events our principal allies, the Fifth Circuit and the White House, had disappeared. I concluded that we had no alternative but to appeal to the Supreme Court immediately. I got the staff together to prepare a petition for expedited review, just as we had in Little Rock, quoting with mock bravado Marshal Foch at the second battle of the Marne: "My center is giving way, my right is in retreat . . . I attack."

In addition to our clients in fourteen Mississippi cases, we intervened in sixteen other cases that the Justice Department had initially tried, but that they hadn't appealed. We wanted to have a say in those cases and not allow Justice to give away the rights of black schoolchildren by putting up less than the best case, and then failing to appeal adverse decisions. First, we filed a motion asking Justice Black to vacate the postponement that the Fifth Circuit had entered. On September 5, he denied the motion, but wrote a stinging opinion rejecting the administration's position, and called for the end of "all deliberate speed." He urged us to appeal right away:

> Deplorable as it is to me, I must uphold the court's order which both sides indicate could have the effect of delaying total desegregation of these schools for as long as a year.
>
> This conclusion does not comport with my ideas of what ought to be done in this case when it comes before the entire Court. I hope these applicants will present the issue to the full Court at the earliest possible opportunity. . . .
>
> In my opinion there is no reason why such a wholesale deprivation of constitutional rights should be tolerated another minute. I feel that this long denial of constitutional rights is due in large part to the phrase "with all deliberate speed." I would do away with that phrase completely.

Then, on September 27, we filed a petition for writ of certiorari and a motion to advance in the Supreme Court. As is customary, I asked the clerk of the Fifth Circuit to send the records in those cases to the Supreme Court. Part of the record, however, was in Judge Harold Cox's court in Mississippi, and his clerk refused to part with it unless we paid fifty cents per page—for thousands of pages. I asked one of our Mississippi lawyers to see Cox himself, but Cox replied only that the price per page just had gone up. I turned to John F. Davis, clerk of the Supreme Court, who called Cox's clerk and ordered him to send up the record. Cox's clerk complied and sent eight big boxes to Washington.

I asked that the Court consider the petition during the Court's first conference of the term, set for October 6, and either grant review and reverse summarily or set an expedited schedule. Ordinarily, the case, *Alexander v. Holmes County Board of Education*, would be heard in December, possibly not till the following year. But the Court acted quickly and set argument for October 23. I asked Louis Oberdorfer, of the Lawyers Committee for Civil Rights Under Law, to take ten minutes of my argument time because I wanted to show that the American legal establishment was on our side.

Instead of facing the friendly Earl Warren, we now had Warren Burger as chief justice. What little was known about him was that he had been chosen because Nixon thought him a fellow conservative. My opponents were Jerris Leonard, Nixon's chief of the Civil Rights Division, and the tiptoeing

John Satterfield of Yazoo City, who had been banished from the courtroom in *Meredith*.

The morning of argument I opened my suitcase and discovered that I had forgotten to pack a shirt, rushed out to search for a store, bought one, and dashed off to court.

My only argument was that defendants should integrate immediately. Litigation over schedule, districting, busing, and other details should take place while the schools were integrated in some fashion, and not, as was done in the past, while schools remained segregated. Districts that had swapped "segregation forever" for "litigation forever" then could litigate to their hearts' content, but "I doubt[ed] that there would be the incentive." Leonard argued that it would take time to work out administrative problems, but Justice Black, picking up on my argument, replied, "Why not put [the plan] into effect and make arrangements afterward?" Leonard had no satisfactory answer. Satterfield tried to make something of segregated schools in the North; the Court wasn't interested. He argued that the Court shouldn't decide the case then because it didn't have the record—unaware that I had managed to get it sent up. That was an opening for my observation on Mississippi justice: "This is the story of the litigation in this case. Judge Cox doesn't let you have the record and Mr. Satterfield says you don't belong in this Court if you don't have it."

I reminded the Court that Medgar Evers, a plaintiff in the Jackson, Mississippi, case was assassinated before he could see the schools desegregated, adding, "The question in these cases is whether the children in these school districts, and indeed, the children in any school districts throughout our beloved land, are at last to learn that there is a supreme law of the land, binding upon children and parents; binding upon school boards; binding upon the states; binding upon the United States."

Leon Panetta, who had come to Court hoping to see the HEW guidelines vindicated, observed that as he heard the argument "it was hard to suppress a chill or a tear."

Six days later we won. On October 29, the Court, in a per curiam opinion, that is, by the Court, not by any identifiable justice, ruled: "The Court of Appeals should have denied all motions for additional time because . . . 'all deliberate speed' is no longer constitutionally permissible."

Then, accepting my argument of integrate first, litigate later, the Court required the court of appeals to order desegregation "forthwith" without "further arguments or submissions." The court of appeals order would remain in effect during district court hearings; only the court of appeals was empowered to make changes, excluding Mississippi district judges from that part of the process. *Alexander* was Warren Burger's first decision, and he went along with the rest of the Court—not an auspicious beginning for the Nixon Court from Nixon's point of view.

We filed *Alexander* motions across the South demanding immediate desegregation. Still some judges didn't get the message.

THE HAYNSWORTH AND CARSWELL BATTLES

One afternoon, as I was driving out of the Coliseum garage, which was under our office building, I was stunned by a radio report that Nixon was planning to nominate Clement Haynsworth of the Fourth Circuit to succeed Abe Fortas. Here was a judge who had been against us just about whenever his vote made a difference. When Prince Edward County, Virginia, closed schools to avoid integrating, Haynsworth, in a two-to-one decision, voted that the plaintiffs opposing the closing had first to take their case to the Virginia courts, which would have delayed reopening for years of inconclusive state court proceedings. The Supreme Court reversed. Haynsworth dissented from a decision holding unconstitutional a Virginia minority-to-majority transfer plan, which brought about resegregation. The Supreme Court made clear that that was wrong. In another case he wrote that students didn't have the right to sue for desegregation of teachers, on which he was held wrong again. He ruled against us in *Green v. New Kent County*, which ended freedom of choice, which the Court reversed, and he dissented in the case that held segregation in federally aided hospitals unconstitutional. There was reason for alarm.

I called Roy Wilkins and described Haynsworth's history as an appellate judge. He asked me to draft a telegram for his signature to the president, which kicked off the Haynsworth battle. Organized labor also opposed Haynsworth for decisions in which he had ruled against its interests. After a long battle, on November 21, the Senate rejected Haynsworth, 55 to 45, ostensibly because he had participated in a case that remotely affected a corporation in which he owned stock. I thought that was a bum rap and that the consistently anti–civil rights and obstructionist positions that made up his judicial record were sufficient and proper grounds for opposing him. At least some senators who agreed with us seemed to have used the ethics issue because it was less controversial.

In an in-your-face response to the rejection of Haynsworth, Nixon countered on January 19, 1970, by nominating G. Harrold Carswell, easily worse than Haynsworth on issues involving race. We earlier had opposed appointing Carswell to the Fifth Circuit because, as a district judge, he had stalled civil rights cases interminably and then made rulings clearly contrary to established law. Marian Edelman, who by then had become head of the Washington Research Project, took the lead in that fight. Marian's staff, particularly Rick Seymour, dug up facts in rural Georgia and Florida that demonstrated that earlier in his career, Carswell had been involved in blatantly racist political activity. Charlie Black wrote an influential article for the *Yale Law Journal*, which demonstrated that the Constitution contemplated that senators should exercise independent judgment on Supreme Court nominations and that even if the nominee had not been involved in any blatantly illegal or unethical conduct, they were not obliged to approve anyone the president offered. After seventy-nine days of debate, the Senate defeated Carswell, 51 to 45.

Nixon, in desperation, then turned for advice to Warren Burger, who suggested his friend Harry A. Blackmun, then sitting on the Eighth Circuit, whom the Senate confirmed. Blackmun's record on the Court is one more confirmation of the fact that at least sometimes there is something to be gained in defeating unsatisfactory appointments. A second or even third choice can turn out to very different from the first.

BUSING BEGINS

Jim Nabrit and Julius Chambers tried and argued *Swann v. Charlotte-Mecklenburg Board of Education*, which addressed the next question in the school struggle: What constitutes effective desegregation? In Charlotte, where blacks were concentrated near the center of town, it wasn't possible to desegregate by drawing simple zone lines. An expert witness, John Finger of the University of Rhode Island, drew a plan that paired center-city and outlying schools into single, noncontiguous zones. The inner-city school would teach some grades and the peripheral school would teach the remaining grades, so that black and white children would attend each school, many by bus. The zones were gerrymandered to achieve a black–white ratio approximating that of the general population, about 71 percent white, 29 percent black. *Swann*, therefore, had to deal with the extent to which a district court might use such percentages to correct a segregated system; whether every all-black and all-white school must be eliminated as such and integrated at least to some extent; the limits on rearranging attendance zones; the limits on busing.

The Supreme Court unanimously approved the Charlotte plan. The 71 to 29 percent ratio was, in Burger's view, "no more than a starting point, rather than an inflexible requirement." Gerrymandering, establishing zones that are "neither compact nor contiguous," indeed "on opposite ends of a city," though "awkward, inconvenient, and even bizarre," was permissible. Busing was appropriate. "Eighteen million of the Nation's public school children, approximately 39%, were transported to their schools by bus in 1969–1970 in all parts of the country," observed Burger. The "existence of some small number of one-race or virtually one-race schools . . . [was] not in and of itself the mark of a system that still practices segregation by law." As a practical matter, sometimes that would be unavoidable.

With *Swann*, I argued another case, from Mobile, very much like it. To prepare for the argument I drove through the streets of the city at about the speed of a school bus, so that I could tell the Court confidently that busing in Mobile would not be too lengthy or onerous. But Burger had a different question on his mind: Must courts continue to rezone after population shifts have resegregated integrated districts? I replied, "In a city like Mobile . . . we have a situation in which the Constitution has been violated . . . from 1954 to 1969. . . . It is not as if they have been thoroughly well-integrated for a hundred years and someone is suddenly calling them into court."

We won the Mobile case in a decision much like *Swann*.

Earl Warren later told me that he had learned that Burger originally had voted against us in this group of cases, and others on the Court had supported him. But, little by little, he lost his support, until "he stood there naked," as Earl Warren put it. So he joined the majority and assigned the opinion to himself, making sure that it included his own answer to his question: "Neither school authorities nor district courts are constitutionally required to make year-by-year adjustments of the racial composition of student bodies once the affirmative duty to desegregate has been accomplished and racial discrimination through official action is eliminated from the system."

In those words lie the conflict in the courts over school desegregation today. Many formerly desegregated systems have become resegregated as a result of shifting populations, and efforts to undo that regression have run into conflict with Burger's dictum.

We filed *Swann* motions in all our pending cases and, for the first time, thoroughgoing desegregation became widespread.

As busing became a national issue, a recorded telephone message of the National Socialist White People's party denounced it as "a massive attempt to mongrelize the white race with the inferior black race. . . . The man most responsible for busing decisions across the country is Jack Greenberg, a Jew."

DELIBERATE SPEED—WAS IT JUSTIFIED?

Was the introduction of the phrase "with all deliberate speed" into *Brown* responsible for the snail's pace of desegregation between 1955 and 1970? Certainly, according to the language in *Brown II*, it couldn't have been. *Brown II* required a "prompt and reasonable start" and permitted delay only for tasks like redrawing zone lines and bus routes, reassigning pupils and teachers, and expressly prohibited delay because of hostility. Criteria of that sort would have been reasonable even if the Court had required desegregation "forthwith." However, the words "deliberate speed" allowed a perception that the Supreme Court had signaled lower courts to tolerate a certain amount of delay. And, if we can believe accounts of conferences among the justices, some indication that delay would be acceptable was the price the majority paid to get a unanimous opinion. Otherwise, there might have been one or more dissents and, some conjectured, opposition to *Brown I* would have been deeper and fiercer.

Furthermore, it's not at all clear that "forthwith" would have produced a quicker pace of desegregation except, perhaps, in a few border areas. The slow pace of desegregation was due almost entirely to factors independent of the language in *Brown II*. The congressional Southern Manifesto, which denounced the Supreme Court for *Brown* and other decisions; a bill in Congress to strip the Supreme Court of its jurisdiction, which failed by a single vote; doctrines of nullification and interposition; state sovereignty commissions; white citizens councils; boycotts and firings of, as well as violence toward, black teachers, civil rights advocates, and parents who tried to transfer their children to white schools—all had the effect of intimidating plaintiffs, white lawyers, and judges.

Other hindrances were that the resources to bring desegregation suits were meager; there were few black lawyers in Southern states; the Justice Department had no jurisdiction to file school cases. LDF was equipped to assist in only a fraction of the school districts of the South. This environment enabled many districts to do nothing, and in those where something was done, plans like twelve-year grade-a-year "stairstep," minority–majority transfer, pupil assignment, and freedom-of-choice arose, if not simply to maintain the status quo, then at least as sops to those in defiance of the law on this issue. The resources—funds, lawyers, political will—to change that situation were inadequate. Not until the American political agenda changed, as a consequence of the civil rights movement, itself partially a product of *Brown*, were the courts—and the country—ready to move to desegregation "forthwith." By the time of the Johnson administration, the LDF had greater financial resources to draw upon, due to increased giving, more lawyers, and more favorable legal doctrine, and the Justice Department and the Department of Health, Education and Welfare joined the struggle.

At the same time, it may well be true that a dissenting opinion, or maybe more than one, might have undercut the decision's moral imperative, possibly leading to even more intensive opposition. If there had been a dissent, would the congressional effort to diminish the Court's jurisdiction, which failed by a vote, have passed? Would violence have been more widespread? On the other side, would more violent opposition have spurred the civil rights movement into existence earlier and made it stronger? Would a "forthwith" decision have made lower courts act tougher sooner? We should not allow speculation to run amok, for there are no authoritative answers to these questions. I would guess that if I were making the decision in 1955, I would have voted for "forthwith." At least the highest court would not be saying, "Yes, black people have constitutional rights, but we will tolerate deferring them." I have to qualify that stance, however: To guess at what each of us might have done is a far different matter from acting when we know that we will bear the responsibility for the consequences of that decision.

THE WAR ON BLACK TEACHERS

We had not anticipated how seriously black teachers would be at risk during desegregation. Many whites found it unacceptable to have their children taught by blacks; the firing, or threat of firing, of black teachers created pressures against desegregation, deterring some black teachers from engaging in civil rights activity. Another unhappy development was the demotion of many black principals to second in command, where they would be supervised by white principals. Others were bumped down out of administration altogether or simply discharged. Southern states moved quickly after *Brown* to repeal teacher tenure laws, which would give the state a freer hand in dealing with the issue of black teachers and school administrators.

We rapidly developed a docket of teacher cases and incorporated into desegregation suits demands that black teachers be integrated into the school system. I won a Supreme Court decision approving a distribution of black teachers throughout the school system. While not based on a fixed quota, this was the first Supreme Court decision to accept a numerical guideline as a standard for measuring whether equality has been established.

By decade's end we had more than twenty-five teacher dismissal cases across the South. We won a lot, but the problem was more widespread than we could handle, and most cases involved unique circumstances, requiring that they be litigated individually. For example, the Orangeburg, South Carolina, School District fired Gloria Rackley because she had engaged in NAACP activities. By 1966 Matthew Perry and Mike Meltsner got her job back. The Court awarded back pay for one of the three years she had been out of a job, but not for the other two, because she had found a new job after a year. The Court's ruling hardly formed a deterrent to such firings nor was it much of a remedy for the plaintiff herself.

The National Education Association (NEA) found, in a study of the years between 1968 and 1970, that school districts in the Fifth Circuit reduced the number of black teachers by 1,072 while increasing the number of white teachers by 5,575. One out of every five black principal positions was eliminated, while the number of white principals increased.

The impact on black communities and morale was severe and in large measure responsible for the disenchantment with the desegregation process felt by many blacks. Nevertheless, it should be noted that black teacher organizations continued to support desegregation and regularly contributed to LDF, a confirmation of their perception of which way the path to equality lay. There is evidence that other factors, such as growing political power and regional shifts in population, offset at least some of the losses.

THE *KEYES* PRESUMPTION

LDF and the NAACP Special Contribution Fund, led by Bob Carter, tacitly divided up school cases: He mostly filed in the North, we stuck pretty much to the South, where we had our hands full until the *Alexander* decision ordered desegregation "forthwith" without "further arguments or submissions." Carter had a theory of de facto school segregation for Northern school suits—that is, segregation brought about by forces other than an intent to segregate—that I thought wouldn't wash, though the argument was entirely logical: School authorities assign students to neighborhood schools; they know when their actions will create distinctly black and white schools; state action therefore always is involved in creating segregation even when there is no articulated intent to separate by race. The theory continues: What is called *de facto* (literally, according to fact) segregation is really *de jure* (literally, according to the law) and is prohibited by the Fourteenth Amendment in both cases because in both cases state action has denied equal protection. Language in *Brown* supported this approach: "To separate them from others of similar age and qualifications solely because of their race generates a feeling of inferiority that may affect their hearts and minds in a way unlikely ever to be undone."

The theory was cost-effective, too. To prove that school boards had the motive of separating blacks from whites would be difficult, sometimes impossible. Decisions on where to draw lines, build schools, schedule bus routes, and assign teachers were made by many people and were often unexplained, unexpressed, concealed, or simply unfathomable. Making a case for intentional segregation could be as hard as making a case based on bank fraud. Demonstrating racial imbalance would be easier and cheaper. The problem was that it was too easy. If courts were required to correct any racial imbalance, they might have to restructure not only schools, but other institutions that were far from being in racial balance at the time—for example, private housing, higher education, employment. Some would have been pleased if the courts had undertaken a task of that sort. But without legislation and a bureaucracy to implement it, the courts would have been getting into difficult, uncharted territory, one that I doubted they wanted to enter. I was sure they wouldn't start down that road.

Bob had some early success before state administrative boards and in federal cases in Manhasset, New York, and Springfield, Massachusetts. But the effort soon crashed. Around this time Bob left the NAACP and was replaced by Nathaniel Jones, now a judge of the United States Court of Appeals for the Sixth Circuit, with whom there was none of the clash Thurgood and I had with Bob. By then the NAACP theory had run its course and there was no likelihood of conflict if we were to try an approach of our own. We, therefore, decided to enter a Denver case, in which blacks and Hispanics, on the one hand, and whites, on the other, had been concentrated in separate schools by a complex of factors, including transportation routes, construction, expansion of overcrowded schools with trailerlike portable classrooms to avoid sending students to schools attended by children of another race, optional zones (children might pick their school), and transfer policies. Minority teachers were assigned to minority schools, white teachers to white schools. A school board that had adopted a policy of integration was defeated by candidates pledged to continue segregation.

Colorado, of course, had no law requiring school segregation. We chose not to rely on the mere fact that there were separate minority and white schools, as the earlier NAACP approach would have done, and set out to prove an intent to segregate out of all these circumstances too conveniently contributing to a pattern of quite rigid segregation. I came up with the name "crypto de facto"—meaning a case ostensibly based on government intent which essentially was a de facto case—for this kind of case, but the term never caught on. The new approach left one major gap: Even if intent could be proved as to some areas within a school system there was no way of knowing how racial concentrations had come about in other areas within the same system. Would it be impossible to win a comprehensive desegregation order covering the areas about which there wasn't enough information?

Gordon Greiner—a burly, red-bearded, and iconoclastic Denver antitrust lawyer in one of Denver's largest firms, a moose and elk hunter in his spare time—along with Vilma Martinez, Conrad Harper, and later Jim Nabrit III, tried and appealed the Denver school case to the Supreme Court in 1973. Jim and Gordon wrote the Supreme Court brief. The decision pointed the way to winning cases across the North. One important part of the decision, which I developed, became known as the *Keyes* presumption: Where a plaintiff establishes that officials segregated in one part of town, the burden shifts to the officials to explain why there are racial concentrations in other parts. Since then, Northern school cases have been winnable because many districts that managed to cover most of their tracks left enough evidence to show some intentional segregation in a local area or two. Such evidence having been uncovered, *they* would have to prove that the rest of the district was segregated by happenstance—something that would be as difficult for them to prove as the contrary would be for us.

INTERDISTRICT INTEGRATION

In the late 1960s and early 1970s a new issue surfaced: Where there is a district line between city and suburban schools, should city children be sent to suburban schools and vice versa to bring about desegregation? If not, as a city became blacker, the boundary would keep segregation insulated from change. That's what happened in Richmond, as whites left desegregated schools and moved to the suburbs. We then won a court order to desegregate Richmond schools, which treated the city and adjacent districts as a single unit for desegregation purposes. But the court of appeals reversed. Bill Coleman argued the case in the Supreme Court, which upheld the reversal four to four. As is the custom with affirmances by an equally divided Court, it wrote no opinion.

The Court's reasoning emerged in an NAACP case involving Detroit one year later, *Milliken v. Bradley*. Opponents of interdistrict integration had argued that where the suburbs had done nothing to segregate they shouldn't compensate for wrongs of the city. They also argued that busing across city boundaries often meant going great distances and that schools work best if parents are in the neighborhood. Moreover, their argument continued, separate tax systems are responsive to their respective constituencies. The decision stated that there would be no interdistrict integration unless there had been an interdistrict violation, meaning that plaintiffs would have to prove that the suburbs and city were in complicity in segregating.

Nevertheless, there was some city–suburban integration. Charlotte, Jacksonville, Nashville, and their environs, among many other school systems that desegregated under court order, are in single districts that encompass city and suburbs. In Indianapolis, towns near Philadelphia, and elsewhere, courts found that there had been city–suburban complicity and ordered integration.

While it's true that many suburbs became a refuge for whites who didn't want to go to school with blacks, it's also true that many parents who chose suburban over city schools and private over public schools did so because of the terrible state of public education in many cities. These families are disproportionately white; whites more readily afford private and suburban education, and housing discrimination keeps many blacks out of the suburbs even when they can afford it.

By 1973 we had 115 school cases where desegregation had been achieved and ninety-nine where we continued to litigate, mostly in rural areas. Thirty-four teacher cases were on the docket.

President Nixon inveighed against busing. The political reaction to busing was hostile; indeed, it became a major national political issue. Congress and state legislatures passed antibusing laws, though few of these laws were effective and we struck some down in LDF cases. By October 1972 the Justice Department, now doing the bidding of an antibusing president, was opposing us in busing cases in Las Vegas, Tulsa, Charlotte, Oklahoma City, and Memphis.

School cases between 1973 and 1984 continued to diminish on the docket as we won greater compliance, and government and other groups also began occasionally litigating educational issues. By 1976 we had ceased filing many new suits and dealt more with issues such as efforts to resegregate, discriminatory discipline, discharge and demotion of black teachers, and a Mississippi board's refusal to use a textbook that depicted the role of blacks in state history. We sued to win admission of blacks to state-subsidized private academies and for counsel fees from our opponents.

FORCING HEW TO OBEY THE LAW

While HEW had power to enforce *Brown* across the board and was, for all practical purposes, the only source of effective national enforcement, for political reasons it sat on its hands. Motivated by politics of the Nixon administration, HEW adopted a lax stance in gathering complaints and evidence of school segregation and in acting upon them when received. Jean Fairfax's Division of Legal Information and Community Services and its deputy director, Phyllis McClure, working with other civil rights groups and a network of black citizens in two hundred districts covering nine Southern states, launched a project to gather facts proving that HEW was not doing its job. Using this information, in 1969, with Joe Rauh and his partners, John Silard and Elliot Lichtman, we filed a case (originally called *Adams v. Richardson*, but with name changes over the years to reflect successive secretaries of HEW) to force HEW to process complaints and withhold federal funds from violators.

At the outset, the case was problematic because administrative agencies, prosecutors, and other law enforcement officials have traditionally had wide discretion concerning where to target their activities, but Joe and his partners persuaded District Judge John H. Pratt and the court of appeals for the District of Columbia that Congress intended to empower courts to enjoin HEW to enforce Title VI. We won an order setting deadlines to act on complaints. When HEW didn't comply the court required it to do so. The second prong of the case—requiring HEW to withhold funds from higher education systems that discriminated—at first attracted little attention. When we filed the case, we expected flak from white schools, not black opposition. Yet this is the opposition we found ourselves facing when some blacks feared that West Virginia might be the model for what would happen when black colleges integrated. Dr. John W. Davis, when he was president of West Virginia State College, even before *Sweatt* and *McLaurin* in 1950, had admitted white students—then in violation of state law. In time the college was no longer majority black, although in some ways it preserved its black identity, with a black president, buildings named after prominent blacks, and a substantial number of blacks in the student body. But to some it seemed that such transformations of colleges from majority black to majority white threatened to destroy centers of black power and influence, identity, and jobs.

In response to these fears, in June 1971 Jean Fairfax convened a group chaired by Julius Chambers, Henry Marsh, and John Walker to study how to address the issue of integrating higher education. They concluded that

Southern states had no commitment to educating poor black students and wanted instead to admit only a few top black students to their formerly all-white colleges. They called for addressing the problems of job loss among black teachers and of ill treatment of black students.

Another problem requiring attention was black higher education and the all-black schools; the status quo was unacceptable. Most of the best black students and faculty were moving to formerly all-white schools, North and South. Black colleges and universities were becoming backwaters. There was an element of illusion at work too: While many blacks felt that public black colleges belonged to black people, in fact they were under state—that is, majority white—control, particularly with regard to appropriations, and were underfunded.

Jean's group advocated what I would call modulated integration, which combined the integration of higher education with enhancement of formerly black colleges. They advocated that blacks should become trustees, administrators, faculty, students, and nonacademic staff in all institutions within the state systems. They advocated numerical guidelines for admissions and appointments. Pointing to the expensive, segregative effect of duplicate programs (identical courses in black and white schools), they called for maintaining, for example, a single racially diverse nursing school, one architecture school or business school, instead of one in a black and another in a white university. But, apart from the political problems involved in closing any program, the proposal suggested other difficulties: What if whites with superior preparation were admitted in disproportionately large numbers to the most attractive programs, shutting out blacks who would have had a program available to them under the old system? Should schools limit white enrollment and use affirmative action in admitting blacks—a solution that would be sure to cause a backlash among whites now shut out? Unraveling segregation in higher education, which Southern states had entrenched even more deeply after *Brown*, was bound to be complicated and controversial.

In 1972, when the government first appealed the order against HEW, the National Association for Equal Opportunity in Higher Education (NAFEO), consisting of heads of black colleges and universities, filed a brief opposing us. The court of appeals, while upholding the judgment, observed that black colleges should be treated with care in the desegregation process. Because the states were making virtually no progress in integrating higher education, in August 1975 we filed a motion asking the court to require HEW to revoke approval of state higher education plans in Florida, Georgia, Maryland, North Carolina, Oklahoma, Pennsylvania, and Virginia, because they had not changed admission requirements to raise black enrollment, reassigned staff, altered faculty distribution, eliminated duplicative programs, upgraded black institutions, or desegregated institutional governance. That proceeding continued into the 1980s. No longer did higher education cases involve the simple issue of whether G. W. McLaurin might be required to sit in a chair designated for blacks only. Jean worked with coalitions of black educators to shape the role of LDF in regard to these complex issues, but it remained an uneasy relationship.

We continued to try to compel HEW to enforce desegregation of schools wholesale. The district court ordered the Office of Management and Budget to hire hundreds of additional civil rights workers to enforce the decree at all levels. While HEW accepted higher education desegregation plans from Arkansas, Florida, Georgia, Oklahoma, and the North Carolina community college system in 1978 and from Virginia in 1979, North Carolina wouldn't submit an acceptable blueprint to desegregate student bodies and faculties, reduce duplicative programs, and enhance black institutions.

In 1979, therefore, HEW began proceedings before an administrative law judge as the first step toward cutting off federal funds for the North Carolina state system of higher education. Hearings went on for nine months, creating a record of fifteen thousand pages and more than five hundred exhibits. This was what enforcement was coming to.

When Ronald Reagan became president, North Carolina, supported by Senator Jesse Helms, entered into a consent decree with HEW in a North Carolina federal court exonerating the state of its obligations under the original *Adams* decree. We filed a motion in the District of Columbia to enjoin HEW from agreeing to the North Carolina consent decree, but lost six to four in the court of appeals, which held that we should have intervened in the North Carolina federal court. We were running up against political limits to what we could accomplish.

BOB JONES

The Reagan administration struck again in an attempt to bestow tax exemption on fundamentalist Christian Bob Jones University, which had a rule prohibiting black students from marrying or dating whites. Because of this racial discrimination, the Internal Revenue Service canceled Bob Jones's tax exemption. Reagan's Justice Department, led by Assistant Attorney General for Civil Rights William Bradford Reynolds, then joined the university in seeking to overturn the revocation. The case reached the Supreme Court in 1982.

At first it was a fixed fight: The opponents, the university, and the Justice Department were actually on the same side. When it became apparent that Justice, which was supposed to defend the IRS, was actually trying to compel it to grant tax exemption to Bob Jones, there was an immense public outcry. So that both sides of the issue could be heard, Chief Justice Warren Burger called Bill Coleman and asked him to argue as a friend of the court in support of denying tax exemption to Bob Jones. Bill agreed readily. Burger suggested, however, that Bill might want the weekend to think it over; perhaps he had a conflict of interest. Bill replied that he didn't, but if there were a conflict, he would shed any other client. Burger warned that the Court wouldn't pay a fee, only expenses, and that since Bill practiced in Washington that would only be taxi fare. He suggested, however, that since Bill was "so fat" he would be better off walking. Bill nevertheless wanted to accept and did. While Bill was appointed as an individual, he was well known as the chairman of LDF. Eric Schnapper and I worked with him in preparing his brief and argument.

In arguing before the Supreme Court, Thurgood had sprinkled his arguments with expressions of courtesy and, similarly, I would always make clear my respect for the justices, but Bill was all business. If a justice harassed him with questions wide of the mark, wasting precious minutes, Bill would brush past the query. At one point during the Bob Jones argument, as a justice hectored him, Bill, raising his voice, interrupted with "hear me out, hear me out" and proceeded to make his point.

The decision completely repudiated the Reagan administration's strategy of warping the tax laws to promote segregation; only Justice Rehnquist dissented. Burger wrote that "entitlement to tax exemption depends on meeting certain common law standards of charity. . . . A charity must serve a public purpose and not act contrary to public policy." He held that the United States has "a firm national policy to prohibit racial segregation and discrimination in public education."

We rejoiced in the victory, but should have been spending our time moving ahead. Instead we were fighting the Civil Rights Division over the Nashville, Baton Rouge, Charleston, and other school cases, winning the first two and losing the third. But, during the same period, after eight appeals, Jim Liebman won an interdistrict school case in rural Pennsylvania and, following years of litigation, a big city school case in Kansas City, Missouri, where the city joined us in suing the state and the suburbs to obtain more money. The city and state had fostered segregation in the city schools while impoverishing them as it directed more resources to the suburbs; the decision ordered city–suburban desegregation to be accomplished by attracting suburban children to well-funded city magnet schools. The trials and appeals cost $1 million, which we ultimately recouped from the state and city. No longer did cases involve basic issues of principle; no longer were they against simple country lawyers.

THE IMPACT OF DESEGREGATION CASES ON EDUCATION

Blacks have made great, though uneven, progress on the educational front during the years following *Alexander v. Holmes County Board of Education* (1970). In 1970 the percentage of blacks aged twenty-five to twenty-nine who had completed high school was 55.4 percent; in 1980, 75.2 percent; and in 1986, 83 percent. At least at the high school level, the percentage of high school graduates among blacks was beginning to approach that of white Americans. For college education black ratios have also gone up, but since the late 1980s, they have been slightly down in comparison to whites. In 1960, 19 percent of black high school graduates were in college whereas 24 percent of their white counterparts were; in 1975 the ratio was 32.5 percent for blacks compared to 33 percent for whites; but in 1985 the number of white high school graduates going on to college had risen to 35 percent, while the percentage for blacks had fallen to 26.5. Between 1980 and 1986, the proportion of blacks aged twenty-five to twenty-nine with college degrees was virtually unchanged at 11.5 percent. The proportion of whites was 22 percent, nearly double that of blacks. The figures for the percentage of Ph.D.'s awarded to black people are sketchy, but it appears that the percentage did rise in the 1970s, only to fall after 1984. All in all a broad advance at the high school level, falling far short at the college level, while a growing number of black college students have moved on to doctoral degrees. But in many disciplines, particularly in the sciences, virtually no blacks have earned the doctorate.

By the mid-1980s, when I left LDF, the South was the most desegregated part of the country. But, according to James Liebman's exhaustive survey of the literature, even in big Northern cities, where resistance and obstacles often have been great, desegregation has worked well in that black and white children generally are attending school together, black children are learning better, and whites are learning no less well. Buffalo, Columbus, Dayton, Denver, Minneapolis, St. Louis, San Diego, and Wilmington, Delaware (which at the time of *Brown* was governed by a segregation statute) all have desegregated schools. In the South desegregation has been particularly successful in Charlotte, Greenville, Jacksonville, Louisville, Nashville, and Tampa. But it has been virtually nonexistent in New York, Chicago, Philadelphia, Detroit, Los Angeles, and Atlanta. The big cities with vast populations and often great distances, ghettoes from which whites and middle class blacks have moved, often to suburbs, have been particularly resistant and physically difficult to desegregate.

Consistently, studies show that blacks who attend desegregated schools achieve higher test scores than blacks who attend segregated schools, and that the performance of whites doesn't suffer under desegregation; black IQ has risen to "eras[e] nearly half the gap between blacks predesegregation . . . scores and the national norm." Blacks who attended desegregated schools do better in society, getting better jobs after graduation, and are less likely to get pregnant while in desegregated schools. Gerald Jaynes and Robin Williams write, "Children who have attended desegregated schools tend to have more friends who are of another race, to work in higher-status jobs, to attend and graduate from multiracial colleges and universities, and to live in integrated neighborhoods. Blacks from desegregated schools appear to make more money."

As with other social situations, explanations are complex. Desegregation has played its part, but better-educated parents (itself influenced by desegregated schools from which blacks graduate at a higher rate), more preschool programs, a decline in poverty, black migration from the South to the West and North and from rural areas to cities and suburbs where schools are better also have had an effect. Moreover, education in the South improved as the economy became better. However, none of this good news applies to ghetto schoolchildren, North or South.

As integration progressed, gerrymandering of school attendance zones and busing to carry children to integrated schools became one of the most heated of national political issues, although nowadays it seems to have faded from the front pages. Allocations by percentage posed the specter of quotas, historically associated with attempts to limit the opportunities of minorities, particularly Jews. Others raised objections that children would travel so far that it would adversely affect their health or ability to learn. Some who opposed busing claimed that parents who were distant from schools wouldn't support school budgets or belong to the PTA. Opponents claimed also that busing led to white flight, which turned cities disproportionately black and contributed to all the problems associated with black ghetto life. But, as Warren Burger wrote, 39 percent of America's schoolchildren were being bused to school at the time of *Swann*, when the Court first approved of it as a means of desegregating. Indeed, pre-*Brown* busing controversies arose when whites were bused but blacks had to walk or were driven by their parents and demanded equal busing—that is how the Delaware elementary school case began. Before *Brown* whites had been happy to bus black children from districts where there was no black school to a segregated school in a distant community. It's hard to conclude that the objections to busing haven't been based mainly on the fact that schools would be desegregated, not busing. As a white woman who objected to busing her child said, "It's not the distance, it's the niggers"—a telling comment, which LDF used as the title of a pamphlet dealing with the busing issue.

Such studies as there have been of the relationship between busing and white flight from the cities show that the exodus began well before busing and did not increase markedly afterward. Whites do not suffer academically and black children do better. Studies also show that a very large proportion of whites whose children were bused were pleased with the results. The issue of busing seems to have faded from the national stage. Perhaps because fears did not materialize and children did not suffer as predicted, opponents gave up. Some, of course, moved elsewhere.

Black higher education in the South has hardly improved in recent years and, in some cases, has become worse. In 1987 Julius Chambers, reviewing the five most important states covered by *Adams*—Arkansas, Florida, Georgia, Oklahoma, and Virginia—concluded that while the physical plants of traditionally black state schools had improved, they lacked facilities, resources, and programs comparable to those of white schools. Moreover, at each successive level of higher education the proportion of blacks diminishes. Altogether, school desegregation has been a story of conspicuous achievements, flawed by marked failures, the causes of which lie beyond the capacity of lawyers to correct. Lawyers can do right, they can even do good, but they have their limits. The rest of the job is up to society.

29

ANGELA DAVIS, THE SAN RAFAEL SHOOTOUT, AND TURMOIL AT LDF

Court victories over racism in education, public accommodations, and other aspects of life, whatever their beneficial effect over time, were no answer to the immediate frustration felt by blacks in the ghetto, especially by those who became enmeshed with the criminal justice system. Militant assertions of black power, violent self-defense and aggression, and even widespread urban riots began to appear during the late 1960s and continued into the 1970s. All of this created a need for legal representation that competed for our limited resources with other commitments that LDF had long honored. At times the new tensions threatened to tear the LDF apart.

MURDER AT THE COURTHOUSE

On August 7, 1970, Jonathan Jackson, brother of George Jackson, one of three prisoners known as the Soledad Brothers, entered the Hall of Justice in San Rafael, California, and handed guns to three San Quentin inmates—James B. McClain, Willy Christmas, and Ruchell Magee—who had been brought to court on a separate matter. The four then took the judge, the district attorney, and three jurors hostages and threatened to kill them if anyone interfered, demanding the release of the Soledad Brothers within the hour. They took their captives to a waiting van, but as the van left the parking area, gunfire broke out between the gunmen and corrections officers. One of the kidnappers killed the judge. Gunfire killed McClain, Christmas, and Jackson. Two hostages were wounded. The nation was outraged. The violence of the past few years was now off the streets and inside the hallowed halls of justice. Many saw it as just one more step on the nation's road to a new civil war.

Angela Davis was a twenty-six-year-old acting assistant professor of English at the University of California, Los Angeles, black, tall, strikingly beautiful, a former student of Herbert Marcuse at Brandeis, and a member of the Communist party. Law enforcement interest focused on her for several reasons. She had been seen several times with Jonathan Jackson, the man who had dealt out the guns in the courtroom. She and Jonathan had been campaigning to free George, with whom Davis was said to be in love, at the same time protesting the oppression of blacks and the cruel conditions at San Quentin. Most important, forms she had filled out when she bought four guns showed that these were the weapons used in the kidnapping; there was evidence that Jonathan accompanied her when she bought two of them. A gas station attendant near the courthouse testified before a grand jury that he saw someone resembling her in the getaway van the day before the trial.

Within a few hours of the shootout Davis flew from San Francisco to Los Angeles and disappeared. FBI agents captured her in New York on October 13, 1970. She had changed her appearance and was known as Mrs. George Gilbert.

On October 20 Margaret Burnham, an LDF staff lawyer, sent me a memorandum saying that for a week she had been, with John Abt (who was counsel for the Communist party), representing Angela Davis, "a long time personal friend," in her effort to resist extradition to California, but had been unable to tell me about it. Burnham was a slight, shy, very soft-spoken black woman who had been at LDF for about a year. "Work with this case will consume a great deal of my time, at least for the next few months," she wrote. "Needless to say, I would like to continue my status as a staff member here at the Legal Defense Fund. Further, I would like to have available to me Legal Defense Fund resources in connection with my work on this case." She concluded, "Fewer problems will arise if the National Conference of Black Lawyers, and not the Legal Defense Fund, continues to be the organization publicly identified with the defense of Angela Davis."

Burnham visited me that day. I had been through plenty of extradition cases, and told her that as far as I knew Angela Davis had no basis to resist extradition. More to the point of our meeting, I was unaware of any issue in her case that would make it the type of case that LDF normally handled; there seemed to be no civil rights component to her case. If there were, we might become involved, but none was apparent.

The next day the entire staff met and voted unanimously, with the exception of Jim Nabrit, that I should authorize LDF to take on significant black militant cases as a matter of general policy and that we should represent Angela Davis. Until then formal votes were virtually unheard of. The staff presented their results to me and I rejected the proposal, making the staff very unhappy. A week later I met with more than twenty staff lawyers. A memorandum I wrote at the time describes the meeting:

I took the position that the case was not one for us because there had not been alleged any denial of legal or constitutional rights; that there was no question of racial discrimination apparent; that the extradition which she sought to avoid was unavoidable under any state of law of which I was aware; that the case was not a run of the mill inconsequential matter such as staff lawyers sometimes handled in their spare time or on Fund time, but presented certain political and ideological questions; that the Legal Defense Fund would not identify itself with the politics and ideology represented by Angela Davis.

This was not merely a case, I said, of a lawyer representing a client who was not otherwise represented. She was represented by John Abt. In the absence of legal or constitutional questions the only justification for our involvement with such a case would be our identification with her as a symbol associated with violent resistance to the Justice system. And the Legal Defense Fund would not do that.

Various arguments were made to the contrary, including such things as: No one would ever find out; only a relatively small amount of our resources would go into the case; that she is being persecuted for her views; that she is the authentic voice of the black revolution; that in the course of representing her, legal and constitutional issues might emerge; that the attempt to extradite is defective on the ground that the warrant is insufficient; and so forth.

After approximately an hour's discussion I stated that I was not persuaded and that neither Legal Defense Fund nor any staff member employing its resources would represent Angela Davis.

A formal vote was taken and every lawyer present with the exception of James Nabrit voted that we should take the case. I replied that, nevertheless the authority and responsibility were mine in the end, and I would not change my decision.

The next morning Margaret Burnham, accompanied by Conrad Harper, another staff lawyer, visited me and asked whether I would permit her to go on half-time status on half salary, so that she could devote her time to representing Angela Davis. I replied that that would be acceptable. Burnham asked whether she could use LDF secretaries and equipment, but I denied this request; LDF would in no way support this case. She asked whether she might make personal arrangements with secretaries and compensate them for work on their own time. To this I had no objection. She then told me that staff lawyers would make personal contributions to her defense of Davis and would support the case in other ways. To which I could only reply that that was their own business. Harper, who became spokesman for the group, prepared and distributed forms for lawyers to commit periodic payments for Burnham's support.

Then, on October 30, as I was leaving the office, my eye fell on a paper in a typewriter that contained a typed signature line for Margaret Burnham and another staff lawyer: "c/o Legal Defense Fund, National Office for the Rights of the Indigent."

We never signed papers this way. Our style always was to place only the names of the lawyers, not of the organization, on pleadings. My name (and, earlier, Thurgood's) also was placed on papers after I had approved them. The paper in the typewriter was a pleading prepared with the National Conference of Black Lawyers, seeking relief against conditions under which Angela Davis was imprisoned, particularly solitary confinement. I asked Ms. Burnham what it was all about. I had never authorized taking the case. Lawyers didn't go off on their own. She said she assumed that I had authorized her to work on the case because I had said we would represent Angela Davis in connection with matters LDF regularly handled and we did handle prison cases. As to the form for the signature, she had made a mistake; she hadn't known the form was improper.

I told her that I rejected her explanation, that she had been with LDF for a year and knew better. She said she had not seen the need to tell me about what she had done. I told her to strike out the names of LDF and NORI. I viewed her action as an effort to associate LDF publicly with the Angela Davis case. But since she had already done the papers she could file them in her own name.

Subsequently, in that aspect of the case, the court ordered that Angela Davis be removed from solitary.

At this point things began heating up. I sensed a rerun of clashes similar to those we had had with the Communists in Scottsboro, *Groveland*, Trenton Six, and other cases. I probably wouldn't have objected if Miss Burnham had asked about filing a prison conditions case, but I had not been asked. Worse, signing the papers "Legal Defense Fund" showed an attempt to link us with Angela Davis and her broader cause.

The LDF staff constituted a remarkable group of exceptionally bright, well-educated, idealistic men and women, black and white. They had the best legal jobs in America, working as lawyers in service of their beliefs. Their self-satisfaction grew, because, as Mike Meltsner (now a psychotherapist and law teacher) observed, they were perhaps the only members of their law school classes who did something others wanted to know about. Their cases were in the *New York Times* almost every day.

But the staff and I differed on a key aspect of the Angela Davis issue: They wanted to be seen as allies of the Black Panthers, students who tore campuses apart and paraded with rifles, draft resisters, and prisoners who fought jailers. While they were attracted and fascinated by Panthers and similar groups, I wasn't. Their activities would harm not only their victims, I thought, but lead to self-destruction, as it did. I reminded them of the injunction that those who live by the sword shall die by the sword, but received blank stares. My views weren't just personal: They had been the traditional views of LDF and were shared by the board.

Especially offensive were the separatist beliefs of the new militants, which ran contrary to the views of NAACP, LDF, SCLC, and, during their early history, CORE and SNCC—the latter two having turned separatist—the groups that had made real contributions to the progress of civil rights. I even doubted that black people generally identified with Angela Davis, but had to wait to be confirmed in this opinion. Years later I learned that Angela Davis's defense team had conducted a survey of black sentiment in California to identify the best site for the trial upon a change of venue. They decided to stay out of Alameda and San Francisco counties because they discovered that the black working-class populations there did not support Angela Davis. Rather, they opted for an upper-middle-class suburban area, where the residents were people like our staff lawyers.

THE STAFF REBELS

Some observers thought that the division between me and the staff was generational. In part it was: I was in my mid-forties, and they were closer to thirty. I wore suits, sometimes with vests, and ties (collar unbuttoned in the office); unless they had a court date many of the staff wore jeans and any old kind of shirt. Never a tie, of course. Dress had very special meaning: They would often mention how pleased they were that at LDF they were permitted to dress as they liked. They generally were far less settled in their personal lives than I, who had kids, a house, and a dog. I had been through *Groveland* and other brushes with Communists and they hadn't. They associated the issue of communism with the Army–McCarthy hearings and the travails of the Hollywood Ten, where anticommunism had been marked by red-baiting and attacks on the reputations of innocent people.

But it wasn't only generational—plenty of people my age were swept up in admiration for the new, even violent, militancy. Panthers and rifle-bearing students were seen as romantic Che Gueveras. I knew a woman TV executive who confided to friends, "I sleep with Panthers." Tom Wolfe has captured some of that adulation in *Radical Chic and Mau Mauing the Flack Catchers,* describing a meeting at the home of Leonard Bernstein, attended by celebrities, who incongruously fawned on violent Black Panthers in the most luxurious of settings. A *New York Times* article recounted the event, much to the embarrassment of the hosts and other Panther well-wishers. Wolfe writes that in deciding what to do next, Bernstein and some of his friends concluded, "They were all now 'too exposed' to do the Panthers any good by giving parties for the Panthers in their homes. They would do better to work through organizations like the NAACP legal defense fund." Bernstein, in fact, was a member of the Committee of 100, but neither he nor other participants at the event ever did anything noticeable for LDF.

Nevertheless, we did enter some cases of militants where there was a constitutional issue of the type that LDF historically had addressed. We also took some borderline cases requiring little time and money where such issues might arise. The problem was that staff lawyers kept wanting to enter cases that would support draft resisters and demonstrators where no such issues existed or were minor. Sometimes I had doubts, but felt that I had to yield. One of our lawyers represented black Columbia College students who had occupied the dean's office (an office I would occupy years later), winning acquittals or suspended sentences for them in campus hearings. Haywood Burns (now dean of the City University of New York Law School), asked by a friend of a friend at Cornell, counseled black students who, armed with rifles, invaded Willard Straight Hall, the student activities building, to protest cross burnings and KKK activity in the area and who were charged with criminal trespass. Protesting KKK activity clearly was an LDF issue. Defending students armed with rifles who invaded the student center was dubious. Nevertheless, the court dismissed most indictments; three students pleaded guilty to a reduced charge and were released.

In August 1969 LDF filed a brief for thirteen Black Panthers who were in jail because they could not afford $100,000 bail each, arguing, as our NORI program had, that high money bail discriminates against the poor. The *New York Times* reported the filing as a policy shift. I issued a public statement that pointed to other cases in which we had argued against excessive bail and promptly received a telegram from Reinhold Niebuhr, one of our oldest supporters: "SHOCKED BY SHIFT IN FUND POLICY AS DESCRIBED IN NEW YORK TIMES TODAY. DO NOT CASH CHECK AS HAVE STOPPED PAYMENT."

We stuck with the case but weren't happy about the reaction.

WE REPRESENT MUHAMMED ALI

Many cases, however, were not easily classified. As Mike Meltsner (who handled the case for LDF) recalls, LDF had a number of reasons for representing Muhammed Ali, the world heavyweight champion, in getting his boxing license back. Ali (who was then still called Cassius Clay by the press) had refused to report for induction into the armed forces because of his religious beliefs, for which he was convicted. Mike believed that race discrimination was unprovable but it seemed obvious that the government could not politically grant an exemption to this highly visible, irreverent, black antiwar Muslim. Indeed, New York and other states stripped him of his title and license as soon as he refused induction, not waiting for trial. Mike recommended that we take the case in 1967, soon after Ali was stripped of the title, relying heavily on work done by the national crime commission, which had made a big point about civil disabilities imposed on convicts by withdrawal of state licenses to practice their business or profession. The commission had in mind licenses for barbering and the like, but the Ali case might make a useful precedent and advance our newly formed program for poor people. Chauncey Eskridge, Ali's Chicago lawyer, who handled his business affairs, also was an LDF cooperating lawyer and finally in 1969 allowed us to go ahead. There was a lot of sentiment on the staff to represent Ali because he was opposed to the war.

Following a hunch based on his New York youth spent playing hooky at Madison Square Garden, Mike went through old copies of *Ring* magazine. It appeared that many great fighters had criminal records. Ann Wagner of our staff spent days digging up facts at the boxing commission, where she discovered that it almost seemed to help a licensee to have a criminal record—so many fighters had one. Mike won Ali's case in federal district court because he was able to show that New York had given at least 244 boxing licenses to applicants who had been convicted of felonies, misdemeanors, or military offenses involving moral turpitude, including grand larceny, rape, sodomy, aggravated assault, and other serious crimes. Indeed, the New York commission recognized Sonny Liston, who had been convicted of armed robbery and assault with intent to kill, as heavyweight boxing champion in the state of New York. The judge granted an injunction and I called Louis Lefkowitz, the New York State attorney general, and persuaded him not to appeal. Then followed the first Ali–Frazier fight, which Ali lost in a unanimous decision.

As Ali's draft conviction was being appealed, Eskridge decided that he wanted LDF to take over that case too. He had been present in the supreme court of Mississippi when LDF assistant counsel Jonathan Shapiro argued a case in which SCLC had been sued for conducting a boycott, and he particularly wanted Jonathan to handle Ali's appeal.

Jonathan wrote Ali's brief and Eskridge argued the case. The case involved a range of issues, including illegal wiretaps, discrimination in selection of draft boards, and whether the Muslim religion satisfied the test for qualification as a conscientious objector. We won on the grounds that Ali met the test for qualification as a conscientious objector.

As the case proceeded Ali came to the office a few times to shake our hands, causing quite a stir, particularly among the female secretaries. Once or twice he invited us to his hotel suite. We became fight fans for a brief period. His manager gave us tickets to a number of fights that were fought in Madison Square Garden or elsewhere and shown on a huge television screen at the Garden. These were the only fights that I or, as far as I know, any other staff members ever attended while I was at LDF. After Ali regained his license he earned vast sums and made a small gift to LDF, which was barely adequate to pay the modest expenses of his cases. Repeated efforts to get a substantial contribution came to naught.

But I wouldn't take some cases. I refused to sue Harvard for injuries suffered by a student during a campus riot. I couldn't imagine what would be accomplished and had visions of an interminable, expensive trial. When the

Georgia legislature wouldn't seat Julian Bond because of his anti–Vietnam War views, I wouldn't allow LDF to represent him, although LDF assistant counsel Steve Ralston sent a memorandum to his lawyer, Howard Moore, which was the basis of the district court decision. The Georgia legislature would have refused to seat a white person for the same reason. More important, although the case might have barely met our regular criteria, I saw Bond's case, like the Ali case, as a high-visibility part of the anti–Vietnam War movement. I had been opposed to the war from its beginning, but didn't want to make LDF part of any movement except the civil rights movement. The Bond decision angered many staff members.

LDF cases always had been selected by the director-counsel after staff discussion, with Thurgood, and later me, making the final decision. Rarely was there a vote. After the Bond rebuff the staff wanted a formal arrangement by which staff consensus would determine which cases we took. I agreed, so long as I retained the ultimate right of decision. When the Angela Davis case erupted, the staff disputed my refusal to represent her and sent the board of directors a memorandum proposing a new standard of case selection:

> The Civil Rights movement—of which we were the legal arm—[has] broadened to become the Black Liberation Movement. . . . The Legal Defense Fund accepts as one of its basic functions the use of its resources to ensure against the misuse of the judicial system and to ensure the proper functioning of the system in cases involving militants. The stature of the Fund and the respect afforded it by the judiciary can be vital in accomplishing these ends.

They submitted that "individual lawyers should be allowed independence of judgment in taking such cases, with the provision that they must inform the Director Counsel concerning them." Should I disapprove of taking a case, two-thirds of the staff could overrule me. They acknowledged that this might adversely affect fund-raising, but thought money could be found elsewhere.

I thought the proposal sheer lunacy. We had a charter, a tradition, a board that defined the role of LDF, and contributors who gave for that program. The staff now proposed that lawyers, most of whom had been at LDF only a few years and some not even that long, and who soon might move on, should be the ones to commit LDF funds and personnel to the litigation of suits. Such a change in policy would place the resources of the LDF at the service of causes of the staff's choice, including violent and separatist ones. I wasn't going along and neither was Jim Nabrit.

Meetings with board members followed, some of which were loud and furious. At one, a bearded white lawyer pounded the table and angrily said to Bill Coleman, "The black people of America demand—" Bill, the gentlest of souls, interrupted, "Don't you tell me what the black people of America demand, you sonofabitch, or I'll punch you in the nose."

On November 16 the executive committee decided unanimously that "the Fund could not apply its staff, professional or other resources to the representation of Miss Angela Davis." They added, "The Director-Counsel is the Chief Executive officer of the Fund and is to determine what litigation the Fund shall become involved in subject to the ultimate responsibility of the . . . Board." They resolved to prepare a general statement of policy on case selection.

While that was in process the executive committee issued another memorandum. It stated our traditional agenda: The Fund should handle cases "of major constitutional or other legal dimension pertaining to the rights of blacks." We might become involved in other cases of not quite such importance where black litigants with substantial legal claims didn't have lawyers. "No person—whether a member of the Board or of the legal staff—may commit the Fund to any form of participation in any law suit without the express assent of the Director-Counsel. . . . The responsibility for decision lies with the Director-Counsel alone [who] is accountable therefore to the . . . Board." At the executive committee meeting of February 11, Bill Coleman observed that Angela Davis had five lawyers and eleven black law professors on her defense team. Tony Amsterdam also assisted in her defense.

A special board committee drafted criteria for case selection:

> [LDF] has rejected any notion of racial separation, even though espoused by those who firmly and sincerely believe that it is the only way to eliminate white racism. . . . LDF . . . believes that drastic changes in our society are called for in order to eliminate segregation and discrimination and to achieve justice for all our citizens, but that these changes should be brought about through non-violent means. . . . LDF abhors violence and threats of violence and also those who would subvert or undermine the law courts and the legal system, or seek changes thereto by violent or destructive means.

The report called upon LDF to handle cases of constitutional dimension involving the rights of blacks and to make resources available to those who support elimination of racial separation and discrimination by nonviolent legal means. We would not be precluded from taking cases of those who advocated separatism or violence where the legal process was directed against them because of their race. The memorandum called for establishing a litigation policy committee to consult with the director-counsel and concluded, "It is to be emphasized, however, that decisional authority lies with the Director-Counsel, subject, however, as is the case with all decisions of the Director-Counsel, to his accountability to the full Executive Committee and in an ultimate sense to the entire Board."

As this was going on the Angela Davis affair was taking almost all of my time. I wrote memoranda to the staff, they wrote to me; they wrote to the board, I wrote to the board. I met day and night with staff committees and individual lawyers. The executive committee held an extraordinary Saturday meeting. Evans and Novak wrote a column stating, "The fund's staff, dominated by black radicals, wanted to defend Miss Davis. . . . The board of directors, dominated by white liberals, refused." They didn't know that the staff, black and white, was unanimously against me, except for Jim, who is black, and that the mostly black board, chaired by Bill Coleman, unanimously supported me. The column provoked mail from contributors and members of the public, which I had to answer, while simultaneously running a program of all sorts of other cases.

On January 12, 1971, Margaret Burnham was back with a long memorandum arguing once more that we should enter the Angela Davis case. I wasn't persuaded, however, and we continued to stay out. Ms. Burnham then received a leave of absence for a year. By April relations with the staff once more had become entirely agreeable. Everyone was involved in cases they cared about. To my astonishment, and that of many others, Angela Davis was acquitted.

Margaret Burnham never returned to LDF. For a time she was a lower court judge in Boston and, as far as I know, is in private practice. Conrad Harper, who spoke for the pro–Angela Davis forces, joined Simpson, Thacher and Bartlett, a Wall Street law firm, where he became a partner, and, later, was the first black president of the Association of the Bar of the City of New York—about a half-century after Frank Rivers had become its first black member.

30

WINNING JOBS

SENIORITY SUICIDE PREVENTION

Remarkable stories of employment discrimination make up a large part of black folklore. Thurgood talked of a good friend, Kip Hilton, who, during the 1930s, went to work at Thompson and McKinnon, a Wall Street brokerage firm. He was so good at the game he trained others as brokers. If he hadn't been black, he would have been a partner. As it was, he never rose above the rank of messenger. Many times I heard Thurgood tell of the Linotypist at the Baltimore *Afro American*, whom the white papers called in for repair jobs no one else could do, but whom they would never hire. The solitary black worker at highway construction jobs—he held the flag to halt traffic or wave it on—was a common subject of ironic joking. Blacks were not seen as fit to dig alongside whites. Organized labor disgraced itself and betrayed its credo of the universal brotherhood of working men by setting up separate black and white locals; those unions that were forced to merge the separate locals under pressure of law usually assigned blacks subordinate roles. Union contracts often reserved the best jobs for whites.

Between 1965 and 1970, LDF brought the cases that cleared away the procedural obstacles to using the 1964 Equal Employment Opportunities Act (Title VII) effectively and later, for some years, brought virtually all the cases that gave the law its bite. We enlisted scholars, economists, and labor experts every step of the way to target industries where lawsuits would do the most good. They also informed courts of legal wrongs and how to remedy them. Our Title VII operation was a major triumph in making legal doctrine and achieving social gain—blacks, other minorities, and women won a dramatic increase in the number of jobs available to them and in the higher pay they received in those jobs. In terms of the impact of the change wrought, it was almost on a par with the campaign that won *Brown*.

LAUNCHING THE CAMPAIGN

Shortly after President Johnson signed the 1964 Civil Rights Act, I decided that on the day the Equal Employment Opportunities Act became effective in July 1965 we should file one thousand complaints with the commission to publicize the law, give it credibility, and get a leg up on the enormous process of interpretation and enforcement that lay ahead of us. We gathered a group of students, community workers, and staff members, who spent that year with NAACP branches, in churches, barbershops, fraternities, civic associations, and elsewhere, telling people about their rights and gathering facts about discrimination. Ruth Abram, a white, seventeen-year-old Sarah Lawrence student, freshly arrived from Atlanta, coordinated this project, arriving on her first day of summer vacation wearing a hat and white gloves, in proper Southern fashion, as her mother had counseled. After observing our counterculture dress code she fell into line.

The team's targets included U.S. Steel, Union Carbon and Carbide, A & P, General Motors, International Paper, numerous unions, and the state employment services of Mississippi, Georgia, Alabama, and North Carolina. While we didn't quite file one thousand cases, we came close. We filed 476 complaints with the Equal Employment Opportunity Commission (EEOC) in July 1965, right after the act went into effect, and another 374 soon afterward. The complaints focused on areas of large black population, high black unemployment, and industrial growth. To moderate turf problems with the NAACP, I gave the complaints to its labor secretary, Herbert Hill, for filing, a gesture that acknowledged the Association's role in the struggle, while we followed up with lawsuits, which is what we were best at. Bill Robinson and those who later directed LDF's employment program worked cooperatively with NAACP staff over the years. We gave the Association other civil rights complaints, particularly those involving discrimination in hospitals, to file as well. Roy Wilkins welcomed the cooperation, telling me that if we hadn't gathered the complaints it wouldn't have been done.

I assigned Bob Belton, who came to LDF after graduation from Boston University Law School (he is now a professor at Vanderbilt), to major responsibility for the initial phases of the Title VII cases between 1965 and 1970. We filed the first Title VII case in October 1965, three months after the law went into effect, and by fall 1966 we had twenty-five cases, far more than the Justice Department. For years, no one had a docket approaching ours.

Title VII was unclear in many ways, creating endless possibilities for narrow interpretations. To guide us through this perilous terrain I decided to find a combination scholar and litigator. I enlisted Albert Rosenthal, a former Frankfurter law clerk who, after more than two decades of private practice, was about to become a professor at Columbia Law School. In 1966 and 1967, with Belton and staff lawyer Gabrielle (Gabby) Kirk (later a federal judge), Al assembled a remarkable group of scholars, and practitioners, like those LDF had gathered for other battles in the past. They developed strategies—even drafting model pleadings—that dominated the field of Title VII litigation for years to come.

THE DIVISION OF LEGAL INFORMATION TARGETS JOB CASES

In 1967 LDF got a $300,000 grant for Jean Fairfax's work from the Rockefeller Foundation. While refusing to support litigation, the foundation decided that pre- and post-litigation activities were safe to support, something like Ford's toe-in-the-water testing of civil rights via NORI. The foundation long had rejected LDF requests for financial support because its counsel, a partner at a Wall Street law firm, advised that we weren't tax-exempt, although we were in fact in the treasury's book of exempt organizations. He simply disapproved of what we were doing.

By fall 1966 Jean Fairfax's staff and others had gathered eighteen hundred charges, which we submitted to the EEOC, often jointly with the NAACP. Many black workers came to meetings clutching wrinkled, decades-old smudged bits of paper—one railroad worker had saved documents for twenty-six years—records of how they had been passed over in favor of whites, denied that most fundamental ideal of democratic capitalism, the opportunity to sell their services in an open and fair marketplace. While many black workers who brought their complaints to us were so aged that winning would mean little to them, they fought to reform the system for others. Some who spoke up were victims of cruel retaliation, like Toby Duhon, who sued Goodyear Tire and Rubber and then found a snake in his tool kit.

We targeted areas where black unemployment and economic growth were high, an indication of discrimination, and focused on semiskilled and skilled blue-collar jobs, which paid well but didn't require much formal education. We surveyed cooperating lawyers to identify industries and practices that fit this profile and zeroed in on steel, railroads, trucking, ship building, tobacco, and paper. Within these industries the cases focused on segregated locals; seniority systems that locked blacks into low-paying jobs; and discriminatory hiring and promotion practices, mainly testing, unnecessary high school diploma requirements, and word of mouth recruiting. But other issues sometimes were irresistible, like segregated toilets and payroll window lines and even, in one case, a segregated YMCA that the company maintained for its employees, with separate Bible classes, although as the plaintiffs meekly admitted in cross-examination, the same Bible was used for blacks and whites.

Jean and I met with the EEOC, led by Franklin D. Roosevelt, Jr., and persuaded it also to target its activities, which focused on the Southern textile and paper industries. Textiles turned out to be a mistake, because the industry was declining and technology was replacing a great deal of labor. It was more effective to make the case that blacks were entitled to a share in a growing pool of jobs than to try to compete with whites in a declining pool. This did not deny the reality that blacks were entitled to equal opportunity in either situation. It was just that it was best to apply our limited resources to cases where they would do the most good.

Jean's field workers Allen Black and Bob Valder generated complaints in the growing paper industry; their efforts eventually matured into about thirty LDF and government suits and many jobs for blacks. We not only didn't hesitate to sue industry giants, such as P. Lorillard, U.S. Steel, and national unions, the AFL-CIO and the Teamsters, but enjoyed showing that we wouldn't be deterred by their strength.

CLASS ACTIONS IN EMPLOYMENT SUITS

Between 1965 and 1970 we cleared away countless procedural obstacles. Employers raised technical objections to class actions, which exposed them to far-reaching restructuring and to back-pay awards to hundreds, sometimes thousands, of black workers. In an effort to keep the size of class action suits with claims of discrimination small, they argued that a suit should include only those who had filed charges with the EEOC and not the complainant's coworkers, no matter how similar their situations were. Sometimes, to avoid class actions, an employer would fire a complainant or even give the complainant the redress he or she sought, arguing either that the discharge was for good cause or that, having obtained what was sought, the plaintiff was no longer a victim of discrimination and had no standing to bring a class action. As part of a series of cases that developed job discrimination class actions, I had one appeal for a black worker who had been promoted and another for one who had been fired, winning for both the right to continue their lawsuits on behalf of others, even though the outcome would not help them personally.

The recently revised class action rules had been written by Al Sachs, a Harvard law professor (later dean) who lectured often at our lawyers' training conferences. He understood civil rights cases and, therefore, wrote the rules so that victims of discrimination would not face unreasonable obstacles in achieving their rights.

One of the first Title VII cases brought by LDF, against the Werthan Bag company, resonates in the popular movie *Driving Miss Daisy*. Morgan Freeman, in the film, fixes a stalled elevator at Werthan Bag that no white employee can repair. As a reward, he doesn't get a wonderful job at the plant, but becomes chauffeur for the owner's mother, Jessica Tandy. Our plaintiff hadn't fixed a stalled elevator, but he was a victim of discrimination at Werthan Bag. When we sued the company right after the act became effective, Helen Buttenwieser, who was on the LDF board, called me. I was surprised that she introduced the call by telling me that one of her sons was married to a Werthan. I told her of the discrimination at the plant; she urged me to get on with the suit vigorously. The district court rejected the defense that Title VII did not authorize filing a class action, and Werthan settled. Later, a member of the family contributed to our scholarship fund.

Between 1965 and 1970 Gabby Kirk and Bob Belton played the major role for LDF in employment cases, all tried with local lawyers, although we usually took over the appeals, many of which I argued. But staff lawyers, like Leroy Clark and Bob Belton, only recently out of school, were also, remarkably, in the court of appeals on a regular basis. In a big firm such an opportunity might be the capstone of a career.

QUARLES: SENIORITY SUICIDE PROHIBITED

Employment relations were constructed, often by union contracts, in ways that institutionalized discrimination. For example, seniority generally was within departments, so that if blacks finally won the right to enter a department from which they had previously been excluded, they would start at the bottom of the ladder of that department. They would be most vulnerable to layoff and last in priority for benefits accorded by high seniority, like choice of shift, opportunities for overtime, promotion, transfer, and pay increases. This would be so even though that black worker might have been an employee in the plant longer than most of the whites who were his or her senior in the department. The solution to that problem would be to allow employees to carry their seniority with them if they asked for transfer to other departments, rather than starting anew as required by union contract; we made that one of the goals of our lawsuits.

Selection standards were another area of our focus. Such standards often had the effect of discriminating even where it might be difficult to show that racial discrimination was their intent. Requiring a high school diploma for employment, even though the diploma might bear no relation to ability to do the job, disqualified otherwise qualified blacks during those years when blacks graduated from high school at a rate lower than whites. Requiring the achievement of a certain score on an IQ test, where the test score might bear no relationship to ability to do the job, might also disfavor undereducated blacks. Restricting recruiting for the job to word of mouth networking would keep out most blacks where current workers were mostly white. Giving preference to children of union members discriminated against those whose parents had had no opportunity to join unions. We targeted job selection standards that worked to discriminate in such covert ways.

Although there were few substantive Title VII decisions before 1970, Henry Marsh, Gabby Kirk, and Al Rosenthal won *Quarles v. Philip Morris*,

Inc., a 1967 district court decision that struck the first blow against departmental seniority. Philip Morris had always hired blacks, but placed them in unpleasant, low-paying jobs, like preparing tobacco leaves for processing, where they had little chance of advancement. Whites mainly operated machinery to make and package cigarettes, and worked in the warehouse, often starting without skill or experience but then being allowed to work their way up. By the time we filed *Quarles*, Philip Morris had stopped discriminatory hiring and allowed some transfer from black to white departments. However, because the union contract provided that layoffs, shift selection, and promotion were determined by length of service in a particular department or job, rather than by plant seniority, longtime black employees were unlikely to elect to transfer to a better department because doing so would require surrendering their seniority rights. Because the transfer would expose them to becoming first to be laid off, such transfers were often called seniority suicide. We maintained that black employees who had been discriminatorily placed in "black" jobs when first hired should be able, upon transfer, to hold on to their seniority. The union fought us on this. Whatever the pro–civil rights position of national labor unions in Washington, in the plants they too often upheld the rights of whites—acquired during periods of overt discrimination—at the expense of blacks.

In defending their position, the unions relied on Section 703(h) of Title VII, which declared that it was not unlawful to apply different standards pursuant to a bona fide seniority system "provided that such differences are not the result of an intention to discriminate because of race." In *Quarles* Judge Butzner rejected the union argument:

> The differences between the terms and conditions of employment for whites and Negroes about which plaintiffs complain are the result of an intention to discriminate in hiring policies on the basis of race before January 1, 1966 [the date Philip Morris ceased its discriminatory practices]. The differences that originated before the act are maintained now. The act does not condone present differences that are the result of intention to discriminate before the effective date of the act.

Butzner gave blacks the right to transfer to better departments, if qualified to do a job within that department, without losing employment date seniority. Blacks could not "bump" whites, that is, take jobs now occupied by whites, a right we disclaimed; they had to wait for vacancies. Logically, there was a pretty good argument for moving to their rightful place immediately, but we knew that would never fly and didn't even make the argument.

Neither the company nor the union appealed. As a consequence, the opinion, *Quarles*, from only a district court, the first on the subject, written by a highly respected judge, became the prevailing law, resulting in improved employment opportunities for thousands of blacks and women before it was overturned by the Burger Court ten years later. *Quarles* was responsible for the Fund's high success rate over the next decade, and our stock took an even sharper turn upward in the civil rights community.

In 1970 Mike Sovern, who had become dean of Columbia Law School, asked me to teach a seminar on civil rights. I developed a course like the one Walter Gellhorn taught when I was a student, except that students worked only on cases for LDF—by then we had enough to occupy an entire class.

GRIGGS V. DUKE POWER

In December 1970, in the midst of the Angela Davis strife, I argued *Griggs v. Duke Power Co.*, winning "the most important case in employment discrimination law," with an opinion by Chief Justice Burger for a unanimous Court. *Griggs* dealt with a typical situation: Duke Power reserved the best jobs for whites; blacks worked only in the labor department in dirty outside work, where the highest-paid worker earned less than the lowest-paid "operating" white employee.

In 1965, after Title VII was passed, the company stopped expressly confining blacks to labor jobs and announced new hiring and promotion standards. They required a high school diploma and test scores equal to those of the average high school graduate on two widely used paper and pencil IQ tests, although neither measured ability to perform the jobs in question. Fifty-eight percent of whites passed but only 6 percent of blacks succeeded. Employees hired before the high school requirement (white, of course) weren't required to have a diploma, they had only to pass the tests. Those already in the operating departments (again, whites) didn't need a diploma either, or to pass a test, yet they performed well, indicating further that testing didn't measure ability to do the job. The IQ tests were supposed to measure academic potential, and sometimes have been defended on the grounds that they predict ability to do well in school, but Griggs wanted only to be a coal handler, which hardly required a special aptitude for school work.

Much of our theoretical approach to testing was developed by George Cooper, of Columbia Law School, and Richard Sobol, as well as Richard Barrett, an industrial psychologist, our expert in *Griggs*, who counseled us on employment cases for many years. They maintained that where a pre-employment test has an unfavorable impact on blacks *and* does not predict ability to do the job, it violates Title VII. In such cases, they asserted, it should not be necessary to prove intent to discriminate, an almost impossible task. Key to this issue was Section 703(h) of the act, which authorized the use of "any professionally developed ability test" that is not "designed, intended or used to discriminate because of race."

Julius Chambers and Bob Belton set out to show that the Duke Power test was not "professionally developed" and that it did not predict well. The EEOC had defined "professionally developed" as "a test which fairly measures the knowledge or skills required by the particular job." Barrett testified that a professionally developed test to predict ability reliably must be "validated" by careful analysis of what a worker must do, and must study enough workers to warrant the conclusion. Duke Power had done none of this. Consequently, the test was not "professionally developed." I thought that *Griggs* was a good case for appealing the testing issue. Some of our academic advisers, Justice Department lawyers, and the EEOC disagreed and advised against appealing the testing issue. I thought that the discriminatory impact of testing would be better understood in a case where an IQ test was being used to evaluate someone who wanted to be a coal handler than in some other kind of case. Moreover, if we won, the payoff could be enormous; if we lost we would be no worse off—a better case was unlikely to arise. I decided to go ahead.

The testing issue was not easy: We are used to tests; we think that people who get higher scores are more capable. Even if a job doesn't require high levels of the kind of intelligence tested, shouldn't an employee have to prove that he or she is smart enough to move up? At oral argument the justices peppered me with questions of this sort: What if "higher jobs require a high school diploma or an ability to pass those tests?" I had prepared in advance: "If the company could demonstrate that blocking up the lines of progression would adversely affect the plant, we would not be urging . . . [this] position. . . . In other words it would be job related." But Duke Power had shown nothing of the sort.

Burger wanted to know about "eligibility to intern in a hospital, the hospital standard required that they be persons whose scholastic training and general aptitude measured by some reasonable test, were such that they were qualified." I answered, "A medical education is or at least ought to be directly related to the ability to practice medicine, and . . . the excellence of one's training and what one has learned as demonstrated by his record would bear some relationship. I would assume that that would be job validated."

Burger's skepticism was nowhere reflected in the unanimous victory. Resorting to metaphors, he referred to the tests as "built in headwinds" and summoned Aesop's fable of the stork and the fox: Congress has "provided that the vessel in which the milk is proffered be one all seekers can use." He concluded, "Congress has commanded . . . that any tests used must measure the person for the job and not the person in the abstract." *Griggs* laid the foundation for much Title VII law, including the use of statistical evidence, the order and allocation of burdens of proof, the requirement that business necessity be demonstrated to justify a test that results in a disparate impact, and the standard of job relatedness and deference to EEOC guidelines.

Bob Belton left LDF in 1970 to join Julius Chambers's law firm. That year, Bill Robinson began directing the Title VII program and argued the first sex discrimination case under Title VII in the Supreme Court for Ida Phillips, a white woman. The company refused to hire her because she had preschool-age children, but hired men who did. It did not even bother to try to justify the distinction as a "bona fide occupational qualification" (BFOQ), permitted under the law. Ida Phillips came to us at LDF because there was no legal defense fund for women, and she had heard that we had been winning job cases for blacks. The BFOQ defense was related to whether a test measured ability to do the job and so I thought the case might turn out to be important for blacks as well. In the end, the Supreme Court held illegal the company's refusal to hire her while it hired men in the same circumstances. The victory advanced women's rights and raised the stature of LDF with a new audience.

We next developed effective remedies, particularly back pay and, for workers for whom there was no place to be promoted, front pay, that is, earnings for jobs they would have had if the jobs had not been given to whites by discriminatory means.

COMPUTERS IN THE COURTROOM

Martin Mador came to LDF in 1971 in alternative service as a conscientious objector. Marty was an unkempt, bearded redhead, who never wore a tie and was happy to get the job even with little pay. We hired him to assist in the preparation of the trial of three big cases against the steel industry. Marty and Barry Goldstein prepared the statistical data by hand; but the company used computer printouts, and the Justice Department, in the cases with us, obtained computer runs from U.S. Steel by discovery. Neither Marty nor Barry relished doing cases by hand while companies were aided by computers. My wife, Debby, got the idea that we should ask IBM, celebrated for its use of computers in the major government antitrust suit against it, whose general counsel, Nick Katzenbach, was on our board, for help in developing computer capability. Nick sent Dick Allphin to our office with a terminal resembling a portable typewriter. He laid a telephone on it and before a clutch of awestruck lawyers called up all sorts of data from the record in *United States v. IBM.* He gave lectures on computers and turned Marty Mador into a computer analyst to assist in Title VII cases.

In one of our earliest cases the defendant used a labor market economist who purported to show that the difference in black–white earnings was due to productivity, not discrimination. We enlisted our own economist, Marc Rosenblum, who helped us plan a strategy based on cross-examination of the company's experts; after this we commonly used our own labor economists, statisticians, and industrial psychologists. To furnish them material for analysis we developed extensive interrogatories to obtain defendants' employment records and subpoenaed their personnel computer tapes. While the company information often had not been collected for the purpose, Marty developed computer programs that could "massage" it to produce analyses comparing black and white jobs, seniority, previous experience, salaries, hires, layoffs, terminations, overtime, promotions, and pay, and to demonstrate disparities explainable only by race that surprised even defendants. With statisticians and labor force economists using multiple regression analysis we prepared evidence for trial. In many cases not even the major American corporations could match us. In a case against Monsanto our staff taught government lawyers how to do computer analyses.

Marty's appearance was more countercultural than that of anyone on the staff—all of the men, at least, wore a suit and tie in going to court; women dressed appropriately. Once John Walker, an early intern who went into practice in Little Rock, used Marty as an expert in a case against International Paper. Marty says, "John made me wear a necktie. It was enough that I was a Jewish conscientious objector with long hair and a beard testifying for the NAACP Legal Defense Fund."

JOE MOODY'S VINDICATION

Bob Belton and Julius Chambers carried *Griggs* a step farther in *Moody v. Albermarle Paper Co.* Blacks had the dirtiest, worst-paying outside jobs, moving wood in the woodyard for grinding into chips while whites operated machinery in higher-paying jobs indoors. Promotions were awarded on the basis of tests, on which blacks fared poorly. On the eve of trial, Albermarle hired an industrial psychologist to do a validation study. His report was no surprise—the tests vindicated the company; they tested ability to do the job.

Bob and Julius showed that segregated lines of progression persisted under the 1968 union contract that tacked formerly black lines to the bottom of white ones, because blacks promoted into a white line lost seniority and faced layoffs. Barrett testified that the tests had not been validated or shown to predict ability to do the job. After we won in the court of appeals, Albermarle requested rehearing by the entire court, rather than the three judges who heard the case originally.

A new issue emerged, so esoteric that it would flabbergast most judges: May senior judges, that is, judges who have reached retirement age but are still active, vote on whether a case should be heard by the entire court (as distinct from participating in the case once it was heard)? We were opposed to the senior judges voting on whether there should be a rehearing by all the judges, simply because, calculating how the judges would vote on the merits, we concluded that we would lose if the case were heard by all. It was even more complicated than that but not worth further explanation. It's hard to convert that issue into one of principle. This question went to the Supreme Court—the arguments on each side are not worth repeating—consuming large chunks of Mike Baller's time.

We won, the court of appeals decision was not upset, and then Albermarle petitioned the Supreme Court for review of the merits of the case. The Court agreed to hear it, and the plaintiff, Joe Moody, came to the Supreme Court in April 1975 for Julius's argument. Moody was illiterate and couldn't sign his name, but as leader of the black workers at Albermarle he had fought discrimination for thirty years. He looked grave and proud as Julius—also from North Carolina and from circumstances not far removed from his own—argued his case.

The Court decided that the company was not entitled to a jury trial, that back pay must be awarded in employment discrimination cases (since then it has been, routinely), and that good faith is no ground for exception. Otherwise, employers and unions would have no incentive to clean up their act; they would await suit and then, only if they lost, eliminate discrimination, cost free. With the meter running, it would become increasingly expensive to continue to discriminate. Julius got a $20,000 settlement for Moody; because he was unskilled he could not benefit much beyond that. He had believed in the law and his lawyers and carried on the struggle for the younger black workers, not for himself.

Between 1971 and 1974 the staff did four to five class action trials and after that one or two each year. At the same time there was pre- and post-trial litigation (briefs, motions, discovery) of earlier cases and those awaiting trial, numerous appeals with local lawyers, and monitoring of many cases. In the first half of 1980 staff lawyers were lead counsel in eight cases in the Supreme Court, twenty-six in courts of appeals, and twenty-nine in district courts. By then, more than half the cases were against state and local governments and there were many against large corporations and unions. Staff lawyers were on the road continuously. We had more cases than the entire Equal Employment Opportunity Commission.

Back pay awards began to grow. In 1972 P. Lorillard secured Senator Edward Brooke to set up a meeting between me and its counsel to negotiate a settlement. We got $725,000. In 1975 we won $1 million from Gilman Paper Company; later we obtained $1.75 million against Cities Service in Louisiana; $820,000 against the world's largest paper mill, owned by Union Camp Corporation in Georgia, and three unions; $1.1 million against Norfolk and Western Railway, and amounts of this magnitude against corporations, unions, and governmental bodies. We did as well in monetary awards as the Office of Federal Contracts Compliance, which had a much larger staff. While the cases won jobs, promotions, and training, and eliminated non–job-related tests, and while the money was welcome, even more welcome was the new message the awards sent: The longer you discriminate the more it will cost you.

During this same period staff lawyers and I also testified before congressional committees that exercised oversight for the EEOC and the Labor and Justice departments, led the winning opposition to a nominee as general counsel of the EEOC, and argued successfully with the EEOC not to change its guidelines on employee selection.

TAKING ON STEEL

The steel industry was among the worst discriminators, with blacks confined to hot, dirty, front-end jobs, handling raw materials, taking ore from railroad cars, and separating iron at open hearths and blast furnaces. Even though the United Steel Workers Union supported civil rights in Washington, locally its white members fought to require blacks to enter seniority lines only at the bottom, which subjected them to layoff during downturns. In 1973 LDF won a case against U.S. Steel and the United Steelworkers Union after a fifty-four-day trial in Birmingham. That was the beginning of a long struggle against steel.

Bill Robinson, who had met Barry Goldstein at Columbia Law School, persuaded me to hire him for six months, just to try the steel cases, which wound up taking twelve years; Barry stayed with LDF for eighteen years, in time branching out into employment cases generally.

District Judge Sam C. Pointer ordered ratios for black promotion to apprenticeship and supervisory positions, red circling (transfer to the bottom of the white seniority line, without reduction in pay, to a job which in time would lead to higher pay), and other relief. The court required defendants to pay 61 of our 361 black plaintiffs over $200,000. The victory was particularly sweet for U. W. Clemon, one of our earliest interns and a lawyer in the case, whose father had worked in Jim Crow jobs in U.S. Steel's Fairfield, Alabama, plant for twenty years. The decision also awarded the highest counsel fee as of that time, $170,000, half against the steel company and half against three locals, for eight years of work, over fifty days of trial, and huge expenses—a rate that would have driven private lawyers into bankruptcy. We would have obtained nothing if we lost, but the lawyers who did lose undoubtedly were paid many times our award.

The Justice Department, which had presented the case for three thousand other black steel workers, obtained the same injunctive relief, but no monetary award. We moved to intervene in its case to ask for back pay for the workers Justice represented. Pointer approved our intervention, but curiously didn't award any money, and we appealed. So did the government.

The steel industry and union faced an expensive prospect. Lawyers all over the country, particularly with the lure of counsel fees, would be filing heavy back pay suits. The longer steel continued its old ways, the more it would eventually cost. So, they took a cue from antitrust enforcement, where the neatest, cheapest resolution has been a not-too-disagreeable consent decree worked out with the Justice Department. The term "sweetheart contract" sometimes describes such arrangements. Nine steel companies, the union, and the Justice Department secretly negotiated two decrees (one for union, the other for nonunion jobs), covering plants across the country.

On April 12, 1974, the department filed its complaint and the consent decrees in United States District Court in Birmingham. Before anyone heard about it, Judge Pointer approved them. In many respects the decrees were good, requiring that jobs, training, promotion, and all aspects of work be open to blacks, women, and Hispanics, using plantwide seniority. They required affirmative action for hiring and trade and craft jobs, more or less parallel to the decrees recently won in Birmingham. The consent order established a fund of more than $30 million to settle back pay claims, but didn't explain how awards would be computed, a worker perhaps receiving much less than he or she was entitled to, but having no way of knowing. Workers who accepted awards had to sign waivers giving up all claims against the company and union.

Bill Robinson, who had left LDF to become chief of litigation for EEOC, negotiated the $30 million settlement, although his influence was limited because Justice was in charge. He now thinks that the amount was far too low; he accepted it then because he was inexperienced and $30 million seemed like a lot of money. Many black workers were undercompensated. On the other hand, most workers would not have sued to win a larger amount, and those that did might not have won.

We were stunned and furious. We were angry at the small amount of back pay, secrecy about how it was calculated, waivers that would permit the effects of past discrimination to continue cost free, and the shifting of some issues from courts to committees appointed by the wrongdoers themselves. We also were irritated about having been excluded from a process we started. I decided to crash their party and in nine days Eric Schnapper and other staff lawyers drafted and filed a petition in which LDF asked to enter the case.

On May 20, Judge Pointer held a hearing in Birmingham. Maybe fifty lawyers were in the courtroom, representing the companies, the government, the union, and LDF. Counsel tables weren't large enough and lawyers overflowed into the jury box. It was the first time in recent years that I saw a federal court jury box with only whites in it. Pointer allowed us to intervene, but then upheld the consent decrees. We went straightaway to the court of appeals.

In October 1975, Barry and I argued the steel cases in the Fifth Circuit in New Orleans. Afterward we went to the Court of Two Sisters, a venerable

New Orleans café, where we drank Sazeracs in the garden and came down from having battled the largest corporations, unions, and the Justice Department. The last time I had been there was when my LST was being outfitted with anti-aircraft guns, before heading to the Panama Canal and across the Pacific.

Barry won his case outright, the court deciding that actions commenced before the decrees were signed weren't affected by them. The black workers could recover back pay and might sue for injunctions should they suffer discrimination in the future. The court held that the rights claimed in my argument were already in the decree—this astonished me, the companies, and the union—and there was nothing to complain about. It decided that they had not agreed to deny workers who signed waivers the right to sue for post-decree discrimination that flowed from pre-decree conduct and that a worker could sue for more if his compensation was a "mere pittance," which wasn't defined. The companies, union, and government returned to district court, saying that the court of appeals had misunderstood their intention, and Pointer allowed them to amend the decrees, from which we appealed. Ultimately that appeal got nowhere.

GAG ORDERS

In Pittsburgh we tried to inform black workers about their rights under the consent decrees at the United States Steel Homestead Works, where Debby and a local lawyer, Bernie Marcus, were suing the company and union. Judge Hubert Teitelbaum imposed a "gag order," prohibiting us from communicating with the employees. Bill Coleman won a writ of mandamus in the court of appeals in Philadelphia, requiring Teitelbaum to allow us to advise the workers—a slap in the face to a lower court judge. Teitelbaum then prohibited us from sending black workers a leaked memorandum, showing how the back pay awards had been calculated. Once more Bill went to the court of appeals, which mandamused Teitelbaum again.

Despite these wins, gag orders were common in employment cases, prohibited us from talking with class members, and hindered preparation for trial. The gag order idea came out of a manual for complex litigation, drawn up by a committee of leading lawyers, mostly counsel for corporate defendants, and some law professors, which judges followed without question. The justification was that it prevented stirring up litigation. I protested to committee members to no avail. Finally we took a gag order case, against Gulf Oil, to the Supreme Court. I argued the case first in the court of appeals in New Orleans, before twenty-two judges, who sat in tiers ranging across the room and fired questions from all directions. Thirteen ruled that the gag order violated the First Amendment; eight that it was invalid under the Federal Rules of Civil Procedure; one dissented. The company went to the Supreme Court, where in 1981 I won unanimously because the gag order conflicted with the Federal Rules of Civil Procedure. That was the end of gag orders.

By April 1976 almost all black steelworkers in the country had signed waivers. It was impossible to tell whether the amounts they received compensated for the discrimination they had suffered. The cases remained pending until 1990, by which time they worked a transformation of employment patterns in the steel industry, although workers never knew whether their back pay awards reflected the loss they had suffered.

By the end of the 1970s, however, the steel industry, and manufacturing generally, was in a recession, battered by foreign competition, and many mills closed. The right to skilled and crafts jobs in steel and other industries often became meaningless because many of those jobs disappeared. But plantwide seniority, sometimes works-seniority (covering several plants in a "works"), protected many black workers from layoff. Many blacks were promoted. In Birmingham, for example, forty blacks in unskilled car-shop jobs moved up to the position of welder. The jobs that remained were well integrated. Moreover, there is another dimension to these suits that should not be ignored. Following a recent LDF victory over Du Pont, a black worker said, "If we didn't get a nickel I felt like justice has been served." When cases ended workers often gave banquets for the lawyers and presented them with plaques and scrolls.

AGAINST THE GOVERNMENT

In 1972 Congress amended Title VII to permit employment suits against the federal government and from then on, cases against federal and state agencies became the most important part of the LDF employment docket. Steve Ralston and Bill Lee, who treated the issue as a personal vendetta, resented the maze of procedural roadblocks the federal government had erected to make suits so difficult that they were almost impossible. Justice Department lawyers obstinately insisted that government workers were bound by the usually inadequate record of hearings before government administrators, and not entitled to a full trial of an employment discrimination complaint, that class actions were not permitted, and that the statute of limitations was very short. Nevertheless, LDF won cases against the federal government involving NASA, the Immigration and Naturalization Service, the Postal Service, the Veterans Administration, the army, navy, and air force, and other agencies. We also won many suits against city and state governments involving policemen, firemen, teachers, correction guards, and other civil servants.

In the Reagan administration, Justice was an opponent also in cases against private employers, which presented the issue of affirmative action, arguing that only proven victims of discrimination, not other black workers, should share in affirmative relief. But the vast number who were affected indirectly by discrimination, those who knew better than to waste time applying, or were disadvantaged by societal discrimination, could never summon the proof needed according to Justice's theory. The Justice Department opposed us in New Orleans, where the black populaton was 55 percent and which, in 1980, had only seven black police officers in ranks above officer and only one black captain. We had similar battles with Justice in the Detroit police case, where Mayor Coleman Young asked LDF to represent the city. After long courtroom battles in both cases we won and increased black representation on the police forces. But we lost against Justice in cases in which blacks had been hired because of affirmative action and then, having little seniority, were laid off during economic downturns.

PACE

Joining forces with Rick Seymour of the Lawyers Committee for Civil Rights Under Law and MALDEF (Mexican American Legal Defense and Education Fund), we sued the United States Civil Service Commission over its Professional and Administrative Career Examination (PACE), which was taken by 200,000 applicants each year competing for up to 8,000 jobs. The test clearly violated EEOC guidelines and kept virtually all minorities out of higher civil service jobs. Twenty-five percent of white applicants but only 1.1 percent of minority applicants scored high enough for career ladder positions in which they might expect to move up and have a lifetime of employment in a government career.

In the last days of the Carter administration we entered into a settlement requiring the government to make "all practicable efforts to eliminate any disproportionately adverse effect of continued use of the PACE during the phase-out period, or of alternative examining procedures . . . against blacks or against Hispanics." When it came to office, Reagan's Justice Department denounced the settlement as requiring quotas. With cocounsel I met Justice officials headed by Charles Renfrew, formerly Carter's deputy attorney general, who was serving in the Reagan administration as a holdover. We argued that the tests were invalid under *Griggs* and that the administration's weakest case against affirmative action would be one in which the parties had agreed to remedy a test like PACE, which was clearly illegal. Finally, I argued that our agreement was not with the Carter administration but with the United States. That won nods and murmurs of assent and the settlement was allowed to stand.

WALK-INS

Many walk-in cases involved New York City employers. Debby was in cases against the *New York Times*, the *Daily News*, the *Wall Street Journal*, and other publications; the Long Island Railroad; the New York City Human Resources Administration; the New York State Department of Corrections; and, with Betsy Bartholet Dubois, against the New York City Board of Examiners. As a legacy of the movement, Wall Street firms were usually cooperating counsel in cases in the New York area. This public interest activity helped attract some of the best new graduates to their firms.

Debby's thirty cases, even though only a handful were active at any time and some were in New York, kept her out of town regularly, which had an unanticipated impact on our personal life. As my work consisted principally of appellate arguments, working on briefs and strategy in the office, I played a more than active role at home. Billy and Suzanne lived with us. Josiah (who went to Columbia College), David (mostly away at Reed College in Oregon), Ezra (at Grinnell College in Iowa), and Sarah (at the Culinary Institute of America in upstate New York) had their permanent home with their mother in Great Neck, but spent substantial stretches of time with us. I cared for the kids, dealt with major crises, usually prepared dinner, and developed into a fair cook. Sometimes I took Sarah to the office, where she became a particularly good pal of Velma Harris, our switchboard operator. When Debby called home from out of town, the kids, to her chagrin, usually seemed to be having a good time. She decided she had to spend more time at home and took a job as president of the Legal Action Center in New York, a public interest law firm dedicated to the reform of the criminal justice system and the rights of those convicted of crime or with histories of addiction. Later she became clinical professor of law at Columbia, the university that, ultimately, five of our six kids attended in various academic programs. It may be that the tuition exemption at Columbia and partial tuition payment elsewhere accorded faculty members and their families, when applied to our six children, made Debby the highest-paid teacher in America.

Unlike our cases down South, in the New York cases we actually observed the appearance of black cops, firemen, city officials, and other workers, who until recently had been almost all white. One of the plaintiffs in the newspaper cases had been unable to get delivery jobs reserved by white old-timers for their sons, through a complex set of rules that kept out virtually all minorities. When he first came to the office seeking help, he was on welfare. After the court approved a settlement with a 25 percent minority hiring goal, almost a thousand blacks and Hispanics got better-paying jobs delivering the papers.

I ran into this plaintiff on the street a few years after the decree, the man who had been on welfare when he came to us. His job now was driving a tractor trailer for the *New York Times* to places like Syracuse and Pittsburgh, receiving overtime pay for remaining out of town overnight. I asked,

"Would you mind telling me how much you're making now, John?" "A hundred thousand a year," he replied, "but next year I'll make more."

By the end of the 1970s our litigation had become in some ways like big law firm cases with none of the frantic excitement that characterized the movement in the early 1960s. But racists continued to hate with the passion associated with the early days of transition from a legally segregated society to a more fully integrated one. My recently partially opened FBI file reveals that the National Socialist Party of America had planned to bomb me in the spring of 1977. The FBI, which knew of the plot, never notified me.

31

THE WAR ON POVERTY: MARTIN LUTHER KING, JR., AND NORI

RESURRECTION CITY AND THE POOR PEOPLE'S CAMPAIGN

With the Civil Rights Acts came the realization that merely prohibiting discrimination would not end the legacy of slavery and segregation that had
divided the country into two societies, one rich, mostly populated by
whites, the other poor, mostly populated by blacks. Poverty affected black
people in ways that made it impossible to achieve educational equality, par-
ity in the job market, decent housing, or to otherwise participate in our
bountiful society at the level most whites did.

Combating poverty, however, was not something that could be done successfully for blacks, or indeed any single group, alone. The effort would
have to transcend race. That was the premise of the Ford Foundation's grant
for the LDF National Office for the Rights of the Indigent (NORI), which
represented the poor among whites and others as well as blacks. Similar
perceptions moved Martin Luther King, Jr., to launch his last great national
effort, the Poor People's campaign.

In March 1968, King invited me to Atlanta to discuss representing SCLC
in that project. Earlier, Marian Wright had brought to him four sharecroppers in their forties who had been driven off their land by government subsi-
dies that paid the landowners to stop farming. Marian argued that if the
government was subsidizing farmers to not grow crops, why were comparable payments not being made to the people who had been forced to give up
their livelihoods, who had been thrown off the land they used to live on as
well as driven from work? Out of that developed an idea of a protest like the
bonus marches of veterans in Washington during the thirties, which had
established a city of shanties and focused the attention of the world on the
plight of the unemployed during the Great Depression. King hadn't had
much success since the Selma to Montgomery march. His efforts in
Chicago—we had represented him, along with Chicago lawyers, in housing

protests—had produced little beyond a mostly symbolic 1966 agreement with the city and the real estate industry.

I met with him and top SCLC staff in Atlanta on March 13, at Paschal's Motel, accompanied by Leroy Clark, Chuck Jones, Lou Pollak, and Mel Zarr. King outlined a program scheduled to begin about April 15 and to continue through the middle of May. He proposed poor people's marches from several locations, including Jackson, Mississippi, which would go on for about a week. The effort would be racially integrated, including other minority groups, and would be committed to nonviolence. He wanted our help because the marchers would need lawyers to defend them against harassment, arrest, prosecution, and other hostile legal action and to get permits for meetings and parades. He planned visits to congressmen to urge public hearings and the passage of legislation. Middle-class demonstrators who held jobs would picket government offices on weekends. A mass demonstration of civil disobedience was planned, including sit-ins at congressional offices that would involve refusals to leave when requested to do so. They planned also to build a shantytown in Washington as a symbol of the living conditions of the poor.

I thought that the proposed shantytown had the potential of turning into great confusion and perhaps even defeat the aim of eliciting sympathy for the plight of the poor. I suggested that instead the SCLC should bring to Washington a typical sharecropper's shack and donate it to the Smithsonian. This could have the effect of focusing on how poor rural blacks lived and avoid the possibility of losing control involved in creating a settlement. Some of King's advisers liked my proposal, but not enough to adopt it.

I observed that civil disobedience, by definition, was a crime and that it might be impossible in many cases to defend them against the substance of the charges; there might, however, be a role for us with regard to refusal of bail or bail set at excessive levels, appropriateness of charges, and sentencing. Martin was willing to plead guilty when he was civilly disobedient and understood that he would have to serve his sentence. Lou Pollak, in particular, probed him as to what the operation was supposed to accomplish, but nothing very clear emerged.

During lunch there was talk about the position he had taken in open opposition to the war in Vietnam, for which he had been criticized a great deal, including by Roy Wilkins and Whitney Young. He said that he understood he was splitting the movement and, therefore, had gone public with his beliefs only after long hesitation, but he had felt that he had to take the moral position. Moreover, he had hesitated to criticize the armed forces, because they were a place where blacks could find upward mobility—a view I hardly would have expected to hear from a pacifist like Martin. I told the LDF executive committee that I did not "see how we could turn our back on [Dr. King] now merely because . . . [the Poor People's campaign] is so controversial." I discussed the possibility of representing demonstrators selectively, with regard to some activities, but not others. We knew how to refuse to handle inappropriate cases: "SNCC groups intruded themselves [during the Selma march] and did such things as urinate in the streets and on the walls of Dr. King's church. We merely refused to represent them and we certainly would refuse to represent anyone conducting himself in a manner inconsonant with Dr. King's proclaimed policy of non-violence."

The executive committee unanimously approved my proposal that we represent SCLC in the Poor People's campaign.

Around the same time, in April, pursuing his newly developing policy of moving beyond classical civil rights issues, Martin supported a sanitation workers strike in Memphis. SCLC enlisted LDF to handle legal matters that might arise out of the strike and a mass march scheduled for April 5. My FBI file recounts that "Jack Greenberg . . . would help to organize this legal staff." Hosea Williams, SCLC director of voter registration, said that they needed lawyers "who will go all the way and who know all the angles."

By April 2, LDF staff lawyers Leroy Clark and Jim Finney put together a plan to coordinate LDF staff, volunteer lawyers and students, and Hispanic and Native American interpreters with regard to a catalog of projects on which they might work in the Poor People's campaign. But on April 4, 1968, before the campaign could get under way, in an event which horrified the world, an assassin's bullet killed the country's most outspoken, committed advocate of nonviolence. The murder occurred in Memphis, where Martin had gone to support the sanitation workers' strike, a strike to improve the conditions and pay of both black and white workers.

The whole world was stunned. Those of us connected with the movement were shattered. But no one thought for a moment of giving up the struggle. SCLC resolved to go forward with Martin's work. On the Sunday following the murder I met with Ralph Abernathy, Andy Young, and other SCLC leaders in Atlanta. Abernathy announced that SCLC had decided to proceed with the Poor People's campaign and wanted LDF to represent it. I sent several staff lawyers, led by Leroy Clark, to Washington to meet with the District of Columbia corporation counsel and lawyers who had volunteered to handle legal matters in connection with the campaign. Leroy negotiated a lease with the National Park Service for a campsite for Resurrection City, recruited lawyers, and arranged to have them trained by law professors at Howard. Unhappily, the campaign proceeded without Martin's guiding hand; the results showed the lack of whatever order he might have impressed upon it.

The campaign constructed Resurrection City, which opened on May 13 and consisted of shanties that housed perhaps two thousand people, in West Potomac Park, under a permit from the National Park Service that was good until the end of June. Jesse Jackson was its mayor. The weather was not kind and heavy rains left the area ankle deep in mud and strewn with garbage. Farm animals wandered freely about. Crossroads, the black squatter campsite near Cape Town in South Africa, was far more habitable. Campaign leaders pointed to Resurrection City as an example of how poor people had to live all over America; these conditions had now been placed under the gaze of the nation's leaders. The problem was that most of the nation's leaders didn't see it; to the extent they were aware of Resurrection City, there is no evidence that they were made more supportive of its aims.

Abernathy and the principals in the campaign led visits to congressional offices, headed marches and parades, and held a mass rally that attracted more than fifty thousand people. They then approached Congress and the cabinet with a series of demands for ending poverty. But these were so numerous and diffuse—ranging over food and agriculture programs, employment policy, welfare, health policy, Northern and Southern school desegregation, rights of Mexican Americans and Native Americans, and many other matters—that they were doomed to defeat. Moreover, the campaign attracted participants who had never been trained in nonviolence, some carrying weapons and others who engaged in a range of antisocial behavior. Legal skirmishes developed, including some felony cases, which volunteer lawyers handled and we monitored.

On June 24, three weeks after after its permit expired, two thousand District of Columbia police shut down Resurrection City. Police arrested Hosea Williams, the "city manager," charging him with breach of the peace. The *New York Times* reported that upon the clearing of Resurrection City a "feeling of good riddance was shared by leaders of the campaign and the police." A sad ending for the last crusade of Martin Luther King, Jr., who, five years earlier, from this very city, had told America, "I have a dream."

Our final legal work for Resurrection City dealt with a government claim of $71,795 for use of equipment, damage to trees, razing the shanties, and so forth. Frank Reeves negotiated it down to $2,197 and I recommended settlement on that basis.

Marian and Martin were right in their awareness that ending poverty was fundamental to changing the status of blacks. But the Poor People's campaign could not have been planned and executed more badly. Its prospects for success were doomed by Martin's death, which could not have come at a worse time for the effort. The key perception, however, that whites and blacks, indeed all groups, have to address poverty and will benefit from change together seems to be central to the Clinton administration's strategy in dealing with race relations. To the extent that Marian is influential within that administration, the campaign was an important learning experience.

THE NATIONAL OFFICE FOR THE RIGHTS OF THE INDIGENT

We did a little better with the National Office for the Rights of the Indigent (NORI). LDF obtained funds that enabled us to increase staff size by almost half and to address the conditions in which the poor lived, particularly poor blacks. These were cases we once carried as LDF cases but put under NORI; however, there was no consistent delineation separating LDF and NORI cases. We always had cases with implications beyond race, for example, forced confession, right to counsel, and capital punishment cases. As we perceived ways in which welfare law and consumer fraud in the ghetto affected blacks adversely we took on such cases for NORI. They might just as well have been called LDF cases. Employment discrimination and education cases had the potential of lifting blacks out of poverty. We continued to call them LDF cases. One of our most important job cases was for a white woman. Because NORI came into being as a fund-raising vehicle, in order to demonstrate that the Ford Foundation grant that launched the program was being spent as Ford wanted it spent, we placed under its rubric whatever cases fit, but these assignments made little difference in how we prosecuted the cases.

Among the earliest NORI projects were cases to improve inferior services in black sections of cities. While they focused on black areas, they might be applicable to any neglected section of a city. If we were successful, cities would have to start pouring resources into areas that they had previously neglected. Selecting small locales to develop the law quickly—no need for massive factual records, as would be necessary for New Orleans or Jackson—we started with three little Mississippi towns: Shaw, Belzoni, and Itta Bena. Shaw was a town of fifteen hundred blacks and one thousand whites. Whites lived in lovely homes along the bayou, with broad porches, wide lawns, and willow trees trailing branches in the water—much as they must have been before the Civil War—and with appropriate public facilities. Black sections were substandard: weatherbeaten small houses, unpaved streets, roadside ditches filled with stagnant water, unlighted streets, distant fire hydrants, nonexistent traffic signs, inadequate sewerage, and low water pressure.

I won *Shaw* after a reargument before sixteen judges of the Fifth Circuit. The majority held that "it is not necessary to prove intent, motive or purpose to discriminate on the part of city officials," and that "there was here neglect involving clear overtones of racial discrimination . . . resulting in the same evils which characterize an intentional and purposeful disregard of the principle of equal protection." Some judges concurred and dissented in part, so the vote was hard to pin down, but only three dissented completely.

Shaw satisfied the decision with a federal grant to pay for equalizing the community. Other public interest groups began like cases; foundations gave grants for similar litigation—to my annoyance—to other groups, not to LDF. But satisfactory answers to questions that had not arisen in *Shaw* and would be bound to come up elsewhere were not found. What of towns where residents paid for their own paving, sewerage, and other facilities by special assessments, not general taxation, and where whites with money assessed themselves while blacks didn't? What about cities where more money was spent in black sections than white, but where population density in black neighborhoods was higher? What if the city cleaned black areas more often than white ones, but black sections remained dirtier because people without jobs or recreational opportunities spend more time on the street? Where would cities get the money to equalize if, unlike Shaw, they couldn't get federal grants? These problems were common.

Moreover, assembling the facts for big cities was often virtually impossible. The *Shaw* case was difficult to apply outside the setting of tiny towns, and the municipal equalization effort soon died. Several years later, in an employment case, Justice White's opinion said that *Shaw* had been wrongly decided and that to establish a constitutional violation the plaintiff must show an intent to discriminate, which would be almost impossible to do in a municipal equalization case, where so many factors interact.

It began to dawn on me that municipal equalization cases might have become impossible for at least one very practical reason: If successful, they would end in enormous financial outlays by government. Deep down the courts probably realized this and resolved that such decisions were for the legislature.

ACCESS TO HOUSING

Connie Motley's early cases established that blacks had to be admitted to white public housing projects. In 1967 we got a court order against evicting a black family from an Atlanta public housing project. In 1969 Jim Nabrit III won a case in the Supreme Court holding that public housing tenants had the right to a fair hearing before eviction. We lost an effort to stop a highway plan in Nashville that would have walled off Fisk University from the rest of the city, but we stopped an urban renewal plan that would have razed black parts of Newark to build a medical school. In 1969 I won a case in the Fifth Circuit, requiring federal courts to hear black residents who desired relocation following eviction to make way for an urban renewal project. The state's slight involvement had consisted only of building a drainage ditch. Perhaps state participation of any kind— way down the road consisting of sidewalk repair, street lighting, fire protection?—would be subject to equal protection rules, a hope that never was realized.

In theory, the 1968 Civil Rights Act (Title VIII), the new fair housing law, passed in the wake of the assassination of Martin Luther King, offered hope of equal access to housing without regard to race. But New York had long had a fair housing law, which didn't give us much encouragement. Cases were difficult to prove, not many blacks used the law; and the State Commission Against Discrimination hardly enforced it. We considered suit to compel the commission to enforce the law, but the prospects didn't seem favorable. Instead, with local fair housing groups, we assembled a lengthy dossier that demonstrated the commission's ineffectiveness. We invented a procedure: We filed with the commission itself a complaint setting forth the facts, stapled it into a handsome blue cover, and announced it at a press conference. The newspapers ran stories, TV covered the announcement, Governor Rockefeller proposed legislative changes, the chairman resigned. In the end, however, the commission's committment to enforcing the law didn't change very much.

One idea for enforcing the federal housing law was to give the law a credible bite by winning lots of cases, because, we thought, large damage judgments and counsel fees would deter discrimination, as we had seen in employment discrimination cases. In 1973 I argued a case to persuade the Supreme Court that jury trials weren't necessary under the law, that a judge alone had the power to decide a fair housing case. We feared that juries would be prejudiced against blacks. The Supreme Court disagreed. The only time he ruled against me, Thurgood wrote for a unanimous Court that Title VIII required a jury. It turned out that I was wrong in anticipating that juries would be unfair to fair housing plaintiffs, who often did well before juries, winning large judgments—prejudice against landlords is pretty strong too. Even so, cases remained relatively few in number compared to the size of the problem and were difficult to prove.

Too large a part of the housing market consists of individual units or small developments, so a single case cannot have the effect of a school desegregation order or judgment against a national employer. The threat of damages, which motivated employers to comply with Title VII, didn't seem real to most small property holders, who thought that they could keep blacks out without being caught. After all, a property owner could refuse to lease for a variety of reasons. Who could say he or she had not used a valid reason rather than a discriminatory reason? Also, marketing of vacant apartments did a lot to determine who applied for them. To cite an extreme example of this, I met a landlord who prefers to rent to Asians, but not to blacks, and so he advertises only in Chinese-language newspapers.

Nevertheless, as a substantial black middle class has developed, the situation has begun to change, and a fair number of middle-class blacks have been buying and renting in areas that were formerly all white. This has served the right of those doing better financially to be able to choose where they want to live (as whites do), but who were formerly denied this choice because of race. It doesn't do anything for poor people, whose choice is restricted by lack of funds.

Still, one of my black colleagues at Columbia reports that whenever she has tried to buy or rent she has initially been rebuffed because of her race. Nevertheless, after some difficulty, she has been successful in obtaining the housing she has wanted. However, not everyone has her knowledge of the law and her determination to fight back.

THE CONSUMER IN THE GHETTO

As part of NORI we launched a consumer protection program. Courts in seventeen states used to be able to order debtors to pay part of their debts, usually by having it withheld from wages, without notice or even a hearing on whether they owed anything. This practice, called garnishment, humiliated the person with his employer as well as adding additional expense of litigation to the amount owed. As a result, garnishing put enormous pressure on poor people to pay claims that they might not have incurred. I won a case—representing a white person—in which the Supreme Court held that before a creditor can garnish a debtor there must be a fair hearing on whether the money is owed.

We also went after installment contracts. High-pressure salesmen would sell overpriced, substandard appliances to ghetto residents, getting them to sign contracts that called for monthly payments. The buyer was never advised that the seller reserved the right to sell the debt to a third party, making worthless the buyer's natural assumption that if the product was unsatisfactory he or she would be able to withhold the remaining payments as leverage to get some satisfaction from the seller.

By the time the buyer realized how little quality had been received for so high a price, it was too late to refuse to pay. By then the seller had transferred the installment loan to a so-called bona fide purchaser (BFP) of the debt who, under conventional law, had to be paid without regard to whether the original deal could be set aside in a lawsuit. The buyer had to sue the seller and try to get back the cost of the purchase, if a lawyer could be found willing to handle the case, while continuing to make payments to the purchaser of the debt. In reality, the BFP was often not so "bona fide." Rather it was a related corporation set up by the fraudulent seller or someone in cahoots with the seller to whom the contract was transferred for the sole purpose of insuring that the payments would have to be paid even though there might be a good defense against the seller. The BFP, then, was hardly an innocent third party to a dispute between buyer and seller. Where the connection between seller and BFP could be demonstrated, the buyer could make the claim—for example, that a washing machine never worked—against the so-called BFP.

LDF assistant counsel Phil Schrag, just out of Yale Law School, tried to fashion a campaign against spurious transfer of installment contracts. But he ran into exasperating delays as big law firms stonewalled, using every procedural device to stall, including lengthy, unnecessary pretrial interrogation of plaintiffs that cost them time lost from work, and shifting of hearings from one courthouse to another. Overworked courts didn't pay attention to Phil's efforts to protect his clients from interminable and exhausting questioning. The cases bogged down and ultimately were lost.

At a bar association supper one night I encountered a partner in a large firm who had been running Phil ragged. Looking like a George Grosz print of an offensively fat lawyer, gorging himself on a plate so full that food tumbled down his shirt and mountainous belly, he chuckled, "I sure taught that kid of yours a lesson or two." It soon became clear that the only effective way to get at inner-city consumer problems would be through legislation and governmental enforcement. Phil went to work for the New York City Department of Consumer Affairs where he could protect consumers more effectively. Now he is a law professor at Georgetown.

WELFARE

We joined welfare rights advocates in attacking a catalog of rules that limited welfare and stripped recipients of dignity. Targets included: denying a woman aid for her children when she lived with a man (the man-in-the-house rule); refusing welfare unless an applicant lived for an extended period of time in the state (residency rules); refusing hearings before terminating eligibility; setting an upper limit on grants so that larger families would receive less support per child than families with fewer children; requiring work as a condition of receiving welfare (the employable mother rule); and requiring blacks to take jobs whites were not required to take.

We soon learned that LDF couldn't dominate welfare law development as we did the law of schools and employment. Lawyers bringing cases sometimes made inadequate records and brought suits with unfavorable facts or in less than the most favorable sequence. Our cooperating lawyer network no longer had a lock on the cases we wanted to file. The Center for Social Welfare Law and Policy, which had been established to litigate welfare issues, couldn't control the cases either. Lawyers connected with the Office of Economic Opportunity and private lawyers went their own ways. Nevertheless, we were successful in a lower court man-in-the-house case and another involving the employable mother rule.

Supreme Court cases brought by others invalidated the man-in-the-house rule and won the right to a hearing before benefits could be terminated. But in other cases the Supreme Court signaled that welfare reform through the judiciary was at an end. One held that the maximum family grant, no matter how many children were in the family, was acceptable rough justice. Another decided that a welfare mother might not refuse a home visit by a caseworker without risking termination of benefits. This judgment came in a case where a child in the home in question had a fractured skull and a possible rat bite, as Justice Blackmun's opinion pointed out. LDF would not have taken the case; bad cases make bad law. We were not in a position to make sure such cases did not reach the appellate level, where their effect would be magnified. Moreover, the cases that might have made a difference wouldn't necessarily have come to us.

EQUALITY IN FINANCING EDUCATION

LDF was not involved very much in cases that some groups began bringing in the late 1960s to equalize financing of education between rich and poor school districts. These cases did not rest on claims of racial discrimination, although they may have mentioned race as an additional factor. Rather, they argued that there is a constitutional duty, under federal and state constitutions, to spend the same amount of money, more or less, on the education of all children. We did file a friend-of-the-court brief in the leading Supreme Court case, but it rejected the argument, holding that education is not a fundamental right and that inequality had not been demonstrated. Some state supreme courts, in cases brought by various groups, have held that their state constitutions mandate equal school financing, but the Fund's one venture into that area was unsuccessful. While the litigation, which continues to this day, has focused public attention on disparities between rich and poor, and while legislatures have as a consequence of the decisions addressed the issue, so far there has not been any marked movement toward equality.

FIGHTING POVERTY IN THE COURTS: A BALANCE SHEET

The effort to reform civil justice for the poor had notable successes. No longer could poor people be evicted from public housing or have their wages garnished or welfare benefits terminated without a hearing. Some unjustifiable intrusions into the personal lives of the poor, as with the man-in-the-house rule, came to an end. Some communities were saved from destruction to make way for public projects. Builders had to think twice before bulldozing black areas and uprooting residents without providing relocation, although the practice hardly came to an end.

But poverty advocates lost cases to equalize public facilities in rich and poor parts of towns, raise welfare payments, and equalize school financing. In the last analysis, what the poor have always needed most is more money. As important as the Fund's role has been in changing the life situation of black people so that they can earn more money by, for example, upgrading job, school, and voting opportunities, neither we nor others have been very successful at redistribution of economic opportunity through the courts.

32

NORI AND CRIMINAL JUSTICE

We developed a criminal justice program under the aegis of NORI. The new program consisted of some kinds of cases we would have taken earlier (jury discrimination, right to counsel, forced confessions, and so forth), but also launched new initiatives in the areas of capital punishment, prisoners' rights, and the right to bail even for those too poor to pay for it.[1] The capital punishment and prisoners' rights cases turned out to make major contributions to developing constitutional rights. In the jury discrimination cases we introduced the use of statistical proof and changed the focus of suits as well—we started to move for injunctions to desegregate jury rolls, rather than waiting to undo a conviction based on discriminatory jury selection. The criminal justice program attracted support but also often lost friends. The public rallies behind someone who has been unfairly accused and contributes to the defense. At the same time, many people disapprove of any organization which frees someone who apparently has committed a horrible crime, even though convicted in violation of the law

RAPE AND THE DEATH PENALTY

Even before NORI came into being in the early 1960s we began exploring ways to attack the death penalty for rape. In time, that developed into a full-scale attack on capital punishment, as arbitrary, cruel and unusual, and racist. We launched the effort because almost 90 percent of the 455 defendants executed for rape since 1930 were blacks convicted of raping white women. Memories of Scottsboro, *Groveland*, and Ozzie Jones demanded that we do something to end this most discriminatory of punishments.

By the 1960s civil rights law was developing favorably and, with more money available, an attack on capital punishment for rape seemed doable.

As this possibility slowly developed in my mind, *Hamilton v. Alabama* came to LDF. The black defendant, who obviously was demented, had been sentenced to death for breaking into a home and exposing his genitals to an elderly white woman. He didn't threaten her; he didn't touch her. She called for help, he was arrested, and, following trial, the court imposed the death penalty. Jim Nabrit wrote the petition for review and brief in the Supreme Court, and Connie Motley argued his case there in 1961, winning on the grounds that Hamilton hadn't had counsel at his arraignment.

Preparing for the second trial, I thought that the case was the ideal vehicle to launch an attack on the death penalty for rape—not only had no life been taken, but no physical harm had been done. Frank Heffron went to Alabama for the second trial, bringing with him as a psychiatric expert witness Robert Coles. Now a Harvard professor, Coles has over the years developed a national reputation as a psychiatrist and social critic. Coles earlier had enlisted my help for a study of Southern black children who had been involved in desegregation. As it turned out, at this trial our defendant, Hamilton, was convicted of a lesser offense and the death penalty issue in his case evaporated.

But we weren't the only ones who were thinking about this problem. In October 1963 Justice Arthur Goldberg, dissenting from the Court's refusal to review a case, wrote what could only be called an invitation to start attacking capital punishment. The defendant had been sentenced to death for rape and, although no one raised the issue, Goldberg asked whether the Eighth (prohibiting cruel and unusual punishment) and Fourteenth Amendments permitted the death penalty for a rapist who had neither taken nor endangered human life. He pointed to the trend away from the death penalty for rape in the United States and worldwide, inquired whether taking a life when no life has been taken is excessive and greatly disproportionate, and whether the aims of punishment, namely, deterrence, isolation, and rehabilitation, could be achieved by punishing less severely. His opinion signaled that the time to launch the effort had arrived. Shortly afterward, I announced to the board that we would launch a full-scale attack on capital punishment for rape. By mid-decade we had seventeen cases.

To gather evidence of discriminatory application, I arranged with the Law Students Civil Rights Research Council (LSCRRC) to send fifty students South to "go into every county in the South and compile records . . . of judicial proceedings [in rape cases] over the past dozen or so years . . . [to use the] information [as] evidence in specific cases." Ultimately, twenty-eight LSCRRC students went to eleven Southern states and researched twenty years of cases in counties selected according to statistical models. Surprisingly, court officials rarely interfered. Each student had a batch of printed twenty-eight–page questionnaires (schedules) entitled "Capital Punishment Survey," which were constructed by Tony Amsterdam and Marvin

Wolfgang, a criminologist at the University of Pennsylvania, and which listed every conceivable factor that might influence sentencing in a rape case, for example, the race, occupation, criminal record, and family background of the defendant and of the victim.

For reasons related to our professional responsibility to our clients, the program didn't develop according to plan. We found that we couldn't ethically limit ourselves to claims of racism if defendants had other good arguments, like objections to the widespread practice of excluding as jurors everyone with religious or moral scruples against the death penalty. This seemed to deny a jury representative of a cross-section of the community. Moreover, jurors who had no problem with capital punishment would be more likely to believe police and prosecutors; they were called "prosecution prone." Limiting capital juries to nonscrupled jurors, therefore, might also violate the Sixth Amendment's right of trial by jury, and the Fourteenth Amendment's due process and equal protection clauses.

Another attack on the death penalty could be based on the fact that judges never charged jurors with criteria for deciding whether to sentence to death, although even in ordinary civil cases they are given standards by which to decide how much money to award. Standardless sentencing arguably violated the due process clause and, because of the inconsistency bound to follow, might constitute unusual punishment—which also inherently was cruel. Closely related was the procedure by which the jury decided guilt and punishment together: In noncapital cases judges have the benefit of probation reports and of hearing the defendant speak for himself before sentencing, but in capital cases juries announce a guilty verdict and the death penalty at one time. Indeed, if in a capital case the defendant were to take the stand to tell the jury of mitigating circumstances (perhaps he had been a battered child or the victim had sexually abused him), he might be forced on cross-examination to incriminate himself, when otherwise he would have had a constitutional right to remain silent.

Finally, there was the question of whether capital punishment was cruel and unusual and, therefore, prohibited by the Eighth Amendment. There was an obligation to argue this issue, and, though the few we had were helpful, Supreme Court precedents defining "cruel and unusual" were meager. One case, decided in 1910, held that in applying the Eighth Amendment courts are to be guided by "contemporary human knowledge," "public opinion enlightened by a humane justice," and "the evolving standards of decency that mark the progress of a maturing society." In another, the Court held that stripping a defendant of citizenship for desertion in wartime was cruel and unusual—the Eighth Amendment required observing the "evolving standards of decency that mark the progress of a maturing society." While in years past it might have been acceptable to turn a defendant into a person without a country, now the Court believed that was too terrible a fate. A 1962 decision held that making drug addiction a crime was cruel and unusual because the defendant had no control over his illness; it was like punishing a common cold. That was about all the case law there was.

Arguments from these precedents ran up against serious historical problems. When the Eighth Amendment was adopted capital punishment was commonplace. The Fifth Amendment refers to the death penalty: "No person shall be held to answer for a capital . . . crime, unless on a presentment or indictment of a grand jury . . . nor . . . be subject for the same offence to be twice put in jeopardy of life or limb . . . nor be deprived of life, liberty, or property, without due process of law."

But when the amendment was adopted, punishments such as branding, slitting the tongue, and nailing the ears, as well as capital punishment, were all accepted. The words "to be twice put in jeopardy of life or limb" were a clear reference to the punishment of amputation. Could it seriously be contended that a court in the mid-twentieth century would permit lopping off a limb as punishment? The Fifth Amendment references to the death penalty ought not to insulate it from contemporary standards any more than its reference to amputation would preserve that eighteenth-century punishment. In response, it would be argued that legislatures, not courts, have abolished colonial punishments such as amputation, branding, and slitting of the tongue. Not so with the death penalty. There had to be an answer to the assertion that the legislature is the judge of contemporary standards of decency and that the courts are without power to second-guess it.

There were issues also related only to individual cases, like search and seizure, forced confession, adequacy of counsel, even alibi. In representing a client, we couldn't forego any defense that might help him, even though it might not advance our goal of outlawing capital punishment for rape.

These arguments against capital punishment could be made in the cases of whites as well as blacks. We knew that if we wanted to persuade the Supreme Court to make law, we needed to control every case possible that involved capital punishment issues, or some lawyer with ideas quite different from ours or who was perhaps not very competent might produce decisions that would tie our hands. So, very soon we got into the capital punishment business generally, in murder as well as rape cases, representing whites as well as blacks, dealing with nonracial issues as well as racial ones.

The transition was precipitated in Arkansas where Governor Faubus signed six death warrants at one sitting and then left the state to attend a conference. Three of the men whose names were on those warrants were our clients, for whom we promptly obtained stays. The other three had no lawyers. We had the knowledge and means to prevent the execution of our clients; conscience would not allow us to permit execution of the others. We contacted their last known lawyers and offered help; they accepted and we obtained stays of execution. We then felt that we should do no less in other states in similar situations.

Perhaps, also, we were driven by an unconscious understanding of how the death penalty worked. As we probed deeply, in time we learned that racism permeated even cases that at first seemed to involve no such issue. Ultimately this led to demonstrating that the single greatest determinant of whether a defendant will be sentenced to death is the race of the victim: Killing a white is much more likely to bring the punishment of death. Only one white ever had been executed for killing a black. These dynamics were not fully appreciated until the 1980s.

Tony Amsterdam's genius and energy led the campaign that, by 1970, had raised the basic issues in thirty-five cases. I assigned to Jack Himmelstein, a recent Harvard Law School graduate, the job of managing the program and working with Tony. (At first, he feared that the "capital" campaign was a fund-raising assignment because "capital campaigns" are what institutions call programs to raise money to build buildings.)

Maxwell v. Bishop (1966) was the earliest case to put the race-of-victim rape study to the test. Maxwell had been convicted of rape and sentenced to death. We challenged imposition of the death penalty in postconviction proceedings. To our surprise, when the challenge to the death sentence came up in the trial court in Little Rock, the prosecutor didn't challenge the accuracy of the schedules or our introduction of them and our conclusions into evidence. The defendant, Maxwell, was there, handcuffed, saying nothing, staring blankly ahead. Marvin Wolfgang testified that the schedules showed that race alone explained the disproportionate number of death sentences for blacks. The federal district court that heard the postconviction attack on the death sentence reported: "A Negro man who is convicted of raping a white woman has about a 50 percent chance of receiving a death sentence, regardless of the facts and circumstances surrounding the crime, whereas a man who is convicted of criminally assaulting a woman of his own race stands only about a 14 percent chance of receiving a death sentence."

I examined John Monroe, the statistician who had designed the survey. Unhappily, not having Maxwell or any particular case in mind, Monroe had selected counties for survey according to a model that did not include the county where Maxwell was tried. Our theory was that Arkansas, not any particular county, was imposing the death penalty. Another problem was that only seven blacks had been sentenced to death in Arkansas for rape of white women, and this number did not represent a majority of those who had been convicted. Although the statisticians were satisfied that the sample and the evidence were sufficient, one might argue whether anything certain could be concluded from seven cases. The district judge offered his own racist explanation of why blacks might have been sentenced to death more often than whites: In interracial rape cases jurors might be more likely to believe that a white woman hadn't consented to sexual relations with a black man.

On August 26, the district judge dismissed the petition and, worse, refused to issue a certificate of probable cause, needed to take the case to the court of appeals. Execution was scheduled for September 2. The court of appeals then also denied the certificate on August 29, indicating the belief that Maxwell's arguments were so thin that they didn't deserve a full appeal. There was nowhere to go but the Supreme Court. Tony, Jim Nabrit, and Norman Amaker flew to Washington and presented a hurriedly prepared petition to Justice White, who, just before Maxwell's scheduled execution, granted a stay until the entire Supreme Court could consider the petition. Then, after the Supreme Court commenced its work that year, it sent the case back to the court of appeals for the serious consideration that court had said it didn't deserve.

When, finally, the Eighth Circuit decided the case in June 1968, it concluded, in a decision by Harry Blackmun, who would later be appointed to the Supreme Court, that while there may have been discrimination in the past, it didn't exist at the time of Maxwell's sentencing. Moreover, there was no proof that Maxwell's jury was influenced by race. We took *Maxwell* back to the Supreme Court.

As death cases increased, how in the world could we handle them all? Florida had more than fifty prisoners on death row and newly elected Governor Claude Kirk promised to resume executions—he visited death row, shook hands with the condemned men, and told them so. Toby Simon and his associate Alfred Feinberg, one of the few white LDF interns, represented several death row inmates. Toby proposed filing a class action habeas corpus application—something never done before—for all death row prisoners in Florida. Toby was an implacable foe of the death penalty. When the Florida state prison got rid of its antiquated electric chair in favor of modern technology, Toby acquired the chair and placed it in his backyard. Once, I suspect deliberately, he filed an appeal in a capital case in the wrong court—the intermediate court of appeals rather than the Florida Supreme Court. Florida's attorney general leaped into the trap with a motion to dismiss, and Toby litigated for years about which court the case belonged in. Sometimes his benign eccentricity unnerved roommates at our lawyers' training conferences when he would stand on his head, clad only in underwear, doing his morning yoga ritual. With all of this he maintained a highly prosperous private practice.

Toby's class action idea wasn't so crazy. In April 1967, shortly after he filed the petition, Judge William MacRae granted a stay.

Tony and I flew to Cambridge to consult with Harvard Law School professor Al Sachs, whose role in drafting the class action rules became so important for Title VII. Al thought that the position was defensible. Tony asked MacRae to allow us to conduct a factual investigation of death row inmates, their intelligence, education, access to counsel, and so forth, to determine whether they had enough in common to file a class action.

MacRae agreed, and we and ACLU lawyers conducted the interviews, which revealed that half the death row inmates who faced imminent execution were without counsel, twenty-one were unskilled or farm laborers, and almost all had no money or less than $100. The mean IQ was in the low-average range. MacRae held that a class action was appropriate and extended the stay of execution.

Years later, Chesterfield Smith, a Florida lawyer who had been president of the American Bar Association at one time and who knew MacRae well, told me that MacRae had always longed for greatness and thought that the case gave him a claim to that title.

In California, Tony won an order requiring the state to notify capital punishment lawyers whenever an execution was scheduled. They then might file a petition for habeas corpus, upon which an individual stay would be granted. Stopping executions in these two big death row states (Florida then had fifty-four inmates on death row, California eighty-three) helped create a national moratorium on executions. The California Supreme Court later, in 1967, stayed all executions in the state. Other lawyers wanted copies of our papers so they might do the same, but we talked them out of it. Two wins in a row was lucky. A loss might create a conflict in which the Supreme Court might become interested and undo the whole thing. Lawyers in other states proceeded case by case, bringing about a de facto nationwide moratorium. Some thought that the Supreme Court might fear that if it upheld the death penalty there would be a bloodbath when executions resumed against inmates on death row whose numbers had grown large. I wasn't so sure. Those who approved executions were generally not fazed by having huge numbers of people put to death. In fact, some would be more pleased by many than by few.

As the Florida and California cases proceeded, Burt Jenner, a leading Chicago lawyer and ex-president of the American Bar Association, represented William Witherspoon, who had been sentenced to death for murder in Illinois. He challenged the death penalty and conviction on the grounds that scrupled jurors had been excluded. We filed a friend-of-the-court brief that supported the argument that the defendant had been denied a jury drawn from a cross-section of the community, but feared that he didn't have adequate proof that nonscrupled jurors favored the prosecution. I had asked Louis Harris to conduct a study to learn whether, indeed, scrupled jurors were prosecution prone. But the study was not complete. So, our brief, which Tony wrote, urged the Court to support Jenner on the cross-section argument, but to do nothing on the prosecution-prone argument for fear that it might be lost in the absence of adequate proof. Lawyers associated with Jenner wrote Tony a blistering letter, suggesting that we took the position because *Witherspoon* was not our case. Tony, who ordinarily has complete equanimity, replied patiently, but concluded by inviting them "singly and collectively, jointly, equally, in common dignity, and hand-in-hand, to take an exceedingly long hike on a very short peninsula."

Witherspoon held unconstitutional the exclusion of jurors with scruples against capital punishment on cross-section grounds and, as we had urged, refused to decide the prosecution-prone issue. Justice Stewart wrote: "Whatever else might be said of capital punishment it is at least clear that its imposition by a hanging jury cannot be squared with the Constitution."

On prosecution proneness he said: "It is not surprising that the amicus curiae brief filed by the NAACP Legal Defense and Educational Fund finds it necessary to observe that with respect to bias in favor of the prosecution on the issue of guilt, the record in this case is 'almost totally lacking in the sort of factual information that would assist the Court.'"

Lower courts initially restricted *Witherspoon* in its application, but we managed to invalidate large numbers of sentences under its principles.

By spring 1968, Tony, on leave from teaching, moved into our office as virtually a full-time unpaid staff lawyer and was giving his incredible energy to the full range of our program. When staff lawyers would bring him a paper for comment, by next morning it would be returned, full of substantive and editorial suggestions, new ideas, and, often, brilliant insights.

On May 3, 1968, we held the first national conference on capital punishment at the Summit Hotel in New York, which developed our network further. Meanwhile, *Maxwell* worked its way back to the Supreme Court on the question of whether the Constitution required the judge to charge jurors with standards for imposing the death penalty and whether there should be a separate penalty hearing. During Tony's argument, in an effort to avert a ruling on those issues, counsel for California, who appeared as a friend of the court, suggested that the Court review the *Maxwell* record for a possible *Witherspoon* error in jury selection. The chief justice then asked Arkansas's lawyer, Don Langston, whether he could provide a copy of the record on jury selection, which until then had not been involved in the case at all. He hesitated, but replied, "I will lodge it with the Clerk, but whenever you finish with it I would like for him to return it." The chief justice said, "You would what?" Langston answered, "Like for him to return it to me so that I can have it filed back in the Supreme Court [of Arkansas]." Earl Warren solemnly promised. The Court set *Maxwell* down for reargument in October 1969. For the time being at least that derailed *Maxwell*, as California had hoped, as a vehicle to hold capital punishment unconstitutional.

Around the same time Tony formulated what became our definitive argument assailing the death penalty as cruel and unusual in an amicus brief in *Boykin v. Alabama*. A jury had sentenced Boykin to death following a guilty plea to five robberies in which no life had been taken, a favorable scenario for litigating the issue. Tony responded to the argument that the legislature had unfettered power to determine whether a punishment meets evolving standards of decency, writing that because capital punishment is applied infrequently and irregularly, against only poor, despised sectors of society, who are largely racial minorities, the statute that authorizes it does not express contemporary standards of decency:

> It is a freakish aberration, a rare, extreme act of violence, visibly arbitrary, probably racially discriminatory—a penalty reserved for wholly arbitrary application because, if it were regularly used against robbers, it would affront universally shared standards of public decency.... The cruel and unusual punishment clause of the Eighth Amendment is directed at the difference between what public conscience will allow the law to say and what it will allow the law to do.

CAPITAL PUNISHMENT UNCONSTITUTIONAL—FOR A TIME

Tony had argued *Maxwell* in March 1968, after which Warren Burger replaced Earl Warren, who retired. Harry Blackmun replaced Abe Fortas, who resigned. Tony then reargued *Maxwell* in May 1970 and won on relatively uncontroversial *Witherspoon* grounds. California's ploy worked. Maxwell was spared; the death penalty survived. The Court at the same time set down for argument two cases brought by lawyers unaffiliated with LDF. They argued that a judge denies due process of law by charging a jury that it may impose the death penalty without giving it standards. Harlan's opinion disagreed: It was "beyond present human ability" to express those characteristics that merit the death penalty and those that don't. He held that "in light of history, experience, and the present limitations of human knowledge, we find it quite impossible to say that committing to the untrammeled discretion of the jury the power to pronounce life or death in capital cases is offensive to anything in the Constitution."

Justice Black wrote a concurrence hostile to any cruel and unusual punishment challenge:

> The penalty was in common use and authorized by law here and in the countries from which our ancestors came at the time the [Eighth] Amendment was adopted. It is inconceivable to me that the framers intended to end capital punishment by the Amendment. Although some people have urged that the Court should amend the Constitution by interpretation to keep it abreast of modern ideas, I have never believed that lifetime judges in our system have any such legislative power.

The capital punishment effort looked hopeless. We filed a supplemental brief in support of petitions for writs of certiorari—Tony was the author—in a case awaiting a decision on a petition for review, to inform the Court about 120 other capital cases pending before it, affecting six hundred death row prisoners. There was a wide range of issues represented: lower courts had been evading *Witherspoon*; the Court had not yet ruled on the death penalty for rape; there remained the issue of the right to counsel in post-appeal stages of capital sentencing; there was no decision on whether the death penalty is cruel and unusual. Hundreds of lives depended on the outcome. We argued that the Court could not allow people to be executed without resolving these issues and had to continue to explore capital punishment.

The Court responded on June 28, 1971, granting review in four cases—all but one were LDF cases—that presented the issue of cruel and unusual punishment. By then we represented more than half of the 640-plus defendants on death row. At the same time the Court reversed thirty death sentences on *Witherspoon* grounds and for other reasons of not general significance, which indicated that there seemed to be an anti–capital punishment mood in conflict with Harlan's recent opinion.

The brief in our case reprised pretty much the *Boykin* arguments: The penalty remains on the books only because it is "rarely and unusually inflicted" and "it is not a part of the regular machinery of the state for the control of crime and the punishment of criminals." By this time we had a judicial opinion to cite for the proposition: a 1970 decision of the Fourth Circuit invalidating the death sentence in a Maryland rape case as cruel and unusual.

We answered the objection that the Bill of Rights and the Fourteenth Amendment accepted capital punishment: "If the Constitution does not forbid capital punishment today upon the theory that it was widely allowed by law and practiced in 1791, then the Eighth Amendment also does not forbid today—and will never forbid—the stocks and the pillory, public flogging, bashing and whipping the bare body, branding of cheeks and forehead with a hot iron, and the slitting, cropping, nailing and cutting off of ears," all employed in 1791.

One of our defendants had been convicted of first-degree murder for two killings and also had committed a third murder and another rape. He had taken one victim, a sixty-year-old woman, to her bedroom, tied her arms behind her back, raped her, and stabbed her to death. He raped the second victim, who was five months pregnant and the mother of two children, and stabbed her to death on a railroad embankment as she tried to flee. Our notion of contemporary standards of decency received a jolt when a couple of secretaries refused to type the briefs because they thought he should be executed.

On January 17, 1972, Tony argued two of the cases, including *Aikens v. California*; I argued another; and a Texas lawyer, Melvyn Bruder, argued a fourth. Tony's main thrust was the argument he developed for *Boykin*. He argued that the states could make their same arguments in defense of boiling in oil. When Tony told the Court that capital punishment had been eliminated in most of the world and virtually had come to a halt in the United States, Warren Burger asked: "It is not a process that one ordinarily does by court decision, is it?" Tony replied that most countries did not have a principle of judicial review of legislation like ours.

I argued that outside the United States capital punishment for rape existed only in South Africa, Malawi, and Taiwan. Of 455 executions in the United States for rape since 1930, when record keeping began, 405 were of blacks. Before the Civil War, in Georgia and other Southern states, the law provided for executing blacks who raped whites; others received one to twenty years in prison. That pattern continued as a matter of practice in the post–Civil War South.

One month later, Tony won *People v. Anderson* in the California Supreme Court, on the grounds that capital punishment violated the California constitution as cruel, degrading, and dehumanizing; unnecessary to any legitimate goal of the state; and incompatible with the dignity of man. Just before the argument, someone stole the skis from the top of his cocounsel Jerry Falk's car by ripping them off, along with part of the car top. Falk never stopped fuming. Halfway through Tony's argument Chief Justice Wright asked: "You're arguing that the death penalty is unconstitutional for the crime of murder . . . let me ask you: Is there any crime, which in your judgment *could* constitutionally be punished by death?" Jerry Falk whispered "ski theft," causing Tony to break out into laughter that the justices couldn't understand, given the gravity of the issues.

Anderson disposed of Aikens's case in the United States Supreme Court, because it was also from California and would be undone by the state supreme court. With *Ralph v. Warden*, the Fourth Circuit case that recently had held capital punishment for rape unconstitutional, *Anderson* showed the Supreme Court that it would not be alone if it too were to hold capital punishment unconstitutional.

With all the progress we had been making, when victory came it came as a surprise. On June 29 the Court decided, as *Furman v. Georgia*, the remaining three cases we argued. While the decisions of a year earlier—holding that unguided discretion did not violate due process—had made winning seem impossible, *Furman*, by a vote of five to four, wiped out capital punishment laws across the country. Each member of the majority—Douglas, Brennan, Stewart, White, and Marshall—wrote his own opinion. The chief justice, Blackmun, Powell, and Rehnquist dissented, each in separate opinions. Nine individual opinions! Three of the majority, Douglas, Stewart, and White, forming the core of *Furman*, stressed the infrequent, capricious, and discriminatory manner in which the death penalty was applied. For them the central vice of capital punishment was its arbitrary application. Stewart used the word "freakish." White wrote:

Based on 10 years of almost daily exposure to the facts and circumstances of hundreds and hundreds of federal and state criminal cases involving crimes for which death is the authorized penalty ... the death penalty is exacted with great infrequency even for the most atrocious crimes and ... there is no meaningful basis for distinguishing the few cases in which it is imposed from the many cases in which it is not.

Douglas, Stewart, and White left open the possibility that states might set standards for the application of capital punishment and save its constitutionality. Douglas wondered whether a mandatory death penalty imposed evenhandedly might not be constitutional.

Brennan would have held the death penalty unconstitutional per se. He summarized: "Death is an unusually severe and degrading punishment; there is a strong probability that it is inflicted arbitrarily; its rejection by contemporary society is virtually total; and there is no reason to believe that it serves any penal purpose more effectively than the less severe punishment of imprisonment."

Thurgood wrote a similar opinion, stressing heavily the death penalty's racially discriminatory impact.

That evening we had the biggest victory celebration ever. Lynn Walker, a staff lawyer, had a kid brother who led a rock band that we renamed "The Eighth Amendment." It set up in the library and filled 10 Columbus Circle with electric guitar and percussion, amplified to the maximum, as we and dozens of friends partied well past midnight.

Furman was in one sense a mystery. Only a year after the Supreme Court had rejected the argument that standardless sentencing violated due process, *Furman* bought the same argument under the Eighth Amendment cruel and unusual punishment clause. I can think of no explanation other than superior advocacy and, perhaps, the decisions in *Ralph* and *Anderson*, which showed that to outlaw the death penalty was not unthinkable.

Following *Furman*, Florida's governor pardoned Freddie Lee Pitts and Wilbert Lee, who had been convicted of murder after someone else confessed to the crime. A new trial acquitted a North Carolina defendant who had been sentenced to death. Four New Mexico defendants got a new trial when someone else confessed; the district attorney dismissed the charges against them. The convictions of all others on death row remained in effect and they were sentenced to life imprisonment.

But public opinion, which only a few years earlier had been 55 percent opposed to capital punishment, turned sharply the other way. Sixty, 70 percent, and even higher majorities endorsed the death penalty. The reasons are not clear. Certainly rising crime rates had an effect. Perhaps the cases focused attention on the issue as it hadn't before. But, while the majority was really expressing a desire for stricter law enforcement, when asked about particular circumstances of a crime and a defendant, majorities were either smaller for the death penalty and often opposed to it as a punishment.

But politically capital punishment became unstoppable. States enacted laws setting standards for administering the death penalty. Every state that had had the death penalty restored it, although capital crimes became fewer—arson, burglary, armed robbery, and rape were no longer on most lists. Some adopted mandatory death statutes for killing a police officer or prison guard. If the Supreme Court said that the problem was that the death sentence was meted out so infrequently and capriciously as to be totally arbitrary, North Carolina's Supreme Court reinterpreted its law retroactively to *require* the death penalty whenever it was permitted, following which North Carolina defendants convicted of arson, burglary, rape, and murder were routinely sentenced to death, with the result that the state's death row population soon comprised one-third of the death row inmates in the United States.

With this rigidity in sentencing, the decision on whether to award death or some lesser punishment came to reside mainly in the prosecutor's discretion. Instead of seeking a lesser penalty, prosecutors charged a lesser crime. There had been thirty thousand burglaries in North Carolina, but only a handful of burglars were sentenced to death—others were charged with some other offense. By 1975, death row, which *Furman* had largely cleared, was back up to a population of four hundred. Of that number, we represented about one hundred.

We kept track of death cases, as the campaign unfolded, with the help of Douglas Lyons, a young death penalty abolitionist, who had established Citizens Against Legalized Murder (CALM). Doug moved into our office, where he set up an operation that gathered the details of capital cases. CALM was nothing more than Doug Lyons, although through his father, Leonard Lyons, a columnist specializing in the comings and goings of celebrities, he enlisted names like Truman Capote and Burt Lancaster for his letterhead. In time, his work developed into an LDF monthly newsletter, *Death Row USA*, which catalogues the state, names, race, and other information about death row inmates. Lyons left LDF and went to law school, but *Death Row USA* continues at LDF as the primary resource of scholars, the courts, journalists, and Congress for tracking the status of capital punishment.

THE DEATH PENALTY COMES TO LIFE

On January 22, 1976, the Supreme Court granted review in five more capital cases. Four hundred and eleven convicts were on death row, 60 percent of them black. Cases from North Carolina and Louisiana dealt with new laws that made the death penalty mandatory in capital cases. Those from Georgia, Florida, and Texas dealt with other new laws that required a jury to weigh in a separate sentencing hearing aggravating against mitigating factors and then decide whether to sentence to death. An aggravating factor in Georgia, for example, would be if the offender had a prior conviction for a capital felony or "a substantial history of serious assaultive criminal convictions." Murders committed for pay and murders of peace officers were aggravating. The North Carolina, Texas, and Louisiana cases were LDF cases. As before, Tony Amsterdam led LDF lawyers in brief and argument.

We argued that *Furman* required treating like cases alike. Mandatory statutes violated it by imposing death on defendants who were quite unlike one another and who had committed very different crimes. Laws requiring guided discretion violated *Furman* by leaving unguided decision-making power with the prosecutor in the form of plea bargaining and charging of a lesser offense; discretion on the part of jurors to enter verdicts of a lesser included offense; and the power of govenors in their unfettered judgment to grant executive clemency violated *Furman* too.

David Kendall and Peggy Davis joined LDF around this time and became mainstays of the capital punishment project. Peggy later became a family court judge and professor at New York University Law School. David was a graduate of Wabash College, where he had been on the wrestling team, was a Rhodes scholar, went to Yale Law School, served a stint in the army and a clerkship with Justice White. He developed a caring relationship with his death row clients, purchasing chess sets for those who wanted to play, setting up a row of miniature boards in his office, and mailing moves back and forth by postcard, moving pieces on his boards accordingly. Most clients usually beat him by the tenth move, maybe because they had more time to study. David's wife persuaded him to give up the games—clients wouldn't have much faith in a lawyer they could beat at chess.

The confidence David inspired in his clients peaked a bit earlier, in 1974. Wallace "Skip" Rhodes, who had been on death row in Montana, called from Las Vegas at 3:00 A.M. to tell David he had escaped. (His first words: "Hello, David. This is Skip," as if David had been expecting to hear from him.) Skip had switched identities with another prisoner who was about to be shipped to Texas to testify as a witness. In Texas he protested that he wasn't the prisoner they thought they had, and when it was clear he was someone else, the jailers released him. David asked Skip to stand by, headed for the office, and concluded that his ethical obligation and Skip's interests were the same. He persuaded Skip to turn himself in to a public defender and newspaper reporter for surrender. But the FBI arrested all three almost immediately, later releasing the lawyer and reporter. Subsequently, David won a case invalidating Skip's death sentence.

On July 2, 1976, five to four, the Court struck down the mandatory laws, which violated the cruel and unusual punishment clause because "the fundamental respect for humanity underlying the Eighth Amendment . . .

requires consideration of the character and record of the individual offender and the circumstances of the particular offense." The decision invalidated the sentences of about three hundred defendants on death row in twenty states. But, in another decision, *Gregg v. Georgia,* the Court, also five to four, upheld the guided discretion laws, reasoning that "the most marked indication of society's endorsement of the death penalty for murder is the legislative response to *Furman.* The legislatures of at least 35 States have enacted new statutes that provide for the death penalty." About 147 defendants remained on death row.

A year later, David Kendall argued *Coker v. Georgia,* which held capital punishment for rape unconstitutional and thus met the original goal of the Fund's capital punishment effort. The win was like a touchdown following a ninety-yard march. We had started a decade earlier with the rape survey, moved ahead with class action stays, and advanced with the decision to prohibit excluding scrupled jurors. *Furman* set up the win by invalidating all capital punishment laws as then written. When the states reenacted the death penalty they took a fresh look. Almost all rejected the death penalty for rape, enabling the Court to conclude that civilized society had repudiated a punishment that existed only in Georgia and virtually nowhere else in the world.

The LDF board began asking questions about our capital punishment docket. It wanted to know what proportion of our energies went into capital cases, something board members asked about no other program. In September 1976 I reported that "we are putting somewhat less than 20% of our energies into the capital punishment program, probably more in terms of manpower and less in terms of money." Forty percent of our time and a much larger share of money went into employment. The board, satisfied, resolved, "The Fund's continued involvement in this area was generally endorsed [by the board] within the limitations of its present allocation of resources. " An endorsement, but one that revealed discomfort.

Foundations began giving for capital cases: The Edna McConnell Clark Foundation gave $300,000, to study race in capital sentencing; Veatch gave $50,000; Field (which had been established by Marshall Field, who had made a large anonymous contribution that supported School Segregation Cases) gave $20,000; Playboy $15,000. We also conducted a successful appeal through the mail.

Into the early 1980s the courts reversed an overwhelming proportion of capital sentences or convictions. LDF lawyers were counsel, or consulted, in every Supreme Court case and many in other courts. Our Supreme Court success rate was 88 percent and, in the courts of appeal, 78 percent. A student in my Columbia seminar, Phil Tegeler, wrote the first draft of the petition for a case in which the defendant had been sixteen years old when he murdered a police officer. Phil, later an ACLU lawyer in Connecticut, argued that executing someone so young would violate international human rights norms. We won because the sentencing judge hadn't taken every mitigating factor into account.

But by 1983 courts began to show impatience with the slow pace of death cases. Jim Nabrit lost *Barclay v. Florida*, the third major death penalty defeat that year. During Jim's argument, his father, Big Jim Nabrit, sat in the courtroom. Thurgood passed him a note, "Big Red, Take it easy, he's doing just fine." But not fine enough to win. The trial judge had overruled a jury recommendation of life imprisonment and took into account the defendant's prior criminal record, a factor not prescribed in the death penalty statute. Nevertheless, the United States Supreme Court held that Florida might allow a departure from the statute and execute the defendant. Doggedly, Jim and Talbot (Sandy) D'Alemberte, later president of the American Bar Association, took the case back to the Florida Supreme Court. There, by a vote of four to three, on the eve of execution, they persuaded the court that the defendant had not been represented effectively on his original appeal in the state court. His lawyer, who also represented a codefendant, had not even mentioned defendant Barclay's name in a single brief filed for the two of them. Moreover, the lawyer was the codefendant's brother-in-law—in effect he had sacrificed Barclay in the interest of his wife's brother. The Florida Supreme Court then held that the trial judge erroneously overruled the jury's recommendation of mercy. Barclay was resentenced to life imprisonment. While in prison, he married a Swiss woman who heard about his case and is the father of their child.

Immersion in hundreds of death cases brought the realization that blacks who killed whites were those sentenced to death most frequently; next were whites who killed whites; blacks who killed blacks seldom received the death penalty. By the mid-1970s we began to realize that no white who killed a black had ever been executed, although by 1993 one was.

As this became clearer, we asked David Baldus, a leading authority on the statistics of racial discrimination, to study racial disparities in capital sentencing. He gathered data on more than two thousand murder cases in Georgia in the 1970s and compared not only race, but also graded the cases according to more than 230 variables, including aggravation of the crime, characteristics of defendant and victim, and every other factor that might imaginably make a difference. In 1983 Baldus testified in *McCleskey v. Kemp*, a Georgia capital case, about his findings, including his key conclusion that defendants charged with killing white victims were 4.3 times as likely to receive the death sentence as those charged with killing black victims. No one seriously challenged him. We lost in the lower courts and took *McCleskey* to the Supreme Court. In 1987, after I left LDF, by a vote of five to four, the Court rejected McCleskey's claim because we had not demonstrated intentional racial discrimination in his case.

PROCEDURAL REFORMS IN DEATH SENTENCING

LDF didn't succeed in defeating the death penalty. But we outlawed its use in rape cases and invalidated it in hundreds of individual cases. Even states that reenacted capital punishment following *Furman* applied it to only a limited number of crimes. Moreover, cases in which we played roles large and small brought about procedural reforms that made application of the death penalty a bit more rational. Scrupled jurors no longer readily could be excluded from death cases. Jurors' discretion no longer was unfettered—they had to weigh aggravating and mitigating circumstances; courts couldn't exclude from consideration any mitigating circumstance. And there were other requirements. On a broader front, our death penalty cases introduced procedural reforms that affected criminal law generally.

CAPITAL PUNISHMENT AS AN AMERICAN SYSTEM

Capital punishment usually is debated as an abstraction. The real issue is, How does it work in the real world? As capital sentencing resumed, the system continued to function like this: For the 20,000 to 25,000 homicides committed each year, 200 to 300 defendants are sentenced to death and 20 to 30 per year (as the 1990s began the numbers continued to rise) are actually executed. Virtually all the executions have taken place in former slaveholding states and virtually all executed defendants (about half of whom are black or Hispanic) are those convicted of having killed white persons.

Of all the countries we resemble in our values and political system, none has capital punishment. All of Western Europe, Canada, Australia, New Zealand, most of Latin America, and even some former Communist nations of Eastern Europe have abolished it. International treaties, by which the United States is not bound, prohibit the death penalty. The biggest executors in the world are countries like China, Iran, Iraq, Syria, and, of course, the United States. What a lot to be associated with! Our system can hardly be a deterrent, and even for those who find satisfaction in retribution, it hardly can serve that purpose well in its uneven application.

It is our history of racism that has kept America from observing the same values that have led all those nations, most of whose ideals we otherwise share with regard to the death penalty. This is demonstrated by the preponderance of executions in the former Confederacy and the disproportionate number of persons on death row who have killed whites. Perhaps, as we move farther from that racist past, the hold capital punishment has on the American public will diminish and the majority in favor will shift, as it has elsewhere in the world, to a majority against.

PRISONERS' RIGHTS

Commonplace beatings, torture, arbitrary discipline, crowded and unsanitary conditions, inadequate nutrition, lack of medical care, and solitary confinement violate the cruel and unusual punishment clause of the Eighth Amendment. As with the death penalty we began to assert the rights of whites who were victims of these practices as well as blacks. (Thurgood liked to tell of having visited a New Orleans police station to complain about beating of black prisoners. To show that he was evenhanded, the chief took him to a back room where the beating of a white man was in progress.) The Fund's NORI program conducted the first trial that asserted the rights of prisoners against cruel and unusual punishment and the first to address a statewide prison system. Suits that reformed prisons across the country followed. Other organizations entered the area and a large body of prisoners' rights law developed.

William Bennett (Bill) Turner, who came to LDF in 1967 from a Wall Street law firm, initiated the program. After graduation from Harvard Law School, he had gone South as a volunteer civil rights lawyer during the summer of 1966 and, as he put it, "never looked back." A fly-fisherman and sportsman who looks like the classic matinee idol, Turner is quiet and introspective. He now lives in San Francisco, where he practices law and is a public television commentator on legal subjects. He entered the prisoners' rights field in 1968 when he tried a New York case that won the right to due process in prison disciplinary matters and regulated conditions of solitary confinement. News of the victory spread through the prisoners' grapevine and led to other cases.

This soon brought on the first statewide prisoners' rights suit. In 1969, not long after I had agreed to pay John Walker and Phil Kaplan, law partners in Little Rock, $200 plus expenses for each civil rights case they tried, the United States District Court appointed Phil as counsel for prisoners who had filed their own complaint about prison conditions. They complained of solitary confinement for long periods and torture by electric impulses to their genitals from a specially wired old-fashioned hand-cranked telephone designed to inflict shocks (the "Tucker telephone"). Hundreds of men, armed with guns, knives, and scissors, slept in large barracks where theft, violence, and homosexual rape were rampant. Some prisoners were confined to overcrowded, filthy, unsanitary isolation cells. Thirty-five paid employees, eight of whom were guards (only two worked at night), along with "trusties" (other prisoners), supervised more than a thousand prisoners, selling favors, drugs, and liquor.

Kaplan called Turner, whom he had met at an Airlie conference, and asked for help. Together, they drafted an "amended, substituted and consolidated complaint" to replace the one the prisoners filed. Bill recruited expert witnesses, including James Bennett, who had retired as head of the

United States prison system. They won a decision that was the first to reform a statewide prison system, ordering decent living conditions, fair discipline, and adequate staffing, and leading the way in reforming systems elsewhere. It finally went to the Supreme Court in February 1978; the decision was the Supreme Court's first to hold that indefinite solitary confinement is unconstitutional.

In 1972 William Wayne Justice, a United States district judge in Tyler, Texas, heard Turner lecture about prisoners' rights at Southern Methodist University. Justice had pending a case, *Ruiz v. Estelle*, which prisoners had filed themselves. Deciding to appoint Bill to represent them "to see what a first-class lawyer could do," he called me to ask whether I would assign Bill to the case. Bill was on a trek in Nepal but took the case over when he returned. Justice also appointed the United States Justice Department as amicus curiae to gather the facts. The case went to trial in 1978, continued into 1979 for 159 days with 349 witnesses and 1,565 exhibits, and transformed the Texas prison from one of the worst in the country to one of the best, with vast improvements in living conditions, security, medical care, employment, and discipline.

By 1975 we were in more than fifty prison and jail cases that considerably reformed prisons in their states. Soon after coming to LDF in 1971, Lynn Walker took charge of a Georgia case. Somewhat resembling a darker version of the classic Breck shampoo girl, she had been Connie Motley's law clerk and the second black and first black woman on the *Columbia Law Review*. Following the brutal suppression of the prison uprising at Attica, the upstate New York prison, she joined lawyers who represented the inmates, courageously meeting alone with those who had been convicted of violent crimes.

Lynn's case against Georgia's prisons, which she tried with assistant counsel Marilyn Holifield, was the longest trial in the southern District of Georgia; it ended in a 1981 consent decree that thoroughly reformed the system. The Georgia state prison had been racially segregated, guards and inmates regularly harassed other prisoners, living conditions were intolerable, discipline was arbitrary, beatings were common (one guard was known as "Clawhammer"), officials confiscated lawyer–client mail. Homosexual rape was commonplace. The day the trial began six prisoners died in a riot.

Much of the enforcement proceedings in the Georgia case dealt with medical care. A prison doctor was incompetent and had been imprisoned for having had sexual relations with addicted patients whom he encouraged to steal so they could buy drugs. He diagnosed one prisoner as a malingerer who, after Lynn intervened, was found to have a brain tumor. He ignored another who complained of an injury to his tongue. Lynn arranged an examination at Emory University: He had been shot, which lodged a tooth in his tongue. Another prisoner, who had been coughing for years, had tuberculosis, diagnosed only after Lynn secured an outside examination. Prison officials did nothing to test his cellmate of two years until Lynn arranged it. Happily, he had not been infected. One prisoner, officials reported, complained that he suffered from "athletic fits." The doctor prescribed foot powder. Lynn explained that he was saying "epileptic." After a while, sometimes without even leaving the prison, she began writing applications for temporary restraining orders for proper medical care; officials began responding without court proceedings.

One prisoner with lupus offered to testify about abuses in medical care. Lynn warned that he might be injured or killed by guards or by another prisoner, but he replied: "If I get out, they'll just lock me up again. I'd like to die for something." Despondent following a contentious cross-examination, he cut his throat, and from his hospital bed wrote to Lynn that he was sorry he'd lost his temper and let her down. Happily, he subsequently recovered.

JURIES

We had pioneered in fighting discrimination in the selection of jurors well before there was a NORI. That's the ground on which we won *Groveland* and many other cases. In 1970 we still had eighteen cases involving discrimination in selecting jurors and thought that there was a better way to deal with the issue than the traditional challenge after conviction, which dealt with isolated cases and had to overcome the obstacle that many judges would hesitate before setting free a guilty defendant and then hear the press describe the reversal as based on the "narrow technicality" that there had been discrimination in selecting the jury. We thought that it would be better to reform the system and, therefore, began suing for injunctions to integrate juries just as one would integrate a school.

I asked Michael Finkelstein, one of the few lawyers who knew enough about it, to teach us how to use statistics to prove jury discrimination. He gave fascinating lectures to Airlie conferences, using a large beaker from a chemistry lab, with a narrow neck, filled with black and white marbles, a dozen of which fell below a certain line when someone shook the jar. Mike had formulas by which one might predict the black–white ratio of the marbles below the line if the grouping were random. If, on successive occasions after the beaker was shaken, ratios indicating that chance was at work did not result, one might conclude that some other factor was at work and set out to find what it was. Similarly, in the context of selecting jurors, where a difference occurred between the black–white ratio of jurors who actually were selected and the ratio that would have occurred through the operation of chance, we would argue that the burden of proof should shift and the jury commissioners would have to explain.

Norman Amaker argued the first such case to reach the Supreme Court. The opinion held:

This is the first case to reach the Court in which an attack upon alleged racial discrimination in choosing juries has been made by plaintiffs seeking affirmative relief, rather than by defendants challenging judgments of criminal conviction on the ground of systematic exclusion of Negroes from the grand juries that indicted them. . . . The State may no more extend it to some of its citizens and deny it to others on racial grounds than it may invidiously discriminate in the offering and withholding of the elective franchise.

We won another case involving how jury commissioners, who selected the group from which the jurors were chosen, were selected, and we were ahead of the times in seeking an injunction against the Louisiana law that exempted women who did not volunteer for grand jury service.

The Court held that "this claim is novel in this Court and, when urged by a male, finds no support in our past cases." Because we won on racial grounds it declined to consider the sex claim, which finally was vindicated in 1975.

I left LDF before I could take part in overruling one of our most deeply felt jury case losses, *Swain v. Alabama* (1965), where the Court wouldn't reverse an Alabama conviction in which the prosecutor had used all his peremptory challenges—those which do not require that he provide any reason—to strike all blacks from the jury. Justice White's opinion held, in essence, that unless a defendant could show a long-standing pattern of using such challenges on a racial basis, the practice was not unconstitutional. In 1986, in *Batson v. Kentucky*, the Court overruled *Swain*, holding that all-white juries created by use of peremptory challenges to rid the jury of all blacks were unconstitutional, unless the prosecutor could offer some nonracial justification for his action. The Court's opinion drew heavily on Steve Ralston's friend-of-the-court brief for LDF.

33

AFFIRMATIVE ACTION

IT DEPENDS ON WHAT YOU MEAN BY MERIT

At a garden cocktail party, as I was balancing a glass in one hand and a plate of canapes in the other, a stylish white woman in her mid-forties walked toward me purposefully, poked her finger into my chest (I almost spilled my drink), and said, "Because of you my son didn't get into Harvard." She claimed that but for Harvard's affirmative action policy he would have been admitted, but instead of admitting her son, Harvard, in her view, took a less qualified black or Hispanic. It was my fault. I asked where he went to college. "Haverford." In some ways, I said, Haverford is better, but in any event Harvard created its policy itself. She remained unconsoled and very bitter.

In a small way the encounter explains much of the antagonism to affirmative action. The very personal feeling that a white—a member of one's own family, perhaps—has been displaced, just because of race, by one perceived as less able raises hackles. But there is no such anger about other policies that give little weight to grades and scores while looking to other factors deemed more important. As dean of Columbia College I took part in giving preference to children of alumni to build loyalty to the college and thereby encourage financial support for the institution, without which we would not be able to admit other qualified students whose families couldn't afford it. Many admissions offices across the country favor the scions of America's great industrial, financial, or political dynasties; there is no other explanation for the presence of some of these students at our most competitive universities. Students from afar or abroad often have priority because they make the campus more diverse and therefore more interesting. Some athletes are admitted for physical, not intellectual, prowess. At the faculty level, in times of reduction in staff, a tenured professor who is a poor scholar and teacher will remain on the faculty while a nontenured, brighter, more frequently published, effective teacher may be laid off. Merit in the sense that it is ordinarily used doesn't always carry the day.

Networks of friends favor whites with connections. Between a white and black applicant of equal qualifications, the white applicant will generally be able to come up with more impressive recommendations. Ironically, I hired Ruth Abram to help coordinate the LDF Title VII campaign after her father, Morris Abram, asked whether I would give his daughter a summer job. She turned out to be terrific. Morris later became president of the American Jewish Committee and one of the most outspoken foes of affirmative action. Ruth, who doesn't mind hearing this story, has described him as an enemy of affirmative action, except where it benefits his family. Affirmative action policies often stand in the place of an influential parent or friend.

EARLY PROGRAMS AND CASES

Lyndon Johnson, in a celebrated 1965 commencement address at Howard University, said that "you do not take a person who, for years, has been hobbled by chains and liberate him, bring him up to the starting line and then say, 'You are free to compete with all the others,' and still justly believe that you have been completely fair." In 1969, the Nixon Labor Department's Philadelphia Plan used goals and timetables for minorities in the building trades. That year, I persuaded the Supreme Court to require distributing black teachers throughout each of the schools within a system in approximate proportion to their numbers within the entire system. In 1971, in the Charlotte desegregation plan, Warren Burger, writing for a unanimous Court, approved assigning black children more or less proportionately.

Opponents summoned images of quotas, which had excluded Jews from American and European universities. They quoted Justice Harlan's dissent in *Plessy*—"Our constitution is color-blind"—and relied on Title VI of the 1964 Civil Rights Act, "No person shall, on the ground of race . . . be excluded from . . . any program or activity receiving Federal financial assistance," and on Title VII, which made it unlawful to "discriminate [in employment] because of . . . race."

But we favored affirmative action because it was frequently the best way to get blacks into schools or jobs from which they had long been unfairly excluded. In many cases it would have been impossible to admit or promote minorities and women if in each instance we had had to mount a full-scale case. Moreover, in many cases, individual discrimination that actually existed might be impossible to prove.

But affirmative action cases presented difficulties for civil rights lawyers. Usually we were on the outside looking in. When a university favored minorities, and a white sued, we had no input into how the program had been formulated or how to conduct the litigation. Usually, we could only file an after-the-fact friend-of-the-court brief. Another major problem presented by these cases was that major Jewish organizations vigorously opposed affirmative action, causing serious conflict between blacks and Jews, which was not in the interest of either group.

In 1974, *DeFunis v. Odegaard* was the first nationally publicized affirmative action battle. The white law school applicant claimed that he would have been admitted to the University of Washington if it hadn't had an affirmative action program. Pending decision, he was permitted to attend the law school. We filed a friend-of-the-court brief, arguing that the case should be dismissed as moot, because the plaintiff was about to graduate and a decision would make no difference to him. The Court followed our suggestion. Our hope had been to make the contentious argument go away, but it didn't.

For the first time in the history of the movement black and Jewish groups were divided bitterly. The Anti-Defamation League of B'nai B'rith (ADL), the American Jewish Committee, and the American Jewish Congress opposed the university's policy in *DeFunis*. At the urging of Joe Rauh, the Washington lawyer who joined us in the demonstration cases, the smaller Union of American Hebrew Congregations and the National Council of Jewish Women filed briefs supporting the university to demonstrate that many Jews approved affirmative action.

ADL became the point man opposing affirmative action. In their ADL brief, Alexander Bickel and Philip Kurland, eminent constitutional scholars, called the university's program a "numerus clausus," using the term for the quota used against Jews who applied to universities in Europe before the Second World War. They argued that the policy stigmatized blacks, impaired their self-esteem, was as "invidious as it is patronizing," and that the program's aims could be achieved by open admissions, larger classes, and special preparation.

For the Jewish organizations, I thought, the primary question should have been whether affirmative action hurt Jews. The answer to that question was that beneficiaries of affirmative action wouldn't displace Jews any more than anyone else. Black representation in law schools has never risen to close to 10 percent. Even if no blacks were admitted, relatively few of those places would be taken by Jews who were, after all, a very small part of the population. For those not admitted to a particular school, like other whites, at worst it would be one law school instead of another. The fundamental issue was whether the country could afford to have a profession in which virtually no blacks were graduates of elite universities. Jews would suffer from that situation along with everyone else. Would it be good for Jews if that condition resulted from Jewish activism? The Jewish organizations didn't realize that they were leading the fight against a policy of paramount importance to blacks and antagonizing black leadership by opposing policies through which a large part of that group—or their relatives and friends—was achieving success.

BAKKE

In mid-1974 Allen Bakke sued for admission to the University of California Medical School at Davis. In 1973 and 1974 there were between 2,600 and 3,700 applicants for 100 places and Bakke's record was not thought to be good enough to warrant admission. Moreover, Bakke was over thirty—he had served in the Vietnam War—and medical schools then preferred younger candidates. But Bakke believed that he would have been admitted if there had not been an affirmative admissions policy: His grades and scores were much higher than those of minority students who had been let in. Davis at that time set aside sixteen places for minorities, and the minority pool of applicants competed only against each other for these sixteen spots, not against whites whose grades and scores were generally much higher.

A Davis admissions officer, who was unsympathetic to the school's policies, encouraged Bakke to sue, writing to him, "You might consider taking my other suggestion which is then to pursue your research into admissions policies based on quota-oriented minority recruiting. . . . It might be of interest to you to review carefully the current suit against the University of Washington School of Law [DeFunis v. Odegaard] by a man who is now a second year student there but who was originally rejected and brought suit on the very grounds you outlined in your letter." He didn't tell Bakke that there was also another affirmative action policy at Davis: The dean could pick up to five members of the entering class on any basis he liked and sometimes selected applicants from influential and wealthy families who had been rejected or wait-listed. If the dean had decided to use only four of his options the year Bakke applied, that might have opened up a place for Bakke. Or, if some of his selections had been evaluated on the same basis as other whites, they might not have been admitted and perhaps Bakke would have been.

Bakke sued. Billy (William K.) Coblentz, an LDF board member and chair of the University of California Board of Regents, called to suggest that I look at the case. I phoned the university's general counsel offering assistance, but he declined. I would have suggested that he attempt to demonstrate that the policy was adopted to counteract discrimination for which the university, the state of California, and the nation was responsible. He might have put on evidence of minority health needs and the society's special need for more minority physicians to serve areas where white doctors had shown a reluctance to practice. While the university presented fragments of testimony on this subject, the showing was not substantial.

Bakke won in the California courts. The university conceded that it could not "meet the burden of proving that the special admission program did not result in Mr. Bakke's failure to be admitted." The California Supreme Court "directed [the trial court] to enter judgment ordering Bakke to be admitted.

Civil rights groups were outraged. The university, under immense pressure, took the case to the Supreme Court. Many believed that the university had thrown the case. NAACP counsel Nathaniel Jones demanded it withdraw its petition to the Supreme Court because the record was so bad that he feared the case would be lost. The university retained new counsel, Paul Mishkin, a professor of constitutional law at the University of California School of Law at Berkeley, to write the brief. Coblentz chose Archibald Cox, a masterful constitutional scholar and former solicitor general, to argue the case. Cox's reputation also might help in so politically controversial a case. Cox told Coblentz that he would have to be paid and asked for the ridiculously low fee, for someone of his stature, of $100 per hour. Mishkin worked closely with LDF and, particularly, Jim Nabrit.

A frenzy of amicus brief writing followed. Fifty-eight friend-of-the-court briefs were signed by more than twice as many organizations, most adding little understanding to the issues. But for the LDF brief, Eric Schnapper unearthed unknown, or certainly unappreciated, legislative history, which showed that the framers of the Fourteenth Amendment had adopted affirmative action programs, passing laws that provided land, buildings, special education programs, a hospital, and other benefits to blacks, while offering no such programs to whites. Opponents in Congress had attacked the Freedmen's Bureau bill, which extended such preferences, in terms used to assail affirmative action today: "A proposition to establish a bureau of Irishmen's affairs, a bureau of Dutchmen's affairs, or one for the affairs of those of Caucasian descent generally, who are incapable of properly managing or taking care of their own interests by reason of a neglected or deficient education, would . . . be looked upon as the vagary of a diseased brain." One congressman of that era said, "We used to talk about having a white man's chance; It seems to me now that a man may be very happy if he can get a negro's chance."

President Andrew Johnson vetoed the Freedmen's Bureau bill with a message that might have been written by contemporary opponents of affirmative action. When the bill was enacted once more, Johnson vetoed it again, writing that the bill established "for the security of the colored race safeguards which go infinitely beyond any that the General Government has ever provided for the white race. In fact, the distinction of race and color is by the bill made to operate in favor of the colored and against the white race."

Congress then overrode Johnson's veto. One reason for enacting the Fourteenth Amendment was to put the Freedmen's Bureau bill beyond constitutional question. Thurgood cited our sources in his concurring opinion.

This evidence so confounded opponents of affirmative action, who otherwise tout "original intent" jurisprudence, that they didn't even try to answer it.

The struggle shifted to a contest for support of the solicitor general, Wade McCree, former judge for the Sixth Circuit Court of Appeals, who was black. Among my friends in Detroit, his hometown, McCree didn't have the reputation of a civil rights advocate at all. Shortly after *Bakke* reached the Court, someone leaked a draft in which the government argued for Bakke's admission. Civil rights proponents went up the wall. White House domestic policy adviser Stuart Eizenstat and counsel Robert Lipshutz urged President Jimmy Carter and Vice President Walter Mondale to enter the situation to prevent the filing of such a brief, which would contradict the government's position on affirmative action. They strongly urged supporting affirmative action, but not "rigid, inflexible racial quotas [which] . . . do not pass constitutional muster." They argued also that the *Bakke* record "may be an inadequate vehicle for determining the limits of affirmative action" and that the government should urge the Court to dismiss its writ agreeing to review the case as having been improvidently granted, or to send the case back for additional fact finding. Cabinet members Joe Califano, and former LDF board members Pat Harris and United Nations ambassador Andrew Young weighed in with the president on the side of the university. Ultimately, the president urged his staff to jump into the drafting process and support affirmative action, but not rigid quotas.

Jim Nabrit mobilized the Black Congressional Caucus by calling Joe Rauh, who got Congressman Louis Stokes to convene a meeting at which Jim and Lou Pollak briefed them. Jim wrote a memorandum for the caucus, which it presented to the president and vice president. Jim and Lou visited McCree and Jim argued the history of the Fourteenth Amendment to him. Lou told him about the LDF case that he had won a year earlier in which the Court had upheld a racial numerical standard used in drawing electoral districts to make it easier for blacks to win. I visited McCree with Bill Coleman and argued what I had told Archie Cox in the sit-in cases: He wasn't writing a law review article or espousing a personal view; he represented the United States and should support the administration if there was a sound legal argument, and there was.

Perhaps our greatest influence was through Bill Coleman, with whom McCree worked, the two of them staying up until 4 A.M., in preparing his oral argument. It may be, however, that the telling blows were struck before our meeting with McCree, because the White House, before that time, had sent him a memorandum ordering him to take the position we advocated. I knew that the solicitor general's brief would go our way when Attorney General Griffin Bell and Vice President Mondale came to the Second Circuit Judicial Conference, which I was attending, in Buck Hills Falls, Pennsylvania. Jim Nabrit had heard that they would visit and called me to suggest that I lobby Mondale. I intercepted him as he descended from his helicopter. He interrupted, "Don't worry, Jack, it's going to be okay."

The brief the government filed led off with the statement that "race may be taken into account to counteract the effects of prior discrimination," but argued against rigid quotas.

The *Bakke* decision was close and complex. By a vote of five to four the Court upheld the use of race as a basis of university admissions, but would not support fixed quotas. Justices Stevens, Rehnquist, and Stewart and Chief Justice Burger thought that Title VI prohibited taking race into account at all. They voted to admit Bakke, but had only four votes against any consideration of race. Justices Brennan, Marshall, White, and Blackmun agreed that the Fourteenth Amendment and Title VI permitted race to be taken into account, even though Davis set aside a fixed number of places for qualified minority applicants. One vote short for the sort of affirmative action that the University of California had employed.

Justice Powell's opinion held that Congress, in adopting Title VI, which outlaws discrimination in institutions that receive federal funding, employed the strict scrutiny standard of the Fourteenth Amendment's equal protection clause. He concluded that a quota could not be justified under that standard. But, he decided, taking race into account in order to create diversity was an aspect of academic freedom. So long as Davis considered race among other factors in considering each applicant and did not admit a fixed number of minority students the university might constitutionally have an affirmative action program. Powell decided that Bakke had been treated unconstitutionally because a fixed number, sixteen places, had been reserved for minorities. Davis had to admit Bakke, even though under a system of nonquota preferences affirmative action would be acceptable. Race-sensitive admissions had survived, for that added up to five votes for an affirmative action program, although not the one Davis had used in rejecting Bakke.

Ironically, Powell's swing vote approved admitting blacks because in part it helped whites. While to my mind the reason is inadequate because it doesn't give full weight to past injustices dealt to blacks and to other purposes served by affirmative action, such as serving the medical needs of the black community, there is a basic truth in it: Whites won't live in a decent society until blacks do.

In 1974 LDF represented Eddie Kirkland against the New York State Department of Correctional Services, which had discriminated against black and Hispanic applicants. There had been virtually no black prison guards in higher positions. One of the guards, because he actively worked against discrimination, was required to patrol on horseback in bitter winter weather outside an upstate New York prison. We won; the court ordered a quota of one black or Hispanic sergeant for every three white sergeants until New York developed a new selection procedure that did not discriminate against blacks and Hispanics.

Once again the ADL weighed in with a brief against affirmative action. While Jewish law school applicants might have felt disadvantaged by affirmative action, I didn't think that many Jews applied for prison guard jobs. I called ADL leaders to express this view and to argue that they would lose anyway; therefore, why make enemies in a futile effort? They replied it was a matter of principle, their constituency felt deeply about the issue, and they were committed to the position.

Affirmative action cases kept coming up. We won a case against one of three Kaiser Aluminum plants in Louisiana and settled for $300,000 back pay, leaving Kaiser and the union facing more of the same at the other two plants. To deal with this situation, Kaiser and the steelworkers union agreed to permit blacks to become apprentices, until then virtually impossible, setting up a training program that would reserve half its places for blacks until the proportion of blacks in skilled positions equalled that in the local work force. Brian Weber, a white with more seniority than blacks who were in the program, tried to enroll, wasn't admitted, and sued under Title VII. The case went to the Supreme Court.

We worked closely with Tom Powers, Kaiser's counsel, helping with his brief and in a dry run of his argument. ADL supported whites who objected to the plan. But this time the American Jewish Committee and the American Jewish Congress took no position, in part out of concern for the frayed relationships between blacks and Jews. The Court, by a vote of seven to two, interpreted the statute to uphold the affirmative action plan.

On September 14, 1981, I was invited with a group of black leaders to visit with Menachem Begin, who was in New York, to discuss black attitudes toward Israel. His was a name I used to hear in my childhood when Zionist family members and their friends denounced him and Vladimir Jabotinsky, who then were leaders of the radical Irgun in Israel, as fascists. In a large parlor at the Waldorf Towers, with security guards standing around the room and a buffet laid out for the guests, Begin commenced by telling us of a black sect that had camped in the Negev desert and was making the claim that it was Jewish, a claim with which the government disagreed. Begin went on at some length to justify his position. We were mystified. I don't think that any of his visitors knew what he was talking about. When my turn came, I offered the opinion that the black community cared deeply about affirmative action and that black leadership disagreed with the positions taken by Jewish groups on the subject. Anger at those organizations could readily be displaced onto the state of Israel. Begin replied that I had raised an internal American issue with which he was not concerned. But, he added, he might say something about it to Jewish organizations if the occasion arose. I have no way of knowing whether he ever did.

In subsequent cases the American Jewish Congress and American Jewish Committee supported affirmative action plans, but the ADL continued to oppose them. It has stated that its objection is to quotas, not affirmative action, although it has objected even to the use of goals as a technique of affirmative action. But ADL, even while fighting affirmative action, has supported civil rights in a variety of ways; its Washington representative, David Brody, chaired the Leadership Conference on Civil Rights committee on employment. Nevertheless, despite the reversal of position by most of the organized Jewish community, and its support for other civil rights measures, the ADL position on affirmative action remains widely perceived as that of organized Jewry, which has obscured its support for other civil rights measures.

34

LDF GOES TO WASHINGTON

THE WASHINGTON OFFICE

In 1969, we set up a Washington office, staffed by Phyllis McClure, who worked with Jean Fairfax. The office had to be careful not to lobby in order to retain our tax exemption. Phyllis was an educational expert, not a lawyer; she stayed on top of what the government was doing about schools. She and Jean wrote a report on Title I of the Elementary and Secondary Schools Act of 1965, a part of the War on Poverty. It showed that government funds were being used to spruce up black schools to discourage black kids from exercising their right under freedom of choice to transfer to white schools and detailed other abuses. The report helped clean up administration of Title I. Phyllis also kept tabs on HEW desegregation plans, and she and Jean prepared influential reports on the school lunch program and rights of Native Americans.

Soon our Washington office would have a new mission and be headed up by Elaine Jones. She was the first black woman graduate of the University of Virginia Law School. In 1970, about to go to work for Mudge, Rose, Richard Nixon's law firm, she told the dean of UVA's law school, Monrad Paulsen, that she really wanted to practice civil rights law, and he recommended her to me. After I interviewed her for about a minute, hearing her rich Virginia accent punctuated by enthusiastic, high energy bursts of emphasis, and knowing what Monrad had told me about her, I hired her then and there, even though I had no position open. It turned out to be a good pick: Today Elaine is director-counsel of LDF.

At first she worked for us on capital punishment and employment. In 1975, when Gerald Ford named Bill Coleman secretary of transportation, Elaine took leave from LDF to become his special assistant. In 1976 Congress amended the tax laws to allow exempt organizations to spend a substantial part of their income on lobbying, which enabled us for the first time to ask Congress for what the courts wouldn't or couldn't do. I persuaded Elaine to rejoin us in early 1977 to head the Washington office and spearhead our lobbying effort; in that role she would become one of Washington's leading lobbyists. Clarence Mitchell, the NAACP veteran lobbyist, to whom tension between NAACP and LDF meant nothing, welcomed Elaine and introduced her to major players on Capitol Hill. We joined the Leadership Conference on Civil Rights (LCCR), a group of civil rights, labor, religious, and other organizations, in which Clarence and the NAACP were the dominant figures. To minimize potential for conflict over turf, I defined Elaine's initial agenda to include lawyers' issues, in which other groups had little interest: access to the courts, whether civil rights lawyers should receive attorney's fees in administrative proceedings, jurisdiction of the Equal Employment Opportunities Commission, appointment of federal judges, and the question of whether the Fifth Circuit should be divided in two.

Her first major battle was over the proposal to split the Fifth Circuit (Georgia, Alabama, Florida, Mississippi, Louisiana, Texas, and the Panama Canal Zone), on which sat some of America's greatest judges—Elbert Tuttle, John Minor Wisdom, John R. Brown, and others who joined them later without whom it would have been impossible to stand up to massive resistance. However, the migration of population and industry to the Sun Belt increased the number of cases in that court as well as the number of its judges, making the circuit unwieldy. The obvious remedy was to divide the circuit. One proposed division, the four–two split—Louisiana and Texas as one part, and Georgia, Alabama, Florida, and Mississippi as the other— would have divided pro–civil rights judges disadvantageously. James Eastland, the most racist member of the Senate, advocated the four–two split, which was reason enough to oppose it. Because at first this was the only division with any hope of being enacted, we opposed any split at all, hoping ultimately for a political climate that might allow a partition that would not impair the effectiveness of pro–civil rights judges.

Elaine mustered support from consumer and environmental advocates, interested because of the oil issues in Texas and Louisiana. Peter Rodino, chairman of the House Judiciary Committee, working closely with Congresswoman Barbara Jordan and Senator Edward Kennedy, refused to allow the four-two bill to move without our approval. Judges on both sides called me and Elaine for support. The alternative to four–two was a three–three division, which would create the Eleventh Circuit, Georgia, Alabama, and Florida, leaving Louisiana, Mississippi, and Texas as the Fifth, but we weren't ready to support it until we were sure it would pass. After the bills were stalled for eight months, Judge Joseph Hatchett of Florida (the Fifth Circuit's only black judge) called Elaine and me on behalf of the other judges, to find out whether three–three was acceptable to us. We agreed, informed Rodino, and the law passed.

Elaine played a major part in Jimmy Carter's appointment of thirty-eight black federal judges (there were only twelve when he took office). Racists opposed some nominees and, of course, there was competition from non-blacks. The Alabama legal establishment opposed U. W. Clemon, one of our earliest interns, who by the mid-1970s had developed into one of the leading lawyers in the state. Local newspapers accused him of failing to report that tax liens had been filed against him and alleged that he had been arrested for speeding. Elaine requested the predominantly black National Bar Association to investigate; it did, and concluded that U. W. was not guilty of wrongdoing with regard to his taxes and had not been arrested. The report played a major role in persuading the Senate Judiciary Committee to reject the charges; U. W. now serves as a district judge.

More racy, though not less racist, was the case of a nominee whose candidacy Senator Strom Thurmond held up. When Elaine asked the senator's aide what the problem was, he asked in return what the candidate had meant by referring to a white woman as his "main squeeze" during interrogation. Elaine explained that the term meant "best girl." She then divined the reason for the delay and informed the candidate. He ended his relationship with the woman. The senator withdrew opposition. The candidate was confirmed and the couple reunited and married. It may have been a "good old boy" system, but Elaine knew how to deal with the old boys.

VOTING RIGHTS GO TO CONGRESS

Through the 1970s LDF voting cases used between 6 and 12 percent of our "lergs," as we called them, or units of legal energy. Typically, one LDF lawyer worked full-time on voting; up to seven others had one or more cases. Often we joined private lawyers and organizations, such as the Lawyers Committee for Civil Rights Under Law and the ACLU. But even though more blacks were voting, black candidates weren't being elected to city councils, school boards, state legislatures, and other local offices because of gerrymandering and the use of a technique known as at-large, sometimes called multimember, districting. An at-large district with a 30 percent black population concentrated in one area, for example, in which everyone in the district could vote for four candidates running at large, would invariably elect four whites and no blacks whenever the voting was racially polarized, which was nearly always. If the district were to be subdivided into four parts, each electing one candidate, and with one of the single units carved so that it included most of the black population, this unit would most likely elect a black when voters split along racial lines, while the other subdivisions elected three whites. Theoretically, in the multimember system blacks would have some influence with the four whites, all of whom needed their support for victory. But in reality blacks carried little weight with white politicians. Certainly that's what blacks living in such districts believed.

Because of an odd quirk in voting patterns in certain parts of New York State, a new issue developed between blacks and Jews. In 1965 voting statistics in parts of New York placed these districts among the jurisdictions covered by the statutory formula devised to target Southern communities: those with a literacy test and where fewer than 50 percent of the voting-age residents had voted in the 1968 presidential election. As a consequence, the state needed approval of its periodic reapportionment by the United States attorney general or the United States District Court in the District of Columbia. New York submitted a plan that increased the size of the nonwhite majority in senate and assembly districts in Williamsburgh, an area of Brooklyn with a substantial Hasidic population. A staff member of the legislative reapportionment committee later testified that in the course of meetings with Justice, he "got the feeling . . . that 65% would be probably an approved figure" for the nonwhite population in the district. To make the district 65 percent nonwhite, some Hasidic Jews were assigned to an adjoining district, thereby diluting the Hasidic influence. A Hasidic Jewish organization sued on the grounds that creating large black and Hispanic majorities constituted illegal quotas that unconstitutionally diluted the Hasidic vote.

The case, *United Jewish Organizations of Williamsburgh v. Carey* (1977), became one of the leading cases dealing with gerrymandering, multi-member districts, and affirmative action. We represented the local NAACP, and I asked Lou Pollak to argue the case. After complex procedural wrangling, the Supreme Court held that a reapportionment does not violate the Fourteenth or Fifteenth Amendments "merely because a State uses specific numerical quotas in establishing a certain number of black majority districts." The Court likened the districting to creating single-member districts out of multimember districts in order to increase minority representation, a practice that it approved.

In 1976 Jim Blacksher, one of a small number of Southern white LDF cooperating lawyers, won a multimember district case in federal district court against the city of Mobile on grounds similar to those later approved in the Williamsburgh case. But by 1980, after Blacksher's case had struggled upward, the Supreme Court changed its mind. It reversed the lower court Mobile decision, writing six separate opinions that, pieced together, concluded that the Voting Rights Act required proof of discriminatory intent. Discriminatory result would not be enough. Intent was especially hard to prove in Mobile because its election system originated in 1819 and went through many changes over the years. As a result of that decision most multimember district cases became no longer winnable.

Blacksher asked for a new trial and set out to prove intent, knowing well that to come up with a smoking gun in such matters is almost impossible. I allocated $20,000 for a team of historians of the South to dig up Mobile's past. They unearthed material from archives in Montgomery, newspaper clippings, and other repositories, tracing Alabama history from the early nineteenth century to the present, demonstrating that, after the Civil War, Mobile's at-large system had been perpetuated to maintain white control. My favorite piece of the history is an 1869 legislative committee report of an attack on black voters during a Mobile election: "One organization known as a 'Fire Company' . . . threw open the doors of their engine house and ran into the street a piece of artillery which had been concealed . . . and actually loaded and trained it upon the crowd at said polls. . . . As may be expected, especially from the timid, hundreds left the place as fast as possible."

The smoking gun, indeed!

In April 1982 the trial judge found that Mobile's at-large system was infected by discriminatory intent. But it would be impossible to win many at-large cases if it were necessary to prove intent. The evidence might not always be found and the expense would be prohibitive. The answer was for Congress to tell the Court that it didn't understand *its* intent in enacting the 1965 Voting Rights Act.

ELAINE JONES, LANI GUINIER, AND THE NEW VOTING LAW

As the Mobile case worked its way up again, the Voting Rights Act approached the end of a seven-year renewal period in August 1982, when Congress would have to reenact it or allow it to lapse. Along with renewal, overcoming the Mobile decision became a top priority. Elaine worked principally with Lani Guinier, a new staff lawyer who had come to LDF from Harvard College, Yale Law School, and a clerkship with Damon Keith, then a United States District Court judge in Detroit. Hers was a university family—her father, Ewart Guinier, was professor of African American studies at Harvard. After leaving LDF Lani became a professor at the University of Pennsylvania Law School. President Clinton later chose her to head the Civil Rights Division, a nomination he then withdrew following unfounded attacks on her as a radical "quota queen."

Lani is tall and dignified and always perfectly tailored, with a soft manner and passionate feelings about race. Her politics are anything but radical; her political manner is as conservative and careful as the business suits she often wore at the office. While in her writing and thinking she has imaginatively explored a wide range of possibilities as remedies for black underrepresentation, I couldn't imagine her taking anything but lawyerlike positions, sound legal arguments buttressed with factual demonstration, which would be persuasive to mainstream judges.

The position for which she was nominated was as an enforcer of civil rights legislation, the kind of role in which we expect and accept more of an advocacy posture than we may want to see in a judge. If we were to deny the office of prosecutor to all those who have theorized about ways to strengthen a prosecutor's hand in law enforcement, we'd have thousands of vacancies to fill across the country.

Elaine and Lani worked with the Leadership Conference on three main voting rights issues: extending the Voting Rights Act; legislatively overruling the Mobile case; and extending the bilingual provisions of the act. While the language sections were not due to expire until 1985, Hispanic and black groups thought we would be more effective by combining forces. The groups had clashed in 1975 when the NAACP opposed extending the act to language groups because Clarence Mitchell had seen bilingual provisions as possibly bringing about the bill's defeat. Bilingualism passed on that occasion but left a legacy of bitterness and mistrust between blacks and Hispanics.

As the 1982 bill loomed, the Reagan administration appeared to want to split blacks and Hispanics once more. Attorney General William French Smith invited black and other groups, but not Hispanics, to a meeting on extending the act. But Elaine was a coalition builder and, not least because LDF and the Mexican American Legal Defense and Education Fund (MALDEF) had been close since we founded it, Elaine invited Antonia Hernandez, their Washington representative, to come along. Elaine introduced her to Smith as someone who was "interested" and probably had not been invited because of an "oversight." Outmaneuvered, Smith could do nothing, and Antonia remained.

Elaine and Lani showed their toughness with allies as well as adversaries in maneuvers over the bailout provision. "Bailout" meant escape from the act's requirement that changes in voting rules must be cleared in advance by the attorney general or the United States District Court for the District of Columbia. Opponents compounded metaphors, arguing that jurisdictions that had complied with the act should be allowed to "bail out" and no longer remain in "the penalty box."

Congressman Henry Hyde drafted a bailout provision that would allow bailout when the "Attorney General had not successfully interposed any *substantial* objection with respect to" a jurisdiction's submissions to the attorney general. The term "substantial" was an invitation to litigation and a concept that invited conservative district judges to make findings of compliance that would be difficult, perhaps impossible, to overturn. Hyde's proposal may have been his price for voting for the act's extension and, as a conservative Republican, his was a very important vote. Bailout and substantiality became the center of a major conflict among civil rights groups.

LDF lawyers, the Lawyers Committee for Civil Rights Under Law, and others who were in the business of trying voting cases immediately opposed

Hyde's bailout idea. But conservatives, whose votes were needed, supported the Hyde proposal. The leaders of the Leadership Conference after long, tense, and painful negotiations accepted a bailout provision containing substantiality as the price of passing the bill. In angry exchanges among proponents, Elaine, Lani, and Armand Derfner and Frank Parker of the Lawyers Committee adamantly refused to go along with Hyde. Principals in the Leadership Conference accused LDF and its allies of trying to torpedo the compromise they had crafted. Under heavy pressure, Lani stepped out of the room, and called me from a pay phone, asking what to do. She has said that the high point of her years at LDF was when I told her to oppose the compromise, adding, "Lani, do what's right." She felt validated as an LDF lawyer.

In place of the Hyde proposal, Congressmen Fish and Sensenbrenner sponsored a provision backed by LDF and the Lawyers Committee that did not include a concept of substantiality. The Judiciary Committee sent it to the floor by an overwhelming vote and it became law. The form in which the bill passed "aim[ed] to ensure that jurisdictions achieving bailout enjoy full minority participation in the electoral process." As one who had made some compromises and had refused to enter many a quixotic fight, I was hardly an ideologue in backing Lani and Elaine. The law would have been weakened. Our resources might have been drained in needless litigation. Besides, I wasn't sure that, if we stuck to our guns, we would lose, and in fact, we won. The strength of LDF lay in large part in the energy and enthusiasm of its lawyers. More than once I said no to a case, but when I felt I could back the staff I did.

During the early stages of the Voting Rights Act renewal effort, the Reagan administration played no role, merely announcing that it was studying the matter. But when the bill came up in the Senate the White House opposed replacing the intent standard with a results test. Senator Orrin Hatch attacked the proposal as requiring proportional representation. Senator Dole advocated language drafted by Armand Derfner that expressly incorporated the Supreme Court's earliest multimember case criteria, including as evidence of violation that the "political processes . . . are not equally open," that members of a protected class "have less opportunity . . . to participate in the political process," and that the courts may take into account the "extent to which members of a protected class have been elected." The draft answered charges of proportional representation by providing that "nothing in this section establishes a right to have members of a protected class elected in numbers equal to their proportion in the population." The White House went along with Dole. Lani and Elaine worked with Senators Kennedy and Dole's staffs in preparing the guide to interpreting the act that appears in the Judiciary Committee report.

As the Mobile case worked its way up again, the Supreme Court got the message. A few days after the amendment passed, a case in which we filed an amicus brief struck down the at-large system of electing the Burke County, Georgia, Board of Commissioners. For all practical purposes it overruled its recent decision in the Mobile case.

But the Reagan administration continued to resist. Following the 1982 amendments, Lani won a case of a gerrymandered electoral district, which the Justice Department had approved, that snaked its way through black neighborhoods in Louisiana, and another dealing with multimember state legislative districts in North Carolina. Justice supported the state with respect to some of those districts.

In a curious irony some Republicans in the late 1980s began advocating creation of majority black districts, because where black voters are zoned compactly fewer can join with white Democrats to create Democratic majorities in white areas, making Republicans even more the party of the white majority area.

35

FINAL SEPARATIONS

From almost the time LDF was born, the relationship with the NAACP oscillated between conflict and cooperation. Thurgood valued our independence, so much so that some Association board members accused him of having contrived to bring about the complete separation between the two organizations the IRS demanded in 1957. He hadn't, of course, though he later said that the IRS had done us a "favor." He clashed with Walter White, and while his relationship with Roy Wilkins was close and mutually supportive, differences between the organizations were inherent in the structure and had nothing to do with personality, as Roy once put it. This reality manifested itself in many ways: The collision over the Association's decision to appeal Texas's judgment against the Association when Thurgood wanted to settle the matter; LDF's willingness to represent sit-in demonstrators without regard to whether they first went to the Association's branches; Thurgood's and my representation of NAACP competitors, Martin Luther King, Jr., CORE, and SNCC, and of other unaffiliated individuals. Nevertheless, we provided almost all the representation in cases brought by NAACP branches. The NAACP initials in our name reflected the glory of our victories on the Association, and we worked well with Nathaniel Jones and Tom Atkins, who became general counsel at the NAACP after Bob Carter resigned.

During the years he was in control, Roy Wilkins deflected calls from within the Association to take control of LDF or force us to drop the initials NAACP from our name. He knew that for all the difficulties, a mutually supportive relationship was best for the promotion of civil rights for black Americans. But others in the Association envied our success; they attributed it to the use of the initials, which they thought Thurgood had hijacked in 1957. Others had the idea that we fooled the big foundations, corporations, and, indeed, the black community into supporting us under the false representation that we really were the Association. Still others believed that our decisions about what cases to take and positions to advance, particularly for NAACP branches, did not always take NAACP policies into account, although it was hard to think of a matter in which we disagreed about substance. Some LDF board members thought that there was a problem with me within the Association because I was white, which the Association, as a group advocating integration, would not articulate publicly. Certainly no one within the NAACP ever offered my race as a reason for difficulties between the groups; the problems had existed even during the period of Thurgood's leadership.

Many at the Association resented not having control over our activities. When Thurgood announced our willingness to defend the movement, the Association took the position, "We cannot commit ourselves to free-wheeling activity planned and launched by another organization. If we are expected to pay the bills, we must be in on the planning and launching, otherwise the bills will have to be paid by those who plan and launch." Of course, the demonstrators never would submit to that control. Bob Carter described the consequences of the separation in a memorandum to the Association board:

> Legal action which may involve NAACP policy (e.g. decision to put up bail and defend all the Freedom Riders) is undertaken by the Legal Defense Fund without clearance with the NAACP National Board. In sum, the NAACP lost control of its main legal machinery and for a while had an insufficient staff and lack of funds to have a legal program in the pre-1956 sense. . . . Since the cases went to the Legal Defense Fund from the lawyer or individual independent of the organization, the NAACP had therefore lost one of its main sources of fund-raising—its legal activities.

Bob deplored the 1957 separation of LDF from NAACP: "The Director-Counsel of the Fund was no longer organizationally subject to the NAACP's Board or Executive Secretary." Of himself, he wrote at this time, "Circumstances resulted in the General Counsel functioning as more than house counsel but never assuming the duties and responsibilities which a General Counsel is generally understood to have."

Bob argued that the separation was not required by the Internal Revenue Code—that Bill DeWind and Thurgood were wrong—and that LDF was, indeed, permitted to fund Association legal activities, adding that if LDF wouldn't support the Association's legal work, the Association could compel it to do so. He brought up one "delicate issue [namely, *me*] . . . the relationship between the present NAACP General Counsel and Fund's General Counsel in the reorganized department." Thurgood's "resignation should remove any deterrent to a clear analysis of the situation in terms of the

NAACP's best interest." Bob followed up by trying to prohibit lawyers with NAACP connections from working with LDF without his permission. In February 1962, he wrote to me: "I understand that you are planning to meet with a number of NAACP lawyers in New Jersey. . . . This is a request that you abandon that plan."

He wrote other letters to me and lawyers throughout the country to the same effect. Generally, they resented his demands and never acquiesced in them, nor did I. The NAACP committee that met with LDF also disagreed with Bob's approach. In April 1962 it recommended that "all units of the NAACP at all levels should secure the assistance of the Inc. Fund in connection with litigation whenever needed and possible." Neither Bob (who was on the West Coast) nor Roy (who was ill) attended that committee meeting. They absented themselves from such meetings so regularly that it became apparent they didn't want to be identified with the committee's work.

Matters continued pretty much the same until January 1964, when the Association got tax exemption for a legal arm, the Special Contribution Fund, which it set up in November of that year. With the creation of this group, relations between the organizations changed further. The boards had not been interlocked since 1957 and, since the advent of the movement, the Association had not been the only source of cases, and now that the NAACP had its own tax-exempt legal unit, we no longer were its only source of lawyers. Not long after this, Bob Carter wrote to me, "I want to make explicit the basic point of my telephone conversation with you on Tuesday, June 9, 1965. . . . I am requesting that you cease any direct contact with any NAACP branches in regard to litigation."

The antagonism continued: In July 1965 the Association board resolved to request LDF to reincorporate under another name "and, if they refuse to do so, the NAACP should go into court and enjoin them from use of the name NAACP." But in September Roy reported that its legal committee had suggested that the threat of suit be stricken from the minutes because "it would have no standing in court." The NAACP board followed that recommendation, proposing only further meetings with LDF. Nevertheless, the rift continued to grow. Though in years past we had counseled members and branches and held lawyer training sessions at NAACP annual conventions, in 1966, for the first time, the Association did not invite us. Indeed, we were expressly disinvited: John Morsell, Roy's top assistant, wrote to Jim Nabrit and me and asked us not to come.

Committees of the two boards continued to meet and LDF continued to represent Association branches, which turned to us without hesitation. We won cases for them, were personal friends, and obtained the money to bring the cases. LDF began placing a legend on press releases, stationery, and literature that evolved over time. In its basic form it stated: "The NAACP Legal Defense & Educational Fund, Inc. (LDF) is not part of the National

Association for the Advancement of Colored People (NAACP) although it was founded by it and shares its commitment to equal rights. LDF has had for ... years a separate board, program, staff, office and budget." The inscription brought further complaints from the Association. Apparently, there were some at least who would have been happy to be associated with our accomplishments.

On January 14, 1966, Roy Wilkins sent me a further NAACP board resolution that stated: "The Committee is of the opinion that the expansion of the activities of the Legal Defense and Educational Fund is evidence of its intent to exacerbate, rather than ameliorate, the very apparent difficulties of our relationship ... all of which is harmful to our efforts, which are beginning to show promise of raising substantial funds for the organization under our tax exempt arm, the NAACP Special Contribution Fund."

Once more, committees met. Stephen Spottswood, chair of the Association board, and Bob Carter led the fresh demand that we drop the initials NAACP from our name. They were particularly upset by a *New York Times* story telling of LDF successes and programs that, in effect, they said, had the potential of poaching on their territory. We responded that the programs were directly related to litigation, that we cooperated closely with the Association and its branches, as for example, in jointly filing Title VII complaints, and responded to branch requests. Nothing was decided. The committees agreed to meet again.

When we announced creation of businessmen's and athletes' committees to raise money for LDF, the NAACP reacted vigorously. Roy told his board: "The Inc. Fund, with a budget of over two million dollars and a grant from the Ford Foundation of over a million, and several smaller grants, is nonetheless reaching out to the people who have been giving to the NAACP." In fact, members of these committees in the past had hardly given to either organization.

NAACP LEGAL DEPARTMENT SELF-DESTRUCTS

The conflict between the two organizations suddenly moderated, for a time, when the Association's board, on October 14, 1968, fired Bob Carter's staff lawyer, Lewis Steel, for having published in the *New York Times* magazine an article attacking the Supreme Court entitled "Nine Men in Black Who Think White." Bob called the firing "personally offensive and demeaning" and resigned, along with all eight lawyers on his legal staff. I didn't know a lot about NAACP internal politics, but the conflict obviously ran deeper than the Steel article. Bob Ming, who was an NAACP board member, said, "We got him." I wasn't sure what that meant, but it suggested that he saw the resignations following the article as a solution to the problem rather than the cause of it. Association dissidents sued the NAACP, and Roy Wilkins asked me to assist their board member Max Delson in the defense.

What a turn of events! Jim Nabrit and I went to Delson's office, but never did a great deal. LDF staff lawyers, out of sympathy with Steel, whom they thought got a raw deal, refused to work on the case, and I was just as happy to stay out of that conflict.

To the extent that clashes with the Association stemmed from Bob's view of the proper place of LDF, the problem was gone for the moment. To the extent that there was what Roy had called a "structural" problem and competition for money and glory, differences would revive. Bob joined a law firm and several years later Richard Nixon appointed him a United States district judge.

Soon, some LDF board members began urging that we drop the NAACP initials, arguing that we did the work that effected change and attracted attention while the Association reaped the benefit. But there was little support for the measure and it died.

In the late 1970s the dispute with the NAACP over the initials, dormant for more than a decade, came back to life. Once more, a few LDF board members proposed that we drop the initials, but the board again rejected the suggestion.

Matters stayed under control until Roy Wilkins suffered a stroke and retired in 1977. He had led an honorable and, in a quiet way, even a heroic life. Among other accomplishments he was a leader of the battle for the Civil Rights Acts, struggling successfully against Southern racists, while fending off competing civil rights organizations and dissidents within the Association who harassed him until the day he left. He had been a friend of LDF, and a personal friend, who kept his good will toward us circumspect lest his critics within the Association think he was consorting with the enemy. Most of all, as far as the relationship between the organizations was concerned, he managed to avert an open break between the NAACP and LDF. Ben Hooks, a Memphis lawyer-preacher, succeeded him and soon the Association renewed the argument over the initials NAACP in the LDF title. Some members of the Association's board continued to believe that we were stealing its contributions. Actually, the opposite occurred. Some who contributed to the Association, after hearing about the latest LDF victory, would ask, "What does the NAACP do?"

There continued to be board members of the Association who objected to my role as director-counsel. Nathaniel Jones, the NAACP general counsel when the dispute revived, thought that some board members believed that Bob Carter or some other black person should be heading LDF, although no one within the Association leadership publicly offered race as a reason. On the fringe of the controversy, however, Louis Lomax, a black journalist, wrote: "The argument invariably comes in these words: 'The Jews would die before they would let a Negro rise to the leadership of one of their organizations; so why should we let a Jew, or any white man for that matter, head our organization?'" A New York City lower court judge, Bruce McM.

Wright, denounced me in similar terms. But, in 1979, running for reelection, when Wright solicited Marvin Frankel's support, Marvin reminded him about his denunciation of me. They arranged a carefully choreographed exchange of letters in return for which Marvin would support him. Wright sent me a draft stating that "there is absolutely no doubt that the assistance and leadership given to the black struggle by whites, and especially those from the Jewish community, have been indispensable to the development and life of the civil rights movement in America. . . . Your own role, over the past twenty years or so has been both exemplary and praiseworthy." I approved of the draft, and he then sent the letter in final form on August 30. Following his reelection, however, Wright resumed his attacks, stating, in a speech at Howard University on September 18, 1981, that "no one yet has ever explained to me why a white lawyer should be leading the Legal Defense Fund."

In early 1978 the Association board voted to demand that we stop using the NAACP initials and decided to sue. Nate Jones argued that the NAACP could not win and reminded the board that Roy Wilkins thought that whatever the problems might be, we could work them out. But a member of the Association's board, Theodore Berry, came up with a magical solution: The Association could somehow revoke the permission to use the initials that it had given in 1939.

Rejecting Jones's advice, the board hired an outside lawyer, Samuel Pierce, later Reagan's secretary of housing and urban development, and plunged ahead. After Pierce joined the cabinet, the NAACP hired former senator Edward Brooke.

Part of the Association's anger stemmed from our plans to commemorate the twenty-fifth anniversary of *Brown*. It felt we were claiming credit to which it was entitled. Recognizing that *Brown* resulted from the combined effort of the Association and LDF, I invited NAACP leaders to join our celebration, but they declined, and held their own ceremony in Clarendon County, South Carolina.

Conflict was exacerbated when an Alabama court convicted a young black man, Tommy Lee Hines, who had an IQ of thirty-nine, of raping a white woman and sentenced him to thirty years in prison. An Association staff lawyer had represented Hines and, improbably, had never raised Hines's mental condition as a defense. Hines's family and SCLC, which was parading and picketing over the case, believed that the defense had been bungled and asked the LDF, U. W. Clemon, and Howard Moore (who had represented Angela Davis) to take over. Outraged by Hines's thirty-year sentence and the incompetence of his defense, I agreed, even though I knew that the Association wouldn't like it. To make matters worse, we argued the only grounds available to win a new trial, which was that counsel at the first trial had been ineffective.

An enormous public controversy exploded. The NAACP lawyer refused to withdraw even though Hines's family wanted him to. The NAACP board denounced us and its staff lawyer threatened to sue us. Ultimately, it all simmered down. Elaine Jones, U. W. Clemon, and Jim Liebman won a new trial and, in a gesture of conciliation, nominally associated the NAACP lawyer with the defense. Then Elaine, U. W., and Jim achieved the almost unbelievable result of persuading an Alabama jury to acquit Hines on the ground that he was mentally incompetent.

Around the end of 1978, Margaret Bush Wilson, the Association's chair, and Ben Hooks wrote and called Julius Chambers, then the LDF president (they wouldn't communicate with me), once more demanding that we drop the initials. Thus began a series of interminable meetings, letters, memoranda, press releases, conferences, and legal maneuvering.

We set up a meeting in Bill Coleman's office, but Ben Hooks requested a change to neutral territory (reminiscent of the shape-of-the-table dispute of the Vietnam peace conference), and we met at the Mayflower Hotel in Washington on May 7, 1979. Rather than conferring in normal fashion, Ted Berry read aloud, word for word, a four-page statement setting forth the Association's grievances. He offered two alternatives: "return to the fold" or "surrender the privilege of using the initials." It seemed to me that the real problem was that the LDF was successful, while the Association had serious financial and organizational problems and was acting like a country setting out on a foreign adventure to distract attention from its domestic difficulties. In the more than two hours of back and forth Ben Hooks kept falling asleep, as he did at subsequent meetings. When I spoke to him privately, entreating him to work out some solution, he replied only that he was controlled by his board and could do nothing.

On June 28, 1979, the Association's convention adopted a formula: The NAACP "hereby rescinds its resolution of October 9, 1939 and revokes the permission granted to use the initials," the first step plotted by its legal gurus to establish a legal claim. Even as this occurred the committees continued to meet. Association board members would read statements about theft of their funds, name, publicity, and so forth. We offered to do anything short of changing our name or merging. Then, thinking that it provided some retroactive advantage, the NAACP registered its initials as a trademark. Finally, in May 1982, the Association sued us and held a press conference trumpeting what it had done. We retaliated with a press conference of our own. The frantic writing of releases, TV appearances, phone calls, the need to calm excited board members, and other activity drained energy that would have been more profitably directed to combating Reagan's war on generations of civil rights progress.

The Association's foray reflected internal tensions and pressures that were the product of its own success and that of the movement, of which it was now only a part. There had been a time when the Association was the only authentic voice of the black community, or at least, a major part of it.

Then came new protagonists, like Martin Luther King, Jr., whom the NAACP viewed as Johnny-come-latelies. It continued to believe that after all the smoke had cleared it would once more be seen as the unquestionable leader in the struggle. Ironically, for all practical purposes, most of the NAACP rivals have disappeared—Martin Luther King, Jr., in tragic circumstances—and the Association has remained. But it remained in weakened shape as a consequence of the conflicts.

Even with these disabilities the Association remained strong in some ways. Clarence Mitchell continued to be known as the 101st Senator until he retired, the most influential civil rights lobbyist of his time. But after he stepped down that title was held by the Fund's Elaine Jones. Some NAACP branches remained powerful in their own areas. But, overall, the organization no longer had the primacy it held in years past, and following passage of the Civil Rights Acts in the mid-sixties it increasingly felt the fall from that position.

There were internal fissures too. Within a year of suing us, Margaret Bush Wilson led an effort that ousted Hooks as executive director and appointed its new general counsel, Tom Atkins, Nate Jones's successor, as acting executive director. Within a week, Hooks fought his way back to reinstatement. Then the board called for Wilson's resignation and curbed her powers.

Most important, I believe, but not recognized within the Association, the Association had been replaced across the country by elected political leaders, who were the exponents of black aspirations and the officially designated representatives of the black community. By the 1990s forty black congressmen and the mayors of major cities spoke for the black community more authentically than could any private association.

Though its motive in suing us was ostensibly to claim and reclaim funds contributed to LDF, the Association spent so much on the lawsuit that it had to launch a special fund-raising effort to rebuild its treasury. For us, the case was financially cost free. Jay Topkis, a partner at Paul, Weiss, Bill Coleman, Vernon Jordan, and Barrington D. (Danny) Parker, all LDF board members, represented LDF without fee. The biggest toll on LDF was the diversion of our energies. We were so sure that the Association's claim was frivolous that we moved for summary judgment, a quick way of disposing of a case without a trial. But Judge Thomas Penfield Jackson, a new Reagan appointee, stunned us in March 1983 when he ruled that we had to give up the name. He concluded that the NAACP "grant[ed] *permission* [emphasis in original]—not the right—to use the initials."

For the first time we were worried and hastened to shore up our defenses in a motion for a new trial. At the time of the split from the Association, Thurgood had told me that during negotiations over the tax-exempt issue, the IRS asked that we drop the initials, and he reminded me of this after the Association sued us. At the time of the split both NAACP and LDF wanted the initials kept in the LDF name and refused to acquiesce in that demand; ultimately the IRS had relented.

When the NAACP sued us we didn't want to involve Thurgood in the messy business of the lawsuit and, consequently, never offered that evidence at the first trial. After the adverse decision, however, I contacted the only member of both boards then still alive, John Hammond, the great jazz impresario. He recalled the episode and gave an affidavit recounting it. I also got an affidavit from Herman Zand, who had worked with Arthur Spingarn when he incorporated LDF. Zand even recalled the name of the official with whom he filed the papers and made clear that the Association did not condition the grant of permission, but gave it outright. We filed these statements with a motion for new trial, which Jackson denied. We appealed.

After I left LDF to join the Columbia law faculty the court of appeals reversed Jackson with "directions that the suit be dismissed." The unanimous opinion by David Bazelon (Abner Mikva and Robert Bork also were on the panel) concluded that "the passage of time coupled with the reliance between the parties leads this court to conclude that laches [failure to assert a claim under circumstances prejudicial to the other party] of over forty years bars the injunctive relief sought by the Association." The NAACP then petitioned the Supreme Court for review, which it denied. That was the last of the dispute over the initials.

Some years later, after Hooks retired, and following the period with which this book deals, Ben Chavis was elected to leadership of the Association. He had been a civil rights activist in the 1960s and 1970s. North Carolina had once imprisoned him on criminal charges of arson in a case that became known as the "Wilmington Twelve." LDF, through James Ferguson and Julius Chambers's firm, had secured his release because he was innocent, as the court held. There now is good reason to believe that a constructive working relationship with the NAACP will develop once more.

36

BEYOND THE RIGHTS OF BLACKS

Because of our success, other groups turned to us—Mexican Americans, Puerto Ricans, Native Americans, gays and lesbians, women, and even some who were being denied human rights elsewhere in the world.

MEXICAN AMERICANS AND NATIVE AMERICANS

As we probed poverty law we early on began taking cases of Mexican Americans (Chicanos) and Native Americans. By 1968 we had a docket of about ten cases for Chicanos, involving classic issues of racial discrimination, and a half-dozen for Native Americans, dealing with esoteric subjects like treaty and fishing rights.

Around 1966, Pete Tijerina, a short, stocky, bouncy, and cheerful Chicano lawyer whose practice in San Antonio, Texas, dealt mostly with criminal matters, real estate, and divorces, began discussing with me, along with some other Chicano lawyers, the idea of setting up a legal defense fund. I invited them to some of our Airlie conferences to give them an indication of what we did and how LDF worked. Pete had roots in the Chicano community and a sense of its needs. While not at all a constitutional lawyer, or one who appeared in federal court very often, he provided the spark that got the Mexican American Legal Defense and Education Fund (MALDEF) under way. Things began moving when I sent Pete and two other lawyers, Roy Padilla and Albert Pena, $500 to travel to New York and asked Bill Pincus of the Ford Foundation to join us at an Argentine restaurant on Broadway—the closest I could come to cuisine appropriate to the occasion.

As we explained the idea, Bill liked it, but needed a detailed proposal. I went to a pay phone and called Les Dunbar at the Field Foundation, who agreed to give us $6,000 to hire someone to write it. I then recruited Mike Finkelstein, who was helping us with statistical analysis of jury discrimination, to travel to the Southwest, gather the facts, and write an application describing the situation of the Mexican American community and what lawyers might do about it.

His study, which I sent to Ford, reported that there were four to five million Mexican Americans in the Southwest; nearly one-third had an income of under $3,000 per year; they suffered from poor as well as segregated education, and virtually none were in higher education. They had legal problems with immigration, voting, consumer fraud, welfare, and as migratory laborers. A new militancy among the group required legal defense, but there were very few Mexican American lawyers and they were concentrated in large cities. *Not one* of these lawyers had a library with federal statutes and cases. Mike proposed creating an office of five lawyers in San Antonio with a budget of between $225,000 and $300,000 per year for five years. The new organization would work closely with us and I would be a member of its board.

Ford responded in May 1968 with an initial grant of $2.5 million over a period of five years, which included $250,000 for law school scholarships. In August 1968 MALDEF opened its doors in San Antonio. MALDEF lawyers began to attend our Airlie conferences regularly, and we conducted training sessions for them in the Southwest, including one at a ranch in Bandera, Texas. We learned about Chicano culture, the poverty and oppression that afflicted it, some of its heroic figures like Emilio Zapata, as well as mariachis, margaritas, guacamole, and how to ride horseback, while they learned federal procedure and constitutional law. Some LDF lawyers today still fondly refer to "the era of Bandera." MALDEF, now based in Los Angeles, has become the single most influential Mexican American organization. After it moved to California, Vilma Martinez, a Texas-born lawyer, whose first job after Columbia Law School had been with LDF, became its president and chief counsel.

Some NORI Native American cases involved fishing rights, to which tribes claimed they were entitled by treaty, and probed the efficacy of the several fishing techniques for the purpose of allocating the salmon catch: nets, traps, spears, hooks, and other means. One celebrated case ultimately was resolved by giving up on influencing the size of the catch by designating the method of fishing, but simply by divvying up the fish caught. Mike Sovern, who had been at an LDF conference at Tahoe, observed fish swimming one by one up the fish ladders at Bonneville dam. He asked: "Why don't we just give this one to the Indians and the next to the whites?" Ultimately, a solution along those lines was worked out.

In 1967 Vine DeLoria, a Native American scholar and executive director of the National Congress of American Indians, asked me to attend a national convention of Indian nations in Laramee, Wyoming, to consult about setting up a legal program. It was an immense gathering, where many participants stayed in tepees, dined on buffalo chili from enormous vats, and listened to me talk about what legal action had done for blacks and was beginning to do for Chicanos. I didn't then appreciate certain important differences between Native Americans and other groups. While Indians were extremely poor (the median family income was $1,500 compared to $6,882 for the general population), had some culture in common, and were viewed by whites as a single group, in fact they were scattered among 263 continental tribes, bands, villages, and pueblos and in 300 Alaskan communities. Members of certain groups tended to assimilate themselves into the general population, or at least integrate into it, while others groups remained closely bound together on tribal reservations, and which of these two courses had been taken very much determined the position of the group on various Native American issues. Treaty rights varied from group to group. There were very different philosophies about relationships with the rest of the United States, as well as inter- and intratribal rivalries. There was disagreement over whether they should form a legal services or an impact litigation organization.

Moreover, funding would not be easy. By the time I submitted a grant proposal, Ford had been burned by a political controversy surrounding MALDEF. Congressman Henry Gonzalez objected to MALDEF activities supporting some highly controversial militant groups in South Texas, causing Ford to fear adverse congressional action; as a consequence of the controversy, MALDEF moved from San Antonio to California. It became impossible to agree on what our proposed Native American organization should do or to devise a program that would satisfy Ford. Ford got rid of the problem by making a grant to California Indian Legal Services for a "small, narrowly focused Indian Rights Fund, with the grant period to be used to shape what may become a bigger national program," doing nothing further along this line. At that time, no other source of funds was in sight and I gave up. Some years later, several Native American legal organizations were created and I joined the board of one, the Indian Law Resources Center. Beyond that, the Fund's contact with Native Americans dwindled.

I helped create the Puerto Rican Legal Defense Fund and the Asian American Legal Defense Fund, where I became a member of the board. Both subsequently moved into the same building as LDF and sometimes shared our facilities. When a gay and lesbian group consulted me about setting up the Lambda Legal Defense Fund I assigned a staff lawyer to help in the process. But, unhappily, prejudice affects some who fight it: I had to ask several lawyers before one would agree to meet with the gay rights group.

RIGHTS IN OTHER LANDS

I felt we could draw upon the law of other countries and international law in our cases, but I was almost completely wrong. In 1963, to encourage interest in international human rights, I wrote one of the first articles about the European Court of Human Rights for the *Columbia Law Review*, but it attracted little attention. Except in *Coker*, which referred to disuse of the death penalty for rape outside the United States, the Supreme Court scarcely referred to the law of other lands. We cited international law in arguing that Oklahoma couldn't execute someone who was sixteen when he committed a murder; the court ignored this argument but ruled with us on other grounds. In the sit-in cases we argued that, except in South Africa and in Franco's Spain, no one would be convicted for peacefully demanding service at a lunch counter. Most of the justices didn't notice, but Justice Black, from the bench, said he didn't care what was done in other countries.

I tried unsuccessfully to obtain funds for African interns to work at LDF; once I hired a student from the British Virgin Islands for a summer. To celebrate the tenth anniversary of *Brown* I proposed a program with speakers to discuss its meaning elsewhere in the world, but it took about fifteen years until we began to have human rights lawyers from Africa, Asia, the Caribbean, and elsewhere at LDF events to discuss rights in their countries. LDF affiliated with the International League for the Rights of Man (later, the International League for Human Rights), but the connection was nominal. No one was very interested. Unless I inserted international human rights material in our briefs personally it wouldn't happen.

We did better exporting the idea of American rights to other lands. The Warren Court was an inspiration all over the world. Because of the LDF role in that constitutional revolution human rights groups invited me to go on missions abroad.

SOVIET JEWS

In May 1976, Debby and I visited Leningrad, Riga, and Moscow for the National Conference on Soviet Jewry, accompanied by Damon Keith, then United States district judge in Detroit (now on the court of appeals), and his wife, Rachel, a physician, to support refusniks who were trying to emigrate. We obtained visas only at the last minute, through the intervention of Bill Coleman, then secretary of transportation, who personally urged the Soviet ambassador to help. In Moscow, Anatoly Scharansky met us outside the synagogue, the focal point of foreign visitor–refusnik contact, and became our guide in Moscow. Wherever we went I got the question in Yiddish asking whether Damon, who was black, was Jewish (he covered his head in synagogue with a ski cap)—he wasn't.

One of our aims was to bolster the refusniks' morale. Just meeting with them was important. They cherished the most meaningless letters from Westerners, recited details of meetings, told of phone calls from abroad, read large meaning into small gestures. We also were charged with protesting to the procurator the treatment of Jews who had attempted to emigrate, among them a Dr. Shtern who was imprisoned for bribery because a patient had given him a chicken as a gift. Damon and I had tried, unsuccessfully, to make an appointment through the American embassy, so we went to the procurator's office. I had just taken several weeks of Russian lessons at St. Sergius, a private Russian high school on Manhattan's Upper East Side. Communicating with a secretary who knew a dozen words of English, my Russian, plus sign language were enough to arrange a meeting that afternoon, but only if we brought our own interpreter. Intourist, the Soviet tourist agency, normally would be the source of translators but we were told none could or would accompany us, undoubtedly because of what we were up to. Anatoly, however, was more than pleased to volunteer for the job. Rather than exposing himself to danger, he thought that role would confer protection on him.

We returned to the procurator's office with him, told an armed guard that we had an appointment and went upstairs. There consternation burst loose. Anatoly had been there often as suspect and defendant, the officials knew him well, but hardly expected to see him in this novel capacity. Heads popped in and out of doorways, which then slammed shut. Someone summoned him to a room, closed the door, and we waited for fifteen minutes. When he emerged, smiling, he said they had asked him whether he was now an Intourist interpreter, all of whom were women. Our discussion with the procurator's assistant went something like this: Did we want to discuss abstract or concrete matters? Damon said both. But, they replied, experts on concrete matters were not available. As to abstract matters, they called for specialists, who weren't available either. We raised the matter of Dr. Shtern and others, but she knew nothing about them. I gave her a letter I had written to the procurator about the cases we were protesting and we left. I was amazed that we had gotten as far as we did. Anatoly was delighted. For him the meeting was a triumph. He was certain that word would reach the top and cause great concern. Later we had dinner with him in the National Hotel, a taboo for refusniks, but he joined us defiantly.

On our last night we visited Andrei Sakharov and Anatoly interpreted; while Sakharov could speak English, he preferred not to. The visit had been discouraged by the National Council because Sakharov, who was not Jewish, was concerned with human rights generally, which its leadership thought might distract from the cause of refusniks. But in the Soviet Union refusniks and civil libertarians, known as "legalists," were close friends. Some members of both groups belonged to a circle that monitored compliance with the Helsinki human rights accords.

Sakharov lived in an apartment in an old building that was littered with debris. We went up in the creaky elevator, but were afraid to use it again and, when the evening was over, walked down. Sakharov occupied the bedroom with his wife, Elena Bonner; his daughter, her husband, and two children slept in the living room; his mother-in-law in the kitchen. Sakharov discussed concern for the Crimean Tatars and, particularly, Mustafa

Dzhemilev, a leader who was in prison. We talked a great deal about capital punishment and the LDF campaign against it. He estimated that in the Soviet Union there were seven hundred to one thousand executions per year; but there were no published statistics. He was worried about particular individuals: A woman living in an extremely cold climate, no longer qualified to occupy her apartment, had been put out in the cold with her child, whom she killed before committing suicide; a teenage boy who had been tortured to death—a photo of his corpse displayed marks of abuse. Sakharov showed us photographs of women engaged in heavy manual labor.

He spoke with pride about his grandson, who was at his dacha when Brezhnev, who lived nearby, complimented him on being a fine-looking child. I invited him to become vice president of the International League for Human Rights, which he accepted, and asked for a letter confirming the appointment. He authorized two friends to accept an honorary degree on his behalf at the University of Jerusalem. Before we left he served a Latvian cake that looked like irregular spokes extending from a hollow cylindrical center. It is made by pouring batter on a broomstick-like core that is rotated over a fire.

On that trip we last saw Anatoly in the Moscow subway, where Debby gave him her wool-lined raincoat to pass on to a dissident who was seriously ill and lived in Siberia under harsh conditions. To avoid suspicion that might be caused by carrying the coat, Anatoly, short and somewhat round, put it on, encasing himself tightly, and left us walking into the dark of the tunnel at Red Square. Not long afterward, shortly after Elaine Jones had visited him at my suggestion, police arrested and imprisoned him. We next saw him in New York, several years later, after his release in a spy-for-dissident swap. I saw Andrei Sakharov again, after Gorbachev released him from exile and permitted him to travel abroad, at the office of Human Rights Watch, where he had gone to meet with friends who had supported him.

SOUTH AFRICA

In 1978 David Hood, a program officer at the Carnegie Corporation, asked Debby and me to visit South Africa for a month to advise lawyers interested in setting up an organization like LDF. Hood had gone to Mississippi during the movement and had a good idea of the Fund's work and an interest in a direct link of the movement experience with the fight against apartheid. South African lawyers, including Arthur Chaskalson and Sydney Kentridge, had heard about LDF and wanted to explore the possibilities of public interest law in South Africa. If a successful plan were developed, Carnegie, Ford, and the Rockefeller Brothers foundations were interested in funding it.

Debby and I brought Billy, then fifteen, and one of his classmates with us and parked them part of the time in St. Barnabas, the first integrated private school in South Africa, in which they were the first whites—so-called "col-oreds" (mixed-race people) and Indians already were enrolled. For a while they also attended King David, a Jewish day school. We lectured to the bar and at universities around the country about the development of civil rights law in America, and spent a great deal of time with Arthur Chaskalson, dis-cussing lessons learned at LDF, which were somewhat, but not always, rele-vant.

Chaskalson, Kentridge, and other South Africans established the Legal Resources Centre (LRC) in Johannesburg with funding from major Ameri-can foundations. Led by Arthur with great legal and organizational skill, it has made a substantial difference in moving South Africa toward becoming a nonracial country. It won cases striking down regulations that prevented black men who were living in urban areas from having their wives and grown-up children living with them. It successfully attacked an official device preventing blacks from having permanent residence after ten years continuous employment with the same employer. It restricted operation of a law under which "idle" blacks could be deported from an urban area. These modest gains had large impact.

With offices in a half-dozen cities, the LRC is funded from within South Africa and Europe—now only some of its support comes from the United States. It now has a national office, six regional offices, and a staff of more than one hundred, including forty staff lawyers and fifteen recent law grad-uates in a fellowship program resembling the LDF internship program. (In 1984 I started a program at Columbia Law School that sends summer human rights interns to agencies around the world. Regularly, Columbia students intern at the LRC.) When we visited Albie Sachs, then a South African exile in Mozambique, following our first trip to South Africa, he chastised us for supporting the enemies of his people. Albie, who has returned to South Africa, soon became a strong supporter of the LRC. Nel-son Mandela, in a letter to the Council of Europe seconding Nadine Gordimer's nomination of the LRC for the European Human Rights Prize, wrote that the LRC "has served the disadvantaged people of our country well during the last 13 years. Millions of our people benefitted by the actions taken by the Centre challenging apartheid's laws and practices. . . . It has an important part to play in support of the rule of Law and the nurtur-ing of the human rights culture in the democratic South Africa that we hope will soon be established." Debby and I continue to return to South Africa to hold seminars on constitutional litigation and to visit friends.

THE PHILIPPINES

In August 1983, the Marcos regime's flagrant abuse of human rights peaked when former Senator Benigno S. Aquino, Jr., was murdered at the Manila airport upon his return from exile to reenter politics. The middle class joined in strikes, demonstrations, and public disruption because they no longer could tolerate the widespread corruption that characterized the regime. The Lawyers Committee for Human Rights asked me to join Marvin Frankel and Diane Orentlicher, who had been my student and was deputy director of the Lawyers Committee, on a mission to the Philippines in September to report on human rights in the wake of the Aquino assassination. The Marcos government, concerned about possible loss of United States support and apprehensive that President Reagan might cancel a projected visit to Manila, allowed us to enter the country; officials met with us and ostensibly allowed us to visit anywhere we wanted to go. We met with Imelda Marcos; Minister of Defense Juan Ponce Enrile; the legal adviser to the president and the chief justice and associate justices of the Philippine Supreme Court; the archbishop of Manila; the American ambassador; political prisoners and victims of government abuse; human rights lawyers; Corazon Aquino, who later would become president; Salvador Laurel, who became vice president under Aquino; and many others. Each day we woke up at dawn and kept a grueling schedule under a hot sun, led by human rights activists who risked their lives and who, like Southern black lawyers, knew they would have to remain behind after we left and took the international spotlight with us.

Enrile entertained us at a lavish lunch in his office, which appeared to be sixty feet square, attended by uniformed, bemedaled officers. As at other banquets we attended, there was a meat and a fish course; the meat was tongue served with a sweet and sour sauce. Following lunch Marvin questioned Enrile about a priest who was being held incommunicado for complicity with Communist guerillas. Enrile assured us that the man had confessed and offered to produce him. A half-hour later soldiers escorted into the room the priest-prisoner, freshly shaved and neatly dressed in an open collar shirt, who admitted that, indeed, he was a Communist. Marvin asked whether we might question the prisoner alone. We stepped to a corner where he said that he admitted to being a Communist only because he feared torture.

On our last day, the American embassy, unable to arrange a meeting with Ferdinand Marcos, set up a strange encounter, a visit to Imelda. She agreed, apparently expecting us to use our influence with Ronald Reagan to persuade him to visit the Philippines during his Asia trip. At dusk we drove in an American embassy car, accompanied by an embassy official, into an eerie medieval scene at the palace compound, past phalanxes of guards in protective masks, carrying shields and batons to fend off demonstrators. We went not to the Malacanang Palace, the presidential residence, but to one across a grassy courtyard, where the Marcoses lived temporarily while the Malacanang Palace was being renovated.

Mrs. Marcos received us at a large coffee table in an enormous room. There, over triangular chicken and mayonnaise sandwiches on crustless white bread accompanied by mango juice, she led off the conversation. Man, she said, is composed of heart, soul, and mind, which demonstrates that he is two-thirds spiritual. She then described how close the Philippines was to Communist China. To compound the danger, the water between the two nations was not very deep. But the Philippines was resolutely anti-Communist and would repel any Communist threat. She urged that we remind President Reagan of this.

Here, I interrupted and reminded her that we had come to discuss human rights. I brought up the padlocking, earlier that day, of the Philippines *Times* and the attempt to arrest its editor, who escaped. She hadn't heard of the incident, but was sure that he must have done something wrong. She proceeded to tell of her role in human rights. When she became mayor of the greater Manila area she was concerned about conditions in which prisoners lived and visited the prison, where she found large numbers of men housed in barracks. She ordered that partitions be erected between beds and gave each prisoner a seedling that he might grow in a window box. She also gave each of them a pet: a chicken, rabbit, duck, or cow. They cared for their pets, which multiplied. Later she suggested that they start a business and sell the animals, but they refused because they had become attached and knew the animals would be killed. The moral was that the most hardened criminals, having something to love, would not harm even an animal.

As we left the palace, Diane asked whether we might have a look at the Malacanang Palace, on the other side of the square. Imelda happily agreed. It was dark and not raining, but an aide carried an umbrella over her as we walked across the square. Workmen were all over the place. There was beautiful furniture, paintings, sculpture, artifacts, and many pictures of the Marcoses and Reagans, some depicting them dancing, dating back to when Ronald Reagan was governor of California. In one niche, a string of rosary beads hung from a small statue of the Virgin Mary. Imelda told us that she had been walking past the icon when she first heard that Benigno Aquino had been shot. She fell to her knees and prayed to God that he would not die and placed the rosary on the Virgin to mark the event.

As we left the palace the embassy aide whispered, "Do we tip the tour guide?" I thought that showed that the embassy had written off the Marcoses, which it had.

We wrote a report that documented political killings, disappearances, torture, arbitrary arrest and preventive detention, relocation of entire villages, the ineffective role of the judiciary, press censorship, and the operation of martial law. The Lawyers Committee reports on the Philippines, of which this was one, helped influence Congress and the administration to withdraw support from Marcos, leading to his flight from the country, the introduction of democracy, and a marked improvement in human rights.

Shortly after our visit to the Soviet Union, Robert Bernstein, then head of Random House, and Orville Schell, a Wall Street lawyer (who had given Debby her first job as the only woman in his firm, Hughes, Hubbard, Blair and Reed), formed Helsinki Watch to support Soviet dissidents who had created a committee of the same name. I became one of its original members—in time it developed into Human Rights Watch—and went on human rights missions for it, including to Poland with Debby and Jay Topkis to observe the trials of Adam Michnik, Jacek Kuron, and other political rebels. We stopped in Paris to meet with exiles who gave us up-to-the-minute information and asked us to smuggle in tightly rolled up messages concealed in cigarettes, which didn't make much sense because any security police who might look for secret messages would look in cigarettes. We just carried the messages and no one interfered.

I wasn't very good at the cloak and dagger business—after I crudely encoded names and addresses of dissidents in my address book, I couldn't decipher my own notes. The American embassy was unsuccessful in attempting to obtain permission for us to attend the Michnik-Kuron trial. So we went to the courthouse anyway. Lech Walcsa came too and we marched up the courthouse steps. But neither he nor we were permitted in. The New York Times carried a story about police turning us away, calling international attention to the suppression of human rights. Whatever else it accomplished, it infuriated the Polish government, which denied me a visa the following year, the consular officer giving as a reason the report of our last visit, which had appeared in the Times.

One afternoon we rented a car and with one of the dissidents as interpreter went to Lowicz, where my father, who died in 1974, had lived until he came to America. My uncle gave me the precise address; he had recently visited the family's apartment. As we poked around trying to find it, a woman inquired about what we were looking for. She remembered my uncle's visit and led us to the flat. I had expected to find a hovel, but it was an apparently middle-class garden lodging, facing a park. Inside was a built-in gleaming white tile floor-to-ceiling stove that the occupant said would be removed to a museum. Lowicz once had been an almost entirely Jewish town. Not a single Jew lives there now. I went to the local Jewish cemetery to look for my grandmother's grave, but the stones were too worn to be legible. Surprisingly, the cemetery had a caretaker, through whose home we entered, and was in good condition, though overgrown with weeds and wildflowers.

OPENING UP PRIVATE CLUBS FOR WOMEN AND MINORITIES

When I worked for the New York State Law Revision Commission after graduation from law school I encountered a strange phenomenon. We would meet at the Association of the Bar and break for lunch, occasionally at the Harvard Club. The club wouldn't admit women, except to a segregated area, which had to be entered through a separate door. Some members of the group preferred the club because they didn't like to lunch with one female senior staff member. She seemed congenial enough to me, but they didn't enjoy her stiff, scholarly manner. After I became director of LDF, I would sometimes encounter the men-only phenomenon at private clubs, where I would be invited to lunch with a foundation officer to discuss the possibility of a grant. Sometimes I would attend evening meetings at such clubs for fund-raising and observe law firms, investment banking firms, advertising agencies, and other business groups meeting in adjoining rooms. Members sometimes confided that their firms paid their club expenses or that they took them as a tax deduction. Members transacted business at clubs, although the clubs stoutly denied it, and some had rules against having papers on the table at lunch and so forth. But even if a word about business was not spoken, advantageous relationships developed. Those who were excluded—women, Jews, and blacks—were at a significant disadvantage.

In the late 1970s Mike Sovern proposed me for membership in the Century, a club on Forty-third Street, whose members included some of the most prominent figures in academic life, the arts, letters, and music. Debby pointed out that while the club had many black members it didn't admit women. I discussed the exclusion with members who said that the ban soon would end. I joined, but nothing changed. There was no written rule that excluded women and so I nominated for membership Joan Cooney, the creator of "Sesame Street" and president of the Children's Television Workshop. By the club's own standards she was at least the peer of any of its members. I received no reply for more than a year when I got a letter from a functionary stating that since the club had been founded as a gentlemen's association in 1857 it could not consider my nomination.

So I decided to do something about it. Clubs defended their right to exclude women, blacks, Jews, and others on the basis of a so-called constitutional right of privacy. No Supreme Court case ever said that clubs had such a right, but the argument had plausibility. I was sure, however, that the Supreme Court wouldn't uphold such a right for clubs with hundreds, sometimes thousands of members, where many members transacted business and where their firms paid club expenses or members took them as tax deductions—hardly private, intimate activity.

I decided to draft a statute to prohibit discrimination by any private club that had hundreds of members and where business was transacted, which I identified as places where 20 percent of the members took club expenses as a tax deduction or where employers paid dues and expenses for their employee members. I asked Carol Bellamy, then president of the New York City Council, to introduce my ordinance.

It ran into a barrage of criticism. Clubs denounced the infringement of their right of privacy. Labor unions claimed that clubs would go out of business, throwing waiters and doormen out of work. In reality, the contrary was true: Clubs were already losing business because companies, universities, foundations, and others were starting to boycott them because they excluded women. The *New York Times* wrote an editorial against the bill. Some denounced the 20 percent test as arbitrary: Why wasn't it more or less? The New York State Club Association hired a leading liberal lawyer, Al Blumenthal, to oppose the bill. Some local benevolent orders, like the Moose, objected that the law would affect them. The city council majority leader sat on the bill and it got nowhere.

I rewrote the law to take out reference to taxes and exclude benevolent orders. Instead of the 20 percent test I substituted any club that "regularly receives payment for dues, fees, use of space, facilities, services, meals or beverages directly or indirectly from or on behalf of nonmembers for the furtherance of trade or business"—much tougher than the 20 percent test. My first draft had covered clubs with more than one hundred members. Opponents held out for five hundred. I proposed settling at four hundred because that seemed to cover any club in New York. The city council majority leader, who had been sitting on the bill, retired. I drafted findings of fact for the city council that declared that discrimination in private clubs interfered with advancement in business and the professions for minorities and women.

I had kept the bill general to minimize attacks on it, which created the danger that it might be too vague to be constitutional. To remedy this, I had students in my seminar draft regulations, which the city later adopted, to make specific the bill's generalities. Mayor Koch endorsed the bill. Women's and civil rights groups supported it. In 1984 it finally passed. The New York State Club Association then sued to enjoin it as unconstitutional. It took the case to the Supreme Court where the city's corporation counsel, Peter Zimroth, once an LDF summer law student, defended it. The Supreme Court upheld the law unanimously. The law, with some variation, has been adopted across the country. Most New York private clubs now have many women members, no longer suffer boycotts over the issue, and are flourishing as never before.

PART VI

CHANGING THE GUARD AGAIN

37

MY LAST YEARS AT LDF

A PERMANENT HOME FOR LDF

As the 1980s arrived, the lease at 10 Columbus Circle ran out. The building faced demolition to make way for a new development and, in the meantime, our rent would triple. Jim Nabrit and I started a hunt for new quarters. In 1983, after a year of looking, we found a lovely old art deco building, 99 Hudson Street, in Tribeca, with Hudson River views, in an area of downtown Manhattan that had been declining over the years and was on the verge of gentrification. The building had once been used by printing plants and other light industry, which by then had moved out of New York. The space would be relatively expensive to purchase, but I thought that while foundations were reluctant to give money for buying bricks and mortar they might help in creating a public interest law center, not for LDF alone, but for a group of legal defense funds that, as neighbors, would share our extensive library, confer on common issues, and enjoy the synergy of working close to one another. Ford Foundation was willing to give and lend money for the project, as were Revson, Carnegie, and others. With their support and that of Bill Scheide, we bought a condominium of five floors, of which LDF took three, at a bargain price in a complex rental-purchase option transaction—the contract was perhaps six inches thick. Skylights illuminated the top-floor library. We built a large conference room; during lunch hour we moved aside tables to hold exercise class. I attended the classes, but for reasons I never could figure out, no other male staff member would.

The Puerto Rican Legal Defense and Education Fund, the Asian American Legal Defense and Education Fund, the NOW Legal Defense and Education Fund, and the Council of New York Law Associates purchased the remaining two floors, all of us constituting the Public Interest Law Center. Other public interest agencies, including the New York Urban Coalition, occupied other floors in the building. LDF bought the roof, from which we could see fireworks in the harbor on the Fourth of July. My own office was too small to accommodate Thurgood's massive desk and so, at last, I got a smaller one. I gave Thurgood's desk to Steve Ralston, who was happy to have it even though it occupied perhaps half of the space in his office.

THE HARVARD BOYCOTT

In early 1982 Jim Vorenberg, dean of the Harvard Law School, asked Julius Chambers to teach a course in civil rights law during the three-week Harvard January semester in which students study a single course intensively every day. Derrick Bell, who had left LDF to take government jobs in 1966, later became a professor at Harvard Law School, where he taught a course in civil rights, a position he had resigned to become dean of the University of Oregon Law School. While our subject—civil rights law—was not given as a substitute for his civil rights course, it would temporarily address some of the same material. Julius couldn't leave his practice for so long a time, and asked me to split the teaching with him, to which I agreed.

Shortly after the course was announced, the Harvard Black Law Students Association (BLSA), joined by the Harvard Third World Coalition, counseled and encouraged by Bell, called upon students to boycott us and demanded that we withdraw. Bell—who had become a vocal critic of LDF, the NAACP school desegregation policies, and Harvard's failure to hire more minority faculty—openly endorsed the boycott. As time went on, BLSA, Bell, and their supporters gave many reasons for their boycott, but the principal one was my color, sometimes expressed, as it was by Bell, in the formulation that Harvard should appoint "a teacher whose credentials include experiences in and with American racism similar to those the students have already suffered." Facing heavy criticism for being racist, BLSA soon backpedaled and stressed the need to hire more black faculty (there was one tenured and one nontenured black faculty member at Harvard Law School) and to make civil rights a permanent part of the curriculum.

Other issues, including the LDF dispute with the NAACP, became entangled. Muhammed Kenyatta, the black student association's president, objected to my "adamant refusal to relinquish directorship of the NAACP Legal Defense and Educational Fund to a Black attorney." In October an NAACP officer attended an open forum at Harvard where Julius and I spoke and attacked LDF over our use of the initials NAACP. The Association's magazine, *The Crisis*, ran a long article sympathetic to the boycotters, approving the students' "high level of sophistication" in bringing up "the NAACP's legal battle with the LDF" and "adamant . . . demands that Greenberg relinquish directorship of the LDF to a black attorney."

Kenyatta and Tony Brown, a columnist who had a TV show dealing with black themes, used the issue to protest the LDF position on higher education, arguing that we threatened to put black colleges out of business.

Kenyatta invented my nonexistent "intervention against the efforts at Cornell University by the Black Students Union to establish an Afro-American–oriented dormitory." I had never said anything on the subject. Duncan Kennedy, a white Harvard law professor and a leader of the Critical Legal Studies movement, who had voted for my appointment, switched to support the boycott after black students announced it. He circulated a letter he had written to the *New York Times*, which it hadn't published, stating that the "point is *not* that he is white, and whites should not teach about racism and civil rights." Rather, it was that "a Harvard Law School with only two blacks on a faculty of sixty-five ought not to entrust its one course on racial issues to a visiting white lawyer."

Some of those who supported the boycott slipped easily from one position to another, taking pains to disclaim race as a reason. Sometimes the language was equivocal: A member of the BLSA executive committee wrote to the *Harvard Crimson* that "the fact that one of these visitors, Jack Greenberg, is white is simply not the animus behind our actions. Rather, we are protesting the complete lack of good faith by the Law School administration in recruiting and retaining minority tenured professors."

During all of this Julius and I met with Harvard students in public and private meetings, trying to persuade them not to boycott us, though we got nowhere. I have a vivid memory of meeting with the Third World Coalition, where a woman student sat on the floor, head buried in her knees, which were drawn to her chest, sobbing. A lot of it was crazy.

Harvard law students overwhelmingly opposed the boycott. So did many important blacks, within Harvard and without. Harvard government professor Martin Kilson wrote that BLSA members "who require ethnocentric crutches as part of their academic regimen must start growing up." Carl Rowan called it "racist, anti-intellectual," and "anti–civil rights." Bayard Rustin denounced it as "nothing more than blatant racism." Randall Kennedy, who soon would join the Harvard law faculty, wrote that I belonged in the category of "Wendell Phillips and Thaddeus Stevens" and other whites who fought for racial equality.

Within the press, the *New York Times* editorialized that "it is hard to think of anyone better qualified to teach such a course" and that "the students unwisely inject themselves into a dispute between the National Association for the Advancement of Colored People and the Defense Fund over the fund's use of the parent group's initials." Editorials in the black press, including the *Pittsburgh Courier*, attacked the boycott. At Columbia, the Law School Student Senate resolved, "We are proud that a lawyer of stature and prominence teaches the Clinical Seminar in Race and Poverty Law at the Columbia University School of Law."

Anti-Semitism came up repeatedly. Kenyatta wrote that making me director of the Legal Defense Fund "was like asking Stokely Carmichael to become the director of B'nai B'rith." Tony Brown remarked on "the controversial Jack Greenberg, the white and Jewish director of the NAACP Legal Defense and Educational Fund, Inc." Brown argued that Carl Rowan had brought religion up first, when he wrote that the dispute arose from Muhammed Kenyatta's anti-Jewish bent as a Muslim, which Brown denied existed, pointing out that Kenyatta was not a Muslim, but in fact a Baptist. While some of these critics might have objected equally to a WASP, it is difficult to conceive of criticism focusing on the fact that he or she was, say, an Episcopalian. To complicate the jumble, a conservative columnist, who objected to my support of affirmative action, wrote that "Greenberg and those students deserve each other."

For two weeks before the course began I was in India, lecturing on public interest law. The night before the course began I flew for about sixteen hours from New Delhi to New York and Boston, joining Julius the following morning for the first session, which we taught together. Pickets from BLSA and the Third World Coalition patrolled the building entrance. Associate Dean Lance Liebman (now dean of Columbia Law School) led Julius and me to the classroom through a line of chanting, sign-holding protesters, where we taught the course to more than forty students, including only one black student, a woman from the graduate school of education. The line quickly dwindled and in a day or two disappeared. At the end, as far as I could tell, it consisted mainly of gay and lesbian students. It may be that they were so marginalized that any sort of alliance was better than none. The course continued without incident.

Perhaps a dozen black students, singly or in small groups, visited me during office hours and expressed disagreement with the boycott. A couple said that their parents wanted me to know that they supported me. I invited them to enroll or audit, but they declined, saying they didn't dare split publicly with BLSA. I recalled the time in my life when at the age of five or six, to go along with the gang, I joined other kids in throwing stones into the Chinese laundry. I also recalled some white Southern lawyers who took me aside and explained quietly that they really wished me well, but could not afford to come out and say so publicly. At least they had the excuse that their practices would be ruined and their families placed in physical danger.

When we completed the course at Harvard a student group at Stanford invited us to teach a summer course there. But the Harvard BLSA objected, informing Stanford's black student association that for us to be allowed to teach there would be an affront to Harvard black students. Stanford's BLSA objected. Julius and I didn't want to go through chaos like that again and declined the offer.

My reaction to all this was that I scorned those boycott leaders and their followers who, caught in their racist enterprise, scrambled for other justifications, and I pitied those who disagreed with the boycott, but wouldn't break ranks and risk retaliation. From which group, I wonder, will we enlist the civil rights leaders of the future?

MY LAST CASES

My last argument before the Supreme Court, against the United States Postal Service, involved the seemingly minor procedural issue of how to prove an employment discrimination claim. Although the case involved the narrow question of what constitutes a prima facie case, I focused on testimony about the plaintiff's supervisors having made statements such as, "All they [blacks] want to do is to lay around and breed like yard dogs and collect relief checks," evidence that showed that employers who discriminated could be hiding behind procedural obstacles. Rhetorically, it would cause anyone to sympathize with the plaintiff. Amazingly, I won unanimously, with Justice Rehnquist writing the opinion. The case had been feared as one that would undo procedural gains of the past, but the Court preserved rules governing how one proves a prima facie case, a small victory in a hostile environment.

At the beginning of the Reagan administration, the Civil Rights Commission continued to be dominated by Carter appointees, who repeatedly assailed Reagan's policies on affirmative action, busing, and other matters. Reagan retaliated in October 1983 by firing the three most critical commissioners, Mary Frances Berry, Belinda Cardenas Ramirez, and Rabbi Murray Saltzman, in order to replace them with members sympathetic to his policies.

Because appointment to the commission requires Senate confirmation, my immediate reaction was that the firings, without Senate agreement, might be illegal. The critical question was whether the law that required Senate confirmation of appointments permitted unilateral discharge of these same appointees. While the statute said nothing on this question, legislative history and comparison with other statutes might make a case. I told the purge victims that if they wanted to sue, we might be able to undo what Reagan had done. Berry and Ramirez wanted to sue; Saltzman didn't.

I suggested my theory to Penda Hair, a new staff member, and asked her to do some quick and dirty research. If she thought I might be right she should, as quickly as possible, file a motion for temporary restraining order to enjoin the president's removal of Berry and Ramirez. Penda was a freckled, redheaded Tennessean who had gone to Harvard Law School, had been Justice Blackmun's law clerk, and who retained a rich, leisurely Southern accent that masked her quick and aggressive approach to legal problems.

Her overnight research confirmed my hunch. Within two days, she filed a complaint and application for a temporary restraining order (TRO). A week later Judge Norma Holloway Johnson denied the TRO but set the case down to hear our application for a preliminary injunction, which receives more careful consideration.

At the same time Elaine Jones and the Leadership Conference lined up members of Congress behind a House bill to make the commission a creature of Congress, taking it out of the president's hands completely. Bill Coleman testified before the House Judiciary Committee that if the president could fire commissioners at will, "traditions of independence and non-partisan continuity have been sacrificed on the altar of political conformity." The Senate resolved to make the commission a hybrid House–Senate body from which members could be removed only for neglect of duty or malfeasance. The president would appoint four members, the speaker of the House two, and the president pro tem of the Senate two. Half would be Republicans, half Democrats.

On November 14, Judge Johnson granted our motion for preliminary injunction, writing that "there is adequate evidence in the legislative record to support plaintiffs' contention that Congress intended the duties of the Commission to be discharged free from any control or coercive influence by the President or the Congress."[28] She enjoined Reagan from "preventing or interfering with plaintiffs' service as members of the U.S. Commission on Civil Rights." The government appealed immediately.

I argued my last case for LDF defending the injunction in the court of appeals. The court dismissed the government's appeal, holding that because the statutory life of the commission had expired while the case was pending the plaintiffs couldn't continue as members of the commission anyway, so there was nothing to decide. But our injunction, which had kept them in place until the law expired, was not upset. We had won a sort of victory. The issue was now political: Would they become members of a new commission created by the recently enacted legislation?

As part of a political deal, Democratic leaders of Congress appointed Berry and Ramirez to the new commission. The White House agreed to appoint two Republican women who were strong supporters of an active federal role in civil rights. It then denied there was a deal and appointed two men who disagreed with the national organizations that had fought the Reagan purge. Civil rights groups and the head of the National Women's Political Caucus, a Republican woman, charged double-cross. But nothing changed. Such was the trench warfare between civil rights advocates and the Reagan administration.

I RESIGN FROM LDF, BEGIN TEACHING FULL-TIME AT COLUMBIA

Not long after the Harvard conflict, Al Rosenthal, then dean of Columbia Law School, called me to extend the faculty's invitation to become a visiting professor for a semester as part of the law school's Samuel Rubin civil liberties program. I wanted to accept, but no matter how I tried to rearrange my schedule I couldn't be absent from LDF for so long. I quipped, "Maybe some day I'll ask you for a full-time job." Al replied, "Any time you ask you can walk right in." About a year later, in February 1984, at a human rights conference at Ditchley Park, a grand eighteenth-century mansion in Oxfordshire, England, I reflected on Al's response as Debby and I walked the extensive grounds. In December I would be sixty, and if I were ever to leave LDF for something else I really wanted to do, like joining the Columbia faculty, it wouldn't remain possible very long. They might appoint me at sixty, but not at sixty-five. I had been at LDF for thirty-five years, director-counsel for twenty-three. My one reservation was that leaving might be perceived as caving in under the pressure of the Harvard boycott and the NAACP lawsuit. But to stay on out of defiance when it made sense to leave would be foolish. I asked Al whether he had been kidding with his offer of a full-time job.

Al replied that he had meant what he said. The faculty, then headed by a new dean, Benno Schmidt, confirmed his response. I told Jim Nabrit and then Bill Coleman and Julius Chambers of my decision, called a staff conference, and announced it to nearly a hundred lawyers, paralegals, researchers, students, secretaries, xerox machine operators, and others.

Jim Nabrit didn't want to succeed me and decided to retire in 1989, thirty years after he arrived. The board appointed a search committee, which unanimously concluded that Julius Chambers, our first intern and then a highly successful lawyer in Charlotte, should be the new director-counsel. On a sunny afternoon in June, two hundred past and present staff and board members, interns, summer students, paralegals, secretaries, telephone and machine operators, cooperating and staff lawyers, occupants of the Public Interest Law Center, and others gathered atop 99 Hudson Street for a party. As music blasted into the sky, with a view of the Hudson to the west, looking down on elegant roof gardens and abandoned, rusty industrial buildings to the east and north, we dined on fried chicken prepared by Jewel Johnson, who administered our lawyers training conferences, and Jamaican meat pies made by Earl Cunningham, who ran the xerox machine. It was the first time we had used the roof on a hot day and didn't realize that the tar surface would become soft and sticky. The footprints we left that night would open leaks in the roof, allowing the next rainfall to drip into Jim Nabrit's office.

On behalf of LDF, Julius presented me with a collage, which Debby had commissioned, created by Barbara Pollack, a lawyer turned artist; it depicted moments in my life at the Fund. Four feet high, five feet wide, it had at its center a large painted photograph of Connie Motley and me walking down the steps of the Supreme Court. Upper left was a light charcoal sketch of Thurgood, one of Earl Warren, and a photograph of the lawyers who argued *Brown* in the library at 107 West Forty-third Street. Elsewhere were photos of me, Martin Luther King, Jr., and Ralph Bunche, G. W. McLaurin sitting in the antechamber from which he observed his class at the University of Oklahoma, staff lawyers, and friends. Newspaper clippings headlined victories in *Brown*; there were captions from briefs in sit-in, capital punishment, and employment cases. A *New York Times* story of my thirtieth anniversary at LDF recounted my decision to remain after the partner at a law firm said I wouldn't be any more valuable if I were to go ahead and argue the University of Delaware case before joining his firm. The only wall space we had large enough to hang the collage was in our kitchen, and Benno Schmidt had a copy made, which hangs in the Columbia Law School library.

We lifted our feet slowly from the sticky tar as we moved about the roof of 99 Hudson Street, as if walking on the moon. It was hard not to be a bit sentimental and think this was what America should be like—black, white, Asian; men and women; lawyers and those who worked with them, working together, joined in friendship and a common cause.

Before my appointment to the law school became effective, Columbia gave me an honorary doctor of laws degree at the May commencement. Walter Gellhorn escorted me to the podium on the steps of Low Library, just below the statue representing alma mater, and Mike Sovern gave me the diploma.

38

A SUMMATION:
VICTORIES AND DEFEATS

In 1949, when I arrived, LDF was only ten years old. Its budget was $121,000. We were five lawyers in New York, a sociologist, and support staff. There was a handful of cooperating lawyers across the country. By 1961, the year I became chief counsel, the budget had increased fourfold, to about a half-million dollars, and we were seven lawyers. Income in 1983, the last full year before I left, was over $6.5 million; there were offices in New York and Washington, staff lawyers numbered twenty-five, cooperating lawyers could be counted in the hundreds; paralegals, a computer specialist, as well as lawyer training and scholarship programs and the department of Legal Information and Community Service, altogether composed a staff of nearly one hundred. The funding base was secure and diverse: tens of thousands of contributors who gave through the mail, a corps of wealthy individuals, black fraternities and sororities, annual dinners, foundations, corporations, counsel fees, the Combined Federal Campaign, and other contributors. We commissioned Romare Bearden, the great black artist, to make a print to commemorate the thirtieth anniversary of *Brown*. Titled "The Lamp," in gorgeous shades of green, blue, black, and red, it shows two black women studying by lamplight. We sold two hundred prints for $1,000 each, posters for less.

VICTORIES

We couldn't have done what we did in a society and world that wasn't ready for it. Neither Thurgood, I, nor anyone else could have won *Plessy v. Ferguson* in 1896. But a half-century later, *Brown v. Board of Education* would not have happened without us, at least not when it did. *Brown* decreed an end to school segregation but also transformed how blacks were seen and treated, by law and by society in general, not only in schools but in many other areas of life. Rural and small town Southern schools are now largely desegregated. Although different economic classes live in separate areas, which often amounts to residential racial segregation, education in many medium-size and large cities North and South is desegregated as well. Clever inventions like magnet schools have brought whites into black areas in some cities, and blacks to the suburbs. A side effect of school integration has been construction of decent schools for blacks, to replace run-down tarpaper shacks, single-room schoolhouses, buildings with outdoor plumbing, and slum school construction. Before *Brown* there may not have been a single black school in the South equal to its white counterpart. Afterward, many schools attended mostly by blacks equaled or at least approximated white schools in physical quality.

LDF cases first opened Southern state-sponsored higher education to blacks and forced every Southern state to admit blacks to their universities (private universities, North and South, followed, many with affirmative action programs); equalized black teachers' salaries; outlawed court-enforced exclusion from housing; and enabled blacks to vote in primary elections. Following *Brown*, we beat off a Southwide vicious, state directed racist backlash against civil rights organizations and lawyers. In *Little Rock* the Supreme Court made clear that the Southern rebellion would fail.

After I became director-counsel, LDF defended the work of Martin Luther King, Jr.'s Southern Christian Leadership Conference, as well as many other elements of the movement in countless sit-ins, Freedom Rides, and other protests, winning more than forty demonstration cases in the Supreme Court and hundreds in lower courts. Shielded and encouraged by these victories, the movement led the country to enacting the Civil Rights Act of 1964, prohibiting discrimination in public accommodations, employment, and federally funded programs. The court order, which we won, and which Jim Nabrit and I then wrote one night in a Montgomery motel, made possible the Selma to Montgomery march, which led to the Voting Rights Act of 1965 and the political transformation it effected in American politics.

At the same time that LDF was defending the movement, we won the admission of James Meredith into the University of Mississippi through gunfire and tear gas; got Vivian Malone and Jimmy Hood into the University of Alabama as Governor Wallace, flanked by the National Guard, stood in the schoolhouse door; and gained entrance for Harvey Gantt into Clemson College in South Carolina. We put an end to that oxymoronic formulation "all deliberate speed," and developed flexible techniques, including busing, as ways of overcoming obstacles to desegregation. Our cases brought school desegregation to the North and forced a reluctant HEW to do its job of administering the desegregation process. LDF breathed life into the Equal Employment Opportunities Act, winning jobs and millions in back pay for tens of thousands of black workers. We led in applying the Voting Rights Act against discriminatory districting and played a key role in extending the act to discriminatory results, not merely discriminatory intent. LDF began the desegregation of hospitals in the South and won the case that created the doctrinal base for Title VI of the 1964 act, which made federal funding of institutions that discriminate illegal. We helped build the foundation of affirmative action law.

An LDF case forbade states to make interracial sexual relations criminal, presaging the unconstitutionality of miscegenation laws. Another ended the death penalty for rape, the original goal of our campaign against capital punishment. Other LDF cases introduced procedural fairness in death sentencing, an improvement over anything goes, although in time the requirement has become less rigorous. We launched the earliest cases to reform prisons, changing how statewide systems treated inmates. LDF led the nation in prohibiting racial discrimination in jury selection and in requiring that coerced confessions be excluded from criminal prosecutions. We extended the right to counsel to misdemeanor cases that carry heavy sentences.

We won the case that gave force to statutes requiring courts to order defendants to pay counsel fees to winning plaintiffs in civil rights cases, which was later extended to other public interest cases. In persuading national foundations to fund our operations, we helped pave the way for the funding of public interest law generally. Our efforts to counter the Reagan administration's efforts to roll back civil rights were not as uniformly successful, but we did establish that the executive branch did not have a right to sack members of the Civil Rights Commission summarily for trying to fulfill the mission given them.

These cases led to changes in the role of the courts in bringing about a just society, and in how civil rights law is practiced. The issues we and the new legal defense funds addressed through this period required many new procedures and remedies, some of which demanded court-ordered revamping of major public institutions and court involvement in activities that had previously been left to legislatures and the executive branch. This in turn has required changes in legal education, teaching students how to use the new doctrines as social engineers, in the manner Charlie Houston envisaged more than half a century ago.

There can be no precise appraisal of the changes LDF wrought in the attitude of a black population that had been isolated and stigmatized by the law, and which once saw all the massive machinery of government arrayed against it. We did indeed contribute, as the Margold Report envisaged, to stirring the "spirit of revolt" among black people. The Freedom Rides, for example, were planned to coincide with the anniversary of *Brown*, Martin Luther King, Jr., held a pilgrimage on another of its anniversaries, and sit-in demonstrators were inspired by *Brown* and *Little Rock*. When LDF lawyers arrived in a town they held high the banner of freedom. Some blacks who are prominent today, Andrew Young, for example, tell of having gone to the local courthouse to hear Thurgood or me or another LDF lawyer present a case, and of coming away inspired. The parent of a black Columbia College student from a small town in North Carolina embarrassed me by saying, "Because of you we always felt safe."

No one who saw blacks denied that most treasured of American ideals, the dream of an unlimited future; who saw blacks shut out of even half-decent colleges or any graduate or professional school in the South; relegated to separate parks and beaches; excluded from hospitals; their teachers, their first role models, paid less than those who taught whites; who watched them forced to stand at lunch counters if served at all; shunted to separate railroad cars, the back of the bus, and segregated waiting rooms; barred from theaters or sent to the balcony; confined to the worst jobs and to black union locals; excluded from the political process; made acutely aware that being black meant that being charged with a crime against a white was synonymous with being convicted; sentenced to death for rape when a white man wouldn't be; imprisoned for interracial sexual relations; convicted by all-white juries; demeaningly called by first name in court; and enjoined from buying homes because potential neighbors who had never met them and knew nothing about them had conspired by means of the law to keep them out—no one who is aware of any part of this black experience can pretend that LDF cases made anything but an enormous difference. Little or nothing would have changed, at least for decades, without our courtroom victories. We laid the experience of a people before the courts of the land to examine for themselves the injustices their pronouncements once had helped imbed in society. Then, pursuing Paul Freund's metaphor of the courts as "the substations that transform the high-tension charge of the philosophers into the reduced voltage of a serviceable current," LDF brought the decisions of these courts back to the people and plugged the current of moral and legal authority into the transactions of everyday life.

DEFEATS

But sometimes, unhappily, we failed. While our National Office for the Rights of the Indigent won a case that required equalizing municipal facilities between rich and poor parts of town, neither we nor anyone else could replicate it widely. Ghetto areas remain run down, dirty, badly serviced. Although our welfare cases were among those establishing minimum levels of procedural fairness, they never established minimum levels of support. Others lost those cases before we could pursue the issue very far; we might not have done any better.

Despite winning judgments in many individual fair housing cases, privately owned housing has remained largely segregated and beyond economic reach of a large proportion of blacks. Prejudice among whites remains potent, and whites by and large continue to move out of integrated neighborhoods when the proportion of blacks goes above a certain point. Moreover, housing that blacks can afford usually consists of individual apartments or houses; housing litigation, which must proceed mostly one house or apartment building at a time, cannot have widespread effect on such widely scattered targets. Some of America's largest cities remain segregated in fact.

Ghetto education is often disgraceful, seemingly hopeless. We failed to persuade courts to employ one possible remedy, to desegregate across urban–suburban lines, beyond which many white families moved, although we did prevail in isolated cases of segregation jointly promoted by city and suburbs. As a consequence of desegregation, many black teachers and principals lost their jobs and there was little, as a practical matter, that we could do about these lost jobs. LDF was only slightly involved in cases that set out to equalize financing between rich and poor school districts; those cases have been lost in the Supreme Court, and where they have been won in state courts produced meager results. Growing out of frustration with all of the problems of society that find their expression in the schools, there is a movement, commenced in the late 1980s among some blacks, the strength of which is not clear, to set up all-black or all-black male schools, which would isolate students who are black or black and male from the rest of their generation.

Our efforts to integrate Southern state systems of higher education made little headway in the face of the complexity of the issue and the hostility of the Reagan administration. As well, there was the perceived threat to the role of black colleges as centers of pride and power, though black colleges were upgraded in the process.

The death penalty persists because, although the Court acknowledged that capital punishment is employed disproportionately against blacks who have murdered whites, it required the unprovable demonstration of racial animus. But while proexecution rhetoric is high, the willingness to execute remains relatively low. Executions remain in the number of about forty per year, these being almost exclusively carried out in former slaveholding states. Almost half have been in Texas. However, the courts are, little by little, tearing down obstacles to accelerating the process of execution and the number of executions will certainly rise. The death penalty has become so politically popular that President Clinton, who has been attacked by some as an unreconstructed 1960s radical, has proposed punishing fifty or so federal crimes by death, which might appease the public's wrath without giving it what it really wants—a reduction in the incidence of crime.

We tried and failed to reform the law of bail, which in practice requires poor people to put up money they don't have in order to stay out of jail while awaiting trial. But these have been legislative reforms.

WHAT LEGAL CHANGES MEANT FOR DAILY LIFE

Our legal victories and related changes in legislation have translated not merely into changes in status, but into a material improvement in the lives many blacks lead. Black educational achievement and job status, measured by grades and scores, level of education completed, jobs blacks hold and how much they earn, has increased markedly over the life of LDF. While the mechanisms of social and economic change are always complex, it is hard to imagine that much of this would have occurred without the *Brown* decision and other courtroom victories. Better education in early grades has led inevitably to better preparation for higher education, leading as inevitably to professional opportunities previously cut off to blacks.

The Equal Employment Opportunities Act has ended a great deal of discrimination in employment; affirmative action has been particularly effective in the federal government contract sector, affecting millions of workers in thousands of private companies under a presidential executive order. In concert with these developments, following the White Primary Cases, the Voting Rights Act, and cases enforcing it, black political participation has grown dramatically, affecting not only who gets elected, but bringing about a very real and practical difference in the way many blacks live their lives. Black lawyers and bankers participate in municipal bond funding; black businesses get city, state, and local contracts; black officials employ staffs and adopt social welfare and affirmative action programs designed to improve the availability of jobs to blacks, and often to the population at large.

Black incomes are coming closer to white incomes, especially in the North. The *Economist* reports that "over the past two decades . . . the proportion of black families earning more than $50,000 a year [in 1990 dollars] increased by 46%, compared with only a 35% increase among white families. A third of the black population is middle class." When I first came to LDF, at day's end we would see a white-only, male-only stream of business suits pouring out of office buildings and factories. Now, as Roy Wilkins would say, it is all pepper and salt. Unfortunately, development of the black middle class has not translated into a perception of economic improvement within the black population as a whole, because the large black underclass remains so economically disadvantaged that it pulls down black averages in all measures of progress.

Moreover, economic improvement has not erased vestiges of the old order: Prejudice and stereotyping afflict middle-class black life. In an episode unhappily quite too typical, a black Ivy League professor friend of mine recently was seized by security guards for shoplifting in an upscale New York department store, handcuffed and bundled into a back room. When he produced the receipt for the purchase he had in a shopping bag they released him. He couldn't help believing that a white customer would have been given an earlier opportunity to produce the receipt. In January 1994, a black New Jersey judge had almost the identical experience, which was widely publicized.

Because they now have the money to do so, many middle-class blacks have moved to white parts of town and to suburbs—often to black suburbs, not as attractive as those in which whites live—further impoverishing center cities. While they often try to remain supportive of those left behind, one may wonder whether that will continue to be true in a generation or two. Along with the gains, there has come into being a large group of unemployed, uneducated ghetto residents, often single mothers and their badly educated, poorly supervised children. The income gaps between upper, middle, and lower classes are growing, faster within the black than in the white community, with the largest concentration among blacks at the lower end. The kinds of people at the lower end are different too. Poor whites tend to be elderly, mentally ill, drug or alcohol addicted; poor blacks more often are single mothers who raise children in the most inauspicious circumstances. Too often children raised in this environment end up in the criminal justice system or pregnant.

The Fund's struggles to improve the criminal justice system have helped make it more equitable and humane. The proportion of blacks convicted of crime, incarcerated, sentenced to death, victimized by police brutality and imprisonment in cruel and inhuman circumstances is so appalling, however, that these gains offer little satisfaction. A recent article states, a "million black men are either behind bars or liable to be put back there if they break their probation or parole."

At the other end of the spectrum, blacks are the principal victims of crime: Homicide is a leading cause of death among young black males. Nevertheless, as bad as things are today, conditions are a far cry from the days when blacks who had no counsel were beaten into confessing or convicted by all-white juries, often on what today would be illegally obtained evidence; unable to testify for themselves against imposition of the death penalty; tortured by the electrical impulses of the "Tucker telephone" attached to their genitals; executed for rape; and otherwise abused by practices that have come to be prohibited or curtailed in large part by LDF cases.

WHAT OF THE FUTURE?

It is forty years since the Supreme Court decided *Brown* in 1954, and despite great achievements since then, there also is reason to despair. But perhaps a more meaningful way of looking at time may be to recognize that a young black man or woman entering college in the early 1990s was likely born in the early 1970s, around the time of *Alexander* (1969), which put an end to "all deliberate speed," and *Swann* (1971), which made possible real school desegregation. In this period the Supreme Court decided *Keyes*

(1973), which first applied *Brown* to the North at the Supreme Court level. The 1964 Equal Employment Opportunities Act didn't become meaningful until the decision in *Griggs* (1971), which prohibited the use of testing or other criteria that did not measure ability to do the job. Only the 1965 Voting Rights Act produced some of, but not all of, its intended effect soon after its passage. The Fair Housing Act of 1968 has never been implemented very widely.

Our hypothetical young person entering college in the early 1990s would be the son or daughter of blacks who most likely were born around 1945, before *Sweatt* and *McLaurin* (1950) opened Southern white universities to blacks, and then only in theory. They likely went to segregated, abysmally equipped schools and, if they were from Mississippi, Alabama, Georgia, or South Carolina, were, despite the Supreme Court decisions, blatantly barred from the state universities for whites. Even in places like Texas, Louisiana, and other parts of the Deep South, where LDF had battered open the doors, schools tried their best to deny blacks of that generation the benefits of a good education, successfully using evasion and stalling techniques for many years. In other Southern states the prospects would have been better only in the abstract. Even in Northern elite colleges, Columbia, for example, where I was in the class of 1945—there were few blacks; I had only two black classmates, only one of whom was an American. Even if these imaginary parents were lawyers or doctors they might have had to make a living as mail deliverers or Pullman porters. If, as is most likely, they weren't professionals, at best they probably had dirty, front-end industrial jobs, in wood-yards, unloading ore, and the like.

So the period of equality of educational opportunity that most people tend to date from *Brown*, decided in 1954, is in reality a very much shorter period, which only *began* in the early 1970s, moved forward fitfully, and whose benefits were never universally enjoyed by black Americans. The period of job equality under law is even briefer.

To me this is a call for action. While this book is a history and not a blueprint for what must be done, a blueprint is what is needed. Now is the time for a new movement, as tenacious, relentless, and idealistic as that of the 1960s, a new Margold plan, or plans, as prescient as the original, and new leaders—a Charles Hamilton Houston, a Thurgood Marshall, a Martin Luther King, Jr.—who will hold high ideals and at the same time keep clearly in mind what is possible and how practically to achieve it. These new leaders will be large people, large in character, large in vision, who will be prepared to plunge into the struggle personally, wrestling with concrete issues as Thurgood and Charlie Houston did in the early Restrictive Covenant, White Primary, and school desegregation cases, and as Martin did in the Montgomery bus strike and in the strategy and tactics of the Selma to Montgomery march.

Now there exists even greater potential for effecting change, although the apparent problems are more diverse, and in some ways more daunting. With a large black vote—which didn't exist in the 1960s—there is a base of political support for racial justice that even Lyndon Johnson did not have when he appointed Thurgood to the Supreme Court over obdurate, mindless opposition and when he brought about enactment of the great Civil Rights Acts of 1964, 1965, and 1968. There has been and there will be opposition, but the need is very real and very urgent. When riots destroyed parts of Los Angeles—the most recent in a long history of racial devastation that has racked the country—following the jury's acquittal of police officers who had been caught on video tape brutally beating a black motorist, Rodney King, others around the country took up the frightening chant "No justice, no peace." That refrain, sorrowfully, expresses a universal truth.

At great moments in our history, America has shown that it can muster the will and strength to change. It must do so again in the generation to come. For, while we should seek justice for its own sake, those for whom that is not reason enough should understand that without justice there will be no peace.

Afterword

THE PEOPLE OF LDF

As I have looked back over these pages there emerges the remarkable picture of a tiny band of lawyers, a cadre of "social engineers," as Charlie Houston called them, which over sixty years has grown to an army, larger and more influential than he could have hoped for. Thurgood graduated from Houston's Howard Law School in a class of about a dozen. Today, thousands of students in law schools across America are being taught by spiritual descendants of those early classes. More to the point: Throughout the judiciary, the legal profession, law schools, and government agencies, a galaxy of present and former LDF staff, board members, and clients has had astounding impact on the law. Many of the most influential practitioners of American law—law school deans and professors, judges, government officials, heads of bar associations, directors of public interest law firms, senior partners of major law firms—are former LDF staff and interns or fellows, board members, cooperating lawyers, and lawyers' training institute teachers—the people of LDF.

Of course, this does not describe some grand conspiracy—it would be absurd to think of this collection of strong-willed people performing the bidding of any single directing force. But they all do share, in large or small degree, a sensibility consonant with the guiding principles of LDF: a commitment to equal justice under law for all Americans, to promoting racial integration, and to enlisting the law in that cause. In a ludicrous malapropism, one Southerner, marveling at the number and diversity of our cases, our victories, and the influence of those with whom we were associated, thought he had us down pat. "LDF is an octopus," he pronounced, "with its testicles reaching in all directions." I almost fell out of my chair, but appreciated his meaning.

LDF people have been deans at more than a dozen law schools. Among the deans of Howard alone, the law school where Houston initiated his effort, have been Jim Nabrit, Jr; Southeast counsel Spotts Robinson; board member and constant adviser Bill Hastie; cooperating lawyer and board member Wiley Branton; John Baker and Charles Duncan. Lawyers' training instructor Paul Bender (he conducted, for many years, the review of that term's Supreme Court cases) has been dean at Arizona State University; assistant counsel Haywood Burns at City University of New York; assistant counsel William Robinson at the District of Columbia Law School. LDF people also have been deans at Columbia (lawyers' training director and board member Michael Sovern, later Columbia's president) and Harvard (lawyers' training instructor Albert Sachs and board member James Vorenberg). Board member Norman Redlich was the dean at New York University; assistant counsel Michael Meltsner at Northeastern. LDF vice president and virtual staff member Louis Pollak was dean at the University of Pennsylvania; Lou also was dean of Yale. Two Stanford deans have been on the LDF staff: student intern John Hart Ely and assistant counsel Paul Brest. Student intern John Kramer has been the dean of Tulane; the dean of the University of Virginia Law School was lawyers' training teacher Monrad Paulsen.

LDF people have populated the law school world as professors. I am at Columbia. Others include: assistant counsel Norman Amaker (Loyola of Chicago); board member John Baker (Albany Law School, Union University); assistant counsel Betsy Bartholet (Harvard); assistant counsel Derrick Bell (Harvard and NYU); assistant counsel Bob Belton (Vanderbilt); assistant counsel Jack Boger (University of North Carolina); Leroy Clark (Catholic); Peggy Davis (NYU); Drew Days (Yale); Debby Greenberg (Columbia); Linda Greene (University of Wisconsin); Lani Guinier (University of Pennsylvania); Marina Hsieh (University of California, Berkeley); Charles H. Jones, Jr. (Rutgers); Pamela Karlan (University of Virginia); former student intern Randall Kennedy (Harvard); assistant counsel Milton Konvitz (Cornell); James Liebman (Columbia); Mike Meltsner (Northeastern); Phil Schrag (Georgetown); Teddy Shaw (University of Michigan); William Taylor (Catholic and Georgetown, in addition to heading the Center for National Policy Review); Steve Winter (University of Miami); Gail Wright (Pace); and Melvin Zarr (University of Maine).

Celebrated scholars have worked closely with us, some virtually as staff members. Anyone in the law school world would rate Charles L. Black, Jr., of Columbia and Yale and Anthony Amsterdam of Stanford, Penn, and NYU as among the great law teachers of our time. Both have spent sabbatical time as unpaid staff members at LDF, have written innumerable briefs, and consulted on scores of cases. Tony has tried and argued some of our most important cases. Vivian Berger of Columbia, an outstanding scholar of criminal law, spent a year at LDF as a staff member working on capital cases.

Some LDF people went into general education: former director-counsel

Julius Chambers has become chancellor of North Carolina Central University. Roger Wilkins, a professor at George Mason University and well-known scholar and commentator on race relations, was our earliest student intern in the 1950s.

On the Supreme Court Thurgood Marshall left a legacy of opinions that are a charter for a more humane America, expressing the goal of a regime marked by abolition of the death penalty and belief in the equality of men and women, black and white, rich and poor. Both before he reached the Court and once he was on it, he worked to realize the maxim inscribed above the Supreme Courts portals, which LDF took as its own credo, "Equal Justice Under Law." Bill Hastie, who was involved in LDF cases and internal affairs for decades, made a notable mark on the Third Circuit Court of Appeals. More than a score of other LDF people are, or have been, on federal and state courts.

LDF lawyers have been leaders in the practice of private and public law, including Bill Coleman, a cabinet member under Gerald Ford, who has headed one of America's leading law firms, O'Melveny and Meyers, and though long a prominent Republican, has never hesitated to criticize Republican administrations on civil rights issues. Vernon Jordan, one of Bill Clinton's confidants and head of his transition team and a senior partner of a large Washington law firm, is on the LDF board, has been an LDF cooperating lawyer, and represented us when the NAACP sued us. There have been cabinet and subcabinet members: board members Bob Weaver (secretary of HUD), Patricia Roberts Harris (secretary of HUD and HEW), and Andrew Young (ambassador to the United Nations). Longtime LDF staff lawyer, Peter Sherwood has been corporation counsel of New York City, heading perhaps the largest law office in the country, as was his predecessor, Peter Zimroth, who worked for LDF while a law student. Corporation counsel of Washington, D.C., Inez Smith Reid was an LDF law student, too. Former assistant counsel Frank White is New York State commissioner of transportation. Earl Warren fellow William Jefferson is a congressman from Louisiana, fellow Melvin Watt is a congressman from North Carolina, and fellow Sanford Bishop has been elected to Congress from Georgia.

Some LDF folks became heads of leading bar associations, which just two generations or so back wouldn't admit blacks: Bernard Segal, a former president of the American Bar Association, became an LDF board member. Talbot (Sandy) D'Alemberte, a cooperating lawyer and board member, became president of the ABA. Conrad Harper, former staff lawyer, has been president of the Association of the Bar of the City of New York, as have board members Cyrus Vance and Adrian DeWind.

Our client list is as impressive as the list of lawyers who worked with us: Martin Luther King, Jr.; Atlanta congressman John Lewis, former head of SNCC, whom LDF represented in the Freedom Rides and on the Selma to

Montgomery march; and Harvey Gantt, who later became mayor of Charlotte and almost beat Jesse Helms in the race for a Senate seat from North Carolina. Charlayne Hunter-Gault, for whom we won entry to the University of Georgia, is a commentator on the nightly "MacNeil/Lehrer News-Hour."

LDF became the model for other public interest institutions like the Mexican American Legal Defense and Education Fund (once run by former assistant counsel member Vilma Martinez); the Lawyers Committee for Civil Rights Under Law (once run by assistant counsel Bill Robinson); the Children's Defense Fund (founded by assistant counsel Marian Wright Edelman); the Legal Action Center (directed by former assistant counsel Debby Greenberg); the Natural Resources Defense Council; the NOW Legal Defense and Education Fund; the Asian American Legal Defense and Education Fund; the Puerto Rican Legal Defense and Education Fund; the Indian Law Resources Center; the Lambda Legal Defense Fund; and various consumer, environmental, and other organizations, such as those for the aged and handicapped. We counseled in the creation of some of the new groups, which adopted our style of name, and I served on the board of some. I helped create the Legal Resources Foundation in South Africa, modeled on LDF, which has been at the forefront in fighting apartheid through the South African courts. Conservative "legal defense funds" have sprung up on the other side. LDF's board has been a particularly influential group. Lynn Walker, informed by her years on the LDF staff, has headed the Rights and Social Justice program at the Ford Foundation, which funds public interest organizations across the country.

LDF didn't seek out celebrities in electing board members or in choosing lawyers who would be associated in one way or another with our work. In most cases these people came to us when they were little known; it was up to Thurgood, or me, or sometimes another board or staff member to spot their talent and assay the genuineness of their commitment to racial equality. Looking at the remarkable record of subsequent achievement of those who dedicated a part of their professional lives to LDF causes, some might say that LDF was a convenient stepping stone to prominence in American law. But it is the obverse that's true. Those very qualities of courage, character, selflessness, and dedication that originally drove these young people to enlist their precious time and talent in the service of others inevitably caused them to stand out as very special people in whatever they attempted.

As the struggle for racial equality continues over years to come, these people of LDF, their students, and colleagues will play an increasingly important role. Just as Charlie Houston's band of freedom fighters fought and won the last civil rights revolution, this new cadre will be among those fighting the battles to follow, the battles for equality in fact, not merely in law.

NOTES

These endnotes include documentation, digressions from, and elaborations of the text. The documentation consists of published and unpublished material. The published material—including case opinions, case records, briefs, oral arguments, statutes, books, and articles—can be found at most university law libraries, much of it through on-line services such as Westlaw and Lexis. The unpublished material comes from various sources, including the Federal Bureau of Investigation, the Harvard University Library, the Schomburg Center for Research in Black Culture, the Kennedy and Johnson presidential libraries, the NAACP, the NAACP Legal Defense and Educational Fund, Inc., and my own personal files. Unless otherwise indicated, NAACP material, including board minutes, may be found at the Manuscript Reading Room of the Library of Congress. To save space and time, I have not indicated the exact Library of Congress location of these materials, but the library has a comprehensive index by which they may be found. The same is true for most LDF material, including minutes, dockets, case matters, correspondence, press releases, and telegrams. These are cited here as "LDF archives." Some LDF material, where indicated, is still at the NAACP Legal Defense and Educational Fund, Inc., 99 Hudson Street, New York, N.Y. 10013. My own files, which include correspondence, interview notes, available FBI materials concerning me, and many other documents cited here as "in author's possession," will be turned over to the Library of Congress when this book is published.

PREFACE

xvii   CHARTER: Charter of Incorporation, NAACP Legal Defense and Educational Fund, on file at the LDF, 99 Hudson Street, New York, N.Y. 10013.
xvii   NAACP AND "INC.": For convenience, the Fund usually drops the periods in N.A.A.C.P. The short form "Inc." Fund (sometimes "Ink" Fund) refers to the "Inc.," which indicated that the Fund was incorporated.
xviii LDF CASES: The Lexis and Westlaw searches were for cases that listed Thurgood or me as counsel. Either or both of us were listed as counsel in all LDF cases while we worked for the Fund.

ix   PRIMARIES: Darlene Clark Hine, *Black Victory: The Rise and Fall of the White Primary in Texas* (Milwood, N.Y.: KTO Press, 1979).

ix   COVENANTS: Clement Vose, *Caucasians Only: The Supreme Court, the NAACP, and the Restrictive Covenant Cases* (Berkeley: University of California Press, 1959).

ix   HIGHER EDUCATION: Mark Tushnet, *The NAACP's Legal Strategy Against Segregated Education, 1925–1950* (Chapel Hill: University of North Carolina Press, 1987).

ix   LITTLE ROCK: Daisy Bates, *The Long Shadow of Little Rock* (New York: David McKay, 1962).

ix   KING IN BIRMINGHAM: Alan F. Westin and Barry Mahoney, *The Trial of Martin Luther King* (New York: Crowell, 1974). See also David Garrow, *Bearing the Cross: Martin Luther King, Jr., and the Southern Christian Leadership Conference* (New York: Morrow, 1986); Taylor Branch, *Parting the Waters: America in the King Years 1954–63* (New York: Simon & Schuster, 1988).

ix   CAPITAL PUNISHMENT: Michael Meltsner, *Cruel and Unusual: The Supreme Court and Capital Punishment* (New York: Random House, 1973).

ix   JAMES MEREDITH: James Meredith, *Three Years in Mississippi* (Bloomington: Indiana University Press, 1966); Walter Lord, *The Past That Would Not Die* (New York: Harper and Row, 1965). The *Griggs* author is Robert Belton.

ix   SCHOOL SEGREGATION: Richard Kluger, *Simple Justice: The History of* Brown v. Board of Education *and Black America's Struggle for Equality* (New York: Knopf, 1976).

ix   NEW BIOGRAPHY: Mark Tushnet, *Making Civil Rights Law: Thurgood Marshall and the Supreme Court, 1936–1961* (New York: Oxford University Press, 1994).

CHAPTER I. PROLOGUE

3   CHARLES HAMILTON HOUSTON: This discussion is based on my recollections and Richard Kluger, *Simple Justice: The History of* Brown v. Board of Education *and Black America's Struggle for Equality* (New York: Knopf, 1976); and Genna Rae McNeil, *Groundwork: Charles Hamilton Houston and the Struggle for Civil Rights* (Philadelphia: University of Pennsylvania Press, 1983), 52, 65, 70–71. Hastie's remarks at Houston's funeral quoted in William H. Hastie, "Charles H. Houston (1895–1950)," *The Crisis,* June 1950, 365; see also William Elwood, Civil Rights Lawyers Project, transcriptions of oral interviews, University of Virginia, Charlottesville, 1990.

5   HOWARD LAW SCHOOL: Brandeis quoted in Kluger, *Simple Justice,* 125.

6   SUPREME COURT, 1954: The last case which Houston was preparing evolved into *Bolling v. Sharpe,* 347 U.S. 483 (1954), which was decided with *Brown.*

9   BLACK FEDERAL JUDGES: There has not so far been a black judge on the Deep South's Fourth Circuit (Maryland, North Carolina, South Carolina, Virginia, West Virginia) or Fifth Circuit (Louisiana, Mississippi, Texas) Courts of Appeals; there had been a black judge on the Eleventh Circuit (Alabama, Florida, Georgia) Court of Appeals, but he has retired.

CHAPTER 2. SOWING SEEDS

14   ORIGINS OF NAACP: Charles Flint Kellogg, *NAACP: A History of the National Association for the Advancement of Colored People* (Baltimore: Johns Hopkins University Press, 1967), 41.

14   DU BOIS: W. E. B. Du Bois, *The Autobiography of W. E. B. Du Bois: A Soliloquy on Viewing My Life from the Last Decade of Its First Century* (New York: International Publishers, 1968), 256.

15   NAACP MEMBERSHIP AND INCOME: Compiled from NAACP annual reports, 1940–1950.

16   CORE: August Meier and Elliott Rudwick, *CORE: A Study in the Civil Rights Movement* (Urbana: University of Illinois Press, 1973); and James Farmer, *Lay Bare the Heart* (New York: Arbor, 1985). SNCC: Clayborne Carson, *In Struggle: SNCC and the Black Awakening of the 1960s* (Cambridge: Harvard University Press, 1981); and James Forman, *The Making of Black Revolutionaries* (New York: Macmillan, 1972). SCLC: David Garrow, *Bearing the Cross: Martin Luther King, Jr., and the Southern Christian Leadership Conference* (New York: Morrow, 1986).

16   WHITE: See his autobiography, *A Man Called White: The Autobiography of Walter White* (New York: Viking, 1948). Lynching discussed on p. 40.

17   ROOSEVELT TO WHITE: Ibid., 170.

17   POSTWAR LYNCHINGS: *Pittsburgh Courier*, June 14, 1947.

17   VOTES IN 1948: Robert Weisbrot, *Freedom Bound: A History of America's Civil Rights Movement* (New York: Norton, 1990), 11.

18   WILKINS ON WHITE'S MARRIAGE: Roy Wilkins with Tom Mathews, *Standing Fast: The Autobiography of Roy Wilkins* (New York: Viking, 1982), 205.

18   WARING TELEGRAM: LDF archives.

19   ROCKEFELLER REFUSAL TO CONTRIBUTE: NAACP minutes, October 9, 1939. See also Arthur W. Packard to Walter White, March 25, 1938, and November 27, 1939, Rockefeller Archives Center, Pocantico, N.Y.

19   ARTHUR SPINGARN: Interview with the author. Years later when the ACLU wanted to set up a "legal defense and educational fund," Paul DeWitt, executive director of the Association of the Bar of the City of New York, told me he would block approval if I opposed those words in its name. I had no objection. Many public interest legal organizations now are called "legal defense and educational fund" or some variant thereof.

19   NAACP RESOLUTION: NAACP minutes, October 9, 1939.

20   LDF INCORPORATORS: They met on March 27, 1940, at 4:00 P.M. and elected the Fund's first board of directors, who met thirty minutes later. See minutes, first meeting of the incorporators, NAACP Legal Defense and Educational Fund, Inc., March 27, 1940, and minutes, first meeting of the directors, NAACP Legal Defense and Educational Fund, Inc., March 27, 1940. LDF was incorporated in 1939 and became tax exempt in 1940. Therefore both years have been used to date its origin.

21   CARTER MEMORANDUM: September 7, 1946, LDF archives.

21   COURTS-MARTIAL: White, *A Man Called White*, 283.

21   WHITE IN SUPREME COURT: Thurgood told me that he tipped off the marshal. In his oral history, on file at Columbia University's Oral History Project (interview with Ed Edwin, June 7, 1977), p. 49, he states that he admonished White not to sit within the rail, but says nothing of having told the marshal.

21   BUDGETS: LDF minutes, October 13, 1941; November 13, 1944; November 12, 1945; February 10, 1947; December 20, 1948; and April 24, 1950. On 1950 shortfall, see memorandum to the board of directors from Thurgood Marshall, May 8, 1951, LDF archives.

22   DETROIT RIOT: White, *A Man Called White,* 224.

23   ORAM: Harold Oram, interview with the author, July 15, 1988. Oram's first appeal, July 28, 1943, in author's possession. Oram to associate on plans for Committee of 100, quoted in NAACP memorandum, n.d., photocopy in author's possession. On Oram's contract with LDF, see letter and memorandum, Eileen Fry to Roy Wilkins, November 17, 1943, in author's possession; LDF minutes, October 11, 1943.

23   ANNA CAPLES FRANK: Interview with the author, August 12, 1988. Reinhold Neibuhr, the world-famous theologian, who married Anna and Karl, later became a supporter of LDF. Virtually from its creation, LDF (and the NAACP) had close ties with social democrats, which fit well with the NAACP and the black community's anticommunism. Gerhard Bly's tribute to Frank in author's possession. On Muriel Buttinger, see Muriel Gardiner, *Code Name "Mary": Memoirs of an American Woman in the Austrian Underground* (New Haven: Yale University Press, 1983). Buttinger's name before her marriage was Gardiner.

23   COMMITTEE OF 100: Fund-raising estimates from LDF financial statements, LDF minutes, various years; Oram, interview with the author, July 15, 1988.

24   NATIONAL LEGAL COMMITTEE'S (NLC) FIRST MEMBERS: See minutes of annual meeting, October 13, 1941, LDF archives. Black members of the NLC included Charles Houston; James M. Nabrit, Jr.; George Johnson, for many years dean of Howard Law School; W. Robert Ming, Jr., the first black law professor at the University of Chicago in 1947; Louis L. Redding, the sole black lawyer in Delaware; Arthur D. Shores and A. T. Walden, for years alone, or nearly alone, as black lawyers in Alabama and Georgia, respectively.

      White members included Karl Llewellyn, who has been called one of the "few American legal scholars [who] ha[s] been unquestionably great." (See Paul Gerwitz's introduction to Karl Llewellyn, "The Case Law System," 88 *Columbia Law Review* 989 [1988]). Incidentally, Llewellyn was my contracts teacher. Walter White first offered him the NAACP position that Houston took after Llewellyn turned it down. The NLC included Francis Biddle, later to become attorney general of the United States and Lloyd Garrison, dean of the law school at the University of Wisconsin, later a member of the law firm of Paul Weiss Wharton and Garrison, as it was then called. Morris Ernst, Arthur Garfield Hays, Benjamin Kaplan, James Marshall, and Steven Spingarn were the other white members. Ernst and Hays were leading civil liberties lawyers and had significant conventional practice; Kaplan became a professor at Harvard and judge of the Massachusetts Supreme Judicial Court; Marshall became chairman of the New York City Board of Education; Spingarn, the son of Joel Spingarn, early NAACP board member, later held important government posts.

CHAPTER 3. FREEDOM HOUSE, 1949

27   ON MARSHALL: See Roger Goldman with David Gallen, *Thurgood Marshall: Justice for All* (New York: Carroll & Graf, 1992); Carl Rowan, *Dream Makers, Dream Breakers: The World of Justice Thurgood Marshall* (Boston: Little, Brown, 1993). On his childhood, early life, work with the NAACP, and, briefly, his tenure on the Supreme Court, see Kluger, *Simple Justice: The History of* Brown v. Board of Education *and Black America's Struggle for Equality* (New York: Knopf, 1976). Other accounts include B. Taper, "Reporter at Large: Meeting in Atlanta," *New Yorker,* March 17, 1956, 80; Louis H. Pollak, "Thurgood Marshall: Lawyer and Justice," 40 *Maryland Law Review* 405 (1981); Mark Tushnet, *Making Civil Rights Law: Thurgood Marshall and the Supreme Court, 1936–1961* (New York: Oxford University Press, 1994); idem, "Thurgood Marshall as a Lawyer: The Campaign Against School Segregation, 1946–1950," 40 *Maryland Law Review* 411; S. E. Zion, "Thurgood Marshall Takes a New Tush-Tush Job," *New York Times Magazine,* August 22, 1965, 11. See also *Who's Who in America,* 44th ed. (New Providence, N.J.: Marquis, 1989), 1089. For a complete bibliography, see George H. Hill and Raymond Trent, "Justice Thurgood Marshall: A Bibliography from the Popular Press," *Bulletin of Bibliography* 42 (June 1985), 105–11.

27   MILLER'S CASE: *Collins v. Hardyman,* 341 U.S. 651 (1951).

27   OKLAHOMA CASE: *McLaurin v. Oklahoma,* 339 U.S. 637 (1950).

28   MITCHELL: Transcript of Mitchell interview arranged by William Elwood as part of his Civil Rights Lawyers Project at the University of Virginia, Charlottesville.

28   STAY OF EXECUTION: Thurgood told this story many times. Recently, when I asked him, he recalled the incident but didn't remember the name of the case.

29   MARSHALL: Carl Rowan's biography, *Dream Makers, Dream Breakers,* quotes Thurgood as regularly using "fucking" as an adjective. I have checked with Monroe Dowling, Thurgood's friend since they went to college together in 1925; Spottswood W. Robinson III and Oliver Hill, who knew him since law school; James Nabrit, Jr., James M. Nabrit III, and Constance Baker Motley, who were closely involved in his work; and Cissy Marshall, his widow. They all agree that he used the word rarely, if at all, and not in the way and to the extent that Rowan reports. I write this not to quibble, but because Rowan, who otherwise gives a good general picture of Thurgood, quotes him as using the word frequently.

30   MARYLAND CASE: *Pearson v. Murray,* 169 Md. 478 (1936).

30   APPOINTMENT BY LDF: Minutes, Special Meeting Board of Directors, NAACP Legal Defense and Educational Fund, Inc., September 9, 1940: "On motion duly made and seconded it was agreed that Thurgood Marshall be employed as counsel on a part-time basis the question of salary to be determined in the future." Not a member of the New York Bar, "special counsel" was supposed to indicate that he was not practicing in New York.

30   MAJOR VICTORIES: White primaries, *Smith v. Allwright,* 321 U.S. 649 (1944); LAW SCHOOL: *Sipuel v. Board of Regents,* 332 U.S. 631 (1948); RESTRICTIVE COVENANTS: *Shelley v. Kraemer,* 334 U.S. 1 (1948), and *Hurd v. Hodge,* 334 U.S. 24 (1948).

32   COLUMBIA, TENNESSEE, CASE: In February 1946, mob violence arose out of a fight between a white repairman and a black ex-GI. The repairman had struck the black's mother in a dispute over the cost of fixing a radio. The State Highway Patrol and National Guard terrorized the black community, and beat and shot black citizens. Someone shot a white patrolman. All but two of the defendants were acquitted; one of the two won on appeal. The State Board of Pardons, Paroles, and Probation commuted the one-to-five-year sentence of the last defendant, Lloyd Kennedy, in 1949, after had he served about nine months. Telephone call to Tennessee Board of Corrections, August 31, 1988.

32   PROCLAIMED HIM SOBER: Rowan, *Dream Makers*, 108–11.

32   409 EDGECOMBE: On Marshall, White, Wilkins, and Du Bois living at 409 Edgecombe Avenue, see Robert Weaver, interview with the author, July 19, 1988. I visited Marshall in the building.

32   TALLULAH BANKHEAD: She wrote, "I . . . carried an emotional banner for Joe Louis." See *Tallulah: My Autobiography* (New York: Harper Brothers, 1952), 21.

32   FRANK WILLIAMS: See *Who's Who Among Black Americans*, 4th ed. (Lake Forest, Ill.: Education Communications Inc., 1985), 900; Enid Gort (Williams's biographer), interview with the author, March 21, 1991; and Williams, interview with the author, July 20, 1988. I knew Williams well.

32   FRANK WILLIAMS: Note from Felix Frankfurter and Williams's scrapbooks, certificates and papers are at the Schomburg Center for Research in Black Culture, 515 Lenox Avenue, New York, N.Y. 10037.

33   DISAGREEMENT BETWEEN WILLIAMS AND MARSHALL: See also Kluger, *Simple Justice*, 249, 272–73, 304.

33   MARSHALL TO WILLIAMS: Date unknown, LDF archives.

34   CONSTANCE BAKER MOTLEY: Connie Motley's oral history is at the Oral History Project, Columbia University. I know her well.

34   BOB CARTER: See *Who's Who Among Black Americans*, 4th ed. Hastie quoted in Gilbert Ware, *William Hastie: Grace Under Pressure* (New York: Oxford University Press, 1984), 152–53. See also Alan Kohn, "Judge Carter's Career Marked by Principle over Pragmatism," *New York Law Journal*, January 2, 1987.

35   PEYSER: Seymour Peyser (brother), interview with the author, July 20, 1988. Annette Peyser's papers are at the Schomburg Center.

35   LEGAL STAFF: U. S. (Ulysses Simpson) Tate was staff counsel for the southwest in Dallas, but he was not as active as the others. Other staff lawyers in the Fund's first ten years included Milton Konvitz, later professor at Cornell School of Industrial and Labor Relations and at Cornell Law School; Edward Dudley, who became ambassador to Liberia and later a New York State Supreme Court judge; Frank Reeves, later a Howard University law professor, who worked in Washington and in 1961 joined the Kennedy White House staff; Marian Perry Yankauer, who left to move to Albany, New York, where her husband took a post in state government. Her leaving created the opening I filled.

35   SEMINARS: Memorandum to legal staff from Robert L. Carter, December 27, 1948, LDF archives.

35   SPOTTSWOOD W. ROBINSON III: Interview with the author, February 17, 1989. See also Elwood, Civil Rights Lawyers Project, transcriptions of oral

interviews, University of Virginia, Charlottesville, 1990.

36   BILL HASTIE: Ware, *William Hastie,* passim. See also William Henry Hastie Papers, Harvard Law School Library. In 1944 President Truman appointed him governor of the Virgin Islands.

36   HASTIE'S JUDGESHIP: There are several types of federal courts, those established under Article III of the U.S. Constitution, which carry lifetime appointments, and those established solely by legislation, such as the customs court and the courts with jurisdiction over U.S. territories, for example, the Virgin Islands and Guam. Hastie was the first black federal judge anywhere, appointed judge in the Virgin Islands in 1937. He was also the first black "Article III" federal judge, appointed for life to the U.S. Court of Appeals for the Third Circuit in 1949, confirmed in 1950. In between, Hernian E. Moore had been appointed (1939), later reappointed (1949), judge in the Virgin Islands, and Irvin C. Mollison was appointed judge of the customs court (1945).

37   WILEY BRANTON: Interview with the author; Kenneth Adelman, "You Can Change Their Hearts," *The Washingtonian* (March 1988), 107–14.

40   SOUTHERN BLACK LAWYERS: Information compiled from the author's personal files, the author's interviews with the lawyers, and transcripts of interviews arranged by William Elwood as part of his Civil Rights Lawyers Project at the University of Virginia, Charlottesville. See also Reuben V. Anderson, "Jack H. Young: A Legacy of Inspiration," 33 *Mississippi Lawyer* 5 (March/April, 1987), 18. This issue contains several articles on black civil rights lawyers in Mississippi. On Carsie Hall being retained by LDF, see LDF minutes, April 4, 1956. Thanks to Linda Kerber for pointing out that many women as well as black lawyers of both sexes "read" law since they could not attend law school. On an earlier period, see J. Clay Smith, *Emancipation: The Making of the Black Lawyer* (Philadelphia: University of Pennsylvania Press, 1993).

41   THURGOOD'S "UNAUTHORIZED BIOGRAPHY": Rowan, *Dream Makers.*

41   MASONIC CASE: For years the Prince Hall Masons were engaged in a struggle against "clandestine Masonry," or bogus groups claiming to be Masons that had no right to use the name. Thurgood told the LDF executive committee that "as a Mason he had no alternative other than to take on the assignment," without fee, and took a leave of absence of ten days. The case went before a special master in Chicago who found facts against Thurgood's client that pretty well determined the outcome of the case. It then went to the United States Supreme Court, which denied review. The Masons felt that Chicago politics had more than a little to do with the special master's findings, and Thurgood's relationship with Bob Ming, the lawyer for his opponents, became badly strained. *Supreme Grand Lodge, Modern Free and Accepted Colored Masons of the World v. Most Worshipful Prince Hall Grand Lodge, Free and Accepted Masons, Jurisdiction of Georgia,* 209 F.2d 156 (7th Cir. 1954), cert. den. 347 U.S. 953 (1954). There were several such cases, but Thurgood was only in one.

CHAPTER 4. WHY ME?

44   HE WOULD TESTIFY: Gellhorn testified in *Sipuel v. Oklahoma*, 332 U.S. 631
      (1948).

44   FRIEND-OF-THE-COURT BRIEF: Gellhorn signed the brief in *Sweatt v. Painter*,
      339 U.S. 629 (1950).

45   ISAAC WOODARD: In 1946, Woodard, a black veteran, was arrested in South
      Carolina because a bus driver thought he had kept the bus waiting too
      long at a rest stop. The police beat and blinded him. The NAACP pres-
      sured the Department of Justice to prosecute the assailant, but he was
      acquitted. Frank Williams and a West Virginia lawyer sued the bus com-
      pany for $50,000 for ejecting Woodard—a feeble, but the only possible,
      remedy. They lost. See LDF minutes, November 1946 and February 1947;
      Pittsburgh Courier, November 11, 1947; and White, *A Man Called White:
      The Autobiography of Walter White* (New York: Viking, 1948), 325.

45   EARLE: A South Carolina lynch mob removed Willie Earle, a twenty-four-
      year-old black epileptic, from jail in February 1947 believing that he had
      stabbed a white taxi driver to death; a member of the mob blew off Earle's
      head with a shotgun blast. The FBI obtained signed statements from
      twenty-six participants, implicating over thirty persons. Surprisingly, the
      local prosecutor brought murder charges against thirty-four defendants.
      The judge dismissed three and a jury acquitted the others. LDF lawyers
      sued the county for damages and settled for $2,000. See LDF minutes, Feb-
      ruary 1948; and *New York Times*, March 18, 1950.

45   INGRAM: During the fight, in November 1947, one of the sons, Wallace,
      fourteen, or Sammie, seventeen, struck the farmer and he died. Ingram
      and the two boys were sentenced to death in January 1948. LDF lawyers
      defended her. The death sentence was commuted to life imprisonment in
      April of that year. See LDF minutes, February 1948. The defendants were
      paroled in August 1959; in September 1964 their sentences were com-
      muted to time served.

45   HAYS: Years later when Hays and I were in a case together, the *Trenton
      Six*, I was appalled by his poor performance; he was unprepared and disor-
      ganized, couldn't answer questions and rambled on. He became a role
      model of a reverse sort—I vowed I never would make a presentation like
      that.

48   MICHNIK AND KURON TRIAL: Michael T. Kaufman, "Walesa Is Barred as
      Trial of 4 Dissidents Begins," *New York Times*, July 14, 1984.

49   VOTE STEALING: *Grovey v. Townsend*, which had upheld the white primary
      was undercut by *Classic v. United States*. *Classic* laid the groundwork for
      the White Primary Cases, which overruled *Grovey*.

51   JEWISH CONTRIBUTORS: Interview with Julius Chambers, former director-
      counsel, LDF, October 22, 1991.

51   GARFUNKEL ARGUMENT: *Wright v. Georgia*, Transcript of Argument,
      November 7, 1962, Supreme Court No. 68, October Term 1962, in tran-
      script captioned *Avent v. North Carolina*, 387.

53   VIOLENCE AGAINST JEWS IN THE SOUTH: See Jack Nelson, *Terror in the Night:
      The Klan's Campaign Against the Jews* (New York: Simon & Schuster,
      1993). I am grateful to Michael Stanislawski, Nathan J. Miller Professor of
      Jewish History at Columbia, and to Arthur Goren, R. & B. Knapp Profes-

sor of American Jewish History at Columbia, for insightful comments on which these passages draw.

CHAPTER 5. THE GROUND IS HARD

54   LOREN MILLER'S CASE: *Collins v. Hardyman*, 341 U.S. 651 (1951).

55   MCCRAY'S CASE: *New York Times*, June 20, 1950; Greenwood *Index-Journal*, January 4, 1950, April 11, 1950; court documents in *State v. McCray*; and documents from the Southern Regional Council made available by Charles Beall, in author's possession.

56   "MARGOLD REPORT": Much of this report, "Preliminary Report to the Joint Committee Supervising the Expenditure of the 1930 Appropriation by the American Fund for Public Service to the NAACP," is reprinted in Jack Greenberg, *Judicial Process and Social Change: Constitutional Litigation* (Minneapolis, Minn.: West, 1977). A complete copy is on file at the New York Public Library. On the American Fund for Public Service, see Mark Tushnet, *The NAACP Legal Strategy Against Segregated Education, 1925–1950* (Chapel Hill: University of North Carolina Press, 1987). The fund's papers are at the New York Public Library.

56   JURY CASE: *Strauder v. West Virginia*, 100 U.S. 303 (1880), 308.

56   STATE ACTION: Civil Rights Cases, 109 U.S. 3 (1883).

57   CHINESE LAUNDRY: *Yick Wo v. Hopkins*, 118 U.S. 356 (1886), 373–74.

57   RAILROAD: *Plessy v. Ferguson*, 163 U.S. 537 (1896), 544, 551, 559.

58   COMPROMISE OF 1877: For more on this period of history see C. Vann Woodward, *Reunion and Reaction: The Compromise of 1877 and the End of Reconstruction* (Boston: Little, Brown, 1951); and Woodward, *The Strange Career of Jim Crow*, 3d ed. (New York: Oxford University Press, 1974). See also Eric Foner, *Reconstruction: America's Unfinished Revolution 1863–1877* (New York: Harper and Row, 1988), chap. 12.

58   CHINESE GIRL: *Gong Lum v. Rice*, 275 U.S. 78 (1927).

58   CHARLES EVANS HUGHES: Charles Evans Hughes, *The Supreme Court of the United States: Its Foundations, Methods and Achievements* (New York: Columbia University Press, 1928), 68.

58   RESIDENTIAL APARTHEID: *Buchanan v. Warley*, 245 U.S. 60 (1917), 81.

59   "MARGOLD REPORT": Quoted in Greenberg, *Judicial Process*, 56–57 (emphasis supplied).

59   DU BOIS–HASTIE EXCHANGE: W. E. B. Du Bois, *The Autobiography of W. E. B. Du Bois: A Soliloquy on Viewing My Life from the Last Decade of Its First Century* (New York: International Publishers, 1968), 298. The 1934 editorial from *The Crisis* is quoted in Wilkins, *Standing Fast*, 152–53, as is Hastie's reply.

60   DEBATE OVER INTEGRATION: *Journal of Negro Education* 4, no. 3 (July 1935). The entire issue is devoted to the debate.

60   STONE FOOTNOTE: *United States v. Carolene Products*, 304 U.S. 144 (1938), 153.

61   JAPANESE CASES: *Hirabayashi v. United States*, 320 U.S. 81 (1943), 100, and *Korematsu v. United States*, 323 U.S. 214 (1944), 216.

61   JEHOVAH'S WITNESSES: *Marsh v. Alabama*, 326 U.S. 501 (1946), 506.

61   WHITE'S VISIT TO WHITE HOUSE: Clement E. Vose, *Caucasians Only: The*

Supreme Court, the NAACP, and the Restrictive Covenant Cases (Berkeley: University of California Press, 1959), 168.

61   MARSHALL'S TESTIMONY: Monthly report of the legal department, April 1947, LDF archives.

61   COMMITTEE APPOINTED: "Executive Order 9808 Establishing the President's Committee on Civil Rights," quoted in *To Secure These Rights: The Report of the President's Committee on Civil Rights* (New York: Simon & Schuster, 1947), viii.

61   GOALS OF COMMITTEE ON CIVIL RIGHTS: *To Secure These Rights*, 166–72.

62   FRIEND-OF-THE-COURT BRIEF: Vose, *Caucasians Only*, 169–71.

62   TRUMAN AT CONVENTION: NAACP, *Annual Report 1947*, 5–6, 53–56.

63   MARYLAND LAW SCHOOL: *Pearson v. Murray*, 169 Md. 478 (1936).

63   MISSOURI LAW SCHOOL: *Missouri ex rel Gaines v. Canada*, 305 U.S. 337 (1938).

63   "DESTROY SEGREGATION": "First Draft Statement Program Legal Department Giving Action for 1945 and Contemplated Legal Action for 1946," December 20, 1945, LDF archives.

64   MEXICAN AMERICAN CASE: *Westminster School District v. Mendez*, Brief for National Association for the Advancement of Colored People, amicus curiae, No. 11,310 (9th Cir. 1946), 161 F.2d 774 (1947).

64   BRANDEIS'S BRIEF: *Muller v. Oregon*, Brief for Defendant, Supreme Court No. 107, October Term 1908, 208 U.S. 412 (1908). Linda Kerber has brought to my attention the fact that the material Brandeis used was assembled and drafted by Josephine Goldmark for the Consumers League.

65   OKLAHOMA LAW SCHOOL: *Sipuel v. Oklahoma*, 332 U.S. 631 (1948), at 633 (emphasis supplied).

66   NOT TO TREAT HER UNEQUALLY: On the Oklahoma local court order, on the roped-off capitol, and on the second try at the Supreme Court, see Greenberg, *Judicial Process*, 70–71; and Kluger, *Simple Justice: The History of* Brown v. Board of Education *and Black America's Struggle for Equality* (New York: Knopf), 258–60.

66   OKLAHOMA SCHOOL OF EDUCATION: *McLaurin v. Oklahoma*, 339 U.S. 637 (1950).

66   STUDENTS PROTESTED SEGREGATION: "Oklahoma Students Protest Negro Ban," *New York Times*, January 30, 1948.

66   DISTRICT COURT DECISION: *McLaurin v. Oklahoma*, 87 F.Supp. 526 (W.D. Ok. 1948)

67   OKLAHOMA LAW AMENDED: *McLaurin v. Oklahoma*, 339 U.S. 637 (1948), 639–40.

67   MCLAURIN'S TESTIMONY: Kluger, *Simple Justice*, 266–69.

67   NEW CASES: *Wilson v. Louisiana State University*, 340 U.S. 909 (1951). *Wrighten v. Board of Trustees University of South Carolina*, 72 F.Supp. 948 (E.D. S.C. 1947). *Brown v. Board of Trustees of LaGrange, Texas, Independent School District, Stephens v. Board of Graded School Trustees of Lumberton, North Carolina*, and *Kelly v. School Board of Surry County Virginia*, LDF Legal Department annual report, 1948, LDF archives.

67   TEACHERS' SALARIES: *Davis v. Cook*, 178 F.2d 595 (5th Cir. 1950), cert. den. 340 U.S. 811 (1950); *Bates v. Batte*, 187 F.2d 142 (5th Cir. 1951), cert. den. 342 U.S. 815 (1951).

68   WARING QUOTE: *Elmore v. Rice*, 72 F.Supp. 516 (1947), 527.

68   CARDOZO QUOTE: Benjamin Cardozo, *The Nature of the Judicial Process* (New Haven: Yale University Press, 1921), 66.

CHAPTER 6. LAW SCHOOLS IN THE SUPREME COURT

70   STATISTICS FROM BRIEF: See *Sweatt v. Painter*, "Brief of Petitioner," Supreme Court No. 44, October Term 1949, 67–74. On the case, see also Jonathan L. Entin, "*Sweatt v. Painter*, the End of Segregation, and the Transformation of Education Law," 5 *Review of Litigation* 3 (1986).

71   *McLAURIN* BRIEF: *McLaurin v. Oklahoma State Regents*, 339 U.S. 637. Brief of Appellant, Supreme Court No. 34, October Term 1949, 12.

71   ACERBIC CORRESPONDENCE: Letter, Marshall to Wesley, January 27, 1950, LDF archives.

72   SEX ISSUE IN BRIEF: *Sweatt v. Painter*, Brief of the States of Arkansas, Florida, Georgia, Kentucky, Louisiana, Mississippi, North Carolina, Oklahoma, South Carolina, Tennessee, and Virginia, amici curiae, Supreme Court No. 44, October Term, 1949, 10.

73   AMERICAN RACIAL PRACTICES: U.S. Brief amicus curiae in *Henderson v. United States*, 339 U.S. 816 (1950), Supreme Court No. 25, October Term, 1949, 27–28, 35–49, 49–64, 60–63.

73   *Sweatt v. Painter, McLaurin v. Oklahoma State Regents*, Memorandum for the United States as amicus curiae, 9–10.

75   "OXYGEN": John P. McKenzie, conversation with the author; "CARPETS": Barbara Underwood, conversation with the author.

76   "THEIR PREJUDICES": "Arguments Before the Court: Racial 'Segregation' Attacked," 18 *United States Law Week* 3277–81 (1950).

77   "SUBSTANTIALLY EQUAL": Quote from *Sweatt v. Painter*, 339 U.S. 629, 634.

77   BLACK TEACHERS: Quote from *McLaurin v. Oklahoma*, 339 U.S. 637, 641.

77   "PUBLIC DINING FACILITY": Quote from *Henderson v. United States*, 339 U.S. 816, 825.

78   ON SWEATT'S FAILURE TO GRADUATE: See Entin, "*Sweatt v. Painter*," 71.

79   STATISTICS ON BLACK HIGHER EDUCATION: George N. Redd, "Present Status of Negro Higher and Professional Education: A Critical Summary," *Journal of Negro Education* (Summer 1948), 400–9; Charles H. Thompson, "Editorial Note: Negro Higher and Professional Education in the United States, *Journal of Negro Education* (Summer 1948), 222; idem, "Some Critical Aspects of the Problem of the Higher and Professional Education for Negroes," *Journal of Negro Education* (Fall 1945), 509–26; Martin D. Jenkins, "The Availability of Higher Education for Negroes in the Southern States," *Journal of Negro Education* (Summer 1947), 459–73; idem, "Enrollment in Institutions of Higher Education of Negroes," *Journal of Negro Education* (Spring 1948), 206–15.

79   CORETTA SCOTT KING'S SCHOLARSHIP: See LDF archives. On Texas's out-of-state grants scholarship programs see Trial Record, *Sweatt v. Painter*, Supreme Court No. 44, October Term 1949, 339 U.S. 629 (1950).

80   LIFE TERMS: "Courts Martial," *Afro American*, February 24, 1951; and "Unfairness Seen in Courts Martial," *New York Times*, March 2, 1951; "Spare Lt. Leon Gilbert," *Afro American*, October 21, 1950; and LDF, legal department monthly report, November 1950, LDF archives.

80   THURGOOD ON KOREA: "Statement by Thurgood Marshall, NAACP Special

Counsel, at Luncheon Meeting," April 5, 1951, LDF archives. TIMES EDITO-
RIAL: *New York Times*, March 4, 1951.

80   ARMED FORCES SEGREGATION: *Pittsburgh Courier*, editorial, January 13,
     1951.

80   KOREAN WAR CASES: Soldier Troubles, various folders, LDF archives. On
     Marshall and black and white snakes, interview with the author, April 5,
     1990. Marshall also referred to black and white snakes during a press con-
     ference after he announced his resignation from the Supreme Court in
     July 1991. A reporter asked if he thought a black person should be
     appointed in his place.

     Some days I would argue several cases consecutively in the Pentagon;
     in many we got reversals or reductions in sentence. One gave particular
     satisfaction. A general court-martial had convicted Frank S. Cole of
     mutiny and sentenced him to twenty years hard labor and a dishonorable
     discharge. There was no showing he had done anything mutinous, or even
     illegal, but the court-martial assumed that evidence about others applied
     to him. He had been imprisoned for three and a half years when I won his
     release and a statutory award of $5,000 authorized by section 2513 of the
     Court of Claims Procedure Act to be paid to anyone convicted with no
     justification. Cole used the money to open a radio repair shop.

80   ARMY ANNOUNCEMENT: LDF archives.

81   CONTACT US FOR HELP: LDF legal department, annual report, 1951; THUR-
     GOOD ON ESCAPED PRISONERS: Memorandum to staff from Marshall, Decem-
     ber 5, 1951, LDF archives.

CHAPTER 7. AN END TO SEGREGATION—NOTHING ELSE

85   PRIORITIES: NAACP annual report, 1951.

86   THURGOOD ON FIGHTING FOR INTEGRATION: LDF executive minutes, Sep-
     tember 11, 1950; ON ATHENS: LDF executive minutes, January 8, 1951.

86   ZOO: NAACP Memphis Branch, "Resolutions," December 18, 1950, LDF
     archives.

87   ON REDDING: Laurie Hays, "Louis L. Redding," *Wilmington Sunday News
     Journal*, November 24, 1985.

89   DELAWARE COLLEGE CASE: *Parker v. University of Delaware*, 31 Del. Ch.
     381 (Del. Ch. 1950).

89   TENNESSEE CASES: *Gray v. University of Tennessee*, 100 F.Supp. 113 (E.D.
     Tenn 1951). See also NAACP press release, "Tennessee Capitulates to
     NAACP in University Case," January 10, 1952, LDF archives.

89   TEXAS COLLEGE CASE: *Battle v. Wichita Falls Jr. College*, 101 F.Supp. 82
     (N.D. Tex. 1951).

89   ON *HAWKINS*: *State ex rel. Hawkins v. Board of Control*, 47 So.2d 608
     (1950), motion den., 53 So.2d 116, cert. den. sub. nom. *Florida ex rel.
     Hawkins v. Board of Control*, 342 U.S. 877 (1951), and motion denied, 60
     So.2d 162 (1952), vacated, 347 U.S. 971 (1954), recalled, vacated, 350 U.S.
     413 (1956), reh'g denied, 351 U.S. 915 (1956), and on remand 83 So.2d 20,
     motion denied, 93 So.2d 354 (1957), cert. den. 355 U.S. 839 (1957),
     Hawkins v. Board of Control, 253 F.2d 752 (5th Cir. 1958), on remand, 162
     F.Supp. 851 (1958).

89   FURTHER ON *HAWKINS*: Darryl Paulson and Paul Hawkes, "Desegregation at

the University of Florida Law School: *Virgil Hawkins v. The Florida Board of Control*," 12 *FSU Law Review* 59 (1984).

90   MARYLAND NURSING CASE: *McCready v. Byrd*, 195 Md. 131, cert. den. 340 U.S. 827 (1950). The state, however, continued to exclude blacks from its teachers college, dental school, and school of engineering. While it accepted Parren Mitchell for graduate study in sociology, it barred him from the white campus at College Park, making special arrangements for him at one of the extension schools in Baltimore. Again we sued, in September, three months after *McLaurin*. Educators and social scientists testified that only by studying with other full-time graduate students in sociology could Mitchell get an equal education. Finally we won. *Whittle v. University of Maryland* (filed in Baltimore City Court and then settled) and *Mitchell v. Board of Regents*, No. 16–126 (Baltimore City Court, Oct 3. 1950). In 1971 Mitchell was elected to Congress from Baltimore. In 1951 we sued the University of Maryland Schools of Engineering and Medicine, and the State Teachers College at Towson. *Roberts v. Maryland State Teachers College*, see report of the legal staff to the board of directors, April 1951, LDF archives. The trustees finally announced in late 1951 that blacks would be admitted to all branches of the university wherever comparable instruction was not offered in separate state schools for blacks. But only after *Brown* did the state teachers colleges desegregate.

90   LOUISIANA LAW SCHOOL: *Wilson v. Board of Supervisors*, 92 F.Supp. 986 (E.D. La. 1950), aff'd 340 U.S. 909 (1951); LDF executive minutes, January 8, 1951.

90   FURTHER LOUISIANA CASES: In 1951 we filed for temporary injunctions to get black applicants into the LSU graduate school (*Payne v. Board of Supervisors*, filed in the U.S. District Court for the Eastern District in June, 1951) and school of nursing (*Foster v. Louisiana State University School of Nursing*, filed in the same court in October). See LDF, legal department annual report, 1951, p. 10. In 1954 another suit got six black students into Southwestern Louisiana Institute; *Constantine v. Southwestern Louisiana Institute*, 120 F.Supp. 417 (W.D. La. 1954). In 1953 we brought another case against LSU to win admission for Tureaud's son to the LSU six-year program of arts and sciences; this case was not concluded successfully until 1956. *Tureaud v. Board of Supervisors*, 351 U.S. 924 (1956). By that time Louisiana had enacted a law requiring applicants to get a certificate of "good moral character" signed by county school officials. Another statute provided, in effect, that officials signing such certificates for blacks would lose their jobs. We won a case overturning this scheme in 1958. See *Ludley v. Louisiana State Board of Education*, 150 F.Supp. 900 (E.D. La. 1957), and *Louisiana State Board of Education v. Lark*, 358 U.S. 820 (1958).

90   NORTH CAROLINA CASES: *Epps v. Carmichael*, 93 F.Supp. 327 (M.D. N.C. 1950), rev'd sub. nom., *McKissick v. Carmichael*, 187 F.2d 949 (4th Cir.), cert. den. 341 U.S. 951 (1951). In 1951, North Carolina admitted Lolita Harrison to its graduate school, then discovered she was black and tried to keep her out of the dorms. We sued; they admitted her to the dorm. But in 1956, well after *Brown*, North Carolina continued to keep blacks out of undergraduate schools. That year we won a decision against the university in the Supreme Court. See *Thomas v. Gray* and *Harrison v. Gray*, filed in 1951, then dropped after admission was granted. See LDF legal department

annual report, 1951, 9. See also Thurgood Marshall, memorandum to Cone, August 1951, 5, LDF archives.

90   GEORGIA LITIGATION: *Ward v. Regents of the University System of Georgia*, dropped without a reported decision; and *Holmes v. Danner*, 191 F.Supp. 385 (M.D. Ga. 1960).

90   VIRGINIA CASE: *Swanson v. University of Virginia*, No. 30 (W.D. Va. September, 1950). See report of the legal department for June, July, and August, 1950, LDF archives.

92   HOLMES: Memorial Day address, May 30, 1884, in Holmes, *Speeches* (Boston: Little, Brown, 1891), 3.

CHAPTER 8. *GROVELAND*

93   *GROVELAND:* The story is put together principally from the Transcript of Record, *Florida v. Irvin*, February 11–14, 1952, the second trial, held in Ocala, Marion County Florida, in the Fifth Judicial Circuit of Florida and materials in LDF files. See also the three-part series in the *St. Petersburg Times* by Norman Bunin, April 7–9, 1950.

93   ALONGSIDE THE ROAD: Norman Bunin, "Time Table, Based on State Testimony, Raises Grave Doubts in Lake Rape Case," *St. Petersburg Times*, April 9, 1950.

94   GREENLEE TESTIMONY: Transcript of Record, *Shepherd v. State*, 46 So.2d 880 (Fla. 1950).

94   HENRY SHEPHERD: Ted Poston, "'They're Out to Get Me,' Wails Father of Negro on Trial," *New York Post*, September 4, 1949.

95   CITIZENS ON OUTCOME OF TRIAL: Orlando *Sentinel Star*, July 19, 1949, quoted in Norman Bunin, "Did Groveland Negroes Get a Fair Trial? Supreme Court to Decide," *St. Petersburg Times*, April 7, 1950.

95   MOBS GATHERED: "Guardsmen Called After Mob Shoots Up Town's Negro Area, *New York Post*, July 18, 1949; "Troops, Gas Save Negroes in Riot," *New York Post*, July 19, 1949.

95   EDITORIAL CARTOON: Orlando *Sentinel Star*, July 19, 1949, quoted in Bunin, "Fair Trial?"

95   CORONER'S JURY: "Jury to Sift Slaying of Hunted Man," *Miami Herald*, July 28, 1949; "Posse Held Justified in Killing Negro," *Miami Herald*, July 29, 1949.

96   TESTIMONY: Ted Poston, "Florida Puts Three Negroes on Life Trial," *New York Post*, September 1, 1949; "State Closes Florida Case—Offers No Medical Testimony, *New York Post*, September 4, 1949.

96   *Groveland* motions and trial: "Trial Shift Sought for Negro Trio," *Miami Herald*, August 31, 1949; "Negro Trio Going on Trial Today," *Miami Herald*, September 1, 1949.

97   CARS CHASE LAWYERS AND REPORTERS: Ted Poston, "Lynch Mob's Breath of Death Scorches Reporter Fleeing Florida," *New York Post*, September 8, 1949.

98   PROHIBITING DEATH PENALTY AT SECOND TRIAL: *Bullington v. Missouri*, 451 U.S. 430 (1981).

98   BILL HASTIE: Letters, Greenberg to Hastie, September 26 and 28, 1950, in author's possession.

98   PROPORTIONAL REPRESENTATION ON JURIES: *Cassell v. Texas*, 339 U.S. 282 (1950).

98 SUPREME COURT DECISION IN *GROVELAND*: *Shepherd v. Florida*, 341 U.S. 50 (1951).

99 MOB DOMINATION: *Moore v. Dempsey*, 209 U.S. 86 (1923). Jackson quoted from in *Shepherd v. Florida*, 51, 55.

99 BLACK QUOTED: *Chambers v. Florida*, 309 U.S. 227 (1940), 241.

99 OTHER LDF CRIMINAL CASES: *Lyons v. Oklahoma*, 320 U.S. 732 (1943) (lost), involved a similar issue. In 1949 Franklin Williams and Thurgood won *Watts v. Indiana*, 338 U.S. 49 (1949), another confession case. *Taylor v. Alabama*, 335 U.S. 252 (1948), upheld the Alabama Supreme Court's refusal to receive evidence that a confession had been coerced following a rape conviction and death sentence. *Patton v. Mississippi*, 332 U.S. 463 (1947), reversed the conviction and death sentence of a black man for murder in a county where no black had served on a jury for thirty years. *Adams v. United States*, 319 U.S. 312 (1943), involved the military base jurisdictional question.

100 "SOUTHERNERS' RAPE COMPLEX": W. J. Cash, *The Mind of the South* (New York: Vintage, 1941), 118–19.

100 SOUTHERN INJUSTICE: An account of Scottsboro and the relationship between ILD and NAACP is in Wilson Record, *Race and Radicalism: The NAACP and the Communist Party in Conflict* (New York: Cornell University Press, 1965), 62–67. See also Dan T. Carter, *Scottsboro: A Tragedy of the American South* (New York: Oxford University Press, 1969).

101 NAACP CRITICIZES COMMUNISTS: *The Crisis* editorial excoriating the Communists' handling of Scottsboro is "Herndon and the Scottsboro Cases," *The Crisis*, December 1935, 369.

101 ON YANCEYVILLE CASE: Prosecutor quoted in the *Pittsburgh Courier*, November 24, 1951, and March 15, 1952, and Court quoted March 7, 1953. See also "North Carolina Supreme Court 'Frees' Mack Ingram," LDF press release, February 27, 1953. See also "'Assault' . . . at 75 Feet," LDF pamphlet, November 1951, LDF archives.

Sex-race issues kept arising. In the *Martinsville Seven Case*, seven black men were executed in 1951 for rape of a white woman in Martinsville, Virginia. I wrote a petition that attacked the death penalty because in rape cases it applied virtually only to blacks convicted of raping white women. The Supreme Court refused to review; *Hampton v. Commonwealth*, 190 Va. 531 (1950), cert. den. 339 U.S. 989 (1950).

Interracial crimes that weren't sex cases also demanded attention. From 1948 to 1953, the *Trenton Six* confirmed the difficulty of working with other organizations where attention and money were at stake, and once more, where there was rivalry with the Communists. See Thurgood Marshall, memorandums regarding the Trenton Six, January 8 and July 31, 1951, LDF archives. Six black men were sentenced to death on questionable evidence and confessions for having murdered a Trenton, New Jersey, shopkeeper. The Civil Rights Congress (CRC), a Communist front, took three defendants' cases to the New Jersey Supreme Court and launched a publicity and fund-raising campaign reminiscent of *Scottsboro*. Arthur Spingarn questioned entering the case at all, saying that "If we lose the case, the Communists will put the blame on us; if we don't go in they will blame us; if we win it, they will take the credit." Nevertheless, we represented two defendants and entered into an agreement dealing with responsibility, publicity, and fund-raising with the groups other than the CRC.

Ultimately charges against all but one of the defendants were dismissed and the last defendant was paroled. The case showed that conflict with non-Communists was possible too. We clashed with the ACLU. It was all in the nature of organizational life. The case was *State v. Cooper*, 10 N.J. 532 (1952).

102 CONFLICT WITH COMMUNISTS: William Patterson to Roy Wilkins, February 14, 1950, LDF archives; Bailey (first name not available) to Bob Carter, August 15, 1952, LDF archives; appeal draft, n.d., LDF archives.

102 SPEAKING TOUR: Roy Wilkins to Gloster Current, December 16, 1949, LDF archives.

102 LAWYER INTIMIDATION: Frank Williams to Gloster Current, October 13, 1949, LDF archives.

102 MISCEGENATION: Thurgood Marshall to J. M. Leflore, May 14, 1951, LDF archives.

102 RIGHTS OF BLACK PEOPLE: Robert Carter to Thurgood Marshall, February 16, 1949, and February 28, 1950, LDF archives.

103 ON BLACKS AND COMMUNISTS: Wilson Record, *The Negro and the Communist Party* (New York: Atheneum, 1971), and Record, *Race and Radicalism*.

103 "COMMIE CONVENTION": Gloster Current quoted in interview with the author, July 22, 1988. Debate over the Marshall Plan, Record, *The Negro and the Communist Party*, 264–65.

104 MARSHALL ON FBI AT CONVENTION: Interview with the author, January 28, 1988. FBI MEMORANDUM ON CONVENTION: Office memorandum from L. V. Boardman to A. H. Belmont, October 21, 1955, NAACP File, Federal Bureau of Investigation Freedom of Information Act (FOIA) Reading Room, Washington, D.C.

104 FBI MEMORANDUM: Office memorandum addressed to Mr. Nichols, dated April 13, 1955, NAACP File, FBI, FOIA Reading Room. On suspension of the San Francisco branch, see NAACP minutes, December 11, 1950.

In January, 1951, the board adopted a report of the Committee on Political Domination that required the president of each unit of the association to "report to the national office any communistic or other political infiltration or domination." NAACP minutes, January 2, 1951. In September of that year the board ordered the Committee on Political Domination to consider the Schenectady, New York, branch's refusal to renew two memberships. See NAACP minutes, September 10, 1951. In June 1952 that committee passed on another applicant in Kingston, New York. See NAACP minutes, June 9, 1952. Appeals from branch action that excluded or expelled persons thought to be Communists sometimes had to be resolved at the national level. In December 1952 the board adopted detailed procedures for dealing with such matters. See NAACP minutes, December 8, 1952. As late as 1954 the convention adopted a resolution "reaffirm[ing] our rejection of Communism . . . call[ing] upon our branches to be constantly on the alert for attempts of Communists . . . to infiltrate . . . any units of our organization," NAACP 45th Annual Convention Resolutions, NAACP archives.

104 INFILTRATION: Marshall's 1952 report to the Select Committee on Foundations, LDF archives.

Ironically, the House Un-American Activities Committee accused Rabbi Stephen Wise (who was deceased) and Reverend John Haynes

Holmes, both founders of the NAACP, of having been under Communist control, despite the fact that at the time the Russian Revolution and the establishment of a Communist state were still in the future. The board characterized the charges as "a reckless and sinister disregard of responsibility"; NAACP minutes, September 14, 1953.

105   *Dennis v. United States*, 341 U.S. 494 (1951). On rejection of Marshall's attempt to file amicus brief, Marshall to Herbert M. Levy, Staff Counsel, ACLU, April 13, 1950, and letter, Philip B. Perlman, United States Solicitor General, to Marshall, November 8, 1950, both in LDF archives. Roy Wilkins's warning not to cooperate in the case, memorandum to NAACP branches, October 18, 1949, LDF archives. Carter and White views on the case, memorandum to White from Robert L. Carter, June 13, 1951, LDF archives.

105   HOOVER ENCOMIUM TO WHITE: April 14, 1947, NAACP archives, FBI, FOIA Reading Room.

CHAPTER 9. PREPARING FOR BATTLE

108   WHITE PRIMARY CASE: *Grovey v. Townsend*, 295 U.S. 45 (1935).

108   BLACK POLITICAL SITUATION IN SOUTH: M. Price, "The Negro Voter in the South" (Atlanta: Southern Regional Council, 1957); "The Negro Year Book," (Tuskegee, Ala.: Department of Records and Research, Tuskegee Institute, 1947), 276; and U.S. Commission on Civil Rights, "Annual Report" (Washington, D.C.: Government Printing Office, 1959 and 1960).

108   PENDING SUIT: *Hasgett v. Werner* [this case has no citation as it was dropped]. See Darlene Clark Hine, *Black Victory: The Rise and Fall of the White Primary in Texas* (Milwood, N.Y.: KTO Press, 1979).

108   LOUISIANA PRIMARY CASE: *United States v. Classic*, 313 U.S. 299 (1941), 317, 319.

108   PENDING CASE DEALING WITH STATE OFFICE: Election to Congress is governed by Article I, Section 2, of the Constitution, which provides that members of the House of Representatives shall be chosen by the people of the several states; Section 4 gives Congress power to regulate the times, places, and manner of holding such elections. These provisions authorized protecting the right to vote against private, not merely state action. Moreover, federal authority to regulate federal elections was, arguably, in other ways greater than authority to control state elections. In addition, the disenfranchised voters in *Classic* were already members of the party; blacks were out, trying to get in. So *Classic*, while powerfully suggesting that *Grovey* was dead, didn't clearly resolve the issue. Curiously, *Classic* didn't mention *Grovey*. *Hasgett*, therefore, might be distinguished from *Classic* in ways that would make overturning *Grovey* more difficult than it had to be.

108   WARNING TO THURGOOD: Hine, *Black Victory*, 206.

109   ON WECHSLER: Richard Kluger, *Simple Justice: The History of* Brown v. Board of Education *and Black America's Struggle for Equality* (New York: Knopf, 1976), 234.

109   REED GETS ASSIGNMENT: Hine, *Black Victory*, 219.

109   WHITE PRIMARY CASE: *Smith v. Allwright*, 321 U.S. 649 (1944), 664–665.

109   SUPREME COURT VICTORIES: The South responded with evasion, which

taught us what to expect later. Eleven days later South Carolina governor
Olin D. Johnston called a special session of the legislature that, in less
than a week, passed 150 acts repealing all laws containing any reference to
primary elections. The South Carolina Democratic party declared itself a
private club. Thurgood then brought *Elmore v. Rice*, 72 F.Supp. 516 (E.D.
S.C. 1947), aff'd 165 F.2d 387 (4th Cir. 1947), cert. den. 333 U.S. 875
(1948), which held the new scheme unconstitutional. South Carolina
appealed to the court of appeals and to the United States Supreme Court,
losing finally in April 1948.

Alabama passed the Boswell Amendment to its constitution, requiring
registrants to be able to read, write, and understand any section of the U.S.
Constitution. Thurgood had the amendment struck down in *Schnell v.
Davis*, 81 F.Supp. 872. (So. Dist. Ala. 1949), aff'd 336 U.S. 933 (1949).
Arkansas repealed all laws regulating state primaries and left intact laws
governing federal primaries, believing that state primaries would be
treated as totally private activities, while federal primaries were a lost
cause, subject to federal regulation in any event. Mississippi passed a
statute permitting anyone who had voted in three previous elections
(guess who) to vote without challenge. South Carolina continued to fight
on. Nevertheless, by 1952 the proportion of blacks of voting age who were
registered to vote was 33 percent in Florida; over 25 percent in Arkansas,
Tennessee, and Texas; over 20 percent in Georgia, Louisiana, and South
Carolina; over 16 percent in Virginia and North Carolina; but still under 5
percent in Alabama and Mississippi. U.S. Commission on Civil Rights,
Annual Report (Washington, D.C.: Government Printing Office, 1959 and
1960).

110   HASTIE'S ARGUMENT: Gilbert Ware, *William Hastie: Grace Under Pressure*
      (New York: Oxford University Press, 1984), 189.

110   BUS CASE: *Morgan v. Virginia*, Supreme Court No. 704, October Term
      1945, Brief for Appellant, 28; 328 U.S. 373 (1946). As usual, the South
      responded with evasion. Bus and rail lines adopted their own segregation
      rules and once more the state action issue surfaced: Were private carriers'
      rules subject to the Commerce Clause and, perhaps, the Fourteenth
      Amendment? On November 16, 1946, staff members and outside lawyers,
      chaired by Bob Carter, put together a catalog of approaches to the private
      regulation ploy. First, the rules inconvenienced passengers and, therefore,
      were burdens on commerce. Enforcing segregation cost carriers money,
      also a burden. Segregation regulations delayed carriers and passengers—
      more burden. State involvement invoked the equal protection clause
      because enforcement involved the state in criminal prosecution. Without
      state licensing the carriers could not function. Carriers adopted segrega-
      tion regulations pursuant to state authority. "Minutes of Meeting of
      NAACP Lawyers on Implications of Irene Morgan Decision and Other
      Transportation Matters," November 16, 1946, LDF archives.

      The group ended by proposing social and political action in addition to
      legal approaches: assembling influential Southerners; getting publicity;
      mounting picket lines; seeking the help of labor unions. But there is no
      evidence that any of the proposed direct action occurred. As the 1960s
      began, segregation in travel remained widespread; ibid.

111   1926 COVENANT CASE: *Corrigan v. Buckley*, 271 U.S. 323 (1926).

111   1945 STRATEGY MEETING: Clement Vose, *Caucasians Only: The Supreme*

Court, the NAACP, and the Restrictive Covenant Cases (Berkeley: University of California Press, 1959), 58.

111 THREE CASES: *Hurd v. Hodge*, 334 U.S. 24 (1948); *Sipes v. McGhee*, 334 U.S. 1 (1948); *Shelley v. Kraemer*, 334 U.S. 1 (1948).

111 HOUSTON TO VAUGHN: "Minutes of Meeting NAACP Lawyers and Consultants on Methods of Attacking Restrictive Covenants," September 6, 1947, LDF archives.

112 IDIOSYNCRATIC ARGUMENT: The Reconstruction statute stressed by Vaughn, the Civil Rights Act of 1866 (42 USCA sec. 1982), is quoted from Chief Justice Vinson's opinion in *Shelley v. Kraemer*, 334 U.S. 1, 11. Did the statute mean that a white could not refuse to sell to a black on racial grounds? Or, did it mean only that when a white agreed to sell to a black, the black had legal capacity to make the deal, that is, the buyers' race would not vitiate the sale, as, for example, that one of the parties was a child might, or, in the days of slavery, that one was a slave? Vaughn offered the Court no help. Vaughn's brief, nevertheless, had an insight vindicated by the Supreme Court twenty years later in *Jones v. Mayer*, 392 U.S. 409 (1968). But there is little doubt that in 1948, the Court, then entering the waters of civil rights law cautiously, would not have accepted the argument that no state action was required. Indeed, in *Hurd v. Hodge* the Court held that the 1866 statute applied only to state action.

112 VAUGHN'S ARGUMENT: 16 U.S. Law Week 3220 (1948).

112 COURT ENFORCEMENT: Following the decision, segregationists sued for damages suffered by the breach of covenants: The court would not have to enforce the covenants, they said; whoever breached merely should pay. *Barrows v. Jackson*, 346 U.S. 249 (1953), held that this evasion enforced the covenants. Apart from covenants, real estate brokers refused to show houses to blacks; banks "redlined," that is, did not give blacks mortgages in certain areas; the Federal Housing Authority and the Veterans Administration refused to insure blacks' mortgages in certain areas; communities zoned certain areas for large lots only, making land too expensive for most blacks. Housing segregation persisted.

113 "THE COLOR BAR": Harry S. Ashmore, "Some Major Problems Involved in Achieving Racial Integration, with Especial Reference to Education in the South," *Journal of Negro Education* 21, no. 3 (Summer 1952), 254.

113 MCKENZIE: "Discussion of Papers—Third Session," *Journal of Negro Education* 21, no. 3 (Summer 1952), 329, 330.

113 GRADUAL CHANGE: John P. Frank, "Can the Courts Erase the Color Line?" *Journal of Negro Education* 21, no. 3 (Summer 1952), 314.

114 THURGOOD: "General Discussion—Third Session," *Journal of Negro Education* 21, no. 3 (Summer 1952), 335.

114 SPOTTS ROBINSON: "Discussion of Papers—Third Session," *Journal of Negro Education* 21, no. 3 (Summer 1952), 332, 333.

115 "BOLD ASSAULT": James M. Nabrit, Jr., "An Appraisal of Court Action as a Means of Achieving Racial Integration in Education," *Journal of Negro Education* 21, no. 3 (Summer 1952), 428, 429.

115 JOHNSON: "Discussion of Papers—Seventh Session," *Journal of Negro Education* 21, no. 3 (Summer 1952), 444.

CHAPTER 10. JIM CROW AND THE VOICE OF
GOD IN KANSAS

116 SCHOOL EXPENDITURES: Harry S. Ashmore, *The Negro and the Schools* (Chapel Hill: University of North Carolina Press, 1954), 153, 156, 160.

117 BECAUSE HE WAS A MAN: Cheryl Brown Henderson, Oliver's daughter, and Leola Brown Montgomery, Oliver's widow, interviews with the author, January 17, 1994.

118 DECISION TO ASK FOR INTEGRATION: Spottswood W. Robinson III, personal interview, February 17, 1989. See Robert L. Carter, "Review of Mark Tushnet's *The NAACP's Legal Strategy Against Segregated Education 1925–1950*," 86 *Michigan Law Review* 1089 (1988).

118 CARTER'S VIEWS: Ibid., 1089.

119 STAFF TO ENCOURAGE INTEGRATION: LDF executive minutes, March 19, 1951; memorandum to Cone, August 1951, LDF archives.

119 CONDITIONS INTOLERABLE: Black schools were wooden buildings on unfenced, unlandscaped grounds, with $1,800 worth of furnishings for 800 students, which meant no desks for some and inadequate ones for others; in one school, seven grades were taught in two rooms by two teachers, and in two other schools, eight grades were taught by four teachers in four rooms; drinking water was brought in from outside pumps in buckets and ladled into glasses; students and teachers used outdoor toilets (at one school, two for 694 students); students were taught nonacademic curriculum featuring agriculture, vocational studies, and home economics. White education was fairly decent, in brick buildings, with inside plumbing, adequate furnishings and equipment, one teacher per grade, and an academic curriculum. Transcript of Record, *Briggs v. Elliott*, 49–58.

119 TOPEKA SCHOOLS: The average black school in Topeka was about six years older than the average white one. The average white classroom was worth about $10,000; the average black one only $6,000. Several of the newer white buildings were luxurious; none of the black ones were. Transcript of Record, *Brown v. Board*, 117–18.

120 PRINCE EDWARD COUNTY: White Farmville High School had a gym, cafeteria, auditorium, locker room, infirmary; black Moton High School had none of these; its teachers were paid less than white teachers. Moton, with capacity for 180, had a student body double that number; three stove-heated tar paper shacks held the overflow of students. Transcript of Record, *Davis v. County School Board*, 327–38.

120 IN DELAWARE: White Claymont school, with 800 students (400 of whom were in high school), was on a lovely thirteen-acre campus, with playing fields and a running track. Black Howard high school, with 1,274 students, was in a congested industrial area, with no play space. Almost 60 percent of Claymont's teachers had master's degrees; only 37 percent of Howard's did. An average Claymont teacher taught 149 pupils per week; an average Howard teacher, 179. Claymont had courses in public speaking, Spanish, sociology, economics, trigonometry, and geography, none of which were taught at Howard; Howard had vocational courses not taught at Claymont.

At the elementary level, white Hockessin School No. 29 was on a beautiful five-acre site, with a pine watershed, a multiflora rose border, bushes and trees, a playground with a baseball diamond, and basketball, volley-ball, and soccer courts. Black school No. 107 was on an unlandscaped two-acre site, its play equipment in need of repair, and had no baseball dia-mond or ball field. White No. 29 had been built in 1932 and had four classrooms; black No. 107 was ten years older and had a single classroom for all grades. White No. 29 had sanitary lavatory facilities; No. 107 had one commode in a closetlike room adjoining storage space for children's lunches and janitorial materials. Whites had buses and blacks did not. Transcript of Record, *Belton v. Gebhart,* A43 et seq.

120 *Hirabayashi v. United States,* 320 U.S. 81 (1943); *Korematsu v. United States,* 323 U.S. 214 (1944).

121 WHITE PRIMARY UNCONSTITUTIONAL: *Rice v. Elmore,* 165 F.2d 387 (4th Cir. 1947), cert. den. 333 U.S. 875 (1948).

121 COMPOSITION OF COURT: Richard Kluger, *Simple Justice: The History of* Brown v. Board of Education *and Black America's Struggle for Equality* (New York: Knopf, 1976), 302–3.

122 EQUAL PROTECTION: Complaint in *Briggs v. Elliott,* LDF archives.

122 WARING AND THURGOOD: Kluger, *Simple Justice,* 295–305, 366; "Dr. Louis T. Wright Cites NAACP Record," LDF press release, July 7, 1952; Judge J. Waties Waring, Waring to Walter White, October 5, 1951, LDF archives; Judge J. Waties Waring, Waring to Ralph Bunche, April 29, 1952, LDF archives.

123 ON PARKER'S NOMINATION: See Kluger, *Simple Justice,* 141–44; Thurgood Marshall, interview with the author, April 5, 1990.

123 FIGG ON EQUALIZATION: Transcript of Record, *Briggs v. Elliot,* 35.

123 McNALLY: Ibid., 74.

123 KNOX: Ibid., 78.

124 CLARK TESTIMONY: Clark interview with the author, January 25, 1989.

124 CLARK TESTIMONY: Transcript of Record, *Briggs v. Elliott,* 88, 89–90, 86.

124 COLEMAN AND MING: Clark, interview with the author, January 25, 1989.

124 SOCIAL SCIENCE EVIDENCE: Two other social psychologists, David Krech, of the University of California, and Helen Trager, a curriculum consultant at Vassar, testified for us. Krech concluded that "legal segregation of educa-tion is probably the single most important factor to wreak harmful effect on the emotional, physical and financial status of the Negro child and may I also say, it results in a harmful effect on the white child." Tran-script, *Briggs,* 133. Trager testified that "a child who expects to be rejected, who sees his group held in low esteem, is not going to function well, he is not going to be a fully developed child, he will be withdrawn, or aggressive in order to win the acceptance he doesn't get." Ibid., 140.

125 KESSELMAN: Ibid., 102–4 (emphasis in the original).

125 E. R. CROW TESTIMONY: Ibid., 113.

125 CROW TESTIMONY: Ibid., 114–20.

125 REDFIELD TESTIMONY: Ibid., 161.

126 PARKER OPINION: 98 F.Supp. 529.

126 EARLY *BROWN* CORRESPONDENCE: McKinley Burnett to Walter White, Kluger, *Simple Justice,* 394; Connie Motley to McKinley Burnett, Septem-ber 7, 1950, LDF archives (emphasis in the original).

127 TELEGRAM: Hugh Speer to Greenberg, May 29, 1951, LDF archives.

128 "SOUTHERN COMMUNITIES": Carter to Marshall, June 13, 1951, LDF archives.

129 SILAS FLEMING: Transcript of Record, *Brown v. Board of Education*, 109–10.
129 SCOTT OBJECTS: Ibid., 139.
130 HOLT TESTIMONY: Ibid., 169–70.
131 HUXMAN OPINION: *Brown v. Board of Education of Topeka*, 98 F.Supp. 797, 800.
131 FINDING ON EFFECTS OF SEGREGATION: Transcript of Record, *Brown v. Board of Education*, 245–46.
131 HUXMAN'S INTENT: Letter, Hugh Speer to Jack Greenberg, January 11, 1994, in author's possession.
132 GOD-GIVEN ELOQUENCE: Louisa Holt, interview with the author, December 5, 1988. Letter to Holt, in author's possession.

CHAPTER 11. *GROVELAND*, DELAWARE, AND DANCERS DRESSED IN FEATHERS

135 THE TRIAL JUDGE: "The Clergymen's Investigation," sponsored by the LDF Committee of 100, LDF archives.
136 COLLINS J. SEITZ: See Richard Kluger, *Simple Justice: The History of* Brown v. the Board of Education *and Black America's Struggle for Equality* (New York: Knopf, 1976), 430–33, 443–50. *Wilson v. Beebe* and *Johnson v. Beebe*, 99 F.Supp. 418 (Dist. Del. 1951).
136 THE WITNESSES: On Jerome Bruner, Otto Klineberg, and Fredric Wertham, see Kluger, *Simple Justice*, 309–10, 439–46.
136 PAY THE BILL: On Wertham and Delaware kids in New York, see Kluger, *Simple Justice*, 440–45.
137 THOMASSON TESTIMONY: *Belton v. Gebhart* and *Bulah v. Gebhart*, Nos. 258 and 265, Court of Chancery for the State of Delaware in and for New Castle County, Transcript of Testimony, 374.
139 WERTHAM TESTIMONY: Ibid., 124, 127, 131, 137, 138, 141, 143, 146.
140 ON BAKER: Lynn Haney, *Naked at the Feast: A Biography of Josephine Baker* (New York: Dodd, Mead, 1981), 255–57; Herman Klurfeld, *Winchell: His Life and Times* (New York: Praeger, 1976), 135, 151–60; articles by Ted Poston, *New York Post*, October 23–26, 29, November 2, 5–9, 13, 15, 16, 30, 1951, and February 1, 1952; articles and editorials in the *Amsterdam News*, October 27, November 3, 10, December 1, 8, 15; and articles and editorials in the *Chicago Defender*, October 27, November 10, 17. See also correspondence between Walter White and Sherman Billingsley in Josephine Baker, A97, Papers of the NAACP, Vol. II, Manuscript Division, Library of Congress; MARSHALL REMARK: Interview with the author, April 5, 1990. Her son Jean-Claude, in his 1994 biography of Baker, describes her in this incident as a provocateur, not a victim of discrimination. See Jean-Claude Baker and Chris Chase, *Josephine Baker: The Hungry Heart* (New York: Random House, 1994), 306 et seq.
143 MOORE BOMBING: "Bomb in Florida Kills Negro Who Led Drive to Try Sheriff," *New York Herald Tribune*, December 27, 1951.
145 EXCLUSIONARY RULE: *Mapp v. Ohio*, 367 U.S. 643 (1961).
149 ON CHEIN: Kluger, *Simple Justice*, 493.
149 ON CLARK: Ibid., 495.
150 ON GARRETT: Ibid., 501–6.
150 VIRGINIA OPINION: *Davis v. County School Board*, 103 F.Supp. 337 (E.D. Va. 1952), 340.

150 DELAWARE OPINION: *Belton v. Gebhart*, 87 A. 2d 862 (Del. Ch. 1952), 864, 870.

151 THURGOOD ON DELAWARE: LDF executive minutes, November 15, 1951.

CHAPTER 12. THE SCHOOL SEGREGATION CASES AND BULLDOGS

152 "NAACP CAN DO NOTHING": LDF minutes, February 2, 1950.

152 HAMMOND: LDF minutes, April 23, 1951.

152 WILKINS ON SALARIES: Memorandum to board of directors, April 23, 1951, LDF archives.

152 STAFF SALARIES: LDF executive minutes, May 7, 1951.

152 ANONYMOUS GIFT: LDF minutes, March 17, 1952.

153 CONTRIBUTIONS: Contributions folder, LDF archives.

153 MASONS, SHRINERS: Contributions folder, LDF archives; LDF minutes, May 14, 1951.

153 BRANCH CONTRIBUTIONS: NAACP, annual reports, 1947–1953.

154 CONTRIBUTION TO HELP WHITE: LDF executive minutes, January 28, 1952; and "Call Meeting of the Executive Committee of the Board of Directors of LDF," February 6, 1952.

154 NEW QUARTERS: LDF executive minutes, April 23, 1952.

155 CONNECTICUT RAPE CASE: *Higgs v. Connecticut*, 143 Conn. 138 (1956); LDF executive minutes, April 8, 1953.

155 BLACK, DOUGLAS DISSENT: *Briggs v. Elliott*, 342 U.S. 350 (1952), 352.

155 FIGG REPORT: Transcript of Record, *Briggs v. Elliott*, 279.

156 THREE-JUDGE COLLOQUY: Ibid., 279, 281.

156 MARSHALL TO THREE-JUDGE COURT: Ibid., 284.

157 "COURT WILL ENTERTAIN A PETITION": *Brown v. Board*, 344 U.S. 1, 3.

157 CERT GRANTED BEFORE JUDGMENT: *Brown v. Board*, 344 U.S. 1, 3.

158 ILLINOIS CASES: Reports of June Shagaloff, LDF archives.

158 KENTUCKY: *Wilson v. Paducah Junior College*, see annual report, LDF legal department, 1951, 9; LDF annual report, 1953, 13. TEXAS: *Battle v. Wichita Falls Junior College*, 101 F.Supp. 82 (N.D. Tex. 1951); LDF annual report, 1953, 13.

158 INGRAM: *State v. Ingram*, 237 N.C. 197 (1953). TRENTON SIX REVERSAL: *State v. Cooper*, 2 N.J. 540 (1949).

158 ALBERT JACKSON: *Jackson v. Commonwealth of Virginia*, 193 Va. 664 (1952).

158 *GROVELAND* EFFORTS: At a meeting on November 13, 1951, Roy, Thurgood, Bob, Connie, myself, and others from the branch and fund-raising departments discussed sending a delegation to call on Florida's governor, sending a letter signed by a bishop to "high-income persons," requesting action from the branches, possibly sending Samuel Shepherd's brother on tour, circulating a petition seeking five million signatures and holding protest rallies sponsored by ministers in Harlem and Brooklyn. See "Memorandum: The Groveland Case," November 13, 1951, LDF archives.

159 LOUISVILLE CASE: *Muir v. Louisville Park Theatrical Association*, 102 F.Supp 525 (W.D. Ky. 1953), aff'd 202 F.2d 275 (6th Cir. 1953), vac'd and rem'd 347 U.S. 971 (1954).

159 FLORIDA GOLF CASE: *Rice v. Arnold*, 54 So.2d 114 (Fla. 1951), cert. den. 342 U.S. 946 (1952).

159 KANSAS CITY SWIMMING POOL CASE: *Kansas City v. Williams*, 104 F.Supp 848, aff'd 205 F.2d 47 (8th Cir. 1953), cert. den. 346 U.S. 826 (1954).

159 MORE RECREATION CASES: *Charlotte Park and Recreation Commission v. Leeper*, 242 N.C. 311 (1955), cert. den. 350 U.S. 983 (1956). See also Spottswood Robinson, "Memorandum Concerning Charlotte, North Carolina Golf Course Cases," LDF archives. *Lonesome v. Maxwell, Dawson v. Mayor of Baltimore,* and *Isaacs v. Mayor of Baltimore,* 123 F.Supp 193 (Dist. M.D. 1954), rev'd 220 F.2d 386 (4th Cir. 1955), aff'd 350 U.S. 877 (4th Cir. 1955).

159 INTERSTATE TRAVEL: *Chance v. Lambeth*, 186 F.2d 879 (4th Cir. 1951), cert. den. (*Atlantic Coast Lines v. Chance*) 341 U.S. 941 (1951), 198 F.2d 549 (4th Cir. 1952), cert. den. 344 U.S. 877 (1952).

159 *Burns v. Lovett*, 346 U.S. 137 (1953).

162 BLACK ON ARMSTRONG: Charles Black, "In Tribute to Charles Black: 'My World with Louis Armstrong,'" 95 *Yale Law Journal* 1595–7 (1986); originally published 69 *Yale Review* 145 (1979).

CHAPTER 13. IN THE HOUSE OF THE LAW

164 CLARK'S STUDY: Kenneth B. Clark, *Effect of Prejudice and Discrimination on Personality Development,* Fact Finding Report, Mid-Century White House Conference on Children and Youth, Children's Bureau, Federal Security Agency, 1950, Columbia University, Social Work Library, New York, N.Y. Some of the findings of this report are updated in Kenneth B. Clark, *Prejudice and Your Child* (Middletown, Conn.: Wesleyan University Press, 1988). SOCIAL SCIENCE APPENDIX: Among the well-known signers were Floyd Allport, Gordon Allport, Jerome Bruner, Hadley Cantril, Kenneth Clark, Allison Davis, Otto Klineberg, Robert MacIver, Robert Merton, Gardner Murphy, and Arnold Rose. The appendix was reprinted as "Effects of Segregation and the Consequences of Desegregation: A Social Science Statement" 37 *Minnesota Law Review* 427 (1953).

165 "SCHOOL-BY-SCHOOL BASIS": *Brown v. Board,* Brief of the United States, 3, 6, 7–8, 17, 18, 27, 30–31. See also Mary L. Dudziak, "Desegregation as a Cold War Imperative," 41 *Stanford Law Review* 61 (1988).

In 1987, in a highly controversial article, Philip Elman, who as assistant solicitor general wrote the U.S. brief, reported that this section on relief was his idea as "a way to end racial segregation without inviting massive disobedience, a way to decide the constitutional issue unanimously without tearing the Court apart." It grew out of Elman's conversations with Justice Frankfurter over a period of many months. Philip Elman interviewed by Norman Silber, "Essays Commemorating the One Hundredth Anniversary of *The Harvard Law Review:* The Solicitor General's Office, Justice Frankfurter, and Civil Rights Litigation, 1946–1960: An Oral History," 100 *Harvard Law Review* 817 (1987), 827.

Mark Tushnet in "What Really Happened in *Brown v. Board of Education,*" 91 *Columbia Law Review* 1867, 1930 (1991), criticizes Frankfurter: "In a sense, the Court was unanimous because Frankfurter's formula overcame objections to desegregation. The objections, however, came primarily from Frankfurter himself; without Frankfurter's formula the Court's opinion might not have been unanimous because Frankfurter would not have joined it." But, I can't think of a race relations case in which Frankfurter did not come down on the pro–civil rights side, except, perhaps in the second *Sipuel* decision, when he didn't join the dissenters. He was the first justice to hire a black law clerk and had been on the NAACP national legal committee. I doubt, therefore, that he would have dissented from a decision for plaintiffs in *Brown*.

166 ON DAVIS: Richard Kluger, *Simple Justice: The History of* Brown v. Board of Education *and Black America's Struggle for Equality* (New York: Knopf, 1976), 103–4, 525–29.

166 RESTAURANT CASE: *District of Columbia v. John R. Thompson Co., Inc.*, 346 U.S. 100 (1953).

169 CARTER'S ARGUMENT: Leon Friedman, ed., *Argument: The Oral Argument Before the Supreme Court in* Brown v. Board of Education of Topeka, *1952–1955* (New York: Chelsea House, 1969), 13, 14.

169 BURTON'S QUESTION: Friedman, *Argument*, 32. *Plessy* had been decided fifty-six years earlier. Burton probably was speaking in generalities.

169 BLACK QUESTION TO CARTER: Ibid., 34.

169 FRANKFURTER TO MARSHALL: Ibid., 48.

170 MARSHALL REPLY TO FRANKFURTER: Ibid., 50.

170 MARSHALL AND JACKSON: Ibid., 50.

171 DAVIS ARGUMENT: Ibid., 55.

171 DAVIS AND FRANKFURTER DEBATING HISTORY: Ibid., 55–56.

171 MARSHALL ON FIGHTING AND LIVING TOGETHER: Ibid., 67.

172 FRANKFURTER ON SERMON ON THE MOUNT: Ibid., 91.

172 FRANKFURTER ON MISCEGENATION: Ibid., 116–17.

173 NABRIT ON BILLS OF ATTAINDER: Ibid., 127.

173 *Dred Scott v. Sandford*, 60 U.S. 393, 407 (1857).

173 NABRIT: Friedman, *Argument*, 142.

173 FRANKFURTER ON DELAWARE: Ibid., 159.

174 REDDING: Ibid., 164–65.

174 GREENBERG ON DELAWARE: Ibid., 168.

174 FRANKFURTER ON SOCIAL SCIENCE: Ibid., 172.

174 GREENBERG'S CONCLUSION: Ibid., 173.

175 NATIONAL CONVENTION: NAACP, *New Blueprint for Legal Action Against Racial Segregation and Discrimination* (New York: NAACP, 1953), and NAACP, "Civil Rights Handbook" (New York: NAACP, 1953).

175 RECREATION: *Lonesome v. Maxwell, Dawson v. Mayor of Baltimore*, and *Isaacs v. Mayor of Baltimore*, 350 U.S. 877 (1955). Roscoe Brown, deposition, dated August 5, 1952, photocopy, LDF archives.

175 OTHER TECHNIQUES: "NAACP Asks Probe of Mississippi Registrar," LDF press release, May 1, 1952, and "No More 'Soap Bubbles' Questions for Mississippi Negro Voters," LDF press release, February 20, 1953, LDF archives.

175 CONNIE MOTLEY'S HOUSING CASE: *Cohen v. Public Housing Administration*, 257 F.2d 73 (5th Cir. 1958).

176 BILLS TO DESEGREGATE INTERSTATE TRAVEL: H.R. 405, 563, 1250, S. 465, 83rd Cong., 1st sess.; H.R. 563, 1013, 7304, 83d Cong., 2d sess.

176 PROCEEDINGS BEFORE ICC: Various LDF monthly reports, 1954.

176 NASHVILLE CASE: *Hayes v. Crutcher*, 108 F.Supp. 582 (M.D. Tenn. 1952).

CHAPTER 14. BACK TO THE DRAWING BOARD

177   THURGOOD'S PREDICTION: LDF executive minutes, April 8, 1953.

178   FIVE QUESTIONS: *Brown v. Board of Education,* 345 U.S. (1953), 972, 973.

178   FRANKFURTER'S ROLE: Richard Kluger, *Simple Justice: The History of* Brown v. Board of Education *and Black America's Struggle for Equality* (New York: Knopf, 1976), 582–616; Frankfurter quoted on p. 615.

178   CARTER'S OUTLOOK: Ibid., 618.

179   DE MILLE'S RELEASE: "Filing of Brief Ends 22 Hectic Weeks for NAACP Lawyers," LDF press release, November 16, 1953, LDF archives.

180   FUND-RAISING: LDF minutes, April 13, 1953, and September 8, 1953; "Los Angeles Church Gives $1,500 to NAACP Legal Fund," LDF press release, August 20, 1953; "Rose Morgan Party Raises $5,000 for Legal Defense," LDF press release, October 29, 1953; "NAACP Va. State Conference Gives $5,100 to School Cases," LDF press release, December 3, 1953.

181   ASSIGNMENTS: Memorandum to National Legal Committee from Thurgood Marshall, Hastie Papers, Harvard Law School Library, box 100, folder 10.

181   COMMAGER: He added that we should consult Leonard Levy, "who has studied this whole issue carefully and who takes a somewhat different view." There is no indication that anyone tried to contact Levy. Carl Swisher wanted first to investigate further and think it over. Kluger, *Simple Justice,* 620.

182   "THERE IS A GOD": Philip Elman interviewed by Norman Silber, "Essays Commemorating the One Hundredth Anniversary of the *Harvard Law Review:* The Solicitor General's Office, Justice Frankfurter, and Civil Rights Litigation, 1946–1960: An Oral History," 100 *Harvard Law Review* 840 (1987).

183   "NORMAL EXERCISE": *Brown v. Board,* Brief for Appellants in Nos. 1, 2, and 4, and for Respondents in No. 10 on Reargument, 21.

184   CONGRESS FINANCING DISTRICT OF COLUMBIA SCHOOLS: Committee on Historical Development, memorandum, LDF archives.

184   "SEGREGATED SCHOOLS": *Brown v. Board of Education* Reply Brief for Appellants in Nos. 1, 2, and 4, and for Respondents in No. 10 on Reargument, 25.

184   THE AMENDMENT: The Civil Rights Act of 1866 is currently codified as 42 USCS 1982.

184   ON BINGHAM'S AMENDMENT: *Brown v. Board of Education* Brief for Appellants in Nos. 1, 2, and 4, and for Respondents in No. 10 on Reargument, 91.

185   "FILIBUSTER TACTICS": Michael McConnell, "Originalism and the Desegregation Decisions," unpublished manuscript, in author's possession.

185   "RATIFYING STATES": Horace Bond Mann to Mabel Smythe on pre-admission constitutions, October 5, 1953, LDF archives (emphasis in original).

186   AFTER RATIFICATION: Committee on Historical Development—States—New York, memorandum, LDF archives.

186   "CONSTITUTIONAL THEORY": Howard Jay Graham, "Proposed Amendment to Appellants' Briefs," 1, 3, 47, LDF archives.

187   "DECISIONS OF THE COURTS": C. Vann Woodward, "The Background of the Abandonment of Reconstruction," LDF archives.

187   SUMMARY OF ARGUMENT: *Brown v. Board of Education* Brief for Appellants in Nos. 1, 2, and 4, and for Respondents in No. 10 on Reargument, 17–18.

187 GOVERNMENT'S BRIEF: "While the legislative history does not conclusively establish that the Congress which ENDNO: the Fourteenth Amendment specifically understood that it would abolish racial segregation in the public schools, there is ample evidence that it did understand that the Amendment established the broad constitutional principle of full and complete equality of all persons under the law, and that it forbade all legal distinctions based on race or color. Concerned as they were with securing to the Negro freedmen these fundamental rights of liberty and equality, the members of Congress did not pause to enumerate in detail all the specific applications of the basic principles which the Amendment incorporated into the Constitution." Brief of the United States as Amicus Curiae, 115.

188 KELLY ON THE BRIEF: Dr. Alfred H. Kelly, "When the Supreme Court Ordered Desegregation," *U.S. News & World Report*, February 5, 1962, 86–88.

188 CLARK STUDY: "Desegregation: An Appraisal of the Evidence," *Journal of Social Issues* 9, no. 4 (1953): 2–76 (entire issue).

189 "FORTHWITH": Brief for Appellants in Nos. 1, 2, and 4, and for Respondents in No. 10 on Reargument, 190.

189 SPOTTS'S ARGUMENT: Leon Friedman, ed., *Argument: The Oral Argument Before the Supreme Court in* Brown v. Board of Education of Topeka, *1952–1955* (New York: Chelsea House, 1969), 187.

190 DAVIS ON AESOP: Ibid., 216–17.

191 THURGOOD'S PERORATION: Ibid., 236, 239, 240.

191 RANKIN: Ibid., 250.

191 RANKIN ON "DELIBERATE SPEED": Ibid., 253, 256.

192 BLACK TO KORMAN: Ibid., 287.

192 NABRIT'S ARGUMENT: Ibid., 308.

192 CARTER'S ARGUMENT: Ibid., 262.

194 THOMPSON RECENTLY RECALLED: Sydnor Thompson, interview with the author, May 13, 1993.

CHAPTER 15. A HISTORIC TURN

198 *Brown v. Board of Education*, 347 U.S. 483, 489, 493–95.

198 D.C. CASE: *Bolling v. Sharpe*, 347 U.S. 497, 499–500.

199 NEWS OF VICTORY: Roy Wilkins, *Standing Fast: The Autobiography of Roy Wilkins* (New York: Viking, 1982), 213. BOWING DOWN: Kenneth Clark, interview with the author, January 25, 1989.

199 "TIME HAD COME": Sydnor Thompson, interview with the author, May 13, 1993.

199 GIFT GIVERS: Stuart Marks, interview with the author, May 14, 1993.

199 CASES VACATED: *Florida ex rel. Hawkins v. Board of Control*, 342 U.S. 877 (1951), motion denied 60 So.2d 162 (Fla. 1952), vacated 347 U.S. 971 (1954), and *Tureaud v. Board of Supervisors*, 351 U.S. 924 (1956), from Louisiana, which had been bouncing around the lower courts on questions of procedure, even though *Brown* hadn't addressed the procedural issues of either case. The Court denied review of a Fifth Circuit case ordering Hardin Junior College in Wichita Falls, Texas, to admit blacks, *Battle v. Wichita Falls Jr. College*, 101 F.Supp. 82 (N.D. Tex. 1951).

199 LOUISVILLE CASES: *Muir v. Louisville Park Theatrical Association*, 102
     F.Supp 525 (W.D. Ky. 1953), aff'd 202 F.2d 275 (6th Cir. 1953), vac'd and
     rem'd 347 U.S. 971 (1954).

199 SHAGALOFF MEMORANDUM: The states were Arkansas, Delaware, Kansas,
     Maryland, Missouri, Oklahoma, Tennessee, and West Virginia, plus Wash-
     ington, D.C.; Shagaloff to Carter, February 1955, LDF archives.

200 FLORIDA, LOUISIANA: "The Florida School Admissions Law," 1 *Race Rela-
     tions Law Reporter* 237 (1956), Section 1, Article xii of the Constitution of
     Louisiana, 1 *Race Relations Law Reporter* 239 (1956).

200 MILFORD CASE: *Steiner v. Simmons*, 111 A. 2d 574 (1955); "Delaware,"
     Southern School News 1, no. 2 (October 1954), 4.

201 WHITE SULPHUR SPRINGS: "West Virginia," *Southern School News* 1, no. 2
     (October 1954), 14; "District of Columbia," 4; and "Maryland," 8.

201 "MORE TO BE GAINED": Constance Baker Motley to Gloster Current, memo-
     randum, February 16, 1954, LDF archives.

201 BYRD, SHAGALOFF, HASTIE EFFORTS: The Mississippi towns were Laurel,
     Columbus, Jackson, Clarksdale, Hattiesburg, Meridian, and Vicksburg.
     One Northern town was Englewood, New Jersey. Concerning gerryman-
     dered school districts, see LDF docket, February 1954. June met with the
     Jamaica and Amityville, New York, NAACP branch members to survey
     school segregation. See LDF docket, March and April 1954. See also LDF
     monthly reports, February–April 1954. Hastie quoted from LDF executive
     minutes, October 6, 1954.

201 ON TEACHERS: Elwood Chisolm, memorandum, October 26, 1955, LDF
     archives.

202 TAX EXEMPTION: LDF executive minutes, September 23, 1954, and Novem-
     ber 2, 1955.

202 GIFTS: LDF minutes, May 11, 1955.

202 RESOLUTION ON THURGOOD'S HEALTH: LDF minutes, March 2, 1955.

203 BOARD ON IMPLEMENTATION: LDF executive minutes, June 1954.

203 IMPLEMENTATION BRIEF: *Brown v. Board of Education*, Brief for Appellants,
     11, 17, 25, 29.

203 FORM OF DECREE: *Brown v. Board of Education*, memorandum Brief for
     Appellants, 13, 15.

204 BLACK'S STYLE: *Brown v. Board of Education*, Reply Brief for Appellants,
     17.

204 U.S. BRIEF: *Brown v. Board of Education*, Brief for the United States on the
     Further Argument of the Questions of Relief, 19, 7–8.

204 NORTH CAROLINA BRIEF: *Brown v. Board of Education*, Brief of Harry
     McMullan, attorney general of North Carolina, amicus curiae, 40.

205 LAKE: Leon Friedman, ed., *Argument: The Oral Argument Before the
     Supreme Court in* Brown v. Board of Education of Topeka, *1952–1955*
     (New York: Chelsea House, 1969), 449.

205 LAKE: Ibid., 452–53.

205 ROGERS AND WARREN: Ibid., 413–14.

205 ASSOCIATION'S POSITION: NAACP annual report, 1954, 86.

206 "ALL DELIBERATE SPEED": *Brown v. Board of Education*, 349 U.S. 294 (1955),
     300–1 (emphasis supplied).

206 MIGRATION: Between 1950 and 1960 the number of black people in the
     South decreased more than 14 percent, in addition to the 16 percent

decline of the previous decade. During the 1950s, the black population of the Northeast increased 26 percent while the black population of the North Central states increased 24 percent. In the previous decade, the figures were 34 percent and 42 percent, respectively. From 1950 to 1960, in New York, New Jersey, Ohio, Illinois, and Michigan the black population increased more than 25 percent, in California, more than 50 percent. See *Statistical Abstract of the United States* (Washington, D.C.: Government Printing Office, 1965), 34. During the same decade, the percentage of white people living in urban areas, North and South, increased from 64 percent to 69 percent, while for black people the percentage rose from 62 percent to 72 percent; ibid., 24.

207 MEASURES OF EDUCATION: By 1950, the median years of school completed by white men between the age of 25 and 29 was 12.4 (equivalent to a high school diploma), while the median years for similar black men was 8.4. By 1960 the situation for whites was the same, but the median years of school completed for black men between the age of 25 and 29 had grown to 10.5. United States Bureau of the Census, *Historical Statistics of the United States from Colonial Times to 1970* (Washington, D.C.: Government Printing Office, 1971), 381. The number of blacks enrolled in higher education nearly doubled, from 90,000 to 174,000. In the 1950s, 80 percent of blacks at this level attended black institutions, but by 1964 that number fell to 51 percent. Increases occurred mainly in Northern white schools. See Richard Freeman, *Black Elite* (New York: McGraw-Hill, 1976), 47–48.

207 COLLEGE, LOWER SCHOOLS: Between May 17, 1954, and April 1955 we had eight college cases in Texas, Oklahoma, and Louisiana. An Ohio judge wouldn't enjoin a school board because he determined it was trying to do something about segregation. I appeared before the New Jersey State Division Against Discrimination to desegregate Englewood's schools. Spotts Robinson represented parents in West Point, Virginia (where there was no black high school), who had been convicted of violating the compulsory school law because they wouldn't send their kids to another town, twenty miles away. LDF monthly reports, January, February, and March–April 1955, LDF archives.

207 CONNIE MOTLEY'S DOCKET: She had cases in St. Louis, Camden, Savannah, Birmingham, Benton Harbor (Mich.), Detroit, and Columbus. Benton Harbor defended on the grounds that it was following community custom. Her most ambitious effort was against Levittown, Pennsylvania, which would include 16,000 homes, asserting that its use of state and federal powers to assemble property and finance construction amounted to state action. Levitt, the world's biggest builder of private homes during this period, led in creating the all-white suburb with governmental assistance, drawing whites out of cities creating inner-city ghettos. The district court dismissed, concluding that no state action was involved, *Johnson v. Levitt*, 131 F.Supp. 114 (E.D. Penn. 1955).

207 RECREATION: One case was under a state civil rights act in Coney Island, Ohio; another, in North Carolina, involved a park that had been deeded to the state on condition that if blacks ever used it the property would revert to the donor. LDF monthly report, March–April, 1955, LDF archives.

207 BALTIMORE DECISION: *Dawson v. Mayor and City Council of Baltimore*, 220

F.2d 386 (4th Cir. 1955), aff'd 350 U.S. 877 (1955).

207   COERCED CONFESSION: *Reeves v. Alabama,* 348 U.S. 891 (1954). Brief for
       Petitioner, 14. See *Canty v. Alabama,* 309 U.S. 629 (1940), and *Vernon v.
       Alabama,* 313 U.S. 547 (1941), both resting on *Chambers v. Florida,* 309
       U.S. 227 (1940), an early LDF case in which Thurgood participated.

208   EXTRADITION: *Dukes v. Hanna, Warden,* 99 A. 2d 452 (N.J. 1954), cert. den.
       347 U.S. 914 (1954); LDF minutes, May 5, 1954.

208   PHILADELPHIA EXTRADITION CASE: *Brown v. Baldi, Superintendent,* 106 A. 2d
       777 (Penn. 1954), cert. den. 348 U.S. 939 (1955). During this period I
       argued the *Higgs* case in the Connecticut Supreme Court (with Peter Mar-
       cuse, a Connecticut lawyer), in which a black man had been convicted of
       rape of a white woman, and won on the grounds that counsel had not been
       permitted to interrogate potential jurors about racial bias, anticipating a
       similar Supreme Court decision by three decades; *Higgs v. Connecticut,*
       143 Conn. 138 (1956).

208   *GROVELAND* IN SUPREME COURT: *Irvin v. State,* 346 U.S. 927 (1954).

209   LDF INCOME: 1954 income was $213,840, increasing to $311,393 in 1955.
       See LDF financial statements, LDF archives; LDF executive minutes, Jan-
       uary 5, 1955, January 11, 1956, and January 18, 1960; LDF executive min-
       utes, April 27, 1959; LDF membership and annual meeting and LDF min
       utes, March 11, 1960.

210   BOARD MEMBERS: Charles Buchanan, a leader of the Harlem community and
       owner of the Savoy Ballroom; Homer Brown, a black judge in Pittsburgh;
       George Cannon, a Harlem physician, who had started the first group med-
       ical practice there; Bill Coleman; Lois Cowles, who had been married to
       Gardner Cowles, publisher of the Cowles newspaper empire; Bill DeWind;
       Dr. C. B. Powell, a successful businessman and publisher of the *Amster-
       dam News;* Walter Gellhorn; Amos Hall, a leading Prince Hall Mason and
       lawyer from Oklahoma City; Bill Hastie; Hans Huber, who owned one of
       the largest private lumber, mining, and oil businesses in the country; Lois
       Jessup, whose husband, Philip, was a professor of international law at
       Columbia and became the U.S. representative on the International Court
       of Justice at The Hague; Ben Kaplan; Paul Moore; Lou Pollak; Charlie
       Thompson; Dorothy Rosenman, wife of Sam Rosenman, who had been
       counsel to presidents Roosevelt and Truman; Catherine Waddell, who was
       Chief Justice Charles Evans Hughes's daughter; and Charles Zimmerman,
       general manager of the New York Dress Joint Board and a vice president of
       the International Ladies Garment Workers Union.

210   RIVERS: Farnsworth Fowle, "Francis E. Rivers Dies; Black City Judge Was
       82," *New York Times Biographical Service,* July 1975, 905. George D.
       Cannon and John W. Davis, remarks at service for Francis Rivers, July 31,
       1975, in author's possession.

211   FUND-RAISING: LDF executive minutes, January 20 and December 15, 1958;
       LDF minutes, October 5, 1955. The Committee of 100 appeals dealt with
       cases like those of Emmett Till, a black teenager who had been kidnapped
       and murdered by whites in Mississippi for whistling at a white woman;
       violent attacks on black leaders by white citizens councils; *Groveland;*
       the Montgomery bus boycott; as well as voting, school segregation, and
       demonstration cases.

CHAPTER 16. THE SPIRIT OF BLACK REVOLT STIRS AND JIM CROW FIGHTS BACK

212 MARGOLD QUOTED: Jack Greenberg, *Judicial Process and Social Change: Constitutional Litigation* (Minneapolis, Minn.: West, 1977), 51.

213 BUS SEGREGATION: In November 1956, Bob Carter also assisted a maverick South Carolina white lawyer, Philip Wittenberg, in representing a black woman who refused to submit to segregation on a bus in Columbia. Wittenberg and his family were harassed because he had the case; we took it over. Citing *Brown* and cases decided in its wake, the Fourth Circuit held unconstitutional South Carolina's bus segregation law, and the Supreme Court refused to hear the appeal, which some interpreted as virtually an affirmance of the circuit court's ruling. But the decision was widely ignored; *Flemming v. South Carolina Elect. & Gas Co.*, 224 F.2d 752 (4th Cir. 1955), app. dism. 351 U.S. 901 (1956). Then, in another LDF case, *Gayle v. Browder*, 352 U.S. 903 (1956), the Court upheld enjoining enforcement of the Montgomery bus segregation ordinance as unconstitutional.

213 MEMPHIS CASE: *Evers v. Dwyer*, 358 U.S. 202 (1958).

213 EISENHOWER: Richard Kluger, *Simple Justice: The History of* Brown v. Board of Education *and Black America's Struggle for Equality* (New York: Knopf, 1976), 753; "Ike Won't Forecast Virginia Role, Backs Up Courts," *Southern School News* 4, no. 12 (June 1958), 9.

213 CONGRESSIONAL MANIFESTO: "Manifesto Protests Court Act" and "'Southern Manifesto' Criticizes Supreme Court," *Southern School News* 2, no. 10 (April 1956), 1–2.

214 ON CONGRESSIONAL MANEUVERING: C. Herman Pritchett, *Congress versus the Supreme Court, 1957–1960* (Minneapolis: University of Minnesota Press, 1961), 3, 31–35.

214 ATTACKS ON THE COURT: Pritchett, *Congress*, 21, 23. James F. Byrnes, "The Supreme Court Must Be Curbed," *U.S. News & World Report*, May 18, 1956, 50.

215 JENNER BILL: Leo Katcher, *Earl Warren: A Political Biography* (New York: McGraw-Hill, 1967), 391–92.

215 "WRITTEN THE OPINION": Herbert Wechsler, "Toward Neutral Principles of Constitutional Law," 73 *Harvard Law Review* 1 (1959), 34.

215 "SCIENTIFIC FINDING": Edmond Cahn, "Jurisprudence," 30 *New York University Law Review* 150 (1955), 166.

216 "JIM CROW SCHOOLS": "8 Southern Legislatures Adopt 35 New Measures," *Southern School News* 4, no. 3 (September 1957), 1.

216 *TRIBUNE* ADVERTISEMENT: NAACP minutes, March 10, 1958.

216 SOUTHERN REACTIONS: "Florida's First Admission Action Is Filed in Miami," *Southern School News* 3, no. 1 (July 1956), 2; "Floridians Debate Effectiveness of New School Laws," *Southern School News* 3, no. 3 (September 1956), 13; "Georgia Ardent Foe of Integration Winner in Governor's Race," *Southern School News* 5, no. 4 (October 1958), 18; "Charlotte Pupils Reject Advice to 'Welcome Back' Negro Girl," *Southern School News* 4, no. 7 (January 1958), 13; "Oklahoma: Displacement of Teachers Shows Drop for 2nd Year," *Southern School News* 5, no. 4 (October 1958), 13; "Little Major Activity Reported in South Carolina During the Month," *Southern School News* 3, no. 1 (July 1956), 11; "S.C. School Month Brings

New Litigation on '56 Law Barring NAACP Membership," *Southern School News* 3, no. 4 (October 1956), 3; "Race Violence, Amity Mix in S.C. During Month," *Southern School News* 4, no. 7 (January 1958), 12; "Tennessee," *Southern School News* 1, no. 9 (May 4, 1955), 10; "West Virginia: Governor Criticizes School Closings," *Southern School News* 5, no. 9 (March 1959), 11.

216 SCHOOL BOARD: *Brewer v. Hoxie School District No. 46*, Brief of Appellees, LDF archives.

217 CLINTON: "One Tennessee School Desegregated; Violence Marks Protests, Picketing," *Southern School News* 3, no. 3 (September 1956), 3.

217 TEXAS: "100-Plus Texas Districts Lower Bars; Flareup in One," ibid., 12.

217 CLAY AND STURGIS: "Peaceful Transition, Mob Activity Mark Kentucky's School Month," *Southern School News* 3, no. 4 (October 1956), 3.

217 REACTIONS TO DESEGREGATION: "2 Tennessee Cities Face 'Showdown' on Schools," *Southern School News* 4, no. 8 (February 1958), 10; "Alabama: Supreme Court Ruling On Placement Law Anticipated in October," *Southern School News* 5, no. 2 (August 1958), 11; "Alabama: Private School Corporation Planned as Anti-Integration 'Standby' Measure," *Southern School News* 5, no. 5 (November 1958), 12; "Georgia: Atlanta Local Option Proposal Stirs Debate Flurry Among Top Officials," *Southern School News* 5, no. 6 (December 1958), 15; "North Carolina: Stiff Penalty Asked for Bomb Scares; Legal Sparring Continues in Durham," *Southern School News* 5, no. 7 (January 1959), 15.

217 POPLARVILLE LYNCHING: "Mississippi: Officials Express Concern at Poplarville Incident," *Southern School News* 5, no. 11 (May 1959), 8.

217 PLANNING DEFENSES: Jack Greenberg, speaking engagements memoranda, LDF archives.

218 REQUIRED TO REGISTER: The NAACP registered in Georgia, Tennessee, Virginia, Missouri, Arkansas, Delaware, and South Carolina. NAACP minutes, November 13, 1956; December 10, 1956; January 7, 1957.

218 ALABAMA INJUNCTION: The legal battle over Alabama's attempt to stop the NAACP from practicing took shape in three cases: *NAACP v. Alabama ex rel. Patterson*, 357 U.S. 449 (1958), 360 U.S. 240 (1959); *NAACP v. Alabama ex rel. Gallion*, 368 U.S. 16 (1961); and *NAACP v. Alabama ex rel. Flowers*, 377 U.S. 288 (1964). In 1958 the Supreme Court held that "the immunity from state scrutiny of membership lists which the Association claims on behalf of its members is here so related to the right of the members to pursue their lawful private interest privately and to associate freely with others in so doing as to come within the protection of the Fourteenth Amendment." See 357 U.S. 449 (1958), 466.
On the final victory over Alabama, see NAACP annual report, 1964, 45.

218 HASTIE PLEA: Memorandum to chairman of the board of directors, September 10, 1956, Hastie Papers, Harvard Law School Library, box 100, folder 7. The NAACP Board authorized Thurgood to make a public statement embodying Hastie's recommendations. NAACP minutes, January 7, 1957. Happily, the Association won the case and never had to face the issue.

218 SOUTH CAROLINA TEACHER LAW: 1 *Race Relations Law Reporter* 600 (1956), 751.

219 ELLOREE CASE REJECTED: *Bryan v. Austin*, 354 U.S. 933 (1957).

219 ARKANSAS: In 1957 and 1958, Arkansas required those who promoted

school desegregation to register, keep records of their contributions, and report to a State Sovereignty Commission. 2 *Race Relations Law Reporter* 491 (1957), 495. The state enacted a law punishing lawyers or firms who sought out clients; required school officials to file affidavits listing organizations to which they belonged; and disqualified NAACP members from public employment, 3 *Race Relations Law Reporter* 1049 (1958), 1053. A Committee of the Legislative Council found that the NAACP "is a captive of the international communist conspiracy," *Southern School News* 5, no. 8 (February 1959), 14. In three cases, Arkansas demanded the Association's list of supporters, employees, and officers, publications, correspondence, deposit slips, and contributors. It sued LDF for doing business in the state without having registered as a foreign corporation. There was one case and appeal after another. A federal court struck down as unconstitutional a provision prohibiting teachers' membership in the NAACP, but upheld a requirement that teachers make available to school administrators a list of any organizations to which they belonged. But, the federal court stayed the remainder of the proceedings because state courts might interpret other anti-NAACP laws in ways not harmful to the Association. State courts struck down Arkansas's new solicitation law. The Arkansas Supreme Court limited the information that the Association was required to produce. The United States Supreme Court reversed a state court order that the Association produce names. The case against LDF lingered for almost a decade and was dismissed. The Arkansas cases were *NAACP v. Arkansas ex rel. Bennett*, 360 U.S. 909 (1959); *NAACP v. Bennett*, 360 U.S. 471 (1959); *Shelton v. McKinley*, 174 F.Supp. 351 (E.D. Ark. 1959).

219 SUPREME COURT BLOCKS LOUISIANA'S EFFORT TO GET MEMBERS' NAMES: *Louisiana ex rel. Gremillion v. NAACP*, 366 U.S. 293 (1961).

219 NORTH CAROLINA: The Association was fined $500; it paid and the case went away. North Carolina's was the only legislature which refused to pass an anti-Association bill. NAACP minutes, March 11, April 8, and June 10, 1957.

219 FLORIDA: 3 *Race Relations Law Reporter* 784 (1958). After J. B. Matthews, a professional anti-Communist, testified before the legislature concerning Communists in the NAACP, it refused to produce names of members. NAACP minutes, February 10, 1958. State courts held NAACP officers in contempt, fined them, and sentenced them to prison. Bob Carter won the case in the United States Supreme Court in 1963 because Florida had shown no relationship between the information sought and subversive activities to justify encroaching upon the Association's First and Fourteenth Amendment rights. The cases were *In re Petition of Graham*, 104 So.2d 16 (Fla. 1958); and *Gibson v. Florida Legislative Investigation Committee*, 372 U.S. 539 (1963).

219 GEORGIA: *Williams v. NAACP*, 2 *Race Relations Law Reporter* 181 (Ga. Super. Ct. 1956); *NAACP v. Pye*, 101 S.E.2d 609 (Ga. Ct. App. 1957); and *NAACP v. Williams*, 359 U.S. 550 (1959).

219 VIRGINIA: *NAACP v. Button*, 371 U.S. 415 (1963); and *Virginia ex rel. Virginia State Bar v. NAACP*, 8 *Race Relations Law Reporter* 1145 (1963). *Button* made possible creation of countless public interest legal outfits that address racial, ethnic, gender, and other discrimination, environmental, consumer, and other concerns. *Button* arose when Virginia, in 1956 and 1957, passed five laws requiring organizations that took positions on

or engaged in litigation of racial issues or that caused racial conflict, to register and file reports. It passed laws punishing "running" and "capping," that is, soliciting business for lawyers or supporting lawsuits without having a direct interest in them. It redefined barratry to cover civil rights lawyers' activities. See 2 *Race Relations Law Reporter* 1015–25 (1957). The legislature began investigating the Association and subpoenaed names of members. The Virginia State Bar Association sued LDF for illegal practice of law. In response, the Association and LDF filed cases against the registration, reporting, and antilitigation laws. Proceedings went on in state and federal courts, at the trial and appeal levels, ultimately resulting in *Button.*

219 TEXAS CASE: That year Texas passed a law requiring organizations that engaged in activities "designed to hinder, harass, and interfere with the powers and duties of the State of Texas to control and operate its public schools" to register and file certain information. 3 *Race Relations Law Reporter* 90 (1958).

220 TEXAS APPEAL ISSUE AND THURGOOD TO HASTIE: NAACP minutes, October 8, 1956. *Texas v. NAACP,* 1 *Race Relations Law Reporter,* 1068 (1956); 2 *Race Relations Law Reporter* 678 (Dist. Ct. Tex. 1957). Memorandum, unsigned, n.d., Hastie Papers, Harvard Law School Library, box 101, folder 1; NAACP minutes, October 8 and December 13, 1956, May 13, June 10, and September 9, 1957.

221 NAACP REGIONAL AND NATIONAL MEMBERSHIP INFORMATION: NAACP annual reports, 1955, 15; 1956, 12; 1957, 15. Financial information, NAACP annual reports, 1955, 75; 1957, 93. Membership and financial information for 1964, NAACP annual report, 1964, 31, 96.

221 BROWNELL: J. W. Anderson, *Eisenhower, Brownell and the Congress: The Tangled Origins of the Civil Rights Bill of 1956–1957* (University: University of Alabama Press, 1964).

221 WARREN'S OPPONENTS DEFEATED: Katcher, *Earl Warren,* 398.

221 BLACK: Charles Black, "The Lawfulness of the Segregation Decisions," 69 *Yale Law Journal* 421 (1960), 424.

222 POLLAK: Louis Pollak, "Racial Discrimination and Judicial Integrity: A Reply to Professor Wechsler," 108 *University of Pennsylvania Law Review* 1 (1959), 30.

222 THURGOOD ON IRS: LDF executive minutes, April 4, 1956.

223 RESOLUTION ON CASES WE TAKE: LDF minutes, November 7, 1956.

223 ENDING INTERLOCK: LDF minutes, special meeting of the board of directors, May 16, 1957. Affidavit of John Hammond, April 8, 1983, quoted in *NAACP v. NAACP Legal Defense and Educational Fund, Inc.,* 753 F.2d 131 (D.C. Cir. 1985), 134.

223 THURGOOD ON MY FUTURE: NAACP minutes, November 10, 1958.

223 BYRD TO IRS: 4 *Race Relations Law Reporter* 490 (1959).

223 THURGOOD'S RELATION TO NAACP: Thurgood continued into the spring of 1957 to assist in the case arising out of Texas's efforts to put the Association and LDF out of business in the state; while he represented only LDF he took part in aspects of the case involving the Association too. As late as November 1958 he attended NAACP board meetings. NAACP minutes, November 10, 1958.

224 TAX EXEMPTION: Our name continued to appear in the "Blue Book," published by the IRS, which lists tax-exempt organizations.

224 FURTHER ON SEPARATION: LDF executive minutes, December 15, 1958, and NAACP minutes, October 13, 1959. Memorandum, Marshall to Hastie (charges against Thurgood), Hastie Papers, Harvard Law School Library, box 101, folder 2.

224 "DID US A FAVOR": Thurgood Marshall Oral History, Oral History Project, Columbia University (interview with Ed Edwin, June 7, 1977), 178.

224 BOB'S BURDEN: NAACP minutes, March 10, 1958.

224 QUOTE FROM *CITIZEN'S GUIDE:* Herbert Hill and Jack Greenberg, *Citizen's Guide to De-Segregation: A Study of Social and Legal Change in American Life* (Boston: Beacon, 1955), 161; Jack Greenberg, *Race Relations and American Law* (New York: Columbia University Press, 1959), 274.

CHAPTER 17. LUCY AND LITTLE ROCK

225 THURGOOD TO BOARD: LDF minutes, June 1, 1955, and LDF executive minutes, April 4, 1956.

226 *Lucy v. Board of Trustees,* 213 F.2d 846 (5th Cir. 1954); *Lucy v. Adams,* 134 F.Supp. 235 (N.D. Ala, 1954), modified 350 U.S. 1 (reinstating injunction in part), aff'd per curiam 228 F.2d 619 (5th Cir. 1955), cert. den. 351 U.S. 931 (1956). On Lucy's arrival at the University of Alabama and the rioting see, among many other sources, "First Alabama Negro Enrollment Brings 3-Day Demonstration," *Southern School News* 2, no. 9 (March 1956), 6; Wayne Phillips, "Tuscaloosa: A Tense Drama Unfolds," *New York Times Magazine,* February 26, 1956, 17; Arthur Carter, "'I'm Ready to Go Back to School,'" and "Ike Calls Mob Action 'Deplorable,'" *Afro American,* February 18, 1956, 1.

226 LUCY: See 350 U.S. 1 (1955) (vacating suspension of injunction); 2 *Race Relations Law Reporter* 350 (N.D. Ala. 1957) (university board not in contempt); Brian Lanker, *I Dream a World: Portraits of Black Women Who Changed America* (New York: Stewart, Tabori & Chang, 1989), 126; "36 Years After the Hate, Black Student Triumphs," *New York Times,* April 26, 1992.

226 THURGOOD ON LUCY, ROY'S RESPONSE: LDF minutes, April 4, 1956 (emphasis supplied).

226 THURGOOD ON MISSISSIPPI: LDF minutes, May 2, 1956.

227 CLAY AND STURGIS: "Peaceful Transition, Mob Activity Marks Kentucky's School Month," *Southern School News* 3, no. 4 (October 1956), 3.

227 "PREACHING": James Crumlin, interview with the author, January 18, 1989.

227 CLAY, STURGIS DECISIONS: "Clay, Sturgis Are Told to File Desegregation Plans," *Southern School News* 3, no. 7 (January 1957), 13; *Gordon v. Collins,* 2 *Race Relations Law Reporter* 304 (1957); *Garnett v. Oakley,* 2 *Race Relations Law Reporter* 303 (1957).

228 BRANTON: Following the Little Rock case Wiley became head of the Southern Regional Council's Voter Education Project, president of the Council of United Civil Rights Leadership (a consortium of the leading civil rights organizations), dean of Howard Law School, and partner in the law firm of Sidley and Austin.

228 LITTLE ROCK CASE: *Cooper v. Aaron,* 358 U.S. 1 (1958). See also "Three

Court Cases Dominate School Scene in Arkansas; U.S. Intervenes," *Southern School News* 2, no. 9 (March 1956), 6.

229 FAUBUS: Daisy Bates, *The Long Shadow of Little Rock* (New York: David McKay, 1962), 81.

229 FAUBUS QUOTED: Bates, *Little Rock*, 61. For a chronology of the legal developments in Little Rock, 2 *Race Relations Law Reporter* 931–65 (1957).

230 EVENTS AT CENTRAL HIGH IN LITTLE ROCK: Bates, *Little Rock*, passim; "U.S. Troops Sent to Little Rock: Three Districts Desegregate," *Southern School News* 4, no. 4 (October 1957), 3.

230 U.S. PETITION: Quoted, 2 *Race Relations Law Reporter* 943 (1957).

231 EISENHOWER'S PROCLAMATION: 2 *Race Relations Law Reporter* 963 (1957), 964. His order quoted, ibid., 965.

232 MINNIJEAN BROWN: Bates, *Little Rock*, 106, 117.

232 BOARD PETITION: 3 *Race Relations Law Reporter* 624 (1958).

232 LEMLEY'S DECISION: *Aaron v. Cooper*, 163 F.Supp 13 (E.D. Ark. 1958).

235 WILEY: Transcript story, interview with the author, July 14, 1988.

235 DOCKETING THE APPEAL: 3 *Race Relations Law Reporter* 618 (1958). See also "Little Rock Program Postponed 2 1/2 Years by Order of U.S. Court," *Southern School News* 5, no. 1 (July 1958), 7.

236 LITTLE ROCK TO SUPREME COURT: *Aaron v. Cooper*, Petition for Writ of Certiorari, 11. Supreme Court's June 30, 1958, decision quoted, 357 U.S. 566, 567.

236 EIGHTH CIRCUIT QUOTE: *Aaron v. Cooper*, 257 F.2d 33 (8th Cir. 1958), 40.

236 GARDNER QUOTED: Ibid., 41.

236 EIGHTH CIRCUIT STAY: 3 *Race Relations Law Reporter* 649 (1958).

237 SPECIAL TERM CALLED: Anthony Lewis, "Warren Calls High Court for Little Rock Decision, Session Starts Thursday," *New York Times*, August 26, 1958, 1; and Bernard Schwartz, *Super Chief, Earl Warren and His Supreme Court: A Judicial Biography* (New York: New York University Press, 1983), 294.

237 EISENHOWER, ROGERS: Russell Baker, *New York Times*, August 28, 1958: "Eisenhower Hints Desire for 'Slower' Integration," 1; "Transcript of the President's News Conference on Foreign and Domestic Matters," 10; "Text of Rogers Speech to Bar Association on Policy of Integration in U.S.," 12. RUSSELL'S TELEGRAM TO ROGERS: Baker, "Eisenhower," *New York Times*, August 28, 1958, 10; Claude Sitton, "Faubus Program Is Voted," *New York Times*, August 28, 1958.

238 FULBRIGHT POSITION: James William Fulbright with Seth Tillman, *The Price of Power* (New York: Pantheon, 1980), 89, 90, 91, 93. FULBRIGHT'S BRIEF: Baker, *Little Rock*, 10.

238 LDF BRIEF: *Cooper v. Aaron*, August Special Term 1958, Misc. No. 1, Brief for Respondents; Brief of the United States, 7.

239 LITTLE ROCK ARGUMENT: Russell Baker, "Courtroom Hushed as Drama Unfolds," *New York Times*, August 29, 1958, 1; "Excerpts from Oral Arguments Before Supreme Court on Question of Integration," *New York Times*, August 29, 1958, 10.

239 "COSTUMES OF THE WOMEN": Baker, "Courtroom."

239 COURT'S ORDERS: *Aaron v. Cooper*, 358 U.S. 27 (1958).

240 BOARD'S BRIEF: "Text of Petition to High Court by Little Rock Board," *New York Times*, September 9, 1958, 24.

240 LDF BRIEF: *Aaron v. Cooper,* August Special Term 1958, Brief of Respondents, 6, 9.

240 BRENNAN: "Excerpts from Oral Argument Before the Supreme Court on Little Rock School Case," *New York Times,* September 12, 1958, 12.

241 FULL LITTLE ROCK OPINION: Per curiam opinion quoted *Cooper v. Aaron,* 358 U.S. 5. This opinion is published as a footnote to *Cooper v. Aaron,* 358 U.S. 1, 5.

241 QUOTE FROM LITTLE ROCK OPINION: 358 U.S. 1, 4, 16, 17, 18.

241 LITTLE ROCK OPINION ON PRIVATE SCHOOLS: Ibid., 4.

242 POST-DECISION EVENTS: "Where Are They Now?," *Southern School News* 5, no. 7 (January 1959), 14; "Where Are They Now?," *Southern School News* 5, no. 11 (May 1959), 6; "State Supreme Court Upholds School Closing Law Used by Faubus," *Southern School News* 5, no. 11 (May 1959), 6. *Aaron v. McKinley,* 173 F.Supp. 944, aff'd *Faubus v. Aaron,* 361 U.S. 197 (1959); "High Schools Are Reopened at Little Rock," *Southern School News* 6, no. 3 (September 1959), 1; "Three Little Rock School Board Members Recalled in Special Vote," *Southern School News* 5, no. 12 (June 1959), 2; "Federal Tribunal Holds School-Closing Laws Unconstitutional," *Southern School News* 6, no. 1 (July 1959), 8; "Two 'Moderates' Are Re-Elected to Little Rock's School Board," *Southern School News* 6, no. 7 (January 1960), 5; "Three Begin Pupil Placement Procedure After Transfer Plea Denied," *Southern School News* 6, no. 5 (November 1959), 6; "Dollarway," *Southern School News* 6, no. 5 (November 1959), 3; "Dollarway's Statement Is Approved by Federal Judge," *Southern School News* 6, no. 12 (June 1960), 6.

242 1960 STATUS: "Arkansas, Segregation-Desegregation Status," *Southern School News* 6, no. 10 (April 1960), 6; "Dollarway's Statement Is Approved by Federal Judge," *Southern School News* 6, no. 12 (June 1960), 6.

243 My thanks to Terrence J. Roberts for his comments on this section.

CHAPTER 18. TRENCH WARFARE

244 DOLLARWAY: "New Anti-Segregation Lawsuit Starts; First Since Little Rock School Crisis," *Southern School News* 5, no. 9 (March 1959), 3. Carter's cases involved picketing in Savannah; segregation on beaches in Mississippi; a criminal prosecution in North Carolina of two black youths who had been kissed by two white girls; park segregation in Montgomery; schools in Prince Edward County, Virginia; voting in Montgomery; bus segregation in Atlanta; schools in Miami. The Miami, Montgomery, and Virginia cases had all originally been LDF cases. Constance Baker Motley to Thurgood Marshall, October 24, 1960, William Henry Hastie Papers, Harvard Law School Library, box 101, folder 2.

245 THURGOOD TO HASTIE: Unsigned memorandum from Thurgood Marshall to W. H. Hastie, December 10, 1958, Hastie Papers, Harvard Law School Library, box 101, folder 1.

245 GRAVES $1,700: Memorandum, Motley to Marshall, LDF archives.

245 THURGOOD ON COORDINATING CASES: Thurgood Marshall to W. H. Hastie, November 10, 1960, LDF archives.

246 NEW ORLEANS LITIGATION: *Bush v. Orleans Parish School Board*, 187 F.Supp. 42 (E.D. La. 1960), 190 F.Supp. 861 (E.D. La. 1961).

247 WRIGHT'S OPINION: *Bush v. Orleans Parish School Board*, 138 F.Supp. 337 (E.D. La. 1956).

248 RIVES: Jack Bass, *Unlikely Heroes* (New York: Simon & Schuster, 1981), 69, 74.

248 WISDOM: Ibid., 46.

249 LOUISIANA LEGISLATION: The state established "special agencies" to govern parks and schools and withdrew permission to sue them; ordered segregation in public recreation under the "police power" and to protect "the public health, morals and the peace and good order"; required a certificate of good moral character signed by an applicant's high school principal and school superintendent to register at a tax-supported college; suspended the compulsory school attendance law for children ages seven to sixteen in integrated schools; in four separate laws required dismissing public school bus drivers, other school employees, and teachers who belonged to organizations prohibited by state law or who advocated school integration; required New Orleans white schools to remain white and black schools to remain black; prohibited teachers from teaching anyone but members of their own race; designated the state as the only legal defendant in any suit that might contest the school segregation law; and required state consent to be sued in any case concerning that law. Finally, another law prohibited interracial social functions or sports contests and required separate seating at "approved" events; 5 *Race Relations Law Reporter* 857 (1960).

249 GREMILLION: 5 *Race Relations Law Reporter* 668 (1960). The order was stayed a few days later by the court of appeals; 5 *Race Relations Law Reporter* 669 (1960).

249 SCREENING: "Governor Calls Special Session of Legislature," *Southern School News* 7, no. 5 (November 1960), 1; "New Orleans Desegregates Schools; Federal Court Bans State Interference," *Southern School News* 7, no. 6 (December 1960), 1.

249 INTEGRATION BEGINS: Claude Sitton, "Two White Schools in New Orleans Are Integrated," *New York Times*, November 15, 1960, 1.

250 NEW ORLEANS REACTION: Claude Sitton, "2,000 Youths Riot in New Orleans," *New York Times*, November 17, 1960, 1.

250 VIRGINIA: One case after another, in Arlington followed quickly by Norfolk, and then by Fairfax, Newport News, Pulaski County, and Charlottesville, defeated grand and petty segregationist strategems. "Segregation-Desegregation Status," *Southern School News* 6, no. 12 (June 1960), 1.

251 PARKER: *Briggs v. Elliott*, 132 F.Supp. 776 (E.D. S.C. 1955), 777 (emphasis supplied).

251 FRIENDS OF PARKER: Bass, *Unlikely Heroes*, 124.

252 PUPIL ASSIGNMENT LAWS: Jack Greenberg, *Race Relations and American Law* (New York: Columbia University Press, 1959), 386.

253 LOST NORTH CAROLINA CASE: *Carson v. Warlick*, 238 F.2d 724 (4th Cir. 1956), cert. den. 353 U.S. 910 (1957); LOST ALABAMA CASE: *Shuttlesworth v. Birmingham Board of Education*, 162 F.Supp. 372, aff'd 358 U.S. 101 (1958). In the Alabama case, the Supreme Court, in affirming, wrote that in some later case the law might be challenged as applied.

253 MARYLAND CASE: *Slade v. Board of Education of Harford County,* 252 F.2d 291 (4th Cir. 1958); 3 *Race Relations Law Reporter* 173 (1958).

254 NASHVILLE: *Kelley v. Board of Education of Nashville,* 159 F.Supp. 272 (M.D. Tenn. 1958), 3 *Race Relations Law Reporter* 180 (1958). "Nashville School Bombed, Clinton Opening Peaceful," *Southern School News* 4, no. 4 (October 1957), 6.

254 RESISTANCE: See various monthly dockets, 1955–1961, LDF archives; "46 Desegregation Cases Listed in 13 Southern States," *Southern School News* 6, no. 12 (June 1960), 1.

255 ACTIVITIES SUPPLEMENTING LITIGATION: LDF monthly reports, 1954; LDF executive minutes, January 5, 1955.

255 PROGRESS?: "Segregation-Desegregation Status," *Southern School News* 6, no. 12 (June 1960), 1.

CHAPTER 19. VIVID MEMORIES

256 CIRCUMCISED RAPIST: *Georgia v. Ozzie Jones,* 75 S.E. 2d 429 (Ga. 1953).

257 STATE APPEAL: *Jones v. Balkcom, Warden,* 79 S.E. 2d 1 (Ga. 1953).

257 SUPREME COURT DENIAL: *Jones v. Balkcom, Warden,* 347 U.S. 956 (1954).

257 AGAINST THE WALL: Ozzie Jones was executed June 11, 1954.

258 *GROVELAND* IN SUPREME COURT: *Irvin v. State,* 346 U.S. 927 (1954).

258 ILLEGAL EVIDENCE: *Wolf v. Colorado,* 338 U.S. 25 (1949).

258 EXCLUSIONARY RULE: *Mapp v. Ohio,* 367 U.S. 643 (1961).

258 REHEARING IN *GROVELAND* DENIED: *Irvin v. State,* 348 U.S. 915 (1955).

258 COLLINS: Tom Wagy, *Governor LeRoy Collins of Florida: Spokesman for a New South* (University: University of Alabama Press, 1985), 65–68; LeRoy Collins, interviews with the author, February 8 and August 26, 1989.

259 FOLLOWING *GROVELAND:* There were some victories in criminal cases. In 1957 I won *Fikes v. Alabama,* 352 U.S. 191 (1957). Someone had raped the mayor's daughter in Montgomery and the pressure to find the rapist was, of course, overwhelming. Police interrogated Fikes, a mentally ill twenty-seven-year-old black man who had left third grade at age sixteen, keeping him in "protective custody" at the penitentiary, not permitting him to see a lawyer. The Supreme Court reversed, with an opinion that for a time was on the cutting edge of the law of confessions, then overtaken by other Warren Court decisions that expanded constitutional protections.

259 CONRAD'S HORSES: Letter to the author from Julius Chambers, February 21, 1991, in author's possession.

259 MCKISSICK AT UNIVERSITY OF NORTH CAROLINA: *McKissick v. Carmichael,* 187 F.2d 949 (4th Cir. 1951), cert. den. 341 U.S. 951 (1951).

260 DURHAM SCHOOLS: "North Carolina: Stiff Penalty Asked for Bomb Scares; Legal Sparring Continues in Durham," *Southern School News* 5, no. 7 (January 1959), 15.

260 DURHAM ADMINISTRATIVE REMEDY: "Seven Districts End First Month Operation in Comparative Quiet," *Southern School News* 6, no. 4 (October 1959), 13.

260 DURHAM SCHOOL CASE: *Wheeler v. Durham,* 210 F.Supp. 839 (M.D. N.C. 1962).

261 DURHAM OPINION: *Wheeler v. Durham,* 210 F.Supp. 839 (M.D. N.C. 1962).

Some North Carolina black lawyers who had not been part of the *Brown* effort did not agree with our strategy of first building a record of how pupil assignment worked, and in 1955 they attacked the North Carolina pupil placement law head-on and lost. Judge Parker wrote that "we cannot hold that that statute is unconstitutional upon its face and the question as to whether it has been unconstitutionally applied is not before us." See *Carson v. Warlick*, 238 F.2d. 724 (4th Cir. 1956), cert. den. 353 U.S. 910 (1957). In 1958 the Court affirmed a similar Alabama decision, noting, however, that "in some future proceeding it is possible that [the pupil placement law] may be declared unconstitutional in its application." See *Shuttlesworth v. Alabama*, 162 F.Supp. 372, aff'd 358 U.S. 101 (1958). I lost a case in the Fourth Circuit in which the school board had repeatedly assigned children to segregated schools initially, although in theory they could transfer out. *Covington v. Edwards*, 264 F.2d 780 (4th Cir. 1959).

261 NATIONAL GUARD: See folder on National Guard, LDF archives.

261 BOXING AND OTHER CASES: *Dorsey v. State Athletic Commission*, 168 F.Supp. 149 (E.D. La. 1958), aff'd 359 U.S. 533 (1959). Other LDF cases involving public facilities in Louisiana during this period involved buses and the airport in New Orleans (LDF press release, January 17, 1958), buses in Lake Charles, Baton Rouge, and Shreveport (LDF docket, December 1960); cases in Georgia involved the restaurant in the Atlanta County building, the City Hall, the State Capitol, the Atlanta airport, and the Savannah public library (ibid.); in Memphis, we had suits involving public transportation (LDF docket, February 1959), the public library, public parks (including the zoo), and the municipal auditorium (LDF docket, December 1960); in Florida, cases involved Tampa's parks and Miami's buses (LDF docket, January 1957); we had a suit against the restaurant in the Wilmington, Delaware, municipal garage (LDF docket, December 1958) and the Greenville, South Carolina, airport (ibid.); in North Carolina, we had cases against the airport restaurant and a swimming pool in Greensboro (ibid.); in Maryland we sued a movie theater in the public auditorium in Fredericksburg (LDF docket, November 1959).

262 WILMINGTON HOSPITAL: *Eaton v. James Walker Memorial Hospital*, 261 F.2d 521 (4th Cir. 1958), cert. den. 359 U.S. 984 (1959).

262 DENTAL SOCIETY CASE: *Hawkins v. North Carolina Dental Association*, 355 F.2d 718 (4th Cir. 1966).

262 ICE CREAM CASE: *Clyburn v. State*, 247 N.C. 455; 101 S.E. 2d 295 (1958).

263 GREENVILLE, SOUTH CAROLINA, AIRPORT: *Henry v. Greenville Airport Commission*, 175 F.Supp 343 (W.D. S.C. 1959), 279 F.2d 751 (4th Cir. 1960).

263 GREENVILLE SWIMMING POOL: J. Hunter Stokes, "2 New Councilmen Seated, and Debate Begins on Swimming Pool Question," *Greenville Piedmont*, October 8, 1963; James W. Thompson, "Council Would Make Marineland of Swimming Pool," *Greenville Piedmont*, October 23, 1963.

263 ATLANTA AIRPORT CASE: *Coke v. City of Atlanta*, 184 F.Supp. 579 (N.D. Ga. 1960).

263 AN EXAMPLE OF A GOLF COURSE CASE: *Cummings v. City of Charleston*, 288 F.2d 817 (4th Cir. 1961).

263 MEMBERSHIP LIST CASE: *NAACP Legal Defense and Educational Fund v. Committee on Offenses Against the Administration of Justice*, 204 Va. 693; 133 S.E.2d 540 (Va. 1963).

CHAPTER 20. OUT OF THE COURTS AND INTO THE STREETS

267 SIT-INS GENERALLY: Fred Powledge, *Free At Last? The Civil Rights Movement and the People Who Made It* (Boston: Little, Brown, 1991), see chap. 12; Robert Weisbrot, *Freedom Bound: A History of America's Civil Rights Movement* (New York: Norton, 1990), see chap. 2.

267 PRAYER PILGRIMAGE: Taylor Branch, *Parting the Waters: America in the King Years 1954–63* (New York: Simon & Schuster, 1988), 214.

267 EARLY SIT-INS: "Pioneer of Sit-In Movement Remembered," Louis Jolyon West, letter to the editor, *New York Times*, March 15, 1990, 22; "Sit-In Movement Had Origins Outside the South," Ronald Walters, letter to the editor, *New York Times*, April 5, 1990, 28.

270 *Boynton v. Virginia*, 364 U.S. 454 (1960).

271 LAWSON: Henry Hampton and Steve Fayer, *Voices of Freedom: An Oral History of the Civil Rights Movement from the 1950s Through the 1980s* (New York: Bantam, 1990), 54.

271 NOT TO PROTEST: Franklin McCain, interview with the author, July 13, 1993.

271 "LEADERSHIP THEY DISPLAYED": Hampton and Fayer, *Voices of Freedom*, 56.

271 SIT-INS: Weisbrot, *Freedom Bound*, chap. 2; Branch, *Parting the Waters*, chap. 7; David McCullough, *Truman* (New York: Simon & Schuster, 1992), 971.

272 ALABAMA EXPULSIONS: *Dixon v. Alabama State Board of Education*, 294 F.2d 150 (5th Cir. 1961). Judge Frank Johnson upheld the suspension. I argued the appeal; the Fifth Circuit reversed.

272 ELLA BAKER: Franklin McCain, interview with the author, July 13, 1993; Nash quoted, Hampton and Fayer, *Voices of Freedom*, 59; Branch, *Parting the Waters*, 291–92.

272 FUND-RAISING: Franklin McCain, interview with the author, July 13, 1993.

273 RAISING MONEY FOR DEFENSE: LDF executive minutes, April 19, 1960.

274 "SHUFFLING" SAM CASE: *Thompson v. City of Louisville*, 362 U.S. 199 (1960), 206.

274 JUSTICE CLARK COMMENT: Conversation with James M. Nabrit, Jr.

275 SIT-IN CONFERENCE: "Thurgood Marshall Calls Lawyers Conference on Lunch Counter Protest," LDF press release, March 10, 1960; "We Must Defend Them—Thurgood Marshall," LDF press release, March 21, 1960.

276 PREPARING DEFENSES: LDF executive minutes, April 19, 1960.

276 CASES IN VARIOUS CITIES, ETC.: LDF docket, April 1960.

276 JEHOVAH'S WITNESSES CASE: *Marsh v. Alabama*, 326 U.S. 501 (1946).

277 JOHNSON C. SMITH CASES: LDF press release, March 9, 1960.

277 CAMERON VILLAGE: *State v. Forbes*, LDF docket, April 1960.

278 CAMERON VILLAGE VICTORY: "Major Sit-Down Victory Won in Court," LDF press release, April 22, 1960.

279 CATALOG OF CASES: "Report of Jack Greenberg," attached to LDF dockets, 1960.

281 TRANSPORTATION CASE: *Boynton v. Virginia*, 364 U.S. 454 (1960), 459, 462–63.

282 KING'S IMPRISONMENT: David Garrow, *Bearing the Cross: Martin Luther King, Jr., and the Southern Christian Leadership Conference* (New York: Morrow, 1986), 135, 143–49; Branch, *Parting the Waters*, 351–70; letter,

Thurgood Marshall to William G. Nunn, November 4, 1960, LDF archives, LDF dockets, January 19, and May 8, 1961.

283   BOOTLE: Charlayne Hunter Gault, *In My Place* (New York: Vintage, 1992), chaps. 14–16. *Danner v. Holmes* (M.D. Ga. 1960), 191 F.Supp. 394 (Mid. Dist. Ga. 1961), 5 *Race Relations Law Reporter* 1069 (1960).

283   STAY DENIED: *Danner v. Holmes*, 5 *Race Relations Law Reporter* 1089 (1960).

284   UNIVERSITY OF GEORGIA CASE: Ibid., 1069.

CHAPTER 21. NEW CLIENTS, NEW CASES, NEW THEORIES

285   CASE LOAD: "Thurgood Marshall Reports on Legal Defense Fund Activities," LDF press release, January 6, 1961. The cases moving upward were *Garner v. Louisiana*, 368 U.S. 157 (1961); *Avent v. North Carolina*, 373 U.S. 375 (1963), and *Fox and Sampson v. North Carolina*, 378 U.S. 587 (1964).

285   THE OTHER RACE: On CORE generally, see August Meier and Elliot Rudwick, *CORE: A Study in the Civil Rights Movement* (Urbana: University of Illinois Press, 1973).

286   "NO GOOD ACHIEVED": Meier and Rudwick, *CORE*, 35.

286   PREVIOUS LDF TRAVEL CASES: *Morgan v. Virginia*, 328 U.S. 373 (1946), *Whiteside v. Southern Bus Lines*, 177 F.2d 949 (6th Cir. 1949), *Chance v. Lambeth*, 341 U.S. 941 (1951), and *Boynton v. Virginia*, 364 U.S. 454 (1960).

286   JOURNEY REVIVED: Meier and Rudwick, *CORE*, 135.

286   FREEDOM RIDE SCHEDULE: Taylor Branch, *Parting the Waters: America in the King Years, 1954–63* (New York: Simon & Schuster, 1988), 427; James Farmer, *Lay Bare the Heart* (New York: Arbor House, 1985), chap. 17.

287   JOHNSON ENJOINS KLAN AND FREEDOM RIDERS: *United States v. U.S. Klans*, 6 *Race Relations Law Reporter* 528 (M.D. Ala. 1961).

287   OUR OWN CASE: *Lewis v. Southeastern Greyhound Lines*, 199 F.Supp. 210 (M.D. Ala. 1961).

287   CALL FOR "COOLING OFF": Meier and Rudwick, *CORE*, 139; Victor Navasky, *Kennedy Justice* (New York: Atheneum, 1971), 204–5.

287   ARREST THE DEMONSTRATORS: Branch, *Parting the Waters*, 433.

288   LOU'S CASE: *Abernathy v. Alabama*, 380 U.S. 447 (1965).

288   I MEET WITH CORE: LDF executive minutes, June 13, 1961.

288   STATE PROSECUTIONS: Louis Lusky to Grenville Clark, October 26, 1961, in author's possession.

288   THURGOOD TO FARMER: LDF executive minutes, October 25, 1961. Around the same time, on June 9, Connie Motley filed, on behalf of Jackson citizens, *Bailey v. Patterson*, which asked for an injunction against segregation in interstate travel, including at bus, rail, and air terminals. A three-judge court ruled against us; we asked the Supreme Court for an injunction against the freedom rider prosecutions pending appeal. We lost once more in December 1961, on the grounds that Connie's plaintiffs didn't include those who were being prosecuted—although as ordinary citizens of Jackson they faced threat enough. Ultimately, we won *Bailey v. Patterson*, 199 F.Supp 595 (S.D. Miss. 1961), 369 U.S. 31 (1962), 206 F.Supp 67 (S.D. Miss. 1962), 323 F.2d 201 (5th Cir. 1963).

289 CLARK PROPOSAL: LDF executive minutes, May 17, 1960.

289 DEFENDANTS' OPTIONS: It would have been possible to plead nolo contendere or waive appeal and go to jail, which a few did, though most would not.

289 CONSEQUENCES OF FAILING TO MAKE BOND: Louis Lusky to Grenville Clark, October 26, 1961, in author's possession.

290 RESOLUTE: James Farmer to Thurgood Marshall, September 16, 1961; James Nabrit III to Thurgood Marshall, September 21, 1961; and Louis Lusky to Grenville Clark, October 26, 1961, all in author's possession.

290 LOANS TO ME FOR BOND: LDF executive minutes, October 25, 1961.

290 INFORMAL TRUST FOR BOND: LDF executive minutes, February 7, 1962.

290 FINALLY FOUND BONDING COMPANY: LDF executive minutes, October 10, 1963.

290 STILL SEEKING BOND MONEY: LDF executive minutes, January 1964.

290 CASES WON: LDF docket, March 1, 1966.

291 NINETY-THREE CASES: LDF docket, September 27, 1961. That fall we worked on twenty demonstration appeals in state supreme courts in five states. The United States Supreme Court scheduled four LDF demonstration cases. We filed two others there in August. See LDF docket, September–December 1961.

291 CASES: I drove from vacation on the Jersey shore to join Thurgood in arguing a motion before Justice Brennan in his chambers, filed by the New Rochelle, New York, school board to stay integration while it filed a petition for review. As we left, we both agreed we had lost, but then Brennan ruled with us. The Court refused to hear the case. *Taylor v. Board of Education of New Rochelle*, 221 F.Supp. 275 (S.D. N.Y. 1963), 294 F.2d 36 (2d Cir. 1961), cert den. 368 U.S. 940 (1961). *Anderson v. Alabama*, 366 U.S. 208 (1961) (jury case). *Anderson v. Courson*, 203 F.Supp. 806 (M.D. Ga. 1962) (voting case). *Anderson v. Martin*, 375 U.S. 399 (1964) (voting case). *Brazier v. Cherry*, 293 F.2d 401 (5th Cir. 1961), in which the court of appeals for the first time applied state law in federal court to allow damages for the family of a prisoner who had been killed by those guarding him.

291 WILMINGTON GARAGE: Lou Redding argued *Burton v. Wilmington Parking Authority*, 365 U.S. 715 (1961), against a Wilmington parking garage and its tenant, a restaurant. The state supreme court had upheld the restaurant management's exclusion of blacks because state law permitted refusing service to persons who "would be offensive to a major part of . . . customers." The United States Supreme Court reversed because the relationship between the restaurant and the garage supplied the requisite state action. The majority, however, had only five votes.

We had other suits against segregation in places where there was some government ownership or control, such as restaurants in airports and courthouses, public parks and playgrounds, municipal bus lines, libraries, and hospitals.

291 DAVIDSON'S OPINION: *Borders v. Rippy*, 184 F.Supp. 402 (N.D. Tex. 1960).

CHAPTER 22. THE NEW CHIEF COUNSEL

292 LDF INCOME: LDF executive minutes, February 24, 1961; LDF minutes, January 10, 1962; LDF minutes, March 10, 1961.

292 BELL ON GREENBERG: Letter to the Editor, 3 *Civil Liberties Review* 7 (April/May 1976).

293 WILDER: LDF executive minutes, February 24, 1961.

293 NAACP CONCERN ABOUT LDF: NAACP minutes, April 1960. In October the committee once more called for cooperation between the two organizations, NAACP minutes, October 1960.

294 JUANITA MITCHELL: Interview in William Elwood, Civil Rights Lawyers Project, transcriptions of oral interviews, University of Virginia, Charlottesville, 1990.

295 THE SUCCESSION: LDF executive minutes, September 27, 1961.

297 *NEW YORK TIMES:* "NAACP Names a White Counsel," *New York Times,* October 5, 1961.

297 *PITTSBURGH COURIER:* "Thurgood's Successor!" *Pittsburgh Courier,* October 14, 1961; "Liked by NAACP Officials—Greenberg Choice Creating No Stir," *Pittsburgh Courier,* October 21, 1961.

297 *AFRO AMERICAN:* "Greenberg Named as NAACP Counsel," *Afro American,* October 14, 1961.

297 *KANSAS CITY CALL:* "A Good Choice—and a Logical One," *Kansas City Call,* October 13, 1961.

297 HOLLOWELL: "Greenberg Succeeds Marshall as NAACP's Chief Legal Council [sic]," *Atlanta Inquirer,* October 14, 1961.

297 EVELYN CUNNINGHAM: *New York Courier,* October 21, 1961.

297 LAWRENCE BAILEY: "Comment," *Amsterdam News,* October 14, 1961.

297 HICKS: Ibid.

297 CRITICISM THAT APPOINTMENT DISCRIMINATED: Bob has said that he wasn't interested in the job. See Derrick Bell, "An Epistolary Exploration for a Thurgood Marshall Biography," 6 *Harvard Blackletter Journal* 51 (Spring 1989), 54.

298 NAACP ON MY APPOINTMENT: The minutes report, "Sharp comment was made upon Mr. Greenberg's reported interview in the *New York Post* which made pronouncements on the NAACP's policy and procedure." NAACP minutes, October 9 and November 13, 1961.

      The *Post* had referred to me as chief counsel of the NAACP Legal Defense Fund and of the NAACP. What I said in the *Post* was that "legal battles pave the way for social changes and social changes create the atmosphere for legal victories." I added, "I think generally attitudes in both the North and South have gotten very distinctly better." Allan Levine, "New NAACP Counsel Sees a Hard Road" *New York Post,* October 5, 1961.

CHAPTER 23. COMPLETING THE CIRCLE

299 EARLY PROTESTS: David Garrow, *Bearing the Cross: Martin Luther King, Jr., and the Southern Christian Leadership Conference* (New York: Morrow, 1986), 143–49; Taylor Branch, *Parting the Waters: America in the King Years, 1954–63* (New York: Simon & Schuster, 1988), 351–70; Thurgood Marshall to William G. Nunn, November 4, 1960, LDF archives; LDF dockets, January 19, and May 8, 1961.

300 CONGRESSIONAL ATTACKS ON COURT: "Manifesto Protests Court Act" and "'Southern Manifesto' Criticizes Supreme Court," *Southern School News*

2, no. 10 (April 1956), 1–2; C. Herman Pritchett, *Congress versus the Supreme Court, 1957–1960* (Minneapolis: University of Minnesota Press, 1961), 3, 31–35.

302 THURGOOD TO DERRICK BELL: Michael Meltsner, interview with the author, April 7, 1991.

302 ARONSON BEATEN: LDF telegram, September 13, 1966, LDF archives.

302 "USUALLY RELIABLE INFORMANT": FBI memorandum, May 28, 1964, FBI file 105-477-2254; ASSASSINATION THREAT: FBI teletype message, May 13, 1964, FBI file 157-1659.

303 OTHER FBI DOCUMENT: May 17, 1964, FBI file 157-478-3.

303 MOBILE SPEECH: John Will, "Negro Rights Suits Urged By Greenberg" Mobile *Register*, May 18, 1964, copy in FBI file 157-6-61-A.

304 FIRST DEMONSTRATION CASES: *Garner v. Louisiana*, 368 U.S. 157 (1961).

304 MORE CASES: Memorandum, Jack Greenberg to LDF board of directors, March 14, 1962, LDF archives.

304 MID-DECADE: LDF docket, December 13, 1961, and November 1965.

304 NUMBER OF DEMONSTRATORS: LDF minutes, October 14, 1965.

304 ROSTER OF DEMONSTRATOR CLIENTS: LDF minutes, October 11, 1962; mailing by the "Committee of 100," March 30, 1962, in author's possession; "Legal Defense Fund Speeds Aid to Selma Voter Drive," LDF press release, February 3, 1965.

304 DEMONSTRATION CASES: Daniel Halberstam, "Demonstrations Cases from 1955 through 1967," research paper, in author's possession; LOSS FOR KING: *Walker v. City of Birmingham*, 388 U.S. 307 (1967).

304 ONLY THIRTY CASES: LDF docket, March 1966.

304 *Meredith v. Fair*, 306 F.2d 374 (5th Cir. 1962).

304 *Clemson v. Gantt*, 320 F.2d 611 (4th Cir. 1963); AUBURN CASE: *Franklin v. Parker*, 331 F.2d 841 (5th Cir. 1964).

304 SCHOOL CASES: LDF docket, December 13, 1961, and November 1965.

304 COURT WARNS ON "DELIBERATE SPEED": *Turner v. City of Memphis*, 369 U.S. 350 (1962); *Calhoun v. Latimer*, 377 U.S. 263 (1964).

304 TRANSFER CASE: *Goss v. Board of Education of Knoxville*, 373 U.S. 683 (1963).

304 TEACHER CASES: LDF docket, May 1966.

305 EMPLOYMENT CASES: LDF docket, March 1966.

305 R. JESS BROWN: *In the matter of R. Jess Brown*, 346 F.2d 903 (5th Cir. 1965).

305 COHABITATION CASE: *McLaughlin v. Florida*, 379 U.S. 184 (1964).

305 HEALTH CASES: *Simkins v. Moses H. Cone Hospital*, 323 F.2d 959 (4th Cir. 1963). *Cypress v. Newport News General and Nonsectarian Hospital Association*, 375 F.2d 648 (4th Cir. 1967). *Rackley v. Board of Trustees*, 310 F.2d 141 (4th Cir. 1962). Michael Meltsner, "Equality and Health," 115 *University of Pennsylvania Law Review* 22 (1966).

305 MISS HAMILTON: *Hamilton v. Alabama*, 376 U.S. 650 (1964).

305 REDUCING SOUTHERN REPRESENTATION: *Lampkin v. Connor*, 360 F.2d 505 (D.C. Cir. 1966).

305 ANTITRUST IN HOUSING: *Bratcher v. Akron Board of Realtors*, 381 F.2d 723 (6th Cir. 1967); "Trenton and Mercer County White Realtors Charged with Conspiracy," LDF press release, June 22, 1965; *Lavelle v. Pittsburgh Multilist*, an unreported LDF case settled in 1966.

307 FIRST SIT-IN CASES: *Garner v. Louisiana*, *Briscoe v. Louisiana*, and *Hoston v. Louisiana*, 368 U.S. 157 (1961).

308   ORAL ARGUMENT: *Garner v. Louisiana,* Oral Argument, Supreme Court No. 26, October Term 1961, 3.

308   *GARNER* DECIDED, DOUGLAS QUOTED: 368 U.S. 157 (1961), 181.

308   NEXT ROUND OF DEMONSTRATION CASES: *Peterson v. City of Greenville,* 373 U.S. 244 (1963); *Gober v. City of Birmingham,* 373 U.S. 374 (1963); *Avent v. North Carolina,* 373 U.S. 375 (1963); *Lombard v. Louisiana,* 373 U.S. 267; *Shuttlesworth v. City of Birmingham,* 373 U.S. 262 (1963). Jim Nabrit III at the same time argued a case representing black young men who had been convicted of unlawful assembly for playing basketball in a white park, *Wright v. Georgia,* 373 U.S. 284 (1963).

309   RAUH'S CASE: *Griffin v. Maryland,* 378 U.S. 130 (1964).

309   EARLIER LOSS: The "ice cream case," *Clyburn v. State,* 247 N.C. 455; 101 S.E. 2d 295 (1958).

309   "LAID HANDS UPON": *Black's Law Dictionary,* 3d ed. (St. Paul, Minn.: West, 1933), 1199.

310   COX'S BRIEF: *Avent v. North Carolina,* Brief of the United States, Supreme Court No. 11, October Term 1962, 42. For more on Cox and the sit-ins, see Victor Navasky, *Kennedy Justice* (New York: Atheneum, 1971), 289–93.

310   *AVENT: Avent v. North Carolina,* Oral Argument, 6.

311   SOUTH CAROLINA CASE: *Peterson v. City of Greenville,* 373 U.S. 244 (1963), 248.

311   BIRMINGHAM CASE: *Gober v. City of Birmingham,* 373 U.S. 374 (1963). The Court also reversed Fred Shuttlesworth's conviction for persuading Gober to demonstrate. Since Gober was innocent there could be no conviction for having urged him to do what he did, *Shuttlesworth v. City of Birmingham,* 373 U.S. 262 (1963).

311   HARLAN: *Peterson v. City of Greenville,* 373 U.S. 244 (1963), 250.

311   SOUTH CAROLINA CASE: *Bouie v. City of Columbia,* 378 U.S. 347 (1964).

311   MOTLEY AND PERRY ARGUE: *Barr v. City of Columbia,* 378 U.S. 146 (1964).

311   TOILETS: *Robinson v. Florida,* 378 U.S. 153 (1964).

311   MARYLAND CASE: *Bell v. Maryland,* 378 U.S. 226 (1964), 286.

312   POWELL'S SECTION: Appendix to Brief for Petitioners, *Bell v. Maryland,* Supreme Court No. 12, October Term 1963.

312   COMPARATIVE LAW ARGUMENT: *Rochin v. California* supported an argument to the effect that the Fourteenth Amendment deals with "personal immunities 'so rooted in the traditions and conscience of our people as to be ranked as fundamental' . . . or are 'implicit in the concept of ordered liberty,'" 342 U.S. 165 (1952), 196, quoting Cardozo in *Snyder v. Massachusetts,* 291 U.S. 97 (1934), 105, and *Palko v. Connecticut,* 302 U.S. 319 (1937), 325.

312   SIT-IN ARGUMENTS: We also argued that the state trespass laws made it a crime to enter property when told to stay out, while defendants had entered first and were told to leave afterward. Such a law, applied in these circumstances, we claimed, was unconstitutionally vague, did not give fair warning and denied due process of law. We didn't have much faith in that argument, because the state courts had interpreted their laws otherwise. Besides, if we won on that ground it wouldn't help where laws did make it a crime to refuse to leave when told to do so after entry. States could readily rewrite their laws for the next round of demonstrations.

312   "POISONED A WELL": *Bell v. Maryland,* Oral Argument, Supreme Court No.

12, October Term 1963, 123, 125.

312 COURT INVITES SOLICITOR: Bernard Schwartz, *Super Chief* (New York: New York University Press, 1983), 509.

313 WHITE MEMO: Lee White to Lyndon Johnson, December 19, 1963, LBJ Library, Austin, Tex.

313 MARSHALL, KENNEDY, AND COX: Burke Marshall, interview with author, June 26, 1992.

314 *BELL* DECIDED: The Court also reversed one of the South Carolina cases, *Barr*, because there was no evidence of disturbance. It reversed the other South Carolina case, *Bouie*, because the statute referred only to entering after exclusion, not refusal to leave after unopposed entry. Black, Harlan, and White dissented, on the grounds that the trespass law long had been understood to prohibit remaining after having been asked to leave. It reversed *Robinson*, the Florida case, because a health regulation required segregated toilets—enough state action.

314 SIX OTHERS: The cases were: *Green v. Virginia*, 378 U.S. 550 (1964); *Harris v. Virginia*, 378 U.S. 552 (1964); *Williams v. North Carolina*, 378 U.S. 548 (1964); *Fox v. North Carolina*, 378 U.S. 587 (1964); *Mitchell v. City of Charleston*, 378 U.S. 551 (1964); and *Drews v. Maryland*, 378 U.S. 547 (1964). *Bell v. Maryland*, 378 U.S. 226 (1964).

315 SIMILAR DISCRETION: *Shuttlesworth v. City of Birmingham*, 376 U.S. 339 (1964).

315 PICKRICK CASE: *Willis v. Pickrick Restaurant*, 231 F.Supp. 396 (N.D. Ga. 1964). The government also argued for the validity of the act in another case which went to the Supreme Court, *Heart of Atlanta Motel v. United States*, 379 U.S. 241 (1964).

315 OLLIE'S RESTAURANT CASE: *Ollie McClung v. Katzenbach*, 379 U.S. 294 (1964).

316 SOUTH CAROLINA PARKS: LDF docket, March 1966.

316 LAST SIT-IN BRIEF: *Hamm v. City of Rock Hill*, Brief of Petitioners, Supreme Court No. 2, October Term 1964, 23. The big obstacle was a highly technical law, the federal "savings" statute. Because Congress had disapproved of the abatement doctrine well before the sit-in cases, it passed the "savings" law, which said that "the repeal of any statute shall not have the effect to release or extinguish any penalty . . . incurred under such statute, unless the repealing Act shall so expressly provide." In other words, if the Civil Rights Act "repealed" state trespass laws, abatement would not apply unless the act "so expressly provide[d]." Charlie wove together a stunning argument that the Civil Rights Act invalidated the convictions not by repealing trespass laws, but by creating a new right.

316 *HAMM* DECISION: *Hamm v. City of Rock Hill* 379 U.S. 306 (1964). The Court held that the "savings" statute applied only to repeals; the Civil Rights Act had transformed the crime of trespass into a right to service.

317 COURT'S MOTIVATION: Schwartz, *Super Chief*, 553.

CHAPTER 24. JIM CROW CRUSHED IN MISSISSIPPI

318 KENNARD: *Kennard v. State of Mississippi*, 242 Miss. 691, 128 So.2d 572 (1961), cert. den. 368 U.S. 869 (1961).

319 MEREDITH'S LETTER: Dated January 29, 1961, quoted in James Meredith,

Three Years in Mississippi (Bloomington: Indiana University Press, 1966), 56.

319 MEREDITH NOT REJECTED BECAUSE HE WAS BLACK: *Meredith v. Fair*, 199 F.Supp. 754 (S.D. Miss. 1961).

320 WISDOM'S OPINION: *Meredith v. Fair*, 298 F.2d 696 (5th Cir. 1962), 701, 703.

320 MIZE: *Meredith v. Fair*, 202 F.Supp. 224 (S.D. Miss. 1962).

320 MAJORITY ORDERS SPEED, TUTTLE DISSENTS: *Meredith v. Fair*, 305 F.2d 341 (5th Cir. 1962).

320 MEREDITH ARRESTED: "Fact Sheet on University of Mississippi Desegregation Suit," LDF press release, September 17, 1962. This press release contains a chronology of the case to that date.

320 "QUINTUS FABIUS MAXIMUS": *Webster's New Biographical Dictionary* (Springfield, Mass.: Merriam, 1988). Hence the term "Fabian."

320 WISDOM REVIEWED THE PRETEXTS: Long delays preceded the registrar's reply to Meredith's letters. Meredith had been rejected because Jackson State was unaccredited. But he also had earned credits while in the air force from Washburn in Kansas and the University of Maryland, both of which were accredited. Besides, Jackson State was run by the same trustees as Ole Miss, and, by the time of the appeal, it was accredited. The alumni recommendation requirement was discriminatory—Ole Miss had no black alumni. He reviewed Mize's delays, repeated postponements because of defense counsel's illness, and numerous other obstacles that caused Meredith to lose the chance to attend two summer terms and two regular terms of 1961 and 1962. He rejected Mississippi's defense that Meredith had committed a crime by registering to vote in Jackson. *Meredith v. Fair*, 305 F.2d 343 (5th Cir. 1962), 344–45, 358.

321 CAMERON'S STAY: *Meredith v. Fair*, 7 *Race Relations Law Reporter* 741 (5th Cir. 1962).

321 COURT OF APPEALS ORDER: *Meredith v. Fair*, 306 F.2d 374 (5th Cir. 1962).

321 CAMERON REINSTATES: For back and forth between Cameron and other members of the Fifth Circuit, see 7 *Race Relations Law Reporter* 742 et seq. (5th Cir. 1962).

321 TRUSTEES DENY POWER: Trustees' order reproduced, *Meredith v. Fair*, 7 *Race Relations Law Reporter* 745 (1962).

321 INJUNCTION: *Meredith v. Fair*, 83 S. Ct. 10 (1962).

321 MIZE TO COX: Constance Baker Motley, interview with the author; *Meredith v. Fair*, 7 *Race Relations Law Reporter* 746 (S.D. Miss. 1962).

322 PROCLAMATION: Reproduced in *Meredith v. Fair*, 7 *Race Relations Law Reporter* 748 (1962).

322 STATE COURT INJUNCTION: 7 *Race Relations Law Reporter* 748–49 (Miss. 1962).

322 COURT OF APPEALS ENJOINS S.B. 1501: The bill is reproduced in 7 *Race Relations Law Reporter* 750 (1962); *Meredith v. Fair*, 7 *Race Relations Law Reporter* 752 (5th Cir. 1962).

322 BOARD INVESTS BARNETT: Resolution reproduced in *Meredith v. Fair*, 7 *Race Relations Law Reporter* 753 (1962).

323 ADMINISTRATION APPROACH: Victor Navasky, *Kennedy Justice* (New York: Atheneum, 1971), 185–92.

323 REBUFFED: See Meredith, *Three Years*, chap. 7.

323 PRESS REACTION: Claude Sitton, "Negro Rejected at Mississippi U.; U.S. Seeks Writs," *New York Times*, September 21, 1962; Hedrick Smith, "3

Acquitted of Contempt in Mississippi U. Dispute," *New York Times*, September 22, 1962; Claude Sitton, "New Crisis Faces Mississippi U.: U.S. Appeals 3 Contempt Cases," *New York Times*, September 23, 1962.

324 STUDENTS SWAMP MEREDITH: Meredith, *Three Years*, 199.

324 BARNETT'S SEPTEMBER 24 PROCLAMATION: 7 *Race Relations Law Reporter* 754 (1962).

324 EN BANC HEARING: "Transcript of Hearing, *Meredith v. Fair*, September 24, 1962," LDF archives.

324 REGISTER MEREDITH: "U. of Mississippi Bows and Agrees to Accept Negro," *New York Times*, September 25, 1962.

325 BARNETT AND ADMINISTRATION EXCHANGES: Navasky, *Kennedy Justice*, chap. 4; all the relevant Justice Department and presidential phone calls are transcribed or summarized here.

325 COURT OF APPEALS RESTRAINS BARNETT: *Meredith v. Fair*, 7 *Race Relations Law Reporter* 756 (5th Cir. 1962).

325 BARNETT'S NEW PROCLAMATION: 7 *Race Relations Law Reporter* 749 (1962).

325 MEREDITH REJECTED: Claude Sitton, "Meredith Rebuffed Again Despite Restraining Order," *New York Times*, September 26, 1962.

325 ORDER TO SHOW CAUSE: Ibid.

326 OPEN DEFIANCE: Anthony Lewis, "U.S., to Avert Violence, Calls Off New Effort to Enroll Meredith; Sends Hundreds More Marshalls," *New York Times*, September 28, 1962.

326 "COST IN HUMAN LIFE": Walter Lord, *The Past That Would Not Die* (New York: Harper and Row, 1965), 169.

326 DRAW THEIR GUNS: Ibid.

326 "EMPLOY THAT POWER": *New York Times*, September 28, 1962.

327 TUTTLE TO SATTERFIELD: "Transcript of Hearing, *Meredith v. Fair*, September 28, 1962," LDF archives.

327 TUTTLE, SATTERFIELD ON EXCEPTIONS: Ibid.

328 RIVES AND SATTERFIELD: Ibid.

329 MOTION DENIED: Ibid.

329 "ADEQUATE SERVICE": Ibid.

329 BARNETT HELD IN CONTEMPT: *Meredith v. Fair*, 7 *Race Relations Law Reporter* 761 (5th Cir. 1962).

329 BARNETT CHANGES MIND: Navasky, *Kennedy Justice*, chap. 4.

330 FEDERAL FORCES: President's proclamation and executive order, 7 *Race Relations Law Reporter* 764 (1964); "Federal Troops Massing at a Base Near Memphis," *New York Times*, September 30, 1962.

330 MARSHALS FIRE: Lord, *The Past That Would Not Die*, chap. 9.

331 MEREDITH REGISTERS: Fred Powledge, *Free at Last? The Civil Rights Movement and the People Who Made It* (Boston: Little, Brown, 1991), 437–42.

331 DOAR: Henry Hampton and Steve Fayer, eds., *Voices of Freedom: An Oral History of the Civil Rights Movement from the 1950s Through the 1980s* (New York: Bantam, 1990), 119–20.

332 MEREDITH ON HIS MISSION: Meredith, *Three Years*, 243.

332 BARNETT'S CONTEMPT CASE: *United States v. Ross Barnett*, 376 U.S. 681 (1964).

332 COURT OF APPEALS ON BARNETT: *United States v. Ross Barnett*, 346 F.2d 99 (5th Cir. 1965).

CHAPTER 25. FREEDOM RIDES, FREEDOM SUMMER, FIGHTING AMONG FREEDOM FIGHTERS

333 CONSOLIDATION DENIED: LDF docket, September 1963.

333 FREEDOM RIDE CASES DECIDED: *Abernathy v. Alabama*, 380 U.S. 447 (1965).

334 LOU'S ARGUMENT: *Abernathy v. Alabama*, Oral Argument, Supreme Court No. 9, October Term 1964. Audio tape, in author's possession.

334 FREEDOM RIDER CONVICTIONS REVERSED: *Thomas v. Mississippi*, 380 U.S. 524 (1965).

334 GASTON MOTEL: A. G. Gaston, a black insurance executive who owned the motel, became an LDF board member and contributor.

334 IN MARTIN'S ROOM: Charles Jones, interview with the author, March 5, 1990.

334 CONNOR WILL PICKET TO JAIL: Alan F. Westin and Barry Mahoney, *The Trial of Martin Luther King* (New York: Crowell, 1974), 66.

335 KING STATEMENT: Ibid., 79.

335 LEWIS CASE: *United States v. United Mine Workers of America*, 330 U.S. 258 (1947).

335 MORE RECENT CASE: *In re Green*, 369 U.S. 689 (1962).

336 RESEARCHING THE LAW: Clark, tall, thin, and restless, was also a Columbia Law School graduate and a student in Kenneth Clark's psychology class at City College when I lectured there once. Kenneth had persuaded him to become a psychologist, but my visit influenced him to change direction and go to law school. He now is a professor at Catholic University Law School.

336 JENKINS HOLDS IN CONTEMPT: *City of Birmingham v. Walker*, 8 *Race Relations Law Reporter* 439 (1963).

337 HARLAN JOINS MAJORITY: Bernard Schwartz with Stephan Lesher, *Inside the Supreme Court* (Garden City, N.Y.: Doubleday, 1983), 241.

337 STEWART'S OPINION: *Walker v. Birmingham*, 388 U.S. 307 (1967), 320.

337 TEST CASE: Chauncey Eskridge to Jack Greenberg, August 8, 1967, in author's possession. The test case was *Shuttlesworth v. City of Birmingham*, 394 U.S. 174 (1969).

338 KENNEDY SPEECH: Tom Wicker, "Kennedy, in South, Hails Negro Drive for Civil Rights," *New York Times*, May 19, 1963.

338 TROOPS: "Exchange of Messages on Troop Disposition," 8 *Race Relations Law Reporter* 442 (1963); "Troops Dispatched," *New York Times*, May 13, 1963; *New York Times*, May 28, 1963.

338 GROOMS ORDERS ADMISSION: Claude Sitton, "Alabama U. Told to Admit Negroes," *New York Times*, May 22, 1963; *Lucy v. Adams*, 8 *Race Relations Law Reporter* 452 (1963).

338 "PREPARATORY": Jack Raymond, "Alabamian Sues on Use of Troops," *New York Times*, May 19 1963; *State of Alabama v. United States*, 373 U.S. 545 (1963).

339 LYNNE STATEMENT: *United States v. George Wallace*, 8 *Race Relations Law Reporter* 453 (N.D. Ala. 1963), 455.

339 FIELDS: FBI memorandum, "National States Rights Party Racial Matters," FBI file 105-66233-100.

339 DEEMED NECESSARY: Presidential proclamation no. 3542, June 11, 1963, 8 *Race Relations Law Reporter* 455 (1963); president's executive order,

June 11, 1963, 8 *Race Relations Law Reporter* 456 (1963).

339 WALLACE REPLIED: Governor's proclamation, June 11, 1963, 8 *Race Relations Law Reporter* 457 (1963).

339 ALLGOOD: *Woods v. Wright,* 8 *Race Relations Law Reporter* 444 (N.D. Ala. 1963), 445.

339 TUTTLE ORDER: *Woods v. Wright,* 8 *Race Relations Law Reporter* 445 (5th Cir. 1963).

340 APPEALABLE: *Woods v. Wright,* 334 F.2d 369 (5th Cir. 1964).

340 EXCHANGE AT SCHOOLHOUSE DOOR: Claude Sitton and Tom Wicker, "Alabama Admits Negro Students; Wallace Bows to Federal Force; Kennedy Sees Moral Crisis in U.S.," *New York Times,* June 12, 1963.

340 FREEDOM SUMMER: William McCord, *Mississippi: The Long, Hot Summer* (New York: Norton, 1965); and *Report of the NAACP Legal Defense and Educational Fund,* II, no. 2 (October–November, 1964), LDF archives.

341 MISSISSIPPI DOCKET: October 22, 1964, LDF archives. The traffic cases included charges of drunken and reckless driving; improper driver's license, registration, and inspection stickers; passing on the right; failure to signal when turning; speeding and passing a stop sign. The free expression cases involved handbills, urging people to vote, walking to the courthouse to vote, carrying a sign without a permit, and obstructing the sidewalk while picketing. The more serious cases involved selling cotton subject to a landlord's lien, bigamy, stealing electricity, carrying a concealed weapon, arson, contributing to the delinquency of a minor, passing bad checks, and peeping into a white woman's window.

342 KINDS OF CASES: Ibid.

342 CASES IN SOUTH: LDF docket, March, 1966.

342 CLARK TO HALL: Steve Ralston, interview with author, April 20, 1990; Tony Amsterdam, interview with author, May 13, 1991.

343 LONG NIGHTS: Mel Zarr, interview with author, May 13, 1991.

344 COUNSEL IN MISDEMEANOR CASES: *Harvey v. Mississippi,* 340 F.2d 264 (5th Cir. 1965).

344 INCENTIVE TO CONVICT: *Hulett v. Julian,* 250 F.Supp. 208 (M.D. Ala. 1966), enforced a long ignored Supreme Court decision, *Tumey v. Ohio,* 273 U.S. 510 (1926), which had held such a practice unconstitutional. Another case, *Bennett v. Cottingham,* 393 U.S. 317 (1969), struck down a similar Alabama policy of paying sheriffs according to the number of arrests they made.

344 ALABAMA CASES: LDF docket, September 1965.

344 FLORIDA CASES: Ibid.

344 AMERICUS, GEORGIA: Ibid.

344 GEORGIA CASES: LDF docket, November 1965.

345 BILOXI: *Mason v. Biloxi,* 385 U.S. 370 (1966); "Supreme Court Gives Negroes Access to Public Facilities Made with Federal, State & Local Cash," LDF press release, December 16, 1966.

345 WATTS: "Legal Defense Fund Intervenes in Behalf of 4,000 Watts Rioters," LDF press release, October 8, 1965. In Maryland we tackled another aspect of criminal law administration. Following the shooting of two police officers, and the death of one of them, police conducted more than three hundred warrantless searches, breaking into homes of black Baltimore citizens, looking for the two suspects, the Veney brothers,

who were suspected of having committed the crime. Jim Nabrit and Tony Amsterdam got an injunction prohibiting the police break-ins. *Lankford v. Schmidt*, 364 F.2d 197 (4th Cir. 1966).

345   "IMPROVIDENTLY GRANTED": *Diamond v. Louisiana*, 376 U.S. 201 (1964).

345   RUNNING DOWN AISLE: *Ford v. Tennessee*, 377 U.S. 994 (1964).

345   CHURCH CASE: *Jones v. Georgia*, 379 U.S. 945 (1964).

346   CRITERIA FOR TAKING CASES: LDF minutes, October 8, 1964.

348   LDF REPRESENTS SCLC: Andrew Young, interview with the author, February 29 and March 1, 1992. See also FBI memos that discuss meetings where SCLC and LDF discussed cooperation, FBI files 100-11180 and 100-73250.

348   OUT-OF-STATE LAWYER: Mel Leventhal, interview with the author, April 2, 1990. I asked one of our Mississippi lawyers to get a transcript of the statement but the stenographer refused to transcribe it.

348   COLEMAN'S CASE: *Anderson v. Cox*, 401 F.2d 241 (5th Cir. 1968); LDF minutes, May 9, 1968.

348   REPRESENTING DEMONSTRATORS: Mississippi docket, n.d. (late 1960s), LDF archives.

349   WORK WITH VOLUNTEERS: LDF minutes, April 14, 1964; "Legal Defense Fund Holds 25th Anniversary Session," LDF press release, June 5, 1964.

349   FLORIDA LAWYERS: Statement of Gustav Heningburg, LDF press release, April 20, 1964.

349   TOBY'S CASE: LDF executive minutes, December 10, 1964.

350   ON THE GUILD: Ann Fagan Ginger and Eugen M. Tobin, eds., *The National Lawyers Guild: From Roosevelt Through Reagan* (Philadelphia: Temple University Press, 1988), 34–35, 84–85.

350   THURGOOD ON THE GUILD: Warren Weaver, Jr., "Marshall's Standing as Lawyer Is Challenged in Senate Hearings," *New York Times*, August 18, 1962; Thurgood Marshall, interview with author, April 5, 1990.

350   DECLINED: Marshall to Simon Schachter, May 27, 1954, LDF archives.

350   "NO REPLY": Royal France to Marshall, March 1, 1956, LDF archives.

350   "COMMIES": Thurgood Marshall, interview with the author, April 5, 1990.

350   REFUSAL TO REPRESENT: LDF minutes, March 9, 1954; Herbert Brownell, Jr., "Address," in *Annual Report of the American Bar Association*, 78 (Baltimore: Lord Baltimore, 1953), 334–40.

350   DROPPED CASE: Ginger and Tobin, *National Lawyers Guild*, 136–60.

351   JOHN LEWIS TO WALTER WHITE: April 28, 1954, LDF archives.

351   NOT GET INVOLVED: LDF minutes, April 11, 1963.

351   VIEW OF BOARD: LDF executive minutes, May 14, 1964.

352   REMOVAL DECISIONS: *Georgia v. Rachel*, 384 U.S. 780 (1966). See also *City of Greenwood v. Peacock*, 384 U.S. 808 (1966).

352   EVERY CRIMINAL TRIAL: Len Holt, *The Summer That Didn't End: The Story of the Mississippi Civil Rights Project of 1964* (New York: Da Capo, 1992), 87–94.

353   DANVILLE MEMORIAL HOSPITAL: *New York Guild Lawyer*, November 1962.

CHAPTER 26. FROM SELMA TO MONTGOMERY

354   SELMA TO NEW ORLEANS: Charles Jones, interview with author, July 19, 1993.

355   ORIGINS OF MARCH: Andrew Young, interview with author, February 29,

1992; Leroy Clark, interview with author, July 22, 1993; personal recollection.

355 KING MEETS WITH JOHNSON: Charles Mohr, "Johnson, Dr. King Confer on Rights," *New York Times*, March 6, 1965; David Garrow, *Bearing the Cross: Martin Luther King, Jr., and the Southern Christian Leadership Conference* (New York: Morrow, 1986), 395.

355 POLICE STOP MARCH: Garrow, *Bearing the Cross*, 397–400; Roy Reed, "Alabama Police Use Gas and Clubs to Rout Negroes," *New York Times*, March 8, 1965.

356 JOHNSON ENJOINS MARCH: *Williams v. Wallace*, 10 *Race Relations Law Reporter* 218 (1965).

356 THREE HUNDRED YEARS: Garrow, *Bearing the Cross*, 402.

357 TROOPERS' LINES: Leroy Collins, interview with author, February 8, 1989; Jack Bass, *Taming the Storm* (New York: Doubleday, 1993), 241.

357 WIRETAPPED: FBI memorandum regarding registrars of voters, Dallas County, Alabama, FBI file 44-12831-520. The document, incidentally, is garbled at points and attributes to me statements that I couldn't have made, such as, "We must by our witness and our own bodies and souls, immobilize the brutality of this police force by absolving—by exposing it and everything else let them be glutted by their own barbarianism [sic]." I never talk like that; perhaps another participant's words were attributed to me. David Garrow in *Bearing the Cross*, p. 403, refers to this FBI document and writes: "Greenberg recommended against any march, and told King that Johnson's order would probably not be upheld if they appealed it." Nowhere does the document say that I "recommended against any march," or words to that effect. I did say that the order would not be upheld. Advice to march or not to march would have been inconsonant with my relationship with Martin Luther King, Jr., and other movement leaders.

357 CONFERENCE CALL: Ibid. See also Garrow, *Bearing the Cross*, 403–5.

358 MARCH ENDS IN PRAYER: Roy Reed, "Dr. King Leads March at Selma; State Police End It Peaceably Under a U.S.-Arranged Accord," *New York Times*, March 10, 1965; Garrow, *Bearing the Cross*, 404.

358 KING IN CONTEMPT: Ben A. Franklin, "Dr. King Says He Did Not Intend March to Montgomery Tuesday," *New York Times*, March 12, 1965.

358 MARTIN BETRAYED: Ibid.

358 NONVIOLENCE: Jack Bass, *Taming the Storm* (New York: Doubleday, 1993), 247.

358 JOHNSON, "BETTER EFFORT": Ibid., 248.

359 MARTIN-COLLINS CONVERSATION: Ibid., 242.

359 NO FURTHER: Ben A. Franklin, "Dr. King Says He Did Not Intend March to Montgomery Tuesday," *New York Times*, March 12, 1965.

359 GREENBERG-JONES CONVERSATION: FBI wiretap, Garrow FOIA request, Clarence Jones, box 14, NY 100-73250, vol. 4, New York Public Library.

359 LUBELL TO HIS WIFE: Ibid.

359 BOMB IN WINDOW: Ben A. Franklin, "Use of Gas on Selma Marchers Called Justified by FBI Agent," *New York Times*, March 13, 1965.

359 "MY PROPERTY": Conversation with Jim Nabrit III, who overheard the remark.

360 JOHNSON AND DOAR: Franklin, "Use of Gas"; Andrew Young, interview with author, February 29, 1992.

360   JOHNSON SPEECH: Tom Wicker, "Johnson Pledges Vote for All; Calls Selma
      'American Tragedy'; Urges Wallace to Support Him," *New York Times*,
      March 14, 1965; "Transcript of the Johnson Address on Voting Rights to
      Joint Session of Congress," *New York Times*, March 16, 1965.
360   PLAN: *Williams v. Wallace*, 10 *Race Relations Law Reporter* 229 (1965).
361   "WANDERING": Ben A. Franklin, "5-Day March Plan Is Given to Court,"
      New York Times, March 17, 1965.
361   MARCH PROCEEDS: *Williams v. Wallace*, 10 *Race Relations Law Reporter*
      230 (1965); Fendall W. Yerxa, "Johnson Calls Up Troops, Deplores Wal-
      lace's Acts; Alabama March on Today," *New York Times*, March 21, 1965.
361   MURDER OF VIOLA LIUZZO: Paul L. Montgomery, "Woman Is Shot to Death
      on Lowndes County Road," *New York Times*, March 26, 1965.

CHAPTER 27. LDF GROWS AS AN INSTITUTION

365   "END OF THE ROAD": This is consistent with Thurgood's recently released
      Columbia Oral History (interview with Ed Edwin, June 7, 1977) in which
      he recalls that Johnson didn't promise him anything.
366   CONNIE TO THE SENATE: LDF executive minutes, February 13, 1964.
366   CONNIE BOROUGH PRESIDENT, JUDGE: LDF executive minutes, March 31,
      1965; Howard W. French, "Guiding Wedtech Trial, a Sure Hand," *New
      York Times*, August 7, 1988.
366   PENSION PLAN: LDF executive minutes, May 14, 1964.
366   STAFF: LDF dockets, April 1974 and February 1975.
367   LDF FINANCES: LDF minutes, October 21, 1965; LDF financial statements,
      various months and years.
367   1970 INCOME: LDF financial statement, December 1970.
367   1975 AND LATER INCOME: LDF financial statement, December 1975; LDF
      minutes, January 27, 1976; LDF minutes, January 27, 1981. The MacArthur
      Foundation prepaid a five-year grant for law school scholarships. In 1980
      pwe received $1.5 million in attorneys fees and expenses from more than
      sixty cases.
         I suggested in 1976 that we might solicit government funding for cer-
      tain programs from the Carter administration and still keep our indepen-
      dence. The board decided that we could solicit government support for
      nonlitigation programs, particularly Earl Warren Legal Training Program
      scholarships; LDF minutes, November 30, 1976, and June 28, 1977. But
      we never succeeded, possibly because we had an adversarial relationship
      with the administration on other issues.
367   CLARK PROPOSAL: LDF executive minutes, April 16, 1964.
367   COMMITTEE OF 100: Some of the more famous Committee of 100 members
      included Leonard Bernstein, Van Wyck Brooks, Ralph Bunche, Grenville
      Clark, James Bryant Conant, Ralph Ellison, John Hope Franklin, Frank
      Graham, Herbert Lehman, Archibald MacLeish, Reinhold Niebuhr, Carl
      Rowan, Lillian Smith, Norman Thomas, and Bruno Walter. Most had lit-
      tle or nothing to do with LDF activities, but gave us visibility and assured
      contributors they were in good company.
         Committee of 100 appeal letters included those in support of freedom
      riders, February 6 and March 14, 1962; Martin Luther King, Jr., and
      Albany, Georgia, protestors, March 23 and 30, 1962; Clyde Kennard,

December 3, 1962. The Committee sent out a story on the mayor of Birmingham's cancellation of surplus food distribution, April 11, 1962, and a letter about the case of a black auto accident victim, whom a white ambulance refused to carry. See, "Report: The NAACP Legal Defense and Educational Fund," Spring 1962. The Committee distributed an Anthony Lewis story that reported that LDF had more cases in the Supreme Court than any law office other than the government. Anthony Lewis, "NAACP Fund Piling Up Suits," *New York Times,* June 18, 1962.

367 INCOME: LDF comparative income statement, November 1963.

367 CONTRIBUTORS: LDF minutes, January 14, 1965.

368 ABEL ESTATE: LDF executive minutes, December 9, 1965; LDF minutes, October 21, 1975.

368 FUND-RAISING: LDF executive minutes, October 25, 1961; LDF executive minutes, February 7, 1962; "Legal Defense Fund Gains Greater Boston Committee," LDF press release, April 20, 1964; LDF executive minutes, May 13, 1965; LDF executive minutes, September 12, 1968; LDF executive minutes, June 9, 1966; LDF executive minutes, February 9, March 16, and September 14, 1967; "Star Athletes Form National Body to Aid Rights Movement," LDF press release, January 23, 1967; "Wealthy Negroes Pledge One Million Dollars to 'Rights Lawyers,'" LDF press release, March 20, 1967.

Boston and Washington raised about $100,000 and $25,000, respectively; LDF executive minutes, April 21, 1966. The San Francisco Foundation gave $100,000 to open an office there; LDF executive minutes, October 19, 1967, and October 19, 1968.

The Prince Hall Masons and the Shriners continued to give over $20,000 per year many lodges contributing parts of the total; "New York Masons Give $1,250 to Legal Defense and Educational Fund," LDF press release, June 13, 1962; see also LDF financial statements, various dates. The Links, a black women's organization gave $75,000 over three years; "Top Links Attend Rights Seminar in New York City," LDF press release, July 22, 1964. Another black women's group, Jack and Jill's Queens, New York chapter, gave $2,000; "Jack & Jill Assist Legal Defense Fund," LDF press release, February 20, 1965. To receive this money I attended a fashion show in Queens, where designers paraded the latest fashions in hats. The black National Conference of State Teacher's Associations (NACOSTA), gave more than $200,000 over a period of years; "Ten-Year Contributions for Negro Teachers Total $202,000," LDF press release, November 6, 1965.

368 STEPHEN CURRIER: John Simon, interview with author, March 5, 1990; Jane Lee Eddy, interview with author, March 6, 1990.

368 TACONIC PLEDGE: Greenberg to Stephen Currier, December 8, 1961, in author's possession; Greenberg to Gentlemen (Taconic Foundation), August 19, 1964, in author's possession.

369 WILKINS ON SCLC AND SNCC: NAACP minutes, October 9, 1961.

369 RESENTMENT AT VOTER PROJECTS: Ibid.

369 WILKINS ON SNCC: Simon, interview with author.

370 WILKINS ARRESTED: Roy Wilkins, with Tom Mathews, *Standing Fast: The Autobiography of Roy Wilkins* (New York: Viking, 1982), 288.

370 MEETING WITH JOHNSON: Memorandum, Lee White to the president, November 18, 1964, diary backup, box 11, Lyndon B. Johnson Library and

Museum, Austin, Tex.; list, unknown author, diary backup, box 11, LBJ Library; and diary entry, November 19, 1964, president's daily diary, box 2, LBJ Library.

370 YACHT TRIP: David Garrow, *Bearing the Cross: Martin Luther King, Jr., and the Southern Christian Leadership Conference* (New York: Morrow, 1986), 447.

371 "LARGE DELEGATION": The fact was that I had hoped to bring others as well, and had invited Roy Wilkins, Whitney Young, and James Farmer; either they could not come, or more likely, each believed he might do better alone.

371 VISIT TO FORD FOUNDATION: Memorandum, Richard Sheldon to Henry Heald, February 11, 1963, Ford Foundation Archives, copy in author's possession.

372 BEGINNING OF NORI: LDF executive minutes, December 9, 1965. The proposal addressed welfare; public housing; slum housing; consumer credit; migrant workers; rural indigents; barriers to employment, such as arrest records; criminal law, including bail and right to counsel; and issues distinctive to Mexican Americans (immigration, bilingualism, school and voting discrimination), Native Americans (fishing and hunting rights, reservation law and rights of nonreservation Indians), and other matters.

372 BOARD MEMBERS: After I became chief counsel new board members included Chauncey Waddell, a pioneer in creating mutual funds (his wife, Catherine, who had been on the board, had died); Tom Dyett, a prominent black member of the New York bar; Thurgood's old friend, Texas lawyer and businessman W. J. Durham; David Feller, general counsel of the United Steel Workers Union, later professor of law at Berkeley, and Jim Nabrit, Jr., then president of Howard University; LDF minutes, January 10, 1962. In 1963 we added William Sloan Coffin, Yale chaplain and Freedom Ride client; Arthur Logan, a prominent black physician, who was Duke Ellington's doctor and a confidant of Martin Luther King, Jr., and A. Leon Higginbotham, later a judge of the United States Court of Appeals for the Third Circuit. In 1965 we elected A. G. Gaston; Damon Keith, a leading black lawyer in Detroit, later a federal judge; Percy Julian, a black scientist who had developed techniques for making cortisone; and A. G. Spaulding, a black insurance executive in Durham, whom I had represented in a school case; LDF minutes, October 14, 1965. Some members, like Connie Lindau and Miriam Allen, were unsung, dedicated toilers who came to all meetings, kept the minutes, ran theater benefits, and held fund-raising meetings.

Clifford Alexander, later to become secretary of the army; Ben Dyett, a leading Harlem lawyer; Christopher Edley, who would head the United Negro College Fund; Marian Wright Edelman; Estelle Osborne, president of the National Nurses Association; and Harvey Russell, vice president of Pepsico were among the new black members. Nicholas Katzenbach, Ramsey Clark, both former attorneys-general; James Vorenberg, later dean of Harvard Law School; Bernard Segal; and William Scheide, founder of the Bach Aria Group, were among the whites who joined. For once we broke into the field of entertainment and celebrities, which SCLC, CORE, and SNCC regularly attracted, but only briefly. Dick Gregory joined the board, attended one meeting where he spoke in unintelligible parables, and never returned.

On Rivers, LDF minutes, October 5, 1971.

372 RELATIONSHIPS: Arthur Logan, Duke Ellington's doctor, took us to the Duke's annual gigs at the Rainbow Room, and when I remarried in 1970 (to Deborah Cole), we had the wedding party in his home.

373 CORPORATE SUPPORT: Richard Gerstenberg, CEO of General Motors, chaired our 1974 fund-raising dinner; LDF executive minutes, October 15, 1974. Lee Iacocca, John Filer, John Riccardo of Chrysler, and Robert Abboud of First Chicago Corporation, raised money for LDF by chairing dinners or heading committees; LDF executive minutes, February 24, 1976; January 25, 1977; January 24, 1978; February 27, 1979. On Kutak, LDF executive minutes, March 25, 1980. On my reservations about accepting money from corporations LDF might oppose in court, and on the board's decisions, see LDF executive minutes, January 18, 1973; December 9, 1975; November 30, 1976; June 28, 1977; and October 28, 1980. Among the possibilities considered were limiting corporate contributions to the Earl Warren Program; that active counsel in a case take no part in fund-raising that might solicit adversaries; that an outside committee headed by someone of stature be informed and consulted on potential conflicts; that plaintiffs be informed of potentially conflicting relationships.

373 PERSONAL SOLICITATIONS: One of my pleasant duties was to visit each year with Iphigene Sulzberger, then in her eighties, widow of Arthur Hays Sulzberger, publisher of the *New York Times*. She invited me to her home for lunch once a year to discuss LDF in a highly informed and lively manner and made substantial contributions.

374 C. B. POWELL: LDF press releases, March 15 and June 11, 1978.

374 *NEWMAN* CASE: *Newman v. Piggie Park*, 390 U.S. 400 (1968), 402.

375 CFC: Charles Stephen Ralston to Jack Greenberg, February 16, 1993, citing *National Black United Fund v. Campbell*, 494 F.Supp. 748 (D.D.C. 1980), rev'd 667 F.2d 173 (D.C. Cir. 1981); *NAACP LDF v. Campbell*, 504 F.Supp. 1365 (D.D.C. 1981); *NAACP LDF v. Devine*, 567 F.Supp. 401 (D.D.C. 1983), 727 F.2d 1247 (D.C. Cir. 1983); *Cornelius v. NAACP LDF*, 473 U.S. 788 (1985).

375 INTERNSHIPS: LDF minutes, October 11, 1962, and January 10, 1963; LDF executive minutes, September 12, 1963.

376 EWLTP: LDF executive minutes, June 1 and July 13, 1971, April 4, 1972; LDF minutes, October 5, 1971, and January 25, 1972.

377 ACHIEVED DISTINCTION: The list included Roger Wilkins (Roy's nephew), professor at George Mason University and journalist; John Kramer, now dean of Tulane Law School; Eleanor Applewhaite, general counsel for Channel 13 in New York City; John Hart Ely, who became dean at Stanford Law School; Elizabeth Holtzman, later a congresswoman and New York City controller; Pierre Leval, judge of the United States Court of Appeals in New York; Peter Zimroth, New York City corporation counsel; Inez Smith Reid, corporation counsel for Washington, D.C.; and Barrington D. (Danny) Parker, senior partner in Morrison and Foerster, one of the country's largest law firms.

In 1963 Taconic and Stern foundations gave funds to hire law students to work in cooperating lawyers' offices in the South.

377 STUDENT PROJECTS: LDF minutes, May 13, 1965.

377 LAWYERS TRAINING: LDF executive minutes, November 8, 1961; March 14, 1962 (see director-counsel's attached written report); February 14, 1963.

August 18, 1963; September 12, 1963; November 14, 1963; and March 12, 1964.

378   MORE ON LAWYERS TRAINING: The sessions covered state action, school desegregation, protecting civil rights lawyers against harassment, protests and demonstrations, the Civil Rights Act of 1964, habeas corpus, confessions, searches and seizures, the right to counsel, bail, *de facto* school segregation, voting rights, urban renewal, and many other subjects. We had practical classes on how to represent the movement, run a law office, get a grant from the government, and so forth. Tony Amsterdam prepared several casebooks on civil rights law, including *The Defensive Transfer of Civil Rights Litigation from State to Federal Courts* and *Civil Rights Law Institutes*, both written for the Civil Rights Law Institutes of the NAACP Legal Defense and Educational Fund, n.d., in author's possession.

378   LEHMAN FUND: LDF minutes, January 10, 1964; LDF executive minutes, February 13, April 16, and October 8, 1964; and Butler Henderson, interview with author, March 30, 1990.

379   PLANNING MEETINGS: Other subjects of the meetings included Northern school cases; the new area called poverty law; suing entire Southern states for school segregation; antitrust cases against real estate boards; using the National Labor Relations Act and the newly enacted Equal Employment Opportunities Act against employment discrimination; fair employment by government agencies; civil suits to desegregate juries; health care; equal governmental services; discrimination in welfare. In criminal law: the death penalty for rape and capital punishment generally; the rights of defendants between arrest and trial, including search and seizure, right to counsel, coerced confessions, plea bargaining; status crime laws, such as vagrancy and loitering. We discussed research programs, internships, and cooperating lawyer relationships in the North. The entire staff, at a final meeting addressed mundane matters: cost cutting, office space, morale of nonprofessional staff, standards for filing cases and appeals.

379   "WHITHER": LDF minutes, January 9, 1969; LDF executive minutes, March 13, 1969.

CHAPTER 28. EDUCATION FOLLOWING THE DEFEAT OF "ALL DELIBERATE SPEED"

381   LEVEL OF DESEGREGATION: U.S. Commission on Civil Rights, *Southern School Desegregation, 1966–1967*, A Report of the U.S. Commission on Civil Rights, July 1967, 6.

381   JUDGE SCARLETT'S DECISION: *Stell v. Savannah-Chatham County Board of Ed.*, 220 F.Supp. 667 (S.D. Ga. 1963), rev. and remanded 333 F.2d 55 (5th Cir. 1964).

382   WISDOM: *Hudson v. Leake County School Board*, 357 F.2d 653 (5th Cir. 1966), 654; "NAACP Attorney Charges Pressure in Leake County," *Southern School News*, 11, no. 4 (October 1964), 9; "Judge Considers Plea to Expand Desegregation in Leake County, *Southern School News* 11, no. 4 (November 1964), 7.

382   WISDOM ON PLANS THAT WORK: He attacked John Parker's phrase, which for a decade had frustrated implementing *Brown*, that "the Constitution . . . does not require integration. It merely forbids segregation" as having "prompted Pupil Placement Laws, the most effective technique for perpet-

uating school segregation," which "drain[ed] out of *Brown* that decision's significance as a class action to secure equal educational opportunities for Negroes by compelling the states to reorganize their public school systems." *United States and Stout v. Jefferson County Board of Education,* 372 F.2d 836 (5th Cir. 1966), 847, 863, 865.

382 LDF SCHOOL CASES: LDF minutes, April 5, 1967. On May 25, 1967, a day after the *Jefferson* argument, I argued the Oklahoma City school case, *Dowell v. Oklahoma City School Board,* 375 F.2d 158 (10th Cir. 1967), cert. den. 387 U.S. 931 (1967), in Wichita. The district court had entered the most comprehensive desegregation order until that time: pupils in predominantly black schools were allowed to transfer, two sets of secondary school zones were combined, and by 1970 black teachers had to be distributed throughout the system. We won *Dowell;* the Supreme Court rejected Oklahoma's petition. In other LDF free choice cases, district courts ordered boards to reconfigure geographic zones: in Franklin County, North Carolina, *Coppedge v. Franklin County,* 404 F.2d 1177 (4th Cir. 1968); Loudon County, Virginia, *Corbin v. County School Board of Loudon County,* 283 F.Supp. 60 (E.D. Va. 1963, Order 1967); and Duval County, Florida, *Braxton v. Board of Public Instruction of Duval County,* 402 F.2d 900 (5th Cir. 1968).

382 COURT IS IMPATIENT: I won *Goss v. Knoxville Board of Education,* 373 U.S. 683 (1963), in which the Court held unconstitutional a plan providing that blacks in a majority white school might freely transfer to a black school and whites in a black majority school could move to a white school. They all were under pressure to switch and did. Indeed, students had transferred without ever setting foot in the school to which they originally were assigned. Connie won *Watson v. City of Memphis,* 373 U.S. 526 (1963), which involved a segregated Memphis park, in which Justice Goldberg denounced the "deliberate speed" doctrine, and the Atlanta school case *Calhoun v. Latimer,* 377 U.S. 263 (1964). The Court also decided *Griffin v. County School Board,* 377 U.S. 218 (1964), writing that "the time for mere 'deliberate speed' has run out." But it still didn't compel any district to desegregate promptly. *Bradley v. City of Richmond,* 382 U.S. 103 (1965), decided that students might sue for teacher desegregation; the Court wrote that integration should speed up. In *Rogers v. Paul,* 382 U.S. 198 (1965), a student who wanted to take a course in a class in which the stairstep plan did not entitle him to enroll was allowed to transfer to white classes.

382 FAIRFAX'S BACKGROUND: Born in Cleveland in 1920, her father was a city employee and her mother a social worker with the county juvenile court. At the University of Michigan she was elected to Phi Beta Kappa, followed by a degree in comparative religion at Union Theological Seminary. In the 1940s she worked in Austria for an AFSC postwar rehabilitation team and in 1953 directed an AFSC international work camp in Israel, presiding over a kosher kitchen—she had grown up with Jewish neighbors and knew what was required. In the 1960s she worked for AFSC in Leake County, in Jackson and Biloxi, Mississippi, organizing black children to enter white schools and acted as liaison between LDF and the Justice Department.

382 FAIRFAX AT LDF: While at LDF she was also, for seven years, a member of the Central Committee of the World Council of Churches, founder of its program to combat racism and encourage divestment from South Africa.

She also was involved in social action programs of the United Church of Christ.

383 FAIRFAX'S WORK AT LDF: Jean Fairfax, memorandum to LDF board-staff committee, January 25, 1983, in author's possession.

383 ATTACK ON FREE CHOICE: *Green v. New Kent County Board of Education* (Virginia), 391 U.S. 420 (1968); *Raney v. Gould County Board of Education* (Arkansas), 391 U.S. 443 (1968); and *Monroe v. Board of Commissioners of Jackson, Tennessee*, 391 U.S. 450 (1968). Sam Tucker argued *Green*, Jim Nabrit argued *Monroe*, I argued *Raney*.

383 VIRGINIA PUPIL PLACEMENT CASES: *Marsh v. County School Board of Roanoke* 305 F.2d 94 (4th Cir. 1962); *Green v. School Board of City of Roanoke* 304 F.2d 118 (4th Cir. 1962).

383 QUOTE FROM MY BOOK: *Raney v. Gould County Board of Education*, Brief for Respondent, Supreme Court No. 805, October Term 1967, 38.

383 BRENNAN REMARK: *Raney v. Gould*, Oral Argument, 159.

383 JUSTICE WHITE: Ibid., 101.

383 DELAY: *Green v. New Kent County Board of Education*, 391 U.S. 420 (1968), 438.

384 FIFTH CIRCUIT CRISIS: Leon E. Panetta and Peter Gall, *Bring Us Together: The Nixon Team and the Civil Rights Retreat* (Philadelphia: J. B. Lippincott, 1971), 249.

384 STENNIS: Ibid., 255.

384 ON JUSTICE, FIFTH CIRCUIT, DISTRICT COURT: See Motion to Advance and Petition for Writ of Certiorari in *Alexander v. Holmes County Board of Education*, 396 U.S. 1218 (1969).

384 FOCH: George Gray Aston, *The Biography of the Late Marshal Foch* (New York: Macmillan, 1929), 122.

385 JUSTICE BLACK: *Alexander v. Holmes*, 396 U.S. 1218 (1969), 1222.

386 "LITIGATION FOREVER": *Alexander v. Holmes*, Oral Argument, Supreme Court No. 632, October Term 1969, 28.

386 MY ARGUMENT ON THE RECORD: Ibid., 73.

386 MEDGAR EVERS: Ibid., 75.

386 PANETTA REACTION: Panetta and Gall, *Bring Us Together*, 299.

386 DECISION: *Alexander v. Holmes County Board of Education*, 396 U.S. 19 (1969).

386 "FORTHWITH": Ibid.

387 DECISIONS FOLLOWING *ALEXANDER*: In an opinion covering fifteen cases from six Deep Southern states, *Singleton v. Jackson Municipal Separate School District*, 419 F.2d 1211 (5th Cir. 1969), the Fifth Circuit delayed desegregation until September 1970 (but ordered teachers to be desegregated by February 1). LDF had some of the cases for which Jim Nabrit wrote the petitions; LCDC and other lawyers had the others. We each pursued slightly different tactics, sped to the Supreme Court, and won an order requiring immediate desegregation. *Alexander* meant business. LDF filed a petition for writ of certiorari and motions to speed decision, arguing that the court of appeals was wrong under *Alexander*. We asked Justice Black for an order requiring desegregation by February 1, 1970, pending decision by the entire Court. The entire Court issued the order. *Carter v. West Feliciana School District*, 396 U.S. 290 (1970).

387 HAYNSWORTH: "Memorandum: Civil Rights Decisions by Judge Clement F. Haynsworth, Jr.," n.d., unsigned (author James M. Nabrit III), in author's possession.

387 PRINCE EDWARD: *Griffin v. School Board,* 377 U.S. 218 (1964). Bob Carter argued this case for the NAACP.

387 TRANSFER PLANS: *Dillard v. School Board of the City of Charlottesville, Va.,* 308 F.2d 920 (4th Cir. 1962), cert. den. 374 U.S. 827 (1963).

387 TEACHER DESEGREGATION: *Bradley v. School Board of Richmond,* 382 U.S. 103 (1965).

387 HOSPITAL DESEGREGATION: *Simkins v. Moses H. Cone Memorial Hospital,* 323 F.2d 959 (4th. Cir. 1963), cert. den. 376 U.S. 938 (1964).

387 HAYNSWORTH REJECTED: Warren Weaver, Jr., "Senate Bars Haynsworth, 55–45," *New York Times,* November 22, 1969.

388 CARSWELL: Richard Harris, *Decision* (New York: Dutton, 1971), passim.

388 EFFECTIVE DESEGREGATION: *Swann v. Charlotte-Mecklenburg Board of Education,* 402 U.S. 1 (1971).

388 CHARLOTTE OPINION: Ibid., 25, 32. Along with *Swann,* Jim Nabrit argued a North Carolina case in which state law prohibited busing students without their parent's consent. The Court held that law unconstitutional, *North Carolina State Board of Education v. Swann,* 402 U.S. 43 (1971).

388 MOBILE: *Davis v. Board of School Commissioners of Mobile County,* 402 U.S. 33 (1971).

389 MY ARGUMENT IN MOBILE: *Davis v. Board,* Oral Argument, Supreme Court No. 436, October Term, 1970, 15.

389 BURGER IN *SWANN: Swann v. Charlotte,* 32.

389 WHITE PEOPLE'S PARTY ON BUSING: FBI file 105-70374-7790.

390 COURT'S DELIBERATIONS IN *BROWN:* For the most recent findings, see Mark Tushnet, "What Really Happened in *Brown v. Board of Education,*" 91 *Columbia Law Review* 1867 (1991).

391 TEACHER AFFIRMATIVE ACTION: *Carr v. Montgomery Board of Education,* 395 U.S. 225 (1969).

391 TEACHER CASES: LDF executive minutes, June 9 and September 24, 1966.

391 THE PLAINTIFF: *Gloria B. Rackley v. School District No. 5, Orangeburg County,* 258 F.Supp. 676 (Dist of S.C. 1966).

391 NEA STATISTICS: Brief Amicus Curiae for the National Education Association in *United States v. State of Georgia,* p. 12. This case is reported as *United States v. State of Georgia,* 445 F.2d 303 (5th Cir. 1971).

391 TEACHER EMPLOYMENT: Richard Freeman has written that "increased black voting power appears to have substantially raised demand for black school teachers, offsetting most of the reduction in demand due to desegregation. In the South, where segregation had created an especially favorable market for black teachers, some teachers and many principals were displaced, but the potentially disastrous effects of desegregation on teacher employment did not occur. In the North, demand increased greatly." "Political Power, Desegregation, and Employment of Black Schoolteachers," *Journal of Political Economy* 85, no. 2 (1977), 299. Freeman adds that "between 1949 and 1969, black male teachers improved their income position relative to white male teachers by 17 percentage points; black female teachers gained 19 percentage points until they had a 4 percent advantage over white female teachers in 1969." Ibid., 302. This trend has continued at least into the early 1970s. See also Freeman, "The New Job Market for Black Academicians," 30 *Industrial and Labor Relations Review* 2 (January 1977), 161–74.

392 NAACP NORTHERN SCHOOL CASES: See Robert L. Herbst, "The Legal Strug-

gle to Integrate Public Schools in the North," *The Annals of the American Academy of Political and Social Science* 407 (May 1973), 43–62. Carter lost three cases: in Gary, Indiana, *Bell v. School City of Gary*, 324 F.2d 209 (7th Cir. 1963), cert. den. 377 U.S. 924 (1964); Kansas City, Kansas, *Downs v. Board of Education*, 336 F.2d 988 (10th Cir. 1964), cert. den. 380 U.S. 914 (1965); and Cincinnati, Ohio, *Deal v. Cincinnati Board of Education*, 419 F.2d 1387 (6th Cir. 1969), cert. den. 402 U.S. 962 (1971).

393 KEYES LAWYERS: *Keyes v. School District No. 1, Denver*, 413 U.S. 189 (1973). Craig Barnes, another Denver lawyer, participated in the case during its early phases. Norman Chachkin wrote the petition for review.

393 KEYES PRESUMPTION: *Keyes*, Brief for Petitioners, Supreme Court No. 71-507, October Term 1979, 89.

394 INTERDISTRICT DECISION: *Bradley v. State Board of Education*, 412 U.S. 92 (1973).

394 COMPLICITY IN SEGREGATING: *Bradley v. Milliken*, 418 U.S. 717 (1974).

394 TEACHER CASES: LDF docket, August 1973.

394 NIXON OPPOSITION TO BUSING: "Strategy to Fight Administration Tactics in School Desegregation Cases Mapped by Legal Defense Fund," LDF press release, May 18, 1972.

394 NIXON OPPOSITION TO BUSING: David Chang, "The Bus Stops Here: Defining the Constitutional Right of Equal Educational Opportunity and an Appropriate Remedial Process," 63 *Boston University Law Review* 1 (1983).

394 JUSTICE DEPARTMENT OPPOSITION: LDF minutes, October 3, 1972.

394 MISSISSIPPI TEXTBOOK CASE: *Loewen v. Turnipseed*, 488 F.Supp. 1138 (N.D. Miss. 1980); LDF executive minutes, June 29, 1976.

395 COURT COMPELS HEW: *Adams v. Richardson.* The history of this litigation is complex. See "A Narrative History of the *Adams* Litigation from October 19, 1970 to December 29, 1977," LDF memorandum, n.d., unsigned, in author's possession; Julius Chambers, "Blacks, Higher Education and the *Adams* Case," LDF memorandum, August 1986 and August 6, 1987, in author's possession; "A Chronology of U.S. Desegregation Actions," *Chronicle of Higher Education*, March 25, 1987, 22; the litigation continued into the 1990s.

396 BLACK EDUCATORS ON HIGHER EDUCATION DESEGREGATION: Jean Fairfax, "The Reorganization of State Systems of Higher Education—Some Black Perspectives," June 1971, in author's possession.

396 LDF MOTION TO REVOKE CERTIFICATION: LDF press release, August 1, 1975.

397 COMPLEXITY OF FASHIONING RELIEF: *Geier v. Blanton*, 427 F.Supp. 644 (M.D. Tenn. 1977), aff'd *Geier v. University of Tennessee*, 597 F.2d 1056 (6th Cir. 1979), cert. den. *University of Tennessee v. Geier*, 444 U.S. 886 (1979), requiring the virtually all-white University of Tennessee in Nashville to merge with black Tennessee State University (TSU), under the governance of TSU. The arrangement promised a nonsegregated combined institution managed in a way that would preserve the integrity of the formerly black institution. Since it would be in control, it could protect itself against duplicative programs, curricula, fund allocation, faculty assignment, and other factors. The *Geier* model offered one way of moving toward integration without squelching the interests of black students, faculty, and administration, but never has been used elsewhere. Tennessee appealed to the Court of Appeals for the Sixth Circuit, where I argued successfully to uphold the district court. The state petitioned the

Supreme Court, which denied review. See also untitled LDF press release, October 1, 1979.

397 AT ALL LEVELS: LDF executive minutes, January 24 and March 28, 1978.

397 NORTH CAROLINA REFUSES TO SUBMIT PLAN: "A Chronology of U.S. Desegregation Actions," 22.

397 NORTH CAROLINA CONSENT DECREE LITIGATION: *Adams v. Bell*, 711 F.2d 161 (D.C. Cir. 1983), cert. den. 465 U.S. 1021 (1984). Skelly Wright's dissent in the Court of Appeals case contains the best summary of the case and questions it involved.

397 BOB JONES CASE: *Bob Jones University v. United States*, 461 U.S. 574 (1983).

398 BURGER TO COLEMAN: Coleman, interview with author, November 11, 1991.

398 COLEMAN ARGUMENT: *Bob Jones*, Oral Argument, Supreme Court No. 81-3, October Term 1981, 50.

398 *BOB JONES* OPINION: *Bob Jones*, 586, 593.

398 CONFLICT WITH CIVIL RIGHTS DIVISION: *Valley v. Rapides Parish School Board*, 646 F.2d 925 (5th Cir. 1981); *Kelley v. Metropolitan County Board of Education of Nashville*, 687 F.2d 814 (5th Cir. 1982); *Ganaway and U.S. v. Charleston County School District*, 738 F.Supp 1513 (Dist. of S.C. 1990).

398 INTERDISTRICT CASES: *Hoots v. Commonwealth of Pennsylvania*, 703 F.2d 722 (4th Cir. 1983); *Jenkins v. Missouri*, 593 F.Supp. 1485 (W.D. Mo. 1984), 807 F.2d 657 (8th Cir. 1986), cert. den. 484 U.S. 816 (1987).

399 BLACK PH.D.'S: In the early 1980s, approximately 6 percent of Ph.D.'s were awarded to blacks; by the late 1980s, the percentage was barely over 3 percent. See U.S. Department of Education, Office of Educational Research and Improvement, National Center for Education Statistics, *Race/Ethnicity Trends in Degrees Conferred by Institutions of Higher Education: 1980–81 Through 1989–90* (Washington, D.C.: Government Printing Office, 1992); National Center for Education Statistics, *Characteristics of Doctorate Recipients, 1979, 1984, and 1989* (Washington, D.C.: Government Printing Office, 1992); and Catherine S. Manegold, "Fewer Men Earn Doctorates, Particularly Among Blacks," *New York Times*, January 18, 1994. According to Manegold, who quotes an unnamed study by the American Council on Education, the number of black women earning doctorates was virtually unchanged during the 1980s while the number of black men dropped 19 percent.

399 STATISTICS: U.S. Department of Commerce, Bureau of the Census, *Statistical Abstract of the United States: 1988* (Washington, D.C.: Government Printing Office, 1987), 125, 140.

399 SOUTH MOST DESEGREGATED: See Gary Orfield, Franklin Monfort, and Melissa Aaron, *Status of School Desegregation 1968–1986*, Report of the Council of Urban Boards of Education and the National School Desegregation Research Project (Chicago: University of Chicago, 1989), 5–6. About 57 percent of black students were in predominantly minority schools in the South, compared to 73 percent in the Northeast. Only 24 percent of black children were in 90 to 100 percent minority schools in the South; 47 percent were in such schools in the Northeast. Conversely, 41 percent of the white students in the South attended schools with blacks, while only 27 percent of whites in the North did.

399   LIEBMAN SURVEY: James S. Liebman, "Desegregating Politics," 90 *Columbia Law Review* 1463 (1990).

399   "NATIONAL NORM": Liebman, "Desegregating Politics," 1624, note 675, quoting Robert L. Crain and Rita E. Mahard, "Minority Achievement: Policy Implications of Research," in *Effective School Desegregation: Equity, Quality and Feasibility,* W. Hawley ed. (Beverly Hills, Calif.: Sage, 1981), 55, 56–70. Elsewhere, Crain concludes from almost "100 analyses of student achievement as a result of desegregation" that "the overall conclusion of the vast majority is that blacks are helped and whites are not hurt"; see Drummond Ayers, Jr., "Civil Rights Groups Fear a Slowdown in Busing for Desegregation of Schools," *New York Times,* December 21, 1980. The National Assessment of Education Progress reports that seventeen-year-old blacks have reduced the difference between themselves and whites in reading scores—the most important indicator of educational achievement—by about 50 percent over the past twenty years. The mathematics gap was reduced about 25 to 40 percent, science 15 to 25 percent. If trends continue, the reading disparity should end in fifteen to twenty years—too long—but at least an end to this terrible discrepancy; see Marshall S. Smith and Jennifer O'Day, "Education Equality: 1966 and Now," in *Spheres of Justice in American Schools,* Deborah Verstegen ed. (New York: HarperBusiness, 1991). Other differences should take longer to erase.

399   BLACKS DO BETTER: Susan Mayer and Christopher Jencks, "Growing Up in Poor Neighborhoods: How Much Does It Matter?" *Science* 17 (March 1989), 1441–42.

399   BLACKS IN INTEGRATED SCHOOLS: Gerald Jaynes and Robin Williams, eds., *A Common Destiny: Blacks and American Society* (Washington, D.C.: National Academy Press, 1989).

399   MORE MONEY: Liebman, "Desegregating Politics," 1626.

400   BUSING AND WHITE FLIGHT: The studies are collected in Liebman, "Desegregating Politics." See also, Gary Orfield, *Must We Bus?: Segregated Schools and National Policy* (Washington, D.C.: The Brookings Institution, 1978), 99–101.

401   CHAMBERS REVIEW: Chambers, "Blacks, Higher Education and the *Adams* Case." Blacks constituted 22 to 36 percent of high school graduates; 12 to 18 percent of freshmen entering college; 7 to 11 percent of bachelor's degree graduates; 6 to 8 percent of graduate students; 5 to 6 percent of professional school students; and 4 to 5 percent of doctoral candidates.

CHAPTER 29. ANGELA DAVIS, THE SAN RAFAEL SHOOTOUT, AND TURMOIL AT LDF

403   BURNHAM DISCUSSIONS: Margaret Burnham to Jack Greenberg, October 20, 1970, in author's possession.

403   STAFF REMONSTRATION: Memorandum, legal and professional staff to board of directors, LDF, n.d., in author's possession.

404   STAFF MEETING: Memorandum from Jack Greenberg, October 28, 1970.

405   NEVER AUTHORIZED CASE: Memorandum, Jack Greenberg to files, November 6, 1970, in author's possession.

406   JUROR SURVEY: Conversation with Jerome Skolnick, who had been associated with the defense.

406   BERNSTEIN PARTY: Tom Wolfe, *Radical Chic and Mau Mauing the Flack Catchers* (New York: Farrar, Straus, 1970), 87. Jerome Skolnick, in *The Politics of Protest* (New York: Simon & Schuster, 1969), 107, listed justifications offered for "the politics of confrontation": confrontation and militancy are ways of arousing militants to action; they educate the public; combative behavior with respect to police and other authorities, while alienating respectable adults, has the opposite effect on nonstudent youth; resistance may have a liberating effect on young middle-class radicals; and the political power of backlash is exaggerated. At the time, while these arguments were not fully articulated, I wouldn't have subscribed to them. The politics of confrontation was, to my mind, not for LDF.

407   CAMPUS HEARINGS: *Columbia v. Denmark*, LDF docket, March 1971.

407   CORNELL CASE: *People v. Meade*, LDF docket, March 1971; Haywood Burns, interview with author, September 17, 1990.

407   STUDENT CASES: We won a case for black Wagner College students who had been expelled for protesting, *Coleman v. Wagner College*, 429 F.2d 1120 (2nd Cir. 1970), and a similar one against the University of Wisconsin where the district court held that summary suspension violated due process of law, *Stricklin v. Regents of the University of Wisconsin*, 297 F.Supp. 416 (W.D. Wisc. 1969).

407   PANTHERS' BAIL: "Rights Groups Aids 13 Panthers Here," *New York Times*, August 5, 1969; LDF press release, August 5, 1969; Niebuhr telegram, copy in author's possession; LDF telegram, August 11, 1969; "Background of the LDF Attack on New York's Bail System," LDF press release, August–September, 1969; "Black Panther Case Prompts LDF to Seek Supreme Court Review of New York Bail System," LDF press release, December 13, 1969. We lost the Panthers' bail case, lost again on appeal, and then the Supreme Court denied review. *Shakur v. McGrath, Commissioner of Corrections*, 303 F.Supp. 303 (S.D. N.Y. 1969), 418 F.2d 243 (2nd Cir. 1969), cert. den. 397 U.S. 999 (1970). To inquire into police shootings of Panthers, I formed a national commission of distinguished citizens headed by Arthur Goldberg and Roy Wilkins, "Statement on Commission of Inquiry into the Black Panthers and Law Enforcement Officials," LDF press release, December 15, 1969; LDF telegram, December 17, 1969.

In other cases for militants, LDF represented Bobby Seale, whom Judge Julius Hoffman had sentenced to four years imprisonment for contempt. We claimed that Seale had been denied a jury trial, right to counsel, a full hearing, and that the judge was prejudiced, and won in the court of appeals, *U.S. v. Bobby Seale*, 461 F.2d 345 (7th Cir. 1972); "LDF to Defend Bobby Seale," LDF press release, February 18, 1970. Tony Amsterdam, for LDF, represented *New York Times* reporter Earl Caldwell, whom the *Times* at first refused to represent (although later it cooperated in the defense), arguing that he had a First Amendment right to maintain the confidentiality of his sources within the Panthers absent a compelling interest on the part of the prosecution. We won in the court of appeals and lost in the Supreme Court, *Caldwell v. United States*, 434 F.2d 1081 (9th Cir. 1970), rev'd 408 U.S. 665 (1972). Mike Meltsner won a case in the Supreme Court for Father James Groppi, an anti–Vietnam War activist, establishing the constitutional right to change of venue in misdemeanor cases, *Groppi v. Wisconsin*, 400 U.S. 505 (1971). LDF also filed a class action seeking reform of prison conditions at San Quentin, where the Soledad Brothers were locked up, winning in December 1970, a preliminary injunction requiring procedural due process in disciplinary cases, *Clutchette v. Procunier*, 328 F.Supp. 767 (N.D. Cal. 1971); LDF San Francisco docket reports, June 1971, September 1972.

407 MELTSNER RECALLS: Meltsner to Greenberg, October 26, 1993, in author's possession.

408 LICENSE CASE, DRAFT CASE: *Ali v. The Division of State Athletic Commission*, 316 F.Supp. 1246 (S.D. N.Y., 1970); *Clay v. United States*, 403 U.S. 698 (1971).

409 MEMORANDUM: Legal and professional staff to board of directors, LDF, n.d., in author's possession.

409 STAFF MEMO: Ibid.

410 EXECUTIVE COMMITTEE MEMO: Memorandum, Francis E. Rivers to members of staff, November 16, 1970, in author's possession.

410 SECOND EXECUTIVE COMMITTEE MEMO: Statement of the executive committee, memorandum, n.d., in author's possession.

410 COLEMAN OBSERVATION: LDF executive minutes, February 11, 1971.

410 BOARD CRITERIA: "Report of Special Committee of LDF Board of Directors Appointed by the Fund's President to Make Recommendations with Respect to Guidelines for Undertaking Litigation and Procedure to Apply Said Guidelines," December 22, 1970, in author's possession. Members of the committee included Bill Coleman, Ramsey Clark, Arthur Logan, Leon Higginbotham, John G. Lewis, Lou Pollak, and Frank Rivers.

411 BOARD CRITERIA: Ibid.

411 "LIBERALS REFUSED": Rowland Evans and Robert Novack, "Angela Davis Case Causes Rift Within the NAACP," *New York Post*, December 3, 1970.

411 ANGELA DAVIS CASE: Memorandum, Burnham to Greenberg, January 12, 1971, in author's possession. She asserted that the case presented civil rights issues: the indictment was based on insufficient evidence; the grand jury was selected in a racially discriminatory way; steps should be taken to assure that the trial jury is untainted by racial discrimination; she is entitled to bail; there is prejudicial publicity; she faces capital punishment, and so forth. The staff sent another memorandum to the board joining in this request; memorandum, legal staff to board of directors, January 14, 1971, in author's possession. I asked Tony Amsterdam and Cecil Poole, both in California, to take a close look at the case and give me their views. Tony wrote a long letter to Cecil Poole, urging that LDF enter the case on the issues of bail, pretrial detention, access of the black media to Davis, and the right to bail; Tony Amsterdam to Cecil F. Poole, January 31, 1971, in author's possession. Cecil disagreed and thought we should stay out; LDF executive minutes, February 11, 1971.

411 STAFF RELATIONS: LDF executive minutes, April 8, 1971.

CHAPTER 30. WINNING JOBS

413 EEOC COMPLAINTS: LDF minutes, May 13 and October 14, 1965.

413 NAACP FILES COMPLAINTS: "Job Bias Laid to Companies, Unions, NAACP Complains," LDF press release, July 29, 1965; "214 Job Bias Complaints

Filed Under Title VI of Rights Act," LDF press release, September 15, 1965.

In 1965, with the Washington Bureau of the NAACP, we filed complaints against hospitals throughout the South. See "First Complaint Filed Under Title VI of Civil Rights Act," LDF press release, February 15, 1965; "29 Southern Hospitals Challenged in Second Complaint Filed Under Title VI of New Civil Rights Act—NAACP and NAACP Legal Defense Fund Move Jointly," LDF press release, March 4, 1965; "Record Number Complaints Against Southern Hospitals Is Filed with HEW Department," LDF press release, April 14, 1965; "Legal Defense Fund Files 12 Complaints Charging Discrimination in Hospitals," LDF press release, July 15, 1965; "Rights Groups Ask HEW to Act on Charges of Racial Discrimination in 16 Hospitals," LDF press release, September 3, 1965. These hospitals, after our victory in *Simkins v. Moses Cone Hospital*, faced cutoff of federal funds if they discriminated against black staff or patients.

413 BOB BELTON: Belton took over from Leroy Clark and Al Feinberg (who became a Florida intern), who had held that responsibility from the time the act was passed in 1964.

413 LDF EMPLOYMENT CASES: Before Title VII was adopted there had been no effective law prohibiting employment discrimination. Regulations against discrimination by government contractors weren't credible because they never had been enforced by canceling a contract. Charles Houston had invented the doctrine of *Steele v. Louisville and Nashville Railroad*, 323 U.S. 192 (1944), requiring labor unions to represent blacks fairly, but it was cumbersome and roundabout. State laws were virtually unenforced. I dreamed up a clever idea: Sue employers who had been lured to the South by state or municipal bond financed construction, claiming the resulting employment was "state action" covered by the Fourteenth Amendment. We filed such a case in Mississippi but my theory never was tested because Title VII soon offered an easier way.

413 SCOPE OF LDF EMPLOYMENT DOCKET: "LDF Attorneys Hit U.S. Steel," LDF press release, September 9, 1966. In 1971, the Employment Section of Justice's Civil Rights Division consisted of a chief, thirty-two lawyers, and ten research assistants, and had filed seventy-five Title VII cases, some interventions in our cases. By then we had twice as many such cases, staffed by five or six LDF lawyers along with cooperating attorneys.

413 TITLE VII UNCLEAR: Robert Belton, "A Comparative Review of Public and Private Enforcement of Title VII of the Civil Rights Act of 1964," 31 *Vanderbilt Law Review* 905 (1978).

413 DEVELOPMENT OF TITLE VII PROGRAM, LAWYERS, AND CONSULTANTS: Much of what follows is from interviews with Al Rosenthal, Bill Robinson, Barry Goldstein, Mike Baller, Bob Belton, Gabby MacDonald, and Marty Mador. Notes in author's possession.

414 GROUP OF SCHOLARS: Scholars included Joe Bishop and Clyde Summers (Yale), Al Blumrosen (Rutgers), Mike Sovern and George Cooper (Columbia), Bill Gould (Wayne State), Jack Kroner and Thomas Christensen (New York University), Peter Doeringer, an economist, David Shapiro (Harvard), Bernard Dunau (Virginia), Michael Piore, an economist (MIT), Dan Pollitt (North Carolina), Ted St. Antoine (Michigan), Mike Trister (Mississippi), Sandy Rosen (Maryland). Practitioners included F. A. O. (Fritz) Schwarz III, Sandy Rosen, and Peter Swords.

414   COMPLAINTS TO EEOC: LDF, *30 Years of Law Which Changed America* (New York: LDF, 1970).

414   RAILROAD WORKER: The case was *Gamble v. Birmingham Southern Railroad Co.,* 514 F.2d 678 (5th Cir. 1975).

414   DUHON: *Duhon v. Goodyear,* 494 F.2d 817 (5th Cir. 1974).

414   BIBLE CASE: *James v. Stockham Valve Co.,* 559 F.2d 310 (5th Cir. 1977).

415   PROCEDURAL OBSTACLES: Robert Belton, "Title VII of the Civil Rights Act of 1964: A Decade of Private Enforcement and Judicial Developments," 20 *St. Louis University Law Journal* 225 (1976).

415   CLASS ACTION STANDING: *Jenkins v. United Gas Co.,* 440 F.2d 28 (5th Cir. 1968), decided that, by promoting individual plaintiffs, employers could not avoid classwide relief—the case would go on. *Huff v. N. D. Cass,* 485 F.2d 710 (5th Cir. 1973), decided that even though the employer wasn't wrong in firing the plaintiff, he still could represent the class of employees—a deterrent to getting rid of plaintiffs as a way of getting rid of lawsuits.

415   OTHER PROCEDURAL ISSUES OF THIS PERIOD: Whether we had to join individually as defendants all white workers whose jobs or seniority might be affected; a charge filed with the EEOC had to be made under oath; an action had to be limited to the precise charge described in the EEOC complaint; charges had to be investigated and conciliated by the EEOC within strict time limits set forth in the act as prerequisite to suit (impossible in view of the tens of thousands of complaints and the small staff of the commission); other remedies, like state or local discrimination laws, National Labor Relations Board or Railway Labor Board procedures, and union grievance procedures and possibilities for arbitration must first be pursued; if decided adversely, whether they would bar Title VII relief. District courts usually ruled against us, but the courts of appeals and the Supreme Court responded in our favor by interpreting the procedural provisions generously. On all these cases, see Belton, "Title VII of the Civil Rights Act of 1964." As one case put it, "Technicalities are particularly inappropriate in a statutory scheme in which laymen, unassisted by trained lawyers, initiate the process [by filing charge with the EEOC]," *Love v. Pullman Co.,* 404 U.S. 522 (1972), 527.

415   *Hall v. Werthan Bag Co.,* 251 F.Supp 184 (M.D. Tenn. 1966).

416   TITLE VII LAWYERS: The local lawyers included Henry Marsh, who was soon to become mayor of Richmond, up to his ears in politics and brilliant in the courtroom; Gabby MacDonald, who, following her marriage, practiced in Houston, where she was a meticulous trial lawyer and later the first black United States district judge in Texas; Oscar Adams, later a judge on the Alabama Supreme Court, who could make the strongest position seem reasonable when proposed in his soft Southern drawl; U. W. Clemon, an early intern, later United States district judge in Birmingham, a formidable advocate because of his careful preparation and intellectual prowess; John Walker, one of Little Rock's leading lawyers, a former intern whose daring insights and tenacity assured that he would prevail in almost impossible cases; and Julius Chambers, my successor at LDF, who mostly did his own cases at trial and on appeal, with support from LDF when he needed it.

417   BUTZNER: *Quarles v. Philip Morris, Inc.,* 279 F.Supp. 505 (E.D. Va. 1967), 517.

418   BURGER COURT OVERRULES *QUARLES: Teamsters v. United States*, 431 U.S. 324 (1977).

418   MOST IMPORTANT CASE; *Griggs v. Duke Power Co.*, 401 U.S. 424 (1971); Belton, "A Comparative Review," 936.

418   TESTS IN *GRIGGS:* Wonderlic Personnel and Bennett Mechanical Comprehension.

418   EMPLOYMENT CASES: George Cooper and Richard Sobol, "Seniority and Testing Under Fair Employment Laws," 82 *Harvard Law Review* 1598 (1969).

419   BARRETT: *Griggs v. Duke Power Co.*, Transcript of Record, Supreme Court No. 124, October Term 1970, 117.

419   "PROFESSIONALLY DEVELOPED": Belton, "Title VII of the Civil Rights Act of 1964."

419   ARGUMENT IN *GRIGGS: Griggs v. Duke*, Oral Argument, 43.

419   BURGER TO GREENBERG: Ibid., 46.

420   WOMAN'S CASE: *Phillips v. Martin Marietta Corp.*, 400 U.S. 542 (1971). Robinson left to join the EEOC in 1973. Barry Goldstein and Mike Baller ran the program from 1973 to 1975. From that point, Peter Sherwood took over increasing responsibility and directed the program until he became solicitor general of the state of New York in 1984.

420   REMEDIES: LDF won the leading remedies case, *Pettway v. American Cast Iron Pipe Co.*, 575 F.2d 1157 (1978), cert. den. 439 U.S. 1115 (1979), which set standards for monetary relief, and *Franks v. Bowman*, 424 U.S. 747 (1976), tried and appealed by Mike Baller, which set standards for injunctive relief. On remedies in general see Bob Belton, *Remedies in Employment Discrimination Law* (New York: Wiley Law Publications, 1992).

420   LABOR MARKET ECONOMIST: *James v. Stockham Valves Co.*, 559 F.2d 310 (5th Cir. 1978), cert. denied 434 U.S. 1034 (1978); LDF minutes, February 26, 1974.

421   *GRIGGS* CARRIED FURTHER: *Albermarle Paper v. Moody*, 422 U.S. 405 (1975).

422   BACK PAY BECOMES ROUTINE: The Court held also that Albermarle had the burden of justifying the tests and that they were invalid. According to EEOC criteria, Albermarle was wrong in comparing test scores with subjective supervisors' rankings, without knowing the job-performance criteria they were considering. The purported validation had focused on the top of the lines, giving no indication of scores employees needed at the bottom. Moreover, it had compared experienced white workers with younger, inexperienced blacks.

422   LDF EMPLOYMENT CASES: LDF docket, January to June 1980. The remainder of the cases were inactive or led by cooperating lawyers.

422   TYPES OF CASES: We were suing U.S. Steel, Republic Steel, and Bethlehem Steel, and the United Steelworkers Union, International and Scott Paper (we had ten paper cases), National Cash Register, Delta Airlines, Continental Can, ITT, General Motors, the Long Island Railroad, Cannon Mills, J. P. Stevens, Goodyear Tire and Rubber, Kaiser Aluminum, to name only some of the best known. There were cases against trucking companies which reserved $15,000 to $22,000 a year over-the-road jobs for whites, leaving inner-city, lower-paying jobs for blacks. By mid-1970 in one way or another we were in eighty-seven Title VII cases. By 1973, when most procedural obstacles had been cleared away, we participated to some extent in almost two hundred. By 1975, there were over 220. See LDF

minutes, October 5, 1971; January 18 and October 23, 1973; and September 23, 1980; LDF dockets, October 5, 1971; August 1973; February 1975; and January to June 1980.

422   LAWYERS ON THE ROAD: Particularly Mike Baller, Barry Goldstein, Debby Greenberg, Clyde Murphy, Ron Ellis, Patrick Patterson, Jeff Mintz, and Bill Robinson.

422   MORE CASES THAN EEOC: LDF minutes, September 23, 1980.

422   LORILLARD: LDF minutes, January 25, 1971.

422   GILMAN, CITIES SERVICE: LDF press release, March 1, 1977.

422   UNION CAMP: *Boles v. Union Camp*, 57 Federal Rules Decisions 46 (S.D. Ga. 1972), LDF docket, December 1977.

422   NORFOLK AND WESTERN: LDF minutes, October 24, 1978.

422   OTHER AWARDS: We won $500,000 for black, Hispanic, and Filipino workers at the Naval Air Rework Facility in Alameda, California; LDF press release, no. 311, 1978. In 1980 Monsanto paid $2.65 million in back and front pay, which brought the total for 1979–80 to $10 million; LDF minutes, April 24, 1980; Title VII docket, January through June 1980, attached to LDF minutes, September 23, 1980. See also LDF minutes, September 25, 1979, and February 26, 1980.

423   STEEL CASES: *United States of America v. United States Steel Corporation; Luther McKinstry v. Same; William Hardy v. Same; John S. Ford v. Same; Elder Brown v. Same; Elex P. Love v. Same; Thomas Johnson v. Same; James Donald v. Same; James Fillingame v. Same*, 5 Employment Practices Decisions (CCH) P8619 (1973); LDF executive minutes, September 18, 1973; *Equal Justice* (an occasional newsletter of the LDF), Autumn 1973, LDF archives. LDF lawyers were Oscar Adams, Jim Baker, and U. W. Clemon of Birmingham and Barry Goldstein, who tried the cases with Justice Department lawyers.

423   BACK PAY: One plaintiff got $9,483, another only $74. The amounts included a front pay 50 percent wage increase to compensate for loss that would be suffered until openings appeared at the black workers' rightful places, that is, where they would have been absent the discrimination.

423   APPEAL OF POINTER DECISION: LDF minutes, October 15, 1974. The steel cases weren't the only ones in which one of our roles was to pressure the government to seek adequate relief. In *Rock v. Norfolk and Western Railroad*, 532 F.2d 336 (4th Cir. 1975), cert. den. 425 U.S. 934 (1976), we recovered $1.35 million for about two hundred workers; LDF minutes, October 24, 1978. The case was identical to a Justice Department case, *U.S. v. Chesapeake and Ohio Rwy Co.*, 471 F.2d 582 (4th Cir. 1972), which involved the same type of coal loading yard. Justice didn't seek or get back pay and settled for less effective seniority. After our victory the company and union had to accept the remedies we won. The pattern existed in many other cases, for example, *U.S. v. Georgia Power Company*, 634 F.2d 929 (5th Cir. 1981), 456 U.S. 952 (1982), 695 F.2d 890 (5th Cir. 1983).

423   STEEL APPEALS: By 1974 we had three cases against the steel industry on appeal as well as, two in which we were preparing appeals, two in district courts for consideration of relief, and two in preparation for trial, LDF minutes, October 15, 1974.

424   STEEL CONSENT DECREES: Bill Robinson, interview with author, August 31, 1991.

424 APPEAL OF CONSENT DECREE APPROVAL: *United States v. Allegheny-Ludlum Industries,* 63 Federal Rules Decisions 1 (1974).

424 ARGUMENT OF CONSENT DECREE APPROVAL: Barry argued *Ford,* now known as *United States v. United States Steel Corp.* 520 F.2d 1043 (5th Cir. 1975), cert. den. 429 U.S. 817 (1976), and I argued the consent decree cases, *United States v. Allegheny-Ludlum Industries,* 517 F.2d 826 (5th Cir. 1975), claiming that they offered inadequate back pay, denied workers who signed waivers the right to sue for the continuing effects of past discrimination practiced after the decree, and other rights.

425 APPEAL OF AMENDED DECREES: LDF press release, October 10, 1975; LDF executive minutes, November 18, 1975.

425 TEITELBAUM MANDAMUS: *Rodgers v. United States Steel,* 508 F.2d 152 (3rd Cir. 1975), 536 F.2d 1001 (3rd Cir. 1976).

426 GAG ORDERS: *Bernard v. Gulf Oil,* 619 F.2d 459 (5th Cir. 1980), aff'd 452 U.S. 89 (1981).

426 BLACK JOB UPGRADING: Similarly, on the railroads, black switchmen were able to finish their careers as conductors. Barry Goldstein, interview with the author, May 26, 1991.

426 "JUSTICE ... SERVED": Rorie Sherman, "Long Du Pont Case Ends— Almost," *National Law Journal,* December 7, 1992.

426 EMPLOYMENT DOCKET: LDF docket, December 1977; LDF minutes, September 23, 1980.

426 CIVIL SERVANTS: A sample of these cases includes *Louisville Black Police Officers' Organization v. City of Louisville,* 517 F.Supp. 825 (W.D. Ky. 1979), 700 F.2d 268 (6th Cir. 1983); *Barrett v. U.S. Civil Service Commission,* 439 F.Supp. 216 (D.C. D.C. 1977) (NASA); *Kirkland v. New York State Dept. of Correctional Services,* 711 F.2d 1117 (2nd Cir. 1983), cert. den. 465 U.S. 1005 (1984) (correction officers); and *Postal Service v. Aikens,* 460 U.S. 711 (1983). LDF counsel in these cases included Clyde Murphy, Gail Wright, Patrick Patterson, Peter Sherwood, Penda Hair, Deborah Greenberg, and me.

427 NEW ORLEANS: *Williams v. New Orleans,* 694 F.2d 987 (5th Cir. 1983).

427 DETROIT: *Bratton v. City of Detroit,* 712 F.2d 222 (6th Cir. 1983). Detroit's affirmative action plan for police by 1984 had increased the proportion of black lieutenants from under 5 to about 30 percent in a city that was 67 percent black. The Sixth Circuit Court of Appeals held that the government had applied too late to submit an amicus brief. The Supreme Court would not allow them in, either.

427 ECONOMIC DOWNTURN: We first lost the layoff battle in the Memphis firefighters case; *Memphis Fire Department v. Stotts,* 467 U.S. 561 (1984). Another similar case was *Wygant v. Jackson Board of Education,* 476 U.S. 267 (1985). See also Jack Greenberg, "Report to the Board of Directors," LDF minutes, April 26–28, 1984; other cases were the Pine Bluff, Arkansas, arsenal case, *Goldman v. Marsh,* 54 Fair Emp. Prac. Cas. (BNA) 1689 (E.D. Ark. 1983); a case involving the Memphis, Tennessee, Corps of Engineers; a case involving the Warner Robbins Air Logistics Center case, *Howard v. McLucas,* 597 F.Supp. 1501 (M.D. Ga. 1984).

427 PACE: *Luevano v. Campbell,* 93 Fair Employment Practices Cases 68 (D.C. 1981); "Suit Filed Charging Civil Service Test Discrimination," LDF

press release, January 29, 1979 (complaint filed in case is included with press release).

427 PACE SETTLEMENT: *Luevano v. Campbell,* 93 Fair Employment Practices Cases (D.C. 1981), 93.

428 WALL STREET FIRMS: Wilkie, Farr took the case against the New York City newspapers and the Newspaper and Mail Deliverers Union, *Patterson v. Newspaper and Mail Deliverers Union,* 514 F.2d 767 (2nd Cir. 1975). We referred the New York City Police Department case, *Guardians Association v. Civil Service Commission of New York City,* 431 F.Supp. 526 (S.D. N.Y. 1977), to Davis, Polk, and the fire department case, *Vulcan Society of the New York City Fire Department v. Civil Service Commission,* 490 F.2d 387 (2nd Cir. 1973), to Nickerson, Kramer. White and Case took the case against the Long Island Railroad, *Capers v. Long Island Railroad,* 429 F.Supp. 1359 (S.D. N.Y. 1977).

429 PLANNED TO BOMB ME: FBI file 185-875-35.

CHAPTER 31. THE WAR ON POVERTY

430 MARIAN WRIGHT: Andrew Young, interview with the author, February 29, 1992.

431 LDF IN CHICAGO: LDF docket (*Bender v. King*), September 1966; LDF executive minutes, September 22, 1966.

431 PROPOSAL: Memorandum, March 20, 1968, FBI file, 157-8428.

431 OPPOSITION TO THE WAR: The antiwar movement was vilifying President Johnson, who had done more for racial justice than any president since Lincoln. As well, Johnson's vision of a poverty-free society had led to his launching the "War on Poverty." Coming out against the war seemed to many in civil rights to be an act of disloyalty to a true friend. Roy Wilkins and Whitney Young urged Martin not to take that position. But King as a Christian preacher started with an adverse view of war, any war. Also, he would see war, the most expensive enterprise government ever undertakes, as competing for resources needed to deal with pervasive poverty.

432 LDF REPRESENTS POOR PEOPLE'S CAMPAIGN: LDF executive minutes, March 14, 1968; Mel Zarr, interview with author, May 13, 1991.

432 HOSEA WILLIAMS: FBI file 157-9146-74.

432 CLARK-FINNEY PLAN: Memorandum, Finney to Clark, April 2, 1968, LDF archives.

432 LDF REPRESENTATION: At the May LDF executive committee meeting Walter Gellhorn warned that we should not become involved in planning the campaign or influencing legislation, lest we jeopardize our tax exemption.

432 RESURRECTION CITY: Ben A. Franklin, "5,000 Open Poor People's Campaign in Washington," *New York Times,* May 13, 1968; "'City' of the Poor Begun in Capital," *New York Times,* May 14, 1968.

433 MASS RALLY: Ben A. Franklin, "Over 50,000 March in Capital in Support of the Poor," *New York Times,* June 20, 1968.

433 CAMPAIGN PROGRAMS: "Statement of Rev. Ralph David Abernathy on Goals of Poor People's Campaign," LDF press release, June 11, 1968, in author's possession.

433 ANTISOCIAL BEHAVIOR: Young, interview with author, February 29, 1992.

433 CLEARING RESURRECTION CITY: "Tear Gas Is Used by Capital Police at

Marchers' City," *New York Times*, June 23, 1968; Joseph A. Loftus, "City of the Poor Shuts Peacefully," *New York Times*, June 25, 1968.

434 MUNICIPAL EQUALIZATION CASE: *Hawkins v. Town of Shaw*, 461 F.2d 1171 (5th Cir. 1972), 1172, 1173.

435 WHITE'S OPINION: The employment case was *Washington v. Davis*, 426 U.S. 229 (1976). Even before *Shaw*, in an earlier LDF case, the Second Circuit required Lackawanna, New York, to permit a church-based housing developer to build homes for blacks outside the ghetto. It had been barred by zoning changes, refusal to hook up sewers, and other strategems. But this was a church developer, not a private business and the impact of the case was limited because not many churches or nonprofit agencies go into the building business; *Kennedy Park Homes v. Lackawanna*, 436 F.2d 108 (2nd Cir. 1970); "Background: *Kennedy Park v. Lackawanna*," LDF press release, December 2, 1970; "Appeals Court Rules That City Discriminated," LDF press release, December 11, 1970.

435 ATLANTA HOUSING: "Statement to Associated Press," LDF press release, March 9, 1967; "Memorandum—Atlanta Reporters," LDF press release, March 17, 1967; "Eviction Procedure of Low Income Public Housing Projects Attacked in Atlanta," LDF press release, March 20, 1967.

435 NABRIT'S CASE: *Thorpe v. Housing Authority of Durham*, 393 U.S. 268 (1969).

435 NASHVILLE CASE: *Nashville I-40 Steering Committee v. Ellington*, 387 F.2d 179 (6th Cir. 1967), cert. den. 390 U.S. 92 (1968); "Routing of Interstate Highway Thru Nashville Negro District Temporarily Halted by LDF Staff," LDF press release, November 18, 1967; "LDF Asks Supreme Court to Review Interstate Highway Construction in Nashville, Tenn.," LDF press release, January 8, 1968; "Supreme Court Has Halted Construction of Federal Nashville, Tenn. Highway," LDF press release, January 12, 1968.

435 NEWARK CASE: After filing complaints with several federal and state agencies, we won agreements that provided more than two thousand new housing units, an "extensive community health program," and that one-third of all journeymen and one-half of all apprentices on the hospital construction would be black or Puerto Rican; LDF National Office for the Rights of the Indigent (NORI) docket, March 1968.

435 RELOCATION REQUIRED: *Arrington v. City of Fairfield*, 414 F.2d 687 (5th Cir. 1969).

436 JURY TRIALS: *Curtis v. Loether*, 415 U.S. 189 (1974). My position was that compensation to plaintiffs in a housing discrimination case was part of equitable relief, ancillary to an injunction, for which a jury was not required, the same as the law for awarding back pay in employment cases.

437 GARNISHMENT CASE: *Sniadach v. Family Finance Corp.*, 395 U.S. 337 (1969).

438 INNER-CITY CONSUMER: Phil Schrag, "Bleak House," 44 *New York University Law Review* (1969), 115.

438 WELFARE CASES: See Jack Greenberg, "Litigation for Social Change: Methods, Limits and Role in Democracy—Thirtieth Annual Benjamin N. Cardozo Lecture Delivered Before the Association of the Bar of the City of New York on October 31, 1973," 29 *The Record* 320 (1974).

438 SUCCESSFUL CASES: "Thousands of Children South and North, Are Presently Affected," LDF press release, January 28, 1966; "Statement of Steve Ral-

ston," LDF press release, January 31, 1966; "Memorandum," LDF press release, January 13, 1967; LDF telegram, April 6, 1967.

438   MAXIMUM GRANT: *Dandridge v. Williams,* 397 U.S. 471 (1970).

438   HOME VISIT: *Wyman v. James,* 400 U.S. 309 (1970).

439   SUPREME COURT ON SCHOOL FINANCE: *San Antonio School District v. Rodriguez,* 411 U.S. 1 (1973).

439   LDF SCHOOL FINANCE CASE: *Board of Education, Levittown Union Free School District v. Nyquist,* 57 N.Y. 2d 27 (1982), app. dismissed 459 U.S. 1139 (1983). California's Supreme Court held that its constitution requires equality in school financing, *Serrano v. Priest,* 135 Cal. 345 (1976), cert. den. 432 U.S. 907 (1977).

CHAPTER 32. NORI AND CRIMINAL JUSTICE

440   NORI: The Eighth Amendment provides, "Excessive bail shall not be required." There was virtually no Supreme Court law on the subject. By the time a case could be appealed the defendant would have been convicted or acquitted and the question would be moot. See Jack Greenberg, "Litigation for Social Change: Methods, Limits and Role in Democracy—Thirtieth Annual Benjamin N. Cardozo Lecture Delivered Before the Association of the Bar of the City of New York on October 31, 1973," 29 *The Record* 320 (1974), 329.

We drew up a profile of the ideal defendant for a test case: no money, no long criminal record, ties of employment and residence to the community, special investigative problems in which defendant might help his lawyer if out on bail. The case that developed involved an assault on a police undercover agent who had been attacked by several persons with cinder blocks and sticks. The judge set bail at $1,000, which required a $100 bail bond premium, but the defendant couldn't provide necessary collateral. Even though a social worker at a poverty law program had offered to supervise the defendant, he went to jail to await trial. Tony Amsterdam's heroic effort did get the case to the Supreme Court before trial, but it denied review with only Justice Douglas dissenting; *Gonzales v. Warden, Brooklyn House of Detention,* 390 U.S. 903 (1968). We gave up. There always had been lurking in the bail effort the possibility that if economic discrimination were abolished there would have to be some system of preventive detention—rich and poor alike might be held before trial without bail, hardly an attractive outcome.

440   CAPITAL PUNISHMENT CAMPAIGN: Michael Meltsner, *Cruel and Unusual: The Supreme Court and Capital Punishment* (New York: Random House, 1973). There are a few points on which our perceptions differ; Meltsner was a staff lawyer at LDF during the early days of its capital punishment effort.

440   STATISTICS: U.S. Bureau of the Census, *Statistical Abstract, 1989* (Washington, D.C.: Government Printing Office, 1989), 187.

441   *Hamilton v. Alabama,* 368 U.S. 52 (1961).

441   GOLDBERG: *Rudolph v. Alabama,* 375 U.S. 889 (1963).

441   CAPITAL PUNISHMENT EFFORT LAUNCHED: LDF executive minutes, November 14 (discussing LDF cases in Georgia and Alabama raising the issue and discussing conference on death cases where victim not killed) and December

12, 1963 (cases in Georgia and Alabama). See also Meltsner, *Cruel and Unusual*, 30, which dates the conception of the campaign several months later. Early in 1965 I proposed a conference for February 15 and 16 in which the lead item was "Expansion of the attack on capital punishment with immediate emphasis on interracial rape convictions, with eventual attack on all capital punishment against Negro defendants, regardless of the crime." See "Confidential" memorandum, n.d., in author's possession.

441 LSCRRC: LDF executive minutes, May 13, 1965.

441 SCHEDULES: Schedules went into detail concerning the victim's reputation for chastity, whether she was pregnant at the time of the assault, other offenses committed upon her, circumstances of the offense, how long she was detained, planning of the offense, collaborators, numbers of assailants, extent of violence, weapons, injuries suffered by the victim, whether she became pregnant or contracted venereal disease, prior relations between defendant and victim, details about the trial and appeal and post-conviction proceedings, clemency, and whether the death sentence was executed. Samples of the questionnaire are in LDF archives. When the students returned, Wolfgang and statisticians analyzed the materials to determine whether the race of assailant and victim accounted for the disproportionate number of executions of blacks who raped white women.

In one case, United States District Judge Robert Hemphill impounded our 355 South Carolina schedules. I argued the appeal in the Fourth Circuit, which reversed. The opinion observed that the survey "might be useful in this and other litigation"; *Moorer v. State of South Carolina,* 368 F.2d 458 (4th Cir. 1966). But the Fourth Circuit undid the conviction on the ground that the jury had no opportunity to determine whether a statement Moorer had made was voluntary.

442 STANDARDS OF DECENCY: *Weems v. United States,* 217 U.S. 349 (1910). Weems, who had embezzled a small sum, was sentenced in the Philippines—then an American possession—to *cadena temporal,* a punishment inherited from Spain when the Philippines belonged to it. *Cadena temporal* consisted of fifteen years in prison at hard labor, chained ankle to wrist, and loss of personal and civil rights, such as parental authority and the right to vote. On appeal, the Supreme Court vacated the sentence.

442 DESERTION CASE: *Trop v. Dulles,* 356 U.S. 86 (1958).

443 ADDICTION CASE: *Robinson v. California,* 370 U.S. 660 (1962).

444 DEATH PENALTY STATISTICS: See *Death Row USA,* the LDF death penalty newsletter, various dates.

444 *Maxwell v. Bishop,* 257 F.Supp. 710 (E.D. Ark. 1966), 398 F.2d 138 (8th Cir. 1968), vacated and remanded 398 U.S. 262 (1970). Maxwell already had been convicted and sentenced to death for rape, had gone through the state courts, and then through the federal courts on habeas corpus, and to the United States Supreme Court, which had declined to hear his case. With the rape survey completed we went back to federal court with proof that capital punishment for rape was used unconstitutionally in Arkansas.

444 POSTCONVICTION ATTACK: Quote from *Maxwell v. Bishop,* 398 F.2d 138 (8th Cir. 1968), 145.

444 DISTRICT JUDGE'S EXPLANATION: *Maxwell v. Bishop,* 257 F.Supp. 710 (E.D. Ark. 1966), 720.

445 STAY: Described in *Maxwell v. Bishop,* 398 F.2d 138 (8th Cir. 1968), 140.

445 CLASS STAY: *Adderly v. Wainwright,* 272 F.Supp. 530 (M.D. Fla. 1967).

447   Amsterdam letter: Letter, Anthony G. Amsterdam to Thomas P. Sullivan, March 16, 1968, copy in author's possession.

447   Stewart quoted: *Witherspoon v. Illinois,* 391 U.S. 510 (1968), 523, 518.

447   Amsterdam at LDF: LDF executive minutes, May 9, 1968.

447   first national conference: LDF telegram announcing press conference, May 1, 1968; "Statement by Jack Greenberg," May 3, 1968, LDF press release; Jack Greenberg and Jack Himmelstein, "Varieties of Attack on the Death Penalty," 15 *Crime and Delinquency* 112 (1969).

447   borrowing the record: *Maxwell v. Bishop,* Oral Argument, Supreme Court No. 622, October Term, 1968, 68; letter, Anthony G. Amsterdam to Jack Greenberg, January 12, 1993, in author's possession.

448   *Boykin* brief: *Boykin v. Alabama,* Brief for the NAACP Legal Defense and Educational Fund and the National Office for the Rights of the Indigent as Amici Curiae, Supreme Court No. 642, October Term 1968, 61. See also *Boykin v. Alabama,* 281 Ala. 659, 207 So.2d 412 (Ala. 1968), rev'd 395 U.S. 238 (1969).

448   *Maxwell* again: *Maxwell v. Bishop,* 398 U.S. 262 (1970).

448   Harlan opinion: *McGautha v. California* and *Crampton v. Ohio,* 402 U.S. 183 (1971), 196–208.

448   Justice Black: Ibid., 226.

449   supplemental brief: *Mathis v. New Jersey,* 52 N.J. 238, 245 A. 2d 20 (N.J. 1968), rev'd and rem'd 404 U.S. 946 (1971).

449   four cases: *Aikens v. California, Branch v. Texas, Furman v. Georgia,* and *Jackson v. Georgia. Aikens* and *Furman* were murder cases, *Branch* and *Jackson* rape cases. *Branch* was the non-LDF case. See also "Statement on U.S. Supreme Court Capital Punishment Decision," LDF press release, May 3, 1971.

449   our brief: *Aikens v. California,* Motion for Leave to File Brief Amici Curiae and Brief Amici Curiae in Support of Petitioners, Supreme Court No. 68-5027, October Term 1971. See also LDF executive minutes, July 13, 1971.

449   *Ralph v. Warden,* 438 F.2d 786 (4th Cir. 1970).

449   answer objections: *Aikens v. California,* Brief Amici Curiae in Support of Petitioners, Supreme Court, No. 68-5027, October Term 1971.

450   Burger to Amsterdam: 10 *Criminal Law Reporter* (1972), 4146.

450   my argument: Ibid.

450   dignity of man: *People v. Anderson,* 100 Cal Rpt. 152 (Cal. 1972).

450   nine opinions: *Furman v. Georgia,* 408 U.S. 238 (1972).

450   Stewart: Ibid., 310, 309.

451   White: Ibid., 313.

451   Brennan: Ibid., 305.

451   events following *Furman:* LDF Executive Minutes, December 9, 1975; Jack Greenberg, "Capital Punishment as a System," 91 *Yale Law Journal* (1982), 908.

452   North Carolina: *Fowler v. North Carolina,* 285 N.C. 90 (1974).

452   mandatory death penalty cases: *Woodson v. North Carolina,* 428 U.S. 280 (1976); *Roberts v. Louisiana,* 428 U.S. 325 (1976).

453   aggravating, mitigating factors: *Gregg v. Georgia,* 428 U.S. 153 (1976).

453   Kendall's chess: David Kendall, interview with the author, September 30, 1991.

453   Kendall: In the late 1970s David left LDF to join Williams and Connally,

where he is a partner specializing in First Amendment rights, and is a member of the LDF board. He also became President Clinton's personal lawyer.

453 MANDATORY SENTENCES: *Woodson v. North Carolina*, 428 U.S. 280 (1976), and *Roberts v. Louisiana*, 428 U.S. 325 (1976).

454 INVALIDATIONS: LDF press release, July 2, 1976.

454 LEGISLATIVE RESPONSE: *Gregg v. Georgia*, 428 U.S. 153 (1976), 179.

454 DEATH ROW: LDF executive minutes, July 26, 1976.

454 DEATH PENALTY FOR RAPE UNCONSTITUTIONAL: *Coker v. Georgia*, 433 U.S. 584 (1977).

454 RESOURCES IN DEATH CASES: LDF executive minutes, September 28, 1976. In 1981 we put only 15 to 16 percent of our energies and little money into capital punishment. Employment suits consumed 50 percent of our time and remained expensive; education cases used about 15 percent and were costly; LDF executive minutes, May 28, 1981.

454 FOUNDATIONS: LDF executive minutes, May 28, 1981.

454 DEATH CASES: LDF executive minutes, September 28, 1981; September 23 and November 23, 1982. One case in 1980 struck down a Texas statute that required jurors to swear that the prospect of the death penalty wouldn't affect their deliberations. Joel Berger argued a case in 1981 where the Court reversed another statute because a state psychiatrist, who appeared in cases so often that he became known as the "killer shrink," testified that from interviews to learn whether defendant was fit to stand trial, he concluded that the defendant appeared likely to kill again. The testimony violated the Fifth Amendment prohibition of self-incrimination and the Sixth Amendment guarantee of right to counsel. *Estelle v. Smith*, 451 U.S. 454 (1981). The next year, in *Enmund v. Florida*, 458 U.S. 782 (1982), the Court held unconstitutional the death penalty, in a case Jim Liebman argued, where the defendant had driven the killer to the place of the crime but didn't otherwise participate. Only eight states had "felony murder" laws that punished by death this degree of involvement and hardly anyone ever was executed under them.

454 SIXTEEN YEARS OLD: *Eddings v. Oklahoma*, 455 U.S. 104 (1982).

455 IMPATIENCE: In *Barefoot v. Estelle*, 463 U.S. 880 (1983), the defendant's lawyer argued that the jury would give undue weight to the expert opinion of a psychiatrist who testified that the defendant was a sociopath who would kill again—testimony which should have been excluded from evidence. But the district court denied habeas corpus. Barefoot's lawyer applied for a stay of execution to the Fifth Circuit, which required him to brief and argue the case in two days, then denied the stay and affirmed the death penalty immediately. With Barefoot's lawyer I argued the case in the Supreme Court. The Court held that neither the right against self-incrimination nor the right to counsel had been denied. Barefoot's counsel could have cross-examined and put on contradictory testimony. My argument was directed at the rush to judgment. The Court decided that counsel had plenty of time. It laid down rules: The petitioner must have a chance to address the merits; the court of appeals must decide the merits; it may adopt rules for expediting cases.

   Zant v. Stephens, 462 U.S. 862 (1983), upheld a death sentence that had been based on a statutory aggravating factor, "a substantial history of serious assaultive criminal convictions," which the Georgia Supreme Court earlier held unconstitutionally vague. But the United States Supreme Court decided that other statutory factors, including a criminal record, justified the sentence. It brushed aside the argument that there might have been no death penalty if the forbidden standard had not been considered.

455 THIRD DEFEAT: *Barclay v. Florida*, 463 U.S. 939 (1983).

455 RACE OF VICTIM: LDF executive minutes, January 25, 1977; January 17, 1978; March 27, 1979; April 29, 1982; November 19, 1983. In June 1976 we held a conference at Howard University with death penalty lawyers and social scientists to explore next steps. By then we knew that of twenty-two people on death row in Mississippi, nineteen were blacks who had killed whites. The other three were whites who had also killed whites. See LDF press release, no. 304, 1976. In Florida a black who killed a white would be sentenced to death 30 percent of the time; a white murderer of a white would get the death penalty 15 percent of the time; when blacks killed blacks juries awarded death in 3 percent of the cases. Juries never sentenced to death whites who killed blacks. Georgia and Texas followed the same pattern.

455 BALDUS STUDY: LDF minutes, April 29, 1982; November 19, 1983.

455 NO INTENT: *McCleskey v. Kemp*, 481 U.S. 279 (1987).

456 SCRUPLED JURORS: *Witherspoon v. Illinois*, 391 U.S. 510 (1968).

456 MITIGATING CIRCUMSTANCES: *Furman v. Georgia*, 408 U.S. 238 (1972), and *Lockett v. Ohio*, 438 U.S. 586 (1978).

456 PROCEDURAL REFORMS: Juries had to have the option of convicting on a lesser included offense—for example, manslaughter instead of murder—that would not involve the death penalty, *Beck v. Alabama*, 447 U.S. 625 (1980); counsel had the right to see evidence that judges reviewed where it played a role in death sentencing, *Gardner v. Florida*, 428 U.S. 908 (1976); the Court abolished the mandatory death penalty, *Woodson v. North Carolina*, 428 U.S. 280 (1976).

The Court eased requirements for proving discrimination in selecting juries and proving that a confession was coerced (*Coleman v. Alabama*, 377 U.S. 129 [1964] and 389 U.S. 22 [1967]; *Sims v. Georgia*, 385 U.S. 538 [1967] and 389 U.S. 404 [1967]; *Beecher v. Alabama*, 389 U.S. 35 [1967]); excluded evidence seized during a warrantless search conducted with consent that was given following a false assurance that the police had a warrant (*Bumper v. North Carolina*, 391 U.S. 543 [1968]); required that for a guilty plea to be valid the defendant had to have a complete understanding of what such a plea connotes and of its consequences (*Boykin v. Alabama*, 395 U.S. 238 [1969]); and prohibited the use of testimony obtained during a psychiatric session devoted to deciding whether defendant was mentally fit to stand trial (*Estelle v. Smith*, 451 U.S. 454 [1981]).

456 DETERRENCE: The principal study purporting to demonstrate that the death penalty is a deterrent is Isaac Ehrlich, "The Deterrent Effect of Capital Punishment: A Question of Life and Death," 65 *American Economic Review* 397 (1975); it has been thoroughly discredited: See Hugo Bedau, *The Death Penalty in America*, 3d ed. (New York: Oxford University Press, 1982), 129–32.

456 PROSPECTS FOR THE DEATH PENALTY: Jack Greenberg, "Capital Punishment as a System," 91 *Yale Law Journal* 908 (1982), and "Against the American System of Capital Punishment," 99 *Harvard Law Review* 1670 (1984).

457 TURNER: William Bennett Turner, interview with the author, January 27, 1992.

457 DUE PROCESS IN DISCIPLINARY PROCEEDINGS: *United States ex rel. Mosher v. Lavallee*, 321 F.Supp 127 (N.D. N.Y. 1970), 460 F.2d 126 (2nd Cir. 1972), cert. den. *McMann v. Wright*, 409 U.S. 885 (1972); LDF NORI docket, November 1968.

457 GRAPEVINE: A Texas lawyer phoned Tony Amsterdam, asking whether something similar might be done there. Tony called Bill who then commenced *Cruz v. Beto*, 405 U.S. 319 (1972), in 1969.

457 ARKANSAS: Phil Kaplan, phone interview with the author, August 16, 1991.

458 ARKANSAS CASE: *Holt v. Sarver*, 309 F.Supp. 362 (E.D. Ark. 1970).

458 CASE IN SUPREME COURT: *Hutto v. Finney*, 437 U.S. 678 (1978).

458 SOLITARY: Turner moved to California to the LDF San Francisco office, and Stanley Bass, an Illinois prisoners' rights lawyer joined us. His first LDF case, *Williams v. Illinois*, 399 U.S. 235 (1970), involved a prisoner who was too poor to pay $505 in costs and fines and instead was required to serve 101 days in jail at $5.00 per day. The Court held that an indigent who can't pay a fine may not be jailed instead.

458 JUSTICE: Frank Kermerer, *William Wayne Justice: A Judicial Biography* (Austin: University of Texas Press, 1991).

458 TEXAS CASE: *Ruiz v. Estelle*, 503 F.Supp. 1265 (S.D. Tex. 1980). At the New York Legal Aid Society (LAS), Joel Berger, who later joined LDF, had long wanted to file suit to reform the Tombs in Manhattan, the most notorious jail in the country. LAS at that time had no policy of bringing affirmative suits of this sort. Joel asked LDF to take on the case. As soon as I agreed, LAS filed the case, which closed the Tombs and replaced it with a state-of-the art modern jail; *Rhem v. Malcolm*, 371 F.Supp. 594 (S.D. N.Y. 1974), aff'd 507 F.2d 33 (2d Cir. 1974). The decision established that pretrial detainees had the right to contact with visitors, recreation, exercise, minimal environmental conditions, sanitation, and windows and became an important national precedent. Joel Berger, interview with the author, July 17, 1991.

458 LDF PRISON CASES: LDF docket, June 1975; Arkansas, *Holt v. Sarver*, 309 F.Supp. 362 (E.D. Ark. 1970); Florida, *Costello v. Wainwright*, 539 F.2d 547 (5th Cir. 1976), 430 U.S. 325 (1977); Georgia, *Guthrie v. Ault*, 423 U.S. 855 (1975); Texas, *Ruiz v. Estelle*, 503 F.Supp. 1265 (S.D. Tex. 1980).

458 LYNN WALKER: But she confesses that when, for her personal safety, she was locked alone in a cell in New York's Riker's Island prison, where she was observing whether there would be retaliation against inmates who had taken guards hostage, she saw a mouse and conducted the rest of her vigil from the safety of a desk top.

458 GEORGIA CASE: *Guthrie v. Evans*, 93 Federal Rules Decisions 390 (S.D. Ga. 1981). Holifield was recently out of Harvard and now is a partner in a large Florida firm.

459 STATISTICAL PROOF: In *Whitus v. Georgia*, 385 U.S. 545 (1967), 552, n. 2, the Supreme Court cited an article by Mike Finkelstein ("The Application of Statistical Decision Theory to the Jury Discrimination Cases," 80 *Harvard Law Review* 338 [1968]), which gave his analysis its imprimatur. In *Alexander v. Louisiana*, a rape case, Steve Ralston argued that the Louisiana grand jury system was unconstitutional because it listed potential jurors by race and a disproportionately small number of blacks served.

Justice White's opinion held the system unconstitutional, referring to the "petitioner's demonstration that under one statistical technique of calculating probability, the chances that 27 Negroes would have been selected at random for the 400-member final jury list, when 1,015 out of the 7,374 questionnaires returned were from Negroes, are one in 20,000"; 405 U.S. 625 (1972), 630, n. 9. The opinion referred to the Court's earlier citation of Mike Finkelstein's work.

460   AMAKER'S CASE: *Carter v. Jury Commissioners of Greene County, Alabama*, 396 U.S. 320 (1970), 329.

460   JURY COMMISSIONERS: Mike Meltsner argued *Turner v. Fouche*, 396 U.S. 346 (1970), which held unconstitutional the method of selecting juries and school boards in Taliaferro (pronounced Tolliver) County, Georgia. The case in which we first raised the issue of exluding women was *Alexander v. Louisiana*, 405 U.S. 625 (1972).

460   EXCUSING WOMEN AS JURORS UNCONSTITUTIONAL: *Taylor v. Louisiana*, 419 U.S. 522 (1975).

460   JURY CASES: *Swain v. Alabama*, 380 U.S. 202 (1965); *Batson v. Kentucky*, 476 U.S. 79 (1986).

CHAPTER 33. AFFIRMATIVE ACTION

462   JOHNSON'S SPEECH: Timothy J. O'Neill, *Bakke and the Politics of Equality: Friends and Foes in the Classroom of Litigation* (Middletown, Conn.: Wesleyan University Press, 1985), 55.

462   SCHOOL TEACHER ASSIGNMENT: *Carr v. Montgomery Board of Education*, 395 U.S. 225 (1969).

462   ASSIGNING BLACK CHILDREN PROPORTIONATELY: *Swann v. Charlotte-Mecklenburg Board of Education*, 402 U.S. 1 (1971).

463   FIRST NATIONALLY PUBLICIZED AFFIRMATIVE ACTION CASE: *DeFunis v. Odegaard*, 416 U.S. 312 (1974).

463   BRIEFS IN *DeFUNIS:* DeFunis v. Odegaard *and the University of Washington: The Record*, 3 vols., Ann Fagan Ginger, ed. (Dobbs Ferry, N.Y.: Oceana, 1974).

463   DEBATE AMONG JEWISH GROUPS: Marc Stern, "Jews and Affirmative Action," in *1990 Survey of Jewish Affairs*, William Frankel, ed. (London: Blackwell, 1990), 143–64.

464   ADMISSIONS OFFICER'S LETTER: *Bakke v. Regents of the University of California: The Record*, 5 vols., Alfred Slocum, ed. (Dobbs Ferry, N.Y.: Oceana, 1978), vol. 2, 353.

465   ORDER TO ADMIT BAKKE: *Bakke v. Regents*, 18 Cal. 3d 34 (Cal. 1976), 64.

465   NATHANIEL JONES: Letter, December 9, 1976, LDF archives.

465   COX TO ARGUE *BAKKE:* William Coblentz, interview with the author, October 15, 1991.

465   LDF AMICUS BRIEF: *Bakke v. Regents*, Brief of LDF, 14, 25, 33–34.

466   SOLICITOR GENERAL AND *BAKKE:* Joel Dreyfuss and Charles Lawrence, *The Bakke Case: The Politics of Inequality* (New York: Harcourt Brace, 1979), 166.

466   LIPSHUTZ AND EIZENSTAT TO CARTER: "Memorandum for the President and Vice President," September 10, 1977, LDF archives.

466   DEBATE WITHIN CARTER ADMINISTRATION: O'Neill, *Bakke and the Politics of*

> *Equality,* 179–91; Bernard Schwartz, *Behind Bakke: Affirmative Action and the Supreme Court* (New York: New York University Press, 1988), 45–47.

466   LDF CASE ON RACIAL NUMERICAL STANDARDS: *United Jewish Organizations of Williamsburgh v. Carey,* 430 U.S. 144 (1977).

466   LDF ACTIVITIES IN *BAKKE:* LDF Executive Minutes, September 27, 1977; Jim Nabrit, memorandum, n.d., *Bakke* file, LDF archives.

467   THE DECISION: *Bakke v. Regents,* 438 U.S. 265 (1978).

467   BLACK PRISON GUARDS: *Kirkland v. New York State Department of Correctional Services,* 520 F.2d 420 (2nd Cir. 1975), cert. den. 429 U.S. 823 (1976).

468   KAISER LOUISIANA CASE: *Burrell v. Kaiser Aluminum* (unreported); Barry Goldstein, interview with the author, May 26, 1991.

468   AFFIRMATIVE ACTION PLAN: *United Steel Workers v. Weber,* 443 U.S. 193 (1979). See also Stern, "Jews and Affirmative Action."

CHAPTER 34. LDF GOES TO WASHINGTON

470   D.C. OFFICE: I also assigned Barry Goldstein to the D.C. office; he wanted to move to the District of Columbia where his wife had been admitted to medical school. At first he mainly worked on litigation.

470   ELAINE JONES: Her first capital punishment case was *Beecher v. Alabama,* 408 U.S. 234 (1972). Her first employment cases were *Patterson v. American Tobacco,* 535 F.2d 257 (4th Cir. 1976), and *Stallworth v. Monsanto,* 558 F.2d 257 (5th Cir. 1977).

471   LDF JOINS LCCR: LDF minutes, April 21, 1979.

471   JONES'S AGENDA: LDF executive minutes, March 22 and September 27, 1977; LDF minutes, April 26, 1977.

471   SPLIT OF THE FIFTH CIRCUIT: Elaine Jones, interview with the author, November 6, 1991.

472   OPPOSITION TO CLEMON: U. W. Clemon interview with the author, November 6, 1991. See also, National Bar Association, "Report of the Judicial Selection Committee on U. W. Clemon, Esq., Candidate for United States District Judge Northern District of Alabama," presented to the United States Justice Department, October 30, 1979, in author's possession.

472   "LERGS": LDF minutes, May 24, 1980, and April 29, 1982.

472   COOPERATION IN VOTING RIGHTS: *Whitcomb v. Chavis,* 403 U.S. 124 (1971), with James Manahan and ACLU as amicus; *White v. Regester,* 412 U.S. 755 (1973), with David R. Richards, who argued the case, and MALDEF; *Zimmer v. McKeithen* 485 F.2d 1297 (5th Cir. 1973), with Stanley A. Halpin, Jr., and Lawyers Committee for Civil Rights Under Law as amicus; *Beer v. United States,* 425 U.S. 130 (1976), with Stanley A. Halpin, Jr.; *Kirksey v. Board of Supervisors,* 554 F.2d 139 (5th Cir. 1977), with Lawyers Committee for Civil Rights Under Law.

472   MULTIMEMBER SYSTEM: The first big at-large case invalidated a Texas law that created at-large districts in Dallas and Bexar County (San Antonio), Texas. There was a history of discrimination in the area and the law required a majority vote to win nomination in the primary. A Chicano or black with a winning plurality against two competing whites would face only the winning white in a run-off and most likely lose. Only two blacks

had been elected since Reconstruction; the dominant political party neither needed minority support, nor exhibited good-faith concern for minority needs. The party also used racist campaign tactics. Chicanos faced a
cultural and language barrier and, like blacks, lived in poverty. Citing
these circumstances, *White v. Regester*, 412 U.S. 755 (1973), held the Dallas and Bexar systems unconstitutional.

In March 1975 LDF challenged the at-large method of electing the
Boston School Committee in *Black Voters v. McDonough*, 565 F.2d 1 (1st
Cir. 1977). In one of the few policy disagreements on the board, Walter
Gellhorn argued, "We should not support a case which would seek to
carve out districts based on race." John A. Davis (who had directed much
of the research for the School Segregation Cases), also expressed reservations. Bill Coleman appointed a committee that recommended going
ahead; LDF minutes, January 21 and February 25, 1975. We lost in the
First Circuit Court of Appeals, "without prejudice to plaintiffs' right to
reopen their claim in the future in the light of circumstances as they may
appear."

473 GERRYMANDERING: *United Jewish Organizations of Williamsburgh v.
     Carey*, 430 U.S. 144 (1977).

473 BLACKSHER'S MOBILE VOTING CASE: *Bolden v. City of Mobile*, 423 F.Supp.
     384 (S.D. Ala. 1976), 571 F.2d 238 (5th Cir. 1978), 446 U.S. 55 (1980), 542
     F.Supp. 1050 (S.D. Ala. 1982).

474 1869 LEGISLATIVE COMMITTEE REPORT: *Bolden*, 542 F.Supp. 1050, 1057.

475 VOTING RIGHTS LOBBYING: Lani Guinier, interview with the author, October
     30, 1991; Elaine Jones, interview with the author, December 7, 1991.

475 HYDE'S BAILOUT PROVISION: 121 *Congressional Record*, 1858–59.

475 BAILOUT: Michael Pertschuk, *Giant Killers* (New York: Norton, 1986),
     chap. 6.

476 THE VOTING RIGHTS ACT OF 1982: Timothy J. O'Rourke, "Voting Rights
     Acts Amendments of 1982," 69 *Virginia University Law Review* 765
     (1983), 784.

476 LANGUAGE OF VOTING RIGHTS ACT: Public Law 97-205, 42 USC 1973b.

477 BURKE COUNTY CASE: *Rodgers v. Lodge*, 458 U.S. 613 (1982). Fifty-three
     percent of the county's population and 38 percent of its voters were black,
     but no black ever had been elected to the county commission. Obstacles
     to black political participation, like those in *Bolden*, existed. The Court
     held these facts supported the trial court's finding of intent. It didn't cite
     the newly adopted section 2, or its results test, instead finding "intent" in
     the result.

477 GUINIER'S LOUISIANA GERRYMANDER CASE: *Major v. Treen*, 574 F.Supp. 325
     (E.D. La. 1983), 700 F.Supp 1422 (E.D. La. 1988); North Carolina case:
     Edmisten v. Gingles, 590 F.Supp. 345 (E.D. N.C. 1984), *Thornton v. Gin-
     gles*, 478 U.S. 30 (1986).

477 REPUBLICANS SUPPORT MAJORITY BLACK DISTRICTS: "The Battle of the Pastry
     Cooks," *The Economist*, May 18, 1991.

CHAPTER 35. FINAL SEPARATIONS

478 THURGOOD ON IRS: Thurgood Marshall, Oral History Project, Columbia
     University (interview with Ed Edwin, June 7, 1977), 178.

479 NAACP ON REPRESENTING FREEDOM RIDERS: NAACP minutes, September 11, 1961.

479 CARTER MEMORANDUM TO NAACP BOARD: "The Legal Program and the NAACP Dilemma," n.d., in author's possession.

479 CARTER MEMORANDUM REGARDING SPLIT: "Memorandum on the Past, Present and Proposed Future Relationship of the NAACP and the Legal Defense Fund," n.d., in author's possession.

480 PROHIBIT LAWYERS WORKING WITH LDF: Ibid.

480 CARTER LETTER TO GREENBERG: February 16, 1962, in author's possession.

480 COMMITTEE REPORT: "Report of the Liaison Committee with Inc. Fund Board," April 6, 1962, in author's possession.

480 NAACP SPECIAL CONTRIBUTION FUND: NAACP minutes, January 6, May 11, and November 9, 1964.

480 CARTER LETTER TO GREENBERG: June 11, 1965, in author's possession.

480 NAACP RESOLUTION: NAACP minutes, July 2, 1965. RESOLUTION WITHDRAWN: NAACP minutes, September 12, 1965.

480 LDF DISINVITED TO 1966 NAACP CONVENTION: M. S. Handler, "Wilkins Says Black Power Leads Only to Black Death" *New York Times,* July 6, 1966.

480 LEGEND: The LDF disclaimer evolved over time. For another slightly different version see "Constance Motley Named Federal Judge," LDF press release, September 1, 1966.

481 WILKINS LETTER TO GREENBERG: January 14, 1966, in author's possession.

481 LDF-NAACP MEETING: "Notes on Meeting Between Members of the Boards of the NAACP and the NAACP LDF, Inc.," February 24, 1966, in author's possession.

481 WILKINS'S REACTION TO LDF FUND-RAISING COMMITTEES: NAACP minutes, April 10, 1967.

481 FIRING OF LEWIS STEEL: LDF minutes, December 18, 1968; Steel, "Nine Men in Black Who Think White," *New York Times Magazine,* October 16, 1968.

481 CARTER ON STEEL'S FIRING: Sylvan Fox, "NAACP Ouster Will Be Fought," *New York Times,* October 16, 1968. CARTER'S RESIGNATION: LDF executive minutes, December 18, 1968; Carter to Wilkins, October 28, 1968, Roy Wilkins Collection, Lewis Steel Dismissal Case 1968, box 31, Library of Congress, Manuscript Reading Room.

481 NAACP STRIFE: Thomas A. Johnson, "NAACP Is Facing Showdown on Ouster," *New York Times,* November 24, 1968.

482 LDF BOARD RELUCTANCE TO KEEP INITIALS: LDF executive minutes, December 11, 1969. In 1979, preparing to sue us, the Association got a memorandum from one of its fund-raisers explaining that he had failed to obtain a grant from the Rockefeller Foundation years earlier because its officials thought that LDF was the NAACP. He reported, "They noted that Jack Greenberg never disabused them of this false notion." Rockefeller, however, was among the most knowledgeable of the foundations. The fund-raiser also accused us of taking money under false pretenses from the Altschul Foundation, but we never received a grant from Altschul. We regularly printed on our releases that we were entirely separate from the NAACP. Inept fund-raising and disappointed expectations made it easy to blame LDF. See memorandum, Gil Jonas to Denton Watson, March 5, 1979, in author's possession.

482   PROPOSAL TO DROP INITIALS: LDF executive minutes, September 28, 1976;
      ITS REJECTION: LDF executive minutes, November 22, 1977.

482   NAACP SENTIMENT THAT A BLACK PERSON SHOULD HEAD LDF: Nathaniel
      Jones, interview with the author, September 26, 1991.

482   LOUIS LOMAX QUOTED: Randall Kennedy, "On Cussing Out White Liber-
      als," *The Nation*, September 4, 1982.

483   WRIGHT'S DENUNCIATION: Bruce McM. Wright letter and drafts to Green-
      berg, with reply, August 30, 1979, in author's possession.

483   WRIGHT'S SPEECH AT HOWARD: Memorandum and transcript, Wiley A. Bran-
      ton to Greenberg, September 23, 1981, in author's possession.

483   NAACP DEMANDS LDF STOP USING INITIALS: NAACP minutes, April 17–18,
      1978; Nathaniel Sheppard, Jr., "NAACP Renews Dispute with Legal
      Defense Fund Over Use of Name, *New York Times*, April 19, 1978.

484   HINES CASE: Thomas A. Johnson, "Rights Units Battle Over Alabama
      Case," *New York Times*, November 16, 1978; "Rape Case Appeal Argued
      in Alabama," *New York Times*, December 13, 1978; "Rights Groups Agree
      on Lawyer in Retarded Man's Rape Appeal," *New York Times*, January 6,
      1979.

484   CORRESPONDENCE, MEETINGS, MEMORANDA: LDF executive minutes, January
      9, February 3, and March 17, 1979; LDF minutes, April 21, 1979.

484   MEETING: Bill Coleman, Jim Nabrit III, and his father, Big Jim, Julius
      Chambers, Wiley Branton, Bill DeWind, and I attended for LDF; Ben
      Hooks, Margaret Bush Wilson, Nate Jones, and several other Association
      board members represented the Association. NAACP statement read by
      Berry, "Statement of NAACP on Issues and Proposals at the Conference of
      NAACP and LDF Special Committees," Mayflower Hotel, Washington,
      D.C., May 7, 1979, in author's possession.

484   NAACP CONVENTION RESOLUTION: "Resolution," June 28, 1979, in author's
      possession.

484   ASSOCIATION SUES: *NAACP v. NAACP Legal Defense and Educational
      Fund*, 559 F.Supp. 1337 (D.C. D.C. 1983).

485   HOOKS SUSPENSION: Sheila Rule, "NAACP Officials Say Director Has Been
      Indefinitely Suspended," *New York Times*, May 21, 1983; Douglas
      McGill, "Chairman of NAACP Says She Is 'Unaware' of Meeting," *New
      York Times*, May 25, 1983; Ronald Smothers, "NAACP Director Is Rein-
      stated After Pressure by Board Members," *New York Times*, May 27,
      1983; Smothers, "Hooks Case: A New Focus," *New York Times*, May 28,
      1983; Sheila Rule, "Board of NAACP Calls for Resignation of Unit's
      Chairman," *New York Times*, May 29, 1983; Rule, "Leadership Conflict
      Just One Problem Facing NAACP at Meeting Today," *New York Times*,
      June 11, 1983.
        Jones left to become a judge of the United States Court of Appeals for
      the Sixth Circuit. The Association later sued him, alleging financial mis-
      deeds, but the case was dismissed. It also sued Atkins and other former
      staff lawyers with a similar outcome. There was a lot of internal turmoil.

485   NAACP SPECIAL FUND-RAISING: Sheila Rule, "NAACP Outlines New Pro-
      gram to Marshal Black Voters," *New York Times*, June 30, 1982.

485   JACKSON'S RULING: *NAACP v. NAACP Legal Defense and Educational
      Fund*, 559 F.Supp. 1337 (D.C. D.C. 1983).

486   APPEAL AND HAMMOND AFFIDAVIT: *NAACP v. NAACP Legal Defense and*

Educational Fund, 753 F.2d 131 (1985), 134 note 22, cert. den. 472 U.S. 1021 (1985).

486 UNANIMOUS OPINION: Ibid.

CHAPTER 36. BEYOND THE RIGHTS OF BLACKS

487 NATIVE AMERICAN AND MEXICAN AMERICAN CASES: LDF minutes, June 15 and September 14, 1967; LDF executive minutes, November 11, 1967; LDF docket, July 26, 1968; LDF NORI docket, November 1968; LDF docket, April 8, 1969.

488 CREATION OF MALDEF: LDF executive minutes, June 15 and September 14, 1967; memorandum to Antonia Hernandez from Pete Tijerina, March 14, 1988, in author's possession; "A Mexican-American Legal Defense and Education Fund: A Proposal to the Ford Foundation, Prepared Under the Auspices of the NAACP LDF," August 7, 1967, in author's possession.

488 FISHING RIGHTS CASE: *Sohappy v. Smith,* 302 F.Supp. 899 (D.C. Ore. 1966), 529 F.2d 570 (9th Cir. 1976). The case became celebrated, partly because of the names of the parties. LDF staff lawyer Mel Zarr selected Sohappy and Smith from among the parties to list first among plaintiffs' names because they sounded like typical Indian and white names.

489 INDIAN RIGHTS AND STATISTICS: "National Fund for Indian Rights: A Proposal to the Ford Foundation Prepared Under the Auspices of the NAACP LDF," September 1969, in author's possession.

489 MALDEF-GONZALEZ CONTROVERSY: Memorandum from Tijerina, in author's possession.

489 FORD GRANT TO CALIFORNIA INDIAN LEGAL SERVICES: Letter, Leonard Ryan to Jack Greenberg, June 30, 1970, in author's possession.

490 HUMAN RIGHTS ARTICLE: Jack Greenberg and Anthony R. Shalit, "New Horizons for Human Rights: The European Convention, Court, and Commission of Human Rights," 63 *Columbia Law Review* 1384 (1963).

490 OKLAHOMA CASE: *Eddings v. Oklahoma,* 455 U.S. 104 (1982).

490 INTERNS: LDF executive minutes, October 11, 1962.

492 1976 SOVIET UNION TRIP: Report in author's possession.

493 LEGAL RESOURCES CENTRE: Letter, Arthur Chaskalson to Jack Greenberg, April 7, 1992, in author's possession.

493 MANDELA LETTER: December 17, 1991, copy in author's possession.

495 PHILIPPINES TRIP: *The Philippines: A Country in Crisis,* A Report by the Lawyers Committee for International Human Rights, 1983.

496 PROTEST WITH WALESA: Michael T. Kaufman, "Walesa Is Barred as Trial of 4 Dissidents Begins," *New York Times,* July 14, 1984.

498 *NEW YORK TIMES* EDITORIALS: June 3, 1980, and September 12, 1984.

498 PROPOSED SETTLEMENT: Justification for the four hundred minimum was said by some to have originated in *Roberts v. United States Jaycees,* 468 U.S. 609 (1984), but it was a simple compromise made without regard to *Jaycees.* I simply thought that number would pick up all the clubs that mattered.

498 LAW AGAINST DISCRIMINATION: Section 8-102 of the New York City Code, December 31, 1986, and Section 8-107, August 31, 1989.

498 SUPREME COURT UPHOLDS CLUB LAW: *New York State Club Association v. City of New York,* 487 U.S. 1 (1988).

498   ADOPTED ACROSS THE COUNTRY: The club law, or a variation of it, was
adopted in the cities of Buffalo, Chicago, Los Angeles, New Orleans,
Sacramento, San Francisco, Washington, D.C., and Wilmington (Del.), and
the states of Florida and Kansas. A version in Boston limits liquor licenses
to clubs that don't discriminate; another, covering California, prohibits
taking a state tax deduction for expenses incurred at clubs that discriminate, using the bill's standards.

CHAPTER 37. MY LAST YEARS AT LDF

502   BELL'S SUPPORT OF STUDENT DEMANDS: Derrick Bell, Jr., "A Question of Credentials," *Harvard Law Record*, September 17, 1982.
502   BOYCOTT OF GREENBERG: "Students Picket Law Course in Rights Protest at
Harvard," *New York Times*, January 6, 1983. BELL QUOTED: Bell, "A Question of Credentials."
502   BLSA DEMANDS: Dave Horn, "Charges Fly Over BLSA Course Boycott,"
Harvard Law Record, September 10, 1982; see also "Black Students at
Harvard Seek Boycott of Law Course," *Chronicle of Higher Education*,
August 4, 1982.
502   KENYATTA: Horn, "Charges Fly."
502   MEETING WITH STUDENTS: Roland Monson, "Boycotted Profs Meet with Students," *Harvard Law Record*, October 22, 1982.
502   CRISIS ARTICLE: Bernadette Manners, "Harvard Boycott Turns Out to Be Refer-
endum on Affirmative Action," *The Crisis* 89, no. 476 (December 1982).
502   TONY BROWN: "Harvard Tokenism, and Chaos, Compliments of the *Washington Post*," *New York Daily News World*, September 7, 1982.
503   KENYATTA'S REFERENCE TO CORNELL: Horn, "Charges Fly."
503   ALL-BLACK DORMITORY ISSUE: Kenyatta may have been thinking of Kenneth
Clark, who had taken such a position.
503   DUNCAN KENNEDY LETTER: "Memo to the Faculty," August 30, 1982, in the
author's possession.
503   BLSA EXECUTIVE COMMITTEE MEMBER LETTER: Donald Christopher Tyler,
"An Ongoing Fight," letter to the editor, *Harvard Crimson*, September 21,
1982.
503   STUDENT OPPOSITION TO BOYCOTT: Dave Horn, "Students Express Opinion
on Boycott," *Harvard Law Record*, October 8, 1982.
503   MARTIN KILSON: "'Ethnic Outbursts' at Harvard," *Des Moines Register*,
August 18, 1982.
503   CARL ROWAN: Carl Rowan, "Bad Behavior at Harvard," *Washington Post*,
August 20, 1982.
503   BAYARD RUSTIN: "A Misguided Protest by Blacks at Harvard," letter to the
editor, *New York Times*, August 9, 1982.
503   RANDALL KENNEDY: "On Cussing Out White Liberals," *The Nation*, September 4, 1982.
503   *NEW YORK TIMES* BOYCOTT EDITORIAL: "Blind Pride at Harvard," *New York
Times*, August 11, 1982.
503   *PITTSBURGH COURIER*: "Harvard Law Boycott," *Pittsburgh Courier*, August
21, 1982.
503   COLUMBIA LAW SCHOOL STUDENT SENATE: Resolution, April 20, 1983, copy
in author's possession.

503   KENYATTA ON GREENBERG AS DIRECTOR OF LDF: Horn, "Charges Fly."

504   BROWN, ROWAN, AND KENYATTA: Brown, "Harvard Tokenism"; Kenyatta, interview with the author, November 21, 1991.

504   CONSERVATIVE COLUMNIST: Max Freedman, "Greenberg Merits a Taste of Reverse Racism," *New York Times*, September 24, 1982.

505   LAST SUPREME COURT CASE: *United States Postal Service v. Aikens*, 460 U.S. 711 (1983). For testimony see Transcript of Record, 219–20.

505   REAGAN FIRES CIVIL RIGHTS COMMISSIONERS: Robert Pear, "Reagan Ousts 3 from Civil Rights Panel," *New York Times*, October 26, 1983.

506   COLEMAN'S TESTIMONY: "Reagan Asks Vote for Rights Panel," *New York Times*, November 5, 1983; Robert Pear, "House Denies Funds for Rights Commission," *New York Times*, November 10, 1983.

506   SENATE RESOLUTION: Robert Pear, "Accord Reported on Appointment of Rights Panel," *New York Times*, November 11, 1983.

506   JUDGE JOHNSON'S DECISION: *Berry v. Reagan*, 32 Empl. Prac. Dec. (CCH) P33, 898 (D.C. D.C. 1983).

506   THE APPEAL: *Berry v. Reagan*, 732 F.2d 949 (D.C. Cir. 1983).

506   BERRY AND RAMIREZ APPOINTED: Robert Pear, "Two Appointees Fill U.S. Rights Panel," *New York Times*, December 17, 1983.

506   REPUBLICAN APPOINTMENTS AND DOUBLE-CROSS: Robert Pear, "Rift Grows Wider Over Rights Panel," *New York Times*, December 9, 1983.

CHAPTER 38. A SUMMATION

509   LDF STAFF GROWTH: LDF executive minutes, January 24, 1984.

512   METAPHOR OF THE COURTS: Paul Freund, *The Supreme Court of the United States* (Cleveland: World Publishing, 1961), 114.

514   PROFESSIONAL OPPORTUNITY: In 1940, there were 3,524 black physicians and 1,052 black lawyers and judges, or one black physician for every 3,651 black persons and one black lawyer for every 12,000 black persons; U.S. Department of the Census, Bureau of the Census, *The Social and Economic Status of the Black Population in the United States: An Historical View, 1790–1978*, Current Population Reports, Population Characteristics, Series P-23, No. 80 (Washington, D.C.: Government Printing Office, 1989), 76. In that year, 80 percent of black people lived in the South, but only 53 percent of black physicians and 31 percent of black lawyers lived there. Thus, in the South, there was one black physician for every 5,509 black persons and one black lawyer for every 31,570 black persons; ibid. That year 3 percent of black employed persons over the age of fourteen were in professional and technical occupations while a total of 6 percent held white collar jobs; ibid., 74. In 1960, the white collar figure had doubled to 13 percent. The number of lawyers had also doubled; ibid., 76. In 1990, 30 percent of black employed men and 58.5 percent of black employed women were in white collar occupations; U.S. Department of Commerce, Bureau of the Census, *The Black Population in the United States: March 1990 and 1989*, Current Population Survey, Population Characteristics, Series P-20, No. 448 (Washington, D.C.: Government Printing Office, 1990), 13.

514   GOVERNMENT CONTRACT EMPLOYMENT: In jobs subject to the order the rate of minority employment grew 20 percent between 1974 and 1980, but

only 12 percent in the noncontract sector. Minorities "experienced significantly greater upward mobility at the companies where the Government enforced affirmative action." Jonathan Leonard, "Employment and Occupational Advance Under Affirmative Action," National Bureau of Economic Research Working Paper no. 1270, February 1984; Leonard, "The Impact of Affirmative Action on Employment," National Bureau of Economic Research Working Paper no. 1310, March 1984; Richard Freeman, "Affirmative Action: Good, Bad, or Irrelevant?" *New Perspectives* (Fall 1984), 23–27.

514   VOTING: In Mississippi, only 7 percent of black people eligible to vote were registered in 1965; 19 percent in Alabama; and 47 percent in North Carolina (the highest for the seven states covered by the original 1964 Civil Rights Act). Even where they were in the majority, no black people registered in many counties. By 1972, 62 percent of eligible black voters in Mississippi were registered. The gap between white and black eligible voters registered was 44 points before the act for the region as a whole, but fell to 11 points by 1972; U.S. Commission on Civil Rights, *The Voting Rights Act* (Washington, D.C.: Government Printing Office, January 1975), 43. None of this could have occurred without the LDF White Primary Cases and other victories, the last case being *Brown v. Baskin,* 80 F.Supp. 1017 (E.D. SC, 1948), aff'd 174 F.2d 391 (4th Cir. 1949). LDF played a major role in passage of the 1965 Voting rights Act, winning at-large cases and enacting the 1982 Voting Rights Act. *United Jewish Organizations v. Carey,* 430 U.S. 144 (1977), set a standard that increased black political power.

Before the Voting Rights Act, there were fewer than 100 black elected officials in the seven Southern states covered by the act. By 1974, there were 963. By 1980, only six years after extensions to the act went into effect, the number of black elected officials had doubled; U.S. Commission on Civil Rights, *The Voting Rights Act: Unfulfilled Goals* (Washington, D.C.: Government Printing Office, September 1981), 11–14. In 1940, Congress had one black member, Arthur W. Mitchell; by 1960 there were five; by 1970 there were nine; and by 1985 there were twenty; *Black Politician* 1, no. 4 (1970), 11; see also U.S. Department of Commerce, Bureau of the Census, *Statistical Abstract of the United States 1987* (Washington, D.C.: Government Printing Office, 1987), 237. In the country as a whole, there were 1,479 black elected officials in 1970. By 1985 there were 6,312; over two-thirds of them in the South; *Statistical Abstract 1988,* 247.

514   BLACK-WHITE INCOMES: Comparing all two-income households in the North and West, the median income of black families in 1987 was 91 percent that of white families. In the South the same year, black two-income households had a median income only 81 percent that of white two-income households; U.S. Department of the Census, Bureau of the Census, *The Black Population in the United States:* March 1988, Current Population Reports, Population Characteristics, Series P-20, No. 442 (Washington, D.C.: Government Printing Office, 1989), 30.

514   "MIDDLE CLASS": "The Other America," *The Economist,* July 10, 1993.

514   AVERAGES: In 1990, while black workers comprised 10.1 percent of the workforce they received only 8 percent of all earnings; Andrew Hacker, *Two Nations: Black and White, Separate, Hostile, and Unequal* (New

York: Scribner's Sons, 1992), 94. But, between 1970 and 1990 the distribution of income among blacks changed, with a higher proportion (29.5 percent compared to 23.8 percent) receiving incomes above $35,000 per year (98). During this period the proportion of black households with incomes above $50,000, Hacker writes, grew by 46 percent, while whites' share grew by 35 percent, although a large part of that change represents more black than white households with two full-time earners (98). Another perspective indicates that from 1947 to 1989 black share of aggregate family income grew from 4.7 to 7.2 percent, reflecting, in part, that more blacks moved into white collar occupations: Between 1960 and 1990 the proportion of black men in white collar jobs grew from 12.1 to 30.4 percent and of black women from 18.2 to 57.7 percent (233). But, overall, blacks remain disproportionately poor: 44.8 percent of black children live below the poverty line, while only 15.9 percent of whites do (99). Blacks are among the poor 3.63 times more than whites (100) and have, over the years, had more than double the unemployment rate of whites (103).

515 BLACK JUDGE: David Margolick, "At the Bar; Falsely Accused: In a Humiliating Arrest, a Black Judge Finds Lessons of Law and Race Relations," *New York Times*, January 7, 1994.

515 SINGLE MOTHERS: Nationally, according to Hacker, more than 3.5 times as many unmarried black women than white have children; more than six times as many blacks die of homicide than whites; black infant mortality is double that of white (Hacker, *Two Nations*, 231–32).

515 "PROBATION OR PAROLE": "The Other America," *The Economist*, July 10, 1993.

AFTERWORD: THE PEOPLE OF LDF

520 SCHOLARS: Marvin Wolfgang of Penn and David Baldus of Iowa have done major work on the death penalty for LDF. David Feller of the University of California at Berkeley (former counsel for the United Steel Workers Union) and Harriet Rabb of Columbia, now general counsel of the Department of Health and Human Services, have served on the board.

521 EDUCATION: John Maguire, a freedom rider client and later a board member is president of the Claremont Graduate School. I have been dean at Columbia College and taught undergraduates.

521 FEDERAL AND STATE COURTS: Spotts Robinson has been on the Court of Appeals for the District of Columbia. Cecil Poole, longtime board member and cooperating lawyer on the Ninth Circuit Court of Appeals in San Francisco. Bob Carter and Connie Motley are district judges in the Southern District of New York. Jack B. Weinstein, who worked on the *Brown* brief, has been the highly praised chief judge of the United States District Court of the Eastern District of New York. Marvin Frankel, who as a law professor directed our lawyers' training conferences, sat on the federal district court in New York for thirteen years, is now in private practice and president of the Lawyers Committee for Human Rights. Pierre Leval, who worked for LDF as a summer intern, is on the Second Circuit Court of Appeals. LDF former vice president Lou Pollak is a United States district judge in Philadelphia. Staff lawyer and Earl Warren fellow Gabrielle McDonald was a federal judge in Texas. Former fellow U. W. Clemon is

on the federal bench in Alabama. Horace Ward, for whom we lost a case to enter the University of Georgia in the 1950s, later became an LDF cooperating lawyer and sits on the federal bench in Atlanta. Matthew Perry, who handled most of our South Carolina cases for decades, is a federal district judge in Columbia. Assistant counsel Ron Ellis and fellow Henry Jones are United States magistrates in New York and Arkansas, respectively.

George Bundy Smith, whom we represented as a freedom rider, became a staff lawyer and is on New York's highest court, the court of appeals. Reuben Anderson and Fred Banks, former fellows, have been on the Supreme Court of Mississippi. Oscar Adams, for years a cooperating lawyer in Birmingham, has been on the Supreme Court of Alabama. George Howard, another cooperating lawyer, is a U.S. district judge in the Eastern District of Arkansas. Earl Warren fellow Gwendolyn Jones Jackson is a judge in Virginia. Other fellows who are or have been state court judges include Charles Becton (North Carolina); LaDoris Cordell (California); Arthur McFarland (South Carolina); and Gene Thibodeaux (Louisiana).

521 PRACTICING LAWYERS: Bill Coblentz, a longtime board member, has been chairman of the California Board of Regents and one of the most powerful lawyers in that state. Danny Parker was a senior partner in another large national firm. Robert Preiskel, for many years a board member and later president of LDF, has been a senior partner of a major national law firm, as has been Jay Topkis. The board has included Cyrus Vance, who later became secretary of state. The board member perhaps least appreciated outside LDF has been Adrian W. (Bill) DeWind, a tax partner at Paul, Weiss, whose wise advice guided us through many perils and brought to our side immensely helpful foundation and business people. He has unassumingly played similar roles with the Natural Resources Defense Council, Human Rights Watch, and other organizations.

521 CABINET MEMBERS: Also, board member Clifford Alexander (secretary of the army) and Ernest Green, one of the Little Rock Nine (assistant secretary of labor).

521 LDF LAW STUDENT: Elizabeth Holtzman was New York City controller and a member of Congress.

521 GOVERNMENT OFFICIALS: Drew Days, former staff lawyer, headed the Civil Rights Division of the Justice Department; he is the Clinton administration's solicitor general. President Clinton nominated former staff lawyer Lani Guinier as head of the Civil Rights Division, then withdrew the nomination when right-wingers criticized law review articles she had written. Later, Clinton selected LDF assistant counsel, Deval Patrick, for that job. Longtime cooperating lawyer Henry Marsh has been mayor of Richmond, Virginia.

521 CLIENT LIST: Ernest Morial, after he won his admission to LSU law school, became mayor of New Orleans. We represented Richard Hatcher, mayor of Gary, Indiana, in a suit to desegregate hospitals there, and Coleman Young, mayor of Detroit, in defending his affirmative action plan to integrate the police department.

522 INFLUENCE OF LDF BOARD: Board members—other than those mentioned elsewhere in this chapter—have included Eleanor Applewhaite, general counsel of Channel 13, New York's public television channel; Alice Beasley, formerly in our San Francisco office; Wiley Branton; Charles

Duncan, who had worked on *Brown*; David Kendall, former staff lawyer, a partner in Williams and Connally, and now President Clinton's private lawyer. Some had been board members from the earliest days: George Cannon, a Harlem physician and one of the leaders in community medicine; Columbia political science professor Charles Hamilton; Harry Kahn, who handled investments for LDF; Connie Lindau, a New York lawyer; Bob McDougal, a Chicago lawyer; Dorothy Rosenman, wife of Sam Rosenman, who was counsel to FDR and Harry Truman and an expert on housing; Harvey Russell, a vice president of Pepsico; Bayard Rustin; Bill Scheide, founder of the Bach Aria Group and one of the nation's great rare book collectors and Bob Weaver. Others were more recent: Jack G. Clarke, senior vice-president of Exxon and former vice-chairman of the Carnegie Corporation; Christopher F. Edley, head of the United Negro College Fund; George Simkins, plaintiff in important North Carolina civil rights cases; Charles Renfrew, deputy attorney-general in the Carter administration; Jack Sheinkman, president of the Amalgamated Clothing and Textile Workers Union; and Karen Hastie Williams, Bill Hastie's daughter, who is a lawyer in Washington, D.C.

INDEX

Note: Cases in which NAACP Legal Defense and Educational Fund lawyers participated are shown with (LDF) after the case title. When LDF was amicus curiae, that is so indicated. NAACP cases are designated as such.